Foundations of Business

Foundations of Business

Andrew Gillespie

OXFORD
UNIVERSITY PRESS

Great Clarendon Street, Oxford, OX2 6DP,
United Kingdom

Oxford University Press is a department of the University of Oxford.
It furthers the University's objective of excellence in research, scholarship,
and education by publishing worldwide. Oxford is a registered trade mark of
Oxford University Press in the UK and in certain other countries

Published in the United States of America by Oxford University Press
198 Madison Avenue, New York, NY 10016, United States of America

British Library Cataloguing in Publication Data

Data available

Library of Congress Control Number: 2023943790

ISBN 978-0-19-884953-7

Printed in the UK by
Bell & Bain Ltd., Glasgow

Links to third party websites are provided by Oxford in good faith and
for information only. Oxford disclaims any responsibility for the materials
contained in any third party website referenced in this work.

To Tor
Still our shining light.

Foreword

With this book we set out to write a text that would provide an excellent introduction to business for university students. We wanted to generate an interest in business issues, introduce the reader to current thinking and help to develop the analytical and critical thinking skills that are so crucial to an effective business student and business practitioner.

We also wanted to produce a text that was more globally focused than others that already existed, not least because we are aware than many of our readers will work at some point in international organisations.

In this book you will find a number of features to help you navigate through it and to help you to reflect on the material we have covered. The features include, but are not limited to:

- **An opening case study:** this highlights many of the key real world business issues in the chapter; we return to the questions linked to this case once the relevant topics are covered so you can appreciate how your understanding is developing by working through the chapter.

- **Business insights:** these feature businesses from around the world and provide valuable insights into the topic being covered. They help to bring theory to life for you.

- **Analysing business data:** An important skill in business is being able to make sense of data and be able to use it to support decision making. This feature will help you to develop these skills whilst also providing useful insights into trends and patterns related to many important business issues.

- **Think about it:** This feature is intended to encourage you to reflect on what you have read and think about its significance.

- **What would you do?:** This feature asks you to imagine you are in a particular situation and consider what you do next. This is a good opportunity to develop your decision-making skills.

Our aim for this book was to produce a business text that you would find "engaging, supportive, and relevant" – I hope we have succeeded.

Preface

Whilst there are many business textbooks on the market, I could never quite find the one I wanted to use with students! I find them to be either too basic or too complex; too UK focused or similarly too narrow; full of all too familiar cases; or a little too dry. I wanted to write a book that was accessible but demanding enough for university students; that provided an engaging and stimulating introduction to business areas; and which gave global insights into some of the many fascinating aspects of the subject. I hope this text will have achieved this. I hope it provokes your interest, stimulates reflection and leaves you wanting to know more!

As part of the learning package this text contributes to, we have produced a wide variety of valuable, digital resources that are embedded within the interactive e-book, to provide further insights, and help you develop and assess your understanding of the material. I particularly enjoyed producing the practitioner interviews which feature a diverse range of experts (including some brilliant past students) sharing their own experiences in applying key concepts in the world of work; as well as career advice for you as you begin to think about your future pathways.

Enjoy the book and all it has to offer; be curious, observant, and excited by business. Thrive.

Acknowledgements

Many thanks to everyone at OUP who has supported this book, with particular thanks to Elena So and Nicola Hartley for their insights, patience, direction and editing skills. Thank you also to all those involved in the practitioner interviews- Christopher, David, Emili, Grace, Mae and Stephen. I enjoyed talking to, and learning from, you all.

Thank you also to all those involved in the reviewing process- we have been delighted with the feedback. Lastly thank you to everyone else involved in bringing together this text and the various resources that accompany it to support students' learning.

From the publisher:

Content Advisory Group

Oxford University Press sincerely thanks all academics who have offered their invaluable time and subject matter expertise in reviewing chapters of *Foundations of Business* during the development period, including those who wish to remain anonymous as well as those who are listed below:

Dr. Sally Kah, Senior Lecturer in Business Management, De Montfort University

Ms. Christine Habib, Lecturer in Business & Entrepreneurship, Leeds Trinity University

Ms. Maja Pulić, Module Leader in Marketing and Management, University of Essex

Ms. Tracy Dixon, Lecturer in Strategic Management, University of Salford

Ms. Heather Kent, Teaching Fellow in Organisational Behaviour, University of Sussex

Ms. Zainab Atta, Teaching Fellow, University of Surrey

Ms. Julie Wilson, Assistant Professor (Education) in the Durham Centre for Academic Development (DCAD), Durham University

Contents

1

2

3

4

5

6

7

8

9

10

11

Contents

Detailed contents

Part 2

The external environment   297

List of case studies

Chapter	Introductory Case	Company	Industry	Sector (Public/ Private/ Third)	Small/ Medium/ Large company	Territory
Chapter 1 Introduction to business	Volkswagen's letter to its shareholders	Volkswagen	Automotive	Private	Large	Germany
Chapter 2 Entrepreneurs and start-up planning	Entrepreneurship in Africa	Multiple	Entrepreneurship	Private	Multiple	Africa
Chapter 3 Marketing management	Disney's growing portfolio	Disney	Media	Private	Large	US
Chapter 4 Managing operations	UK fashion industry	Multiple (only one specific brand mentioned)	Fashion	Private	Large	UK
Chapter 5 Managing finance	Walmart	Walmart	Hypermarket	Private	Large	US
Chapter 6 Managing people: Human Resource Management	BP's focus on employee diversity and engagement	BP	Oil and gas	Private	Large	UK
Chapter 7 Analysing the external environment of business	Ford	Ford	Automotive	Private	Large	US
Chapter 8 Business strategy	Tesla's business strategy	Tesla	Automotive	Private	Large	US

Chapter	Introductory Case	Company	Industry	Sector (Public/ Private/ Third)	Small/ Medium/ Large company	Territory
Chapter 9 Growth and international business strategies	Netflix goes global	Netflix	Streaming service	Private	Large	US
Chapter 10 Change, culture, and organizational structure	Culture at 3M	3M	Multiple, including heatlhcare	Private	Large	US
Chapter 11 Business ethics and Corporate Social Responsibility	Sony	Sony	Technology/ media	Private	Large	Japan

List of Business Insights

Business Insight	Company	Industry	Sector (Public/ Private/Third)	Small/ Medium/Large company	Territory
Business Insight 1.1 The importance of family businesses in economies around the world	Illy, Miele, Mars, Al_Shirawi, Walmart, LMVH, Hanwa Group, Tata	Multiple	Multiple	Multiple	Multiple
Business Insight 1.2 Carillion goes into liquidation	Carillion	Construction	Private	Large	UK
Business Insight 1.3 Uber sells its shares on the stock exchange	Uber	Service/ride-hailing/delivery	Private	Large	US
Business Insight 1.4 The market capitalization of Microsoft	Microsoft	Technology	Private	Large	US
Business Insight 1.5 The flotation of Facebook	Facebook	Technology	Private	Large	US
Business Insight 2.1 Starting up: motives and fears	N/A	N/A	N/A	N/A	Multiple
Business Insight 2.2 The story of two gym entrepreneurs: Julian Torres and Fitpal	Fitpal, Gymshark	Fitness	Private	Medium	Colombia, UK
Business Insight 2.3 Entrepreneurs in China	N/A	Entrepreneurial activity	Private	Small	China
Business Insight 2.4 The focus on start-ups in South Korea	N/A	Start-ups	Private	Small	South Korea

Business Insight	Company	Industry	Sector (Public/ Private/Third)	Small/ Medium/Large company	Territory
Business Insight 2.5 **Zumba**	Zumba	Fitness	Private	Large	Colombia
Business Insight 3.1 **The Fyre Festival**	Fyre Festival	Music/Festival	Private	Small	US
Business Insight 3.2 **Socially responsible marketing at Coca-Cola**	Coca-Cola	Food and drink	Private	Large	US
Business Insight 3.3 **Changes in emerging markets**	N/A	Marketing trends	N/A	N/A	Multiple
Business Insight 3.4 **Pandora**	Pandora	Jewellery/ fashion	Private	Large	Denmark
Business Insight 3.5 **Market segmentation by Sport England**	Sport England	Sport	Public	Medium	UK
Business Insight 3.6 **AdMov uses technology to target advertising**	AdMov	Transport Marketing	Private	Small	Philippines
Business Insight 4.1 **Re-shoring**	N/A	Process of re-shoring	N/A	N/A	US
Business Insight 4.2 **3M and GSK**	3M, GSK	Healthcare, service, pharmaceuticals	Private	Large	UK [GSK] and US [3M]
Business Insight 4.3 **Managing the supply chain**	N/A	Multiple	Private	Large	Asia
Business Insight 4.4 **Supply chain management**	Walmart	Hypermarket	Private	Large	US
Business Insight 4.5 **Environmentally friendly whisky packaging**	Diageo, Coca-Cola, Carlsberg	Food and drink	Private	Large	UK [Diageo], US [Coca-Cola] and Denmark [Carlsberg]

Business Insight	Company	Industry	Sector (Public/Private/Third)	Small/Medium/Large company	Territory
Business Insight 4.6 Amazon	Amazon	E-commerce	Private	Large	US
Business Insight 4.7 Digital operations in Africa	WeBuyCars	E-commerce	Private	Medium	South Africa
Business Insight 5.1 Online delivery businesses struggle to make a profit	Uber, Lyft, DiDi, DoorDash, Delivery Hero	Service/ride-hailing/delivery	Private	Large	US, China, Germany
Business Insight 5.2 Shein develops thousands of products a day	Shein	Fashion	Private	Large	Singapore
Business Insight 5.3 Airlines in debt	Easyjet, Norwegian	Aviation	Multiple	Multiple	Multiple
Business Insight 5.4 Buy now, pay later (BNPL)	Klarna, AfterPay, Mastercard Instalments, Apple Pay Later, Affirm	BNPL	Multiple	Multiple	Multiple
Business Insight 5.5 Evergrande in debt	Evergrande	Property development	Private	Large	China
Business Insight 5.6 Entegris decides to invest more	Entegris	Manufacturing	Private	Large	US
Business Insight 6.1 Intel and Diversity	Intel	Technology	Private	Large	US
Business Insight 6.2 Netflix put people before process	Netflix	Streaming service	Private	Large	US
Business Insight 6.3 EA's Core Values	EA	Gaming	Private	Large	US
Business Insight 6.4 The successful management of people at Pal's	Pal's	Food and drink	Private	Small	US

Business Insight	Company	Industry	Sector (Public/Private/Third)	Small/Medium/Large company	Territory
Business Insight 6.5 Working in an Amazon warehouse	Amazon	E-commerce	Private	Large	US
Business Insight 7.1 Online food delivery	Private	Food and drink	Private	Multiple	US, China, Germany, UK
Business Insight 7.2 Chickens	N/A	Food and drink	N/A	N/A	UK and US
Business Insight 7.3 Moore's Law	Intel	Technology	Private	Large	US
Business Insight 7.4 Disney	Disney	Technology	Private	Large	US
Business Insight 7.5 Lego	Lego	Toys	Private	Large	Denmark
Business Insight 8.1 A strategic decision to build a new shopping mall in Bangkok	Iconsiam (shopping mall)	Construction/Retail	Private	Medium	Thailand
Business Insight 8.2 How the strategy of Inditex is changing as the external environment changes	Inditex	Fashion	Private	Large	Spain
Business Insight 8.3 Nadella's strategic direction at Microsoft	Microsoft	Technology	Private	Large	US
Business Insight 8.4 A strategy of diversifying	Toleram	Multiple	Private	Large	Singapore
Business Insight 8.5 HSBC withdraws from US	HSBC	Banking	Private	Large	UK
Business Insight 9.1 The growth of Amazon	Amazon	E-commerce/streaming service	Private	Large	US

Business Insight	Company	Industry	Sector (Public/ Private/Third)	Small/ Medium/Large company	Territory
Business Insight 9.2 Legislation in India limiting Chinese takeovers	N/A	Start-ups	N/A	Large	India
Business Insight 9.3 Vietnam's Vingroup aims to export cars	VinGroup, VinFast	Automotive	Private	Medium	Vietnam
Business Insight 9.4 The growth of Jollibee	Jollibee	Food and drink	Private	Medium	Philippines
Business Insight 9.5 Facebook in India	Facebook	Multiple	Private	Large	Multiple
Business Insight 9.6 The growth of US food in India	Burger King, McDonald's, KFC, Domino's, Wendy's	Food and drink	Private	Multiple	India, US
Business Insight 9.7 Russian food prices	N/A	Food and drink	N/A	N/A	N/A
Business Insight 10.1 Strikes in French schools	N/A	Education	N/A	N/A	France
Business Insight 10.2 Johnson and Johnson	Johnson and Johnson	Healthcare/ pharmaceuticals	Private	Large	US
Business Insight 10.3 Comparing the stated cultures of ByteDance, Etsy, Tencent, and Shoprite	ByteDance, Etsy, Tencent, and Shoprite	Retail/e-commerce/ technology	Private	Multiple	China, US, South Africa
Business Insight 10.4 DaimlerChrysler	DaimlerChrysler (now Mercedes-Benz Group)	Automotive	Private	Large	Germany/ US
Business Insight 10.5 South Korean working culture	N/A	N/A	N/A	N/A	South Korea

Business Insight	Company	Industry	Sector (Public/ Private/Third)	Small/ Medium/Large company	Territory
Business Insight 10.6 Japanese business culture	N/A	N/A	N/A	N/A	Japan
Business Insight 10.7 Pandora	Pandora	Jewellery/ fashion	Private	Large	Denmark
Business Insight 11.1 GSK plc says how you achieve your objectives matters as much as the objectives themselves	GSK	Pharmaceuticals	Private	Large	UK
Business Insight 11.2 Opioids and ethics	Purdue Pharma	Pharmaceuticals	Private	Large	US
Business Insight 11.3 Chocolate with social impact	Tony's Chocolonely	Food and drink	Private	Medium	Netherlands
Business Insight 11.4 XPCC and alleged forced labour	XPCC	Multiple	Public	Large	China
Business Insight 11.5 Black Rock stresses the importance of climate change and business purpose	BlackRock	Investment	Private	Large	US
Business Insight 11.6 The dangers of forcing companies to be socially responsible	Kitex	Fashion	Private	Medium	India

List of figures and tables

Part 1

The internal environment

Chapter 1

Introduction to business

Why am I studying this?

- You are interested in business and think you will probably be in business for your career. As a result, you want to know more about what business involves. This chapter will give you an overview of what is involved in business so you start to understand the language and key concepts.
- You know that there are different forms of business but want to understand more about them. You have noticed, for example, that some businesses in the UK have 'ltd' and some have 'plc' after their names. This chapter will explain the difference between these.
- When you are working you will pay money into a pension to provide income for when you retire. These funds will almost certainly be invested into shares. In this chapter you will learn what a share is and what determines the price of a share.
- You have seen references in the news to the market value of a company and changes in share prices and the FTSE 100. This chapter will explain what these terms mean.
- You want to understand why some managers seem to have been allowed to make major mistakes. How a business is governed is known as 'corporate governance' and the importance of this is explained in this chapter.

Learning objectives

By the end of this chapter, you should be able to

- Understand what businesses do
- Understand the different functions of a business
- Understand the different roles of a manager
- Evaluate the different legal forms of a business and the advantages and disadvantages of each
- Understand that companies are owned by shareholders. Shareholders have limited liability.

- Analyse the significance of corporate governance
- Understand the difference between a mission and vision
- Understand the importance of objectives

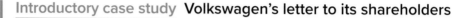

Introductory case study Volkswagen's letter to its shareholders

In 2018 the Chairman of the German car manufacturer Volkswagen (VW) published a letter to the shareholders of the firm. The letter provided an overview of the company's trading performance. It also highlighted some market challenges that VW faced. The letter tried to reassure shareholders that VW was responding appropriately to these challenges. The aim was to encourage investors to continue to hold shares in VW.

Letters to shareholders such as this and other information in annual reports by businesses give us an insight into the strategic visions of the senior management team within an organization.

According to VW's chairman shareholders choose to invest in companies for a range of different reasons. Some shareholders will be looking solely for financial returns. Others are more interested in the way in which organizations behave. However, they are all interested in companies that add value and have values. This is the kind of company that Volkswagen says it aims to be.

In 2018 fiscal year (often denoted as 'FY') VW performed well. It launched more than 70 new models across its range of brands (which include Volkswagen, SKODA, SEAT, and Audi). It increased its sales revenue to a total of €235.8 billion, and its operating profit to €17.1 billion. However, even with good financial performance VW recognized it needed to make some improvements.

Volkswagen logo. *Source:* Wikimedia/Ivan Radic.

The company was clear that Bentley, Audi, and also the core Volkswagen brand had to become more efficient. For example, at the main plant in Wolfsburg, the company wanted to increase productivity by 25 percent by 2020. Of course, ambitions such as these have been impacted by the COVID-19 pandemic. Efforts to become more efficient were thought to be necessary due to greater political uncertainty and a struggling global economy.

Despite these market challenges VW felt it was still able to keep its shareholders happy. For example, it proposed a significant increase of €0.90 in the dividend to €4.80 per ordinary share.

Looking ahead, VW said the situation remained challenging. It stated that the car industry is undergoing massive change with digitalization, connectivity, new mobility solutions, and automated driving. To meet these challenges the company will require investment in time and resources. VW has to review its activities to become more competitive.

VW says that the coming years will be guided by its move to electric vehicles. It is committed to the Paris Agreement and to making its contribution to protecting people and the environment. It is planning investments of around €30 billion in electric vehicles in the next five years. By 2025, VW aims to have 50 new electric models on the road. By then, every fourth car in its range should be an electric model. With the Volkswagen ID, the company will offer the first vehicle with a CO_2-neutral supply chain and production. This will also change the face of its plants: Zwickau, Emden, and Hanover will be transformed into solely electric car plants, forming Europe's largest electric production network. In China, too, the conversion of the Anting and Foshan plants is also occurring. The production launch of electric cars in North America is expected in 2022.

The transformation of the car will go far beyond its energy source, according to VW. A car is becoming a highly complex, connected device, like a 'tablet on wheels'. From assistance systems through infotainment to fully autonomous driving: software is increasingly shaping the car of tomorrow. To be globally successful, companies need scale, and as a leading company in the sector, VW has the necessary size. However, the chairman acknowledged that VW was lacking software expertise. He said that VW is taking steps to acquire these skills by forging alliances with partners, increasing resources at full speed, revising its structures, and changing its workflows. The VW brand has established a separate Board of Management position for software, which will also be responsible for the Digital & Software Services Group division.

The company says it is keeping a close eye on its goal to become the global leading provider of sustainable mobility. This will be possible if it continues to improve. It wants to achieve sustainable growth and create value.

Source

www.volkswagenag.com/en/InvestorRelations/shares/letter-to-our-shareholders.html

To find the letters to shareholders from public companies (plcs) you can search on their websites in the investor relations sections. In the annual report you find an overview of the position of the business from the directors.

Introductory case study questions

Think about the following questions as you read through the chapter. You may not yet be able to answer these questions, but as we progress through the chapter, we will revisit them at key stages. By the end of the chapter, you should be confident in answering them.

▶

1. What does the case suggest about the reasons why people invest in businesses?

2. What are the objectives of VW?

3. What is the transformation process that VW provides?

4. In what ways does the case suggest the performance of a business is partly out of control of the managers?

5. In what ways do you think is the world of VW is changing?

6. Why do you think the Chief Executive of a company such as VW writes to shareholders each year?

Critical thinking

1. Do you think the increase in dividends could have been a way of VW keeping shareholders happy rather than what was best for the long-term interests of the business?

2. Do you think VW could have acted faster to changes in the market?

3. How much do you think investors should trust the Directors' report in VW's annual report?

4. Research the current position of VW. Discuss the reasons why its position may have changed from that outlined in the 2018 report above.

1.1 What is a 'business'?

1.1.1 Defining 'business'

We often refer to 'business' in conversation. A friend is 'in business' or going 'into business'; some of our relations have a 'business' or want a career 'in business'. But what do we mean by 'business'? A business is an entity involving one person or multiple people whose activities are organized in order to produce goods or services to sell for financial gain. There are some key features to pull out of this definition—ultimately 'business' involves:

- People
- Organized activities
- Creation of goods and/or services
- Selling those goods and/or services for financial gain.

A business takes inputs (also called factors of production) such as land, labour, people, and capital and transforms them into outputs—which may be goods or services—in exchange for a financial reward. This transformation process is shown in Figure 1.1. A good is a tangible item—something you can physically touch such as a car. A service is an intangible item which you cannot physically touch such as a haircut. An exchange occurs when there are buyers and sellers who trade. Many businesses provide a combination of goods and services; you choose to eat in a restaurant, for example, for a combination of the food (a good) and the environment (service).

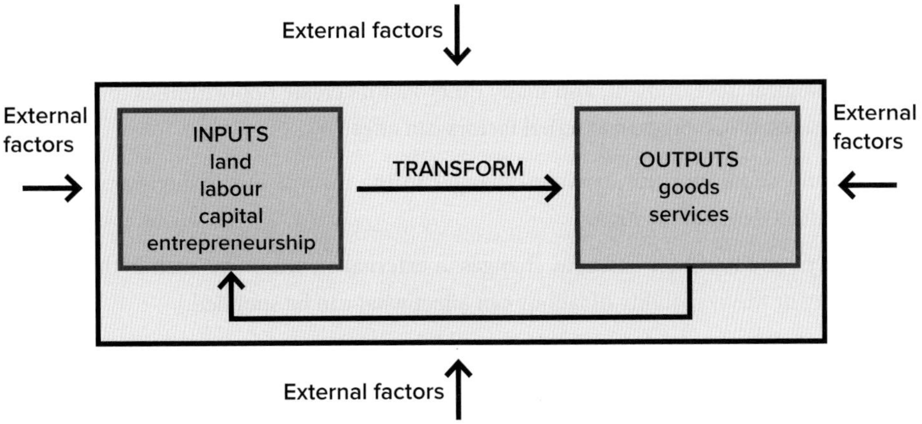

Figure 1.1 The transformation process. *Source:* Author.

1.1.2 How businesses add value

The aim of a business is to create output worth more than the inputs; this is known as adding value.

This desire to add value leads to creativity and innovation (see Chapter 4 for more detail on these topics). Businesspeople seek new ways to do things and new things to do. New markets develop, new industries are created, and new technologies invented. Changes in the way businesses do things and what they do can occur because of internal factors such as a new management team or external factors such as changes in economic or social factors. Take the year 2020, for example: the global pandemic resulted in some new markets being created at a rapid speed as many people had to fundamentally change the way they worked, creating the need for new technologies to support remote working, and new ways of managing supply chains. The year 2020 was unusual but the desire for businesses to create value is longstanding and leads to an exciting and dynamic world where change can happen at breath-taking speed. Google (now part of Alphabet) is viewed by some as an old business even though it was set up in 1998. Facebook started in 2004 and Instagram in 2010. Each of these organizations has evolved extremely quickly. And businesses do not stand still; they adapt and change over time if they want to thrive. The content platform Netflix, for example, began life renting out DVDs from its stores before moving into streaming. Disney moved from films to theme parks. Amazon has moved into healthcare. Meta is investing heavily in the meta verse. The drive to make profits generates choice and innovation for us as consumers.

- What we buy and how we buy it is constantly evolving. This can be shown in the UK by the changes in the shopping basket used by the Office of National Statistics to measure price changes year on year; this basket shows the typical products bought by UK families. Products which were once popular but are not popular anymore include condensed milk, corned beef, mashed potato granules, cassettes, and vermouth. In 2019 the ONS added new items to their basket which included smart speakers (such as Amazon Echo, Google Home), flavoured teas, and popcorn. (ONS, 2019). In 2022 additions to the basket included meat-free sausages, sports bras, and pet collars. In the same year removals were doughnuts, men's suits, and coal.

The transformation process does not take place in isolation, however; it is affected by external factors outside of the business' control. Changes in customer tastes, in social values, technological development, and many other factors create opportunities for new and existing businesses. Changes in external factors can affect:

- demand conditions; for example, changes in the income of the buying population will affect demand for items
- supply conditions; for example, changes in external environment such as the costs of energy or the availability of labour can affect what can be supplied.

The impact of external factors on the valued adding process are shown in Figure 1.1.

Can you now answer these questions from the introductory case study?

What is the transformation process that VW provides?

In what ways does the case suggest the performance of a business is partly out of control of the managers?

In what ways do you think is the world of VW is changing?

The people involved in running a business will decide on:

- Which potential customers to target
- What to produce, i.e. what the outputs will be
- How to produce the product, i.e. the transformation process
- What resources to use, i.e. the inputs used.

Changes in the external environment in the UK in recent years include:

- a growing interest in selling to emerging economies such as China as incomes there increase (changing who to target)
- increased demand for electric cars rather than diesel (changing what to produce)
- increased pressure to produce in an environmentally friendly way (changing how to produce)
- growing interest in using local resources reducing the costs and environmental impact of shipping products long distances (changing what resource to use).

Businesses may operate in the private sector—this means they are owned by private individuals—or they may be part of the public sector—this means they are fully or partly owned by the government. Trends in private sector businesses in the UK are shown in Analysing the Business Data 1.1.

Key concepts

A **good** is a tangible item which you can physically touch, e.g. a car.

A **service** is an intangible item which you cannot physically touch, e.g. financial advice.

Think about it

Do you think that if an organization is not profit making it can be or should called 'a business'?

Analysing the business data 1.1 Private sector businesses in the UK

The chart in Figure 1 shows the number of businesses in the UK owned by private individuals (rather than the government). The data in Figure 2 gives us an insight in the number and size of UK businesses.

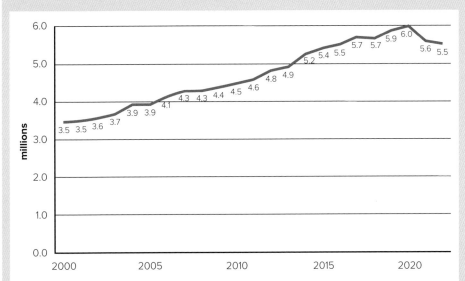

Figure 1 The number of private sector businesses in the UK. *Source:* Department for Business, E.& I.S. (2020) Business Population Estimates 2020, GOV.UK. GOV.UK. Available at: https://www.gov.uk/government/statistics/business-population-estimates-2020 [Accessed 2 April 2023].

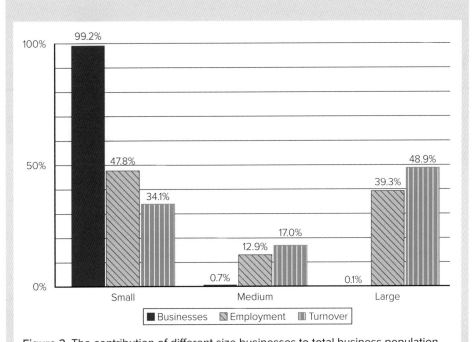

Figure 2 The contribution of different size businesses to total business population, turnover and employment. *Source:* Business population estimates for the UK and Regions 2022: Statistical release (HTML) (no date) GOV.UK. Available at: http://www.gov.uk/government/statistics/business-population-estimates-2022/business-population-estimates-for-the-uk-and-regions-2022-statistical-release.html [Accessed 2 April 2023].

The UK private sector comprises largely of non-employing businesses and small employers. At the start of 2022:

- there were estimated to be 5.5 million UK private sector businesses

- 1.4 million of these had employees and 4.1 million had no employees

- therefore, 74% of businesses did not employ anyone aside from the owner(s)

- there were 5.47 million small businesses (with 0 to 49 employees), 99.2% of the total business population

- there were 35,900 medium-sized businesses (with 50 to 249 employees), 0.7% of the total business population

- a further 7,700 businesses were large businesses (with 250 or more employees), 0.1% of the total business population

Questions

1. Why do you think the number of businesses in the UK might have fallen in 2018?

2. Compare the contribution of micro, small, medium, and large businesses in terms of number of businesses, employment, and turnover (revenue). Did you discover anything interesting?

Source

www.gov.uk/government/statistics/business-population-estimates-2022/business-population-estimates-for-the-uk-and-regions-2022-statistical-release-html

1.2 The functions within a business

Within a business there will be many different activities. These might all be carried out by one person in a small business or, in a bigger business, there may be specialist departments. These activities are sometimes categorized as the functions of a business.

The key functions of a business include:

- Marketing: this function deals with the interaction between the business and its customers. The marketing function will involve identifying customer needs, advising production on the right product features, setting the price, promoting the product, and ensuring it is distributed effectively. Marketing is examined in more detail in Chapter 3.

- Operations: this function deals with the development and production of the product. It may include, for example, decisions regarding where to produce, how to produce, what stock levels to hold, and what levels of quality to aim for. Operations management is examined in more detail in Chapter 4.

- Human resources: this focuses on managing people. It includes decisions regarding recruitment, training, and pay. Human Resource management is examined in more detail in Chapter 6.

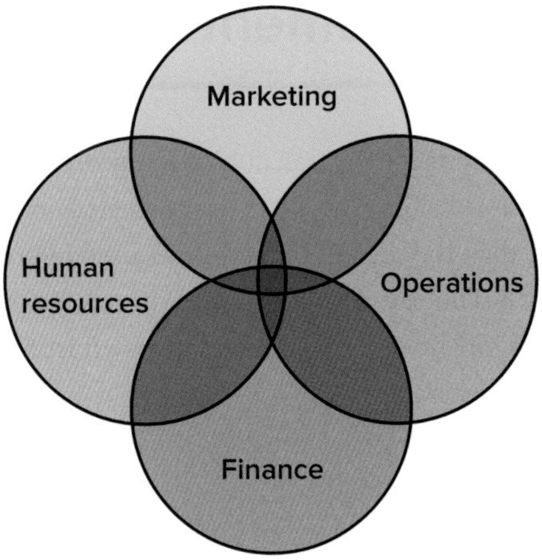

Figure 1.2 Diagram of key business functions. *Source:* Author.

- Finance: this function focuses on issues such as raising finance, managing how money is spent, and reporting on the financial performance of the business. Financial management is examined in more detail in Chapter 5.

The functions of a business are interlinked. A decision to expand, for example, may involve:

- More investment in promotional activities to generate demand (Marketing)
- The raising of funds for greater marketing spending (Finance)
- An increase in the scale of facilities to enable more to be produced (Operations)
- Staff recruitment (Human Resources).

The key functions of business are shown in Figure 1.2. Aspects of one function of a business may influence decisions elsewhere within the business:

- The skills of the staff may be used in the marketing of the business (think of football clubs)
- The facilities available may limit the demand that can be met (think of a music venue)
- The finance available may limit the scale of production possible (think of many start-ups)
- The strength of the brand may make it easier to expand into new areas (think of Apple).

What would you do?

Imagine that you have an objective to increase profits in your supermarket by 20% within a year.

What objectives would you set for different functions within your business?

1.3 What is management?

Managers are the people who manage the transformation process of a business and try to ensure it adds as much value as possible. Managers try to create goods and services which have a higher value to the buyer than the costs of the resources used in producing them. Given how important management is, it is not surprising that there have been many studies of what management involves. Below are the theories of some well-known writers on management:

1.3.1 Fayol

Henri Fayol was a French mining engineer but he was also one of the first people to study and write about management. According to Fayol (1917) managers have five main roles. These roles are shown in Figure 1.3.

The roles of managers outlined by Fayol are:

- **planning** ahead to decide how the business might develop over time
- **organizing** the various resources and the structure needed to undertake the transformation process successfully
- **commanding** i.e. directing and putting the plan into action and maintaining activity among the staff
- **coordinating** the resources to make sure they are where they should be at the right time
- **controlling** what is happening to ensure that things are on time and on target and appropriate actions are taken if not.

Fayol's writings provide a particular view of management which sees it very much as a 'command and control' approach. Managers tell employees what to do and direct their activities. More modern business writers such as Tom Peters and Jim Collins tend to focus more on the role of managers in working with teams, encouraging and supporting using the skills and abilities of others rather than 'telling'.

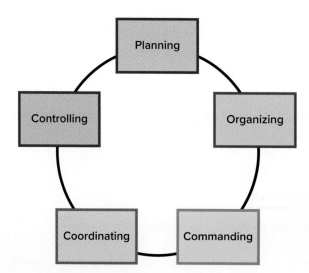

Figure 1.3 The role of managers. *Source:* Author.

Think about it

Why might the approach to management have moved from more of a 'tell' approach to a more supportive, facilitating approach?

1.3.2 Drucker

Peter Drucker was an Austrian-born American management consultant. He has been referred to as 'the founder of modern management' In 1973 in his book *Management: Tasks, Responsibilities, Practices* Drucker defined the role of a manager in terms of five basic functions (Drucker 1973):

1. *Setting objectives*—the manager sets goals and decides what work needs to be done to meet them.

2. *Organizing*—having divided the work into achievable tasks, the manager chooses people to carry them out.

3. *Motivating and communicating*—the manager uses both incentives and his or her relationship with staff to motivate them to achieve objectives.

4. *Measuring*—the manager establishes appropriate targets and measures, and both monitors and assesses performance.

5. *Developing people*—in a knowledge economy, employees are the organization's most important resource, and it is up to the manager to train and develop them.

This view of management highlights that an important part of the work of the manager is working with people and helping them to deliver what is required. Whereas Fayol focused on controlling people, Drucker focuses more on involving employees and working with them.

How people manage and what we expect our managers to do will vary over time as societies change. For example, Fayol's command and control approach may be the norm in some situations but with a well-educated workforce that wants to be involved in decisions a more consultative style may be more effective. Pistrui and Dimov are two management writers who have described how the role of managers has been changing over time.

1.3.3 Pistrui and Dimov

In their article in the Harvard Business Review in 2018 Pistrui and Dimov argued that the role of management has changed significantly since Fayol's work which outlined the role of a manager as planning, organizing, staffing, directing, and controlling.

Pistrui and Dimov (2018) highlighted a number of key changes that they think managers must make to be effective nowadays. These involve a change for managers:

1. **From being directive to being instructive:** Employees are increasingly being replaced with robots which are taking on manual and repetitive jobs. Managers need to focus on working with employees to develop new ideas rather than spend time supervising staff.

2. **From being restrictive to being expansive:** Many managers try to control everything that is done by subordinates; they micromanage. They don't delegate enough or let

Think about it

'Let's fire all the managers' said Gary Hamel in *Harvard Business Review* (Hamel and Zanini 2018). 'Think of the countless hours that team leaders, department heads, and vice presidents devote to supervising the work of others.'

Do you it is likely that there are too many managers in most organizations?

direct subordinates make decisions. This can restrict employees' ability to develop their thinking and decision-making.

3. **From exclusive to inclusive:** The best managers create or join groups of their peers from across the firm, to gain more perspective about problems and solutions rather than try and decide everything in isolation.

4. **From repetitive to innovative:** Managers often encourage predictability—they want to know what is happening and how it is going to be done. This means there are 'no surprises'. The problem with this approach is it can prevent employees from trying new ideas and being innovative.

5. **From problem solver to challenger:** Managers need to make sure they are not spending all their time fighting fires and fixing problems. They need to challenge employees to show what they can do.

Whereas Fayol and Drucker examined the process of management, Henry Mintzberg considered the different roles that managers play and how, in reality, they use their time.

1.3.4 Mintzberg

Henry Mintzberg is a well-known Canadian management writer. Mintzberg's work focused on what managers actually do rather than what they think they do or would like to do.

In his study, Mintzberg (1975) examined the work of five North American chief executive officers. Before Mintzberg the theory that had been outlined by other writers was that management involved taking rational decisions having analysed all the data. Mintzberg found that, in reality, life was characterized by frequent interruptions and reacting to events. Managers spent a lot of time fighting fires rather than long-term planning. They spent a significant amount of time in planned and unplanned meetings.

Mintzberg described the role of a manager in terms of ten behaviours shown in Figure 1.4. The management roles identified by Mintzberg are as follows.

Interpersonal roles

These are:

- Figurehead—a manager performs ceremonial duties as head of the organization.
- Leader—a manager motivates and encourages staff and reconciles individual needs with those of the organization.
- Liaison—a manager networks and maintains relationships with stakeholders both inside and outside the organization.

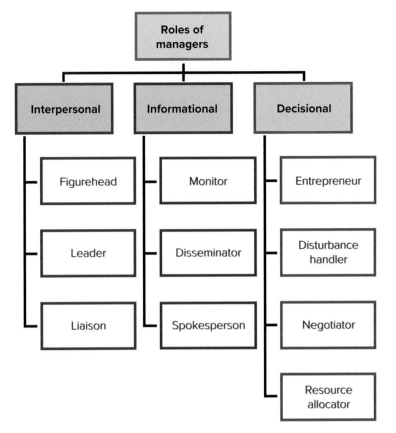

Figure 1.4 Mintzberg's management roles. *Source:* Mintzberg, H. (1989). *Mintzberg on management: Inside our strange world of organizations.* Simon and Schuster.

Informational roles

These are:

- Monitor—a manager gathers information relevant to the organization.
- Disseminator—a manager acts as a conduit, disseminating information to staff.
- Spokesperson—a manager reports to the outside world on matters relating to performance, legislative compliance, and social responsibilities.

Decision-making roles

These are:

- Entrepreneur—a manager designs and initiates change in pursuit of continuous improvement.
- Disturbance handler—a manager deals with crises and unexpected events.
- Resource allocator—a manager controls and authorizes the use of organizational resources, but also determines how work is allocated and coordinated.
- Negotiator—a manager negotiates with others regarding how organizational resources are used.

Think about it

'If you ask a manager what he does, he will most likely tell you that he plans, organizes, coordinates, and controls. Then watch what he does. Don't be surprised if you can't relate what you see to these four words.' (Mintzberg 1975, p. 47.)

Why do you think that what you see when you watch a manager is not the same as they say they do?

Effective management is an important aspect of business success. Managers make the decisions, they determine the direction the business is heading, they organize the resources, and they oversee the implementation of any plan. Find any successful organization and it is the likely to be the quality of management that will be driving its success. Not surprisingly, then, businesses work hard to develop effective managers and many writers study them.

In some businesses the people who own the business also manage it. In other businesses the managers may be specialists employed by the owners. We now look at different forms of business ownership.

1.4 Different forms of business ownership

There are several different forms of business ownership. These include sole proprietorship, companies, partnerships, cooperatives, and social enterprises. This section will consider each of these different forms of business in turn.

1.4.1 Sole proprietorship

A sole proprietorship (or sole trader) occurs when a business is owned and run by an individual. Plumbers, electricians, and hairdressers are often sole proprietors. Sole proprietors can employ other people but the business is owned by one person and in law there is no difference between the person owning and running the business and the business itself. The assets and liabilities of the business (i.e. what it owns and owes) are the assets and liabilities of the individual whose business it is.

The owner of a sole proprietorship has unlimited liability. This means that if she/he is sued there is no limit to the amount they might be liable for; all of their personal assets are at risk. When the sole proprietor dies or retires, the business ends.

Sole proprietorships are popular because they are easy to start up—you simply start trading. There is no need to register the business as a separate entity. The earnings of the business are the personal earnings of the individual concerned.

1.4.2 Company

A company is a separate legal entity that is distinct from its owners. To set up as a company a business must be 'incorporated'; in the UK this means that certain legal documents such as the Memorandum and Articles of Association have to be completed and registered at Companies House.

A company is owned by shareholders. Shareholders invest money into a business. They are liable for the amount of money they have invested and no more, i.e. their liability is limited.

Having limited liability is an important aspect of a company's legal structure. It enables companies to sell shares to investors who are willing to take a risk investing because they know the limit to how much they can lose; if all their personal possessions were at risk people and other businesses would be much less willing to invest and so raising funds would be difficult for companies.

There are different types of limited companies which will each be explored in turn: private company limited by shares, private companies limited by guarantee and public limited companies.

Private company limited by shares

Most limited companies are this type. The company is owned by shareholders who are liable up to the amount of money invested. Private companies tend to be smaller than public ones. They cannot advertise their shares to the general public. Most private limited companies are relatively small partly because they are not raising funds by selling shares to the general public. However, there are exceptions. Mars now employs 80,000 Associates in 78 countries around the world in its food and petcare business. It remains a private, family-owned business.

Private company limited by guarantee

In this type of company there are no shareholders. The business is owned by members who control it and provide a guarantee up to a certain amount of money. This structure is often used for not-for-profit organizations.

Public limited company

This is similar to a private company limited by shares but there are additional requirements such as the information that must be made available to the public. A public limited company's shares may be available to be traded on a stock exchange.

The profits of a company can be distributed to the shareholders in the form of dividends. Dividends are usually paid once or twice a year. The directors of a business recommend how much of the profits to pay as dividends. The shareholders then vote on this proposal. Businesses usually pay a proportion of their profits as dividends and retain the remaining profit for investment.

The dividend per share is, as its name suggests, the amount of dividend paid out for each share owned; for example, 10 pence. The dividend yield shows the dividend as a percentage of the current share price. For example, if the dividend was 10 pence and the price of a share was 500 pence, the dividend yield is $[10p/500p] \times 100 = 2\%$.

Corporation tax (rather than income tax) must be paid by the company on the profit made in each tax year. Dividends received by the shareholders will be taxed as income.

Key concepts

The **dividend** per share is the amount of money paid out to shareholders for each share they hold as a reward for their investment; this is usually paid annually or twice a year.

Dividend yield = ([dividend per share/share price] × 100); this represents the dividend per share as a percentage of the current share price.

Income tax is the amount individuals have to pay on their earnings to the government as tax.

Corporation tax is the amount businesses have to pay on their profits to the government as tax.

All companies need to file annual accounts at Companies House. These accounts are available to the general public. The accounts of a public limited company are far more detailed than those of a private company.

The shares of a private limited company cannot be advertised for sale; they can only be sold privately. The shares of a public limited company can be advertised. Public limited companies (plcs) can have their shares sold on a stock exchange. When a company goes from selling shares privately to selling them on a stock exchange this is known as a 'flotation'. The first time a company sells shares on the a stock exchange to the general public is known as an IPO: an Initial Public Offering. In 2020 AirBnB sold its shares for the first time on the stock exchange; the share price valued the business at over $100bn. Once shares are issued on the stock exchange these can then be resold; this creates a secondary market for the shares, i.e. a market in which shares can be regularly bought and sold.

Business insight 1.1 The importance of family businesses in economies around the world

Family businesses are often an important part of an economy. Many family businesses are quite small but there are some large businesses such as Illy, Miele, Mars, and the Al_ Shirawi group which remain family-controlled.

Figure 1 shows the percentage of companies in different countries that are family-owned in 2017. Figure 2 shows the rate of growth of revenues of family compared to non-family businesses. You will see that the revenue of family businesses has grown faster than non-amily according to this research.

Family businesses are a vital part of a vibrant economy in many countries according to recent research by Credit Suisse Research. Family businesses create jobs, innovate, and generate high returns. According to the Credit Suisse report, family companies—where the founders or descendants hold at least 20% in direct shares or where voting rights held by the founders or descendants is at least 20%—tend to generate higher revenue growth than non-family businesses. They also have higher profitability and less borrowing. At the heart of this successful financial performance seems to be the fact that family businesses take a longer-term view to investment. They are planning for future generations rather than aiming for short-term financial rewards.

Large family businesses include Walmart (owned by the Walton family), LMVH (owned by the Arnault family), Hanwa Group (owned by the Kim family), Mars (owned by the Mars family) and Tata (owned by the Tata family).

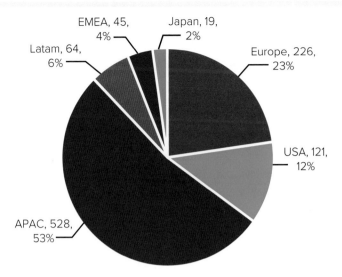

Figure 1 The number of family-owned companies in a region. *Source:* Pricewaterhouse-Coopers (no date) Family business survey 2018, PwC. Available at: https://www.pwc.com/gx/en/services/family-business/family-business-survey-2018.html [Accessed 2 April 2023].

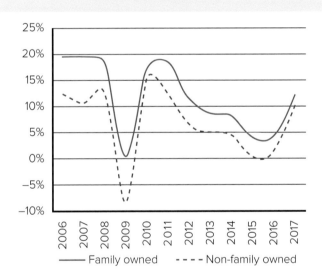

Figure 2 Revenue growth of family-owned companies compared to non-family owned. *Source:* PricewaterhouseCoopers (no date) *Family business survey 2018, PwC*. Available at: https://www.pwc.com/gx/en/services/family-business/family-business-survey-2018.html [Accessed 2 April 2023].

Questions

1. Why do you think family businesses might be more profitable than non-family businesses?

2. Why do you think the proportion of family businesses varies between regions?

3. What else would you want to know about the data provided on family businesses?

Sources

www.credit-suisse.com

www.pwc.com/gx/en/family-business-services/assets/pwc-global-family-business-survey-2018.pdf

Key concepts

Shareholder is an owner of a company; he/she owns a 'share' of the business.

Company is a business that has its own legal identity; it can own assets and be owed money.

What would you do?

You are the Chief Executive of a family business. It is a private limited company. You and other members of the family are considering turning the business into a public limited company. Should you do it or not? What factors would you consider before making a decision?

1.4.3 Partnerships

Partnerships occur when two or more people join to together to create an organization aimed at making profits. There are two types of partnership in the UK: general partnerships and limited liability partnerships.

General partnerships

A general partnership occurs when one or more people join together to do business. All of the partners are personally responsible for both the profits and the losses of the business. Typically, the partners sign a 'Partnership Agreement' which defines how the ownership, profits, and liabilities are divided. The partners are all personally liable for the debts of the business; the liability is divided between them. Each partner is self-employed and is responsible for paying his/her own taxes.

In a general partnership:

- each partner has an equal vote
- profits are divided equally between the partners
- the partners have unlimited liability.

The liability of each partner is not just for his or her own actions but also for the actions of other partners; this means people need to be very careful who they are going into partnership with.

Partnerships are a very common extension of the sole trader model; for example, it may exist when two individuals work together to build the business. A partnership has the benefit over sole proprietor of having two or more people to help make a decision, and it is easier to cover if one of the people is sick or needs a holiday.

Limited liability partnerships (LLP)

A limited liability partnership (LLP) is a separate legal entity which is distinct from its partners. In an LLP all partners have limited liability. Each partner is only liable up to the amount of money they initially invested and they all have management responsibilities.

The partners' responsibilities are usually outlined in an LLP agreement that is created when the business is established. This agreement will decide how the profit is split between partners, which partners need to approve which decisions, what the responsibilities of each partner are, and how partners can leave or join the LLP. LLPs are common in sectors such as financial services. As in an ordinary partnership, the members' share of profit is taxed as income.

1.4.4 Comparisons of different forms of business

The different forms of business all offer advantages and disadvantages. Tables 1.1–1.3 outline the advantages and disadvantages of each.

Sole proprietor

Table 1.1 Advantages and disadvantages of being a sole proprietor

Advantages	Disadvantages
No fees to register or set up as a sole proprietor; quick and easy to set up	Unlimited liability
Make all decisions yourself—quick to make decisions	Business ends when the sole proprietor retires or dies
Keep all the rewards yourself	No outside investors or advice
	Do not have to produce financial reports; simply pay tax

Source: Author.

Partnership

Table 1.2 Advantages and disadvantages of being a partnership

Advantages	Disadvantages
No fees to register or set up as a partnership; quick and easy to set up	Unlimited liability in traditional partnerships
More investors and decision-makers than sole proprietor	Share rewards
Partners share all rewards	Have to agree decisions
	Can be complex if one partner wants to leave

Source: Author.

Company

Table 1.3 Advantages and disadvantages of being a company

Advantages	Disadvantages
Have to register	Administrative and regulatory demands heavier
Limited liability	Annual accounts and financial reports must be placed in public domain
Can attract investors more due to limited liability	Have to employ an auditor to check the accounts
Business continues after managers leave or die	

Source: Author.

1.4.5 **Co-operatives**

Co-operatives are organizations that are owned, controlled, and run by and for their members to realize their shared goals. The members may be the customers, employees, or the residents of a community. Co-operatives are democratically managed with each member having one vote. The profits generated are either reinvested in the enterprise or returned to the members. There are over 3 million cooperatives worldwide employing over 280 million people.

1.4.6 **Social enterprises**

Social enterprises are businesses that have a social purpose although they may also be profit-making. Social enterprises have a goal which will benefit society, a community, or the wider good.

According to the *Financial Times*, in Japan there were estimated to be more than 200,000 social enterprise companies in 2022 employing close to 6 million people. They contribute ¥16tn ($116bn) to Japan's economy, more than 3% of GDP, according to government data. These social enterprises aim to find solutions for social problems, such as poverty, lack of job opportunities, and racial discrimination. They include businesses delivering food to schoolchildren whose families cannot afford three meals a day, at-home haircuts for elderly people suffering from dementia, and the repurposing of abandoned houses to create care homes.

The key characteristics of a social enterprise are:

- There is a clear mission statement with a focus on benefiting society
- The majority of the profits are reinvested to achieve the social objective.

1.4.7 **Deciding on the right legal form for a business**

When deciding on which form of business is most appropriate individuals should consider:

- What degree of control they want to have. If the founders of a business sell shares to raise finance, for example, this means they will lose some control as the outside investors will have votes.

- The degree of regulation they are prepared to accept. A company has more regulation than a sole proprietor, for example. In return for the right to have limited liability, companies have to produce financial information which is recorded at Companies House and is accessible to anyone. This can include information on sales, costs, profits, details of directors, and their rewards.

- The degree of financial risk they are willing to take. In the case of sole traders, for example, the risk is high because there is unlimited liability whereas companies have less risk with limited liability.

Where are we now?

So far, we have examined different forms of business. We now examine the role of shareholders as owners of a company.

1.5 Shareholders

Shareholders are the owners of a company. There are different types of shares but typically most shareholders own 'ordinary shares'. An ordinary share has one vote per share owned.

1.5.1 What is the role of shareholders?

A shareholder can:

- Influence the strategy of the business through his or her votes.
- Benefit from dividends. Shareholders vote on how much the dividends should be, usually every 6 months. Dividends can provide an income for shareholders.
- Benefit from an increase in the value of the share. A share represents a part ownership of the company. For example, if you owned one share out of 1000 this means you own 1/1000th of the company. The value of one share depends on the perceived value of the company. The more the value of the company, the more the share will be worth. A shareholder can buy a share and then, assuming the value of the company increases, she can sell it for more. However, investors do need to be aware that the value of a company and therefore the share price can fall as well as increase. The value of a share depends partly on the number available and the demand for them.

If there are any major decisions to be made, the shareholders will vote on them. It is important, therefore, to consider who the shareholders of a company are and what their objectives might be. For example, the shareholders may be:

- Family members wanting to maintain the values of the founder.
- Suppliers: this means they are likely interested in the long-term success of the business.
- A pension fund that is eager to earn sufficient short-term rewards for its own pensioners and may be less interested in the long-term success of the business.

Can you now answer this question from the introductory case study?

What does the case suggest about the reasons why people invest in businesses?

1.5.2 The agent and principal relationship

Shareholders are the owners of a company. They are known as the 'principals' of the business. They may also be involved in the day-to-day running of the business or, more commonly, employ managers to do this for them.

Managers are the 'agents' of the company—they are responsible for day-to-day decision-making. This means the agents are making decisions on behalf of the principals. This has risks because managers may not share the same objectives and values as the shareholders. The agents have more information about what is actually happening in the business and the danger is they pursue their interests and what suits them rather than what is best for the shareholders.

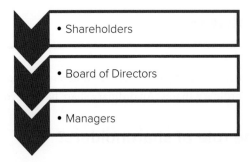

Figure 1.5 Directors-shareholders–managers. *Source:* Author.

To protect their interests, shareholders elect Directors to represent them and oversee the work of the managers. The shareholders are invited to an Annual General Meeting (an AGM) but the Directors typically meet monthly. If a major decision has to be made in between the AGMs, an Extraordinary General Meeting (EGM) may be organized. The relationship of shareholders, directors and managers is shown in Figure 1.5.

1.6 Corporate governance

The systems of checks and controls to monitor the behaviour of managers, including the composition and role of the Board of Directors, is called 'corporate governance'. How businesses are governed is important—it ensures the business is run properly and that decisions are made in the interests of the shareholders.

When considering corporate governance it is important to consider the composition of the Board of Directors. The directors play a vital role in setting the direction of the business and in ensuring it is well managed. The quality of the people on the Board is, therefore, important and shareholders will want to consider the experience and powers of the directors. Shareholders will also want to consider whether all or some of the directors are managers in the business. The advantage of this is that the managers bring direct insight into what is happening; the danger is that the board may end up supporting the managers' interests more than the investors. Directors who are from outside of the business are called 'non-executives'. These 'non-executives' can bring valuable experience from other businesses; they can also provide some valuable questioning of the managers. In a few businesses the Chief Executive who manages the business on a day-to-day basis is the same as the Chair of the Board of Directors; this can create high risks in the system because the Chair is supposed to hold the Chief Executive to account.

When a business has problems it usually comes down to its leadership and the system of governance. Poor governance allows poor management because it does not have the right systems of checks and balances in place. In 2008, for example, banks in the UK and other parts of the world were taking huge risks with their lending. This was due in part to changes in the legislation that made this possible but ultimately it was for the directors to monitor what was happening; unfortunately, too many lacked the necessary expertise to appreciate the risks involved in what the banks were doing.

Key concept

Corporate governance is the system by which companies are directed and controlled.

What would you do?

You are the managing director of a business. The Chair of the Board of Directors has just resigned. You are considering applying for this role as well as being Managing Director. Is this a good idea?

1.6.1 Corporate Governance Codes

In UK law there is a Corporate Governance Code. This was first published in 1992 by the Cadbury Committee. It defines corporate governance as 'the system by which companies are directed and controlled. Boards of directors are responsible for the governance of their companies. The shareholders' role in governance is to appoint the directors and the auditors and to satisfy themselves that an appropriate governance structure is in place.'

At the heart of the current Corporate Governance Code is a set of principles that emphasize the value of good corporate governance to the long-term sustainable success of a company.

Can you now answer this question from the introductory case study?

Why do you think the Chief Executive of a company such as VW writes to shareholders each year?

1.6.2 The principles of corporate governance

The UK Code of Corporate Governance sets out various principles which they think companies should follow. These include:

1. The board should establish the company's purpose, values, and strategy, and satisfy itself that these and its culture are aligned. All directors must act with integrity, lead by example, and promote the desired culture.

2. The board should establish a framework of prudent and effective controls, which enable risk to be assessed and managed.

3. The board should ensure that workforce policies and practices are consistent with the company's values and support its long-term sustainable success. The workforce should be able to raise any matters of concern.

   The board should include an appropriate combination of executive and non-executive (and, in particular, independent non-executive) directors, such that no one individual or small group of individuals dominates the board's decision-making.

4. The board and its committees should have a combination of skills, experience, and knowledge.

5. The board should establish procedures to manage risk, oversee the internal control framework, and determine the nature and extent of the principal risks the company is willing to take in order to achieve its long-term strategic objectives.

6. Remuneration policies and practices should be designed to support strategy and promote long-term sustainable success. Executive remuneration should be aligned to company purpose and values, and be clearly linked to the successful delivery of the company's long-term strategy.

Source: www.frc.org.uk/getattachment/88bd8c45-50ea-4841-95b0-d2f4f48069a2/2018-UK-

Business insight 1.2 Carillion goes into liquidation

In 2018 the company Carillion went into liquidation. Liquidation occurs when a business cannot pay its financial obligations and a legal process is started to claim back what can be recovered for the people and companies that are owed money. Carillion was a large business and its closure affected many employees and many other businesses which were its customers and suppliers. Information on Carillion is provided in the following Figures 1 to 4.

According to a report to the UK parliament about the failure of Carillion:

1. 'Carillion's business model was an unsustainable dash for cash. The mystery is not that it collapsed, but how it kept going for so long. Carillion's acquisitions lacked a coherent strategy beyond removing competitors from the market, yet failed to generate higher margins. Purchases were funded through rising debt and stored up pension problems

Figure 1 The business activities of Carillion. *Source:* Carillion: Six charts that explain what happened (2018) BBC News. BBC. Available at: http://www.bbc.co.uk/news/uk-42731762 [Accessed 2 April 2023].

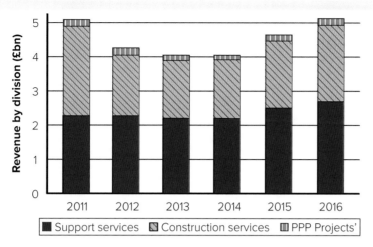

Figure 2 Carillion's revenue. *Source:* Carillion: Six charts that explain what happened (2018) BBC News. BBC. Available at: http://www.bbc.co.uk/news/uk-42731762 [Accessed 2 April 2023].

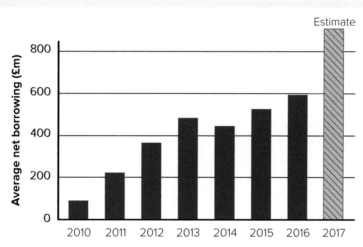

Figure 3 Carillion's debt. *Source:* Carillion: Six charts that explain what happened (2018) BBC News. BBC. Available at: http://www.bbc.co.uk/news/uk-42731762 [Accessed 2 April 2023].

for the future. Similarly, expansions into overseas markets were driven by optimism rather than any strategic expertise . . . in acquisitions, debt, and international expansion, Carillion became increasingly reckless in the pursuit of growth. In doing so, it had scant regard for long-term sustainability or the impact on employees, pensioners and suppliers.'

2. 'The perception of Carillion as a healthy and successful company was in no small part due to its directors' determination to increase the dividend paid each year, come what may. . . . Directors rewarded themselves and other shareholders by choosing to pay out more in dividends than the company generated in cash, despite increased borrowing, low levels of investment, and a growing pension deficit. . . . Carillion's directors chose short-term gains over the long-term sustainability of the company. We too can find no justification for this reckless approach.'

▶

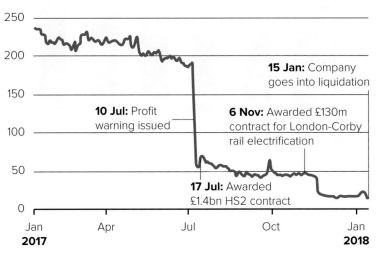

Carillion's share price has collapsed since July 2017

Price in pence (Sterling)

10 Jul: Profit warning issued

15 Jan: Company goes into liquidation

6 Nov: Awarded £130m contract for London-Corby rail electrification

17 Jul: Awarded £1.4bn HS2 contract

Figure 4 Carillion's share price. *Source:* Carillion: Six charts that explain what happened (2018) BBC News. BBC. Available at: http://www.bbc.co.uk/news/uk-42731762 [Accessed 2 April 2023].

3. 'Carillion relied on its suppliers to provide materials, services and support across its contracts, but treated them with contempt. Late payments, the routine quibbling of invoices, and extended delays across reporting periods were company policy. Carillion was a signatory of the Government's Prompt Payment Code, but its standard payment terms were an extraordinary 120 days. Suppliers could be paid in 45 days, but had to take a cut for the privilege . . .'

4. 'The board was either negligently ignorant of the rotten culture at Carillion or complicit in it.'

5. 'Non-executives are there to scrutinize executive management. They have a particularly vital role in challenging risk management and strategy and should act as a bulwark against reckless executives. Carillion's Non-Executive Directors were, however, unable to provide any remotely convincing evidence of their effective impact.'

6. 'Philip Green was Carillion's Chairman from 2014 until its liquidation. He interpreted his role as to be an unquestioning optimist, an outlook he maintained in a delusional, upbeat assessment of the company's prospects only days before it began its public decline. While the company's senior executives were fired, Mr Green continued to insist that he was the man to lead a turnaround of the company as head of a 'new leadership team'.'

7. 'In the years leading up to the company's collapse, Carillion's remuneration committee paid substantially higher salaries and bonuses to senior staff while financial performance declined. It was the opposite of payment by results.'

8. 'Major investors in Carillion were unable to exercise sufficient influence on the board to change its direction of travel. For this the board itself must shoulder most

responsibility. They failed to publish the trustworthy information necessary for investors who relied on public statements to assess the strength of the company. Investors who sought to discuss their concerns about management failings with the board were met with unconvincing and incompetent responses. Investors were left with little option other than to divest.'

Questions

1. Outline the failure of the Directors in the case of Carillion.

2. How do you think this could have been allowed to happen?

Sources

publications.parliament.uk/pa/cm201719/cmselect/cmworpen/769/76908.htm

www.bbc.co.uk/news/uk-42731762

1.7 The price of a company's shares

The price of a company's shares will depend on market forces of supply and demand. At any moment in time there will be a given number of shares in a company issued. There will be a demand for these shares depending on the returns that investors think they will get and how these compare with alternatives. If the returns look relatively high, demand will be high and this will pull the share price up. If the returns are regarded as low this will make demand low and the share price will fall.

Shares on a stock exchange are traded regularly. This part of a stock exchange is sold in the secondary market. The shares have been issued initially (on the primary part of the stock exchange) and are then being bought and sold in the secondary market. On the main market of the London Stock Exchange, for example, there are over 2600 companies from 60 countries listed. Other large stock exchanges include NASDAQ in New York and the Nikkei in Tokyo. Details of who owns shares in UK companies is shown in Figure 1 in Analysing the Business Data 1.2.

The change in the price of a share on the secondary market affects those who are buying and selling it; it does not directly change the amount of the money the company has.

Changes to the share price could be caused by many different things such as:

- an announcement of a new product or strategy

- rumours about the Chief Executive leaving

- a warning about future profits

- changes in the economic climate which might affect sales.

The share price determines the market capitalization of the business. The market capitalization is the current market value of all the shares in the company. If the share price increases this increases the market capitalization. According to Statista Apple had the largest market capitalization in August 2022 with a value of over $2,640 billion.

Key concept

The **market capitalization** is the current market value of all the shares in the company.

Analysing the business data 1.2 Share ownership of companies in the UK

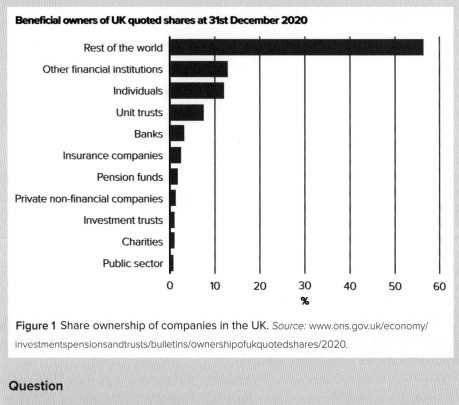

Figure 1 Share ownership of companies in the UK. *Source:* www.ons.gov.uk/economy/ investmentspensionsandtrusts/bulletins/ownershipofukquotedshares/2020.

Question

Discuss the possible consequences of the pattern of share ownership outlined above for UK companies.

1.7.1 Why does the share price of a company matter?

Changes in the share price of a company do not affect the current finances of the business. A company raises money when shares are sold initially. Changes in share price occur as the shares are traded from one owner to another.

Shareholders will be interested in the share price because this affects the value of their holdings. If the share price for a company is falling the wealth of the shareholders is getting less and they are likely to put pressure on the managers to make the share price increase.

Many people put money each week or month into their pension schemes. This means they save some of their earnings and these savings are usually invested in shares to generate the returns to pay for their pensions later. If share prices fall this means that pensioners may receive less valuable pensions.

Managers will also be interested in the price of a share because they may have their own rewards linked to this price. Often managers' rewards include share options. This means they have the right to buy shares at a fixed price at a given time. If the actual share price is higher than this on the set date, managers can buy the shares and immediately sell them making a profit.

Managers may also be concerned about the overall value of the business. The share price determines the market value of the company. If the market value falls this will make the company more vulnerable to takeovers. Managers may worry about the impact of this on their own jobs.

You will often find share indexes which show the performance of the share prices of the biggest companies or particular types of company. One of these indices in the UK is the FTSE; information on this is shown in Analysing the Business Data 1.3.

When investors are considering whether to buy shares one of the factors they might consider is the overall purpose of the business and what it is trying to be. This is shown in its mission statement.

What would you do?

You are the managing director of a public limited company. The share price of your company has fallen by 20% in the last 12 months. Would you worry?

Think about it

The following companies went public in India in 2021: Zomato (food delivery), Freshworks (enterprise software), Paytm (payments), Policy Bazaar (insurance), and Nykaa (fashion). According to The Economist the share prices of each of these had fallen by over 59% by early 2023. Why do think this might have occurred? Does it matter?

Business insight 1.3 Uber sells its shares on the stock exchange

In 2019 Uber, the ride hailing app, was floated on the stock exchange. The company was valued at $82bn (£63bn). Uber had not made a profit and had warned that it may never do so. Since its foundation in 2009 and its flotation, the company had lost about $9bn by 2019. Uber had originally suggested a price for its shares of between $44 and $50, valuing the company at up to $120bn.

Investors who bought Uber shares hope that Uber will grow successfully as it diversifies into several other sectors. As well as the original 'ride-hailing' business, Uber is developing driverless cars, and has a food delivery operation, Uber Eats. Uber's chief executive emphasized that the firm's future is not as a ride-hailing company, but as a wide technology platform shaping logistics and transportation.

Question

Why would anyone buy a share in a company that does not make a profit?

Source

www.bbc.co.uk/news/business-48222567

Analysing the business data 1.3 The FTSE 100 share price index

The FTSE 100 is an index of the share prices of the largest 100 companies on the London Stock Exchange according to their market capitalization. Changes to the FTSE 100 reflect changes in the value of these businesses. Figure 1 shows changes in the value of the FTSE 100 over time.

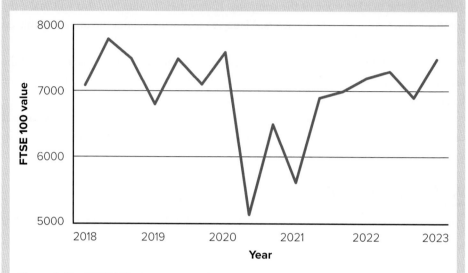

Figure 1 The FTSE 100 share price index. *Source:* www.londonstockexchange.com/indices/ftse-100?lang=en; adapted by the author.

Question

Consider why the FTSE 100 might have changed in the way that it has over the last few years.

Business insight 1.4 The market capitalization of Microsoft

The market capitalization of a company is the market value of all its shares. It shows how much it would cost to buy 100% control of the business.

The market capitalization of a business will change with the perceptions of investors of how well it is doing or is likely to do. In 2019 Microsoft became, once again, the world's most valuable company listed on a stock exchange having had a disappointing few years previously. Microsoft's market capitalization was over $1 trillion. This was an incredible turnaround because at one point Microsoft had been viewed as been a company in decline because it had failed to exploit the opportunities of social media and smartphones. This was said to be because Microsoft had remained too focused on Windows which had been at the centre of the company for years. When a new Chief Executive, Mr Nadella, came in, he deprioritized Windows and focused on 'the cloud'. He also changed the way Microsoft did business, encouraging staff to see suppliers as partners that Microsoft could collaborate with rather than continually push them for lower prices.

1.8 Mission statements

The owners and managers of an organization often want to express what it is they are there to do. They sometimes do this by producing a mission statement. A mission sets out the reason why a business exists at the moment.

Consider the following examples of mission statements:

- McKinsey is a management consultancy firm. 'Our mission is to help our clients make distinctive, lasting, and substantial improvements in their performance and to build a great firm that attracts, develops, excites, and retains exceptional people. We believe we will be successful if our clients are successful. Solving the hardest problems requires the best people. We think that the best people will be drawn to the opportunity to work on the hardest problems. We build our firm around that belief. These two parts of our mission reinforce each other and make our firm strong and enduring.'

- The mission of Alibaba, the Chinese online business, is 'to make it easy to do business anywhere. We enable businesses to transform the way they market, sell, and operate, and improve their efficiencies.'

- Amazon wants to 'be Earth's most customer-centric company.' Its mission is 'to continually raise the bar of the customer experience by using the internet and technology to help customers find, discover, and buy anything, and empower businesses and content creators to maximize their success.'

- The mission of IKEA, the Swedish home furnishings business, is 'to provide a better everyday life for people.'

- Nike's mission is to bring inspiration and innovation to every athlete* in the world (* if you have a body you are an athlete).

- Electronic Art which produces computer games such as FIFA, Battlefield, and The Sims says that 'everything we do is designed to inspire the world to play'.

- L'Oreal says that 'Our goal is to offer each and every person around the world the best of beauty in terms of quality, efficacy, safety, sincerity, and responsibility to satisfy all beauty needs and desires in their infinite diversity'.

- The mission of Fast Fashion Retailing which owns Uniglo is

  - To create truly great clothing with new and unique value, and to enable people all over the world to experience the joy, happiness, and satisfaction of wearing such great clothes

  - To enrich people's lives through our unique corporate activities, and to seek to grow and develop our company in unity with society.

Think about it

1. Think about your university—why does it exist? What are its priorities? is it focused mainly on teaching and learning/or research/or supporting businesses in the community?
2. What if the BBC changed its mission 'to entertain'; what effect might this have on the organization?

Key concepts

A **mission** sets out the reason why a business exists at the moment.

A **vision** is a view of what the business wants to be in the future.

Think about it

UK retailer John Lewis is a cooperative owned by its employees (called partners). What do you think its mission is?

[You can find out if you visit the 'About Us' section on John Lewis' website.]

1.8.1 What is the value of having a mission statement?

Owners and managers often write a mission to set out that they think is important about the business.

A mission statement can:

- Identify the plan, values, and cultures of the business. It can set out how the business wants to compete, how it wants to position itself, and how it wants employees to behave.

- Set out the relationship the business wants in relation to other groups such as employees, the community, suppliers, and shareholders.

- Unify people within the business so they know what the business stands for.

A mission statement is all about 'the big picture'. The process of producing a mission statement can in itself be useful. It brings together different stakeholder groups to get their view of what an organization is and what it should be. Having these conversations in the open can highlight differences and help shape an organization that has a clear sense of identify where employees know what it is they are supposed to do and why.

The true value of mission statements is determined by what actually happens within the business. Mission statements can be an impressive sounding statement but have no link to how people are actually expected to behave. On the other hand, the mission statement may drive what actually happens—what targets are set, how the performance of people is assessed, and how resources are allocated.

Think about it

Barclays is a bank owned by shareholders.

NatWest is a building society owned by people and organizations that save money in it.

How might this difference affect the decisions managers make?

Business insight 1.5   The flotation of Facebook

Facebook was set up at university. Its approach from the start was to build things. Then break them. Then try again . . . and again. This was known as 'the hacker way'. Mark Zuckerburg, the founder, believed that if you are not breaking things you are probably not moving fast enough. In 2012 the company was floated and shares sold to outside investors. Mark Zuckerburg was determined to keep the way that Facebook did things the same. He did not want investors' scrutiny and questioning to slow the business's innovative approach down.

The mission of Facebook, according to Zuckerburg, has always been 'to make the world more open and connected'; profits, he says, are secondary.

To ensure Facebook remained true to its mission Zuckerburg held on to 57% of the votes within Facebook.

Question

Why might selling shares to the public affect the mission of a business?

Source

www.bbc.com/news/technology-18116233

1.9 Vision statements

A vision is a view of what the owners want the business to become. It sets out the future 'vision' for the business. This can inspire and provide a sense of direction.

- British American Tobacco says: Our vision remains clear: while combustible tobacco products will remain at the core of our business for some time to come, we understand that long-term sustainability will be delivered by our transforming tobacco ambition.

- Sainsbury's, the UK retailer, says 'Our vision is to be the most trusted retailer, where people love to work and shop. We'll do this by putting our customers at the heart of everything we do and investing in our stores, our colleagues, and our channels to offer the best possible shopping experience.'

- EE, the telecommunications business, says 'Our vision is to provide the best network and best service so our customers trust us with their digital lives.'

Sometimes businesses produce both a mission and a vision statement; sometimes they combine the two. Sometimes they focus on one rather than the other.

What would you do?

You have just taken over as Managing Director of a large multinational electronics business. You want to produce a new mission statement for the business. How would you outline to your employees why this would be a useful thing to do?

The mission and vision statements are broad and often inspiring statements. They need to be turned into more specific objectives for managers to start planning exactly what to do.

1.10 Business objectives

The objectives of a business are quantifiable targets. The objectives set out what the business wants to achieve and when it wants to achieve it. For example, according to the *Financial Times*, in 2023 the Chinese fashion retailer Shein set an objective of doubling its revenue in the next two years, aiming to achieve nearly $60 billion of revenue per year.

Objectives are often expected to be SMART. This means they are:

- **S**pecific: they set out exactly what is the focus such as sales or profits.
- **M**easurable: they set out how much the desired change is or what the target is, e.g. £100,000.
- **A**greed: this means that those who have to achieve the objectives have agreed to them rather than being expected to achieve something forced on them.
- **R**ealistic: this means the target is believed to be achievable.
- **T**ime specific. This means it is clear when the target has to be achieved.

A business will usually have many different objectives and these will often be inter-linked. There is often the overall corporate objective which is linked to the mission. There are then functional objectives which are the targets each area of the business sets to help it achieve its overall targets. The relationship between the mission, corporate objectives, and functional objectives are shown in Figure 1.6. For example, to achieve an overall profit of £3.5 million within the next year it may be that sales have to increase by 20% and costs can only increase by 5%. To increase sales it may mean five stores must be open within six months. To cut costs by this much staff numbers may need to be reduced by 200 by the end of June. Each employee may have his/her own objective and together they work together to achieve the overall objectives of the organization.

Typical corporate objectives of business include:

- Sales growth. This is often seen as an important target. With more revenue more profit may come (depending on what is happening to costs). A greater volume of sales shows progress and a bigger business may have more power and a greater presence in the market.

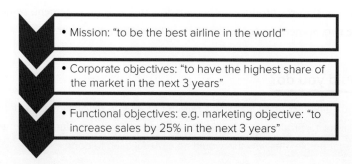

Figure 1.6 The relationship between mission, corporate, and functional objectives.
Source: Author.

Key concept

Market share measures the sales of one business or brand as a percentage of the total sales in a market.

- Market share. Simply setting a sales target may not be enough. Owners and managers may want to set a target for the sakes of the business (or one of its products) relative to the total sales in the market; this is called market share. By setting a market share target the business is ensuring its sales relative to others are increasing.

- Profits. This may be linked to sales growth but may also be linked to efforts to control costs. Profit is a very common measure of business success. Dividends can be paid out of profits to reward investors. Profit can be retained to finance business investment.

- Social objectives. These may relate to supporting charities, investing in the community, or helping disadvantaged groups in society.

- Environmental objectives. These may relate to areas such as emissions or noise.

- Employee objectives. This could relate to achieving certain rates of employee representation in the business, reducing the number of accidents, or increasing diversity within the workforce.

Can you now answer this question from the introductory case study?

What are the objectives of VW?

 ## Now you should know

- Businesses transform inputs into outputs.

- Businesses aim to add value during the transformation process.

- Managers plan, organize, coordinate, and control the use of resources.

- A company has its own legal identity and is owned by shareholders.

- Corporate governance refers to the oversight of the management of the business.

- A mission sets out why a business exists; a vision sets out what the business wants to be in the future.

- An objective is a quantifiable, time-specific target.

- The dividend per share is the amount of money paid out to shareholders for each share they hold as a reward for their investment; this is usually paid annually or twice a year.

- Dividend yield = ([dividend per share/share price] × 100); this represents the dividend per share as a percentage of the current share price.

- Income tax is the amount individuals have to pay on their earnings to the government as tax.

- Corporation tax is the amount businesses have to pay on their profits to the government as tax.

- A shareholder is an owner of a company; he/she owns a 'share' of the business.

- Shareholders have limited liability.

- A company is a business that has its own legal identity; it can own assets and be owed money.

 # Review questions

Quick check

1. State the difference between a private limited company and a public limited company.

2. Explain the difference between limited and unlimited liability.

3. State two reasons why people might buy shares.

4. Describe why effective corporate governance is important.

5. Explain the difference between a mission and an objective.

6. Outline the difference between the dividend per share and the dividend yield.

7. Explain the difference between a mission and an objective.

8. State two features of an effective objective.

Analysis

1. Analyse the advantages and disadvantages for a sole trader of forming a company.

2. Analyse the benefits of setting objectives for the different functions of a business.

3. Analyse the reasons why someone buys a share in a business.

Evaluation

1. Some people argue that 'limited liability' has been critical to the growth of businesses. What do you think?

2. Do you think you can train someone to be a good manager or do you think they are born with these skills?

3. Do you think mission statements are usually just a public relations exercise?

∿➙ Find out more

For more reading on management and corporate governance you might want to look at:

Boddy, D. (2019). *Management*. Harlow, United Kingdom: Pearson Education Limited.

Buchanan, D. A. and Huczynski, A. A. (2017). *Organizational Behaviour*, 9th edition. London: Pearson Publishing

Goergen, M. (2018). *Corporate Governance*: A Global Perspective. Cengage Learning

Robbins, S. P., Bergman, R., and Coulter, M. (2017). *Management*. Melbourne: Pearson Australia.

For more online research you could look at:

- The Drucker Institute which celebrates the work of Peter Drucker at www. drucker.institute
- Office of National Statistics (ONS).
  You can find out more about the number and type of businesses in the UK if you search for the Business Population Survey by the Office of National Statistics. You can find the ONS's website at www.ons.gov.uk

- Jim Collins
  Jim Collins has written some excellent, highly engaging books on what makes a successful company. You can find out more about Jim and his work at www. jimcollins.com/

- John Kotter
  Some writers think there is a difference between managing and leading. For example, it is argued that managing may focus more on managing the here and now; leading may focus more on the future. You can watch the famous business writer John Kotter talk about the difference between managing and leading on YouTube.
  You can find Kotter's website at www.kotterinc.com/

- Henry Mintzberg
  You can watch a video of Henry Mintzberg on You Tube. Search for 'Mintzberg on Managing'. Mintzberg's website can be found at www.mintzberg.org/

- Tom Peters
  Tom Peters is a world-famous management writer and speaker with some highly thought-provoking and inspiring ideas. Find out more at tompeters. com/

For more reading on study skills you might want to look at:

Mind map techniques: www2.open.ac.uk/students/skillsforstudy/mind-maps.php
Note-making skills: www2.open.ac.uk/students/skillsforstudy/notetaking-techniques.php
Cornell note taking technique: lsc.cornell.edu/how-to-study/taking-notes/cornell-note-taking-system/

☰ Bibliography

BlackRock (2022). *The Power of Capitalism*. https://www.blackrock.com/corporate/investor-relations/larry-fink-ceo-letter

Eisenmann, T. (2013). Entrepreneurship: A Working Definition. *Harvard Business Review*, Jan. hbr.org/2013/01/what-is-entrepreneurship

Fayol, H. (1917). Administration Industrielle et Générale : prévoyance, organisation, commandement, coordination, contrôle. H. Dunod et E. Pinat, Paris.

Hamel, G. and Zanini, M. (2018). The end of bureaucracy. *Harvard Business Review*, Nov–Dec.

McKinsey (n.d.). www.mckinsey.com/about-us/overview/our-mission-and-values

Mintzberg H. (1975). The manager's job: Folklore and fact. *Harvard Business Review*, Jul–Aug, 51.

Mintzberg, H. (1989). *Mintzberg on management: Inside our strange world of organizations*. Simon and Schuster.

Office for National Statistics (2019). Consumer price inflation basket of goods and services: 2019. Available at: www.ons.gov.uk/economy/inflationandpriceindices/articles/ukconsumerpriceinflationbasketofgoodsandservices/2019#the-shopping-basket

Office for National Statistics (2023). Consumer price inflation basket of goods and services. https://www.ons.gov.uk/economy/inflationandpriceindices/datasets/consumerpriceinflationbasketofgoodsandservices

Open University (n.d.). www.open.edu/openlearn/money-business/leadership-management/discovering-management/content-section-1.1.2

Rhodes, C. (2020). *Business Statistics*. [online] House of Commons Library. Available at: <https://commonslibrary.parliament.uk/

The Economist (2023). The Painful Development of India's startups. Available at: https://www.economist.com/business/2023/01/19/the-painful-development-of-indias-startups [Accessed 18 February 2023].

Ward, M. and Hutton, G. (2022). Business Statistics. [online] House of Commons Library. Available at: researchbriefings.parliament.uk/ResearchBriefing/Summary/SN06152

www.volkswagenag.com/en/InvestorRelations/shares/letter-to-our-shareholders.html

Chapter 2

Entrepreneurs and start-up planning

 ## Where are we now?

In this chapter we focus on individuals who identify a business opportunity and start up in business for themselves. Many people who study business go on to start a business themselves and this chapter should provide you with useful insights into the world of entrepreneurs.

Why am I studying this?

- You have a great idea for a business and want to know whether you have what it takes to be an entrepreneur. This chapter considers the characteristics of entrepreneurs.
- You are interested in starting up your own business and want to know some 'dos' and 'don'ts'.
- You admire people such as Bill Gates, Jack Ma, and Mark Zuckerburg who have started their own businesses, made a fortune and changed the world; you want to know how they did it!
- You want to understand the appeal of being an entrepreneur.
- You want to know more about the risks and challenges of being an entrepreneur.
- You want to understand why and how governments support entrepreneurs.

 ## Learning objectives

By the end of this chapter you should be able to

- Analyse the features of entrepreneurship
- Understand the different forms of risk facing entrepreneurs
- Analyse the motives of entrepreneurs
- Analyse the characteristics of a successful entrepreneur
- Evaluate the challenges of being an entrepreneur
- Analyse the financing and planning involved in a start-up
- Understand how entrepreneurs can protect their intellectual property

Introductory case study Entrepreneurship in Africa

Africa is a diverse geographical area, and recently greater emphasis has been placed on examining the role of entrepreneurship due to the significant rise of African entrepreneurs in the worldwide economy.

Entrepreneurship in Africa

Africa's entrepreneurship rate is said to be the highest in the world. According to the African Development Bank (AfDB) in 2020, 22% of Africa's working-age population are currently in the process of starting their own businesses. This growth is encouraged by greater access to markets around the world made possible by increased digitalization, greater awareness of entrepreneurship, and more of a culture of innovation and entrepreneurship within countries. Within an overall increase in the amount of entrepreneurship in Africa there are a number of trends.

1. **Younger entrepreneurs**

   Generation Zs (i.e. people born between 1995 and 2015) seem to have more interest than those before them in becoming entrepreneurs. This group of the population are more likely to see entrepreneurship as an option for their future careers than previous generations. More digital opportunities and more global opportunities create greater possibilities to succeed as an entrepreneur than any preceding generation has had. Although barriers exist such as limited access to finance, there is an ambitious group of Gen Zs ready to become entrepreneurs. These young entrepreneurs could not only create more jobs but also improve society as a whole and increase social mobility.

2. **A greater emphasis on social responsibility**

   Entrepreneurs can always claim to be socially responsible because they create jobs in their countries. However, what is happening recently is a more explicit focus by start-ups in Africa on helping their communities. The entrepreneurs themselves and their investors

Bethlemen Tilahun Alemu, founder of soleRebels. *Source:* soleRebels.

seem to want their start-ups to have a clear social impact. Bethlemen Tilahun Alemu's shoe company soleRebels (based in Ethiopia) is one example of this. soleRebels is an eco-friendly footwear business which uses green production methods and sustainable resources. Alemu's business also created hundreds of local jobs for people formerly living in poverty in Addis Ababa.

3. **More female entrepreneurs**

According to the World Bank, Africa is the only region in the world where there are more female than male entrepreneurs. Divine Ndhlukula is just one example. She is the founder and Managing Director of SECURICO, a security company she started in the late 90s in her cottage with four employees and very little capital. Today, SECURICO is one of the largest security firms in Zimbabwe, with more than 3500 employees. Although finance is often an issue (typically men have access to six times as much funding) the numbers of female-run start-ups keeps increasing. The difficulty in gaining finance to start up also is made worse by challenges gaining funding later for growth. However, there have been a number of recent financial initiatives to help women entrepreneurs raise money. For example, the African Development Bank's Affirmative Finance Action for Women in Africa (AFAWA) initiative supports investment projects that exclusively for women in Africa.

4. **More specialized business education**

There is increasing provision of business education at schools, colleges, and higher education in Africa. This increased focus on studying business aims is giving more people the knowledge and skills they need to be successful entrepreneurs.

Challenges to entrepreneurship in Africa

Economic growth comes from three possible sources: (i) an increase in the amount of inputs of factors of production such as land, labour, and capital or the quality of these factors; (ii) improvements in the way in which these resources are used; and (iii) innovation creating new products and new uses for products that already exist. The biggest differences in the growth of developed and developing countries is due to differences in innovation. Entrepreneurship is an important source of innovation and so if this entrepreneurship can be encouraged this may stimulate growth in the economy as a whole.

In Africa there are some governmental and infrastructure factors that limit growth of entrepreneurship. These factors include corruption, a poor infrastructure system (including the digital infrastructure such as broadband), high levels of unemployment, and inadequate education provision.

According to the World Bank governments in Africa need to consider how they: (i) support innovation to develop new products and processes; (ii) encourage entrepreneurs and develop entrepreneurial skills; (iii) make finance more readily available to entrepreneurs; and (iv) develop networking systems to enable entrepreneurs to link to others such as other entrepreneurs to share ideas and experiences and investors to gain access to funds.

Sources

ieg.worldbankgroup.org/sites/default/files/Data/reports/innovation_eval.pdf

www.modernghana.com/news/1000411/4-entrepreneurship-trends-impacting-african-busine.html

www.mckinsey.com/featured-insights/middle-east-and-africa/africas-overlooked-business-revolution

https://www.solerebels.com/pages/about

Introductory case study questions

Think about the following questions as you read through the chapter. You may not yet be able to answer these questions, but as we progress through the chapter, we will revisit them at key stages. By the end of the chapter, you should be confident in answering them.

1. Why do you think people want to be entrepreneurs?
2. Why do you think entrepreneurship is so high in Africa?
3. Where do entrepreneurs tend to get funding for their ideas?
4. Why do you think governments are keen to support entrepreneurs?
5. How can a government support entrepreneurs?
6. How can entrepreneurs raise finance?
7. What do you think entrepreneurs can do to improve their chances of their business surviving?
8. What do you think determines the level of entrepreneurship in an economy?

Critical thinking

1. The introductory case highlights the role that governments can play in influencing the level of entrepreneurship in a country. To what extent do you think the number of successful entrepreneurs in an economy depends on the government?
2. The introductory case focuses on Africa. To what extent do you think the reasons for becoming an entrepreneur are likely to vary around the world? Why?

2.1 Entrepreneurs

The business world is constantly changing with new businesses starting up and new products and services being offered. A driving force for change and progress comes from the entrepreneurs in an economy. Entrepreneurs are risk takers who set up a new business. They find new ways of meeting customer needs, and sometimes they identify needs customers didn't even know they had. They create, they innovate, and they move economies forward. It is true that many entrepreneurs fail in their first few years but there are others who go on to create huge businesses. People such as Mark Zuckerburg, who founded Facebook, Jack Dorsey, who founded Twitter, now known as X, and Elon Musk of Tesla, are well-known names but there are thousands of other highly successful entrepreneurs around the world. For example, Akiko Naka, the founder of Wantedly, a social networking service for professionals, is the youngest female founder ever to take a company public in Japan. Gaurav Gupta is a co-founder of Zomato, which helps you order food from restaurants and book tables and is now available as a service in 24 countries and over 1000 cities. Henry Motte-Muñoz is the founder of edukasyon.ph which now helps over 10 million students in the Philippines a year find courses they want to study. Entrepreneurs bring new ideas to fruition and create more choice for consumers—just look at this list of

Shiho Azuma, CEO of Lily MedTech Inc. *Source:* EY.

some of the winners of management consultancy EY's Asia Pacific Winning Women Entrepreneur Awards in 2020 to get a sense of the variety of business ideas that entrepreneurs bring to consumers.

- Rina Akimoto, Vivid Garden Inc. (Japan)**:** An e-commerce business that enables individuals and restaurants direct access to purchase farmers' produce
- Shiho Azuma, Lily MedTech Inc. (Japan): A business selling a medical imaging device to detect breast cancer without exposure to radiation
- Grace Yehuai Chen, Grace Chen (China): A high-end fashion brand based on Chinese culture
- Brianne West, Ethique (New Zealand): A sustainable cosmetics company which produces plastic-free, ethical and cruelty-free cosmetics and personal care products.

2.1.1 Entrepreneurship

To be successful, entrepreneurs need to master the skills of entrepreneurship. Entrepreneurship refers to the capability to exploit successfully innovative ideas and make them commercially successful. According to the venture capitalist Fred Wilson entrepreneurship is the art of turning an idea into a business. At Harvard Business School the definition of entrepreneurship that is used was formulated by Professor Howard Stevenson. According to Stevenson and Sahlman (1991), entrepreneurship can be defined as 'the pursuit of opportunity beyond resources controlled'.

Think about it

Entrepreneurship largely depends on potential entrepreneurs identifying opportunities that may lead to them creating a business. The 2019 Global Entrepreneurship Monitor (GEM) research shows that Japan has the lowest proportion of adults identifying good start-up opportunities, at around one in 10. By comparison, almost nine out of 10 adults in Poland and eight out of 10 in Sweden and India see good opportunities to start a business.

Why do you think these differences occur between countries?

Key features of Stevenson's definition of entrepreneurship include:

- The word **'pursuit'**. This suggests there is a clear focus on a business opportunity and highlights a sense of urgency. Entrepreneurs chase the opportunities that exist.
- **'Opportunity'**. An opportunity is defined by Stevenson as 'a proposed venture to sell a product or service for which customers are willing to pay more than the required investments and operating costs.' Entrepreneurs discover opportunities throughout their personal and professional lives. They identify ways they think they can deliver value to customers. There are many different types of business opportunity open to entrepreneurs. These include: 1) developing a truly innovative product; 2) developing a new business model; 3) creating a better or cheaper version of an existing product; or 4) targeting an existing product to new sets of customers.
- **'Beyond resources controlled'**. This highlights that there are resource constraints facing entrepreneurs. At the start of a new business venture, the founders control only their own human, social, and financial capital. There is a lot not under their control!

2.1.2 Risks

Given that entrepreneurs are pursuing a new opportunity while lacking access to many resources, they face considerable risk. Risk means there is a danger that something can go wrong. Risk occurs in business because there is the possibility that the actual situation is different from what was expected.

The risks for entrepreneurs can come in different forms such as:

- Demand risk. This relates to the danger that demand won't be high enough. Entrepreneurs are often trying out new ideas and it can be difficult to estimate what demand will actually exist.
- Technology risk. This type of risk occurs if new technology is needed. The risk is that it may not work. An entrepreneur may have a new way of doing things or a new idea for a product. In reality, the technology may not work as or when expected.

Key concepts

Entrepreneurs are risk takers who set up a new business.

Entrepreneurship refers to the capability to exploit successfully innovative ideas and make them commercially successful.

Risk means there is a danger that something can go wrong.

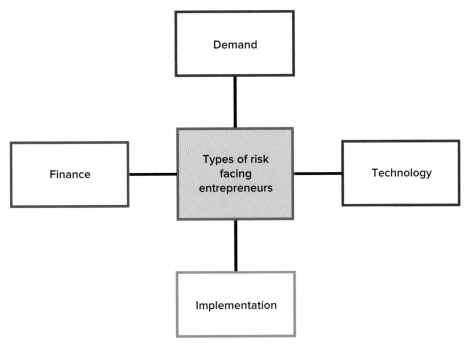

Figure 2.1 Examples of the different types of risks which entrepreneurs face. *Source:* Author.

- Implementation risk. This relates to the danger that the idea won't be implemented effectively. What may seem like a great idea may be difficult to actually bring about and turn into reality.

- Finance risk. This relates to the danger that sufficient finance may not be available to keep the business going and pursue the opportunity. New businesses often struggle with raising and managing finance and so can run out of funds.

The different types of risk faced by entrepreneurs are shown in Figure 2.1.

2.1.3 Why do people start up in business?

People will start up in business for a variety of reasons. A recent report by the management consultancy PWC on the motives for starting a business showed the key reasons were:

1. **To pursue an interest or passion.**
   People may well have a hobby and want to turn this into their business; for example, someone who enjoys cooking might open a catering business or a pet lover might start a dog-walking business.

2. **To run their own operations.**
   Some people prefer to run their own businesses and make their own decisions. Rather than be told what to do, some individuals would like to have the freedom to decide for themselves.

3. **To pursue an opportunity in the market.**
   The ideas for new businesses often come when someone is dissatisfied with what is being provided in the market already or cannot get what they want. Imagine you want a certain style of clothing but cannot find anywhere that provides this;

this is the opportunity to provide it yourself by starting a business. New opportunities also come through new technology. For example, one of the world's youngest billionaires is the entrepreneur Vijay Chehkar Sharma. Vijay set up the online financial services business Paytm in India in 2011. Technology allowed him to provide banking, insurance, and other financial services to hundreds of millions of people in India.

4. **To take a new direction in their lives.**
   Some people may be forced to rethink their careers because they have lost their previous job. Others may rethink because they are bored with their existing job or just want a change.

5. **To create a job.**
   Some people may start up because they need work and cannot easily find a job another way.

6. **To earn money and become rich!**
   An advantage of being your own boss is you can keep all the rewards. The Global Entrepreneurship Monitor (GEM) study of 2019 found that more than eight out of 10 entrepreneurs starting a new business in Iran, Qatar, Pakistan, India, and Italy agree with the motive to build great wealth or income. Assuming the business is successful an entrepreneur may end up with more earnings than she would have done being employed by someone else. However, remember that very few new businesses survive more than a few years let alone generate high earnings.

7. **To address a problem in their social community.**
   People may set up businesses to improve the community they are part of. For example, people may see that their village lacks a shop or a café and use this opportunity to help by setting up a business to meet this need.

8. **To address a fundamental problem in society.**
   Entrepreneurs may want to contribute to society in general. For example, someone might set up a business to raise money to help those with mental health problems or those who rely on food donations from others. In the 2019 Global Entrepreneurship Monitor study there were some countries such as South Africa, Guatemala, Panama, and India where 7 out of 10 entrepreneurs mentioned a social purpose involved in their desire to be an entrepreneur. Social entrepreneurship refers to new enterprises set up to benefit society. For example, an entrepreneur might want to help a particular group that is disadvantaged or to help her local community. The objective of this type of enterprise is to help society rather than to make a profit.

9. **To continue a family tradition.**
   It may be that someone's family has been in business for many years and she is expected to continue this tradition. Family businesses are very common in many countries and continuing a family tradition is a particularly strong motive for becoming an entrepreneur in Poland and India.

The various motives for people starting their own business in Europe in PWC's 2018 study are highlighted in Figure 2.2.

Motivation to start own business

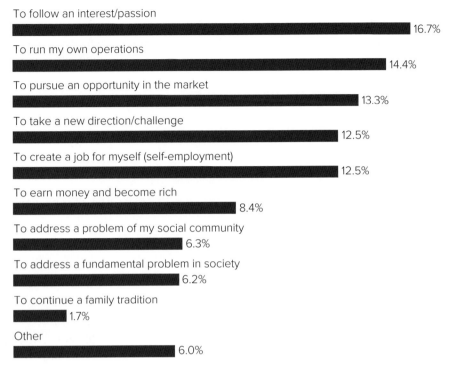

To follow an interest/passion — 16.7%

To run my own operations — 14.4%

To pursue an opportunity in the market — 13.3%

To take a new direction/challenge — 12.5%

To create a job for myself (self-employment) — 12.5%

To earn money and become rich — 8.4%

To address a problem of my social community — 6.3%

To address a fundamental problem in society — 6.2%

To continue a family tradition — 1.7%

Other — 6.0%

Figure 2.2 Why people start up in business in Europe according to PWC study.

Source: PWC.

Business insight 2.1 Starting up: Motives and Fears

In the GEM 2019 survey of entrepreneurs it was found that in 38 out of the 50 economies, more than half of the adults in the population felt they had the skills, knowledge, and experience to start a new business. However, in Egypt, Jordan, Pakistan, Israel, Portugal, and Croatia there were significant proportions of people who felt they could identify an opportunity but did not want to pursue it for fear of failure. In Chile, nearly 75% of adults believed they had the capability to start a business but at the same time nearly 60% of those who could identify a good opportunity did not want to pursue it because they were worried about failure.

In terms of the motivations driving entrepreneurs this differed around the world. More than eight out of 10 people starting a new business in Iran, Qatar, Pakistan, India, and Italy said that their motive was to build great wealth or income. This compares to less than two people in 10 in Norway or Poland. These are indicators that creating wealth is not the only reason why entrepreneurs set up in business.

Continuing a family tradition is stated as a motive for starting the business by more than eight out of 10 entrepreneurs in Poland and India, but less than one in 10 entrepreneurs in the United Kingdom or Republic of Korea. Again, this demonstrates how much motives vary between regions.

▶

Questions

Why might people worry about starting a business and failing?

Why do you think the main motives for starting up in business differ between countries?

Source

gemconsortium.org/report/gem-2019-2020-global-report

Think about it

In the Global Entrepreneurship Monitor (GEM) survey of 2021 there are four economies in which the female rate of entrepreneurship exceeds the male rate; these were Togo, Indonesia, Qatar, and Poland. The biggest differences between male and female entrepreneurship occurred in Serbia, Lithuania, Croatia, Latvia, and the UAE.

In 37 of the 49 countries surveyed the involvement of the 18 to 34 age group was higher than the participation of the 25–64 age range.

Question

Why do you think these gender and age disparities exist when it comes to entrepreneurship?

Can you now answer this question from the introductory case study?

Why do you think people want to be entrepreneurs?

2.1.4 What makes a successful entrepreneur?

There are many entrepreneurs who have gone on to create extraordinarily successful businesses. Think of Jeff Bezos who set up Amazon, Amancio Ortega who set up Zara, Jack Ma of Alibaba, and Steve Jobs of Apple. Not surprisingly, would-be entrepreneurs, but also investors and governments, would like to be able to identify what it is that made these entrepreneurs successful. After all there are many more who have failed, or only been moderately successful, so what makes the difference between success and failure?

There have been many studies over the years trying to identify the characteristics of an entrepreneur and sometimes the results are not clear-cut. One well-known study by the Massachusetts Institute of Technology (MIT) by Jeffrey Timmons and colleagues (Timmons et al. 1977) identified 14 important entrepreneurial characteristics of successful enterprise owners.

These characteristics of an entrepreneur are:

1. drive and energy
2. self-confidence
3. high initiative and personal responsibility
4. internal locus of control
5. tolerance of ambiguity

Key concept

A **high internal locus of control** means that entrepreneurs believe that their behaviour determines what happens to them and that they can control their own behaviour.

6. low fear of failure

7. moderate risk taking

8. long-term involvement

9. money as a measure of success not merely an end

10. use of feedback

11. continuous pragmatic problem solving

12. use of resources

13. self-imposed standards

14. clear goal setting.

Few entrepreneurs are likely to possess all of the traits above but strengths in one area may compensate for weaknesses in others.

One quality that successful entrepreneurs are said to have is known as a high internal locus of control. This means that entrepreneurs believe that their behaviour determines what happens to them and that they can control their own behaviour. This belief is linked to the need for autonomy and personal independence expressed by many entrepreneurs as their prime motivation for setting up their own firms (Gray, 1998).

The concept of internal locus of control implies that entrepreneurs believe the outcome of an event or situations can be affected by their intervention. They believe that they have the skills and the ability to intervene in a situation to influence the outcome positively. Whereas some people may think that things happen to them, entrepreneurs think they can make things happen and influence the outcomes.

Entrepreneurs tend to want to get involved because they think this can have positive effects. A belief in the internal locus of control is regarded by many as a central aspect of the entrepreneur's self-concept.

The proportion of adults in different countries who think they have the skills, experience, and knowledge to be an entrepreneur is shown in 'Analysing the business data 2.1'.

Identifying a business opportunity

The famous Austrian economist Joseph Schumpeter was writing in the 1930s and 1940s, but his theory of the ways an entrepreneur can find opportunities to create new businesses are still relevant today (Schumpeter 1934, 1942). According to Schumpeter, business opportunities can be created by:

1. using a new technology to produce a new product

2. using an existing technology to produce a new product

3. using an existing technology to produce an old product but in a new way

4. finding a new supply of resources

5. developing a new market for an existing product.

Analysing the business data 2.1 The proportion of adults in different countries who think they have the skills, experience, and knowledge to set up in business

Entrepreneurs need to identify an opportunity but for them to pursue it they need to feel they have the skills, experience, and knowledge to take the risk. Figure 1 shows the proportion of people in different countries who feel they have these qualities.

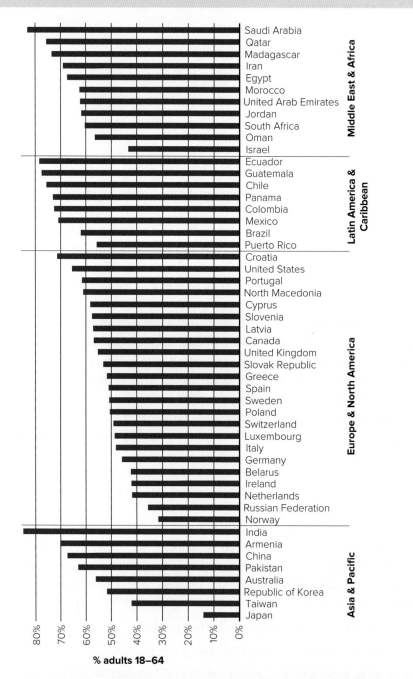

Figure 1 The proportion of adults in different countries who think they have the skills, experience and knowledge to set up in business. *Source:* Gem Consortium.

2

Questions

Why do you think the proportion of people who think they have the knowledge, skills, and experience to start a new business varies so much from country to country?

How could a government increase the proportion of people in its country who feel they have these qualities?

Source

Gem global entrepreneurship monitor. (n.d.). Retrieved April 04, 2021, from https://gemconsortium. org/report/gem-2019-2020-global-report

Think about it

Do you think you have the qualities to be a successful entrepreneur? What evidence do you have of this? If not, what qualities do you think you are missing?

Do you think you could develop these skills?

The ideas for these new opportunities can come from many sources including listening to what others are saying, as this may identify where they are dissatisfied, watching and observing the word around you, and analysing a situation to identify a new solution.

An opportunity may be internal—it comes from within the entrepreneur—or external, which is where it comes from circumstances outside the entrepreneur. For example, an entrepreneur setting up a business linked to her hobby is internal; an opportunity that was created by the COVID-19 pandemic, such as personalized face masks, is external. External opportunities can be created in many ways; for example, a decline in the economy may create an opportunity for budget items or a greater social focus on environmental issues may create the opportunity for a product made from recyclable items.

According to the famous business writer Peter Drucker (1993) an entrepreneur is someone who 'always searches for change, responds to it, and exploits it as an opportunity.' Entrepreneurs want change because this is where their opportunities lie.

In terms of the type of business entrepreneurs set up this can vary considerably Economies vary considerably between regions and will change over time as economies change. People will tend to start their business in a sector where there is easy access to resources whether these be natural resources or people or money and where there is a growing market with easy access. Other factors such as government support may also play a role in the sectors where entrepreneurship thrives.

Think about it

Can you think of a recent example for each of Schumpeter's five ways of creating business opportunities?

Do you have any ideas for a new business?

Why do you think this business is needed?

Into which of Schumpeter's five categories do you think your idea fits?

The GEM Adult Population Survey (APS) analyses entrepreneurship in four broad sectors:

- Extractive, including agriculture and mining
- Transformative, including manufacturing and logistics
- Business Services, including ICT and professional services
- Consumer Services, such as retailing, restaurants, and personal services.

Of the 50 economies examined in 2019, 29 had less than 5% of their new entrepreneurs in the Extractive sector. However, there are significant variations; for example, one in four or more entrepreneurs started in the extractive sector in Madagascar and Armenia.

The results for the Transformative sector have greater variation, from around one in 10 in Switzerland and Germany to one in four in Latvia and Egypt.

Consumer Services are a popular sector for entrepreneurs because they are relatively low-cost and with low entry barriers (for example, coffee shops, taxi businesses, and hairdressers). However, these markets are highly competitive, with low profit margins and considerable movement in and out of them. New entrepreneurs starting up in consumer services are often at the expense of an existing business.

By comparison, Business Services are usually more technology or knowledge intensive; this makes the sector more difficult to enter but once in businesses tend to last longer.

Emerging economies tend to have lower proportions of Business Services entrepreneurs; less than one in 10 entrepreneurs are in Business Services in many countries such as Madagascar, Egypt, Jordan, Morocco, South Africa, Armenia, Pakistan, Mexico, Brazil, Ecuador, Guatemala, the Russian Federation, and Saudi Arabia.

Feasibility study

Once a possible business idea is identified entrepreneurs will want to assess its feasibility. A feasibility analysis determines whether a business idea is viable. It involves an initial evaluation of the proposal, which is undertaken to decide whether to pursue the idea or not. A feasibility analysis will consider factors such as the feasibility of producing the product, what this will cost and the likely levels of demand at different price points. It will consider the attractiveness of the industry and the target market as well as allowing the entrepreneur to evaluate whether she has sufficient managerial experience. What may be right for one person to pursue may not be right for everyone. The end result of a feasibility study is a decision whether to continue developing the business idea.

Assuming the feasibility study shows that the concept has potential, the next stage for an entrepreneur is often raising the finance needed to develop the idea further.

2.1.5 How do entrepreneurs raise finance?

In theory, there are many possible sources of finance for entrepreneurs. However, the funds that are actually available will depend on the entrepreneur and attitude of financial institutions to entrepreneurship. For many entrepreneurs this will be their first business and they may lack experience or a proven track record. Banks may be reluctant to lend in this situation because they perceive the risk is too high. This means many entrepreneurs have to self-finance. They use their own savings or are financed by friends and family. This is an

Business insight 2.2 The story of two gym entrepreneurs: Julian Torres and Fitpal

Julian Torres is the entrepreneur behind Fitpal, an app that links hundreds of gyms in Colombia. Torres is also the author of a best-selling book 'La Estupidez Colectiva' ('The Collective Stupidity') which, he claims, is the first book on start-ups in Colombia. Torres' book aims to dismiss any idea that there are few problems when starting up a business.

Before his business success Torres had a number of failures himself. When he was at university Torres dreamt of being a rock star but his band's singles failed to sell on any scale. An attempt to make money from city tours also failed as did a restaurant he set up. One of his classic mistakes was trying to sell heated toilet seats from South Korea back home in Colombia. The only problem was that the size didn't match Colombian toilets! However, perseverance and a continual search for 'the right idea' eventually led to Fitpal. This is an application that, through various subscription plans, gives customers access to a network of gyms and fitness centres. It offers face-to-face or virtual classes at more than 700 gyms located in 13 cities in Colombia. Torres describes the service as being like Netflix for gyms; you can book the type of class you want at any gym and then stream the class online.

Fitpal's services also include:

- Physical services such as access to classes in: functional, rumba, dance, boxing, and nutrition.
- Emotional services such as meditation, coaching, and yoga.
- Community services such as family cooking and entertainment spaces.

According to Julian Torres 'everyone has ideas, but only some have the courage to put them to the test.' He felt the time was right in Colombia for his business idea. According

Julian Torres, CSO and Co-Founder of Fitpal. *Source:* Julian Torres.

▶

to a 2017 survey by the Ministry of Health, 60% of the adult population in Colombia suffered from obesity and, therefore, were more prone to some illnesses. This meant there was a target population to whom he could appeal. Torres' research also showed that more than half of the people leave their gym because they get bored of the equipment and the same exercises and trainers. If Torres could offer much more choice to gym users he felt this would prove attractive; he was right. Like Netflix, Fitpal uses technology to analyse customers' behaviours and develop what the business offers as it learns more about them.

According to Torres the key to success as an entrepreneur includes 'resilience, discipline, understanding that failures can produce positive results, changes in perspective, and more efficient business models that last over time.'

Ben Francis and Gymshark

In 2020 Ben Francis sold his sports clothing business Gymshark for around £1bn. He was 28 years old. His stake in the business was worth around £700m.

Ben had started Gymshark from his parents' garage in 2012 when he was 19. To help finance his business Ben worked for Pizza Hut at night delivering pizzas. Ben started the business because he couldn't find sportswear that appealed to him. Along with his brother and some friends he bought a sewing machine and screen printer, and started to make gym vests and t-shirts. By 2020 the business had 499 staff and offices in the UK, Hong Kong, and Denver, Colorado. It manufactured all over the world.

One reason for the company's success is its large social media following. It has 4.6 million followers on Instagram. Ben says that it was one of the first businesses to sponsor influencers. The coronavirus pandemic in 2020 also helped. With lockdowns in many countries it led to more people running, cycling, and doing workouts at home than before and more people ordering sportswear online.

Ben's aim is to make the brand a global phenomenon.

Question

Do we learn anything about what it takes to be a successful entrepreneur from the case studies above?

Sources

www.ft.com/content/6122628d-a309-4c33-a664-3fc799b0dee8

www.panamericanworld.com/revista/startups/julian-torres/

www.bbc.co.uk/news/business-53781515

attractive way of financing a business idea for an entrepreneur because it means she keeps full control of the business (and any rewards) and doesn't pay interest. However, it may restrict the entrepreneur's options as there may be limited funds available.

Other sources of finance for entrepreneurs include:

- **Business angels**
  These are wealthy individuals who invest their own funds to start-up businesses in return for part ownership. The entrepreneur has to be willing to give up some control.

- **Venture capitalists**

   Venture capitalists also fund start-ups but unlike business angels they do not use their own money; venture capitalists use investment funds from a range of investors. Venture capitalists will want a proportion of the ownership of the business in return for these funds. As with businesses angels the advantage to an entrepreneur of using venture capitalists is that she can gain access to their experience, their contacts, and network. However, the entrepreneur does lose some control of their business.

- **Bank loans**

   If a business takes out a loan it means it borrows a sum of money for a fixed period of time and pays interest on the amount borrowed. The advantage of this form of finance is that the business does not lose any control to the bank. The bank wants to be paid back but does not get directly involved in the running of the business. The problem with financing the business via a loan is that the entrepreneur is committed to the payment of interest regardless of how well the business is doing.

- **Crowdfunding**

   This occurs when an entrepreneur advertises her business proposal online and many different individual investors commit money to fund the idea in return for a share of the business.

- **Government funding**

   Governments are often eager to support new businesses and may provide some initial start-up money for selected projects or in selected regions.

The advantages and disadvantages of different forms of finance for entrepreneurs are shown in Table 2.1.

The sources of funds used by entrepreneurs in Europe in 2019 according to a study by management consultants, PWC, is shown in Figure 2.3.

Table **2.1** Advantages and disadvantages of different forms of finance for entrepreneurs

Source of finance	Advantage	Disadvantage
Own finances	No interest payments and keep complete control of the business; keep all the rewards	May not have the funds available; may limit plans
Loan	Do not lose any ownership or control; fixed repayments	Have to pay interest regardless of how the business is doing
Business angel/ venture capital	Do not have fixed repayments (usually); can gain from advice and expertise of the angel/venture capitalist	Lose control of some of the business. The angel/venture capitalist usually want some ownership and influence on decisions made
Crowdfunding	Tests public reaction to the idea May get investment from people who are not traditional investors	May not appeal to enough people Shows idea to the public before it is developed so need to ensure it is protected

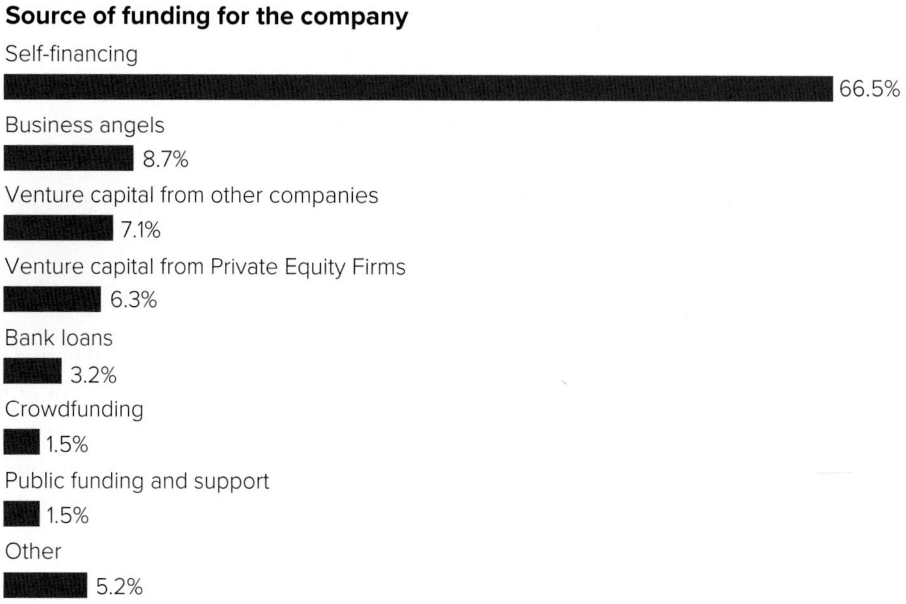

Source of funding for the company

Self-financing

66.5%

Business angels

8.7%

Venture capital from other companies

7.1%

Venture capital from Private Equity Firms

6.3%

Bank loans

3.2%

Crowdfunding

1.5%

Public funding and support

1.5%

Other

5.2%

Figure 2.3 Sources of finance for European entrepreneurs. *Source:* PricewaterhouseCoopers.

Can you now answer this question from the introductory case study?

How can entrepreneurs raise finance?

What would you do?

You are trying to raise money for your new business. Would you take out a loan rather than use venture capital? Explain your reasoning.

2.1.6 What determines the level of entrepreneurship in an economy?

According to a study by the Organisation of Economic Cooperation and Development (OECD) the critical factors affecting entrepreneurship within an economy are:

The regulatory framework

The nature of government rules and regulations will affect the ease of starting up in business. In some countries such as Cuba and China private enterprise was not allowed by the government until relatively recently. The amount and nature of regulations affect how long and how easy it is for a business to start up. Entrepreneurs often complain of the paperwork required to start up (sometimes referred to as 'red tape'). For example, according to the World Bank, in 2020 there were 12 procedures required to set up a business in Algeria.

Market conditions

The size and growth of the market will influence the appeal of a market. For example, highly competitive markets with some large well-established businesses, markets in decline, or markets with high entry costs are not likely to be attractive to entrepreneurs. By comparison, start-ups might be more common in a growing market than in an economy facing decline.

Access to finance

The availability of finance will be important to start-ups. Entrepreneurship is more likely if there is a good banking system and if there are financial institutions willing and able to take the risk to invest in new businesses.

Creation and diffusion of knowledge

This refers to the business environment in terms of the support for innovation and research and development. For example, if governments fund research and ensure adequate protection for their ideas this will encourage start-ups.

Entrepreneurial capabilities

This refers to the quality of the education system and the training provided for entrepreneurs. The better the business education system the more likely it is that entrepreneurship will flourish.

An entrepreneurship culture

This refers to the culture of society. For example, is being an entrepreneur and being in business regarded as a 'good thing'? Are people encouraged to set up their own business? Is failure accepted and understood or does it prevent you from trying again?

Other factors

Other factors to consider that will affect the level of entrepreneurship in a country include:

- The taxes on the profits of business; this will affect how appealing it is to set up and run a business
- The availability of resources such as skilled labour and energy
- The infrastructure of the region or country as a whole such as the ease of transporting items around, the availability of good broadband
- The extent to which corruption exists which can obviously make it more difficult to do business in any fair way.

The ease of setting up in business in different countries is measured in an Ease of Starting a Business Index produced by the World Bank. Information on this index is given in Analysing the Business Data 2.2. The ease of doing business will change over time. This is highlighted in Business Insight 2.3 on entrepreneurs in China which highlights how it has become much easier to start a private business in that country in the last 50 years.

Analysing the business data 2.2 The ease of starting a business

The data in Table 1 below from the World Bank shows the ease of starting a business and the ease of doing business in different countries. It is ranked by the easiest countries in which to start a business.

Table 1 The ease of doing business in different countries

Economy	Ease of Doing Business Rank	Starting a Business
New Zealand	1	1
Georgia	6	2
Singapore	2	3
Canada	22	3
Hong Kong SAR, China	4	5
Jamaica	75	6
Australia	18	7
Armenia	41	8
Azerbaijan	25	9

Questions

Why do you think the ease of starting a business varies between countries?

What might be the impact of this data for a) entrepreneurs b) consumers c) governments?

What else would you want to know about this data?

Source

World Bank. (2021). Retrieved April 04, 2021, from http://www.doingbusiness.org/en/rankings

Can you now answer this question from the introductory case study?

What do you think determines the level of entrepreneurship in an economy?

Business insight 2.3 Entrepreneurs in China

The People's Republic of China allowed its first private business in 1980 when a street seller, Zhang Huamei, registered her stall to sell buttons and toys in Wenzhou. Since then, the Chinese government has made it clear what people are not allowed to produce or sell, such as tobacco, and then let entrepreneurs operate within a clear framework of rules. The result in the past 40 years has been a huge expansion of the private sector. By 2017 close to 6m businesses were registered; this was more than three times the number in 2010. Private firms now account for nearly 60% of national income and nearly 80% of urban employment. In Wenzhou, government officials claim that 99% of the region's businesses are now privately owned and one in five locals has set up a company.

However, the failure rate of new businesses is high. The Asian Development Bank believes that the average life expectancy of small businesses in China is less than four

Part 1

years; this, according to *The Economist*, is half that seen in America. Research by Renmin University in Beijing in 2016 found that only 2% of graduates who began a first business succeeded. Yet the same survey found that four in five still wanted to try their hand at starting one. Partly this is because they are inspired by successful entrepreneurs such as Jack Ma of Alibaba and Pony Ma of Tencent. Would-be entrepreneurs are also encouraged by the value that some start-ups have achieved. China has 206 privately held companies valued at over $1bn. This is more than any other country.

Question

What benefits do you think entrepreneurs bring to the Chinese economy?

Source

The Economist (2020). Private companies have put down strong roots in China. Retrieved April 04, 2021, from https://www.economist.com/business/2020/04/30/private-companies-have-put-down-strong-roots-in-china

Entrepreneurs and governments

Entrepreneurs create new products and new ways of doing things. They create jobs and help stimulate economic growth. They challenge existing ways of doing business and existing providers, ensuring there is competition to win customers, which helps ensure efficiency and quality. Amazon, Tata, Bitcoin, Skype, Quora, SnapChat, Alibaba, Uber, AirBnB, and Tik Tok were all set up by entrepreneurs. Governments are usually eager to encourage entrepreneurs because of the potential benefits that they can provide for an economy.

The ways that governments might encourage entrepreneurship include:

- subsidies to encourage start-ups
- advice and guidance for entrepreneurs
- investment in business and entrepreneurship education at school and university
- a reduction in the regulations that might make it difficult for businesses to start up

As part of this effort to promote entrepreneurship governments will want to promote an entrepreneurial culture within the country. This means creating a business environment where it is easy to set up in business and where entrepreneurs are valued. This requires an acceptance of failure by other businesses, friends, and banks; entrepreneurs take risks and some failure is inevitable—what is important is that the business environment allows them to try again rather than making it very difficult to do so.

Key concept

An **entrepreneurial culture** in a country means there is a business environment where it is easy to set up in business and where entrepreneurs are valued.

Can you now answer this question from the introductory case study?

Why do you think governments are keen to support entrepreneurs?

Business insight 2.4 The focus on start-ups in South Korea

In South Korea the government is placing a great deal of emphasis on start-ups to help drive economic growth. The government has invested huge sums of money into supporting potential entrepreneurs. It has encouraged banks and the massive conglomerates (called chaebol) such as Samsung and Hyundai to do the same. The government has made it easy for small businesses to borrow money, guaranteeing a large portion of bank loans.

The aim of the government in South Korea is to support the long-term growth of the economy. In the past this growth has come from the conglomerates but this has not been the case in recent years and the government see entrepreneurs as the solution.

The South Korean economy faces a number of structural problems in relation to entre- preneurs. It has a rapidly ageing population and a shrinking working age population. It struggles to finance the pensions for its older population. To maintain, let alone improve, its welfare provision the government needs growth that will increase its tax revenue. Exports still account for over two-fifths of national income and are dominated by the *chaebol*, with semi-conductors, cars, and smartphones being the most important products for export. However, all of these are vulnerable both to competition from abroad and to the introduction of trade barriers.

The recent government focus on start-ups has already had a significant impact. In 2016 there were only 80 start-ups in South Korea that had raised more than $1m from in- vestors. In 2020 there were nearly 700 start-ups, including around 200 that have raised more than $10m.

The culture of society in South Korea is also said to be changing. Joining the civil ser- vice or a chaebol are no longer the only 'acceptable' careers. This is helped by the exam- ples of successful entrepreneurs, such as Bom Kim of Coupang and Bang Si-hyuk of Big Hit Entertainment.

Questions

Why do you think the South Korean government is eager to promote entrepreneurship within the country?

How do you think the South Korean government could encourage entrepreneurship?

Source

www.economist.com/special-report/2020/04/08/startups-offer-a-different-future-for-south-koreas-economy

2.1.7 What makes an entrepreneur successful?

In 1974 Jeffry Timmons published a highly respected book on entrepreneurship called *New Venture Creation: Entrepreneurship for the 21st Century*. The Timmons Model of Entrepre- neurship identifies three critical factors in entrepreneurship: opportunities, teams, and resources. An entrepreneur will search for an opportunity and then hopefully turn it into a successful venture by bringing together the right team and resources. All these three ele- ments must be aligned for an entrepreneur to be successful.

According to Timmons' model the key to success for an entrepreneur is to find the right opportunity and develop a product that can add value, and remains attractive and appropriate.

The team factor refers to the need for leadership to manage the resources in the most effective manner. In terms of resources Timmons argues that having more resources does not necessarily reduce risk. He advocates 'bootstrapping', whereby entrepreneurs start with a minimum amount of resources; this forces the entrepreneur to focus on keeping costs low. Successful entrepreneurs balance the valuable resources they have with the opportunity and potential of the team.

According to the management consultancy, McKinsey, the businesses that are most likely to succeed from a start-up focus on talent, customer-centricity, and their core principles. From the beginning these new start-ups work hard at attracting and keeping customers and responding quickly to market changes. In a McKinsey interview, James Bilefield, one of the founders of Skype, says that the company has always remained focused on its mission—to let the world talk for free. Throughout its growth it has made sure it kept its values by being obsessed with delivering value for customers and avoiding hierarchy. At Skype the company set a simple target: 'to become a verb'.

One of the dangers Bilefield identifies is trying to scale up the business before there is a proper fit with the market. A number of dockless bike companies have found this. They grew fast but there was not sufficient demand for all of them and there was a backlash against bikes being abandoned all over a city. A start-up has to grow at the right speed and, like any business, it has to be sure the demand is there.

Business insight 2.5 **Zumba**

Beto Perez is the co-founder of exercise class company Zumba Fitness. The idea for a Zumba-based business actually came about by accident. Beto was running an aerobics class and one day forgot his usual music and had to base a class around some Latin music that he had available. The response was so good that Beto decided to stick with music such as salsa and merengue. The classes proved popular and Beto went on to set up his business Zumba Fitness.

Although Beto was running very successful classes he did not think he could turn Zumba into a business until one of his students introduced him to her son Alberto Perlman, and his friend Alberto Aghion. They saw the potential of the idea and the three went into business together. The brand name Zumba, a made-up word, was created in 2001.

The three men initially sold home fitness videos starring Beto. Then people started contacting them to know how they could become Zumba trained instructors, with 150 people signing up in 2003. This then rose to 700 a year later and grew fast after that after that.

About 14m people now attend Zumba classes (Figure 1) each week, in 140,000 locations worldwide. Today Zumba has more than 100,000 instructors around the world. To get official certification each has to pay from $225 (£180) to do a training course. Instructors then have to pay a monthly fee of around $30, for which they receive continuing training, CDs, DVDs, and choreography guidance. Whilst classes remain at the core of the business, about half the revenue comes from the extension of the brand name to music collections, clothing, and footwear.

The company is continuing to expand, and is currently growing rapidly in other countries such as South Korea and Indonesia.

▶

Figure 1 A trainer teaching a Zumba class. *Source:* iStock/reddees.

When the pandemic hit and people had to stay at home Zumba moved online and allowed customers to take virtual classes with trainers.

Question

What do we learn about what makes a successful entrepreneur from the Business Insight above?

Sources

www.ft.com/content/7584c828-6ecc-11e2-8189-00144feab49a

www.cnbc.com/2020/11/10/zumba-fitness-ceo-on-the-biggest-mistake-business-owners-make.html

www.zumba.com/en-US

www.bbc.co.uk/news/business-49111612

2.1.8 Entrepreneurs and business planning

All businesses face uncertainty. Uncertainty occurs when there are unknowns. In the business environment there are many unknowns; for example, what will happen to interest rates, what competitors will do, what might happen to weather patterns. Businesses have to take a view on what they think is most likely to happen based on whatever information they have and their own experience. Entrepreneurs typically have fewer funds to pay for expert opinion and have limited experience. This makes coping with uncertainty a particular problem for entrepreneurs and increases the risks they face. One way to reduce the risks that uncertainty can bring is to plan given what you do know.

Where are we now?

Having looked at various aspects of being an entrepreneur we now look at some of the planning tools that can help people when starting up a business. We begin with the business plan and go on to consider some of the financial planning tools an entrepreneur can use.

2.2 Business plans

Entrepreneurs are advised to develop a business plan when they are setting up their business. A business plan is a document that sets out what the business is going to be and what it plans to do. It is usually created by entrepreneurs to help raise finance and to help them think through their idea to ensure it is viable. The plan should then be reviewed regularly.

A business plan will usually include:

- A statement of the mission and objectives of the business.
- An analysis of the industry, the target market, and competitors.
- A value proposition. This should state what benefit the business provides, who the target audience is, and how the business does what it does better than others.
- Details of the people involved in the business, their experience, and their responsibilities.
- Details of the goods or services the business will provide.
- A plan of marketing activities.
- Revenue and cost forecasts.
- Cashflow forecasts.

The business plan is important to show potential investors or lenders. If it looks positive and the investors and lenders believe in it, the entrepreneur is more likely to be able to raise funds.

Producing a business plan makes the entrepreneur think ahead and consider all the issues that will be involved in making the business successful. It makes the entrepreneur evaluate the different aspects of the business, and think carefully about the assumptions being made and what actions can be taken to reduce risks.

A business plan should be reviewed on an on-going basis. This is to assess the progress of the business against targets and means the entrepreneur can take action accordingly. Business planning is a process which involves analysing the various elements of the business and reviewing them to measure how the business is doing and to develop the plan over time.

Key concepts

A **business plan** is a document that sets out what the business is going to be and what it plans to do.

Business planning involves analysing the various elements of the business and reviewing them to measure how the business is doing and to develop the plan over time.

A **value proposition** sets out the target audience of the business, what it offers, and how this is better than competitors.

What would you do?

You need to raise funds for your new business. You want to spend time producing a business plan. Your business partner does not see the value of doing this as she says 'things never go according to plan'. How would you explain the value of having a business plan?

Where are we now?

We have now outlined the various elements usually found in a business plan. An important section of the plan will be the financial analysis. This will generally include calculations to show how many units need to be sold to break even and details for the expected cashflow position of the business in the coming months. We now examine these aspects of financial analysis needed by start-ups.

2.2.1 Break-even analysis

A business breaks even when it does not make a profit or a loss. Break-even analysis estimates the number of units that need to be sold for the business to break even. If the break -even output is 100 units a week this means this is the number of units that the business would need to sell for its revenue to cover its costs. If it sold less than 100 units it would make a loss. If it forecasts it will sell more than 100 units it will make a profit.

A business can categorize its costs as:

- Fixed costs; these are costs those that are not related to the output such as the rent on premises. Fixed costs can change over time but are not related to the amount being produced.

- Variable costs; these are costs which that change with output; the more that is produced the higher the variable costs will be. For example, variable costs could include the costs of materials.

2.2.2 Calculating break-even output

When considering the benefit from selling a unit an entrepreneur can calculate the difference between the selling price and the variable costs per unit. This is called the contribution per unit.

$$\text{Contribution per unit} = \text{selling price of a unit} - \text{variable cost per unit.}$$

Imagine we sell cups of coffee for £3 and the variable costs (such as the take-away cup, the coffee, the water, and the milk) are £1. This means there is a contribution per unit of £3 − £1 = £2.

This £2 per cup provides a contribution to pay off the fixed costs.

If a business has fixed costs of £1000 a month, this means it would need to sell £1000 / £2 = 500 units a month to break even. If each cup of coffee pays for its variable costs and generates an 'excess' over variable costs of £2 we need 500 cups of coffee to earn a total contribution of £1000 (= 500 × £2); this will just pay off the fixed costs and the business will break even.

The break-even output can be calculated using the following equation:

$$\text{Break-even output} = \text{Fixed costs} / (\text{Price} - \text{Variable Cost per unit})$$

For example:

$$£1000 / (£3 - £1) = £1000 / £2 = 500 \text{ units}$$

Estimating the break-even output is important when starting a business or considering the viability of a project. If market research suggests the business can sell more than break-even output it will make a profit. If it is likely to sell less than break-even output it will make a loss.

2.2.3 Calculating the profit or loss at different outputs

To calculate the profit or loss earned at a given level of output the following equation can be used:

$$\text{Profit} = \text{Total contribution} - \text{Fixed Costs}$$

For example:

Assume the contribution per unit is £2.

If sales were 800 units this means the total contribution from these sales is £2 × 800 = £1600. This contributes to the fixed costs of £1000 and this means that once the fixed costs have been paid, the business makes a profit of £1600 − £1000 = £600.

By comparison, if sales were 300 units the total contribution would be £2 × 300 = £600.

This £600 contributes to the fixed costs of £1000 but cannot cover them; this means the business will make a loss of £400.

Using the equation: Profit = Total contribution − Fixed Costs

$$\text{Profit} = £600 - £1000 = -£400 \text{ i.e. a loss of } £400 \text{ is made}$$

Earlier, using the contribution per unit method, we calculated break-even output was 500 units. We can now check this is correct.

At 500 units the Total Contribution = £2 × 500 = £1000.

This £1000 contributes to the fixed costs of £1000 and just pays them off. The business will, therefore, break even and make a profit of £0.

Using the equation, Profit = Total contribution − Fixed Costs

$$\text{Profit} = £1000 - £1000 = £0.$$

2.2.4 Reducing the break-even output

If the break-even output is too high (e.g. on current sales forecasts the business would make a loss) the entrepreneur may consider different options:

(a) She may look to reduce the fixed costs. For example, she could look for cheaper premises to rent or reduce marketing expenditure.

(b) She may look to reduce the variable customer unit. For example, she may look to use cheaper suppliers or provide a more basic product.

Think about it

Imagine you sell a product for £50 a unit. The variable costs are £30 a unit and the fixed costs are £40,000 a year.

What is the break-even level of output?

What is the profit or loss if sales are i) 1000 units a year ii) 3000 units a year?

Think about it

How could a manufacturer of boxes of chocolate sweets reduce the cost per box but end up with lower profits than before?

When considering options (a) and (b) the business needs to consider if these decisions will have an impact on the quality of what it offers and therefore sales.

Another option is to increase the price per unit. This will generate a higher contribution per unit and so provided sales are not affected too much this may enable a business to break even. However, if sales do fall too much a loss will still be made despite the higher contribution per unit.

2.2.5 Constructing a break-even chart

Another way of undertaking break-even analysis is to draw a diagram showing total revenues and total costs and, on this diagram, finding the level of output at which total revenue = total costs.

To plot the total revenue line we use the equation:

Total revenue = price per unit × number of units

The total revenue line will begin at the origin; if nothing is sold there is no revenue.

If we assume a constant price per unit then the more units that are sold the higher the total revenue will be.

To plot the total costs line we use the equation:

Total costs = fixed costs + variable costs

Fixed costs do not change with output so this is shown on the diagram in Figure 2.4 as a horizontal line.

Variable costs do change with output. When output is zero the variable costs are zero. As output increases so do the variable costs. The total cost for any level of output equals the fixed costs plus the variable costs. An example of break-even chart calculations is shown in Table 2.2.

An example of a break-even chart is shown in Figure 2.4.

Table 2.2 Profit and loss analysis

Output (units)	Total revenue (TR) = price × output Assume price = £3 £	Fixed costs (FC) £	Variable costs (VC) = variable cost per unit × output Assume VC = £1 per unit £	Total cost (TC) = FC +VC £	Profit/(Loss) (TR–TC) £
0	0	1000	0	1000	(1000)
100	300	1000	100	1100	(800)
200	600	1000	200	1200	(600)
300	900	1000	300	1300	(400)
400	1200	1000	400	1400	(200)
500	1500	1000	500	1500	0
600	1800	1000	600	1600	200
700	2100	1000	700	1700	400
800	2400	1000	800	1800	600

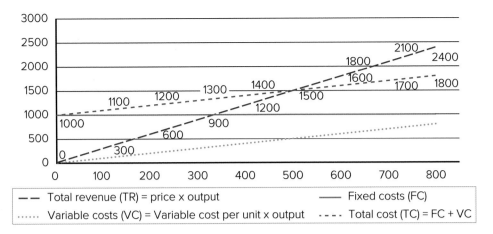

Figure 2.4 An example of a break-even chart. *Source:* Author.

The margin of safety is the difference between the current level of sales of a business and its break-even level of sales. For example, if a business is selling or expecting to sell 700 units and the break-even output is 500 units the margin of safety is 200 units. This means that sales could fall by 200 units before the business started to make a loss.

Think about it

What do you think would happen to the break-even chart and the break-even output if

- fixed costs fell (e.g. perhaps cheaper premises were found)
- the variable cost per unit was lower (perhaps cheaper suppliers were found)
- the price was increased?

What would you do?

You run a city centre restaurant. You are making a loss. What would you do to make a profit? How could you show your options on a break-even chart?

Key concepts

Break-even output is the level of an output at which the revenue of a business equals total costs.

Variable costs are costs that change with output.

Fixed costs are costs that do not change with output.

Contribution per unit equals the price minus the variable cost per unit.

The **margin of safety** measures the difference between the current level of sales and the break-even level of sales.

Profit or loss is measured by the difference between total revenue and total costs.

Where are we now?

Managing finances can be difficult for all businesses but can be a particular challenge for entrepreneurs. We now look at how entrepreneurs plan their spending through budgeting and their cashflow through cashflow forecasts.

2.2.6 Budgeting

A budget shows forecast levels of revenue and expenditure over a period of time. To set budgets entrepreneurs will need to think through what they are trying to do and how much this will earn or cost. Setting financial targets helps entrepreneurs to plan as it gives a financial measure of the sales expected and the resources that are required to generate this revenue.

Once the business is up and running entrepreneurs can compare the actual revenues and expenditure with the targets they set. This is known as variance analysis. If there is a difference between the budgeted figure and the actual and this would increase the expected profits, this is known as a favourable variance. For example, if the budget (target) revenue was £10,000 in a given period and the business actually earned £12,000 this would be a favourable variance of £2000.

If, however, the difference between the budgeted figure and the actual outcome would reduce the profits this is known as an adverse variance.

For example, if labour costs were budgeted at £3000 but the actual figure was £4000 there is an adverse variance of £1000.

By undertaking variance analysis entrepreneurs can consider why these differences occur and take this into account when planning for the future. An example of variance analysis is shown in Table 2.3.

Key concepts

A **budget** is a financial target for revenue and expenditure over a period of time.

A **variance** occurs when there is a difference between a budgeted figure and an actual figure.

A **favourable variance** occurs when the actual revenue is greater than the budgeted revenue or the actual costs are less than budgeted.

An **adverse variance** occurs when the actual costs are greater than the budgeted or the actual revenue is less than the budgeted revenue.

What would you do?

Your small team has been used to spending what they needed but being 'careful'. You want to introduce a more formal budgeting system. How would you explain to your team the benefits of this?

Table 2.3 An example of variance analysis

Item	Budget £000	Actual £000	Variance £000
Revenue	100	120	20 favourable
Labour costs	20	32	12 adverse
Materials costs	30	35	5 adverse
Other costs	10	8	2 favourable
Profit/loss	40	45	5 favourable

Table 2.4 A cashflow forecast

	January £000	February £000	March £000	April £000
A. Opening Balance	100	120	110	60
B. Cash inflows	60	80	90	90
C. Cash outflows	40	90	140	160
D. Net inflows (B–C)	20	(10)	(50)	(70)
E. Closing balance (A + D)	120	110	60	(10)

2.2.7 Cashflow forecast

Cashflow forecasts estimate the future inflows and outflows of cash over a given period and identifies when cashflow problems may occur. This allows an entrepreneur to take action to arrange appropriate finance if possible; for example, through short-term borrowing from a bank in the form of an overdraft.

Cash inflows measure when the money is actually received by the business rather than when orders are placed by customers. Cash outflows measure when money is paid out rather than when the orders are placed with suppliers by the business.

A simplified cashflow forecast is shown in Table 2.4.

The opening balance shows the funds available at the start of the month. The net inflow is the difference between the inflows and outflows in that month. The closing balance is the result of the opening balance plus the net inflows for that month. The closing balance is the money left at the end of the month. This becomes the opening balance for the following month.

By undertaking a cashflow forecast an entrepreneur can identify when cashflow problems may occur; in Table 2.4 the closing balance becomes negative in April. The entrepreneur can take action to avoid this if it is a problem. For example, she could look to delay payments to reduce outflows. Alternatively, she could organize for an overdraft or loan to cover the outflow in that month.

Key concept

Cashflow forecasts estimate the future inflows and outflows of cash over a given period and identifies when cashflow problems may occur.

Where are we now?

Having a business plan and being clear on what you are going to offer is important but entrepreneurs also need to consider how they are going to protect what they do. If their idea is successful, what is going to stop others doing exactly the same and take away their customers? We now look at how entrepreneurs may be able to protect their business idea.

2.3 **Protecting the business idea**

Businesses of all sizes need to be able to protect some aspects of what they have done. In many countries, businesses can protect their 'intellectual property' from being copied by others for a period of time. Intellectual property refers to something that has been created by someone using their mind—for example, a song, an invention, an artistic work, or a symbol. The intellectual property of a business can be protected to stop others stealing or copying it.

Intellectual property refers to:

- the names of products and brand names
- inventions
- the design or look of products
- things that someone has written, made, or produced.

Some types of protection, such as copyright, occur automatically; others such as patents have to be applied for.

The fact that intellectual property can be protected acts as an incentive to businesses to develop their ideas and come up with inventions. If this protection was not in place entrepreneurs would be less likely to want to start in business because of the fear that their ideas would be copied and therefore their rewards would be low.

Intellectual property rights allow a business to make money from the intellectual property it owns. For example, a business may sell the right to another business to use its invention or its name.

The forms of intellectual property rights protection available to a business include patents and copyrights.

2.3.1 **Patents**

Businesses can use a patent to protect an invention. A patent gives a business the right to take legal action against anyone who makes, uses, sells, or imports the invention without its permission. In 2021, for example, Ericsson sued Samsung for infringement of its mobile phone patents.

To get a patent, an invention must be:

- something that can be made or used
- new
- inventive—not just a simple modification to something that already exists.

2.3.2 **Copyrights**

A copyright protects the work of a business and stops others from using it without the creator's permission.

You automatically get copyright protection when you create:

- original literary, dramatic, musical, and artistic work, including illustration and photography

- original non-literary written work, such as software, web content, and databases
- sound and music recordings
- film and television recordings.

Whoever creates any of the above gets copyright protection automatically—there is no need to apply or pay a fee. In the UK it is possible to add a copyright symbol (©) but whether this is there or not does not actually affect the level of protection that the creator has.

In most countries copyright lasts a minimum of life plus 50 years for most types of written, dramatic, and artistic works, and at least 25 years for photographs.

If someone infringes the copyright the owner can sue. In 2018, for example, the band Radiohead sued Lana Del Rey claiming that her Get Closer song was based on their song, Creep, and therefore they should get some of the royalties.

2.4 Protecting a design

In some countries such as the UK it is possible to register the look of a product that has been designed to stop people copying or stealing the design.

The look of the design includes the product's:

- appearance
- physical shape
- configuration (or how different parts of a design are arranged together)
- decoration.

By registering a design, the creator can prevent others from using it for up to 25 years (although the creator has to renew the registered design every five years).

2.4.1 Trade marks

A business can register a trade mark to protect its brand, for example, the name of its product or service.

When a business in the UK registers its trade mark, it can:

- put the ® symbol next to the brand—this shows that it belongs to the business and has been registered
- sell and license the brand to others for a fee.

An example of a successful and, thereby valuable, trademark is Pop Mart's 'blind boxes'. According to the *Financial Times* the Chinese company Pop Mart has had huge success with its character figures which range from canine astronauts to wide-eyed alligators. Launched in 2010, Pop Mart had more than 288 outlets and 1800 vending machines by 2022 and had revenues of over 4.5 bn renminbi (RMB). Its 'blind boxes' sell for RMB 59–69 each and have an unidentified character in them.

Intellectual property can be important assets of a business. They can be listed on a balance sheet and form a significant part of the value of a company. Businesses will fight hard to keep control of their intellectual property but this can be difficult to protect in some

Key concepts

Intellectual property refers to something that has been created by someone using their mind.

A **patent** provides legal protection for an invention.

A **trademark** is legal protection for a brand.

A **copyright** is legal protection for the work of a business and stops others from using it without its permission.

Think about it

What do you think the consequences would be if patents did not exist?

countries. Part of Trump's decision while President of the USA to impose barriers for Chinese firms wanting to sell to the US was in retaliation for what he claimed was the infringement of US intellectual property in China.

Where are we now?

We have now examined the qualities of an entrepreneur and the importance of planning and using financial tools such as break-even analysis, budgets, and cashflow forecasts. Even with a business plan and the planning techniques we have outlined, entrepreneurs face many challenges. In this next section we consider some of the difficulties facing entrepreneurs.

2.5 The challenges of being an entrepreneur

Setting up in business can be a challenge in itself; keeping the business going is often an even bigger challenge. The difficulties of being an entrepreneur should not be underestimated.

These problems facing entrepreneurs include the stress of having the responsibility for the business as a whole. Entrepreneurs' skills may be strong in some areas but not necessarily in all aspects of business. If the business grows the entrepreneur may bring in others with expertise in different aspects of business. Entrepreneurs will often have to work long hours to make the business a success. Taking a holiday often means the business will have to close for this time and so entrepreneurs may have to minimize any breaks they take. As an entrepreneur there is often insecurity. This may be uncertainty over the future of the business but also earnings. Often entrepreneurs have unpredictable earnings in the early years. Entrepreneurs also face the risk of failure and the danger that they will lose the funds invested, which in many cases will be the entrepreneur's own savings.

Think about it

Do you think you would you be good at coping with the responsibility of running your own business? Why?

2.5.1 Cashflow problems for entrepreneurs

A particular challenge facing entrepreneurs is managing the cashflow of the business. Profit measures the revenue minus the costs from selling products over a given period. However, the revenue is not necessarily the same as cash coming in. Many products are sold on credit; this counts as a 'sale' and revenue but the cash for the sale may not be received for weeks, even months. New businesses and small business are particularly prone to this problem because they often need to offer long credit terms to win the sale. They are also in a weak bargaining position with customers. Customers are able to demand long credit terms because the newly set up business needs their orders and so the entrepreneur is likely to agree to those terms.

New and small businesses are also in a weak bargaining position with suppliers; in most cases the entrepreneur needs the supplier more than the suppliers need the business because they have other customers. This means that suppliers often have to be paid relatively quickly.

The result of these trading conditions is that the new business is likely to have the dual problem of customers paying relatively slowly whilst having to pay suppliers quickly. In the published accounts the amount owed by customers at any moment is called 'receivables'; the amount owed to suppliers at any moment is called 'payables'. Entrepreneurs are likely to have relatively high receivables and low payables. This means entrepreneurs often have cashflow problems (even if they are making a profit); this is also described as having liquidity problems.

2.5.2 Managing cashflow

To improve the cashflow of the business an entrepreneur can aim to take the following actions:

- **Insist on being paid in cash or offer relatively little credit.**
  The difficulty here is that offering credit is often a way of winning business. 'Buy now, pay later' can be an effective promotional technique but is not good for cashflow.

- **Negotiate to take longer to pay suppliers.**
  The problem with this approach is that it can be difficult for an entrepreneur as she is likely to be buying small quantities and therefore have little bargaining power.

- **Reduce inventory.**
  If the business can reduce inventory such as raw materials or semi-finished and finished goods this would free up some cash. However, reducing inventory brings with it the dangers of running out of materials if there are any delays with supplies arriving.

- **Use a cashflow forecast.**
  Producing a cashflow forecast can help a business anticipate any potential cashflow issues and ensure funding is in place if possible to cover any potential deficits.

Key concepts

Receivables represent the money owed to a business by customers.

Payables represent the money owed to suppliers.

What would you do?

You are considering delaying payments to suppliers to improve your cashflow. Should you do it?

Where are we now?

So far, we have discussed entrepreneurs and the valuable skills they have. Bigger organizations often want to keep the spirit of entrepreneurship alive in their organizations. This is called intrapreneurship. We now consider the importance of intrapreneurship.

>>> Can you now answer this question from the introductory case study?

What do you think entrepreneurs can do to improve their chances of survival?

2.6 Intrapreneurship

Entrepreneurship is associated with the creation of new businesses. However, older, more established and bigger businesses are often eager to retain an entrepreneurial approach. One problem facing businesses as they grow is that they often become more bureaucratic with more rules and regulations to ensure that senior managers keep control. Whilst more rules and procedures enable the managers to know what is happening, it may encourage employees to simply follow orders and do what they are told; it may discourage entrepreneurial thinking and risk taking. Intrapreneurs are people within larger businesses who retain an entrepreneurial approach—they look for opportunities and new ways of doing things. Bigger businesses often try hard to encourage intrapreneurship. This can be through finding new ventures, rewarding those who try new things, and encouraging cross-functional thinking.

In Amazon's 2016 Annual Report its founder, Jeff Bezos, wrote that whilst he wanted the company to be big he also wanted it to be an invention machine. He wanted all the benefits of large scale but also to keep the features of small businesses such as nimbleness, speed of movement, and a willingness to take risks. This desire to act small whilst being big is common in many organizations as they grow but is not always easy to achieve. To keep control of a larger organization decisions often involve more people and become slower and there are more rules to control and limit risk taking.

Analysing the business data 2.3

In the 2019 GEM survey individuals were asked whether the entrepreneurial activity they are involved with is their own or whether it is linked to an employer (which is called 'sponsored entrepreneurship'). This gives an insight into how much of entrepreneurial activity is actually linked to peoples' existing jobs.

The proportion of sponsored entrepreneurial activity varies from just under 6% in Brazil to more than 98% in Oman (Figure 1). In 13 out of the 50 economies, more than half of those who are starting or running a new business are sponsored by their employer.

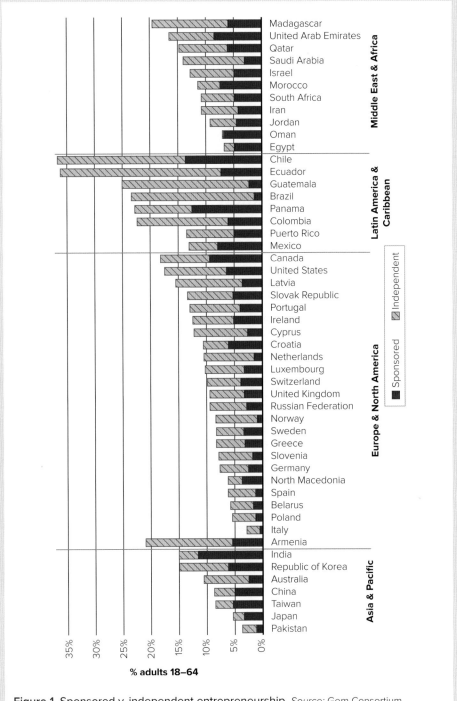

Figure 1 Sponsored v. independent entrepreneurship. *Source:* Gem Consortium.

Question

Why might businesses sponsor entrepreneurial activity?

Source

gem-2019-2020-global-report-rev-280520-1590656414%20(3).pdf

Where are we now?

We have now studied entrepreneurs and entrepreneurship. In the next four chapters we will examine what happens within a business. We will study the marketing, operations, human resource, and finance functions to analyse how these need to be managed to achieve business success.

Now you should know

- An entrepreneur is prepared to take risks to exploit a business opportunity.

- Entrepreneurs may set up in business to pursue a passion, to run their own operations, to pursue a business opportunity, to create jobs, or to help society.

- A high internal locus of control means that entrepreneurs believe that their behaviour determines what happens to them and that they can control their own behaviour.

- Entrepreneurship refers to the capability to exploit successfully innovative ideas and make them commercially successful.

- Risk means there is a danger that something can go wrong.

- The characteristics of an entrepreneur may include drive and energy, self-confidence, a strong internal locus of control, a high tolerance of ambiguity, and a low fear of failure.

- Break-even output occurs when the revenue equals costs.

- Break-even output is the level of an output at which the revenue of a business equals total costs.

- Variable costs are costs that change with output.

- Fixed costs are costs that do not change with output.

- Contribution per unit equals the price minus the variable cost per unit.

- The margin of safety measures the difference between the current level of sales and the break-even level of sales.

- Profit or loss is measured by the difference between total revenue and total costs.

- The margin of safety is the difference between the current level of sales of a business and its break-even level of sales.

- An entrepreneur can protect her intellectual property through trademarks, patents, and copyrights.

- Governments tend to favour entrepreneurs because they create jobs and growth in the economy.

Review questions

Quick check

1. State two types of risk facing an entrepreneur.

2. State two reasons why an entrepreneur starts a business.

3. State the key elements of a business plan.

4. Explain the difference between a patent and copyright.

5. Explain the difference between receivables and payables.

6. State what is meant by the break-even output.

7. Explain the difference between a business angel and a venture capitalist.

8. What is meant by the contribution per unit?

Analysis

1. Analyse the benefits and challenges of being an entrepreneur.

2. Analyse the actions a business might take to reduce the break-even output.

3. Analyse the ways a business might improve its cashflow.

Evaluation

1. Do you think people are born with the skills they need to be an entrepreneur or do you think people can learn how to become one?

2. Do you think the success of an entrepreneur is more due to luck than skill?

3. What more do you think your government could do to encourage entrepreneurship?

Find out more

To find out more about global trends in entrepreneurship you can visit the Global Entrepreneurship Monitor website www.gemconsortium.org/

You might also want to read about entrepreneurship in more detail. Some useful books are:

Barringer, B. R. and Ireland, D. (2019). *Entrepreneurship: Successfully Launching New Ventures* (6th edn). London, Prentice Hall.

Bessant, J. and Tidd, J. (2015). *Innovation and Entrepreneurship* (3rd edn). Chichester, London, John Wiley & Sons.

Burns, P. (2016). *Entrepreneurship and Small Business: Start-Up, Growth and Maturity* (4th edn). Basingstoke, UK, Palgrave Macmillan.

Drucker, P. (2007). *Innovation and Entrepreneurship Classic Collection* (2nd edn). New York, Routledge.

You might also want to look at articles in the *Journal of Entrepreneurship and Entrepreneurship Theory and Practice*.

☰ Bibliography

Drucker, P. (1993). Innovation and Entrepreneurship: Practice and Principles. New York, Harper Collins.

Global Entrepreneurship Monitor (n.d.). *Global Press release*. https://www.gemconsortium.org/reports/latest-global-report.

Gray, C. (1998). *Enterprise and Culture*. London. Routledge,

McKinsey (2020a). [online] Available at: <https://www.mckinsey.com/business-functions/mckinsey-digital/our-insights/what-start-ups-need-to-scale-and-succeed> [Accessed 29 December 2020].

McKinsey (2020b). Digital transformation: The three steps to success. (2020, February 13). https://www.mckinsey.com/business-functions/mckinsey-digital/our-insights/digital-transformation-the-three-steps-to-success [Accessed 4 April 2021].

The Economist (2020). Private companies have put down strong roots in China. https://www.economist.com/business/2020/04/30/private-companies-have-put-down-strong-roots-in-china [Accessed 4 April 2021].

Porter, M. E. (1980). *Competitive strategy*. New York, The Free Press.

Timmons, J. A., Smollen L. E., and Dingee, A. L. M. J. (1977). *New Venture Creation: A Guide to Small Business Development* (1st edn). Homewood, IL, RD Irwin.

World Bank (2021). Retrieved April 03, 2021, from http://www.doingbusiness.org/en/rankings

Chapter 3

Marketing management

3

Where are we now?

In this chapter we are going to examine the relationship between a business and its customers and the role of the marketing function. We will show how understanding customers and then meeting their needs and wants is key to business success.

Why am I studying this?

- You want to understand how businesses decide who to target and how to target them.
- You are interested in what the marketing function of a business does. In this chapter we outline the purpose and activities involved in marketing.
- You are thinking of a career in marketing. In this chapter we outline different aspects of marketing which might help you decide on your future path.
- You want to understand the difference between sales and marketing.

Learning objectives

By the end of this chapter you should be able to:

- Understand what is meant by marketing and marketing management
- Understand the difference between product, production, sales, and marketing orientations of a business
- Understand the difference between marketing objectives and strategy
- Analyse the value of market segmentation, targeting, and positioning
- Analyse the meaning and uses of marketing research
- Evaluate the influences on the marketing mix

Introductory case study Disney's growing portfolio

In 2019 Disney took over 21st Century Fox. This takeover deal cost Disney $71bn but gave it access to well-known global brands such as X-Men, Deadpool, The Simpsons, and Fantastic Four characters to name a few.

As part of 21st Century Fox Disney also acquired the Fox film and TV studios, National Geographic, and the Indian TV business, Star India. The Fox acquisition followed other key takeovers. In 2009 Disney purchased Marvel Entertainment for $4bn giving Disney the rights to brands such as Iron Man, and in 2012 Disney's takeover of Lucasfilm brought with it the rights to Star Wars.

The logo of Disney+, an online video streaming subscription service owned and operated by Disney Streaming Services, a subsidiary of The Walt Disney Company. *Source:* The Walt Disney Company.

The then Chief Executive Officer of Walt Disney, Bob Iger, said that the Fox deal would 'create significant long-term value for our company and our shareholders'.

The deal between Disney and 21st Century Fox immediately reduced the number of major Hollywood film studios. Disney, Warner Bros, Universal, Sony Pictures, and Paramount Pictures were now the Big Five studios. In addition, Disney gained more access to valuable data on customers and their entertainment-viewing habits. Disney can use this data as part of its marketing research to develop an effective marketing strategy, and further develop its marketing mix.

Figure 3.1 is an illustration of the Walt Disney Company's assets.

Disney's strategy to invest heavily in online streaming platforms was to offset the decline in its pay tv businesses. The purchase of Fox (in addition to earlier acquisitions) gave Disney more content to offer on these platforms. The next step in Disney's plan was the launch of Disney + in 2021; this streaming service was intended to directly compete with Netflix.

Disney now owns a wide range of highly popular content and can distribute these shows and films through its television channels, cinemas, streaming services, and other ways in which people receive their entertainment.

Although Disney Plus was not expected to be profitable until 2024, it was extraordinarily successful in terms of attracting subscribers soon after the launch. Continued success will require continued investment into developing content to match Netflix's offering. In 2020 Netflix added more than 370 television series and movies according to Variety data. Disney has initially relied heavily on its back catalogue (which admittedly is extensive). To match Netflix, Disney planned to invest around $15bn a year into developing new content.

Extracts from Disney's 2019 annual report to its investors identified potential business risks for the company. These include:

- **Finding that what it offers no longer matches what people want.**
  Disney offers a range of entertainment, travel, and consumer products (see Figure 3.2). The success of these depend on consumers' tastes and preferences. These tastes can sometimes change in unpredictable ways, and, if they do, this can have a negative impact on Disney. Disney must monitor and respond to changes in consumer tastes and ensure it is developing the ways consumers can access its offerings—for example,

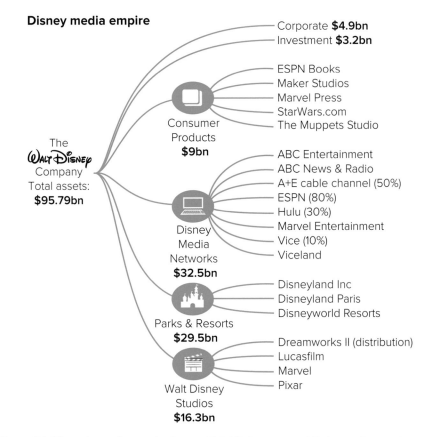

Figure 3.1 Disney's media assets. *Source:* BBC, US Securities and Exchange Commission.

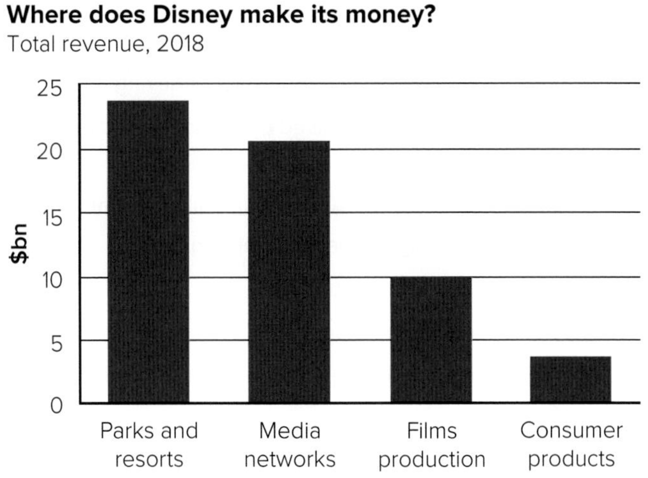

Where does Disney make its money?
Total revenue, 2018

Figure 3.2 The sources of Disney's revenue 2018. *Source:* BBC, Walt Disney Company.

through broadcast tv, cable, internet or cellular technology, theme parks, hotels and re-sorts, travel experiences, and consumer products. It is particularly aware of the need to keep up with technological developments.

• **Finding that competitors are taking sales away from Disney or Disney's costs have to increase to compete against them.**

Disney operates in several product and regional markets. It faces substantial competition in each of their businesses from alternative providers of the products and services Disney offers and from other forms of entertainment, lodging, tourism, and recreational activities. This includes, among other types, competition for human resources, programming, and other resources they require in operating their business.

- **Finding that Disney's reputation or brand image are damaged.**
  The Disney brand is well known globally. It has very strong values and any damage to this brand reputation could affect sales and future business opportunities.

- **Coping with the effects of the seasonality of certain parts of its businesses.**
  Each of Disney's businesses usually faces seasonal variations and other variations in demand. The number of people attending Disney theme parks and resorts, for example, is closely linked to school holidays.

Sources

www.ft.com/content/001b5d08-91a9-11e8-b639-7680cedcc421

www.ft.com/content/f6e79a8e-a7b0-11e9-90e9-fc4b9d9528b4

ft.com/content/3dd18690-6a10-4a3b-ab04-2c608ebff174

www.thewaltdisneycompany.com/wp-content/uploads/2020/01/2019-Annual-Report.pdf

www.theguardian.com/film/2019/mar/20/disney-seals-71bn-deal-for-21st-century-fox-as-it-prepares-to-take-on-netflix

www.bbc.co.uk/news/business-47671266

Introductory case study questions

Think about the following questions as you read through the chapter. You may not yet be able to answer them, but we will revisit these questions at key stages throughout the chapter. By the end of the chapter you should be confident in answering all of them.

1. What are the benefits to a business such as Disney of having a portfolio of products?
2. What do you think would be the criteria used by Disney to decide to target a particular group of customers?
3. How can Disney ensure that its business remains aligned with public and consumer tastes and preferences? Why might it become misaligned?
4. What do you think the Disney brand stands for?
5. How might Disney use marketing research?
6. What changes to the marketing mix might Disney take to reduce the seasonal risk that faces its business?

Critical thinking

1. The case study highlights the benefits to Disney of broadening its portfolio by acquiring Fox. Can you think of any potential disadvantages?
2. To what extent do you think the challenges highlighted in the case study are the main challenges facing Disney? Do these differ from the threats facing other organizations?
3. Research the current position of Disney. Can you analyse the reasons for changes since its position outlined above in 2020?

3.1 **What is marketing?**

Marketing activities provide the link between a business and its customers. The marketing function of a business identifies which customers to target and how the business can meet their needs as well as its own objectives. To do this the marketing function must work closely with the other functions of the business; for example, marketing decisions must be linked to what the business can actually provide (operations) and a budget must be available to undertake the desired marketing activities (finance). The interrelated nature of the business functions is shown in Figure 3.3.

Marketing involves an exchange process. A business supplies a good or service in return for something, often money. This exchange process is shown in Figure 3.4. Marketing aims to create value for its customers, i.e. to provide benefits that customers think are worth more than the price paid. However, the business must also benefit from the exchange—if the exchange is not worthwhile for the business then resources should be used elsewhere in a different exchange process.

To create value for customers a business must understand their needs and wants.

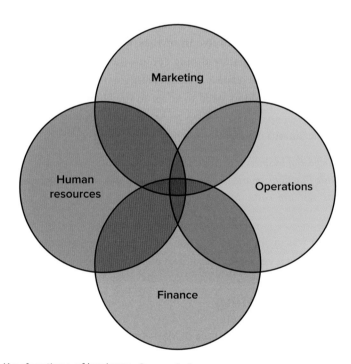

Figure 3.3 Key functions of business. *Source:* Author.

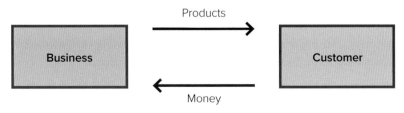

Figure 3.4 Business is an exchange process. *Source:* Author.

Key concept

Effective demand represents what customers want to buy and, crucially, are able to afford.

Think about it

'Marketing is about making customers happy'. Can you identify any problems with this statement?

Needs are what customers must have—for example, people need food and water to survive. A want is a choice of how to fulfil the need; for example, you may need food but want a burger or a sandwich. The marketing function must consider not only what customers want and need but also what they can actually afford. **Effective demand** represents what customers want to buy and are able to afford. Businesses need to be able to identify and meet the effective demand of customers.

Businesses also need to be ready and able to adapt. What people need, want, and are willing to pay for is likely to change over time. For example, let us look at the housing market in the UK compared to twenty years ago: people don't generally want a garage anymore, they want more space to live in or they want an indoor gym instead. They don't want a kitchen and a separate dining room—the general preference now is for open-plan kitchen space. They expect central heating, and they want it controlled by a smart thermostat. House builders need to adapt to the changing requirements of their customers.

According to the famous management writer Peter Drucker (1954):

Because the purpose of business is to create a customer, the business enterprise has two – and only two – basic functions: marketing and innovation. Marketing and innovation produce results; all the rest are costs. Marketing is the distinguishing, unique function of the business.

Essentially Drucker was saying that if you don't have a customer, you don't have a business, which is why marketing is critical to the success of any organization.

3.1.1 Defining marketing

According to the UK's Chartered Institute of Marketing (CIM) (2015) marketing is:

the management process that is responsible for identifying, anticipating, and satisfying customer requirements profitably.

There are some important aspects to this definition that are worth noting. The definition states that marketing involves:

- Identifying: this highlights the need to understand existing customer needs, wants, and demand. This is likely to include market research activities.

- Anticipating: this highlights that marketing is not just about the here and now. It is also about the future and trying to foresee what customers' wants and demand will be. Again, market research will be important.

- Satisfying: this means that customers' demands must be met in a way that creates values for them. Some would argue that merely satisfying customers these days is not enough; businesses need to exceed expectations.

- Being profitable: this highlights the importance of marketing in meeting not only customer demands but also the objectives of the business itself.

Another definition of marketing comes from the American Marketing Association (AMA) (2020). It defined marketing as the 'activity, set of institutions, and processes for creating, communicating, delivering, and exchanging offerings that have value for customers, clients, partners, and society at large.'

Philip Kotler is a well-respected American author, consultant, and professor and regarded by many as the guru of marketing theory. According to Kotler (2006) marketing is 'a science and an art that explores, creates, and delivers value to satisfy the needs of a target market at a profit'. It is a science in the sense that it is based on data and evidence; managers will develop a hypothesis and test it with data. It is an art in that it is creative; for example, marketing involves developing promotional campaigns and brands. Notice that in Kotler's definition marketing is about exploring what people want, creating goods and services to meet these needs and wants, and delivering and ensuring the business meets its needs as well.

There are many definitions of marketing but a study by Crossier (1988) which analysed over 50 different ones identified two broad themes:

1. Marketing is described as a process

   Marketing represents a process where an organization 'markets' its products. This process consists of a number of activities which encourage the analysis of marketing opportunities, researching the market, deciding which segments to focus on, and so on. From this perspective, marketing represents a structured and standardized approach to marketing management.

2. Marketing is seen as a philosophy

   This approach does not necessarily view marketing as a process but as a collection of underlying theories or principles. These definitions place an emphasis on areas such as customer satisfaction with perhaps the most important principle being marketing orientation. This refers to how an organization reflects on, responds to, and views its customers as being important to its existence. Viewing marketing as a philosophy encourages an organization to view all its activities as a collection of principles or values that motivate it to satisfy its customers' needs; this is sometimes described in terms of the 'orientation' of a business. We will now look at different types of business orientation, including marketing orientation.

Think about it

Look at the two definitions of marketing we have provided by the CIM and the AMA. Do you think there are any differences in the definitions? How significant do you think these differences are?

3.1.2 Types of business orientation

Although understanding and focusing on customer needs and wants may seem obvious, the way that businesses actually operate in reality can vary significantly. Some businesses adopt (not necessarily consciously) a certain type of orientation, and we will now explore four different types: product, production, sales, and marketing.

Product orientation

These businesses develop something unique and different, or have exclusive rights to provide a good or service. They focus on the product itself but are not very customer conscious because they don't think they need to be. This approach may be successful if a business offers a product that people want and no-one else provides. For example, the government may be the sole provider of trains or energy in some countries. However, problems come if competition enters the market and customers switch to a business that is more focused on their requirements. The Trabant was a somewhat basic car produced in East Germany between 1957 and 1990; it was a government monopoly. For as long as East Germany restricted imports of cars from the West the Trabant proved popular as customers had no other options. Once Germany was reunited in 1991 and customers could choose from a range of cars the limitations of the Trabant were all too clear.

Production orientation

This approach occurs when a business focuses on growing the scale of its operations. Managers with this perspective think the key to success is to make the business bigger so that it can produce more efficiently—for example, by using production-line technology. With lower unit costs enabling lower prices the business can appeal to many customers who will be able to afford their products. This production orientation was the approach famously adopted by the car company, Ford, in the early 1900s when it created a production line to produce the Model T. The Model T was the first mass-produced car; between 1908 and 1927 Ford sold 16.5 million of these cars. The use of production-line technology enabled Ford to drop the price so much that cars became affordable to the mass market. Ford offered 'any colour you want . . . as long as it's black' because it focused on producing as many cars as possible as quickly as possible. Again, this orientation can work provided competition is limited but once more producers adopt similar technology and start to offer more choice and better customer service the original provider may struggle.

Sales orientation

This approach occurs when a business focuses on persuading customers to buy their products. The emphasis is on sales techniques, such as buy one get one for free or reduced prices for payment in cash. A sales approach focuses on selling a product that already exists. You will find some businesses that constantly seem to be offering '10% off', 'two for the price of one', or 'buy now, pay later' offers.

Marketing orientation

Businesses with a marketing orientation start with the needs of the customers and develop a product to match this. Marketing is not about selling what you have already but developing what the product should be and then determining the price, the distribution, and the

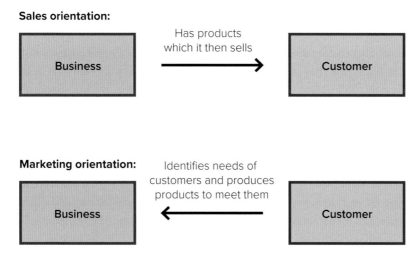

Figure 3.5 Sales orientation and marketing orientation. *Source:* Author.

way in which it is promoted. 'Selling' the product is a small part of marketing activities; marketing begins by thinking about what it is the business wants to sell in the first place.

The difference between sales orientation and marketing orientation is shown in Figure 3.5.

Kotler explained the difference between sales and marketing orientations when he said that marketing is not about finding better ways to disposing of what you make. It is to do with creating genuine value for customers, so they feel better off and will pay for that benefit.

In many organizations there will be a marketing team and a sales team. The marketing activities focus on understanding what is required by customers, developing this, and promoting it. The sales activities focus on taking what has been developed and finding ways to get customers to buy—for example, through offers and promotional incentives. You will often find 'sales' shown as a separate function within a business.

3.1.3 **The importance of a marketing-oriented approach**

An example of the importance of being marketing orientated was highlighted by Theodore Levitt (1960). Levitt argued that the decline of the American railways came about not necessarily because people did not want to travel by train, but because of the fundamental failure of the train companies to recognize their customers' needs, i.e. convenience and comfort. Levitt said that the railways were guilty of 'marketing myopia' (i.e. marketing short-sightedness) by losing sight of consumer needs and allowing other methods of transport to gain sales at the expense of the railways. The train companies failed to appreciate that people were not buying trains—they were buying a way of getting from A to B. If a different way of doing this which is better value for money starts to be offered, customers will switch. The vital message for businesses is that you should not define yourself by what you offer but you should consider the benefits customers are getting from what you do. Some people buy chocolate as a gift for others; some buy it to reward themselves when things have gone well; some to comfort themselves when things have gone badly. Some buy chocolate to eat it immediately; some to eat over time; some to share it with others. Chocolate producers can identify these needs and develop different products to meet them.

Do people buy Rolex watches to tell the time or to show they have achieved a certain level of success or to hand down to their children as a legacy?

Understanding customers is, therefore, key to business success and businesses should be careful not to assume they always know how customers think or how they will behave. The US business Home Depot and the UK business B&Q failed in China because they assumed Chinese customers would embrace 'Do It Yourself' repairs and improvements to their homes. That may have been true in the US or the UK, but it wasn't in China. In China most people don't do much DIY—they either rent property (so repairs are done for them) or employ others to do the work for them. Professional builders want a very different experience from amateur buyers. For example, professional builders want trade accounts rather than paying for each item each time; they know what they want to buy and don't need as much advice; and they want to pick up goods early in the morning before going off to a job.

Understanding customers and markets can prove particularly challenging when going abroad because of differences in language, culture, and buying habits. Even the name of the brand can create issues. In the 1970s, for example, American Motors launched its Matador model of car to create images of strength and courage; in Puerto Rico it was less popular as Matador means 'killer' in Spanish. In 1987 American Airlines promoted its new leather seats in its planes with a slogan 'Fly leather'. The Spanish 'Vuela en cuero,' worked well in much of Latin America but in Mexico the phrase means 'fly naked' and was not so appealing to potential passengers. Idioms, cultural references, and jargon can all create challenges abroad; as do colours—white is associated with purity and weddings in the West; it is linked to death in other cultures. Lifestyles must also be considered. In the US many homes have a big utility room and they have washing machines and dryers that are top-loaders. In many other countries space is at a premium and so these appliances load from the front—the top is needed as workspace. As a result, washing machines have to be designed differently. In the UK a kettle would be in almost every kitchen to make tea and coffee; that is not the case around the world. International marketing is explored further in Chapter 9.

Think about it

Think about a 'typical' family home in any countries that you have visited. How do they differ in terms of size, layout, appliances, and décor. What implications does this have for marketing of household items?

Key concepts

A **marketing orientation** refers to businesses which focus on identifying consumer needs and wants in order to develop products which address those needs.

Marketing myopia means marketing short-sightedness.

What would you do?

You believe your business is too sales-orientated rather than being marketing-orientated. How would you explain to your staff what the difference is and how they might change the business?

Where are we now?

Our view of what marketing involves has evolved over time. For example, these days the importance of relationship marketing for businesses is often emphasized, as is the importance of social media, and promoting the role of the business in society. Some of the most notable recent developments in marketing are considered next.

3.2 Recent developments in marketing

3.2.1 Relationship marketing

In the modern world simply developing and selling a product to a customer is not enough. A business will usually want to develop a relationship with its customers. According to Berry (2000) relationship marketing is a marketing activity for enterprises 'to obtain, maintain, and promote effective relationships with customers'. According to the Association of National Advertisers (ANA), relationship marketing refers to strategies and tactics for segmenting consumers to build loyalty. It focuses on getting customers to come back and buy more rather than having a 'one-off' transaction. It is much cheaper to retain a customer than continually find new ones. According to the *Financial Times* the Chinese fashion retailer Shein set a target in 2023 of doubling its revenues to nearly $60 billion. To do this a key element of the plan was to increase the number of repeat customers. In 2022 around 60% of its 142 million customers shopped with the business for the first time. Its target was that within two years 60% of an estimated 262 million customers will have shopped with the company before.

By building a relationship a business can also cross-sell its products. For example, a bank may want to sell its customers banking, personal insurance, home insurance, investment advice, travel insurance, and mortgages.

Developments in technology have enabled businesses to monitor what customers look at on their websites and what they search for. They can also analyse their databases much more effectively to identify patterns of behaviour and identify other products that existing customers might want and occasions when certain products may appeal. This enables businesses to understand their customers better and build a long-term relationship by meeting their needs more effectively.

3.2.2 Influencer marketing

According to the Association of National Advertisers (ANA), influencer marketing focuses on certain key people who have influence over potential buyers and orienting marketing activities around these individuals to drive a brand message to the larger market.

In influencer marketing, rather than marketing directly to a large group of consumers, a brand inspires or compensates key influencers (who could be celebrities, content creators, customer advocates, or employees) to spread the message on their behalf. In 2020 Dwayne 'The Rock' Johnson was the top earner for a sponsored post on Instagram according to Hopper HQ which estimates the social media earnings of celebrities. The Rock, who has 187 million followers on social media, charges over $1 million per post. Influencers can now have a major impact on the success of new products and can create new trends especially in areas such as fashion, music, clubs, and restaurants and food. According to pressmedia the top 30 social influencers in 2020 included the Portuguese footballer Cristiano Ronaldo, the Brazilian footballer Neymar, the Indian-American actress and film producer Priyanka Chopra Jonas, and the singer Ariana Grande.

The power of influencers can be seen in the numbers who booked to go to the Fyre Festival; the promotion of this event is explored in Business Insight 3.1.

Business insight 3.1 The Fyre Festival

The Fyre Festival has been labelled 'the greatest party that never happened'.

The 2017 festival (now the subject of a Netflix documentary, FYRE) was promoted as a luxury party on a remote island in the Bahamas. The promotion of the event relied heavily on influencers. Many high-profile personalities, such as Kendall Jenner, Bella Hadid, and Hailey Baldwin were paid hundreds of thousands of dollars to promote the festival on social media. In the end the festival was a complete disaster. The festival promised luxury villas and gourmet meals; guests actually got pre-packaged sandwiches and tents! On arrival there were

The Fyre Festival logo. *Source:* Wikimedia/Fyre Media.

problems with security, food, and medical services and the festival was postponed indefinitely.

The failure of the festival raised the question of how accountable the influencers should be for its failure. The influencers promoted a very different picture of what the festival would be like compared to what actually happened. There was also the issue of disclosure. Kendall Jenner was reportedly paid $250,000 for a single Instagram post about Kanye West's G.O.O.D Music family performing at event. Jenner did not disclose that this was an advert. Her posts about the event seemed to be a personal recommendation rather than a paid-for ad.

Following the scandal of the festival the Advertising Standards Authority (ASA) has brought in tighter rules and regulations. The ASA has warned social media influencers that they have to ensure that all sponsored or paid-for content is clearly labelled.

Questions

Do you think influencers should be held responsible for the performance of the goods and services they promote?

Who would you have chosen as an influencer for this type of event? Why?

Sources

https://www.bbc.co.uk/news/46945662 'Has Fyre Festival burned influencers'?

https://www.forbes.com/sites/sap/2019/02/09/fyre-festival-fiasco-a-truly-unforgettable-customer-experience

What would you do?

Imagine you run a business that produces:

- a new vaping product
- a new health drink
- a new electric bicycle
- a stairlift to help people get up the stairs in their homes
- a shampoo.

You are looking for a celebrity to use in a social media campaign for each of these products. Who would you choose? Why?

3.2.3 Viral Marketing

Viral marketing is a marketing phenomenon that facilitates and encourages people to pass along a marketing message. It is called 'viral' because it spreads in a way that is similar to a virus. For example, fidget spinners went viral in 2018 as interest spread rapidly in the playgrounds and on social media.

3.2.4 Guerrilla marketing

This is a marketing activity that aims to use surprise and unconventional approaches to promote a product. The phrase: 'Guerrilla marketing' was made popular by Jay Conrad Levinson's 1984 book of the same name. This type of marketing aims to use originality and creativity to attract interest; this can be particularly useful when budgets are limited. It is called Guerrilla marketing because there is a sense of surprise, sabotage, and raids! The aim is to generate a social buzz and media coverage.

Examples of guerrilla marketing include use stealth marketing when people are 'undercover' and promote the product. For example, Sony ran a campaign in which actors were hired to go around different cities, asking strangers to take a photo of them with their

Publicity stunt by Universal Studios Hollywood to promote the new King Kong movie.

Source: ZUMA Press, Inc./Alamy Stock Photo.

phone. Whilst this was being done the actors would be busy telling everyone how great their new phone was.

Another approach is to use flash mobs when a group of people come together to perform—for example in the middle of a shopping centre. This can generate lots of postings by onlookers on social media.

Other examples of guerrilla marketing include:

- To promote the film *King Kong 3D* huge 'King Kong' footprints were left on Santa Monica beach (California, United States) overnight much to the surprise of those going to sunbathe the next day!
- To attract the attention of holiday makers arriving at the conveyor belt at Gulfport–Biloxi airport (Mississippi, United States) to collect their luggage a local hotel resort put graphics so that the conveyor belt looked like it was a swimming pool with someone swimming along.
- To promote shark week the Discovery Channel put surfboards with a 'shark bite' taken out of them along surfing beaches in Australia.

However, by doing something different there is a risk the idea will flop or not be well received. It may also have unintended consequences. For example, in 2007 Turner Broadcasting promoted a new TV show by placing LED devices around Boston. At night the LED devices lit up. However, some people thought they were explosive devices and it caused panic across the city which Turner had to apologize for.

3.2.5 Societal marketing

Some businesses now aim to undertake societal marketing. This means that they aim to meet the needs of customers and the business itself but also society as a whole. Societal marketing thinks about the environmental impact of the actions of the business and the ethical implications of its activities and tries to improve society through the products it promotes. An example of socially responsible marketing is shown in Business Insight 3.2.

Business insight 3.2 Socially responsible marketing at Coca-Cola

Coca-Cola has been manufacturing drinks for more than 130 years and has brands that are consumed by millions of people across the world every day (Figure 1).

The Coca-Cola Company says that it has always taken its commitment to marketing responsibly seriously, in every country and across all advertising media.

Its Responsible Marketing Policy includes providing easy-to-access nutritional information both on product labels and online, as well as providing individuals with information about the different portions so they can make informed choices.

Figure 1 The Coca-Cola Company. *Source:* Wikimedia/The Coca-Cola Company.

Coca Cola has also committed to not placing any of its brands' marketing in any media which directly target children under 12. This includes television shows, print media, websites, social media, movies, and email marketing. Coca-Cola defines media that directly targets children under 12 as media in which 35% or more of the audience is composed of children under 12. The company says it will not design its marketing communications in a way that directly appeals to children under 12 (under 13 in the U.S.).

The company also says that it will not offer its drinks for sale in primary schools unless requested to do so by parents or school authorities to meet hydration needs. In such cases, it will aim to meet those requests with a full portfolio of beverages, including water, juices, and other beverages in both regular and low-calorie/calorie-free versions.

Questions

Why would Coca-Cola be interested in pursuing 'socially responsible' marketing?

The information above is produced by Coca-Cola and published on its website. It may, therefore, give a particular view of its activities. Can you think of other aspects of Coca-Cola's operations which might be criticized for not being socially responsible?

Source

www.coca-cola.co.uk/about-us/responsible-marketing

3.2.6 Word-of-mouth marketing (WOM marketing)

This occurs when consumers become interested in a product because of what others are saying about it. According to the market research business Nielsen, 92% of consumers believe recommendations from friends and family over all forms of advertising. If businesses can make customers loyal but also ambassadors this can generate more sales from others. How often when you are going to buy something do you look to see what others have said about it? Do you read reviews of books and other products when deciding whether to buy? Many businesses now actively encourage you to rate their products or the experience you have had using their services as online reviews and ratings can form an important part of the buying process for customers.

Where are we now?

So far, we have considered the definitions of marketing, the importance of adopting a market orientation, and recent developments in marketing. We will now consider what marketing management involves.

Think about it

When would you ask a friend for advice about whether to buy a product?

Key concept

> **Marketing management** involves planning, organizing, coordinating, and controlling the activities and resources involved in the marketing process.

3.3 Marketing management

Marketing management involves planning, organizing, coordinating, and controlling the activities and resources linked to the marketing process. In small organizations marketing activities may be developed and managed by one person. In larger businesses there are specialist departments focusing on the various aspects of marketing.

The process of marketing management involves:

- Gathering information through marketing research to understand customers and the market. This is to help the business make informed decisions. This identifies what could be done.

- Developing the marketing strategy through segmentation, targeting, and positioning (STP). This identifies what should be done.

- Developing an integrated marketing plan. This is to develop how the marketing strategy is implemented through the marketing mix.

- Reviewing the outcomes to decide on the next actions. This determines whether to use the same marketing strategy and plan again or whether to do it differently.

The marketing management process is shown in Figure 3.6.

As with all aspects of business, marketing management will change over time. An example of this is the changes in emerging markets outlined in Business Insight 3.3. One of the

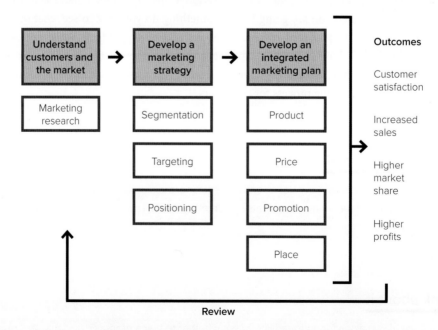

Figure 3.6 The marketing management process. *Source:* Author.

Business Insight 3.3 Changes in emerging markets

Marketing teams need to be aware of changes in market conditions and the opportunities this creates for them. Sometimes these changes will be at a local level; sometimes they are a major change in societies and economies, known as a 'megatrend' (Figure 1). Emerging markets are of particular interest to many businesses because, although the income per person is relatively low in these countries at the moment, they are growing fast. According to the Boston Consulting Group there are four significant megatrends in emerging markets. These are:

Figure 1 Consumers in emerging markets have increasingly greater access to the internet. *Source:* Indranil Mukherjee/AFP via Getty Images.

1. **Population growth.** The population of emerging markets is expected to increase in total by around 1 billion in the next ten years. In many countries the population remains quite young. About half of India's nearly 1.4 billion people are under the age of 25, for example. This creates huge numbers of potential customers for businesses.

2. **The growth of the 'consumer class'.** The average spending per household in emerging markets is increasing at about three times the rate of more developed markets. Hundreds of millions of households are entering the higher income levels of the middle and affluent classes. A key part of the strategy of Unilever, which makes everyday products for hygiene, personal care, and nutrition, has been to target emerging markets where it thinks the growth in sales lies.

3. **Rapid urbanization.** This means that more and more people are moving to the cities from rural areas. Over500 million people have moved from the countryside to the cities in emerging markets since 2007. This trend is continuing. This increase is increasing demand for housing and infrastructure.

4. **Digital adoption.** Over 2.6 billion people in emerging markets are now using the internet. Consumers in many emerging markets are very technology aware. The adoption of smartphones is extensive (see Figure 1) as is digital rather than cash payments.

Question

What implications do you think these megatrends have for marketing teams?

Source

www.bcg.com/en-gb/capabilities/international-business/emerging-markets

most notable changes in marketing management is due to the growing role of technology. Technology allows businesses to understand customers and their behaviour in detail. It allows businesses to target their messages very specifically to the needs of customers and can even provide customers with information on what they might want to buy. It also enables the effectiveness of marketing activities to be tracked much more closely than in the past. For example, the reach of an online ad, the number of impressions, the amount of customer engagement, the number of click-throughs, and online purchases can all be measured. Technological developments in operations also allow more customization of the product.

The results is that marketing is increasingly personalized and businesses are providing more of a one-to-one marketing experience. An excellent example of a business that embraces a marketing orientation is Amazon. When Amazon.com launched in 1995, it was with the mission 'to be Earth's most customer-centric company, where customers can find and discover anything they might want to buy online'. This mission has driven Amazon's actions ever since it started. To be so customer centric Amazon invests heavily in technology to gather and analyse vast quantities of data about its customers' behaviours.

3.3.1 Understanding customers and markets: Marketing research

The marketing management process begins with marketing research. In order to develop a marketing strategy and marketing plan, managers will want to have information or data to help them make the right decisions. Having information should enable better marketing decisions to be made. The desire for information is likely to be particularly strong if the decisions are high risk, involve significant sums of money, or must be approved by others. To gather the information or data needed managers may undertake marketing research. Marketing research will also be used to assess the effectiveness of any strategy and plans so the business can adapt accordingly.

Marketing research is the function that links the consumer, customer, and public to the marketer through information. Marketing information is used to:

- identify and define marketing opportunities and problems
- generate, refine, and evaluate marketing plans and activities
- monitor the implementation of the marketing plan
- review marketing performance.

A current example of how market research might be used in relation to market opportunities is the personal healthcare market. Technological developments allow people to wear devices that monitor their health. This can be linked to a business to interpret the data, recommend what needs to be done, and monitor the impact. Higher incomes and growing awareness of health issues means there is growing interest by individuals in well-being and technology is creating market opportunities for business. Market research can help identify the scale of this opportunity, which customers are likely to buy a product and what they actually want, how best to reach and communicate with these customers, and, once a product is launched, assess its success.

The uses of marketing research in the making of marketing decisions are shown in Figure 3.7.

One use of marketing research will be to identify the sales in a market and sales over time. This can be shown in the video gaming industry around the world in Analysing the Business Data 3.1.

According to Kotler and Armstrong (2017) the marketing research process will:

- specify the information that is required for the marketing decision that needs to be made
- design the method required to collect the information
- manage the data collection process
- analyse the data
- communicate the findings and their implications.

Figure 3.7 The uses of marketing research. *Source:* Author.

Analysing the business data 3.1 Global gaming industry

The video gaming industry was estimated to be worth $159.3 billion in 2020. The biggest areas of growth are in Latin America and the Asia Pacific (APAC) region. In 2020 spending in APAC was approximately $78billion; spending in China was around $41 billion and the USA was around $37 billion (Figure 1).

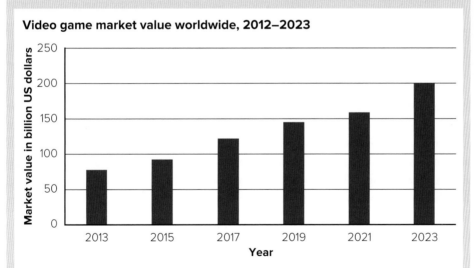

Figure 1 Video gaming industry sales. *Source:* J. Clement (2023), Video gaming market size worldwide 2020-2025. Available at: https://www.statista.com/aboutus/our-research-commitment/408/j-clement [Accessed 21 June 2023]. Adapted by the author.

Questions

1. Analyse the possible reasons for the growth in the global video gaming industry.

2. How might the trend above affect other industries?

3. Is further growth inevitable?

Sources

www.wepc.com/news/video-game-statistics/

www.statista.com/statistics/292056/video-game-market-value-worldwide/

There may, in fact be several 'rounds' of the market research process. For example, research may be used to help identify the cause of a problem such as falling sales. Further research may be required to understand in more detail the different aspects of the cause before any possible actions to be taken and then further research to determine what a solution might be.

Primary and secondary marketing research

Marketing research may be primary, which uses first hand data, or secondary, which uses data already collected. Usually primary research data takes longer and is more expensive to gather. It is more likely to be used when the information needed does not exist already or when there is a high risk involved in the decision being made and so it is worth investing money to get up-to-date and precise information. The ways in which primary data may be gathered are shown in Figure 3.8.

Primary market research data can be gathered in various ways such as:

- Observational data. This involves gathering primary data by observing people, actions, and situations.

- Surveys. This involves gathering primary data by asking people questions. This may be about their knowledge, attitudes, preferences, and buying behaviour.

- Experimental data. This involves gathering primary data by selecting similar groups, giving them different treatments, controlling the related factors, and analysing any differences in responses.

When gathering primary data a business will be interested in what is happening in all of the target market—this is known as the 'population'. However, gathering information from the whole target population may be very slow and expensive. To overcome these problems a business may use sampling. A small amount of the population is sampled with the intention that the findings will represent the population as a whole; the aim is to make the process cheaper and quicker. When there is a political election, for example, market researchers will interview a relatively small number of people to try to predict the result.

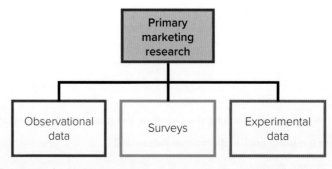

Figure 3.8 The ways of gathering primary marketing data. *Source:* Author.

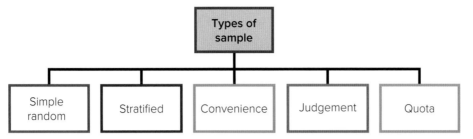

Figure 3.9 Types of sample. *Source:* Author.

Types of samples include:

- A simple random sample. This occurs when every member of the population has an equal chance of selection.

- A stratified random sample. This occurs when the population is divided into mutually exclusive groups (such as age groups) and random samples are taken from each group.

- A convenience sample. This occurs when the business chooses the easiest samples from which it can gather information.

- A judgement sample. This occurs when the business uses its judgement to select a sample.

- A quota. This occurs when a business finds and interviews a set number of people of people in different categories.

These types of sample are shown in Figure 3.9.

When deciding on the sample size and the method of sampling, marketing managers will need to consider the time they have, the budget they have, and how accurate they would like the findings to be. There is no guarantee that any sample will accurately represent the population as a whole, but, depending on the size and the way the sampled is selected and gathered, the market researchers will be able to give a degree of confidence associated with their findings. For example, a 95% confidence level means that 95% of the time (i.e. 19 times out of 20) the actual results for the population as whole will fit within the estimates provided. Market research findings will often be provided with a confidence interval and confidence level. For example, there may be a 95% confidence level that the sales of a business next year will lie in the interval of £2m to £3m. If the marketing manager wants a more specific estimate the researcher will be less confident. For example, she may only be 68% confident that sales will lie between £2m and £2.4m. The confidence level is lower because the interval is smaller.

Secondary marketing research can be gathered from a number of sources such as government publications, annual reports by companies, and academic journals. It is now relatively easy to access secondary data. Secondary market research, for example, is using Statista to tell us that in 2021 the largest global toy companies (in order) were Lego, Bandai Namco, Hasbro, Mattel, and JAKKS Pacific. However, the data may not be exactly in the format that a business wants it or address the specific questions that a business wants answered. Typically, secondary data is not current information. It is also important that businesses consider the source of any secondary data. Wikipedia, for example, provides access to a huge wealth of information but there is not a rigorous process of checking this. By comparison, material published in an academic journal will have undergone more robust examination and should have greater validity.

Technological advances are enabling marketing research to analyse trends and patterns much more effectively than in the past. This is aided by the fact that so much data can be

Key concept

Data mining occurs when businesses identify patterns and correlations within large data sets to predict outcomes.

captured about our behaviours online (although this does bring with it issues of data protection). For example, businesses can track when we search online, what search terms we use, how we navigate their websites, how we respond to promotional initiatives, what we buy, and what we don't buy, and by combining this with all kinds of other data they can develop a detailed insight into their customers. Businesses now have the ability to undertake highly effective data mining (which is explained further in Chapter 4). Data mining occurs when businesses identify patterns and correlations within large data sets to predict outcomes. For example, by considering a whole range of factors such as the weather patterns, time of the year, income levels in a region, media coverage of accidents, social media patterns, trip searches, and holiday bookings, airlines can build up a picture of likely bookings to a given destination at a given time.

Can you now answer this question from the introductory case study?

How might a business such as Disney use marketing research?

3.3.2 Understanding customers

At the heart of marketing is an understanding of who buys the products of a business, why they buy it, when the need or demand occurs, when they start looking to buy, where they look for information, what else they consider when deciding, and what influences their views after the purchase.

In terms of who buys, this can be relatively straightforward—you may want a drink and you go to the shop, buy a can of Coca-Cola and drink it. In this case the marketing manager would be very interested in the factors that affect your decision. You are the person who buys the product—the customer—and the person who actually uses the product—the consumer. However, there may be many occasions when the person buying the product is not the one who consumes it. A parent may be the customer but the child may be the consumer, for example. The person buying a Pandora charm (see Business Insight 3.4) may be doing so to give it to someone else.

In other situations, there may be a group of people involved in the buying decision rather than just one. For example, when a business is buying new equipment there may be:

- a purchasing manager responsible for major expenditure
- the Chief Executive who may need to sign off very significant items of spending
- the head of the department where the equipment will be used
- the person who uses the equipment.

The marketing team will want to understand the views of these different people and their relative importance in the decision-making process.

Marketing managers need to be able to consider the people involved in the buying group and what they are looking for. They also need to think about the stages involved in the buying process.

Business insight 3.4 Pandora

The Pandora story began in 1982 when Per Enevoldsen and his wife Winnie set up a small jeweller's shop in Copenhagen, Denmark. Over time the business became more of a wholesaler selling products to other retailers. In 1987 the company employed its first in-house designer and then in 1989 it started to manufacture jewellery in Thailand. The concept of a charm bracelet, whereby you buy the chain and then add on different charms as you buy them, was launched in 2000 and has been a phenomenal success as the business entered new international markets. Pandora's products are now available in more than 100 countries on six continents through more than 7000 points of sale, including around 2700 concept stores.

Pandora says it is now the world's largest jewellery brand. Its bracelets are from high-quality materials and provide endless possibilities for personalization. Its slogan is 'We give a voice to people's loves'.

Visit the Pandora website and you will see how well the business understands its customers: you can identify an occasion you are celebrating; the amount of money you want to spend; you can even keep track of what you have bought already to ensure you don't buy the same thing twice. Pandora appreciates that you are not buying 'a charm'; you are celebrating a moment in life such as an anniversary, a birthday, or the birth of a child. When you buy the product it is beautifully wrapped in an expensive-looking box because what you are buying is a gift not 'a piece of silver'.

The Pandora model is shown in Figure 1.

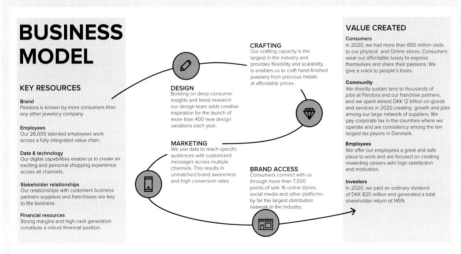

Figure 1 Pandora's business model. *Source:* Pandora.

Questions

If Pandora charms are bought as gifts, who is the customer and who is the consumer?

What difference might it make to the marketing activities of Pandora if many of its sales are gifts?

Pandora could say 'we make jewellery'. In fact it says 'We give a voice to people's loves'. What is the significance of this?

Source

pandoragroup.com/products/jewellery-materials

3.3.3 **The customer buying process**

Marketing managers will be very interested in the decision-making process of buyers. This means they want to understand:

- When exactly does a potential buyer recognize that they have a need to fulfil? At what point does she start to think about fulfilling a need?

- Where do potential customers gather information on their options? In some cases, a customer may know immediately where to go to buy what she wants (such as a local café); in other situations customers may seek the advice of others, in which case who do they ask? When you were choosing a university to go to, for example, did you immediately know where to apply or did you ask other people for information? The marketing department of your university would be very interested to know who you asked as they would want to make sure that they are working with these people to ensure they are good ambassadors.

- How do customers assess the alternatives? When you were choosing a university what influenced your decision—the location? The accommodation? The lecturers? This information will be key to the university in terms of what to promote in its communications.

- How do customers decide whether to buy or not? This may be affected by the payment terms—for example, can you pay in instalments? Or the delivery terms or the guarantee provided? A business will want to understand the relative importance of the many factors that can affect a customer's decision to buy.

- What is the reaction of customers after they have bought an item? The feedback of customers can clearly affect whether others buy the product in the future—for example, what people tell their friends, and the reviews they post online can be powerful influences on future purchases.

The typical stages in the customer buying process are shown in Figure 3.10.

Marketing research provides the information that managers need to decide what to do and assess the effectiveness of marketing activities. For example, managers may use data on different markets such as that in Analysing Business Data 3.3 to decide which to target. In the next section we examine the marketing mix, which describes the collection of marketing decisions managers take to implement their strategy.

Think about it

How did you choose the course you are on and the institution where you are now studying?

What factors did you consider?

Where else did you look?

How did you find out about it?

Where did you look for further information?

When did you start looking?

How might the answers to the questions above affect the marketing activities of the institution where you are now studying?

Figure 3.10 The stages of the customer buying process. *Source:* Author.

Of course, marketing research cannot always be guaranteed to give the right information. The effectiveness of research depends in part on whether the right questions are asked and how the data is interpreted. A classic example of this is the disappointing sales of new Coke when it was launched in April 1985. All the research showed this new formula for Coke was going to be popular. What the researchers didn't ask about was how people would feel if 'traditional' Coke was taken off the shelves. There was outrage when it happened.

Analysing the business data 3.2 Sales of energy drinks around the world

Figure 1 shows the litres of energy drinks consumed in different regions and the annual growth rate of the market (AGR) as a whole.

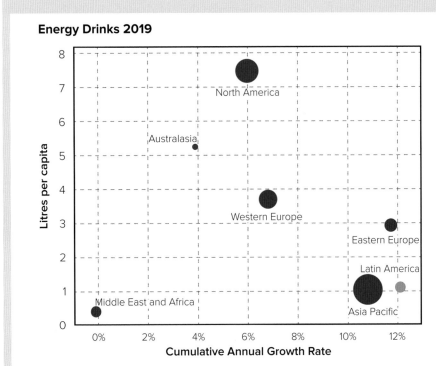

Figure 1 Sales of energy drinks and marker growth rates in different regions of the world. *Source:* Author.

Question

Analyse the significance of this data for the marketing manager of an energy drinks business.

People said it was the equivalent to burning the US flag because traditional Coke was such an iconic brand. The old formula was quickly reintroduced. Marketing research also relies on the way it is conducted and the answers it generates. In the 2001 census in the UK nearly 400,000 people stated as their religion as Jedi (after the Jedi Knights in Star Wars); this was not previously regarded as a religion with the UK. In the 2011 census nearly 6000 people in the UK gave their religion as 'Heavy Metal'.

3.3.4 Developing a marketing strategy

As we have seen, the marketing management process is likely to begin with marketing research to provide the information needed to make marketing decisions. The next stage in the process is to set marketing objectives and develop a marketing strategy. This is shown in Figure 3.11.

Typical marketing objectives include:

- Sales targets. A business may set a certain target level of sales. Sales can be measured in terms of the number of units sold (volume) or the amount spent (value). These measures can move in different ways. For example, if the volume of sales remains the same but the price of a unit falls then the sales value will also fall.

- Market share. This measures the sales of a business or a product as a percentage of total sales in that market. For example, if the market share of a business is 10% this means its sales are 10% of the total sales in that market. The sales of the product and market may be measured in terms of the value of sales or the volume of sales. According to Statista, in 2022 Nike had a market share of nearly 28% of the global athletic shoe market in terms of the value of sales. Market share is often used instead of sales because it takes

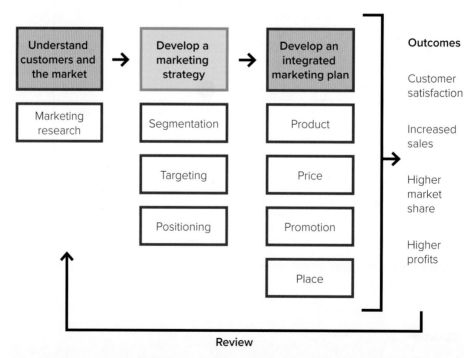

Figure 3.11 Developing the marketing strategy is part of the marketing management process. *Source:* Author.

Analysing the business data 3.3 Market shares of smartphone

The data in Figure 1 shows the global market shares of different smartphones.

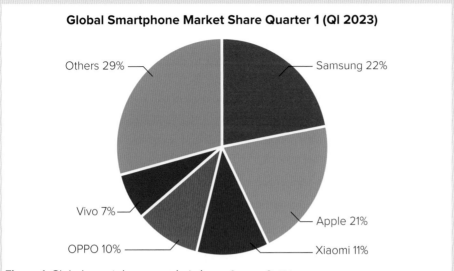

Global Smartphone Market Share Quarter 1 (QI 2023)

- Others 29%
- Samsung 22%
- Vivo 7%
- Apple 21%
- OPPO 10%
- Xiaomi 11%

Figure 1 Global smartphones market share. *Source:* Statista.

Question

What factors do you think influence the market share of any particular brand?

Source

Harmeet Singh Walia, Amulya Pulstya (2023) *Mobile Devices Monitor—Q1 2023 (Vendor Region Countries)*. Available at: https://report.counterpointresearch.com/posts/report_view/Monitor/3866 [Accessed 21 June 2023]. Adapted by author.

account of what is happening in the market as a whole. An increase in sales of 3% in one year may sound appealing but if market share is falling this signals that the sales in the market as a whole are growing at an even faster rate which may, therefore, be a concern. An example of market share data is shown in Analysing the Business Data 3.3.

- Brand awareness. A business may be keen to increase the awareness of its brand by customers. This may influence customers' propensity to purchase and generate customer loyalty and repeat purchases.

When setting a marketing objective, managers will need to consider the resources of the business (for example, does it have the necessary capacity?) and the costs of achieving it. The business will want to evaluate the likely return on any marketing investment. Remember that marketing activities cost money; managers will want to measure the benefits they bring.

Key concepts

Sales value measures the amount spent in a market.

Sales volume measures the number of units sold in a market.

Market share is measured by (sales of a product/total sales in a market) × 100.

Figure 3.12 Developing a marketing strategy: Segmentation, Targeting, Positioning. *Source:* Author.

Having set an objective, a business will need to decide on the strategy to achieve its targets.

To develop an effective marketing strategy, managers will want to:

- Identify segments that exist within a market. Segmentation is the process of dividing markets into groups with people with needs and wants that are similar to each other, but different to the other groups.

- Decide which of these segments the business wants to target.

- Decide how to position the business within its targeted segments.

This process of developing a marketing strategy which involves Segmentation, Targeting, and Positioning (STP) is shown in Figure 3.12.

3.3.5 **Market segmentation**

According to the Market Research Society in the UK, market segmentation is 'the process of dividing markets into groups with people or occasions that are similar to each other, but different to the other groups'.

Markets may be segmented in different ways. For example, there is:

- Demographic segmentation; this includes identifying different groups of people with similar needs and wants according to their age, income, or gender. Toys, for example, may target different age groups. After the fifth edition of the first Harry Potter book the publishers decided to have different covers to target adults and children separately. The children's versions had bright, colourful covers whereas the adult version had a more sophisticated design and was published in black and white. Research had shown that adults would have been embarrassed being seen reading a children's book so a different cover overcame this problem.

- Geographic segmentation; this differentiates customers according to where they are based. For example, the specifications for a car to drive around Norway compared to Monaco could be very different because of very different driving conditions. The menu in McDonald's will be adapted according to the eating and drinking habits of people in that region of the world.

- Psychographic segmentation; this divides a market into different segments based on their social class, lifestyle, or personality characteristics. For example, communications aimed at extroverts may be different from those aimed at introverts. In 2004 Allied Domecq undertook research to understand why sales of the liqueur drink, Kahlua, was low in bars and clubs but relatively high at home. Its research showed its drinkers were mainly women and mainly mothers. They usually drank a glass of Kahlua in the evening. Further research showed that its consumer saw the evening as a time they could be themselves and have some 'me time'; this was marked by a glass of Kahlua. Allied

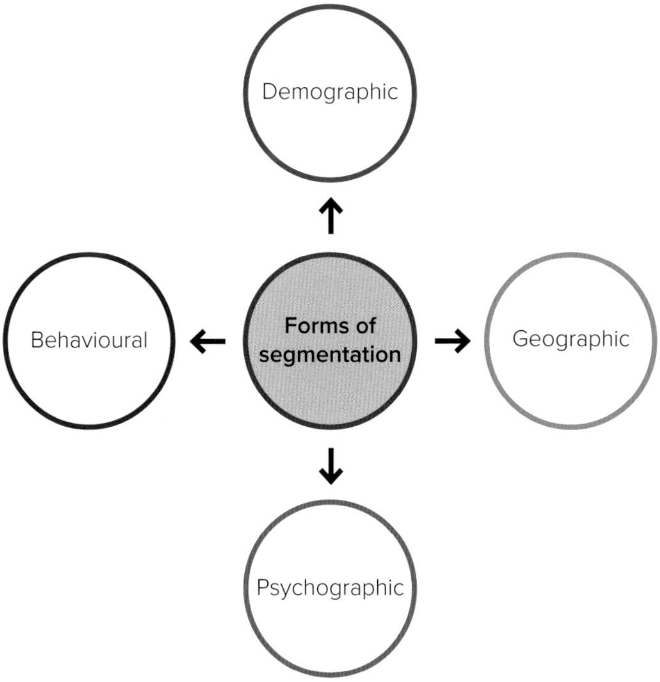

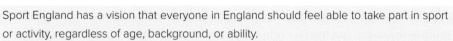

Figure 3.13 Forms of market segmentation. *Source:* Author.

Domecq based a $10 million promotional campaign based on the idea that Kahlua was not associated with the daily routine; it featured women walking alligators and tigers.

- Behavioural segmentation; this divides a market into segments based on factors such as the occasions that people buy, the benefits they seek when they buy the products, how loyal they are, and how much they use the product. For example, are customers buying flowers for peoples' birthdays, to celebrate particular festivals, or when someone is unwell? Are people buying a bike to commute in the city or to get out into the country and exercise at the weekends?

A business will want to understand what segments exist in its markets. It will then decide which of these segments it wants to target, i.e. which segments it wants to compete in. Forms of businesses segmentation are shown in Figure 3.13.

Business insight 3.5 Market segmentation by Sport England

Sport England has a vision that everyone in England should feel able to take part in sport or activity, regardless of age, background, or ability.

It wants everybody to experience the benefits that taking part in sport and physical activity brings, including:

- Mental well-being
- Physical well-being
- Individual development
- Economic development
- Social and community development.

▶

Sport England has used market research to segment its market. Its market segmentation has been designed to help understand the life stages and attitudes of different population groups—and the sporting interventions most likely to engage them. This segmentation identifies the different reasons why groups of people undertake sport—some like to compete, some want to keep fit, some feel they have to do it for health reasons, some like the team element, some like the social element. Sport England identifies very different segments linked to factors such peoples' age, interests, personalities, and their stage in the life cycle. This affects their motivations, the types of sports they want to do and how often and where and they want to take part.

Questions

Do you do any sport? Why? Why do you choose that particular type of sport to do?

How is market segmentation useful for the marketing function of Sport England?

How does market segmentation help Sport England achieve its vision?

Source

www.sportengland.org/research/understanding-audiences/market-segmentation/

3.3.6 Targeting

Market targeting is the process of evaluating each market segment's attractiveness and selecting one or more segments to enter.

The appeal of a particular market segment will depend on factors such as:

- Its size and potential growth.
- The degree of competition and the likely reaction of competitors if the business enters.
- The likely returns on investment.
- The ease with which the business thinks it can meet the demands of customers in this segment.

A business will target the segments where it thinks it can earn an appropriate return on its investment.

A niche strategy occurs when a business targets a relatively small segment of the market. A mass market strategy occurs when a large segment is targeted.

Once certain segments have been selected as targets a business will want to decide on where it is positioned within a market—for example, does it want to offer a premium product or a budget one? Think of the hotel market—there are many different hotels which target different markets (such as family holiday v city break v business) and position themselves differently, such as basic and cheap or luxury and expensive.

Once a target market is selected the business will need to decide on how it fits within that market in the eyes of customers compared to rivals; this is known as positioning.

What would you do?

Your company is developing space flights for private individuals. Who would you target?

Key concepts

Segmentation is the process of dividing markets into groups with people with needs and wants that are similar to each other, but different to the other groups.

Targeting is the process of evaluating each market segment's attractiveness and selecting one or more segments to enter.

Positioning is the arranging for a product to occupy a clear, distinctive, and desirable place relative to competing products in the minds of target consumers.

A **niche market strategy** occurs when a business targets a relatively small segment of the market.

A **mass market** strategy occurs when the market as a whole is targeted.

3.3.7 Positioning

Market positioning is the deciding on a clear, distinctive, and desirable place in the market that the business wants a product to occupy relative to competing products in the minds of target consumers. Think of how McDonald's and Burger King battle for a position in the fast food market or how Apple and Samsung try to shape customers' perceptions of their brand in the smartphone market.

It is important to remember that the positioning of a business depends on how customers see the business not how the business sees itself or would like to see itself. The perception of customers is key to positioning: a business may want to be premium but if its products are badly made and if its customer service is inefficient this is not how customers will see it.

Can you now answer this question from the introductory case study?

What do you think would be the criteria used to decide to target a particular group of customers?

Where are we now?

We have considered two elements of the process of marketing management: marketing research and developing the marketing strategy. In the next section we consider how this strategy is implemented in the form of a marketing plan and the marketing mix.

3.4 Developing an integrated marketing plan

Once a marketing strategy is developed and the business has identified the target segment and the desired position, it can now implement this strategy through a marketing plan. This involves developing the marketing mix in line with the strategy to achieve the objectives of the business. This is shown in Figure 3.14.

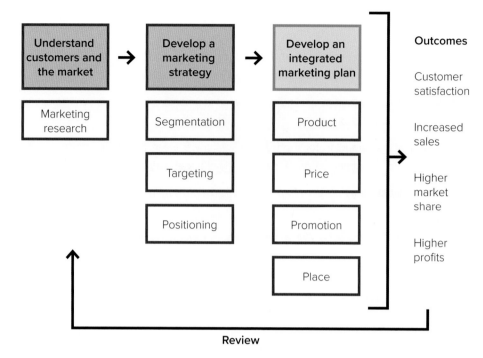

Figure 3.14 A business will implement its marketing strategy by developing an integrated marketing mix. *Source:* Author.

3.5 The marketing mix (4Ps)

The marketing mix refers to the collection of marketing activities related to a product which contribute to its overall ability to satisfy customers. According to Kotler the marketing mix is made up of tactical marketing tools which are blended together in an integrated programme that targets customers and delivers the intended customer value.

The marketing mix is typically described in terms of the 4Ps:

- product
- price
- promotion
- place.

The combination of factors that make up the marketing mix known as the 4Ps is shown in Figure 3.15.

As we will see later, some marketing analysts extend these 4Ps to 7Ps by adding in People, Process, and Physical Environment.

The key to successful marketing is to have an integrated marketing mix that is appropriate for the chosen strategy and target group.

An integrated marketing mix means that the different elements of the 4Ps complement each other. For example, imagine your product is a Rolex watch. This is a speciality product

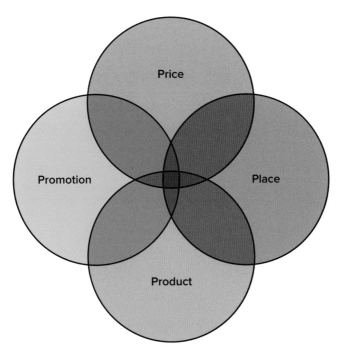

Figure 3.15 The four Ps of the marketing mix. *Source:* Borden, N. (1984). The Concept of the Marketing Mix. *Harvard Business School Journal*, 2, 7–12.

and customers would expect a high price, limited distribution in quite exclusive outlets, and promotion targeting high-income individuals. By comparison, if a business was positioned as a budget airline, customers would expect a basic level of service, low prices, and promotion focusing on low price and targeting price-sensitive buyers.

If the marketing mix is not well integrated this is likely to affect sales. Imagine that a management consultant describes herself as the expert in her field but only charges £25 an hour. There would be a mismatch between what the product is supposed to be and the price charged. Customers would be suspicious and may be less likely to buy.

The design of the mix depends on a clear understanding of:

- Who are your customers?
- What they are buying, i.e. what benefit do they want?
- What do they consider when deciding whether to buy?
- Who is involved in the buying process?
- What is the decision-making process?

We now examine the four elements of the marketing mix: the product, the price, the place, and promotion in turn.

Key concept

The **marketing mix** refers to the collection of marketing activities related to a product which contribute to its overall ability to satisfy customers.

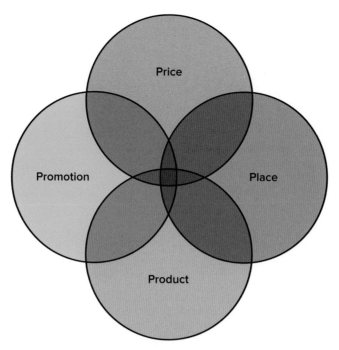

Figure 3.16 The product is one element of the marketing mix. *Source:* Borden, N. (1984). The Concept of the Marketing Mix. *Harvard Business School Journal*, 2, 7–12.

3.5.1 The product

In this section we will examine the product element of the marketing mix in detail. The product as part of the 4Ps is shown in Figure 3.16. We will consider the different types of products that exist, the different ways products can provide value to customers, the importance of the benefits of a product relative to its price, and the significance of the brand.

Types of products

According to the American Marketing Association, 'A product is defined as a bundle of attributes (features, functions, benefits, and uses) capable of exchange or use; usually a mix of tangible and intangible forms'. The different types of product are shown in Figure 3.17.

This means that a product may be an idea, a physical entity (a good), or a service, or any combination of the three.

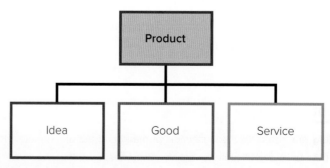

Figure 3.17 Types of product. *Source:* Author.

Key concepts

B2C marketing occurs when businesses target their end customers.

B2B marketing occurs when businesses target other businesses.

Marketing activities can also relate to any of the three (or combinations of them); think about a political party promoting its policies (idea), a business launching a new mobile phone (good), or an accountant attempting to generate more clients (a service). A product exists for the purpose of exchange with the aim of satisfying the individual and organizational objectives.

There are many different types of products and these can be categorized in different ways. For example, products may be divided into:

- consumer products; these are bought by the end user, for example, a McDonald's burger. If businesses are targeting the end consumer this is called B2C or Business to Customer marketing.

- producer (or industrial) products; these are bought to be used by another business in its operations process. For example, machinery. If businesses are targeting other businesses this is called B2B or business 2 business marketing.

Consumer products can be subdivided into:

- **Convenience products.** These are products where consumers realize that they have a need but will not travel far to fulfil this. They will go to the nearest store for this type of product. Managers must focus on ensuring that these products are widely distributed so they are as convenient as possible for customers. An example of a convenience product is chewing gum.

- **Shopping products.** These are products that customers shop around for when they are looking to buy them. For example, if customers are thinking of buying a new washing machine they might look at different models and compare prices. They probably won't go to the nearest shop and buy the first one they see. There is, therefore, something of a time lag—which could be days or weeks—between the decision to buy a product and actually deciding what to buy.

- **Specialty products.** These are exclusive products such as Ferrari sports cars. Customers may have an idea that they want to buy this product for many years and will be willing to travel some distance to buy them. Customers will want an 'experience' of this special purchase so businesses will often focus on well-designed outlets and a high level of personal service.

The different types of consumer product are shown in Figure 3.18.

The differences in these products and the implications for marketing are shown in Table 3.1.

The value of a product

The value of a product measures the satisfaction that customers get from buying it. This depends on the perceived benefits and the price. An expensive product may be good value for money provided the benefits offered justify the price. Similarly, a low-price product could be poor value for money if the benefits are not even worth the low price charged.

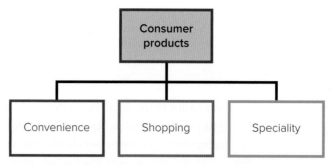

Figure 3.18 Different types of consumer product. *Source:* Author.

Table 3.1 Features of different consumer products

Marketing activities	Convenience	Shopping	Speciality
Buying behaviour	Customers buy regularly, look for nearest outlet, little time comparison with alternatives	Less frequent purchases, compare brands, features and prices	Clear brand preference, rarely bought by a customer (could be 'once in a lifetime')
Price	Low	Higher price than convenience items	High
Distribution (place)	Wide distribution, convenient locations	Selective distribution in retail outlets	Exclusive distribution; very limited distribution
Promotion	Mass promotion	Promotion by producers and retailers	Very targeted promotion
Examples	Newspaper, chewing gum	TVs, washing machines	Rolex watch and Ferrari

The three ways in which a product may provide benefits are:

- **The core product.** When a business develops a product it should consider the core need it is fulfilling. As Theodore Levitt said no one buys a drill, they buy the hole!— They only buy a drill because it drills a hole. The hole is what is demanded.

    Products often fulfil more than one need at once. A car provides transport allowing you to get from A to B; there may also be other benefits such as sense of status—there is a difference driving a Volvo from A to B and driving a Lamborghini. Marketing managers aim to understand what people are looking for and why they want it. For example, a Mont Blanc pen is usually bought as a gift; people are not buying it for themselves but to reward others.

- **The actual product.** This involves aspects of the product itself—for example, in terms of its specifications, its design, its packaging, its features, and its brand name. Think of the appeal of Apple-designed products or the success of IKEA offering self-assembly packed furniture—it is the way that the core needs are being met that are creating value.

- **The augmented product.** This offers additional services and benefits for customers. For example, you might be offered free delivery, after sales service, guarantees, or product support on some products. Think of businesses that offer free home delivery or free home installation.

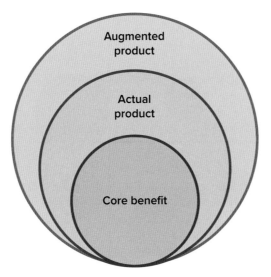

Figure 3.19 The benefits of a product. *Source:* Author.

The different benefits of a product are shown in Figure 3.19.

Product portfolio

Most businesses will have more than one product. Managers will want to assess the position of all of these products to plan what to do next. The collection of products a business offers is known as its product portfolio.

One way of categorizing these products is known as the Boston Matrix. This is a model developed by the Boston Consulting Group. This analyses products in terms of their market share and the growth of the market.

- **Cash cows:** these products have a high market share in a slow-growth market.
- **Problem children** (also called question marks or oil rigs). These products have a low market share of a fast-growth market. They have these names because they highlight that these products may become more successful in the future but may fail. Their future is uncertain.
- **Stars:** these are products with a high market share of a fast-growing market.
- **Dogs:** these are products with a low share of a slow-growth market. These products are not attractive in their existing position. Managers will decide whether to try and revive them, sell them off, or simply stop producing them.

These products can be shown on the Boston Matrix as seen in Figure 3.20. Each circle represents a product in terms of its market share and its market growth. The area of the circle represents its turnover.

A balanced product portfolio

A balanced portfolio occurs when a business has an appropriate mix of products. For example: cash cows are well established and need relatively low levels of promotion. Cash cows generate high funds which can be used to invest in new products that can provide profits in the long term. The problem with cash cows is that the markets are mature and are

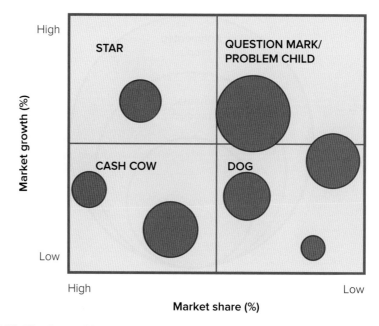

Figure 3.20 The Boston Matrix. *Source:* BCG Global.

well established so they do not offer the opportunity of high growth. Money from cash cows can be used to support products such as question marks and help them become more successful in fast-growing markets.

If there was a lack of balance in the portfolio this could cause problems for the business. For example, if a business has mainly

- Cash cows. This would suggest the current inflow of funds should be high because there are a number of well-established products. However, the business may be concerned about the future because its products are not in fast growth market.

- Dog products. Managers would be concerned about the business because its products are in slow-growth markets and do not have a large market share.

- Question marks: these might have promise but are likely to need investment and support to help them to gain market share.

>>> Can you now answer this question from the introductory case study?

What are the benefits to a business such as Disney of having a portfolio of products?

Key concepts

The **product portfolio** of a business refers to its collection of products a business offers.

The **Boston Matrix** shows the product portfolio of a business in terms of relative market share and market growth.

Where are we now?

So far, we have looked at the types of product a business could offer, the value of these, the concept of the competitive threshold, and the product portfolio. The final topic we will look at in relation to products will be the brand.

3.5.2 **Brand**

According to the American Marketing Association a brand is a 'name, term, design, symbol or any other feature that identifies one seller's good or service as distinct from those of other sellers'. The International Standards Organization (ISO) states that a brand 'is an intangible asset' that is intended to create 'distinctive images and associations in the minds of stakeholders, thereby generating economic benefit/values'.

A brand is, therefore, something that identifies a product. Businesses may protect their brands by taking out legal protection for the name and logo through a trademark.

A brand will convey something about the product. A brand's value proposition is the set of benefits or values it promises to deliver to customers to satisfy their needs. Customers may value it because it may reassure them about the quality of the product or they may identify with the values of the brand and want to be associated with it.

Some brands are global. Just think of brands such as Netflix, Google, IKEA, Amazon, eBay, Nike, H&M, McDonald's, Epic Games, and Nintendo that are huge brands in many (but not all) countries. However, the brand awareness and loyalty will vary from country to country and some brands are more regional. Jinro soju, for example, is one of the world's best-selling spirit brands. It is huge in some markets such as South Korea but in others for example, within Europe, it is far less well known. According to Statista these were the biggest brands in Mexico in 2022: Corona, Claro, Pemex, Modelo Especial, Bodega Aurrera, Cemex, and Telcel—how many of these do you know?

By developing a strong brand, a business may be able to:

- charge more for its products as demand may be less sensitive to price
- spend less on promotional costs as the brand will already be known
- launch and sell other products under the same brand name more easily and more cheaply as customers may be more willing to try them.

However, the brand has to fit with the offering. Levis—well known for its jeans—struggled when it launched a range of suits; Bic—associated with disposable plastic pens and lighters—found its brand did not transfer to small disposable bottles of perfume.

Brand equity refers to the value of the brand. Nike, Adidas, and Zara have high brand equity. These brands have a very high level of high awareness and consumer loyalty. Although it is difficult to value how much these brands are worth it is clear they are valuable. A pair of trainers with the Nike logo is worth considerably more than a pair without it. According to the marketing consultancy Interbrand the most valuable brands in 2022 were (in order) Apple, Microsoft, Amazon, Google, Samsung, Toyota, Coca-Cola, Mercedes-Benz, Disney, and Nike.

Key concepts

A **brand** is a name, term, design, symbol, or any other feature that identifies one seller's good or service as distinct from those of other sellers.

A **brand's value proposition** is the set of benefits or values it promises to deliver to customers to satisfy their needs.

Brand equity refers to the value of the brand.

The value of a brand can be 'leveraged', i.e. built on to generate more revenue by:

- Line extension. This occurs when a business adds more products to existing product lines by adding new versions; for example, new flavours.

- Brand extension. This occurs when a brand is extended on to a different product; for example, Virgin started in the music business but has extended its brand into many other areas such as airlines, banking, trains, and mobile phones.

 ## Can you now answer these questions from the introductory case study?

What is meant by a brand?
Why are brands so important to Disney?

 ## Where are we now?

Now that we've explored the various elements of the 'first P', product, let's now turn to look at the 'second P', price.

3.5.3 **Price**

Price is an element of the marketing mix as shown in Figure 3.21. There are many factors that will influence the price of a product as shown in Figure 3.22.

The influences on price include:

- Costs. To make a profit the price will need to be higher than the unit costs to make or provide it.

- The prices of competitors. A business will need to consider the price of what it offers relative to the benefits and relative to what competitors are offering. A business may be able to compete with a product if it has a higher price provided it has more benefits.

- The sensitivity of demand to prices. If demand is very sensitive to price a low price will generate so many sales that revenue will be higher than a high price. If demand is

 ## Key concepts

Line extension occurs when a business adds more products to existing product line by adding new versions.

Brand extension occurs when a brand is extended on to a different product.

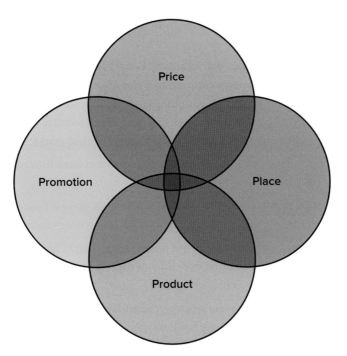

Figure 3.21 The price is an element of the marketing mix. *Source:* Borden, N. (1984). The Concept of the Marketing Mix. *Harvard Business School Journal*, 2, 7–12.

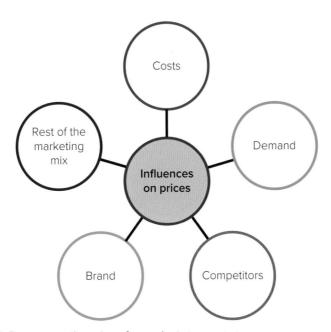

Figure 3.22 Influences on the price of a product. *Source:* Author.

not very sensitive to price a business can earn a higher revenue with a higher price than with a lower one. When the travel restrictions started to be lifted by governments in 2021 for people wanting to travel to other countries airline ticket prices soared in many cases as demand rose. Given the lack of travel possibilities during the pandemic many passengers were so eager to travel that they were not particularly sensitive to prices.

- The brand. The brand values will influence the appropriate prices; for example, if the brand is positioned as a premium product the price should be relatively high. In 2020, although many retailers were cutting prices to clear stocks because of the fall in demand due to the pandemic, for example, the Chief Executive of Superdry felt the brand image was more important even if it temporarily lost market share.

- The rest of the marketing mix. For example, if a product has a limited distribution in upmarket stores the price is likely to be relatively high.

When deciding what price to charge, a business will take all these influences into account and consider the strategy it wants to adopt. Types of pricing strategy include:

- Price skimming. This occurs when the price is set relatively high when a product is first launched and then lowered over time to expand its appeal. This is most likely when demand is not very sensitive to price.

- Penetration pricing. This occurs when a product is launched with a low price to gain sales. This is most likely when the business wants to gain market share quickly.

- Cost plus pricing. This occurs when a business adds on a percentage of profit to the costs. This is often used when a business buys in materials and sells them on; for example, a retailer buying from a wholesaler.

- Price discrimination. This occurs when a business charges one price for a product in one market. For example, the price of a train ticket may depend on the time of day.

These pricing approaches are shown in Figure 3.23.

Of course, there is rarely one price for a product. Prices will vary according to where and when it is sold, who is buying (e.g. there may be a discount for members of a loyalty scheme). There may be, for example, often a list price which is the stated price but then

Figure 3.23 Approaches to pricing. *Source:* Author.

there may be discounts for situations such as large orders and cash payments. With more ordering online businesses can use dynamic pricing (or surge pricing) more easily; this means they change the price according to demand and supply conditions at any moment in time. Dynamic pricing is commonly used by businesses such as hotels, airlines, and passenger hailing companies, such as Uber, that change the price depending on when you book and how many rooms or seats they have left.

One key factor in pricing is how sensitive the demand for a product is in relation to price changes. The price elasticity of demand measures how sensitive the demand is to a change in price. If demand is not price sensitive (which means that the percentage change in the quantity demanded is less than the price change), demand is described as being price inelastic. If demand is price sensitive (which means that the percentage change in the quantity demanded is greater than the price change), demand is described as being price elastic.

The price elasticity of demand for a product will be affected by factors such as:

- The availability of similar products. If customers can easily switch to an alternative, demand will be sensitive to price changes.

- The perceived benefits of the brand. If the consumers are attached to the brand this will make demand less sensitive to price changes.

- The proportion of income spent on the product. If a relatively small proportion of income is spent on a product then price changes will not be perceived as having a significant effect and demand will be price inelastic.

- Who is paying for the product. People are more sensitive to price changes if they pay themselves and less sensitive if someone else pays for them. Demand for air travel is likely to be less price sensitive if the business rather than the individual pays for the tickets.

The price elasticity of demand will affect the price charged for a product and any potential price changes. If demand is price inelastic the business is likely to increase the price because the fall in sales will be proportionately smaller than the price increase. This means revenue can actually increase due to the higher price.

If, however, demand is price elastic then an increase in price would lead to a fall in revenue. The fall in quantity sold is so great that the higher price does not compensate for this.

The relationship between price, the price elasticity of demand, and revenue is shown in Table 3.2.

Businesses should consider the sensitivity of demand to price when setting prices. Marketing teams may focus on developing the brand and try to distinguish the product from

Table 3.2 The relationship between price, the price elasticity of demand, and revenue

Price change	Price elasticity of demand	Impact on revenue
Price cut	Price elastic	Increases
Price rise	Price elastic	Decreases
Price cut	Price inelastic	Decreases
Price rise	Price inelastic	Increases

competitors to make demand more price inelastic and enable price increases and higher profit margins.

Business may also identify different price elasticities in different markets and charge different prices for the same product as a result. This is called price discrimination. For example, the demand for train travel during the rush hour to get to work is less sensitive than later in the demand and fares rise as a result.

Where are we now?

We have now covered the product and price elements of the marketing, and will move on to consider the third 'P': promotion.

3.5.4 Promotion

Promotion refers to ways in which businesses communicate about itself and its products to customers. Promotion is part of the marketing mix, as shown in Figure 3.24.

The promotional mix refers to the combination of activities that are involved in communicating about a product. Elements of the promotional mix are shown in Figure 3.25.

Promotional activities may be used to:

- Inform customers about new features or special offers

- Persuade customers to buy the product

- Remind customers of why they bought it and reassure them they made the right decision.

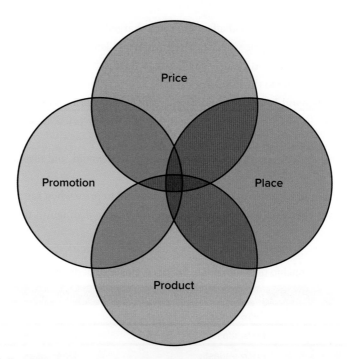

Figure 3.24 Promotion is an element of the marketing mix. *Source:* Borden, N. (1984). The Concept of the Marketing Mix. *Harvard Business School Journal*, 2, 7–12.

Figure 3.25 Elements of the promotional mix. *Source:* Author.

Promotion can take many forms including:

- **Advertising:** This is paid-for communication. Advertising may be broadcast, print, online, mobile, or outdoor. Businesses are also switching more funds into paid-for online advertising such as Google adwords. In 2021 digital advertising on platforms such as Google, Facebook, and Alibaba overtook the spending on traditional media for the first time ever. Global advertising spending was estimated by the media business Group M to be over $530 bn in 2020; digital marketing was estimated to account for over half of this. In the year 2000 online advertising was just 2% of total spending, so this shows how fast this change towards digital is occurring. The appeal is clear. With traditional print it can be difficult to measure the impact—content is static and the message is the same for everyone who sees it. Digital advertising can be very targeted—messages can be adjusted according to who receives it and the impact of the ad such as Click Through Rates (CTRs) can be easily measured.

- **Public relations:** This occurs when a business builds good relations with the various groups involved in or interested in the organization by gaining favourable publicity, building up a good business image, and responding to or preventing unfavourable media coverage.

- **Sales promotions:** These are short-term incentives to encourage customers to try a product; for example, special offers, discounts, coupons, and in-store displays. The Association of National Advertisers (ANA), defines sales promotions as 'tactics that encourage short-term purchases and influence the trial and quantity of purchase, and are very measurable in volume, share, and profit.'

- **Personal selling:** This occurs when a business has a salesforce that communicates, negotiates, and works with customers to generate business and build customer relationships. For example, the sales force of a food manufacturer will try to win orders from retailers. Personal selling is very common in B2B or Business-to-Business marketing. When you have a relatively limited number of customers, who are probably professional buyers with a focus on technical issues, it is likely that a business will have a sales force to meet and negotiate with the business buyers.

- **Sponsorship.** This occurs when a business financially supports an event or an individual. It uses this association to promote its own business. For example, many sports events have business sponsors. Red Bull has used sponsorship on extreme sports rather than advertising to promote its brand image and reach its target audiences.

- **Social media marketing.** Using digital marketing tools such as websites, social media, mobile apps and ads, online video, email, and blogs that engage consumers anywhere, anytime via their digital devices. For example, businesses are increasingly promoting their brand through social media—their Facebook, Instagram, and Twitter accounts, their Linked In profile ad, their business blog, for example, are important ways of informing existing and potential customers and shaping the brand. The number of people online and using social media is shown in Analysing the Business Data 3.4.

The composition of the promotional mix adopted will depend on factors such as:

- The target market and the most efficient way of targeting them.

- The financial resources available, e.g. a national television campaign is expensive and not likely to be viable for a small business.

Analysing the business data 3.4 Global digital population

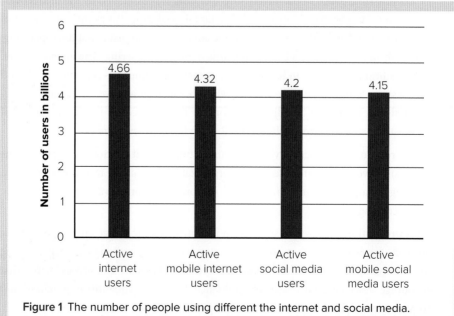

Figure 1 The number of people using different the internet and social media.

Source: Statista.

Question

Analyse the significance of the data in Figure 1 for marketing decisions.

- The nature of the business, e.g. if the business sells to other businesses it is likely to rely on its sales force to generate orders.

- Technology. The growth of social media and increasing options in targeted online advertising are creating many new opportunities for businesses wanting to promote their products. *The Economist* highlighted in 2023 how the internet has changed how younger buyers discover new brands. It stated that print, billboard, and TV advertising has given way to social media. Instagram is where the young look for inspiration, especially for goods such as fashion, beauty, and sportswear. Tik-Tok is another key source of information. These sites are getting better at enabling you to make a purchase without leaving them. According to McKinsey, by 2021 six out of ten Americans under the age of 25 had completed a purchase via a social media site.

Technology is changing the promotional activities of many businesses quite significantly. More businesses are using their budgets more for online activity rather than print. With online advertising it is easier to track what has been seen, when, and what action has been taken. It also allows much faster changes in campaigns. The highly successful Chief Marketing Officer of Burger King, Mr Machado, said that people may be talking about one thing online today but tomorrow will be talking about something else. He said that whereas in the past, a business would work on producing a campaign for about a year before launching it and then look for a new campaign a year later, these days messages are changing much more quickly.

The impact of technology on promotional activities can be seen in Business Insight 3.6.

Business insight 3.6 AdMov uses technology to target advertising

The growing number of smartphone and broadband users has had a significant effect on the advertising industry. There has been a major shift away from traditional media such as television, newspapers, and magazines and radio towards digital advertising.

In the Philippines Ellard Capiral started AdMov which is a technology-driven advertising company.

AdMov is an advertising company that provides technology-driven solutions to brands by showing their adverts through the tablets installed inside Grab cars. With AdMov's features such as artificial intelligence, lead generation, facial detection, real-time analytics, survey polls, and campaign reports, brands are able to target the right audience at their preferred time slots and locations. Currently, AdMov is working with leading brands such as Unilever and Coca-Cola.

The technology within AdMov enables the business to scan the passenger as they enter the vehicle and use various data points to estimate a person's age, gender, and mood. The system can also detect features such as a person's hair colour, the accessories he or she is wearing, and their hair length. All this data influences the adverts that are shown in the vehicle. The software also uses geo-fencing so it can identify where the taxi is and show content relevant to the area and the passenger. What this means is that everyone has personalized and interactive adverts including augmented reality options which allow passengers to try on products such as clothes whilst in the car.

▶

Ellard Capital says that compared to advertising such as billboards AdMov is much more targeted. AdMov describes itself as a sniper rather than the traditional advertising approach which it sees as a shotgun.

Questions

How is technology helping AdMov?

How has more use of technology in marketing affected you as a consumer?

Sources

www.pwc.com/ph/en/ceo-survey/2020/pwcph-start_up_survey_2020.pdf

manilastandard.net/mobile/article/294431

Developing promotional campaigns

To develop a promotional campaign, managers will:

- Identify who they want to communicate with; what is the target group for this communication?
- Determine what the aim of the communication is; for example, is it to make people aware of a new product launch, boost sales of an existing product, or to change their perceptions of a brand?
- Develop the message.
- Choose which media to use; for example, how will funds be allocated between print and online media?
- Send the communication.
- Review whether it has had the impact required and if not consider whether the message or media should be changed.

The stages involved in developing a promotional campaign are shown in Figure 3.26.

3.5.5 Place (distribution)

The final 'P' we will explore is known as 'place'; this is part of the marketing mix as shown in Figure 3.27. The place element of the marketing mix refers to the distribution of product.

Key concept

The promotional mix refers to the combination of activities involved in communicating about a product.

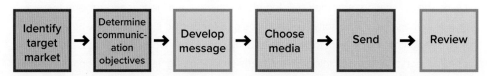

Figure 3.26 The stages in a promotional campaign. *Source:* Author.

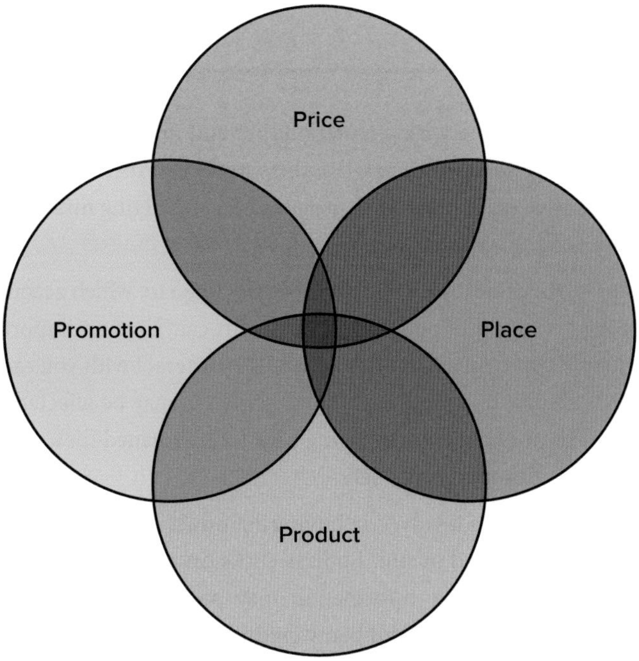

Figure 3.27 Place (distribution) is an element of the marketing mix. *Source:* Borden, N. (1984). The Concept of the Marketing Mix. *Harvard Business School Journal*, 2, 7–12.

This includes how ownership of the product is transferred as the product moves from the producer to the customer. For example, is the product sold directly or via intermediaries such as retailers? If there are no intermediaries, this is a zero-level channel. Using intermediaries may allow a business to reach more customers but will increase costs and means the producer loses some control over pricing and promotion. One consequence of there being more and better internet access is that there are more opportunities for customers to buy direct from a business without using intermediaries. There has also been growth in multi-channel distribution whereby customers can buy direct online but pick up and return products in store. In 2021, according to the *Financial Times*, the German sportswear business, Adidas, announced it was focusing on selling direct to customers rather than through retailers. Its target was for 80% of sales to be online or through its own stores by 2025. By this year Adidas aims to sell every other product direct to customers rather than one in three in 2019.

Developments in technology have also led to growth in digital distribution when the product is distributed in digital form. When Netflix first started it distributed films in the form of physical CDs to peoples' homes—now you obviously stream films direct. Similarly, the book and music industry has been changed significantly by digital options.

What would you do?

Sales in your clothes retails high street chain are falling. Would you move all your business online?

3.6 The 7Ps

With the growth of services marketing writers Bitner and Booms (1981) argued that other Ps needed to be added to the traditional 4Ps; they argue that these additional Ps are often very significant in service marketing. They proposed the marketing mix should be extended to 7Ps and include:

- The People. When deciding on which university to go to, which accountant to use, or which nail bar to use, the people you deal with can have an important role. Their qualifications, their experience, and the way they interact with you can be a big influence on your choice. In a retail store, your purchase may be affected by whether the assistant does or does not approach you, how well informed they seem, and whether you feel they are they to assist or sell.

- The Process. The process involved in buying a product can be important in determining whether you go ahead or not. Endless clicks on a website and requests for what may seem like unnecessary information may put you off. Features such as long queues, excessive form filling, and many credit checks will deter customers. By comparison, if the process is easy this might appeal. Many energy companies and banks have tried to make it much easier to switch from one provider to another to try and steal market share.

- The Physical evidence. This refers to the tangible aspects that customers experience in relation to a service. For example, business cards, business stationery, and website design all create an impression of the business. Similarly, store design and layout can affect your buying patterns. Changing where products are in a supermarket has an impact on sales, as does the width of the aisles, the music playing (or not playing), and even the smells in the store. Many car show rooms are designed to make the buying experience as appealing as possible. The floors are shiny, the cars are polished, there is a waiting area with drinks and snacks, all to make spending your money feel better. These are all physical aspects of a service experience and are important to customer experience.

 Can you now answer these questions from the introductory case study?

What changes to the marketing mix might Disney take to reduce the seasonal risk that faces its business?

 Where are we now

We have now examined the 4Ps in some detail. The marketing mix will change over time as market conditions change and as the position of the product in the market changes. We now consider how the marketing mix might change over time due to the product life cycle.

3.6.1 The product life cycle

The product life cycle model highlights how the sales of a product might change over time. Typically, sales will be relatively slow when a product is launched in a market. This is known as the introduction phase of the product life cycle. Sales may then grow faster in the growth phase. In maturity sales will grow but at a slower rate. In the decline phase sales are falling.

The precise duration and shape of a product life cycle will depend on the product itself. A successful film may have high sales on launch but sales may not last very long. Some food brands such as Heinz tomato ketchup may have sales that continue steadily for many years but even there the business will continually be monitoring sales, competitors, and customer views. Track back over the history of Heinz tomato ketchup and you will find changes to the branding, the containers, the messaging, and the price.

An example of a product life cycle is shown in Figure 3.28.

The marketing mix will be adapted at different stages of the product life cycle. For example:

In the introduction phase of the product life cycle:

- The promotional activities may focus on informing customers about the new product
- The price may be set high (price skimming) or low (price penetration)
- distribution may be relatively limited.

In the growth phase of the product life cycle:

- Promotion may focus more on the benefits of this product compared to rivals
- The price may fall (if a skimming strategy had been adopted)
- Distribution may grow.

In the maturity phase the business might:

- Reduce distribution to key outlets
- Cut the price to maintain interest
- Reduce promotional spending if sales are not expected to rise again.

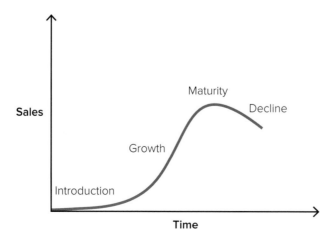

Figure 3.28 Product life cycle. *Source:* Author.

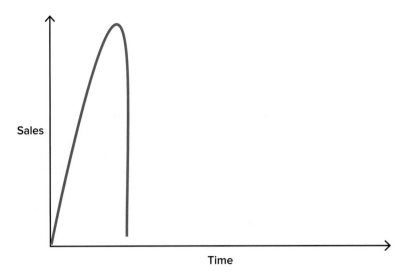

Figure 3.29 An example of a product life cycle. *Source:* Author.

Think about it

Can you think of any products which might have product life cycles similar to the ones in Figure 3.29?

What do you think the product life cycle for a new movie release on Netflix would look like?

3.6.2 Extension strategies

Managers will take action to shape the product life cycle in the way they want. Marketing activities to prolong the maturity phase of the product life cycle are called extension strategies. For example, to prevent the decline phase managers may use extension strategies such as:

- targeting a new market segment
- changing the marketing mix, e.g. lowering prices to sustain sales or seeking more distribution channels.

The effect of an extension strategy on sales is shown in Figure 3.30.

3.7 The 4Cs

In 1990 the marketing writer, Bob Lauterborn, argued that the 4Ps were dead and that we should be looking at marketing from the perspective of the consumer. He proposed the 4Cs instead of the 4 or 7Ps (Figure 3.31).

What would you do?

Your new action adventure film is finally ready and you are ready to launch in cinemas around the world. You are aware that films tend to have a very limited life span. What actions would you take to prolong the life cycle of your new film?

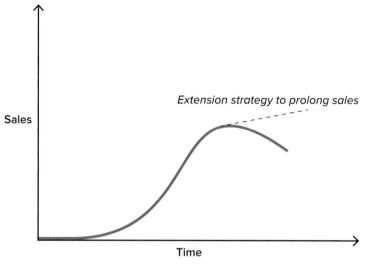

Figure 3.30 Extension strategies used to maintain sales. *Source:* Author.

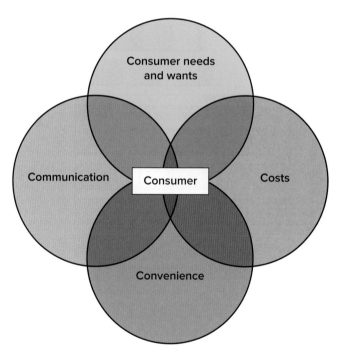

Figure 3.31 The four Cs. *Source:* Author.

Where are we now?

So far we have considered the marketing plan in terms of the marketing mix and the 4 or 7Ps. However, Bob Lauterhorn (1990) argues that we should think of the plan in terms of the 4Cs. We now consider this approach.

Analysing the business data 3.5 Video games consoles

The video games industry has been growing rapidly in recent years. Figure 1 shows the sales of different consoles over time. This highlights the product life cycle of each console.

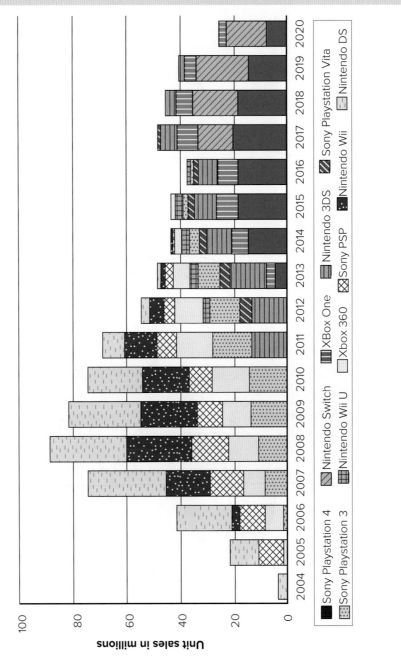

Figure 1 Sales of video games consoles over time. *Source:* Author.

Question

Analyse the significance of the data above in relation to marketing of a computer games console.

Think about it

Do you think the 4Cs is a better way of thinking about marketing activities rather than the 4 or 7Ps?

These 4 Cs are:

Customer needs and wants

As we have seen, a business must understand these to be competitive. If you produce a product that does not meet these needs and wants as effectively as its rivals it won't sell.

Cost

This highlights that what customers pay is a cost to them so businesses should think of the price in relation to the impact on a customer's costs. This should also include the additional and ongoing costs that might be involved—if you buy a phone it is not just the initial price of the handset but also perhaps the cost of buying headphones, a screen protector, the data usage charges and insurance charges. Buying a car involves running costs, repair costs, and insurance costs, not just the price of the car.

Convenience to buy

This refers to how easy it is for customers to access the product. Where can they buy it from? How easy is it to access the product, order it, and receive it? We can see how in an online world there is increasing convenience for the customers of most products and if you cannot offer this you may lose competitiveness.

Communication

Whereas promotion sounds rather one way, Lauterborn uses communication to suggest there can be more of a dialogue between a business and its customers. We have seen earlier how relationships marketing is growing and this provides more of an ongoing two-way link between the business and its customers.

 ## Now you should know

- A market-oriented business focuses on developing a product to meet customer needs; a sales-oriented business aims to persuade customers to buy a product.

- A marketing objective is a market target such as an increase in sales by 5% over 3 years.

- A marketing strategy is a long-term marketing plan to achieve the marketing objective.

- A market segment is a cluster of similar customer needs and wants.

  Markets can be segmented by age, by income, or geographically.

- Primary marketing research occurs when information is gathered for the first time; secondary research uses information that exists already.

- Marketing research can be used to identify who buys a product, how much is bought, when it is bought, and why it is bought.

- The marketing mix is the combination of factors such as the product, the price, the promotion, and the distribution that influence a customer's decision to buy.

- A marketing orientation refers to businesses which focus on identifying consumer needs and wants in order to develop products which address those needs.

- Marketing myopia means marketing short-sightedness.

- Line extension occurs when a business adds more products to an existing product line by adding new versions.

- Brand extension occurs when a brand is extended on to a different product.

- Data mining occurs when businesses identify patterns and correlations within large data sets to predict outcomes.

- Effective demand represents what customers want to buy and, crucially, are able to afford.

- The promotional mix refers to the combination of activities involved in communicating about a product.

- The product portfolio of a business refers to its collection of products a business offers.

- The Boston Matrix shows the product portfolio of a business in terms of relative market share and market growth.

- The marketing mix refers to the collection of marketing activities related to a product which contribute to its overall ability to satisfy customers.

 ## Review questions

Quick check

1. What is the difference between marketing and sales?

2. What is the difference between market growth and market share?

3. Distinguish between consumer and industrial products.

4. Outline three ways of segmenting a market.

5. Outline the elements of the marketing mix.

6. State the four categories of product in the Boston Matrix.

Analysis

1. Analyse the factors that might influence the price of a product.

2. Analyse the advantages and disadvantages of using primary market research when starting up a business.

3. Analyse the ways in which the promotional mix for an industrial product may differ from that of a consumer product.

Evaluation

1. Do you think marketing is a science or an art?

2. Steve Jobs, the founder of Apple, is said to have felt that marketing research was a waste of money because customers would not know what they wanted. Do you agree?

3. Do you think marketing is just another word for selling?

Find out more

For further reading on marketing you could look at:

Armstrong, G. and Kotler, P. (2020). *Principles of Marketing,* 18th edition. Harlow, Pearson. Education, Harlow, United Kingdom.; Philip Kotler is a widely re-spected marketing writer and his books are well worth a read.

Baines, P., Fill, C., Rosengren, S., and Antonetti, P. (2021). *Fundamentals of market-ing*. Oxford (UK), Oxford University Press.

Another good introduction to marketing is Blythe, J. and Martin, J. (2019). *Essen-tials of Marketing,* 7th edition. Pearson Education.

If you would like to know more about the power of a brand why not read 'Shoe Dog' by Phil Knight. Knight was the founder of Nike and the book considers the lessons learned when building the Nike brand. Knight, P. (2018). *Shoe dog*. Simon & Schuster.

For further online research on marketing you could look at:

Kotler. You can watch Kotler on You Tube. He has many videos there. Start with one called Marketing at the Chicago Humanities Festival. You can find Kotler's website at www.pkotler.org/

Viral advertising. You can see some adverts that went viral at www.disruptivead-vertising.com/video-advertising/viral-video-marketing-examples/

American Marketing Association. This website includes a number of articles on marketing you might find interesting. www.ama.org

You may also want to search on the ***Harvard Business Review*** website as this has some excellent articles on marketing. For example, you can find Levitt's classic articles such as 'Marketing Myopia' (July–August 1960), 'After the Sale Is Over. . .' (September–October1983), 'Marketing Success Through Differentiation-of Any-thing'(January–February1980), 'Production-Line Approach to Service' (September–October 1972), 'The Globalization of Markets' (May–June 1983), and 'Creativity Is Not Enough' (May–June 1963).

You might also want to read the HBR's Marketer's Toolkit or its '10 must reads on strategic marketing.' Another useful source for articles is *The Journal of Marketing.*

⬛ Bibliography

McKinsey (2021). [online] Available at: <https://www.mckinsey.com/business-functions/marketing-and-sales/our-insights/modern-marketing-what-it-is-what-it-isnt-and-how-to-do-it> [Accessed 8 May 2021].

American Marketing Association (2020). *What Is Marketing?—The Definition Of Marketing—AMA*. [online] Available at: <https://www.ama.org/the-definition-of-marketing-what-is-marketing/> [Accessed 20 September 2020].

Berry, L. L. (2000). Cultivating service brand equity. *Journal of the Academy of Marketing Science*, 28 (1), 128–37.

•Bitner, M. J. and Booms, H. (1981). Marketing Strategies and Organization: Structure for Service Firms. In Donnelly, J. H. and George, W. R. (eds), *Marketing of Services, Conference Proceedings*. Chicago, IL. American Marketing Association. pp. 47–52.

Borden, N. (1984). The Concept of the Marketing Mix. *Harvard Business School Journal*, 2, 7–12.

Chartered Institute of Marketing (2015). Definition of marketing [online], http://www.cim.co.uk/resources/understandingmarket/definitionmkting.aspx [Accessed 16 January 2020].

•Crossier, K. (1988). 'What exactly is marketing?', in Thomas, M. J. and Waites, N. E. (eds), *The Marketing Digest*, London, Heinemann.

Drucker, P. F. (1954). *The Practice of Management*. New York, Harper & Row.

Kotler, P. (2006). *Marketing Management: Analysis, Planning, Implementation and Control*, 12th edition. London, Prentice Hall.

Kotler, P. T. and Armstrong, G. (2017). Principles of Marketing, 17th edition. Harlow, Pearson.

Lauterborn, B. (1990). New marketing litany; four P's passe; C-words take over. *Advertising Age*, 41, 26.

Levinson, J. (1984). *Guerilla marketing*. Boston, Houghton Mifflin.

Levitt, T. (1960). Marketing Myopia. *Harvard Business Review*, 38, 45–56.

The Economist (2023). *How the young spend their money*. Available at: https://www.economist.com/business/2023/01/16/how-the-young-spend-their-money [Accessed 19 February 2023].

Chapter 4

Managing operations

Where are we now?

So far, we have considered the nature of business and have started analysing the functions of a business beginning with marketing. Marketing identifies the needs and wants of consumers; these need to be fulfilled by the operations function. In this chapter we consider how businesses manage the operations function.

Why am I studying this?

- Most people end up working in operations—they are involved in producing a good or service. This may well be your career in the future and so it makes sense to understand what operations management involves. This chapter provides an overview of operations management, and possibly your future career.
- You are interested in how products are made and delivered. This chapter considers the key aspects of operations and the ways in which different operations can be categorized.
- You want to know more about how businesses can add value for customers. You know this is a key to business success.
- You hear a lot about productivity in relation to business and the economy and you want to understand why it matters.
- You want to know how technology is changing business operations.

Learning objectives

By the end of this chapter you should be able to

- Explain what is meant by the transformation process
- Explain operations management
- Analyse typical operations objectives
- Analyse new technologies that are affecting business operations
- Evaluate the importance of operations management in business

Introductory case study UK fashion industry

The fashion industry is big business in the UK. Consumers in the UK buy more clothes per person that any other country in Europe. In 2017 the UK fashion industry was worth over £32 billion. The industry employs nearly 900,000 people in the UK in retail, manufacturing, brands, and fashion design. The garment industry is said to be the world's third biggest manufacturing industry after automotive and technology. The consumption of clothes creates jobs and growth in developing nations. However, it also leaves these countries with the majority of the environmental and social costs that are created by the fashion industry.

According to many business commentators the biggest clothing retailers in the UK have been 'chasing the cheap needle around the world'. This means they have been searching for the lowest production costs they can find. This means that they have bought materials from countries with low pay, little employee protection, and little environmental protection.

There are also concerns about the industry in relation to:

- The use of child, prison, or forced labour. For example, forced labour is used to pick cotton in two of the world's biggest cotton-producing countries: Turkmenistan and Uzbekistan. The label 'Made in the UK' should mean employees get at least the minimum wage but it is alleged many working in garment factories in cities such as Leicester do not.

- The amount of clothing being consumed in a world of fast fashion. Fast fashion involves increased numbers of new fashion collections every year, the rapid replacement of items in store and often low prices. Stores hold low levels of inventory and buy new designs in regularly. Clothes are all too easily thrown away and replaced by more purchases. This is causing waste and encouraging what could be regarded as unnecessary production.UK citizens discard over a million tonnes of textiles a year. Some of this goes to charity stores but over 300,000 tonnes of textile waste in the UK ends up in household bins and is sent to landfill or incinerators each year. Less than 1% of material used to produce clothing is recycled into new clothing at the end of its life.

- The destruction of inventory that has not been sold. In 2018, the British luxury brand Burberry faced a great deal of criticism when it revealed in its Annual Report for 2017/2018 that the cost of finished goods physically destroyed in the year was £28.6m (2017: £26.9m), including £10.4m of destruction of items in their Beauty inventory. Burberry had incinerated unsold clothes, accessories, and perfume to protect its brand and prevent unwanted stock from being sold cheaply.

A particular concern regarding the clothes industry is its impact on the environment. Textile production is a major contributor to climate change:

- It produces around 1.2 billion tonnes of CO2 equivalent (CO2e) per year; this is more than international flights and maritime shipping combined.

- The fashion industry consumes an estimated 79 billion cubic metres of fresh water annually. The growing and production of fibres consumes the greatest quantity of water. Water is also used when dyeing, finishing, and washing clothes. Adding rips and tears to jeans by applying chemicals is also harmful to workers and the environment. One kilogram of cotton—equal to the weight of a short skirt and a pair of jeans—can take as much as 10,000 to 20,000 litres of water to produce. The Aral Sea was formerly one of the four largest lakes in the world but has now almost entirely dried up due to cotton production.

- Textile production is responsible for high volumes of water containing hazardous chemicals being discharged into rivers and water courses. Twenty per cent of industrial water pollution globally is attributable to the dyeing and treatment of textiles, according to the Ellen MacArthur Foundation.

- The use of land to produce natural fibres can also cause deforestation and the loss of biodiversity. Between 2018 and 2030, for example, the fashion industry is expected to use 35% more land to produce fibres—an extra 115 million hectares that could be used to grow crops for the growing world population or to preserve forests to store carbon.

- Synthetic fibres. Most samples of water in the world's oceans contain tiny pieces of plastic. As much as 20% to 35% of all primary source microplastics in the marine environment are said to be from synthetic clothing.

Introductory case study questions

Think about the following questions as you read through the chapter. You may not yet be able to answer these questions, but as we progress through the chapter, we will revisit them at key stages. By the end of the chapter, you should be confident in answering them.

1. Which stakeholders are affected by the operations of the fashion industry?

2. If you were a manufacturer of clothes, what operations objectives might you set?

3. Why is efficiency so important to fast fashion?

4. Why do you think fast fashion is often associated with low inventory levels by retailers?

5. Why are suppliers important in the fashion industry?

6. Why might there be ethical issues when working with suppliers?

7. How do you think changes in the external environment might have affected the fashion industry?

Critical thinking

The article above is highly critical of the fashion industry.

1. How might the fashion industry defend itself?

2. Do you think the fashion industry would come under the same attacks in all countries?

4.1 Introduction to operations management

Everything you eat, everything you wear, everything you watch, and everything you use has been produced. It is the result of an operations process. Operations management manages the transformation of resources from inputs into outputs. It creates the value that makes the process worthwhile. When you buy an item online this has to be produced, which will often involve many businesses, it has to be ordered, and it has to be stored and delivered. Just think how many different 'operations' are involved in this whole process to get an item delivered to your door—often within 24 hours!

All kinds of things can be transformed in an operations process. These include:

- Materials. For example, different materials can be combined to produce food

- Customers. For example, someone going to a leisure centre may enter stressed but hopefully leaves relaxed; ideally you leave a hairdresser's looking better than when you went in.

- Information. For example, you may give your accountant a lot of financial data and they transform this into a set of finished accounts. Market researchers, consultants, and data analysts all process information.

The transformation of inputs into outputs is shown in Figure 4.1. What is fascinating about business is the number of ways in which value can be created, with business constantly seeking new customer needs and wants and new ways of meeting these needs. Even in an industry in which the transformation process may seem relatively straightforward, such as a coffee shop, the range of ways in this is done is extraordinary as businesses seek to create their own markets: different shop layouts, different ways of making the coffee, different blends, different ways of ordering, of queueing, and of being served. This variety of operations makes it a fascinating area of business.

What is also so interesting about operations is that transformation processes will be continuously reviewed to see if they can be improved, if different resources are needed, and if the output produced needs to be altered in any way. Business does not stand still.

The precise nature of the transformation process will vary from industry to industry so that whilst many principles of operations are transferable the specifics will depend on the context.

For example:

- An airline uses aircraft and staff to move passengers and freight around and transform them by taking them from location A to B.

- A retailer has products, stores, and staff to enable customers to access items they want to buy and consume.

- A management consultancy has specialists to take information and turn it into advice.

The output of operations processes will include:

- Physical goods, such as houses; these are tangible

- Intangible services, such as professional advice

- Waste and by-products; for example, when cutting fabric to make clothes there may be some 'off cuts' which may be thrown away or recycled.

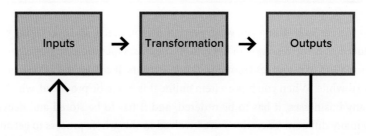

Figure 4.1 The transformation process. *Source:* Author.

Table 4.1 Examples of different types of transformation processes

Examples of operations process that transform materials	Examples of operations that transform customers	Examples of operations processes that transform information
Manufacturers	Tattoo artists	Management consultants
Mining businesses	Hairdressers	Market researchers
Delivery businesses	Theme parks	Accountants
Restaurants	Dentists	School inspectors

Examples of different types of transformation processes are shown in Table 4.1.

Operations management involves managing all the stages of this process, such as acquiring the resources needed, bringing them together successfully, developing the processes to manage their transformation, and distributing the final output.

Operations management will aim to add value through the transformation process and ensure the value generated by the sale of the output exceeds the value of resources used up. This means that a business must understand what customers want and are willing to pay for. It must deliver this output in a way in which it generates a surplus.

Meeting the needs of the market is, therefore, an essential part of operations management.

There is no point producing something that is not demanded. However, it may not be possible to meet each and every consumer's requirements precisely—it may not be technically possible or financially viable. Operations managers must consider the resources they have in relation to the demand of the market and develop the best match in terms of meeting the overall corporate objectives. Time, equipment, materials, and space are all limited at any time and decisions have to be made about how best to use these to meet customers' needs. The operations function and the marketing function are, therefore, closely interlinked and dependent on each other as shown in Figure 4.2.

What makes studying business so fascinating is the constant changes and developments in operations as organizations find new ways of doing things and new things to do. The global pandemic demonstrated the flexibility, resilience, and creativity of many businesses. They switched their operations from being sit-down restaurants which were forced to close in lockdown to takeaway cafes; they moved from physical retail outlets to

Key concept

Operations management manages the transformation of resources from inputs into outputs.

Figure 4.2 The activities of the operations function and the marketing function should be closely linked. *Source:* Author.

online businesses; they switched from making clothes to making face masks where demand was booming; they moved staff from the office to home. They found ways of reducing costs so they could still survive financially, they changed their operations to ensure there was social distancing and they found new ways we could order, pick up, or collect. Innovation in operations constantly changes how our needs are met: for example, streaming music rather than buying a vinyl record, being recommended what to buy through artificial intelligence systems rather than have to work it out for ourselves, and using direct debit rather than cash. Managing and improving operations is key to maintaining a competitive business.

4.2 Categorizing operations systems

At the heart of all operations systems are the concepts of transformation and adding value—whenever a business converts inputs into outputs, the value of the output should be worth more than the cost of producing it to be worthwhile. However, whilst all businesses want to add value, the actual nature of the transformation process can vary significantly.

One way of categorizing operations processes is to consider them in terms of their volume, their variety of output, their visibility, and their variation as shown in Figure 4.3. Differences in these areas have implications for costs and for the range of skills an equipment needed in the operations process.

Each of these aspects of operations will now be examined.

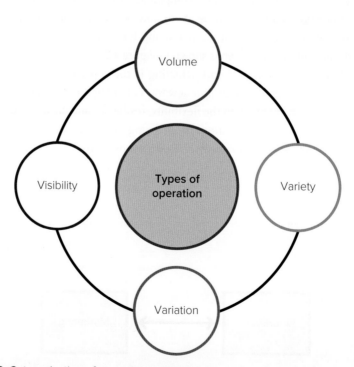

Figure 4.3 Categorization of operations systems. *Source:* Slack, N., Chambers, S. and Johnston, R. (2010). *Operations management.* Harlow, England: Financial Times Prentice Hall.

4.2.1 The volume of production

Operations processes will vary in terms of the volume of output produced in a given period.

For example, Ford produced over 4 million cars in 2020; Lamborghini produced less than 8000. Coca-Cola produces around 108 billion bottles a year whereas a musician, such as Billie Eilish, will probably record less than twenty albums in her lifetime.

In businesses where there is a high-volume production there is likely to be a high level of specialization and repeatability in production. The operations are likely to be capital intensive and, because of these high volumes, the cost per unit is likely to be relatively low as the initial investment costs can be spread over many units.

4.2.2 The degree of variety in production

A business that offers many varieties of a product is likely to be popular with customers because of the choice offered, but producing a range will often be more complex and expensive to provide compared to a more standardized offering. For example, an advertising agency will produce different campaigns for each client and this requires a flexibility and range of skills which will usually be expensive. By comparison, mass producing cans of beans is likely to be cheaper per unit. According to the *Manchester Evening News* the Heinz factory in Wigan, UK is the largest food processing factory in Europe and it produces more than one billion cans a year. By comparison, a restaurant that has a wide variety of menu options cooked exactly how the customer wants it will have higher unit costs than a fast food restaurant where customers have a limited range of options and have to accept how the food is cooked.

Examples of different combinations of 'volume' and 'variety' in operations can be seen in Figure 4.4. Job production describes tailor-made, individually produced items. This means that there a high level of variety as each item is personally made (for example, a tailor-made suit or personally made birthday cake); however, volumes are low because the items are so specific to individual requirements. Job production requires a range of skills and equipment. The unit cost will tend to be high in job production because costs cannot be spread over high levels of output.

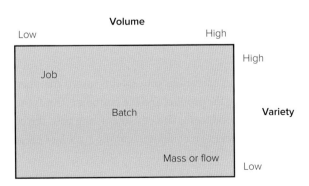

Figure 4.4 Combinations of volume and variety in operations. *Source:* Slack, N., Chambers, S. and Johnston, R. (2010). *Operations management.* Harlow, England: Financial Times Prentice Hall.

Key concepts

Job production describes tailor-made, individually produced items.

Batch production occurs when items move in groups (batches) from one stage of the operations process to another.

In **flow production** an item moves from one stage of a process to the next continuously.

Batch production occurs when items move in groups (batches) from one stage of the operations process to another. For example, when making bread or brewing beer there will be batches produced at one time. This means there is the opportunity for some variety as each batch can be made with different inputs (e.g. a different recipe) but the volume of production is higher than with job production.

In flow production an item moves from one stage of a process to the next continuously (for example, a chemicals plant). The output is standardized and so there is little variety but volumes are high. An example of flow production is the float glass process. According to Glass for Europe a typical float glass factory produces 650 tonnes of glass a day in furnaces that are over 60 metres long, 25 metres wide, and 12 metres high and hold around 2000 tonnes of molten glass. A float glass process is expected to produce 24 hours a day, 7 days a week for around 16 to 20 years.

The desired mix of volume and variety will depend on the need to vary output to meet customer demands and the likely levels of demand.

4.2.3 The degree of variation in demand

In some industries output will be produced on a constant basis because demand is always present. For example, a chemicals factory may be producing the same product 24 hours a day. By comparison, the demands on a car breakdown service or the accident and emergency service at a hospital will vary enormously during the day or at certain times of year. This means that operations need to be flexible to respond to sudden increases and decreases in demand. Where possible the business will attempt to anticipate demand—for example, the breakdown service will look at weather forecasts to estimate the future demand for its services.

However, having to vary output to meet fluctuations in demand is likely to be relatively expensive because resources that are required for the high demand period may not be used all the time.

4.2.4 Visibility

If there is high visibility in an operations process this means that there is close contact between the business providing the product and the customer. This is the case for dentists and doctors, for example—the producer is directly interacting with the customer. There is less visibility between the producer of a computer and the customer because of the intermediaries that sell the product.

If there is high visibility in the operations process this usually means that the production can be adapted for each customer but it is expensive as it is labour intensive. It also means that customer relationship skills need to be good because of the high levels of direct interaction.

Where are we now?

We have looked at how to categorize different types of operations by considering the volume, variety, and visibility of different processes. Now we will consider typical objectives that businesses set. This will provide another insight into what operations management involves.

4.3 Operations objectives

As with all the functions of a business, managers responsible for operations will be set or set themselves objectives. Businesses will decide how they want to compete against rivals and this will determine the relative importance of different objectives.

Typical operations objectives include:

- Volume. A business will need to produce certain quantities of goods or be able to provide a certain level of service at a particular moment. Lego sells over 70 billion bricks a year and needs to have the capacity to produce this volume. For some processes the volume produced will be constant; for others it will vary at different times of day, different days of the week, or different times of year. If a business cannot produce the quantity required this can lead to queues, waiting lists, and dissatisfied customers.

- Quality. Managers will set certain quality standards which can help to differentiate the business. When Dyson develops prototypes for its new models of vacuum cleaners it subjects them to intensive quality testing so that customers know they are reliable. For example, the cleaner heads are slammed into a steel table leg at 30 km an hour to check they won't break! A robot arm pushes the vacuum cleaner backwards and forwards for the equivalent of 21 years and also drops it onto a hard floor 5318 times. High quality can contribute to a strong brand image and customer loyalty.

- Costs. Managers will want production to achieve certain cost levels. These objectives are often set in terms of unit costs, i.e. the cost of providing one unit. Lower costs may enable more competitive pricing; for example, you may be able to claim that customers cannot find the same product cheaper elsewhere and use this in your promotions. The strategy of the giant retailer Walmart is to offer 'everyday low prices (EDLP)' for its customers. To do this, it is committed to 'everyday low cost (EDLC) so that its cost savings can be passed on to its customers.

- Speed of delivery. Managers will need to decide how quickly the business needs to respond to demand. It may decide to compete by being faster than rivals. For example, Pizza Hut aims to deliver its pizzas to your homes within 30 minutes of you ordering. In terms of actually producing the pizza the fastest producer in 2022 at Pizza Hut was Zagros Jaff who produced three pizzas in 70 seconds.

- Product range and flexibility. For example, managers will want to decide on how many versions or variations of their products they need to provide. McDonald's provides a certain number of items cooked a certain way whereas in a restaurant the customer has more flexibility to determine how something is cooked. Being more flexible may be more expensive in terms of production but may add more value for customers and can justify a higher price. Sunseeker, by comparison, produces to order. It builds hand-built and hand-finished luxury yachts to meet the specifications of their customers. Buyers can create a yacht personalized in any way they wish. This flexibility of production is reflected in the price and differentiates the business from more standardized boats.

- Speed of developing products and getting them to the market. In the mobile phone industry or the games industry, for example, new versions of phones are coming out regularly and a business may well set targets relating to new product development so that it stays ahead of rivals.

- Environmental targets. Businesses are increasingly concerned about their environmental impact because of the impact on society and their stakeholders. Targets may include reductions in pollution or carbon emissions. For example, Microsoft has set the target of being carbon negative by 2030. By 2050 Microsoft says it will remove all the carbon the company has emitted either directly or by electrical consumption since it was founded in 1975. Strong environmental value can enhance a brand.

- Dependability. This refers to the extent to which the business delivers the item at the time it promises. Dependability can attract and retain customers; if you know that deliveries will arrive as and when you say they will, this may lead more people to order from you. According to Bloomberg in 2022 the most punctual airline in the world (i.e. the highest proportion of flights that took off and landed within 15 minutes of the stated time) was Garuda Indonesia; over 95% of its flights were punctual.

Typical operations objectives are shown in Figure 4.5.

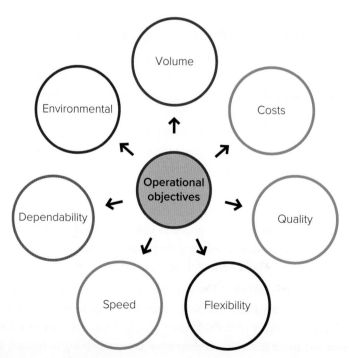

Figure 4.5 Typical operations objectives. *Source:* Slack, N., Chambers, S. and Johnston, R. (2010). *Operations management.* Harlow, England: Financial Times Prentice Hall.

Table 4.2 Comparing operations objectives in a restaurant and a hospital

Operations objective	Restaurant	Hospital
Productivity	How many customers it can serve per hour	How many patients are treated per hour
Capacity utilization	How many tables are booked each evening	What proportion of beds are occupied at any moment?
Speed	How fast does it intend to service customers?	How fast will patients receive treatment after arrival?
Quality	How does it intend to ensure that the food and drinks meet the required levels of quality?	To what extent are the treatments appropriate and accurate?
Costs	How can it manage costs whilst still providing the quality of food it wants? How can it reduce the waste to control costs?	To what extent are costs controlled and is waste reduced?

These operations objectives can be applied to any operations system but the precise nature of them will vary depending on the context. An example of how some of these objectives might apply in three very different operations processes is shown in Table 4.2.

Some of the different operational objectives may overlap. For example, by producing larger volumes a business may have more power over suppliers and may be able to push their prices down, reducing the costs per unit. Higher volumes and lower unit costs may be compatible. However, other objectives may conflict. For example, focusing on producing an item more quickly or transporting items faster may cost more. The Emma Maersk is one of the world's largest container ships. It transports huge quantities of products around the world. It does this cheaply but relatively slowly. Faster transportation would require a different form of transport and would be more expensive. In this case a business may have to decide which objective is the priority.

The importance of particular operations objectives will vary as new sources of competitiveness develop. The car industry, for example, has been revolutionized in recent years by the growing interest in electric vehicles and the drop in the demand for diesel fuel; environmental concerns are now dominant in the industry, requiring a change in engine design. This has created an opportunity for new producers such as VinFest from Vietnam. In food retailing the success in some countries by low cost providers such as the German-owned retailer Aldi has changed the focus of the more established players to ensure they can offer product lines that provide outstanding value for money.

A business will consider which of the operational objectives fit best with their capabilities, with market requirements, and which will provide sustainable sources of competitiveness.

Can you now answer this question from the introductory case study?

If you were a manufacturer of clothes, what operations objectives might you set?

4.4 Operations and the changing business environment

Operations managers will be operating within an external environment that will affect their decisions. Significant external changes that have implications for operations management include:

- Increasing expectations of quality and better service by customers. Customers now have access to more information online and this gives them more choice. To remain competitive businesses therefore have to provide better quality. They also have to keep developing their product range to ensure it meets their customers' needs.

- Increasing demands for more information by customers about how and where a product was made. Customers are increasingly interested in the supply chain. For example, when buying eggs customers may want to know how the chickens are looked after.

- Greater regulations on businesses. For example, more rules about customer safety and product labelling.

- More concern over the environmental impact of the production or consumption of a product. This is a growing issue as concerns over climate change grow and awareness of these issues are increased by activists such as Greta Thunberg.

External changes such as these have affected how businesses produce and have led to greater focus on objectives such as lower unit costs and better quality. Given the competitive nature of the environment in which they operate there is a constant pressure on businesses to improve their operations.

As we have seen, operations lie at the heart of the business and the key operational objectives that a business aims for will be influenced by the business environment. For example, there is growing pressure on business to recycle, to be more sustainable, and to reduce their levels of wastage. In the next section we examine how operations are managed to achieve these objectives.

Figure 4.6 shows the different aspects of operations we will examine.

Can you now answer this question from the introductory case study?

How do you think changes in the external environment might have affected operations management within the fashion industry?

Where are we now?

So far, we have identified typical operations objectives and some of the influences on them. We now consider each of these objectives and how a business might achieve them in more detail.

Figure 4.6 Different aspects of operations management. *Source:* Author.

4.5 **Managing operations: making location decisions**

One important strategic decision for a business is where to base its operations; this is shown in Figure 4.7. The location decision will depend on a range of factors such as:

- Costs. Obviously, the cost of resources such as labour and land will affect the likely returns on a particular location. With greater globalization it is easier to operate overseas and so this means some businesses can cast their net wider when looking at locations. For example, many of the operations in the clothing and footwear industry involve labour-intensive tasks such as stitching and so businesses will often seek low-wage economies. In the past this was often China but rising wages there mean many companies have now moved to South-East Asia and Bangladesh. Nike and Adidas now produce more training shoes in Vietnam than China. A popular destination for businesses more recently has been Ethiopia. This is because it has very low wage costs According to the World Bank the average annual income per person in Ethiopia was around $925. In the US it was over $70,000. However, businesses need to be aware of the potential ethical issues involved in choosing a low-wage location. Managers need

Figure 4.7 Managing operations includes managing location decisions. *Source:* Author.

to be aware of how employees are treated and whether this is acceptable to them or their stakeholders.

- The availability of resources. The appeal of a particular location will depend on how easy it is to access key resources, such as labour, with the appropriate skills and suppliers. Some regions become hubs to particular industries as producers and suppliers locate there; for example, Hollywood for the US film industry or Surat in India, which cuts 90% of the world's diamonds. The management writer Michael Porter wrote in a *Harvard Business Review* article in 1998 about clusters. These are geographical concentrations of interconnected companies and institutions including specialist providers of machinery and services and training colleges. He used the wine industry in California as an example.

- The location of the customer. This will be vital in businesses which need to locate near to their customers such as hairdressers and dentists.

- Infrastructure. A location may or may not be suitable depending on the quality of the infrastructure. For example, can a business easily receive supplies and transport products to its distribution outlets? Developments in communications technology have allowed many businesses in recent years to encourage more working from home (this trend was accelerated by the pandemic).

What would you do?

You run a call centre business. You are deciding where to locate your next call centre. What factors would you consider?

- Government policies. By locating in a certain region a business may be within a trading area and not incur taxes (tariffs) imposed on products coming from outside of the area. When the UK announced it was leaving the European Union, Nissan, the car producer, announced it would review the location of its manufacturing plants. Nissan only confirmed production would continue in the UK when it was confirmed that cars could continue to be sold without additional restrictions to the European Union.

One location trend in the last twenty year has been for businesses with production in developed economies to move production out of the country. Off-shoring production occurs when a business moves all or some of its operations overseas.

This off-shoring is to benefit from:

- Lower costs abroad; for example, due to lower wages.

- Less regulation abroad; for example, less intensive health and safety regulations or environmental restrictions.

- To overcome trade barriers; for example, by producing within the European Union a business can avoid the taxes that would have to be paid if it produced outside that trading area but sold into it. According to the World Bank the highest tariffs in 2021 were in Bermuda; taxes on foreign goods and services were set at over 20%.

- Specialist resources; for example, a region may have a well-developed infrastructure for a particular industry or have developed a particular expertise. For example, most drum cymbals are produced in Turkey. According to Forbes magazine over 90% of semiconductors whose components are smaller than 10 nanometres were produced in Taiwan in 2022.

    The major goods exports from countries around the world in 2014 are shown in Figure 4.8; this highlights the specialist production of different regions and where businesses may base production of different goods.

In recent years, however, there has been a move to bring production back to the 'home' country. This is known as reshoring. Re-shoring has been occurring because:

- The differences in wages costs between the home country and the overseas economies have been getting smaller. China has been a low-wage economy for the last twenty years but more recently wages have been growing faster, making the cost savings of producing there reduce.

- Government policies in some countries have switched to support local producers and penalizing those which produce abroad. President Trump's 'Make American Great Again' policies added taxes to any producer producing in China whilst offering tax incentives to companies producing within the US. In 2022, President Biden introduced major rewards for businesses that produced within the USA.

Part 1

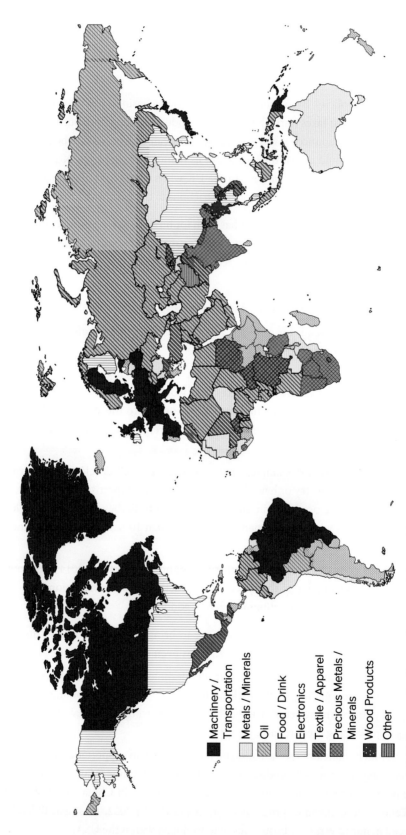

Figure 4.8 Major exports of countries around the world. *Source: Joe Myers.*

Machinery / Transportation

Metals / Minerals

Oil

Food / Drink

Electronics

Textile / Apparel

Precious Metals / Minerals

Wood Products

Other

Business insight 4.1 **Re-shoring**

In 2018, the number of US companies reporting new re-shoring was at its highest level ever. This growth in re-shoring activity was driven by reductions in corporation tax and changes in regulations making it easier to do business within the US as part of Trump's 'Made in the USA' policy. The move was also affected by rising wages and prices in China. Other factors quoted by businesses were part of the 'hidden costs' of off-shoring such as the freight costs, the cost of holding and moving stock, the costs of ensuring product quality, and the impact on the green credentials of the business importing.

Question

Do you think re-shoring makes sense given the current global business climate?

Source

www.industryweek.com/the-economy/article/22027880/reshoring-was-at-record-levels-in-2018-is-it-enough

- Concerns over the vulnerability of producing abroad and transporting products back to meet tight deadlines. Businesses want frequent and reliable deliveries; this can be trickier if production is based a long way away. The impact of the pandemic and lockdown in certain regions highlighted the fragility of some supply chains and the impact of any delays on production in many industries.

- Concerns over quality. In some cases, producers have been concerned over quality standards overseas. For example, many UK businesses shifted call centres overseas for cost reasons. In some cases, the quality of service has not been felt to be as high as it might be locally.

4.5.1 Managing operations: produce or outsource

One strategic operations decision a business will make is how much of the transformation process it wants to undertake itself and how much it wants to outsource to other producers; this is shown in Figure 4.9. Outsourcing occurs when a business uses another producer to produce for it. The decision whether to outsource will involve a consideration of factors such as:

- Cost. Although the other business will want to make a profit on any activity it undertakes, which may increase costs, it may be a specialist in this area and able to undertake the activity more cheaply that the outsourcing business could do it itself.

- Control and quality. A business may have more control over its quality if it produces the product itself.

Key concepts

Off-shoring production occurs when a business moves all or some of its operations overseas.

Re-shoring involves moving production back to the 'home' country.

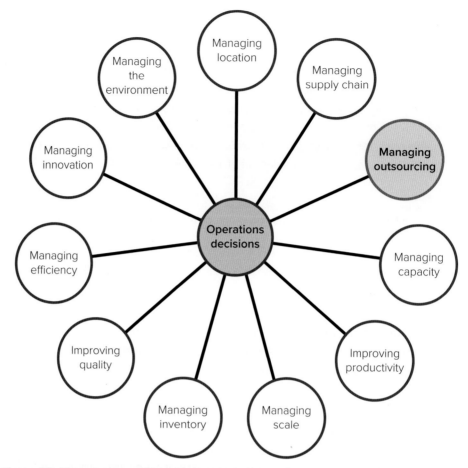

Figure 4.9 Managing operations: produce or outsource. *Source:* Author.

What would you do?

You have the option of outsourcing part of your production. This would reduce costs. What would you consider before making the change?

- Skills and expertise. It may make sense to outsource activity where the business itself has little experience in the area.
- Risk. The business will want to consider whether the activity is crucial to its success and the risk if there are any issues with quality or delivery.

4.6 Managing operations: capacity

Managing capacity is one aspect of managing operations; this is shown in Figure 4.10. The capacity of a business measures the maximum output it can produce at a given moment. The capacity of a business will depend on the resources the business has and how these are managed. The capacity of a business will affect its sales potential. For example. the expansion of Eat Just, a US business which creates 'meat' in laboratories, has been limited by the

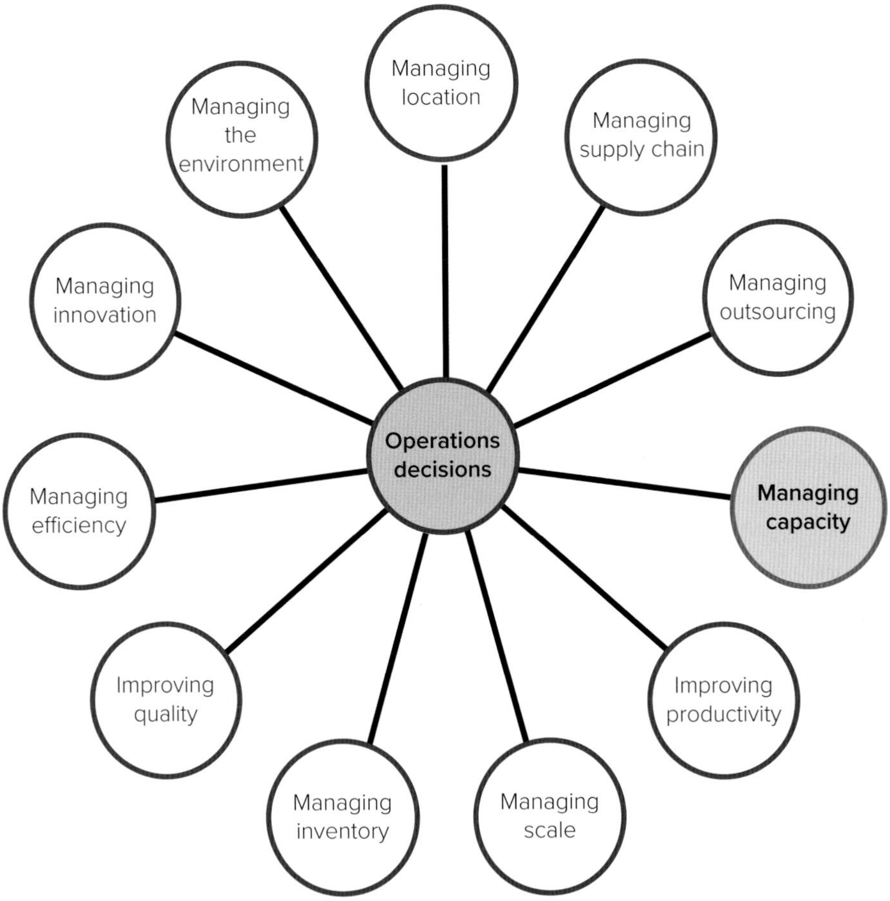

Figure 4.10 Managing operations includes managing capacity. *Source:* Author.

time taken to build capacity. Eat Just cultivates meats from real animal cells in bioreactors enabling people to eat meat without slaughtering animals. However, the technology is new and this has limited production capacity despite hundreds of millions of dollars being provided by investors.

Capacity utilization measures the actual output of a business in a given period as a proportion of the maximum it could produce given its resources.

Capacity utilization can be calculated using the equation:

$$\frac{\text{Actual output}}{\text{Maximum output}} \times 100$$

For example, if a business produces 20 units an hour but has the capacity to produce 80 units an hour this means its capacity utilization = (20/80) × 100 = 25%.

One of the largest stadia in the world is the Narendra Modi Stadium in Gujarat. It has a capacity of 132,000. If 66,000 people turned up at the stadium, its capacity utilization would be (66,000/132,000) × 100 = 50%. An ultra-large container ship these days can carry over 15,000 20-foot containers; if it had, say, only 1000 containers on it the capacity utilization would be less than 7%.

A business may worry if its capacity utilization is low because this means its resources are not being fully utilized. More could be being produced and sold. Low capacity

Key concepts

The **capacity** of a business measures the maximum output it can produce at a given moment.

Capacity utilization measures the actual output of a business in a given period compared to the maximum it could produce.

What would you do?

You produce high fashion shoes. Demand for your shoes is exceeding your ability to produce them. What would you do?

utilization will also increase the cost per unit. Imagine a telecommunications network that has to invest heavily to set up the network. With more users the network costs can be divided between more people bringing the cost per user down. If capacity utilization is low, the investment costs are not spread over many users and so the unit cost is high. In many industries with high fixed costs, such as pharmaceuticals, cars, and airlines, high volumes are essential to most producers to bring down the unit costs. This is further examined when we look at the scale of production.

If a business has low capacity utilization, demand is too low relative to the capacity. To improve its capacity utilization a business might try to increase demand through intensified marketing efforts such as increased promotional expenditure and lower prices. If, however, demand is likely to be low permanently, a business may decide to reduce its capacity. It could, for example, close part of the business. Alternatively, it could try to seek orders to produce for someone else.

If demand is too high for the capacity a business might:

- try to reduce demand through higher prices
- control orders through a waiting list system
- outsource production to other producers
- increase capacity in the long term.

Whilst the volume of production can be important, managers must also consider the quality of what is being produced. This is examined next.

4.7 Managing operations: improving quality

Achieving high quality is a typical operations objective; this is shown in Figure 4.11. For example, Lego, the global toymaker, says that 'quality has always been one of the company's key values—right from the day Ole Kirk Kristiansen set up the business in 1932'. Quality occurs when a business provides product that is 'fit for purpose'. This means that the product meets the standards that the operations department has set. These standards should be set having taken into account the needs of customers. For example, an operations manager at a hotel might set targets for how quickly a call is answered, how often washroom facilities and the

Figure 4.11 Managing operations includes improving quality. *Source:* Author.

pool are checked, and how long it takes to clean a room. The actual performance outcomes then need to be measured and compared with these targets. Producing a quality product can literally be a matter of life and death. In October 2018 the Lion Air flight JT 610 crashed; five months later Ethiopian Airlines flight ET 302 also crashed. Investigators believe these accidents were caused by the failure of a single sensor that sent inaccurate data to the flight control software in Boeing 737 Max planes. These planes had to stop flying until December 2020 when changes to production and the sensors meant they passed the necessary regulations.

Operations managers must decide what is an acceptable performance and at what point action needs to be taken. A quality system therefore has well-defined, measurable targets and a system of review and action.

It is important to differentiate the way that the word 'quality' is sometimes used in marketing—meaning a premium product—and the way it is used in an operations context to mean that the process meets its set targets consistently. For example, McDonald's products may not be expensive but they are generally regarded in terms of operations as high-quality products because the process is carefully designed to produce the same thing again and again. One of the appeals of McDonald's is its quality assurance; you know exactly what you will get when you visit one of its stores. By comparison, you could visit an expensive restaurant and find that what was produced varied significantly each time and it did not always produce what it or you wanted; this would be low quality assurance.

The quality of products and services is, therefore, based on the requirements of the customer. Any product which meets the set standards determined by customer needs can be considered a quality product. A business has to understand precisely what the customer expects—which is what marketing should be doing—and then developing an operations process to deliver exactly that in a way that meets both customer objectives and the business objectives. The process developed should enable a consistent and reliable delivery of the product at the required levels, in the required quantity, and at the right time.

The dabbawalas in India provide a good example of a quality process. The dabbawalas are a group of people who provide a collect and delivery food service in some of the big cities in India, especially Mumbai. The dabbawalas collect an individual's lunchbox and then using a system of bicycles and trains take it to have the order fulfilled and returned to the owner. A system of colours and symbols put in the lunchbox identify where it has come from and needs to be returned to as the box is passed from one person to the next to get it from the home to where the food is prepared and back again. According to the Mumbai Tiffenmen's Association in 1998 less than one mistake is made in the delivery of every 6 million lunchboxes—an impressive level of quality for a very low-tech operation.

To improve quality a business needs to ensure that the process meets the required standards.

This can be done through:

- Quality control. This occurs when items are inspected to find any products that have defects that have arisen from any mistakes in the process. For example, at the end of a production line the finished products may be sampled and tested to try and prevent flawed items leaving the factory. L'Oreal, the global cosmetics business, sells more than six billion products annually; it says there are more than 100 quality controls in place for each of its products.

- Total Quality Management. This is a preventative approach to quality assurance. It aims to prevent errors occurring (whereas quality control aims to identify errors that have occurred). Total Quality Management (TQM) occurs when everyone within the business is regarded as part of the process of achieving quality. This is why it is called 'total' quality management. Quality is not regarded as something that is the responsibility of a quality control department that inspects to find any faults. Instead everyone is expected to take responsibility to prevent errors from occurring in the first place. Under TQM a focus on quality occurs throughout the organization from the minute materials arrive at the business through to the completion of the finished item.

According to the European Foundation for Quality Management (EFQM) TQM involves:

- a culture of continuous improvement throughout the business.

- a belief that an improvement in quality leads to cost advantages and more profit.

- the involvement of everyone.

The concept of TQM was developed in Japan in the 1950 and 1960s, although some of the most famous writers on this are Americans such as W. Edwards Deming. Deming became a specialist in quality systems and ended up much admired in Japan, a country that was a pioneer in its focus on improving the quality of operations.

Key concepts

Quality control occurs when items are inspected to find any products that have defects or any mistakes in the process.

Total Quality Management (TQM) occurs when everyone within the business is regarded as part of the process of achieving quality.

Deming stressed the importance of developing a process that could consistently deliver a set standard of quality. Once a given level of quality was established, changes could then be made to try to improve the quality further. The results of changes would be measured to ensure that they led to better standards. Once this new approach is reliably delivering higher standards the process to improve begins again.

Deming developed the PDCA cycle that highlighted this approach:

- Plan: this is to identify a problem or opportunity and develop potential improvements
- Do: this is to test the potential improvements
- Check: the results of the test
- Act: if the new system seems to improve standards then it can be implemented.

Deming saw quality as an ongoing process. The PDCA process would be used to identify, test, and then implement a change if it worked. The next stage would be to be identify another area of improvement and develop this to improve quality even more. The PDCA process is shown in Figure 4.12.

Some people associate higher quality with higher costs. This could be the case if improving quality involves more inspection and more spending on quality control. However, business writers such as David Crosby argue that better quality actually reduces costs.

This is because better quality means:

- Fewer defects and therefore less spending on collecting returned items
- Less spending to fix any mistakes in products
- Fewer legal costs if the business was sued for any errors.

Ensuring the operations process has a high level of quality is important to the competitiveness of a business. It is also important to control costs and to be as efficient as possible, given the standards you are trying to achieve. The cost of producing a

Figure 4.12 Deming's PDCA cycle. *Source:* Author.

hand-made suit will always be higher than the cost of producing a standard white T-shirt. However, in both cases the business will want to achieve a given standard of quality as efficiently as possible. Improving efficiency is, therefore, often another key focus of operations management.

4.8 Managing operations: improving efficiency

The efficiency of operations considers the value of inputs used relative to the output produced. A business is more efficient if it can product the same output with less inputs or using the existing inputs to produce more outputs. The efficiency of an operation is usually measured by the cost per unit. Improving efficiency is a typical objective in operations; this is shown in Figure 4.13.

One way of increasing efficiency is through reducing waste by adopting a lean approach to operations. Lean production involves a focus on reducing all forms of waste within a business.

Figure 4.13 Managing operations includes improving efficiency. *Source:* Author.

Waste can happen in terms of materials that are wasted, the number of people being used on an activity, or the time that is being spent on an activity—or the time spent but not generating output. Just think of an aircraft waiting at an airport—every minute spent is time being paid for that is not earning any revenue. Figure 4.14 shows how reorganizing the operations process can speed up the turnaround time enabling the business to be more efficient and generate more sales.

Lean production aims to find ways of reducing inputs, of recycling and reusing materials. This increases efficiency. Elements of lean production includes Just In Time inventory control and kaizen techniques; both of these are examined later.

Can you now answer this question from the introductory case study?

Why is efficiency so important to fast fashion?

Minutes and seconds per step for Airbus A320 single-aisle medium-range airliner (disguised example)

Turnaround time between flights

	Average	Best practice	Potential reduction[1]	Lean techniques
Unload passengers[2]	6:14	4:38	1:36	Stricter controls on carry-on bags, fewer passengers moving back in aisle to find bag
Wait for cleaning crew to board aircraft	0:24	0:18	0:06	Cleaning crew in position ahead of time
Clean airplane	11:48	9:40	2:08	Standardized work flow, timing, and methods, such as cleaning supplies in prearranged kits
Wait for transmission to gate of cabin crew's approval to board	4:11	0	4:11	Visual signal from cabin crew to agent when plane is ready to board–for example, light flashing at top of ramp
Wait for first passenger to board	4:06	0	4:06	
Load passengers	19:32	16:00	3:32	Active mangement of overhead storage bins by flight attendants
Wait for passenger infromation list	1:58	0:13	1:45	Passenger-information list delivered by agent following last passenger to board
Close aircraft door	0:57	0:09	0:48	Agent ready at aircraft to close door
Detach boarding ramp	1:39	0:43	0:56	
Total time (including initial steps[2])	**52:18**	**33:11**	**19:07**	

[1]Assumes rudimentary application of lean techniques; further reductions may be possible.
[2]Time for initial steps (attaching boarding ramp, opening aircraft door, and waiting for first passenger

Figure 4.14 The effect in efficiency of reorganizing activities when a plane lands. *Source:* Duncan, E. and Ritter, R. (2014). *Next Frontiers for Lean*, McKinsey & Company.

Standardizing procedures saves time

Service steps for fulfilling order (example: hot chicken sandwich)

Before lean improvements

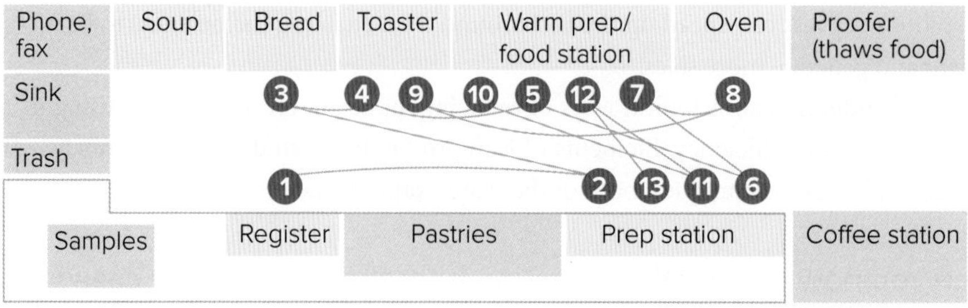

Phone, fax	Soup	Bread	Toaster	Warm prep/ food station	Oven	Proofer (thaws food)

Sink

③ ④ ⑨ ⑩ ⑤ ⑫ ⑦ ⑧

Trash

① ② ⑬ ⑪ ⑥

Samples	Register	Pastries	Prep station	Coffee station

After lean improvements

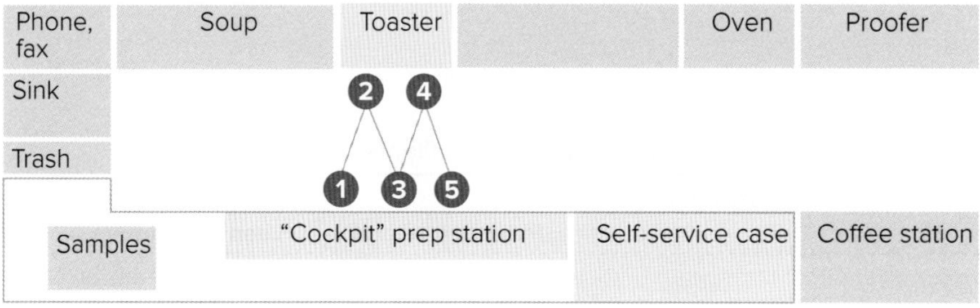

Phone, fax	Soup	Toaster		Oven	Proofer

Sink

② ④

Trash

① ③ ⑤

Samples	"Cockpit" prep station	Self-service case	Coffee station

Reduced preparation time for ...	... a breakfast sandwich by 51 seconds	... a lunch sandwich by 1 minute, 11 seconds

Figure 4.14 *Continued*

4.9 Managing operations: improving productivity

Productivity measures the output of a business relative to the inputs. A common measure of productivity is labour productivity. This measures output per employee in a given period.

It can be measured using the equation: $\dfrac{\text{Output in a given period}}{\text{Number of employees employed}}$

Productivity is important to managers because it affects output and costs; it is part of operations management as shown in Figure 4.15. Greater labour productivity means that either more output can be produced from the same workforce or fewer employees are needed for the same output.

Productivity is not just measured in a manufacturing context. In a call centre, for example, the number of calls taken per hour by any operative will be measured. In an order fulfilment centre the number of items picked, packed, and despatched by an operative on a shift will be monitored.

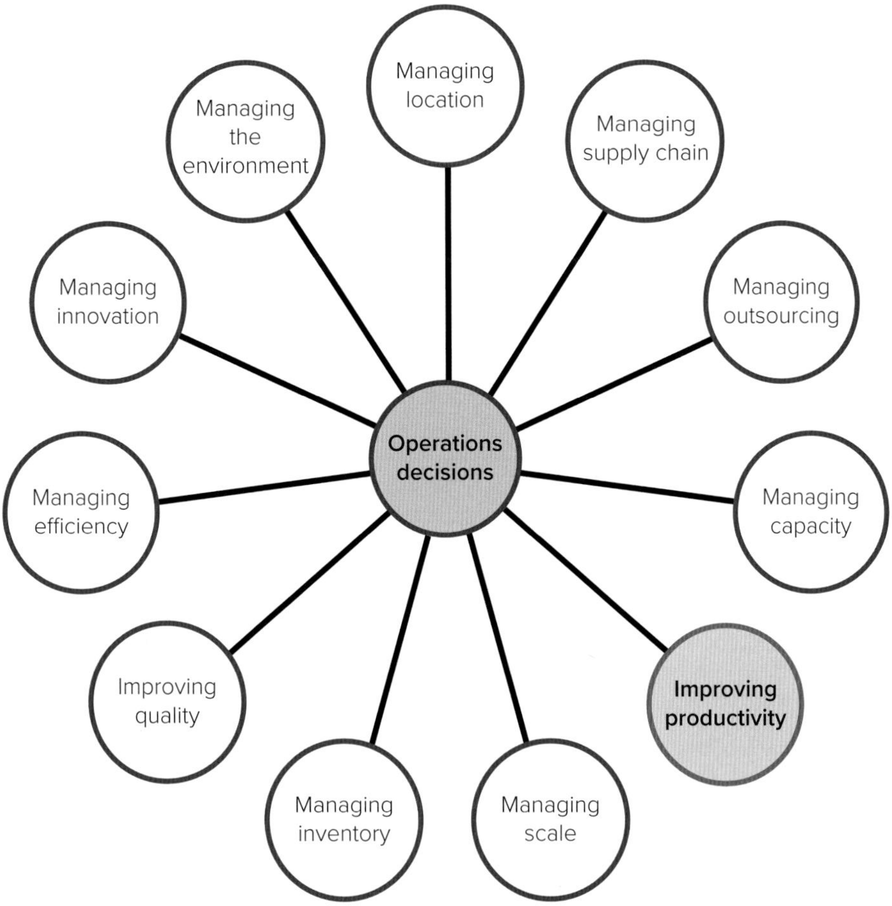

Figure 4.15 Managing operations includes improving productivity. *Source:* Author.

Labour productivity may be increased by:

- Motivating employees so they try harder
- Providing more training so employees have the necessary skills
- Investing in more capital equipment or technology so employees have better resources to work with.

What would you do?

You have recently announced that you want productivity within the business to increase in the coming year. Employee representatives are resisting any changes to increase productivity on the basis that you are simply trying to work them harder. What would you do to convince them that greater productivity was needed?

Key concept

Labour productivity measures the output per employee in a given period.

Analysing the business data 4.1

The data in Figure 1 shows the labour productivity in the UK over time.

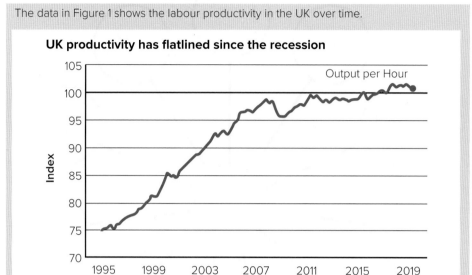

Figure 1 UK labour productivity over time. *Source:* BBC.

Questions

Explain why labour productivity has risen over the period.

What do you think are the implications of the data above for UK businesses?

 Analysing the business data 4.2

The World Bank measures labour productivity in terms of the income earned for each hour worked measured in dollars. The chart in Figure 1 shows the labour productivity of different countries in 2019 compared to a base of 2015, i.e. it shows the percentage change in value of each hour worked over that period.

Discuss the possible reasons for the difference in the change labour productivity since the base year of 2015 in the countries below.

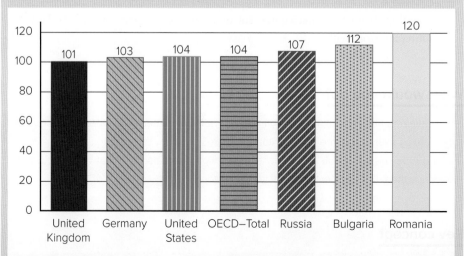

Figure 1 Changes in labour productivity in different countries 2015–2019. *Source:* OECD.

4.10 Managing operations: managing scale

A significant decision for managers involves deciding on the scale of operations they want. This is a key aspect of managing operations as shown in Figure 4.16. The decision regarding scale will be influenced by the expected levels of demand but also by the cost implications of producing at different scales. In many businesses the unit cost will fall as output expands up until a certain point; after that unit costs may rise. This is due to internal economies and diseconomies of scale.

Internal economies of scale occur when the unit cost falls with a greater scale of production. For example, if a business sets up a mobile network this will be incredibly expensive per customer if there are only a few customers. However, as more and more customers join the network the costs can be spread over more people and the unit (or average) cost falls. See Figure 4.17.

Internal economies of scale are very important in many industries; if they do exist for a business, they provide an incentive to expand so to reduce the unit costs. If unit costs fall due to expansion, a business may be able to lower the price and still be profitable. Scale is vitally important in industries, such as car manufacturing, pharmaceuticals, and

Figure 4.16 Managing operations includes managing the scale of the business. *Source: Author.*

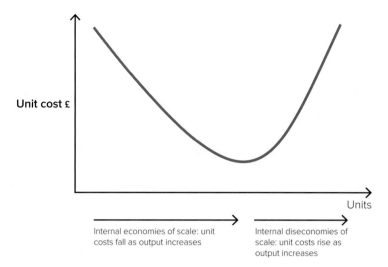

Figure 4.17 Internal economies and diseconomies of scale. *Source:* Author.

telecommunications, which is why you often see mergers and takeovers as businesses combine to increase their scale and bring down their unit costs.

Internal economies of scale occur as a business expands its capacity. External economies of scale occur when the unit costs at all levels of output are reduced.

Types of internal economy of scale include:

- Technical economies. These are cost benefits a business can experience by adopting more production-line production enabling costs to be spread over many units. They also include specialization. As output expands individual employees can specialize in particular areas of production, and so become more productive and more efficient. The benefits of scale can be seen in relation to online businesses. Take Zoom, for example—the computing power required and the associated costs do not rise proportionately with additional users so the more users it gets the lower the unit cost. As Zoom says 'Our cloud-native platform was purpose-built to scale with organizations as they grow in size and complexity. Our platform delivers the highest quality experience for organizations of all sizes and for meetings, whether with two or thousands of users.' As the scale rises from, say, two to thousands of users the unit costs fall.

- Purchasing economies. These occur when a business operates on a large scale and is able to negotiate lower prices of inputs because it is buying in bulk.

- Financial economies. As a business gets larger it is likely to have more assets and using these as collateral may be able to gain from lower costs of borrowing.

Types of internal economy of scale are shown in Figure 4.18.

Whilst unit costs may fall with expansion due to internal economies of scale, a business may become too big and experience rising unit costs. This is due to internal diseconomies of scale.

Internal diseconomies of scale may occur because of a lack of motivation. As a business gets bigger employees may find it difficult to feel part of, and associate with, the aims and values of a large organization. There may also be difficulties controlling and communicating in a larger organization and this can lead to inefficiency. Furthermore, in an attempt to control a big business numerous policies and procedures may be introduced; this can lead

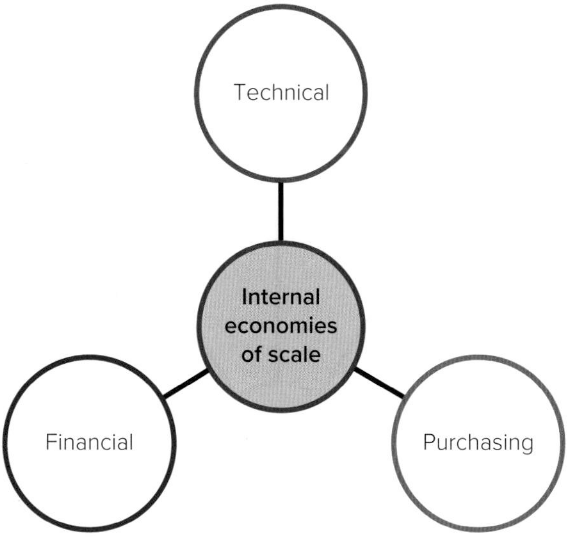

Figure 4.18 Types of economy of scale. *Source:* Author.

to a bureaucratic organization that has many overheads and can be slow to make decisions. T. Boone Pickens, a geologist who went on to a successful career in the oil business, wrote about diseconomies of scale in his 1987 autobiography: 'It's unusual to find a large corporation that's efficient. I know about economies of scale and all the other advantages that are supposed to come with size. But when you get an inside look, it's easy to see how inefficient big business really is. Most corporate bureaucracies have more people than they have work.' To avoid diseconomies of scale managers might limit output or limit the scale of any one operations facility.

4.11 Managing operations: managing inventory

Inventory is another name for stocks. A business will hold different forms of inventory such as:

- Raw materials and supplies. These are held to enable production to occur.
- Work in progress. This refers to items that are still being worked on during the production process.
- Finished products. These are items held to show to customers and to sell.
- General supplies. These are items such as paper and cleaning equipment.

Inventory is important because it enables a business to keep producing and selling. Without raw materials and the required components a business cannot produce. If it has no finished goods customers may be unwilling to wait whilst they are produced and may go somewhere else. This means there are very good reasons for holding inventory, and managing inventory is an important aspect of managing operations as shown in Figure 4.19.

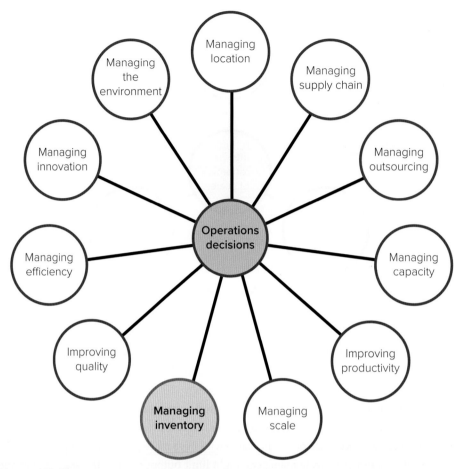

Figure 4.19 Managing operations includes managing inventory. *Source:* Author.

However, holding inventory has disadvantages:

- Inventory represents money that is 'tied up'. Money in the form of inventory is not generating any interest. A business may want to sell the inventory to generate money which can be invested.

- Inventory may need to be looked after and this will incur warehousing and other maintenance costs. For example, some foods may need refrigeration.

- Some inventory may be stolen and this generates a cost, e.g. theft from retailers can create significant costs. In 2019 the UK Centre for Retail Research estimated that the shrinkage in retail (i.e. the difference between the inventory used up and the recorded sales) was worth around £5.5 bn. To prevent or reduce thefts incurs other costs such as paying for more security.

- Inventory may reduce in value over time; for example, if a style of clothing becomes less fashionable the value of this inventory will fall. In 2018 Burberry burnt hundreds of millions of pounds of inventory. It would rather destroy this than have it sold at a discount because this would damage the brand name.

This means that there are pressures to hold inventory and pressures not to hold inventory and a business will have to decide on what is the right level to hold.

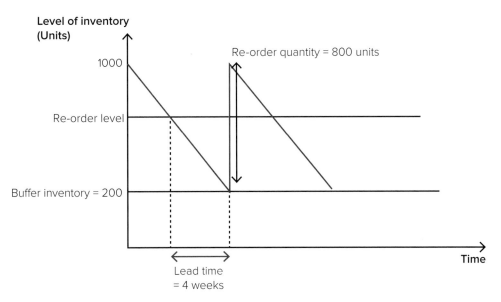

Figure 4.20 Inventory control chart. *Source:* Author.

The usage of inventory can be seen on an inventory control chart. An example of such a chart is shown in Figure 4.20.

In this figure we can see that inventory is being used up at a constant rate between weeks 1 and 4. The buffer level of inventory is the minimum amount a business wants to hold, in this case 200 units. At the end of week 4 new inventory arrives. The amount that arrives is 600 units; this is known as the 're-order quantity'. This quantity will have been ordered in advance. The amount of time it takes for product to arrive when ordered is known as the 'lead time'. The length of the lead time determines when items have to be ordered to arrive at the right time.

Toyota is one of the pioneers in lean production. It describes the Toyota Production System (TPS) as an approach 'based on the philosophy of achieving the complete elimination of all waste in pursuit of the most efficient methods'. One key element of TPS is Just in Time Production which Toyota describes as making only 'what is needed, when it is needed, and in the amount needed'.

This is how Toyota fulfils an order for a vehicle:

1. When a vehicle order is received, production instructions are issued to the beginning of the vehicle production line as soon as possible.

2. The assembly line is stocked with the required number of all necessary parts so that any kind of ordered vehicle can be assembled.

3. The assembly line replaces the parts used by retrieving the same number of parts from the parts-producing process (the preceding process).

4. The preceding process is stocked with small numbers of all types of parts and produce only the numbers of parts that were retrieved by an operator from the next process.

To produce 'just in time' a business needs excellent links with its suppliers so that when it starts to produce the products it needs can be delivered quickly. As example of just in timeis

What would you do?

You manage a chain of clothes retailers. Your Operations Director wants to reduce the amounts on inventory held in stores. What would you want to know to make a decision about this?

Think about it

What are the implications for cashflow of adopting a just in time approach?

Key concepts

A **just in case** approach to inventory control occurs when a business holds inventory as a precautionary measure.

A **just in time** approach to inventory aims to hold as little stock as possible. Inventory is ordered or produced 'just in time 'when it is needed.

Made.com. This is an online furniture retailer. It has an in-house design team. It works with the makers, suppliers, and independent designers and orders straight from the source. The company puts designs online and when it has a certain number of orders it will get them produced. It only makes an item once a customer has bought it. This means it does not have high levels of inventory in its warehouses.

By comparison, a just in case approach to inventory control (as opposed to a just in time one) occurs when a business holds inventory as a precautionary measure; for example, just in case there is a sudden increase in demand a business may hold additional materials and/or products. This enables production and sales to continue but brings with it all the costs of holding inventory.

Can you now answer this question from the introductory case study?

Why do you think fast fashion is often associated with low inventory levels by retailers?

4.12 Managing operations: managing improvement and innovation

Businesses need to innovate and improve to keep competitive and managing this innovation is part of operations management as shown in Figure 4.21. Kaizen is a Japanese term meaning 'continuous improvement' and for many businesses this is an important part of innovation. If a business adopts a kaizen approach it involves employees working together to find new and better ways of doing things. A kaizen approach aims to achieve progress through a series of ongoing small improvements rather than major transformational change. To be successful kaizen requires those doing the work to have the skills and the interest in improving the business. It requires a culture where improvement is valued and

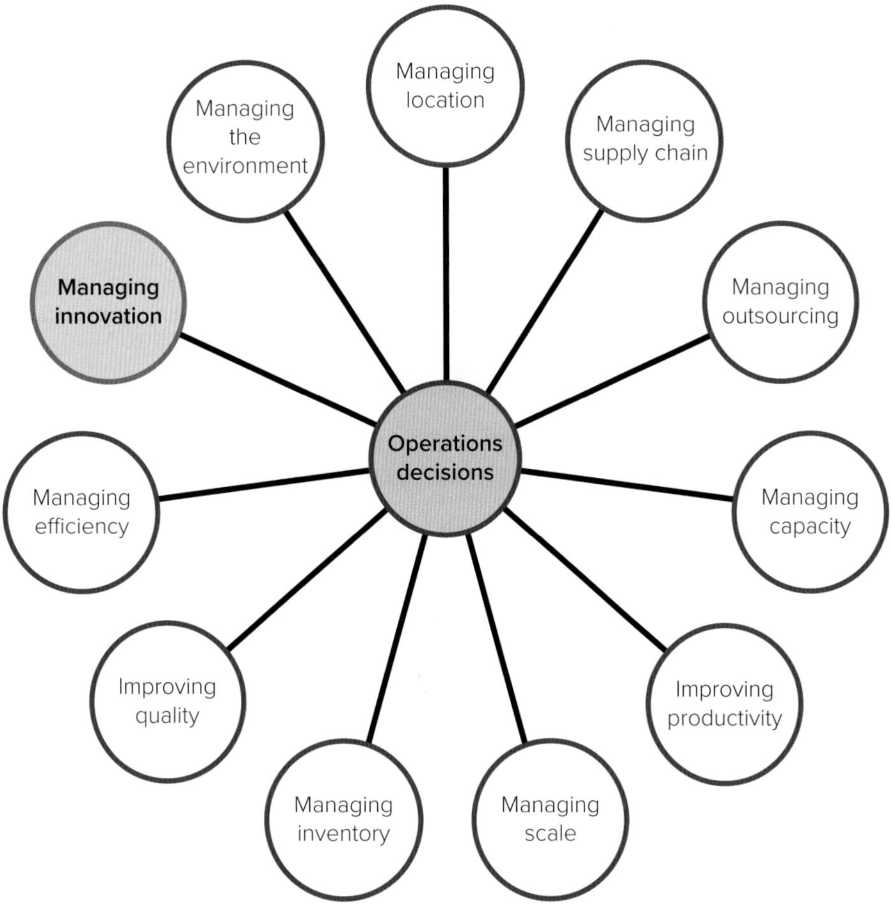

Figure 4.21 Managing operations includes managing innovation. *Source:* Author.

where employees feel able to express their views. This is turn requires managers willing to listen and act on employees' ideas.

A kaizen approach, therefore, believes that:

- the human resources of a business are vitally important
- processes evolve through gradual improvement rather than by radical change.

A kaizen approach is another important element of the TPS system at Toyota as shown in Figure 4.22. To achieve such ongoing improvements the company looks for any issues with production and when these occur it stops production—this is known as jidoka—until a way of solving problems is found. This new approach is introduced and tested and once proven becomes the new way of operating.

Kaizen does not just relate to business. This approach has also been used in many other areas including sport. Dave Brailsford was one of the most successful coaches in British cycling ever. He was famous for his concept of 'marginal gains'. He argued that if you broke

Think about it

Given the speed of change these days do you think that kaizen is no longer appropriate?

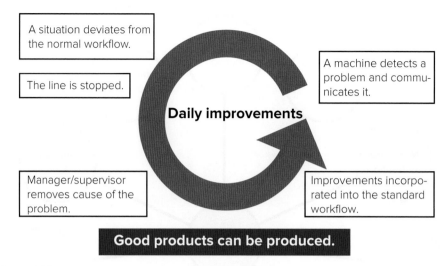

Figure 4.22 Toyota's approach to improving production. *Source:* Toyota.

everything involved in riding a bike at a competition into its different parts and improved each part by 1% you would get an amazing improvement in overall performance. Brailsford constantly measured and monitored data and took action to improve areas where gains could be made. These changes affected all aspects of the cyclist's life. For example, Brailsford argued that how you wash your hands can influence the probability of getting ill for a tournament. How you sleep on the coach between events or at your hotel will influence how you ride on the day of a race. Brailsford improved many areas in small ways. For example, cycle tyres were sprayed with oil so they did not pick up as much dirt and cyclists were kept warm between races so their muscles did not get cold. Under Brailsford, Great Britain led the cycling medal table at the 2008 and 2012 Olympic Games, winning eight golds at both games.

The changes Brailsford made were process innovations. They improved the way things are done. By comparison, product innovations occur when there are developments in the actual product. Product innovations often occur as a result of research and development.

Research and development (R&D) refers to scientific activities that innovate and develop new products. R & D may be linked to the findings of market research, i.e. businesses may seek to develop new products in response to a need they have identified. Alternatively, businesses may invest in R&D and then find how to make use of their discoveries. The Post-It note, for example, came out of work on adhesives by Dr Spencer Silver. Having developed an adhesive with a 'removability characteristic', Silver struggled for years to know what to do with it! Meanwhile Art Fry, another 3M scientist, saw a use for the adhesive if he

Key concepts

Process innovations occur when there are developments in the way a process is undertaken.

Product innovations occur when there are developments in the actual product.

Research and development (R&D) refers to scientific activities that innovate and develop new products.

A **patent** provides legal protection for a new invention.

Business insight 4.2 **3M and GSK**

Item 1

3M describes itself as a science-based technology company that is committed to improving lives and doing business in the right way. It applies science to creating products that make things better in some way. Its products help people to be safe, make them more productive, protect their health, and help safeguard the environment.

The company says it is relentless in its pursuit of solutions to customers' problems—one third of its revenues come from products that did not exist five years ago. It has a culture based on curiosity, problem-solving, and collaboration.

3M has five business units. In each one it has a strong research and development unit. It has thousands of scientists and invests around 5.8% of its sales revenue into R&D. This investment helps the company produce over 3000 patents a year (Figure 1).

Item 2

GSK is a science-led healthcare company. R&D is at the very centre of the business. The company seeks 'the brightest minds' to enable it to discover and develop new medicines, vaccines, and consumer healthcare products (Figure 2).

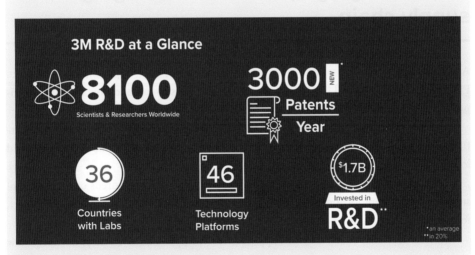

Figure 1 3M's Research and Development at a glance. *Source:* 3M US.

R&D in numbers

£4.3bn	**16,000**	**1,500+**
adjusted R&D investment in 2019	R&D employees globally	collaborations with academia, public-private partnerships, biotech and other pharmaceuticals

Figure 2 GSK's research and development in numbers. *Source:* GSK: www.gsk.com. (n.d.). *Home | GSK*. [online] Available at: https://www.gsk.com/en-gb/?gad_source=1&gclid=CjwKCAjwv-2pBhB-EiwAtsQZFlrJOU5RRpBBjxMZuVB5dj0oT_6H8sbY50rgVZC0GvU0I4hCzqe0WBoCF4AQAvD_BwE&gclsrc=aw.ds.

Questions

What do you think is significant about the fact that one third of 3M's revenues come from products that did not exist five years ago?

Why do you think research and development is so important to GSK?

put it on paper and used it to mark the hymns that were going to be sung in his local church. Together Spender and Fry developed the Post-It concept and it went on to global success.

Research and development is critical in some sectors such as the pharmaceutical industry; businesses here will spend millions of pounds and many years developing new products. Successful innovation and then successful protection of the products through patents is the key to success for pharmaceutical businesses. A patent provides legal protection for a new invention as we saw in Chapter 2.

4.13 Managing operations: managing the supply chain

An important part of operations management is managing the supply chain as shown in Figure 4.23. Managers will have to decide which suppliers to use and how much the business wants to know about the operations of suppliers.

Many supply chains are now global. A business can find experts in the provision of particular goods and services elsewhere in the world and can benefit from better quality and lower costs.

Many supply chains are very extended in that there are many hundreds or thousands of suppliers in different locations contributing to the final product. The supplier of any part, for example, will have their own suppliers who might have their own suppliers and so on.

Just look at the list of some of the suppliers for the Apple iPhone 6 and you will see how global supply chains are these days:

- **Audio chips:** Cirrus Logic, based in the US with locations in the UK, China, South Korea, Taiwan, Japan, and Singapore

- **Battery:** Samsung, based in South Korea with locations in 80 countries

- **Camera:** Qualcomm, based in the US with locations in Australia, Brazil, China, India, Indonesia, Japan, South Korea, and more than a dozen locations through Europe and Latin America

- **Chips for 3G/4G/LTE networking:** Qualcomm

- **Compass:** AKM Semiconductor, based in Japan with locations in the US, France, England, China, South Korea, and Taiwan

- **Glass screen:** Corning, based in the US, with locations in Australia, Belgium, Brazil, China, Denmark, France, Germany, Hong Kong, India, Israel, Italy, Japan, South

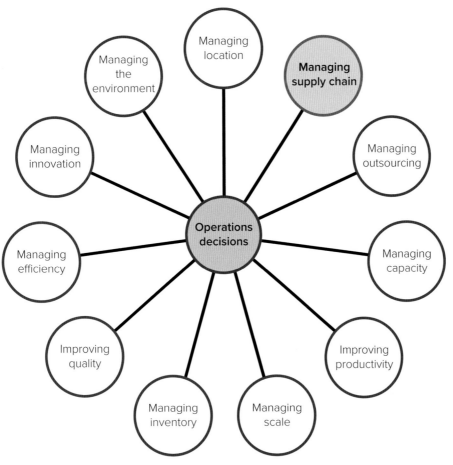

Figure 4.23 Managing operations includes managing the supply chain. *Source:* Author.

Korea, Malaysia, Mexico, Philippines, Poland, Russia, Singapore, South Africa, Spain, Taiwan, The Netherlands, Turkey, the UK, and the United Arab Emirates

- **Gyroscope:** STMicroelectronics, based in Switzerland, with locations in 35 countries
- **Flash memory:** Toshiba, based in Japan with locations in over 50 countries
- **Flash memory:** Samsung
- **LCD screen:** Sharp, based in Japan with locations in 13 countries
- **A-series processor:** TSMC, based in Taiwan with locations in China, Singapore, and the US
- **Touch ID:** Xintec, based in Taiwan
- **Touch-screen controller:** Broadcom, based in the US with locations in Israel, Greece, the UK, the Netherlands, Belgium, France, India, China, Taiwan, Singapore, and South Korea
- **Wi-Fi chip:** Murata, based in the US with locations in Japan, Mexico, Brazil, Canada, China, Taiwan, South Korea, Thailand, Malaysia, Philippines, India, Vietnam, The Netherlands, Spain, the UK, Germany, Hungary, France, Italy, and Finland.

Trying to manage these suppliers based globally can bring a number of risks such as delays occurring due to transportation issues or the introduction of domestic protectionist policies.

To overcome some of the risks of global supply chains managers might:

- Use suppliers that are close by to reduce the risk of problems transporting products around the world. When Toyota pioneered lean production techniques in Japan in the 1970s it built close links with suppliers that were located close to the production facilities. Car manufacturers are now looking to locate electric car production near to battery producers.

- Hold more stocks in case of disruption to the supply chain. This incurs various costs such as holding and warehousing costs but this may be offset by the benefits of keeping production going. The need for stocks will depend on how easy it is to find alternative suppliers and how long the product takes to produce. Novo Nordisk, which manufactures half of the world's supply of insulin at its Kalundborg, Denmark, facility, has five years' worth of stock.

- Use more than one supplier. As part of the lean approach many businesses choose one supplier for any part. This is to build a strong relationship between the business and the supplier. Close collaboration of information and systems is a key part of being lean. However, this is high risk and a business may want either more than one supplier or perhaps for the supplier to have more than one production base in different locations. Following the disruption to supply chains during the pandemic some companies moved away from single suppliers and just in time and stockpiled to enable production to continue even if suppliers were disrupted. In the bicycle industry, for example, in 2022, according to the *Financial Times* the Japanese company Shimano controlled an estimated 65% of the market for high-end gears and brakes;

Business insight 4.3 Managing the supply chain

A survey conducted in April 2019 of 600 multinationals around Asia by Baker McKenzie, an American law firm, found that nearly half of them are considering 'major' changes to their supply chains, and over a tenth a complete overhaul. In many sectors this will involve a rethink of the relationship with Chinese suppliers. It has increasingly become clear that having extended supplier chains brings risks. Part of the problem is that suppliers don't know who supplies the supplier.

Another is the impact of external events such as Brexit which may increase costs or make importing more difficult. The US tariffs on Chinese goods were costing American consumers $1.4bn a month by the end of 2018 according to the National Bureau of Economic Research.

Question

What are the dangers of having extended supply chains?

Source

www.economist.com/special-report/2019/07/11/multinational-companies-are-adjusting-to-shorter-supply-chains

Business insight 4.4 Supply chain management

Strawberries have around 12 days of life after picking so getting them to the store quickly is essential. This has led companies such as Walmart to change its approach to inventory of this type of products. This sort of item is now sent direct to the retailer rather than via a wholesaler. This can save days in the process.

Walmart is replacing all its supply chain systems, both physical and digital, to shift from processing items in batches to continuous replenishment. The firm is also investing in technologies that will allow it to track individual stock-keeping units (skus) through the supply chain. Its warehouses are introducing automatic storage and retrieval systems and autonomous vehicles.

The firm is moving faster downstream, too. It is working with Alert Innovation, an automation start-up, to develop a robot that can fill online grocery orders more quickly for dispatch from its retail outlets.

Question

What are the benefits to Walmart of better supply chain management?

What would you do?

You currently use a Just in Time (JIT) approach to production. However, you are increasingly aware of the dangers of managing your global supply chain and think you should move away from JIT as a result. How would you convince your Board of Directors?

some bicycle companies sought alternative suppliers to avoid overreliance on this one company. This was prompted by disruptions at Shimano caused by the pandemic which meant lead times reached 400 days.

- Rethink the scale of production and production bases. Manufacturers have typically produced a particular model in one location to achieve economies of scale. However, this approach incurs a huge risk if production there is stopped for whatever reason. It may be that businesses operate more bases in different locations around the world. This may be more expensive per unit but be worth doing because it lowers the risk of disruption.

4.14 Managing operations: managing sustainability and the environment

Businesses are increasingly concerned about the impact of their actions on the environment and how sustainable their operations are. This increasing interest in becoming more sustainable is because:

- There is greater understanding of the long-term damage being done to the planet and the problems this can create for future generations

- There is greater awareness that action needs to be taken quickly because the problems are so severe

- There is greater interest from customers, investors, and employees in the behaviour of businesses and how sustainable their activities are. To attract funds, better employees and customers, businesses may need to make their operations more sustainable. With improvements in communications, the actions of businesses are more visible and quickly transmitted around the world. This affects the importance of being seen to be 'doing the right thing'.

Managing the impact of the activities of the business on the environment is, therefore, part of operations management as shown in Figure 4.24. For example, the clothing manufacturer Uniglo states:

> We believe we can turn the power of clothing into a force for good. By designing, making and selling good clothing, we can make the world a better place. Good clothing means simple clothing, high in quality, and built to last. It's clothing that enriches the lives of people who wear it by giving them comfort, protection and pleasure. It is produced in a way that is harmonious with nature, without excessive burden on the environment. Good clothing is made by people of diverse backgrounds working with energy and enthusiasm,

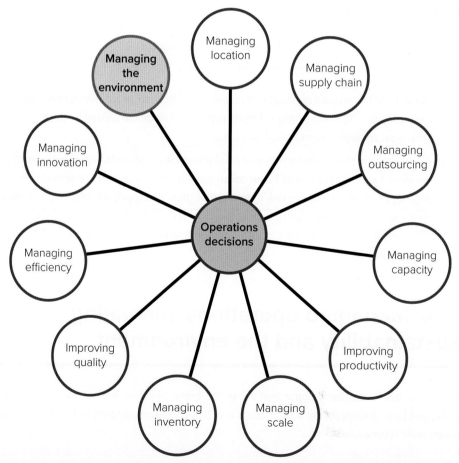

Figure 4.24 Managing operations includes managing the impact on the environment.

Source: Author.

under conditions where their health, safety, and human rights are respected and upheld. And we will extend this same spirit to our customers and all our stakeholders, working with them to aspire to a better society where we all thrive. This is our promise: to always work toward a better, more sustainable society.

Operations actions being taken by businesses to be more sustainable include:

- Reducing the use of some inputs, such as water and energy, from non-renewable sources.

- Recycling waste materials from the production process and recycling the final products. Businesses are increasingly being asked to take responsibility for the products they produce and what happens to them when the customer has finished using them. According to the Ellen Macarthur Foundation businesses have been used to taking resources from the ground to make products, which are then used, and, when customers no longer want them, they throw them away. The Foundation describes this as a linear economy in which we 'Take-make-waste'. The Foundation puts forward a vision of a circular economy. In this approach waste and pollution are reduced at the design stage. Waste has to be seen as a design flaw and new materials and technologies used to reduce both waste and pollution when items are being created. Products need to be designed so they can be reused, repaired, and remanufactured. The features of a sustainable approach are shown in Figure 4.25.

One study by the BBC showed that between 2004 and 2012, the proportion of major household appliances that stopped working and were thrown away within five years rose from 3.5% to 8.3%. In the past manufacturers simply produced and sold; what happened after that was nothing to do with them. Increasingly manufacturers are being expected to take responsibility for issues such as how long their products last, how easy they are to repair, how they can be collected if consumers want to get rid of them, and how many parts can be recycled or reused. In 2021 the furniture retailer Ikea announced

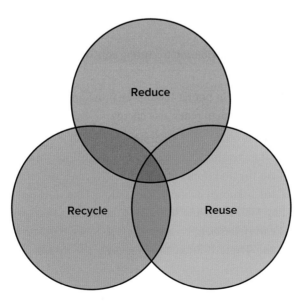

Figure 4.25 Features of a sustainable approach. *Source:* Author.

that it would start selling spare parts such as sofa legs, arm rests, and replacement nuts and bolts for its furniture. It said its aim was to prolong the life of its products and end the idea that it makes disposable goods. In 2020 Ikea started to buy back unwanted bookcases, and some other furniture items. People were offered vouchers worth up to 50% of the original price, to be spent at its store. Ikea said that any items which cannot be resold will be recycled. It aims to become 'a fully circular and climate positive business by 2030'.

- Reusing materials. Think of all the things you throw away each day. How many of these could be re-used? Businesses are gradually looking for more items to be re-used not discarded. Supermarkets in a number of countries now charge for bags to encourage customer to re-use bags. Coffee shops are encouraging you to reuse your own container. Universities encourage you to re-fill your own bottles. All of this reduces waste.

An example of a commitment to sustainability can be seen in the operations of UK clothing manufacturer John Smedley. According to its website the company is working on:

- Reducing the volume of paper and plastic packaging.
- Reducing waste yarn in the knitting process.
- Assessing sustainability of alternative packaging materials to plastic.
- Using tissue paper and cardboard made from only FSC-certified forests.

As well as greater focus on sustainability there is greater government action to bring in measures to make producers change what and/or how they produce to reduce their impact on climate change. For example, in 2016 around 200 governments signed the Paris Agreement; this required countries to take a number of ambitious actions to combat climate change in order to

- keep global temperatures 'well below' 2.0C (3.6F) above pre-industrial times and endeavour to limit them even more, to 1.5C
- limit the amount of greenhouse gases emitted by human activity to the same levels that trees, soil, and oceans can absorb naturally, beginning at some point between 2050 and 2100
- review each country's contribution to cutting emissions every five years so they scale up to the challenge
- ensure rich countries help poorer nations by providing 'climate finance' to adapt to climate change and switch to renewable energy.

The greater focus of businesses on more environmentally and more sustainable production is shown by the fact that increasing numbers are now using different ways of assessing their performance other than the traditional profit and loss (or income) statement. One way of reporting on operations is known as the Triple Bottom Line method. The Triple Bottom Line was developed by John Elkington in his 1997 book *Cannibals with Forks: The Triple Bottom Line of 21st Century Business*.

Businesses using the Triple Bottom Line measure the impact of their activities in terms of:

- Profit: revenue minus costs in a given period
- People: this measures the social impact of the activities of the business on peoples' lives
- Planet: this measures the environmental impact of the business' operations.

Elkington's approach takes a broader view of performance than the traditional approach which focuses on profits.

Business insight 4.5 Environmentally friendly whisky packaging

Johnnie Walker, the whisky brand that has been on sale for 200 years, is now available in paper bottles. Diageo, the huge drinks business that owns the brand, is producing the whisky in environmentally friendly packaging. While most Johnnie Walker is sold in glass bottles, which is less harmful to the environment than plastic, Diageo is conscious that the production of glass consumes energy and creates carbon emissions. Diageo's paper whisky bottle is made from wood pulp and is fully recyclable.

Drinks companies have been developing paper bottles to try to cut down on pollution and make products more sustainable. Many cartons made out of paper have a plastic coating inside to stop the drinks leaking out. Diageo's drinks bottles do not have that plastic coating. Meanwhile Carlsberg is developing a paper beer bottle.

Companies are coming under increasing pressure to reduce the amount of plastic in packaging as consumers increasingly focus on damage to ecosystems. In Europe, 8.2 million tonnes of plastic were used to package food and drink in 2018, according to ING analysts.

Not all companies are dropping plastic bottles. The Head of Sustainability at Coca-Cola says that it will not drop single-use plastic because customers like them because they reseal and are lightweight. The firm, which is one of the biggest producers of plastic waste, has pledged to recycle as many plastic bottles as it uses by 2030. Coca-Cola produces about three million tonnes of plastic packaging a year—equivalent to 200,000 bottles a minute. In 2019, it was found to be the most polluting brand in a global audit of plastic waste by the charity Break Free from Plastic.

Coke has pledged to use at least 50% recycled material in its packaging by 2030. It is also partnering with NGOs around the world to help improve collection. However, Coca-Cola said it could not ditch plastic completely, saying this could alienate customers and hit sales. It said that using only aluminium and glass packaging could push up the firm's carbon footprint. Coca-Cola argues that businesses wouldn't be in business if they ignore what customers want.

Questions

Why do you think Diageo is developing paper bottles?

Do you agree with Coca-Cola's decision not to stop sales of single-use plastic?

Sources

www.bbc.co.uk/news/business-51197463

www.bbc.co.uk/news/business-53361579

www.bbc.co.uk/news/business-53392949

4.15 Managing operations: using technology in operations

The operations of many businesses are clearly being affected by developments in technology and using technology appropriately is part of operations management as shown in Figure 4.26.

Key technological developments in recent years include:

- 3D printing. This is the process of creating a three-dimensional object by successively printing layers of materials on top of each other until an object is formed. This can be used to construct spare parts, architectural models, complex manufactured items, and prototypes. It allows for quick, cheap small-scale production. 3D (or additive) printing involves building up layers of material such as plastic, metal, and resin and bonding them together through layers of printing until the product has the final shape. This process is increasingly used by manufacturers. In 2018, 1.4 million 3D printers were sold worldwide, and that is expected to rise to 8 million in 2027, according to Grand View Research. Boeing is using 3D-printed parts in its spacecraft and commercial and defence aircraft, while BAE Systems uses the technology to

Figure 4.26 Managing operations includes managing the use of technology. *Source:* Author.

make components for the Typhoon fighter. There is even a 3D printer on the International Space Station, where it is used to create spare parts.

Even food can be 3D printed. Spanish company Nova Meat recently produced a plant-based steak derived from peas, rice, seaweed, and other ingredients. Using 3D printing allows the ingredients to be laid down as a criss-cross of filaments, which imitate the intracellular proteins in muscle cells. One of the most exciting fields for 3D printing is

Business insight 4.6 Amazon

Amazon's use of data is at the heart of its success. It uses data to analyse customers' spending patterns and recommend what else they might want. It uses computers in its operations to be more efficient than its rivals.

This efficiency can be seen in its fulfilment centres. These are huge warehouses that store and dispatch Amazon's products. Products are picked, packed, and sent out at tremendous speeds. There are remarkably few people working in the warehouse. Inside fulfilment centres areas are divided into 'pods' which comprise thousands of shelving units around six feet tall. Hundreds of robots move around these units and pull them around to allow products to be quickly selected and packed. Employees (associates) help pick and pack items to fulfil each order. The algorithms used to select where items are stored and how robots move the pods around enable the business to continually improve and become faster and more efficient.

More recently Amazon has started using machine learning technology to track the movement of products in the warehouse. AI cameras and scanners automatically track which products go into which bins. The use of AI means that employees do not have to hold a scanner and again speeds up the processing of an order.

In 2020 Amazon announced it would offer its till-less technology to other High Street shops. This was just over two years after Amazon had launched its own Go Grocery chain which has no tills. Go Grocery shoppers scan a smartphone app when they arrive and this allows them to pay via their Amazon account. When shoppers are in store everything they put into their baskets or trolleys is tracked and when they leave they are billed for this. Amazon had to develop very sophisticated technology to identify exactly what is put in the basket and cope with shoppers putting things back on the shelves.

Amazon has now adapted its Just Walk Out system for other retailers so shoppers register a payment card on entry and are automatically billed as they leave.

Amazon's system involves fitting a shop with hundreds of cameras and depth sensors. This data is then remotely analysed on Amazon's computer servers.

Questions

How do you think technology is helping Amazon achieve its operational objectives?

How will the use of till-less technology affect the operations of an Amazon store?

Why do you think Amazon might offer its till-less technology to competitors?

Sources

www.economist.com/business/2019/04/11/amazons-empire-rests-on-its-low-key-approach-to-ai
www.ft.com/content/ce0a7828-97bd-11e9-8cfb-30c211dcd229

medicine. For some time now, medical professionals have been 3D printing prosthetics, which can be made for a fraction of the usual price. In the construction industry 3D printing is being used to build houses by building walls layer by layer.

- Artificial Intelligence (AI). AI is something of an umbrella term for 'smart' technologies that are aware of and can learn from their environments to assist or augment human decision-making. Machine learning, recommendation software, chatbots, and image recognition are all examples of AI.

- Augmented Reality (AR). This occurs when data or information is 'overlaid' on the physical world. For example, AR can be used to visualize the design of a room or for customers to experience what a piece of clothing might look like on them.

- Blockchain technology. This is a distributed shared ledger where financial transactions are recorded and confirmed without the need for a central authority. It is used for supply chain traceability, financial processes, identity verification, and digital currencies.

Business insight 4.7 Digital operations in Africa

WeBuyCars which buys and sells used cars in South Africa became South Africa's largest second-hand car retailer by going digital. WeBuyCars started simply as a hobby for brothers Faan and Dirk van der Walt two decades ago. The brothers learnt how to fix cars from their father and did this in their own time. Faan trained to be a teacher but it became clear that the used car business offered more opportunities.

The business now employs hundreds of staff, with more than 124 buyers around the country, and more than 200 drivers who pick up cars daily and deliver them all over South Africa. The company trades around 7000 cars a month and has eight offices and eight warehouses located across Gauteng, the Western Cape, the Eastern Cape, and KwaZulu-Natal.

Until November 2018 much of WeBuyCars' data, including its inventory information, was held on Excel spreadsheets. As the number of transactions grew, maintaining and checking this data was very time consuming. WeBuyCars decided to employ a chief digital officer, along with developers and a data scientist and began to invest more in data systems starting with its inventory management. WeBuyCars also began recruiting more technically skilled workers with more of a 'problem-solving' mind-set.

After implementing the inventory management system, the company developed a database that enabled it to produce real-time statistics on the buying and selling of cars. This helped the company to make decisions faster and review the business more effectively. More recently, WeBuyCars started using artificial intelligence to analyse data and help to set the price of vehicles.

The brothers say that one of the most significant effects of the changes has been on the working lives of their employees. Previously, employees were used to spending long hours on routine administrative tasks. Automating the business has allowed them to deal with far larger volumes of trade and has freed up time for them to work with solutions to improve the business.

Question

How has technology changed the WeBuy business?

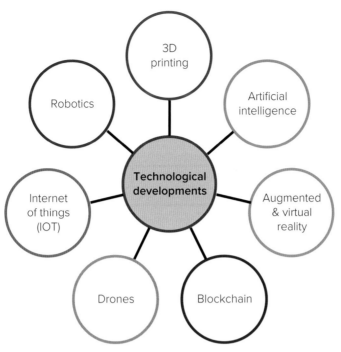

Figure 4.27 Developments in technology in operations. *Source:* Author.

- Drones. These are devices that fly or move without the presence of a pilot and can be used to collect a wide range of data or execute tasks remotely, e.g., remote delivery, infrastructure maintenance, security provision, or video capture.

- The Internet of Things (IoT). This involves extensive network connectivity and enables a range of devices to collect, process, and send back data. It is used in asset tracking, smart metering, fleet management, and predictive maintenance.

- Robotics. This is the combination of engineering and computer science to create, design, and operate mechanical devices, i.e., robots. It is used in industrial manufacturing, medical procedures, transportation operations, and product fulfilment.

- Virtual Reality (VR). This is a simulation of a 3D image or complete environment where a user can interact in a seemingly realistic way. It can be used for training, virtual tours, prototyping, and design.

Some of the technological developments are shown in Figure 4.27.

4.16 **Operations management and stakeholders**

Operations management will involve managing the relations with stakeholders. This is because operations decisions will affect several different groups. For example, an operations decision to relocate a business to provide lower cost facilities will affect:

- The communities where the business was originally based and where it is relocating to. For example, the move could create jobs around the new location.

Table 4.3 Examples of stakeholders and their objectives

Stakeholder groups	Typical objectives
Suppliers	Ongoing orders
	Prompt payment
Employees	Continued employment
	Fair rewards
	Good working conditions
	Career development
Shareholders	High financial returns
	Behaviour in line with shareholder values
Society	High levels of employment
	Operations that are environmentally friendly

- Investors as the move may reduce profits in the short term due to relocation costs but increase profits long term.
- Suppliers; this is because orders may be switched to new suppliers nearer the new location.
- Local and national governments; this is because it may influence the taxation revenue generated from business activity.

Different stakeholders will have their own objectives in relation to operations and their ability to meet these will be affected by what is happening with operations. Examples of stakeholders and typical objectives are given in Table 4.3.

Can you now answer this question from the introductory case study?

What stakeholders are affected by the operations of the fashion industry?

Where are we now?

We have now analysed one of the key internal functions of the business—the operations. In the next two chapters we will consider human resources and finance to complete our understanding of the internal functions of business.

Now you should know

- businesses transform outputs into inputs
- operations management manages the process of transformation
- typical operations objectives include unit costs, quality, and flexibility

- operations can be often categorized in term of their volume and variety

- lean production involves minimizing waste

- kaizen involves continuous improvement

- process innovations occur when there are developments in the way a process is undertaken.

Product innovations occur when there are developments in the actual product:

- Research and development (R&D) refers to scientific activities that innovate and develop new products.

- A patent provides legal protection for a new invention.

- The Triple Bottom Line measures business performance in terms of People, Planet, and Profit.

- A quality product is fit for purpose.

- Managing inventory involves managing stock levels within a business.

- Capacity measures the maximum output of a business given its resources.

- Capacity utilization measures the current output as a percentage of the maximum output.

- Economies of scale occur when unit costs fall as a business expands; types of economy of scale including technical, marketing, and financial.

 ## Review questions

Quick check

1. Explain what is meant by a transformation process.

2. State two typical operations objectives.

3. State two factors that might influence the location of a business.

4. Explain the difference between kaizen and research and development.

5. Explain the difference between just in time and just in case approaches to inventory management.

6. Give the equation for unit costs.

7. Explain what is meant by economies of scale.

8. Explain what is meant by innovation.

Analysis

1. Analyse the benefits and challenges of lean production.

2. Analyse the factors that would influence the levels of stock held by a retailer.

3. Analyse the factors that influence the unit costs of a business.

Evaluation

1. Do you think operations managers should always aim to get costs as low as possible?

2. Do think operations is the most important function of a business?

3. Why do you think productivity is so important in business?

∿ Find out more

- An excellent writer about operations management is Nigel Slack. If you want to explore operations management in more detail why not look at this book? Slack, N., Chambers, S., and Johnston, R. (2010). *Operations Management*. Financial Times/Prentice Hall.

- You can find out more about patents in the UK at www.gov.uk/patent-your-invention.

- Toyota is world famous for its lean production and pioneered many of the techniques associated with it. You can find out more about the Toyota Production System at global.toyota/en/company/vision-and-philosophy/production-system/.

- You can read more about Michael Porter's work on clusters if you look at 'Clusters and the new economics of competition' (2014) in *Harvard Business Review*. Available at: https://hbr.org/1998/11/clusters-and-the-new-economics-of-competition [Accessed 19 February 2023].

☰ Bibliography

Anon (2003). The hidden value in airline operations. *McKinsey Quarterly*, November 2003.

Bekker, H. (2021). *2020 (Full Year) Global: Lamborghini Sales Worldwide—Car Sales Statistics*. [online] Car Sales Statistics. Available at: <https://www.best-selling-cars.com/brands/2020-full-year-global-lamborghini-sales-worldwide/> [Accessed 2 April 2021].

Bozarth, C. and Handfield, R. B. (2008). *Introduction to Operations and Supply Chain Management*. Harlow, Pearson Education.

Brown, S., Lamming, R., Bessant, J., and Jones, P. (2000). *Strategic Operations Management*. Oxford, Butterworth-Heinemann.

Buchholz, K. (2023). *Advanced Microchip Production Relies on Taiwan [infographic]. Forbes* Magazine. Available at: https://www.forbes.com/sites/katharinabuchholz/2023/01/13/advanced-microchip-production-relies-on-taiwan/?sh=20474e44371d [Accessed 18 February 2023].

Cirium (2021). *Delta Air Lines named as the world's best performing airline of 2021; All Nippon Airways as the most on-time globally*. Available at: https://www.cirium.com/thoughtcloud/delta-air-lines-worlds-best-performing-airline-2021-all-nippon-airways-most-on-time/ [Accessed 18 February 2023].

Crosby, P. B. (1979). *Quality is Free: The Art of Making Quality Certain*. New York, McGraw-Hill.

Dale, B. G. (ed.) (1994). *Managing Quality*. Prentice Hall.

Deming, W. E. (1986). *Out of the Crisis*. Cambridge, MA, MIT Press.

Deming, W. E. (2000). *Out of the Crisis: Quality, Productivity and Competitive Position*, 2nd edn. Cambridge, MA, MIT Press.

Elkington, J. (1997). *Cannibals with Forks: The Triple Bottom Line of 21st Century Business*. Oxford, Capstone.

Farmbrough, H. (2021). *Coca-Cola Reveals it Produces 3m Tonnes of Plastic Packaging a Year in Ground-Breaking Report*. [online] *Forbes*. Available at: <https://www.forbes.com/sites/heatherfarmbrough/2019/03/15/coca-cola-reveals-it-produces-3m-tonnes-of-plastic-packaging-a-year-in-ground-breaking-report/?sh=17919fc3670f> [Accessed 2 April 2021].

Garvin, D. (1983). Quality on the Line, September–October, *Harvard Business Review*, 61, 64–75.

Glass for Europe (2022). *Hot hold operations in the flat glass sector*. Available at: https://glassforeurope.com/hot-hold-operations-in-the-flat-glass-sector/ [Accessed 19 February 2023].

GlaxoSmithKline (n.d.). *Home | GSK*. [online] Available at: https://www.gsk.com/en-gb/?gad_source=1&gclid=CjwKCAjwv-2pBhB-EiwAtsQZFlrJOU5RRpBBjxMZuVB5dj0oT_6H8sbY50rgVZC0GvU0I4hCzqe0WBoCF4AQAvD_BwE&gclsrc=aw.ds [Accessed 27 Oct. 2023].

Harrison, M. (1993). *Operations Management Strategy*. Bath, Pitman.

Investors.zoom.us (2021). [online] Available at: <https://investors.zoom.us/static-files/f74354f8-d7de-46fa-a519-c41d6733886a> [Accessed 2 April 2021].

Juran. J. J. and Gryna, F. M. (1988). *Juran's Quality Control Handbook*, 4th edn. New York, McGraw-Hill.

L'Oréal (2021). *L'Oréal Group: Our Product Quality and Safety*. [online] Available at: <https://www.loreal.com/en/commitments-and-responsibilities/for-our-products/product-quality-and-safety/> [Accessed 2 April 2021].

Lifewire (2021). *Where Is the iPhone Made? (It's Not Just One Country!)*. [online] Available at: <https://www.lifewire.com/where-is-the-iphone-made-1999503> [Accessed 2 April 2021].

Lythgoe, G. (2023). Bosses at Wigan's Heinz Factory want to create new 'Cookhouse'. *Manchester Evening News*. Available at: www.manchestereveningnews.co.uk/news/bosses-wigans-heinz-factory-want-26253836 [Accessed 19 February 2023].

McKinsey (2021). [online] Available at: <https://www.mckinsey.com/industries/travel-logistics-and-infrastructure/our-insights/the-hidden-value-in-airline-operations> [Accessed 1 April 2021].

Oag.com (2021). [online] Available at: <https://www.oag.com/hubfs/Free_Reports/punctuality-league-2020/Punctuality-League-2020.pdf> [Accessed 1 April 2021].

Ohno, T. (1988). *Toyota Production System Beyond Large Scale Production*. Productivity Press.

Pickens, T. B. (1987). *Boone*. New York, Houghton Mifflin.

Pine, B. J. (1992). *Mass Customization: The New Frontier in Business Competition*. Harvard Business School Press.

Porter, M. E. (1998a). *Competitive Strategy: Techniques for Analyzing Industries and Competitors*. New York, Free Press.

Porter, M. E. (1998b). Clusters and the New Economics of Competition. *Harvard Business Review*, Dec.

Saunders, M. (1997). *Strategic Purchasing and Supply Chain Management*. Pitman Publishing.

Schonberger, R. J. (1986). *World Class Manufacturing: The Lessons of Simplicity Applied*. New York, Free Press.

Slack, N., Chambers, S., and Johnston, R. (2010). *Operations Management*. Financial Times/Prentice Hall.

Slack, N., Chambers, S., Johnston, R., and Betts, A. (2009). *Operations and Process Management: Principles and Practice for Strategic Impact*. Pearson Education.

Sloan, A. P. (1990). *My Years with General Motors*. Doubleday.

Statista (2021). *Ford—Vehicle Sales 2020*. Statista. [online] Available at: <https://www.statista.com/statistics/297315/ford-vehicle-sales/> [Accessed 2 April 2021].

Terazono, E. and Telling, O. (2022). Lab-grown meat maker eat just unable to capitalise on Malaysia Chicken Ban. *Financial Times*. Available at: https://www.ft.com/content/f986f084-9bb7-4f3a-a91b-1a5c783fc257 [Accessed 18 February 2023].

Vision (n.d.). *Vision|FAST RETAILING CO., LTD*. Available at: https://www.fastretailing.com/eng/sustainability/vision/statement.html [Accessed 18 February 2023].

Walmart (2021). [online] Available at: <https://corporate.walmart.com/media-library/document/2020-walmart-annual-report/_proxyDocument?id=00000171-a3ea-dfc0-af71-b3fea8490000> [Accessed 2 April 2021].

Womack, J. P. and Jones, D. T. (1996). *Lean Thinking: Banish Waste and Create Wealth in Your Corporation*. Simon and Schuster.

Womack, J. P., Jones, D. T., and Roos, D. (1990). *The Machine that Changed the World*. Rawson Associates.

Www2.deloitte.com. (2021). [online] Available at: <https://www2.deloitte.com/content/dam/Deloitte/ch/Documents/consumer-business/ch-en-consumer-business-made-to-order-consumer-review.pdf> [Accessed 2 April 2021].

Chapter 5

Managing finance

Where are we now?

So far we have studied some of the different functions of a business such as marketing, operations, and human resources. Another key business function is finance and accounting. In this chapter we examine different types of accounting and how they can help managers. We then go on to examine the external environment of business and how a business forms its strategy.

Why am I studying this?

- You know that profit is important because businesses frequently talk about it, but you want to know what profit actually is. In this chapter we examine the meaning of profit as well as explore some common misconceptions about its meaning.
- You want to know what is meant by liquidity; how can a profitable business run out of cash? This chapter will explain the difference between cash and profit.
- You want to be able to understand the financial accounts of a business. You want to be able to assess how well a business is doing financially. This chapter will help you to analyse the key financial statements of a business.
- You want to know how using financial data can help management decision-making. In this chapter we examine key concepts such as break even and cashflow management which are essential to managing a business.

Learning objectives

By the end of this chapter, you should be able to:

- Distinguish the difference between management and financial accounting
- Analyse why stakeholders might be interested in financial information
- Explain the different financial statements a business produces
- Analyse the difference between a balance sheet (statement of financial position), income (profit and loss) statement and cashflow
- Classify different forms of profit such as gross, operating, and net

- Discuss how to increase profits

- Assess the financial position of a business using ratio analysis

- Evaluate the value of inter- and intra-firm comparison of financial ratios

- Analyse the limitations of ratio analysis

- Analyse the benefits of budgeting

- Evaluate the various ways of improving cashflow

- Assess the different investment appraisal techniques

Introductory case study Walmart

The US multinational firm Walmart started as a small, single discount store based on the simple idea of 'selling more for less'. Over the last 50 years Walmart has grown into the largest retailer in the world, according to the Fortune 500 list. Each week, over 240 million customers visit approximately 10,590 stores in 26 countries and the company's e-commerce websites.

In the financial year 2022 Walmart had a revenue of $572.8 billion, a net profit of $13.7 billion and an operating cashflow of $24.2 billion. The company's gross profit margin in 2021 was 24.3%; its operating profit margin was 4.1%.

This information can be found in the company's annual report. All companies have to produce financial data for existing and potential shareholders. This information is checked by independent accountants called 'auditors'.

The financial data produced includes:

- The income statement which shows the profit of the company over the last year (see Appendix 1)

- The statement of financial position which shows what the business owns and owes (see Appendix 2)

- The cashflow statement which shows how much cash the business has.

The annual report also includes:

- Detail on the policies used to produce these accounts. These are important because various assumptions have to be made in accounting such as how long any asset will last. An example of accounting policies at Walmart is shown in Appendix 3.

- An outline of future risks facing the business. See Appendix 4.

In its 2021 Annual Report Walmart says its objective is to prioritize strong, efficient growth. To achieve this, the company is focusing on increasing the number of stores, accelerating its sales through e-commerce. When appropriate, Walmart plans to make strategic investments focused on the long-term growth of the company.

The company says it operates its business with discipline by managing expenses, ensuring it is efficient, and creating an environment which focuses on low cost. Walmart measures its operating discipline by ensuring that sales are growing at a faster rate than operating, selling general, and administrative ('operating') expenses. The company is well known for its tight control of costs. However, the effects of the COVID-19 pandemic meant that in the financial year 2021 sales only grew by 6.8% compared to operating selling, general, and administrative expenses growing by 6.9%. Like many other businesses the pandemic created financial challenges for Walmart. ▶

Table 1 Capital expenditure financial year 2021

Area of capital expenditure	$ million
e-commerce, technology, supply chain	5681
Remodelling of stores	2013
New stores	134
International investment	2436
Total	**10,264**

Walmart's objective is to improve its customer-facing initiatives and create an omni-channel experience. Walmart wants it to be easy for you to buy from its stores by visiting in person or ordering online via your phone or other device, having products delivered to you or picking them up yourself, However you want to shop, Walmart wants to make it easy for you do to so whilst also making sure it is tracking your shopping history so it can tailor some of its offerings and promotions to you. To achieve a better all around (or 'omni-channel') experience the company is investing more capital to e-commerce, technology, its supply chain, and store remodelling and openings. Table 1 outlines the capital expenditure Walmart spent on different areas of the business to improve its offering. By investing in improving the business now the company expects higher returns later.

The returns generated by Walmart are invested into the business or used to pay dividends to shareholders. The dividend was $2.20 per share in 2022; in 2021 it was $2.16 per share and in 2020 it was $2.12 per share.

Appendix 1 Extracts from Walmart's income statement for the financial year 2021

	$ billion
Total revenue	559.2
Cost of sales	420.2
Operating, selling, general, and administrative expenses	116.3
Operating income	22.5
Income before income tax	20.6
Net income	13.5

Appendix 2 Extracts from Walmart's statement of financial position (Balance sheet) 2021

	$ billion
Current assets	90.1
including	
Cash	17.7
Receivables	6.5
Inventories	44.9
Total assets	252.5
Current liabilities	92.6
Long-term debt and other obligations	72.3
Equity	87.5

Appendix 3 Extracts from Walmart's accounting policies

In its accounting policies the company states that inventory is valued at the lower of cost or market value using a last in first out (LIFO) policy. Property and equipment are depreciated on a straight-line basis. Buildings are depreciated for between 3 and 40 years. Fixtures and equipment are depreciated for between 1 and 30 years. Transportation equipment is depreciated for between 3 and 15 years.

Appendix 4 Extracts from the list of factors and uncertainties affecting Walmart

Walmart's business operations are subject to numerous risks, factors, and uncertainties, domestically and internationally, outside of its control. These risks, factors, and uncertainties, which may be global in their effect or affect only some of the markets in which the company operates and which may affect it on a consolidated basis or affect only some of our reportable segments, include:

- Competition
- Economic factors
- The impact of the COVID-19 pandemic
- Technology problems
- Changes in trade laws.

Overview

The annual accounts of a company such as Walmart can, therefore, provide an insight into the financial position of the business. This information will be of interest to many different groups such as: suppliers, who will want to know if the business is financially secure; employees, who will want to know if they could be paid more; and the government who will be interested in the tax due. In this chapter we will learn how to interpret the financial accounts and consider other financial information we might need to assess a business. We will also consider the limitations for such reporting—, e.g. in terms of predicting the future and whether they do really give a broad enough insight into enough areas of the business. For example, many commentators are now interested in the social and environmental impact of a business not just its financial results.

Sources

The Fortune 500 list. https://fortune.com/fortune500/2021/search/ [Accessed March 2021]

s2.q4cdn.com/056532643/files/doc_financials/2022/ar/WMT-FY2022-Annual-Report.pdf

s2.q4cdn.com/056532643/files/doc_financials/2021/ar/WMT_2021_AnnualReport.pdf

Introductory case study questions

1. Why is profit important to Walmart?

2. Table 1 shows some of Walmart's strategicW capital expenditure. How might Walmart decide which projects or business areas to invest in?

3. How would you assess the financial performance of Walmart in 2021 using the data provided?

4. To what extent do you think the shareholders of Walmart would have been satisfied with the company's performance?

5. With reference to Appendix 3, explain why accounting policies matter.

Critical thinking

1. If you were a potential investor, what other information would like to have about Walmart which is not provided above?

2. How else might Walmart judge its performance apart from assessing its financial position?

5.1 Introduction: the finance function of a business

As we saw in Chapter 1, at the heart of business is its transformation process: businesses take inputs, transform them, and produce an output. This process involves the transformation of ideas, energy, commitment, and time. One of the key responsibilities of managers is to decide which activity or activities the organization should invest its resources into. Usually, this means businesses will look for the activities which will generate the highest return on those investments. Managers are responsible for the resources in their organization and need to allocate these appropriately to have the maximum impact. In 2023, for example, the global drinks business Diageo, whose brands include Captain Morgan, Baileys, and Guinness, announced the takeover of Don Papa rum, a premium brand from the Philippines, for over £230 million. Managers will have considered whether this acquisition fitted with their overall strategy and whether it would generate sufficient financial returns relative to alternative investments.

To assess the returns they make, managers will want to measure the value they have added through the transformation process. Questions they might ask include: 'How much is the output worth relative to the resources used to produce it?'; and 'Does the excess value generated justify the investment of time, money, and other resources?' Accurately measuring the value of certain activities will help managers make better decisions in the future about which activities to invest in to generate the highest returns.

There are many ways of measuring the value of something, but businesses often place a monetary value on the costs of resources and the worth of sales. The finance function plays a vital role in determining the activities of a business and assessing their worth.

The finance function of a business will be involved in all aspects of the transformation process including:

- raising the funds needed to undertake business activities

- allocating funds within the business; this will include setting budgets for different departments

- monitoring how funds are used

- reporting on the financial position of the business.

In this chapter we are going to explore the very important role that the finance function plays in an organization. We will start by defining the two main types of accounting (management and financial) before moving on to examine each of these in more depth.

5.1.1 Management and financial accounting

Finance activities are often categorized into two broad areas: **management accounting** and **financial accounting**. This is shown in Figure 5.1.

Management accounting refers to the use of quantitative techniques to provide data that helps managers make decisions. This form of accounting helps managers by providing financial data on issues such as whether to accept an order or whether to invest in a project or not.

The process of management accounting was described by Atrill and McLaney (2021) as a process of identifying what financial information is needed by managers, recording this data, analysing this data, and then reporting the findings to support decisions. This process is shown in Figure 5.2.

Management accounting will enable managers to:

- identify and control costs; this should help to reduce waste and increase efficiency
- evaluate and control the financial performance of parts of the business such as the various products, divisions, stores, or regions
- assess investment proposals.

Management accounting drives decisions and helps assess the finances of operations, control costs, and assess the finances of different options.

Management accounting techniques include:

- budgeting
- investment appraisal
- cashflow management.

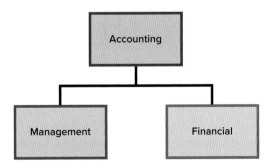

Figure 5.1 An overview of the two main types of accounting. *Source:* Author.

Figure 5.2 The management accounting process. *Source:* Author.

These techniques will be examined in detail later in the chapter in the management accounting section.

Whereas management accounting helps provide information for future decision-making; financial accounting focuses on reporting what has happened.

Financial accounting involves producing the financial reports and accounts for investors and regulatory bodies such as the government. For companies in the UK, for example, financial accounts have to be produced and audited (i.e. checked by independent external accountants) annually and these accounts are filed at Companies House. The legal requirements for the accounts in the UK are specified in the Companies Acts of 1981, 1985, and 1989. Bhimani et al. (2019) highlight that financial accounting focuses on reporting to external parties whereas management accounting is for internal users. Figure 5.3 and Table 5.1 provide more information on the difference between management and financial accounting.

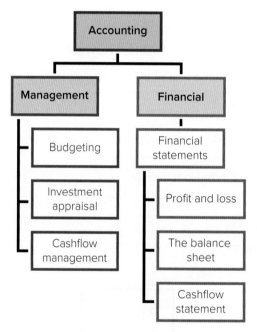

Figure 5.3 The key areas of management and financial accounting. *Source:* Author.

Table 5.1 A comparison of financial and management accounting

	Management accounting	Financial accounting
Regulation	None	Have to meet accounting standards
Frequency of reporting	As and when needed; regular	Usually annual
Time focus	Assessing past and future information	Usually historical
Users	Internal	External

Key concepts

> **Management accounting** refers to the use of quantitative techniques to provide data that helps managers make decisions.

> **Financial accounting** refers to the financial reporting on the activities of the business to external parties.

5.1.2 Stakeholders and financial information

Finance managers work with a wide range of stakeholder groups, both externally and internally. Within the business investors will want accurate information on the financial position of the business. Externally, suppliers may want to assess the financial position of a business before accepting an order. The government will want certain financial records maintained as part of compliance requirements, and banks will want to see financial data if they are approached for a loan. Figure 5.4 shows some of the main users of financial information.

Finance managers will record and present data to appropriate stakeholders in a format that is suitable for these different stakeholder groups. They will also negotiate, for example, the terms and conditions of loans, and plan ahead to identify financial opportunities and risks the business might face in the future. Financial managers might be called 'Chief Financial Officers' (CFOs), Finance Director, or Accounts Assistant depending on the size of the business and extent of their responsibilities.

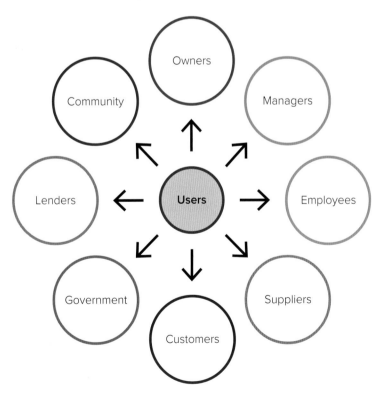

Figure 5.4 The main users of financial information in a business. *Source:* Author.

Where are we now?

Now we've covered the differences between the two main types of accounting and looked at the role of finance managers, we will move on to explore financial accounting in more detail and, having done this, explore management accounting.

5.2 Financial accounting

Financial accountants produce reports on the financial position of the business.

Every country has regulations about what information must legally be produced. Under current UK company law, for example, the financial accounts of a company should contain:

- A directors' statement. This will show who the directors of the company are, and will include comments on the company's performance over the previous 12 months and the directors' expectations for the next trading year.

- Financial statements. These will include an **income statement** (sometimes called a statement of financial position), **a balance sheet**, and **cashflow statement**.

- Notes on the accounts. These are necessary to explain the policies the company has adopted in its accounting and to give more detail to some of the items.

These financial statements will help us to answer key questions about a business such as: What does it own? How did it perform last year? What cash does it have available? Not surprisingly these financial statements will be of interest to many stakeholders. For example, current and potential investors will want information on the financial position of the business to decide whether to invest or maintain their investment. Suppliers may want to assess the financial position of a business before accepting an order; they will want to be sure they will be paid. The government will want certain financial records maintained as part of compliance requirements, and banks will want to see financial data if approached for a loan to assess the risk of lending.

5.2.1 Financial statements

As mentioned in the prior section, there are three key financial statements that a company may typically be expected to produce as shown in Figure 5.5.

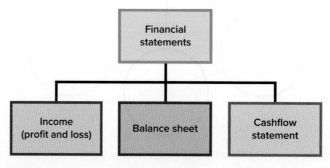

Figure 5.5 Types of financial statements. *Source:* Author.

Let's now look at each type of financial statement in more detail:

- **The income (or profit or loss) statement**

  This shows the revenue earned and the costs incurred generating this revenue over a given period of time, usually a year. For example, according to Forbes, the revenue of the Chinese utilities business State Grid was over $386 billion in 2021. In 2022, following a surge in energy prices, the Saudi oil company Aramco's profits rose to over $161 billion. The income statement is known as a flow concept as it shows the income and costs over the course of a year.

- **The balance sheet (or statement of financial position)**

  This is a statement showing what the business owns—called **assets**—and how the acquisition of these assets was financed. For example, according to Forbes the Industrial and Commercial Bank of China had assets of over $5,110,000 million in 2021. A balance sheet is known as a 'stock' concept because it shows aspects of the financial position of a business on a given day; this is stated at the top of the balance sheet.

- **The cashflow statement**

  This statement shows the inflow and outflow of cash through the business over a given period of time. For example, in January 2021 CNBC reported that Apple had cash amounting to $195 billion.

Each of the financial statements that a business produces offers a different insight into its financial position. For example, a well-established but poorly performing business may have a high level of assets on its balance sheet but a loss on the income statement because of a poor trading year. By comparison, a new but successful start-up may have high profits in its first year but may have limited total assets because it has not been trading for long. A business that is owed money by customers could have profits but not a positive cashflow.

To assess the overall position of a business all three financial statements need examining in conjunction with one another. Assessing one financial statement in isolation could present an inaccurate picture of the financial position of a business. This is worth remembering as you read about each financial statement in turn. We'll move on to look at the importance of the profit and loss statement first.

5.2.2 The income or profit and loss statement

As you are likely already aware, profit is a very important concept in business. It measures the value of the sales of a business in monetary terms compared to the financial value of the resources that are used up to produce and generate these sales over a given time period, usually a year.

The profit of a business over a period is measured using the equation:

Revenue (this is also known *as* 'turnover' or 'sales' or 'sales revenue') – Costs = Profit

Note: if the costs were greater than the revenue, a loss would be made,

There are some important things to note about the equation for profit:

- **Revenue** measures the value of sales generated in a given time period. This does not mean that the cash has been received for these sales but simply that the sale has occurred and been recorded. For example, imagine you sell a product for £2000 and the customer agrees to pay for this in one month's time. The revenue figure can be recorded now because the sale has been agreed. The cash will flow in later, but the revenue is recorded when the sale is completed.

- **Costs** refer to the value of the resources used up in the process of generating sales in a given time period. These costs may have been paid for in cash or may have been bought on credit. What is recorded is the value of what has been used up. Imagine, for example, that £2000 worth of materials is bought on credit and used up in the process of producing the items sold. The cash outflow at this time is £0 (because the items were bought on credit) but the cost of the items used up is £2000; this £2000 will be recorded as a cost. Now consider a situation where a business pays for £2000 of items in cash and uses up £250 of them on one product. Although the cash outflow is £2000, the costs recorded are only £250.

Understanding that costs relate to the value of the resources that have been used up and not necessarily what has been bought or what has been paid for in cash is essential to understanding the income statement. For example, if a business buys a piece of equipment for £50,000, the cost in year 1 will only be how much of this equipment has been 'used up' in that year. If, for example, it is assumed that the equipment will last 5 years and then be worth nothing, then—assuming it is used in equal amounts each year—this means the cost is £10,000 a year. This is known as a **depreciation cost**.

This approach to costing is used for any capital item such as equipment. Businesses will make assumptions about how long any equipment lasts, what it is worth at the end of its life, and the rate at which it is used; from this they will determine the cost per year. Some businesses assume that assets depreciate by a constant amount each year—this is called the **straight-line method of depreciation**. For example, in its 2022 annual report, Nintendo states that it depreciates its buildings and structures by a constant amount each year for between three and 60 years depending on what it is. Intangible assets such as the value of its software are typically depreciated over five years using the straight-line method. However, businesses

Think about it

Imagine a business buys a piece of equipment for £50,000. Managers expects it to last three years and then be sold for £5,000. What is the annual depreciation cost for this equipment if it depreciates by a constant amount each year?

What is the cost of the asset in Year 1 if the equipment was assumed to last for five years instead of three?

Key concepts

Revenue is the value of sales over a period of time.

Costs is the value of the resources used up to generate sales in a period of time.

Straight-line depreciation allocates the cost of an asset in equal amounts over its expected working life.

Reducing balance depreciation allocates the cost of an asset by an equal proportion over its expected working life.

Think about it

> You are thinking of launching a successful promotional campaign in which cash sales are 20% cheaper than buying on credit. How would this affect the business' cash and profits?

Analysing the business data 5.1

> Calculate the profit or loss of a business and its cash position in the following situations. Assume no other costs apart from supplies.
>
> **1.** A business buys £10,000 of supplies in cash. 50% of these are used up generating sales of £14,000. The sales are made on credit.
>
> **2.** A business buys £20,000 of materials on credit and uses up 75% of these. It generates sales of £12,000 in cash.

may also depreciate some assets by a constant percentage each year—this has the effect of depreciating by a bigger amount in the early years than later years. This is called the **reducing balance method of depreciation**. Nintendo uses this method for its equipment. To ensure you understand these concepts, read the next 'Think about it' box and answer the questions.

Profit versus cash

It is important to appreciate that measuring profit is measuring the financial added value generated by a transaction in a given time period. This is different from measuring cashflow. Many people assume that profits and cash are the same thing and that a profitable business must have plenty of cash: this is not the case! For example, if many sales are on credit the business will generate 'revenue' and potentially profit but this does not mean there are cash inflows. For example, when Tesla first launched it sold its cars before they had actually been produced but customers only paid a deposit not the whole sum; according to Bloomberg, Tesla could have (and nearly did) run out of cash before it actually produced and sold the cars.

Types of profit

So far in this chapter we have referred to 'profit' in quite a general sense but there are, in fact, many different types of profit depending on which costs have been deducted. Different measures of profit will be relevant for different stakeholders. For example, managers often consider profit before interest and tax. This is because managers cannot control interest rates or taxation rates and therefore want to measure the profit figure that they do have control over. By comparison, shareholders may be interested in profit after interest and tax because this shows the profit available to pay dividends.

An income (or profit and loss) statement will show different forms of profit earned over a given period of time. For example, it might show:

Revenue

minus

Cost of sales (these are the costs directly linked to the generation of the sales; for example, they include production and material costs; they are sometimes called 'Cost of goods sold')

= **Gross profit** (sometimes called Gross income)

minus

Overheads (sometimes called expenses) i.e. costs not directly linked to the production of the sales such as administrative costs or general marketing costs for the organization

= **Operating profit** (or earnings) before interest and tax (sometimes called Operating income)

minus

Interest

= **Profit (or earnings) before tax**

minus

Tax

= Profit (or earnings) after interest and tax; this is also called **'net profit'** or 'net income'

By measuring different types of profit a business can identify if there is an issue with a particular type of cost. For example, if gross profit is growing at a high rate but operating profit is not, this suggests there is an issue with the level of overheads. This might lead managers to make cuts in the levels of administrative support, for example. By comparison, an increase in the costs of supplies would have an impact on gross profit.

The different forms of profit can be seen if we look at the accounts in a company's annual reports. The accounts of public limited companies can usually be found online in a section of a company's website called Investor Relations.

To see an example of how profit may be broken down into different elements take a look at Table 5.2 which shows data from Starbucks' annual report for 2022.

The annual reports of a company will often include further details about its profits such as where in the world the income and profits occurred, or details of the income and profit of different divisions of the company. This information will be valuable to existing and potential investors.

For example, the information in Table 5.3 was provided in Prada's accounts for the six months ending 30 June 2021. This breaks down the overall sales of the company by brand, by region, and by product line. The company itself will also analyse profits by brand, Region, and product line but this information will not usually be made public.

Now we know more about the different types of profit businesses measure, let's look at why measuring profit is so crucial to organizations.

Table 5.2 Data from Starbucks' 2022 annual report

	$ million
Operating income (profit)	4, 617.8
Interest income	97
Interest expense	(482.9)
Earnings (profit before tax)	4,231.9
Income tax expense	948.5
Earnings (profit) after tax	3,283.4

Source: Starbucks

Table 5.3 Data from Prada's annual report, 2021

Sales by brand	'000 euros
Prada	1,264,829
Miu Miu	190,938
Church's	15,752
Other	6137
Sales by region	**'000 euros**
Europe	372,707
Asia Pacific	644,716
Americas	262,738
Japan	135,905
Middle East and other	61,590
Sales by product line	**'000 euros**
Leather goods	793,647
Clothing	372,074
Footwear	290,229
Other	21,706

Source: www.pradagroup.com/content/dam/pradagroup/documents/Shareholderinformation/2021/inglese/e-Interim%20Report%202021.pdf

Why is profit so important?

Although there are other measures of business success—for example, the social impact of the activities of a business may be an important indicator of performance and there are many not-for-profit organizations—as seen in Chapter 1, profit remains one of the most indicators of business performance. This is because it places a financial value on the rewards from business activity and it expresses these in a way that can easily be compared with other businesses. Profit shows the financial surplus generated from the activities of the business in a given period. It provides a source of finance for growth and it generates rewards for investors. Not surprisingly, then, making a suitable level of profits is regarded by many businesses as a vital objective. Of course, what is a 'suitable level 'of profits depends on the context of the business and so it is important to assess profits relative to some other indicator. Simply measuring profit is not in itself necessarily meaningful. If a business makes a profit of £2 million, it is not clear if this a good return until it is measured relative to something else. For example, if a £2 million profit was made in a year by a business the size of Starbucks, this would be a very small rate of return.

Can you now answer this question from the introductory case study?

Why is profit important to Walmart?

Increasing profits

Given the importance that businesses place on generating profits, the key question now is: how do they increase their profits? Put simply: profits can be grown by increasing revenue, decreasing costs or a combination of the two.

Increasing revenue may be linked to several different functions of the business. For example, the activities of the marketing function could have a positive impact: a business may launch a successful promotional campaign that results in higher sales. Higher revenues may also be linked to the operations function—for example, through the improvement or development of a new product.

Efforts to reduce costs are also likely to be linked to the activities of the operations function—for example, choosing cheaper suppliers, or finding ways of being more efficient. However, once again other functions may be involved; for example, human resources may try to meet staff requirements more efficiently and marketing may look to reduce promotional costs.

When making changes to increase revenue or decrease costs managers must consider the overall impact on profits. For example, a decision to reduce the amount of chocolate in a chocolate bar or put fewer crisps in a packet of crisps will cut the cost of producing a product which could increase profits. However, having less ingredients may reduce customer satisfaction which could reduce sales and profits. According to the *Financial Times* (2021) the chocolate manufacturer Mondelez announced in 2020 that all of its Cadbury chocolate bars such as Crunchie, Twirl, and Wispa that were sold in multipacks would be shrunk in size by the end of 2021. It was claimed this was to reduce their calorie count but there were complaints from some customers. This reduction in the content of products has become known as 'shrinkflation'. Other examples of shrinkflation that occurred in that year included fewer crisps in a bag of Doritos, fewer sheets in a Cottonelle toilet roll, and smaller bottles of Dove body wash. In the service sector, businesses such as Hilton, Marriott, and Hyatt along with many other hotel chains have removed many of their free gifts and encourage towel reuse. Businesses introducing such cost reductions will have forecast that the cost savings will be greater than any fall in revenue.

Efforts to boost revenue must also be treated with some care to ensure they do actually increase profits; this is because activities to generate more sales may cost money—for example, higher spending on an advertising campaign. If costs increase more than revenue, profits would actually fall. Increasing profits can obviously be difficult for some organizations and may take several years—Business Insight 5.1 explores how several delivery or ride-sharing firms have struggled to make a profit.

What would you do?

You manage an exclusive hotel chain. Profits have been falling.
Would you focus on increasing revenues or cutting costs? Justify your answer.

5.2.3 The balance sheet (or statement of financial position)

A **balance sheet** (sometimes referred to as a statement of financial position) is a financial statement which shows the value of the assets owned by a business at a given moment in time. It is a financial snapshot of a business. The **assets** of a business are items which it owns.

Assets can be divided into two types:

- **Non-current assets/fixed assets.** These are assets that are likely to be held for over a year such as buildings, equipment, and transport.

Business insight 5.1 Online delivery businesses struggle to make a profit

In the last few years a number of firms involved in delivery or ride-sharing apps such as Uber, Lyft, DiDi (Figure 1), DoorDash, and Delivery Hero have become public limited companies. In most cases the reason to float the business was to raise additional funds to enable rapid growth. This money was often used to subsidize discounts to try and gain market share. This sometimes led to very bizarre situations—for example, at one point restaurants could order their own food online at a discounted price because of the subsidies that existed from the delivery businesses and then resell it at a profit!

Figure 1 DiDi Taxi, Tokyo, Japan. *Source:* Shutterstock/Nayuki Minase.

Most of these app businesses have grown fast but they have struggled to make a profit. Customers regularly switch between apps looking for the best price. Delivery drivers also switch who they work for depending on the best rates they can get. The bargaining power from both drivers and buyers squeezes these delivery firms and makes it difficult to make a profit. Regulators have not helped either—for example, in London they forced Uber to pay drivers minimum wages and pensions which increased costs; in San Francisco regulators limited the fees DoorDash could charge restaurants for delivering their meals.

Question

If it so difficult to make a profit as an online delivery business, why set one up?

Sources

www.economist.com/business/uber-doordash-and-similar-firms-cant-defy-the-laws-of-capitalism-after-all/21806198

https://pages.stern.nyu.edu/~adamodar/New_Home_Page/datafile/margin.html\

www.google.com/search?q=profit+magins+across+industries&oq=profit+magins+across+industries&aqs=chrome..69i57j0i13j0i390l3.13915j0j4&sourceid=chrome&ie=UTF-8

Part 1

Where are we now?

We have now examined the income (or profit and loss) statement and the significance of profit in business. Profit is generated over a period of time as a result of the activities of a business and is usually measured annually. Analysing the profits of a business relative to its sales or assets over time and in relation to competitors provides useful insights for stakeholders. However, they will also want to know what a business owns and what it owes. This is shown on a balance sheet.

- **Current assets.** These are assets that are likely to change during the next year such as stock (or inventory) which will hopefully be sold in the future, debtors (this is money owed to the business which should be paid in the future), and cash (which will probably be spent).

The current assets of a business plus its non-current assets are called its total assets.

The nature of the assets of a business will vary according to the industry it is in. For example, according to BusinessKorea, Samsung Electronics owned more than 205,000 patents in 2021; these are assets of the business worth trillions of won. According to *The Economist*, in the same year the patents for the inventions of Fredrick Shelton who works for a subsidiary of Johnson and Johnson were valued by Patent Vector at $14 bn. By comparison in the music industry assets include the rights to the music that a company owns. According to the *New York Times*, in 2021 Bruce Springsteen sold the rights to his back catalogue to Sony for an estimated $550 million.

The value of the **total assets** of the business shows the value of what the business owns at a given moment in time.

The other part of the balance sheet shows how these assets were financed.

In order to acquire assets a business must raise funds. The sources of finance to buy the assets are:

- **Short-term borrowings:** such as an overdraft, or items purchased on credit.

  These represent borrowings that must be repaid within 12 months. They are also called **current liabilities**.

Think about it

How might the nature of the assets owned by a manufacturing business differ from a service business?

Can you think of assets that a business might have that are difficult to value?

Key concepts

A **balance sheet** is statement of the value of the assets owned by a business at a given moment in time.

The **assets** of a business are items which it owns.

Total assets equal current assets plus non-current assets.

- **Long-term borrowings:** such as loans and mortgages.

  These are called **non-current liabilities.** They represent borrowing that has to be repaid in more than 12 months' time. Some loans are 'secured' to reduce the risk for the lender. A secured loan means it is guaranteed by some of the assets of the business; if the business cannot repay the loan the assets can be taken instead. In 2021, according to *Global Finance* magazine, AT&T, the communications and telecommunications business, had long-term borrowings of over $147 billion.

- **Reserves**

  These are made up of retained profits and capital reserves.

  Retained profits represent the total profits the business has earned which have been kept. Profit will exist in the form of assets; for example, the business may hold the profits as cash or equipment. Capital reserves represent an increase in the value of a capital item such as a building.

- **Issued share capital**

  This is money raised from selling shares. To raise additional finance more shares may be sold to existing shareholders (this is called a rights issue), to the general public, or to institutional investors. In 2020 the Indian company Reliance Industries raised a massive Rs 53,124 through a rights issue.

Analysing the sources of finance chosen by a business is important because it shows how the assets have been acquired. For example, a company that has financed all its assets through its own profits is in a different financial position than a business which has bought all of its assets with debt; in the case of debt the business will be committed to interest repayments. It is important, therefore, in order to gain a good insight into the financial position of a business, not just to consider what a business owns but also how it financed the purchase of these assets.

The different elements of a balance sheet can be shown in Figure 5.6.

Obviously, the assets that a business owns must have been paid for in some way so this means that the total assets of a business are matched (or 'balanced') by the sources of finance.

This means that:

$$\text{Non-current assets} + \text{current assets} = \text{current liabilities} + \text{non-current liabilities} + \text{retained profit} + \text{issued share capital}$$

This equation can be re-organized.

For example, it may be presented as:

$$\text{Non-current assets} + \text{current assets} - \text{current liabilities} = \text{non-current liabilities} + \text{retained profit} + \text{issued share capital}$$

This version of a balance sheet is shown in Figure 5.7.

Auditors

The accounts of a company need to be checked by an independent accounting business; this is called an auditor. The auditor writes a report on the accounts. The biggest four auditing businesses in the world in 2022 were Deloitte, KPMG, EY, and PwC. In the UK, if the accounts produced by the business are judged to be acceptable, the auditor will sign them off

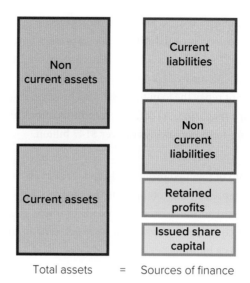

Total assets   =   Sources of finance

Figure 5.6 A balance sheet. *Source:* Author.

Balance sheet for ABC Ltd as at XXXXX

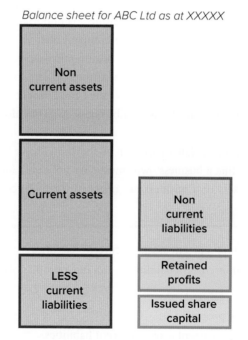

Figure 5.7 Balance sheet for ABC ltd as at a given moment in time. *Source:* Author.

 Think about it

Consider the following situations:

Business A has financed all its assets using non-current liabilities.

Business B has financed all its assets using retained profits.

Why do you think differences in the way the assets were financed matters?

Key concepts

A **liability** is something that is owed by a business.

Current liabilities represent borrowing that need to be paid back within 12 months.

Long-term liabilities represent borrowing that need to be paid back after more than 12 months.

saying they present a 'true and fair view' of the company's finances. If the auditor has any concerns about the accounting practices or the financial viability of the business it should state this so existing and potential shareholders are aware. Investors place a great deal of trust in the auditor's report and so it is important that they are conducted effectively. In 2022 the *Financial Times* reported that the accounting firm EY was being sued for over $2.5 bn because of alleged negligence in its audits of NMC Health, a hospital group that collapsed with suspicions of major fraud. More than $4 bn of debt was apparently hidden from NMC's balance sheet and this was allegedly not spotted by EY meaning the accounts were very misleading.

Where are we now?

We have now considered two of the key financial statements in business: the income (or profit and loss statement) and the balance sheet (statement of financial position). One shows what the business earns over a period of time. The other show what it owns at a given moment. We will consider cashflow information later in the chapter. We now consider how these financial statements can be analysed using ratios.

5.3 Financial ratio analysis

As we have seen, a number in isolation has little meaning. We do not know whether a profit of £20,000 is regarded as good or bad until we understand the context. A profit of £20,000 generated from sales of £30,000, for example, is very different than a profit of £20,000 earned from sales of £3,000,000. Comparing one number with another is a valuable way of getting a sense of the significance of the figure; this process is called **ratio analysis**.

Financial ratios are typically used to analyse the profitability of a business, its liquidity, its debt, and its returns to shareholders. The main types of financial ratios are shown in Figure 5.8.

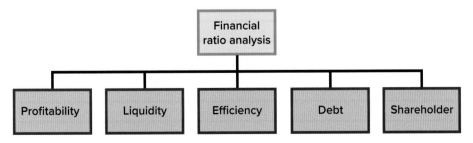

Figure 5.8 Types of financial ratio. *Source:* Author.

5.3.1 Profitability ratios

When we measure profits in relation to something else this is a measure of **profitability** rather than profit. Profitability is measured as a percentage rather than in a particular currency unit, such as pounds or dollars.

To assess the profitability of a business we may measure profits in relation to its sales.

This is known as the profit margin and is measured by (profit/sales) × 100. For example, if the profit is £10 and the sales are £50 this means the profit margin is (£10/£50) × 100 = 20%. This means that for every pound of sales 20 pence is profit.

It is possible to calculate different forms of profit margin such as the 'gross profit margin', the 'operating profit margin' and the 'net profit margin' using the following formulas:

Gross profit margin = (gross profit / sales) × 100
Operating profit margin = (operating profit / sales) × 100
Net profit margin = (net profit / sales) × 100

Differences in these profit margins will depend on what is happening with various costs. For example, according to the *Financial Times* in the financial year 2020 the sportswear business Adidas had a gross margin of 49.7% but an operating profit margin of just 3.8% which was down from 11.3% the year before. This was due to rising operating expenses.

The profit margin earned by a business will depend on the price charged and the unit cost. It will depend on many factors including market conditions. For example, according

Analysing the business data 5.2

The data in the following table was shown in the annual reports of Zoom, the online communications business.

Table 1 Revenue data from Zoom's 2019–2022 annual report.

	2022 $000	2021 $000	2020 $000	2019 $000
Revenue	4,099,864	2,651,368	622,658	330,517
Cost of revenue	1,054,554	821,989	115,396	61,001
Gross profit	3,045,310	1,829,379	507,262	269,516
Operating expenses				
Research and development	362,990	164,080	67,079	33,014
Sales and marketing	1,135,959	684,904	340,646	185,821
General and administrative	482,770	320,547	86,841	44,514
Income from operations	1,063,591	659,848	12,696	6167
Net income after interest and tax	1,375,639	672,316	25,305	7584
Gross profit margin %	?	69	81	82
Operating profit margin %	?	25	2	2
Net profit margin %	?	25	4	2

Source: Zoom

Consider the revenue for Zoom 2019–2022. Why do you think it might have changed over this period?

For 2022, calculate Zoom's:

- Gross profit margin

- Operating profit margin

- Net profit margin

Comment on your findings.

Source

investors.zoom.us/static-files/9a9d91bf-5c62-45fd-9573-fb03159c8a93

Another measure of profitability measures profits in relation to the long-term funds in the business. One measure of the long-term funds in the business is known as the capital employed. This comprises issued share capital, retained profits, and long-term liabilities. Profit in relation to the capital employed is known as the return on capital employed (ROCE). The ROCE provides an insight into how effectively managers are using the long-term funds they have available. If the funds are not generating a sufficient return they should be used elsewhere.

$$ROCE = (net\,profit\,/\,capital\,employed) \times 00$$

Another measure of profit in relation to long-term funds is known as Return on Equity (ROE). This measures profit in relative to the funds provided by or belonging to shareholders (e.g. issued share capital and reserves).

$$ROE = (net\,profit\,/\,equity) \times 100$$

The ROCE and ROE that a business generates depend on the sales it generates and the profit margin from each sale. For example, a business may have a small profit per sale but if the sales are high enough the overall returns on the capital employed or equity may be relatively high. A business can increases its returns on long-term funds if it can use its funds to generate more sales and/or it can generate a higher profit margin for each sale.

Analysing the business data 5.3

Below there is financial data which you can use to calculate profitability ratios.

	Business A	Business B
Sales	20	2000
Capital employed £m	50	50
Net Profit £m	10	10

Calculate the net profit margin and the return on capital employed of each of the businesses above.

Analyse the differences in the financial performances of the two businesses.

8 What would you do?

In January 2020 Helena Helmersson, who had recently been appointed chief executive of H&M, announced that she wanted to achieve an operating profit margin of above 10% within three years, up from less than 2% in 2020 and 7.7% in 2021. How would you do this?

Source: The Economist. (2022). *After expanding in 2021, fast fashion may be squeezed again*. [online] Available at: https://www.economist.com/business/2022/02/19/after-expanding-in-2021-fast-fashion-may-be-squeezed-again

to the *Financial Times,* in 2021 TSMC, the world's biggest contract semiconductor maker based in Taiwan, announced it expected gross profit margins of 50% following a global shortage of semiconductor chips. The shortage meant that customers were willing to pay more for chips allowing TSMC to increase its gross profit margin. By comparison, in the highly competitive supermarket industry in the UK typical profit margins are 3%.

 ## Analysing the business data 5.4

VF Corporation is one of the world's largest apparel, footwear, and accessories companies. Its brands include Vans, Kipling, and The North Face.

Table 1 VFC's balance sheet for March 2021

	£
Revenue	9,238,380
Cost of sales	4,370,780
Operating profit (income)	607,631
Net profit (income)	407,869
Current assets	4,785,870 (of which receivables = 1,298,020, inventory = 1,061,839)
Current liabilities	2,210,477
Equity	3,056,164

Source: VFC

VFC's balance sheet for March 2021 shows the following financial information.
  Using this data calculate the following ratios for the company:

1. Net profit margin

2. Return on capital employed

3. Return on equity

4. Current ratio

5. Inventory turnover.

  Comment on your findings.

Where are we now?

Understanding the profitability of a business is important as it measures the financial surplus the business has generated over a given period relative to something else such as sales or capital employed. However, we are also interested in the ability of a business to pay its bills. It is possible to have high profits but still have problems paying bills if, for example, the revenue has not yet been paid for in cash. We now look at liquidity ratios.

5.3.2 Liquidity ratios

Liquidity ratios measure the ability of a business to pay its short-term liabilities using its current assets. Stakeholders will want to know this ratio because they will want to be assured the business is financially solvent. For example, a potential supplier will want to consider the liquidity of a business for fear that it might not get paid. If a business cannot pay its bills it may be taken to court and forced to sell off its assets to pay its debts.

One liquidity ratio that is commonly used is the current ratio, as shown in Figure 5.9. This measures the current assets of a business compared to its current liabilities.

If the current ratio is bigger than 1 this means the business has more current assets than current liabilities. For example, if the ratio is 1.7 this means the value of current assets is 1.7 times as big as the current liabilities.

To be liquid a business will need sufficient current assets to be able to pay off its current liabilities; however, it won't want to hold too many assets in the form of cash, stock, or debtors as this money could be earning better returns if it was invested elsewhere. Cash and debtors do not earn returns and stock (inventory) can lose value so businesses will not want too many of their funds in these forms. Many businesses operate with a current ratio of less than one knowing that they can raise funds if necessary to pay off current liabilities.

Another common liquidity ratio is known as the acid test ratio.

This is measured by: Current assets excluding inventory: current liabilities.

The acid test ratio is a tougher test of liquidity than the current ratio because inventory is not included. The acid test ratio is measuring the ability of the business to pay its short-term bills without using its inventory. If the acid test is around 0.8 this means that without counting the value of its inventory the business' current assets can pay 80% of its short-term liabilities.

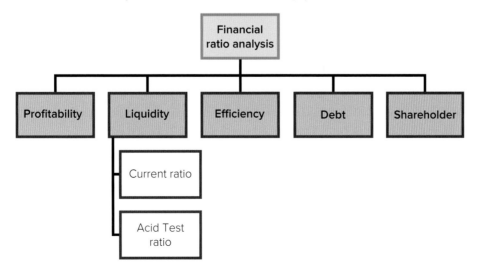

Figure 5.9 Liquidity ratios as part of ratio analysis. *Source:* Author.

What would you do?

Would you make liquidity or profitability the priority for your business?

Analysing the business data 5.5

Below we show financial information from two different businesses. You can use this data to analyse the liquidity position of these organizations.

	£m Business A	£m Business B
Inventory (Stock)	50	20
Debtors	20	10
Cash	10	5
Current liabilities	60	70

Using the data above, calculate the current ratio and acid test ratio for both businesses. Comment on your findings.

Where are we now?

We have now analysed the profitability of a business using ratios as well as its liquidity. We have highlighted the importance of distinguishing between a profits and cash. We now look at how ratios can help a business assess its efficiency.

5.3.3 Efficiency ratios

Efficiency ratios are part of ratio analysis as shown in Figure 5.10. They measure how well resources in the business are being managed.

Efficiency ratios include:

Inventory turnover ratio

A business will hold inventory such as the stocks of materials, works in progress, and finished goods. Inventory is useful to keep production going and to have stocks of finished items ready to sell. In the financial year 2020, for example, Adidas held nearly 4.4 billion euros worth of inventory out of total assets worth around 21 billion euros.

However, holding inventory also has a cost. It can cost money to store and keep the inventory secure. Inventory also represents money 'tied up'; this money could be used elsewhere to earn a return so there is an opportunity cost. There is also the danger that a business may end up holding inventory that does not sell. In 2018, for example, Burberry revealed in its annual report that it had burned £28.6 million of clothing and cosmetics which was unsold; the company did not want to cut prices to sell this inventory because of the impact this might have on its brand.

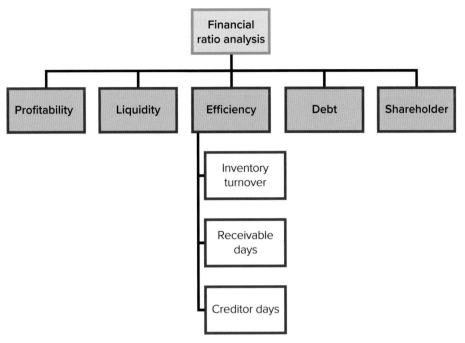

Figure 5.10 Efficiency ratios are part of financial ratio analysis. *Source:* Author.

Analysing the business data 5.6

As of 30 March 2020 Nintendo held the following inventory:

	Million Yen
Finished goods	71,815
Works in progress	19
Raw materials and supplies	17,158

Source: www.nintendo.co.jp/ir/pdf/2021/annual2103e.pdf

Questions

1. Explain why Nintendo holds inventory.

2. What are the costs of holding it?

The inventory turnover ratio considers how much inventory is being held relative to the cost of the items that are sold in a year.

For example, if the inventory held on a given day is £20,000 and in a year the cost of sales is £400,000 then the inventory would have been replaced or 'turned over' 20 times during the year.

$$\text{Inventory turnover} = \frac{\text{cost of sales}}{\text{value of inventory}}$$

Think about it

What do you think the impact of adopting a Just in Time approach to production would be on the inventory turnover ratio? For more on Just in Time production see Chapter 4.

Business insight 5.2 Shein develops thousands of products a day

Shein is a very successful online fashion retailer. According to its website the company focuses mainly on women's clothing although it does also sell men's and children's clothes plus shoes, fashion accessories, and bags. Shein's main markets are in Europe, America, Australia, and the Middle East. The brand was set up in 2012. The company says that 'everyone can enjoy the beauty of fashion'. It operates in over 150 countries and territories around the world.

Shein offers a constantly updated product range at very low prices. According to *The Economist* (2021), Zara—often thought of as a leader of fast fashion—launches about 10,000 new designs every year. Shein releases 6000 new products or colours every day! Some are quickly discontinued. The typical price of its items is between $8 and $30. The company has algorithms to trawl the internet to identify what is trending. It then sends these designs to its designers and produces them in batches as small as 100 items. The company tracks demand in real time. If a design is selling well, Shein orders more. If it's not, Shein simply does not place more orders. The company holds inventory centrally in large warehouses and then sends them direct to customers. By doing this it holds on average just 30 days' worth of inventory compared to an industry average of 150 days.

Shein offers suppliers better terms than rivals by paying within 14 days rather than the 90 days that are often common in the industry; this favourable treatment is to guarantee supply. The company is very active on social media with 250m followers across Instagram, Tik Tok, and other social-media platforms.

Whether the company makes a profit is as yet unclear. Financial information about the business is not readily available.

Questions

Do you think Shein's inventory turnover will be high or low? Why?

Do you think Shein's profit margins will be high or low? Why?

Source

www.economist.com/business/shein-exemplifies-a-new-style-of-chinese-multinational/21805217

According to CSIMarket, in the financial year 2020–21 Amazon's average inventory turnover was 10.46. The rate of inventory turnover will depend in part on the nature of the business, the type of product, and its strategy. Zara aims for fast fashion and, therefore, you would expect its inventory turnover to be higher than a business that holds a season's worth of clothing rather than a few weeks' worth.

Receivables days ratio

Receivables represent money owed to the business. The receivables days ratio measures how much is owed to the business on a given day in terms of the typical day's sales by the business. For example, if receivables days is 14 days this means the amount owed to the business is equal to two weeks' worth of sales.

To calculate receivables days we:

i. work out the average sales per day using the equation: sales/365 days

ii. work out how much the receivables figure is in terms of average days' sales.

What would you do?

For example, if the annual sales of a business are £7,300,000 this means that on average the business sells: £7300000/365 = £20,000 per day.

If the value of the receivables on a given day is £60,000 this is equal to £60,000/£20,000 = 3 days' worth of sales.

To calculate the receivables days, we therefore use the following equations:

Average days sales = sales / 365

Receivables days = receivables / average days' sales

Some business may deliberately use credit to attract customers to increase sales—this is the basis of promotional campaigns saying 'buy now, pay later'; this could lead to a relatively high debtor (receivables) days ratio. In other industries businesses may focus more on cash payments which would lead to a low debtor days ratio.

Creditor days ratio

A business owes money to its creditors. For example, these are suppliers that are owed money. The value of the creditor days measures the size of the amount owed to creditors relative to the costs involved in the sales of a business over a year.

For example, if the costs of sales over a year are £547,500 this means that the average costs of sales per day are £547,500/365 = £1500 per day.

If the amount owed to creditors is £60,000 this is equal to £60,000/£1500 = 40 days' worth of sales.

To calculate the average cost of sales per day we use: Cost of sales/365.

To calculate creditor days, we use the equation: Creditors/average cost of sales

If a business has a high level of power over suppliers it may delay payments which would increase its creditor days.

Managers may want to compare the relative size of receivables days and creditor days. If, for example, the business is owed the equivalent of 14 days' worth of sales and owes the equivalent of 40 days this should be good for the liquidity of the business as it takes longer to pay out than it takes to be paid. If, however, the creditor days were 14 days and the receivables days were 40 days, this means that the business is owed is more than it owes; this could create liquidity problems.

What would you do?

Analysing the business data 5.7

1. The financial data below shows information that allows you to calculate creditor and debtor days.

	£m
Sales	200
Cost of sales	120
Debtors	12
Creditors	36

Using the data above, calculate the business' creditor days and debtor days. Comment on your findings.

2. The following shows financial ratios for three well-known businesses for the financial year 2020–2021.

Table 1 Financial ratios for Nike, Astra Zeneca, and Walmart

	Nike	Astra Zeneca	Walmart
Current ratio (times)	2.7	0.96	0.97
Gross profit margin	45	80	24.68
Net profit margin %	12.8	12	2.41
Inventory turnover (times)	3.58	1.3	9.35
Debtor days	38.57	101.28	4.25
Gearing (%)	42	53	34

Source www.macrotrends.net/stocks/charts/NKE/nike/financial-ratios
www.macrotrends.net/stocks/charts/AZN/astrazeneca/financial-ratios

Question

Using the data above compare and contrast the

- profit margins
- liquidity
- gearing
- debtor (receivables) days
- inventory turnover

for these businesses.

 Where are we now?

We have now used ratios to consider the profitability, liquidity, and efficiency of a business. We now consider how a business raises its long-term finance by looking at the proportion of debt it has.

5.3.4 Debt ratio

Many stakeholders will be interested in the long-term sources of funds for the business; in particular they will want to know how significant the debt of the business is. Gearing is a ratio that measures how much debt a business has, as shown in Figure 5.11.

As we have seen the total long-term funds of a business are called its capital employed. Stakeholders will be interested in the composition of these funds. In the example in Table 5.4 all three businesses have the same total capital employed of £50 million but they have raised this money in very different ways. Business A relies heavily on debt, Business B has used its own profits, and Business C has raised a significant proportion of funds through selling shares.

Gearing measures the long-term debt of the business as a proportion of its capital employed. Debt may be in the forms of loans or bonds. Bonds are corporate IOUs which a business sells to raise money. A bond will have a date when it is repaid; each year the business will also pay a sum to the holder on the repayment date and return for annual payments. Final repayment is on a set date.

There are several versions of the gearing equation so it is important to always check which one has been used.

One of the most common versions of this ratio is

$$\text{Gearing} = \frac{\text{long-term borrowing}}{\text{capital employed}} \times 100$$

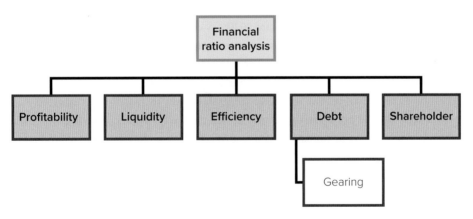

Figure 5.11 Gearing is part of ratio analysis. *Source:* Author.

Table 5.4 Examples of how the composition of capital employed can vary

	Business A £000	Business B £000	Business C £000
Non-current liabilities	40	3	5
Retained profit	8	45	10
Issued share capital	2	2	35
Capital employed	50	50	50

So, with reference to the three businesses in Table 5.4:

	Business A	Business B	Business C £000
Gearing	(£40,000/£50,000) × 100 = 80%	(£3,000/£50,000) × 100 = 6%	(£5,000/£50,000) × 100 = 10%

Another common measure is the debt: equity ratio. With reference to Table 5.4 this means:

	Business A	Business B	Business C
Debt: equity	(£40,000/£10,000) × 100 = 400%	(£3,000/£47,000) × 100 = 6.38%	(£5,000/£45,000) × 100 = 11.11%

An increase in the gearing of the business means that a higher proportion of its long-term funding is from debt. If all else is unchanged this means that the interest repayments will be higher. This can create a risk for the business: if its profits are not high enough it may not be able to pay the interest it owes. Stakeholders—particularly potential lenders—will want to be aware of the gearing ratio so that they can consider the risk to them in terms of the business meeting interest payments. In 2020, for example, according to the *Financial Times*, Chinese companies delayed payment on $7.3 bn of dollar debt and $22.7 bn worth of renminbi-denominated bonds because of the challenges of paying the interest; this led to concerns from some investors about further lending to these businesses in China.

One of the problems many businesses faced during the pandemic was that they had debt to pay but their income was reduced due to fewer sales. In fact, in many cases businesses had to borrow more to survive because their income was much lower than usual. For example, the *Financial Times* reported that in July 2020 US companies owed a record $10 trillion. Meanwhile in the UK the Office of National Statistics reported that in March 2021 the private debt of private companies was around £105 bn. Businesses were helped by the fact that interest rates were extraordinarily low at the time but, even so, this amount of debt put a great deal of pressure on their finances and they were vulnerable to any increase in interest rates.

However, this does not mean that a business should always avoid borrowing. Borrowing enables a business to raise funds to invest in projects such as developing new products or taking over a competitor. The key is to make sure that the additional earnings or benefits generated from using the borrowed funds cover any additional costs. For example, many of us borrow money to buy our car or to buy property; we do this because we would rather own the asset now than wait until we had saved enough to buy it from our own funds. We want the benefits of ownership now, not later. Provided we can repay the loan this is not a problem. Similarly, provided a business can meet its interest repayments then borrowing may make sense to enable it to pursue its growth objectives. Financial managers will, therefore, want to consider the terms and conditions of different loan options before deciding whether to go ahead and which option to take.

 ## Key concepts

Liquidity ratios measure the ability of the business to pay its short-term liabilities.

The **gearing ratio** measures the long-term debt of the business as a proportion of its capital employed.

Business insight 5.3 Airlines in debt

In 2021 it was reported that the world's largest airlines had accumulated over $300 bn in debt and faced massive bills paying interest and repaying finance they were given to help them survive. Another problem some of the airlines faced was a lack of liquidity. The Chief Executive of the airline easyJet said that liquidity was of great importance to make sure that the company always had enough cash to manage any situation. According to the *Financial Times*, although the biggest airlines did have cash of around $140 bn their debt was nearer $320 bn.

Before the pandemic the big airlines were in relatively good financial health. This allowed them to borrow relatively easily according to the credit rating agency, Moody's. The problems faced by airlines were significant because of the collapse in air travel during the pandemic.

In 2021 the International Air Transport Association (IATA) stated that cash was essential to the airlines to survive. IATA said that passenger numbers needed to pick up to enable airlines to start repaying their debt. An animation analyst at Bernstein said that the airlines needed to reduce their balance sheet 'scars' before they became attractive again to investors. Norwegian, which had long been one of Europe's most vulnerable airlines because of its high debt, filed for bankruptcy on 18 November that year.

Questions

Explain why the airlines might have had high gearing during the pandemic.

Explain how the liquidity of the airlines might be affected by their gearing.

Sources

www-ft-com.ezproxy01.rhul.ac.uk/content/0a334f3e-3bb3-4ff3-96ed-39a5b3fe821b

www-ft-com.ezproxy01.rhul.ac.uk/content/0a334f3e-3bb3-4ff3-96ed-39a5b3fe821b

Analysing the business data 5.8

Below is financial data on a business and its sources of funds.

	£m
Long-term loans	20
Retained profits	10
Issued share capital	30

Calculate the gearing ratio for this business.

What would the gearing ratio be if borrowing increased by £30 m?

What is the debt-to-equity ratio for this business?

The advantages of debt and share issues are shown in Table 1.

Table 1 debt v share issue

Advantages of debt	Advantages of share issue
Interest payments will not increase if profits are high; more retained profit	Payment is via dividends; if profits fall dividends can be lowered
Do not lose control	No fixed interest payments

Where are we now?

So far, we have analysed ratios used to assess the profits, liquidity, and borrowings of a business. We now consider some of the ratios that shareholders might use to analyse the financial position of a business, as shown in Figure 5.12.

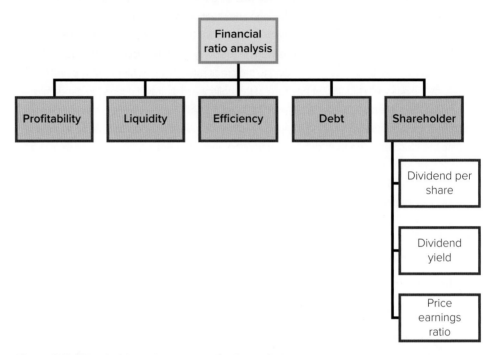

Figure 5.12 Shareholder ratios as part of ratio analysis. *Source:* Author.

Shareholder ratios are ratios which might be of use to help investors analyse the financial position of the business.

As shown in Figure 5.12 shareholder ratios include the following.

Dividend per share

The **total dividends** paid by a business represents the amount of money that shareholders vote to be paid to them. This will be divided amongst all the shares.

The **dividend per share** is the amount of dividend paid on each share. It is calculated using the equation:

$$\frac{\text{Total dividend payments}}{\text{Number of shares}}$$

For example, if the total dividend paid out is £10,000 and the number of shares is 50,000

The dividend per share is £10,000/50,000 = £0.20 per share

Companies will take different approaches to dividend payments. For example, Alphabet (owner of Google) and Amazon, historically, have not paid dividends, preferring to hold on to the funds for investment. They would argue that shareholders benefit from this investment into the business through higher share price over time.

Dividend yield

The **dividend per share** will usually be compared to the price of buying a share. This gives the yield (or return), i.e. it shows how much the dividend is as a percentage of the share price. This gives some sense of the relative scale of the dividend.

The equation for **dividend yield** is: (dividend/current share price) × 100

For example, if the dividend per share is £0.20 per share and the share price is £2.00 the dividend yield is (£0.2/£2.00) × 100 = 10%. Investors will consider these returns (or likely returns in the future) along with the other rewards from investment such as an increase in share price and compare this with other potential rewards elsewhere taking account of factors such as the likely risk involved.

Price-to-earnings ratio (P/E)

The earnings (or profits) per share are calculated by dividing the profits of the business for the year by the number of shares.

$$P / E = \text{profit for the year} / \text{number of shares}$$

For example, if the profits of the business are £20,000 and the number of shares is 50,000 this means the earnings per share are (£20,000/50,000) = £0.40 per share.

The P/E ratio is calculated using: current share price/earnings per share.

If the current share price is £4.00 this means the price to earnings ratio is £4.00/£0.40 = 10.

If there is high level of interest in a business and demand for its shares is high this is likely to increase the share price. All other things staying unchanged, this will increase the P/E ratio. If, however, the demand for a company's shares is low, a fall in the share price will lead to a fall in the P/E ratio. The P/E ratio therefore provides some indication of the confidence that investors have in the company.

Analysing the business data 5.9

Here we show some financial data in a business. You can use this data to calculate shareholder ratios.

Profits	£4m
Dividends	£2m
Number of shares	10 million
Current share price	£1.20

Calculate the:

- Dividend per share
- Dividend yield
- P/E ratio.

What would you do?

Your business is a games developer. Some investors have complained about the fall in dividends paid by your company in recent years. They have asked for all of this year's profits to be paid out. If it was your decision, what would you do?

Where are we now?

We have now examined profitability, liquidity, gearing, and shareholder ratios. We now consider efficiency ratios which are often used by managers to assess the efficiency of the business' operations as Figure 5.13.

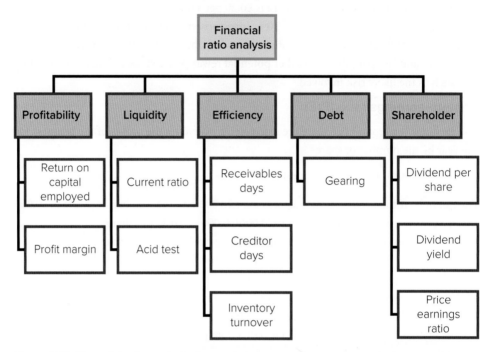

Figure 5.13 Financial ratio analysis. *Source:* Author.

We have now analysed several of the most common financial ratios that help us to analyse the financial position of a business. A summary of these ratios is shown in Figure 5.13.

Summary of key ratios

A summary of key ratios is shown in Table 5.5.

Inter- and intra-firm comparison of financial ratios

When comparing financial ratios, it is important to consider:

- **The trends over time**
  A decrease or increase in a ratio any one year may or may not be significant but if there is a trend it does suggest something is changing and managers would want to analyse why. Comparing how ratios change within a business over time is called 'intra-firm' comparison.

- **How the ratios compare with others in the industry**
  Comparing ratios amongst businesses is called 'inter-firm comparison'. This is important because industries will vary significantly and it is important to compare like with like. For example, food retailing is a low profit margin business whereas sports cars are high margin. In manufacturing and retailing there are likely to be relatively high levels of stocks of finished products whereas in services stocks may be relatively low.

Table 5.5 A summary of key financial ratios

Type of ratio	Ratio	Equation	How measured
Profitability	Return on capital employed	net profit/capital employed) × 100	%
	Return on equity	net profit/equity) × 100	%
	Profit margin	(gross or operating or net profit/ sales) × 100	%
Liquidity	Current ratio	current assets/current liabilities	Number of times
	Acid test	current assets (without inventory)/current liabilities	Number of times
Debt	Gearing	(long-term borrowing/capital employed) × 100	%
Efficiency	Inventory turnover	cost of sales/value of inventory	Number of times
	Receivables day	receivables/average days' sales	Number of days
	Creditor days	creditors/average cost of sales	Number of days
Shareholder ratio	Dividend per share	total dividends/ number of shares	pence
	Dividend yield	(dividend per share/current share price) × 100	%
	Price/earning ratios	market price of share/earnings per share	

- **The context of the numbers**

  It is always important to consider the context that lies behind the numbers. For example, if the economy is booming a business might expect higher profitability than if incomes generally are falling. If a business is growing rapidly it may have high gearing as it borrows to expand and acquire others.

Where are we now?

We have examined the nature of the financial accounts that can be produced for various stakeholders. We now consider how management accounting can be used to inform managers' decision-making.

5.3.5 Limitations of financial ratio analysis

The use of financial ratios must be treated with some caution.

This is because:

- **The published financial data in company accounts will be out of date**

  The numbers in a company's financial accounts will refer to the past and what has happened in the business. Whilst this will give some information on where the business has come from, it does not necessarily show where the business is headed. Using ratio analysis from published figures has sometimes been compared to driving by looking in the rear view mirror. For example, ratio analysis would not have anticipated the effect of the pandemic on most companies' finances or the effect of the increase in energy prices in many countries in 2022. Analysts will want to project forward to what the financial position of the business might be in the future but this will not be published in information available to the public. Looking backwards may help give a context but won't show all of the picture needed to plan ahead.

- **The published data may not reflect reality.**
  According to the BBC, in 2020 Wells Fargo, a major US bank, agreed to pay $3 bn (£2.3bn) following a government investigation into its sales practices, including the opening of millions of fake customer accounts. Wells Fargo admitted it had wrongly collected millions of dollars in fees, misused customer information, and damaged the credit rating of customers. These fines related to activities between 2002 and 2016 but only affected the accounts several years after when it was discovered. Ratio analysis at the time would not have shown the serious problems that existed at the business. In 2023 the *Financial Times* reported that France's financial prosecutor was investigating food retail group Casino for financial manipulation and insider trading that allegedly occurred in 2018 and 2019 when the group was struggling with significant debts. These irregularities would not have shown up in the published accounts at the time.

- **Non- financial factors**
  Financial ratios can only measure what can be turned into a monetary value. They will not show qualitative factors such as the morale of the workforce, the suitability of the strategy, or how ethical behaviour has been. Ratios will not show if, for example, the chief executive is about to leave and yet this could have a significant impact on future performance.

- **The financial position of a business will depend in part on the accounting policies of a business and differences in these can make it difficult to compare ratios between businesses**
  We have already seen how assumptions about how long an asset will last, and the rate at which it depreciates, can affect the costs of an asset and its remaining value in any given year.

Other assumptions will also have an impact on the financial position of a business in any given year. For example, assumptions about which inventory is being used will affect the costs in a particular period and the value of the current assets of the business. Imagine, for example, a business has two identical items of raw materials delivered at different times of the year. The price of one was £200 when bought at the start of the year; the second one cost £300 a few months later. If the business now uses up one of these items it could assume that the item used up was the first one delivered (this is called a First In, First Out (FIFO) approach). In this case the 'cost of sales' was £200 (and this would be the cost on the income or profit and loss statement) and the £300 item is assumed to be left in stock (which would be shown on the balance sheet). Alternatively, the business could say that it had sold the unit that has been delivered last. This is called a Last In First Out (LIFO) approach. In this case it is assumed that the cost of sales would be £300 on the income statement and the £200 would be the value of the stock listed in the balance sheet. Another approach would be to take the average of the two prices of the materials bought and use this to estimate the costs and value of the assets left. A change in assumptions in the accounting policies changes the costs and profits of the business and the value of assets it still has. We can see here how

Where are we now?

We have now analysed how financial ratios can be used to assess the financial position of a business. However, these ratios must be treated with some caution. We now consider why.

different accounting policies can lead to different costs and asset values for a given year. This is why analysts need to look at the notes to the accounts carefully to ensure they have understood the policies used and the implications of these. This also explains why companies often have pages of notes about the accounting policies it uses so this is clear to everyone.

Can you now answer these questions from the introductory case study?

How would you assess the financial performance of Walmart in 2021 using the data provided?

To what extent do you think the shareholders of Walmart would have been satisfied with the company's performance?

With reference to Appendix 3, explain why accounting policies matter.

5.4 **Management accounting**

Management accountants provide the financial information that managers need to make decisions. This information could help with decisions such as whether to outsource or produce internally, whether to invest in a new process or product, or whether spending in a particular division needs to be controlled more. Management accounting techniques include budgeting, cashflow management, and investment appraisal decisions as shown in Figure 5.14.

5.4.1 **Budgeting**

Budgeting is the process of setting financial targets. Managers within different parts of a business will be asked to produce estimates of the expected revenue and expected costs

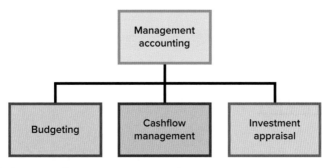

Figure 5.14 Techniques of management accounting. *Source:* Author.

Table 5.6 An example of budgeting

	Budgeted £000	Actual £000	Variance £000	Type of variance
Revenue	200	220	20	Favourable
Labour costs	50	45	5	Favourable
Material cost	20	30	10	Adverse
Other costs	10	12	2	Adverse
Profit	120	133	13	Favourable

(and therefore the expected profit). To do this, managers must think ahead to what sales they think will occur in the coming year and what resources will be used up.

Budgeting enables the senior management team to have an overview of the financial position of the business. If the actual revenues and costs are different from the budgeted ones this means there is a variance.

A favourable variance occurs if actual profits are higher than budgeted. This may be because actual costs are lower than budgeted or actual revenue is higher than budgeted. An adverse variance occurs when there is a difference between budgeted and actual figures that reduces profits. This may be because actual revenue is less than budgeted or actual costs are higher.

Examples of variance are shown in Table 5.6.

The process of budgeting makes individuals throughout the organization look ahead to what they think will happen and estimate the financial impact of this. It makes them responsible and accountable for their actions.

Budgets will usually be agreed by one manager with their line manager. It is usually a process of discussion and negotiation as departments justify what they want their targets to be. Budgets should be set in line with the objectives and strategies of that manager.

According to Antrill and McLaney (2021) the main benefits to business of budgeting include:

- promoting forward thinking and identification of short- term problems
- helping coordinate the various sections of the business
- providing a system of control
- motivating managers to better performance.

Key concepts

Budgeting is the process of setting financial targets.

A **variance** occurs when there is a difference between the budgeted figure and the actual figure.

What would you do?

Your manager has just given you the budget for your team in terms of expected sales and costs for the coming year. You think they are unrealistic figures but are not sure whether to say anything. What would you do?

5.4.2 Cashflow management

As we have seen earlier, there is a difference between cash and profit. Profit measures the financial value of a transaction; this can show whether the activity is worth undertaking. However, because of the timings of payments it is possible for an activity to be profitable but have cashflow problems. Cashflow is important to be able to pay for materials, staff, and other resources. If cashflow is poor, this may mean a business cannot pay suppliers or staff and this could halt operations if it is declared insolvent or bankrupt. For example, according to the *New York Times* in 2020 the retailer, Forever 21, declared it had liquidity problems and needed further investment to keep its 448 stores in the US open. Forever 21 declared liquidity problems in September 2019 as its stores struggled. Another high-profile cashflow crisis, according to Reuters, occurred in November 2022 when FTX, the crypto-currency exchange and trading business, went spectacularly bankrupt almost overnight due to problems with timings with cash incoming and outgoings. According to the *Financial Times* FTX had been valued at $32 bn at the start of 2022. In December 2022 Elon Musk said that he had to make dramatic cost reductions at Twitter, the social media company he had just taken over, or the business would have a net cashflow of minus $3 bn unless he had taken action.

A cashflow statement will show the inflows and outflows over a period of time.

Examples of cash inflows and outflows are shown in Table 5.7.

Managing cashflow is, therefore, very important to business. One aspect of this management will be to produce a cashflow forecast to anticipate future inflows and outflows and identify if actions needed to avoid cashflow problems.

An example of a cashflow forecast can be seen in the Table 5.8.

We can see in the cashflow forecast that the opening balance for one month is the same as the closing balance for month before.

In the example above the outflows in February and March are greater than that month's inflows; this creates a negative net inflow. The results of this is that in both of

Table 5.7 Examples of cash inflows and outflows

Examples of cash inflows	Examples of cash outflows
Cash sales	Paying for supplies
Cash coming in from earlier sales on credit	Paying salaries
Overdrafts, loans	Rent
Sale of current assets, e.g. inventory	Repaying loans
Sales of non-current assets, e.g. land and buildings	Paying dividends

Table 5.8 An example of a cashflow

	January £000	February £000	March £000
Opening balance (A)	100	130	110
Inflows (B)	50	60	90
Outflows (C)	20	80	120
Net inflows (D= B−C)	30	(20)	(30)
Closing balance (A + D)	130	110	80

these months the closing balance is less than the opening balance and the cashflow position is worsening over time. This may require action such as arranging an overdraft or loan.

Some businesses offer extended credit terms to generate more sales as shown in Business Insight 5.4; however, whilst this might increase revenue, it delays cash inflows.

Cashflow problems

Problems with the cashflow position of a business could occur because:

- Items are sold on credit and so the cash inflow has not yet occurred. Businesses may sell on credit to encourage sales; if successful, credit terms will generate sales and therefore revenue, but the cash inflow will be later.

- The business is acquiring items such as materials which it is paying for in cash but is not yet using up (e.g. they are stockpiled).

- The business has acquired capital equipment which it has paid for. The cost of this equipment will be spread over a number of years in the profit and loss statements as the equipment is used even though the payment may already have occurred.

The cash position of a business is the result of the actual inflows and outflows of money into the business. Managing cashflow is important because without sufficient cash to pay suppliers

Business insight 5.4   Buy now, pay later (BNPL)

A recent phenomenon in the finance sector has been the growth of 'buy now pay later' (BNPL) options for customers online. When customers get to the payment section of a website they are increasing offered the opportunity to pay over time. The market is dominated by Sweden's Klarna and Australia's AfterPay but more businesses are now entering the market. For example, Mastercard has launched a product called 'Mastercard Instalments' and Apple and Goldman Sachs are joining together to offer a service called 'Apple Pay Later'. Meanwhile the BNPL business Affirm in is partnership with Amazon allowing US customers to split the cost of any purchases over $50. BNPL is growing rapidly although this is from a low base: BNPL still only represents about 2% of the e-commerce market globally. This means there is plenty of room for growth.

Using BNPL means that retailers continue to get paid at the time of purchase but customers then repay on a short-term fixed-payment schedule, and interest-free. Most providers will charge a fee for any missed payments, and these can accumulate if more are unpaid. The BNPL providers make their profits from the retailers who pay for their services to encourage customers to buy more than they might otherwise do. Critics of BNPL worry that customers end up spending more than they can actually afford. There is no regulation of BNPL in many countries, which may lead to excessive encouragement of consumers to spend.

Questions

Do you think BNPL should be allowed? Explain the reasoning behind your thoughts.

Sources

www-ft-com.ezproxy01.rhul.ac.uk/content/ddb2e207-2450-4ca8-bad0-871290d80ea7

www-ft-com.ezproxy01.rhul.ac.uk/content/eaf53314-d72b-4dba-9110-87a27dce01a2

Figure 5.15 Cashflow through the production process. *Source:* Author.

a business will have liquidity issues and this could lead the operations of the business being halted to raise the cash required or in exceptional cases may lead to government intervention.

Managing cashflow is often a challenge for small businesses. This is because they tend to lack the power to delay payments to suppliers and they often struggle to chase early payments from buyers.

The problems of cashflow can also be particularly acute when there is a long production cycle. Consider a housebuilding business. It may have to pay to buy the land and then pay for staff and materials to build the houses over a period of many months. Throughout this period cash is flowing out of the business and it may be some time before the houses are sold and cash comes in. This is shown in Figure 5.14.

Some focus on cashflow is always going to be present because is liquidity is so important to a business. However, interest will be particularly high at certain times. In 2022, with many economies in decline, high energy prices linked to the Russia–Ukraine war, and high interest rates in many economies there were real concerns about the ability of businesses to pay their bills. Suppliers and contractors were worried they might not get paid. Having a good cashflow also became important to investors who worried their investment might fall in value. According to *The Economist* businesses that had had difficulties in generating a positive cashflow in the past subsequently experienced a major fall in their share prices in 2022. Ride-hailing businesses were a prime example. The share prices of Uber and Lyft, two US firms, and Grab, based in South-East Asia, were all down by 40–60% between January and June 2022. In May 2022 Uber's chief executive told employees that the company would now focus explicitly on generating positive cashflow.

Improving cashflow

The approaches that a business might take to improve cashflow include:

- Reducing the terms of credit. By reducing the credit offered the business may have better cash inflows but there is a danger that sales are damaged if customers prefer to pay over time.

- Providing incentives for cash payment (for example, a lower price for a cash sale). This improves cashflow but reduces profit margins.

- Negotiate more extended periods to pay suppliers. This means the business can hold on to its cash for longer. However, this may limit which suppliers the business can work with.

- Using debt factors. Debt factors are financial organizations that will provide cash to a business based on its debtors. For example, if a business is owed £100 a debt factor may provide £90 in cash and then when the customer pays the £100 that is owed this goes to the debt factor. Some organizations use debt factors on a regular basis. This enables them to offer credit to customers but get cash soon after the sale enabling them to re-order items. The debt factor makes a profit because it gives less cash than it eventually receives. The business using the debt factors benefits from better cashflow than it would otherwise have but it reduces its profit margins.

Business insight 5.5 Evergrande in debt

In 2021 Evergrande, one of the largest property developers in China, experienced serious financial problems. There were major concerns about its ability to pay the interest on its debts. Many bond (debt) holders were not paid on time. Evergrande had total liabilities of more than $300 bn and initially missed an interest payment in September 2021. Evergrande had to announce that there was no guarantee it could meet its financial obligations. Other major developers, such as Kaisa, also defaulted on their debts afterwards. This crisis was a concern to investors generally as the real estate sector in China accounted for more than a quarter of economic activity. The central bank of China responded to this financial crisis by making it easier for banks to lend.

Evergrande was founded by businessman Hui Ka Yan in 1996 in Guangzhou, southern China and was formerly known as the Hengda Group. By 2021 its property division, Evergrande Real Estate, owned more than 1300 projects in more than 280 cities across China. The broader Evergrande Group included businesses ranging from wealth management, producing electric cars, and food and drink manufacturing.

Faced with the challenges of repaying its debt Evergrande sold assets to raise the money it owed to customers, investors, and suppliers.

Following the financial problems at Evergrande the Chinese central bank, the securities regulator, and the banks regulator all issued statements stating that the developer's woes stemmed from management errors and that its crisis would not destabilize the financial system. The government said that it would intervene to support the housing market.

Question

Explain how high levels of debt can cause liquidity problems.

Source

www-ft-com.ezproxy01.rhul.ac.uk/content/21acda99-ee35-4f6d-8cfa-017d55e1bb10

www-ft-com.ezproxy01.rhul.ac.uk/content/a19d7092-1582-446e-98d7-b7db6f01d34d

Where are we now?

We have now analysed some aspects of management accounting in which we use ratio analysis to assess the financial health of the business. We now consider how management accountants might assess possible investments to decide on which one to choose.

Investment appraisal

Capital expenditure refers to the money invested by a business in long-term projects; for example, a business may invest capital into new product development, an expansion of its facilities, or the takeover of another company.

What would you do?

A supplier who works for you relies heavily on your business. At the moment you pay this supplier within 30 days of delivery.

Your finance officer has suggested you change the terms to 90 days. Would you do this?

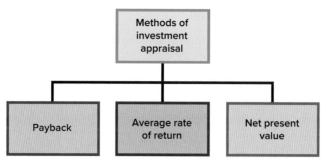

Figure 5.16 Methods of investment appraisal. *Source:* Author.

At any moment there may be several possible investment options facing a business. To assess an investment, managers will consider factors such as:

- the initial cost of the project
- the likely returns the project is expected to generate
- the timings of these returns
- the risk of the investment.

Managers will use investment appraisal techniques to decide which project(s) to invest in.

There are various methods of investment appraisal; these are shown in Figure 5.16.

Business insight 5.6 Entegris decides to invest more

In 2021 US chip material maker Entegris announced it was going to more than double its investment in Taiwan and build its largest manufacturing site there. Entegris said it would invest $500m in Taiwan over the next three years, up from previous plans of $200m. The facility will make filtration and deposition materials for use in 3-nanometre and 2-nanometre chip production processes, the industry's most advanced chipmaking technologies.

The investment occurs when there are many calls from US and other major economies to bring more of the chip supply chain closer to home. There is a desire by many for shorter supply chains. This factory would be close to customers in Taiwan, South Korea, Japan, and the US.

Major chipmakers are in the middle of major expansion as more and more industries such as automobiles and consumer electronics are increasing their demand. The world's top three chipmakers—TSMC, Intel, and Samsung—have allocated more than $350 bn for capital spending. Some commentators think the rush to invest in more production facilities may lead, eventually, to oversupply in the industry.

Entegris supplies all the world's chip leaders, including Intel, Samsung, Kioxia, Micron, and SK Hynix. The company said it would also spend $11m expanding its technology centre in Taiwan.

Question

What factors might Entegris have considered before deciding to increase its investment in a new Taiwan factory?

Source

www-ft-com.ezproxy01.rhul.ac.uk/content/3d254834-1d0c-4bb1-b870-1efd158d1149

Methods of investment appraisal

There are three main methods of investment appraisal:

- **Payback method**

  The payback method determines the length of time it is expected to take for a project to pay off the initial investment in a project. The outcomes of this method are measured in years and months or days. Managers may decide to only invest in projects that pay back within a given period of time.

- **Average Rate of Return (ARR)**

  The ARR calculates the average profit of a project as a percentage of the initial investment. It is measured as a percentage return. Managers may decide to invest only in projects that achieve a certain level of returns.

- **Net Present Value (NPV)**

  The NPV calculates the benefits of investing in this taking account of the returns available elsewhere. It is measured in pounds or a relevant currency. Managers may decide only to invest in projects that achieve a certain level of net present value.

Payback method

This method measures the number of years and months that a project takes to pay back the amount initially invested.

To calculate the payback period, we consider the expected net return each year and how many years are needed to pay off the initial sum invested.

In the example in Table 5.9, we can see:

- In year zero the project costs £50,000.

- In year one the project has a net cashflow of £10,000 which means there is still £40,000 to pay off.

- In year two the project earns £15,000 which means there is still £25,000 to pay off.

- In year three the project earns £20,000 which means there is still £5,000 to pay off.

- In year four the business earns £25,000 but only £5,000 of this is needed to pay off the initial investment. We now need to work out the amount that still has to be paid as a percentage of the total earnings that year.

The amount of money required in year 4 to pay back the initial investment fully is (£5000/£25000) × 100 = 20% of the year's earnings.

Table 5.9 Expected net returns from a project

Year	Net cashflow £000	Cumulative net cashflow £000
0	(50)	(50)
1	10	(40)
2	15	(25)
3	20	(5)
4	25	20

There are 365 days in a year so we need 20% of a year = (20/100) × 365 = 73 days

This means the payback period for this project is 3 years and 73 days.

The payback period is commonly used as a method of investment appraisal because it has a natural common-sense appeal. We can immediately understand why a business would want to know when it will recover its initial investment. Payback is relatively simple to calculate and managers can take a view of whether it can wait for that period of time to recoup its investment or not.

However, this method of investment appraisal has limitations. It simply adds up the payments made regardless of when they occur. In the example above it makes no difference if the inflows are £10,000 + £15,000 + £20,000 or if they are £20,000 + £15,000 + £10,000; in reality the timings will be important and managers are likely to prefer the bigger payments earlier.

Secondly, the payback method does not take any account of what happens after the initial sum has been recovered. In the example in Table 5.9 it makes no difference whether the net returns in Year 5 are £50,000 or £500,000; this would not affect the payback period. This is a limitation of the payback method because it does not take an overview of all the net returns expected from the project.

Average rate of return (ARR) (%)

The average rate of return (ARR) method of investment appraisal calculates the average net profits per year for the project as a percentage of the initial investment. This means that unlike the payback method it does consider all the net returns of the project over its expected life.

To calculate the ARR of a project we:

1. Calculate the total net profit of the project after the initial investment has been repaid.

2. Calculate the average profit per year.

3. Calculate the average annual profit as a percentage of the initial investment.

Analysing the business data 5.10

Using the data provided, calculate the payback period for the following two projects:

Year	Net inflow £m Project A	Net inflow £m Project B
0	(50)	(100)
1	10	20
2	10	80
3	20	5
4	30	5

Which project has the shorter payback?

Why might a manager choose the other project even though it has a longer payback?

Table 1 Investment appraisal data

Year	Net annual profit £000
0	(50)
1	10
2	15
3	20
4	25

Example, using the figures in Table 1

1. Total profit = (£50,000) + £10,000 + £15,000 + £20,000 + £25,000 = £20,000
2. Average profit per year = £20,000/4 years = £5000 per year
3. Average Rate of Return = (average profit per year/initial investment) × 100 = (£5000/£50,000) × 100= 10%

Unlike the payback method, the average rate of return method considers all inflows from the project over its expected lifetime.

Analysing the business data 5.11

Using the data provided, calculate the average rate of return for the following projects:

Year	Net inflow £m Project A	Net inflow £m Project B
0	(50)	(50)
1	10	20
2	10	30
3	20	3
4	30	2

Project B has a lower ARR than project A. Why might a manager choose project B anyway?

Table 1 Comparing payback and average rate of return figures

	Payback (years and months)	ARR %
Project A	2 years 6 months	10%
Project B	3 years 8 months	15%

Looking at the table of findings in Table 1 we can see that, based on the payback period alone, Project A is more attractive because it pays back more quickly. However, the rate of return for Project B is higher than Project A, which means that in terms of overall profitability it is more attractive. The decision of whether to choose Project A or B will depend on whether the business can wait for an additional one year and 2 months to repay the initial investment. If liquidity is an issue and a business needs its returns relatively quickly it will choose Project A.

Key concepts

> The **payback method** of investment appraisal measures the number of years and months that a project is takes to pay back the amount invested initially.

> The **average rate of return (ARR)** method of investment appraisal calculates the average net returns per year for the project as a percentage of the initial investment.

However, like the payback method, the ARR does not take account of when the payments are, i.e. the amounts matter but not the timings.

The Net Present Value (NPV) method

Imagine you are considering an investment. It would make sense to also consider what else could be done with the money and take into account the interest rate that could be earned elsewhere. The NPV method of investment appraisal takes account of the interest rate and the alternatives available before deciding whether to go ahead with an investment. This method uses a 'discount factor' to calculate the present value of the future expected earnings of a project.

A comparison of the different investment appraisal techniques is shown in Table 5.10.

Table 5.10 Summary table of advantages of different types of investment appraisal

Payback	Average Rate of Return	Net Present Value
Advantages	Advantages	Advantages
Relatively simple	Takes into account all net inflows	Takes into account the time value of money
Disadvantages	Disadvantages	Disadvantages
Does not consider net inflows after payback has occurred	Does not take into account the time value of money	More complex to undertake

>>> **Can you now answer this question from the introductory case study?**

> Figure 5.1 shows some of Walmart's strategic capital allocations. How might Walmart decide which projects or business areas to invest in?

Analysing the business data 5.12

> Table 1 shows the discount factors used in the NPV method if the interest rate is 10%.

Table 1 Discount factors if the interest rate is 10%

Year	Discount factor
1	0.909
2	0.826
3	0.751
4	0.683

The discount factor shows how much has to be invested now in an alternative project to become £1 in the future given the interest rate. For example, if the interest rate is 10%, £0.909 would grow to become £1 in one year. £0.909 is the present value of £1 in one year's time given this interest rate. Similarly, £0.826 would grow over 2 years to become £1. £0.826 is net present value of £1 in two years' time. From the table we can see that £0.751 is the present value of £1 in three years' time and £0.683 is the present value of £1 in four years' time.

The discount factor can be applied to the expected net earnings of any project to calculate how much would need to be invested now to earn the same amount of money as the project offers. For example, in the project in Table 2, the expected earnings are £100,000 in year 1. However, given an interest rate of 10% this means that 0.909 would grow to become £1 in the future. If we multiply the discount factor and the expected net earnings we get 0.909 × £100,000 = £90,900. This is the amount that would need to be invested today elsewhere to earn £100,000 given a 10% interest rate. The £90,900 is the present value of the earnings of the project in year 1.

Similarly, looking at year 2's expected earnings, these are £200,000. However, in today's terms 0.826 × £200,000 = £165,200 is the present value. £165,200 invested today at 10% would grow to become £200,000 in 2 years' time.

Adding up all the present values it is possible to calculate the sum of money today that would grow to match all of the expected earnings of the project. The present value for this project is £90,000 + £165,200 + £150,200 + £204,900 = £611,200. This Present Value needs to be compared with the cost of the project. If the investment costs £500,000 then it is a good investment. To earn the same returns as the project offers for £500,000 the business would need to invest £611,200 elsewhere at 10%.

The Net Present Value (NPV) measures the difference between the present value of the projects and its supply price. In this case the Net Present Value = £611,200 − £500,000 = £111,200. If the Net Present Value is positive it means the proposed project is cheaper than the amount of money needed elsewhere to earn the same returns. The bigger the value of the NPV the better the investment is in financial terms.

Imagine, however, that the Present Value was £611,200 but the project would cost £711,200. In this case it would be possible to earn the same returns as the project for £100,000 less than the project itself costs. The New Present Value is negative in this case, which shows that the alternative is better value than the project:

The Net Present Value of the project = £611,200 − £711,200 = −£100,000

Table 2 Net Present Value calculations of an investment project

Year	Expected net earnings £000	Discount factor @ 10%	Present Value £000
1	100	0.909	90.9
2	200	0.826	165.2
3	200	0.751	150.2
4	300	0.683	204.9

The key to the Net Present Value technique is that it takes into account the fact that money grows over time and, therefore, the value of future expected earnings depends on when they occur as well as the interest rate. This method recognizes, for example, that £100,000 in 5 years' time is worth less than £100,000 in 1 year's time. This is shown by the present value and highlights 'the time value of money'.

The size of the discount factor depends on the interest rate. For example, if the interest rate is 20% this means £0.833 could be invested and would grow to £1 over a year. By comparison, if the interest rate was only 5% this means more money has to be invested now to become £1; at this interest rate £0.952 would need to be invested. We can see that the discount factor gets smaller over time; this is because money has longer to grow so less has to be invested now to become £1 in the future.

Table 3 Table of discount factors

Year	5%	10%	20%
1	0.952	0.909	0.833
2	0.907	0.826	0.694
3	0.864	0.751	0.579
4	0.823	0.683	0.482

Think about it

What would happen to the size of the discount factors of the interest rate was very low? Explain your answer.

Analysing the business data 5.13

1. The data below shows the initial cost and expected net returns from an investment project.

Calculate the net present value for the following project:

Year	Net inflow £m	Discount factor 10%
0	(80)	1
1	10	0.909
2	20	0.826
3	25	0.751
4	30	0.683

2. Below is data on three investment projects.

	Project A	Project B	Project C
Payback (years and months)	2 years 3 months	4 years 6 months	5 years 10 months
Average Rate of Return %	5%	15%	25%
Net Present Value £	£100,00	£200,000	£180,000

Which of the three projects would you invest in? Why?

Now you should know

- Revenue: this is the value of sales over a period of time.

- Costs: this is the value of the resources used up to generate sales in a period of time.

- Straight-line depreciation allocates the cost of an asset in equal amounts over its expected working life.

- Reducing balance depreciation allocates the cost of an asset by an equal proportion over its expected working life.

- A balance sheet is a statement of the value of the assets owned by a business at a given moment in time.

- The assets of a business are items which it owns.

- Total assets equal current assets plus non-current assets.

- A liability is something that is owed by a business.

- Current liabilities represent borrowing that need to be paid back within 12 months.

- Non-current liabilities represent borrowing that need to be paid back after more than 12 months.

- Types of financial ratio include profitability, liquidity, debt, efficiency, and shareholder.

- Liquidity ratios measure the ability of the business to pay its short-term liabilities.

- The gearing ratio measures the long-term debt of the business as a proportion of its capital employed.

- Efficiency ratios measure how well resources are used by the business.

- The payback method of investment appraisal measures the number of years and months that a project is takes to pay back the amount invested initially.

- The average rate of return (ARR) method of investment appraisal calculates the average net returns per year for the project as a percentage of the initial investment.

- Budgeting is the process of setting financial targets.

- A variance occurs when there is a difference between the budgeted figure and the actual figure.

Review questions

Quick Check

1. Identify three stakeholders who would be interested in the financial performance of a business.

2. State three financial statements a company produces.

3. State two ways a business might improve its cashflow.

4. Explain the difference between management and financial accounting.

5. Explain the role of an auditor.

6. Explain the difference between cashflow and profit.

7. Explain one reason why businesses use budgeting.

8. Explain the difference between payback, average rate of return, and net present value as methods of investment appraisal.

Analysis

1 Analyse how ratio analysis can be used to examine the financial position of a business.

2 Analyse the ways in which the cashflow position of a business may be improved.

3 Analyse the factors a manager might take into account before deciding whether to go ahead with an investment.

Evaluation

1. To what extent do you think financial ratio analysis is useful for potential investors?

2. A business needs funds to expand. Do you think it would be better to borrow or raise money from investors?

～➤ Find out more

If you want to learn more about accounting for business why not read

- Accounting for Business by Peter Scott. This book provides a thorough coverage of key accounting concepts with plenty of real world examples
  Scott, P. (2018). *Accounting for Business* (3rd edn). Oxford University Press.

- If you want to know how companies can make their accounts say almost anything they want read Terry Smith's Accounting for growth. You will be surprised at the extent to which accounting can be an art as well as a science!
  Smith, T. (1996). *Accounting for growth*. London, Century Business.

- If you want to know more about interpreting financial reports you could read this book. Tracy, J. and Tracy, T. (2020). How to read a financial report: *Wringing vital signs out of the numbers* (2nd edn). Hoboken, New Jersey, John Wiley & Sons. This highlights the importance of the different financial statements and the need to assess the financial position as a whole.

- Most businesses these days measure performance using a much broader range of indicators than just profits. The importance of considering factors such as the impact of business activity on the environment and people is examined in Chapter 11 on Corporate Social Responsibility. In the meantime you may want to read John Elkington's book which highlights the value of measuring the impact on People and the Planet as well as Profits. Elkington, J. (2002). *Cannibals with forks*. Oxford, Capstone.

Where are we now?

In this chapter we have analysed the finance function of a business. In the next chapter we analyse the human resource function. We will then examine the external environment of a business and then go on to consider strategic planning.

≡ Bibliography

Asgari, N., Oliver, J., and Chipolina, S. (2022). 'lightning fast': Liquidity crisis hits Sam Bankman-Fried's crypto empire. *Financial Times*. Available at: https://www.ft.com/content/dcea81b9-70c3-486d-9622-b9cdd84da3fc [Accessed 11 December 2022].

Atrill, P. and McLaney, E. (2021). *Management Accounting for Decision Makers* (10th edn). Pearson. [online] Available at: <https://www.pearson.com/uk/educators/higher-education-educators/program/Atrill-Management-Accounting-for-Decision-Makers-10th-Edition/PGM100003045696.html> [Accessed 14 May 2022].

BBC News (2020). *Wells Fargo reaches $3bn fake accounts settlement* Available at: https://www.bbc.co.uk/news/business-51594117 [Accessed 14 January 2023].

BBC News (2023). *Aramco: Saudi state-owned oil giant sees record profit of $161bn*. Available at: https://www.bbc.co.uk/news/world-middle-east-64931074 [Accessed 12 March 2023].

Bhimani, A., Datar, S., Horngren, C., and Rajan, M. (2019). *Management and Cost Accounting* (7th edn). Pearson [online]. Available at: <https://www.pearson.com/nl/en_NL/higher-education/subject-catalogue/accounting-and-taxation/Bhimani-Management-cost-accounting.html> [Accessed 13 May 2022].

Businesskorea (2021). *Samsung Electronics Holds More than 200,000 Patents Worldwide*. [online] Available at: <http://www.businesskorea.co.kr/news/articleView.html?idxno=74626#:~:text=Samsung%20Electronics%20holds%20more%20than%20200%2C000%20patents%20worldwide.,at%20the%20end%20of%202020.> [Accessed 18 December 2021].

Camino Financial (2021). *Average Profit Margin by Industry|Business Profit Margins*. [online] Available at: <https://www.caminofinancial.com/profit-margin-by-industry/> [Accessed 11 December 2021].

Csimarket.com (2021). *Amazon Com Inc (AMZN) Inventory Turnover Ratio, from third quarter 2021 to third quarter 2020, current and historic results, rankings and more, Quarterly Fundamentals—CSIMarket*. [online] Available at: <https://csimarket.com/stocks/singleEfficiencyit.php?code=AMZN> [Accessed 11 December 2021].

Fortune (2022). *Fortune 500*. [online] Available at: <https://fortune.com/fortune500/> [Accessed 14 May 2022].

Financial Times (2021). TSMC predicts gross profit margins of 50% after global chip shortage. [online] Available at: <https://www.ft.com/content/6fbb6aaf-f022-4e3c-a3e0-2f2887429f8d> [Accessed 11 December 2021].

Financial Times (2022a). Why 'shrinkflation' means you are paying the same for less. [online] Available at: <https://www.ft.com/content/042af8db-a201-4d9d-9f61-cc783be0d725> [Accessed 14 May 2022].

Financial Times (2022b). EY faces $2.5bn lawsuit over NMC Health audits. [online] Available at: <https://www.ft.com/content/4314e1e2-3418-48b9-bd86-49f1c2c1a7ce> [Accessed 15 May 2022].

Global Finance Magazine (2021). *Global Finance Magazine—Corporate Debt Kings: The World's Most Indebted Companies 2020*. [online] Available at: <https://www.gfmag.com/global-data/economic-data/companies-largest-debt-world-2020> [Accessed 11 December 2021].

Hale, T. and Lockett, H. (2021) Chinese companies' dollar bonds hit as Beijing tightens credit. *Financial Times*. Available at: https://www.ft.com/content/fa577173-1d7d-4a44-8614-2326835d1969 [Accessed 14 January 2023].

Haqqi, T. (2022). 5 most indebted companies in the World in 2022. *Insider Monkey*. Available at: https://www.insidermonkey.com/blog/5-most-indebted-companies-in-the-world-in-2022-1094730/ [Accessed 11 December 2022].

Klasa, A. and Smith, R. (2023). Retailer casino probed over alleged financial manipulation and insider trading.*Financial Times*. Available at: https://www.ft.com/content/41060b52-fc3b-4b48-97ea-a8c922e101c5 [Accessed 12 March 2023].

Maheshwari, S. (2019). Forever 21 bankruptcy signals a shift in consumer tastes. *The New York Times*. Available at: https://www.nytimes.com/2019/09/29/business/forever-21-bankruptcy.html [Accessed 14 January 2023].

McLaney, E. (2017). *Business Finance* (11th edn). New York, Pearson.

New York Times (2022). *Bruce Springsteen Sells Music Catalog in Massive Deal*. [online] Available at: <https://www.nytimes.com/2021/12/15/arts/music/bruce-springsteen-sells-music-catalog.html#:~:text=Sony%20Music%20Entertainment%20buys%20the,for%20an%20estimated%20%24550%20million.&text=Bruce%20Springsteen%20has%20sold%20his,single%20

artist's%20body%20of%20work.> [Accessed 14 May 2022].

Nintendo (2021). [online] Available at: <https://www.nintendo.co.jp/ir/pdf/2021/annual2103e.pdf> [Accessed 11 December 2021].

Readyratios.com (2021). *Industry ratios (benchmarking): Current Ratio*. [online] Available at: <https://www.readyratios.com/sec/ratio/current-ratio/> [Accessed 11 December 2021].

Reuters (2022). *Crypto markets in turmoil over FTX bankruptcy*. Available at: https://www.reuters.com/technology/crypto-markets-turmoil-over-ftx-bankruptcy-2022-11-11/ [Accessed 14 January 2023].

Robinson, S. I. (2018). *Book-keeping and accounts*, (9th edn). New York, Pearson.

Starbucks (2021). [online] Available at: <https://s22.q4cdn.com/869488222/files/doc_financials/2020/ar/2020-Starbucks-Annual-Report.pdf> [Accessed 15 December 2021].

Storbeck, O. (2022). Adidas shares tumble after second profit warning in three months. *Financial Times*. Available at: https://www.ft.com/content/71137c24-83b7-4dfc-a366-afccb3c093af [Accessed 14 January 2023].

The Economic Times (2021). Stocks in News Today—Latest News on Stocks, Stock in News [online] Available at: <https://economictimes.indiatimes.com/markets/stocks/news> [Accessed 11 December 2021].

The Economist (2021a). *A new way of understanding the high but elusive worth of intellectual property*. Available at: https://www.economist.com/business/2021/12/04/a-new-way-of-understanding-the-high-but-elusive-worth-of-intellectual-property [Accessed 11 December 2022].

The Economist (2021b). Shein exemplifies a new style of Chinese multinational. Available at: https://www.economist.com/business/shein-exemplifies-a-new-style-of-chinese-multinational/21805217 [Accessed 14 January 2023].

The Economist (2022). *Tech investors are prizing cash generation again*. Available at: https://www.economist.com/finance-and-economics/2022/06/09/tech-investors-are-prizing-cash-generation-again [Accessed 14 January 2023].

The Guardian (2022). *A ponzi scheme by any other name: The bursting of China property bubble* Available at: https://www.theguardian.com/business/2022/sep/25/china-property-bubble-evergrande-group [Accessed 11 December 2022].

Vandevelde, M. (2020). The leveraging of America: How companies became addicted to debt. *Financial Times*. Available at: https://www.ft.com/content/c732fded-5252-4333-a3f8-80b767508bbc [Accessed 14 January 2023].

Zutter, C. and Smart. S. B. (2021). *Principles of Managerial Finance, Global Edition*, (16th edn). New York, Pearson.

5

Chapter 6

Managing people: Human resource management

Where are we now?

In the last few chapters, we have been focusing on the internal functions of business. We continue this analysis in this chapter where we consider the human resource function. Having analysed these internal functions, we will analyse the external environment, and then go on to look at how both the internal and external environments affect business strategy.

Why am I studying this?

- You want to know what is meant by Human Resource Management. In this chapter we will consider the various aspects involved in managing people.
- You want to know more about how managing people can help a business to succeed. In this chapter we look at how managing people effectively supports business performance and how managers can best support and develop their staff.
- You are interested in what motivates people. In this chapter we examine intrinsic and extrinsic motivators.

Learning objectives

By the end of this chapter, you should be able to:

- Understand the importance of managing people effectively
- Explain what is meant by Human Resource Management (HRM)
- Analyse situational factors that influence HR decisions
- Evaluate how stakeholders can affect HR decisions

- Analyse the different aspects of managing people including managing the flow of people, designing jobs, structuring the organization

- Evaluate different HR policy decisions and outcomes

- Evaluate the changing HR environment

- Evaluate the different ways of motivating people

- Analyse how the outcomes of human resource decisions can affect individuals, the business, and society as a whole

Introductory case study BP's focus on employee diversity and engagement

BP is a major energy business that operates globally. It says that its success relies on its employees' creative and scientific thinking to solve some of the world's biggest problems. It concentrates on attracting innovative and capable individuals whilst also ensuring it maintains safe and reliable operations. The company has a group people committee that helps to oversee policies that relate to people. This committee discusses issues such as the company's remuneration policy (i.e. salaries), progress in its diversity and inclusion programme, how to increase its attractiveness as an employer, its talent and learning programme, and its long-term priorities.

In 2019 a total of 296 graduates joined BP. The company invests heavily in employee development—with an average spend of around $3200 per person. This includes online and classroom-based courses and resources, supported by a wide range of on-the-job learning and mentoring programmes.

BP retail gas station. *Source:* Shutterstock/jon lyall.

Equality, diversity, and inclusion

With respect to diversity, BP says it is committed to making its workplaces reflect the communities in which it is based.

The gender balance across BP as a whole is steadily improving, with women representing 38% of BP's total population (2018 35%, 2017 34%, 2016 33%). BP continues to work to improve these numbers further by, for example, developing mentoring, sponsorship, and coaching programmes to help more women advance. However, the company acknowledges it still has work to do at the executive and senior levels.

BP says that it is committed to creating a positive and empowering workplace in which all employees feel valued for the work they do and the impact they make. Its goal is to create an environment of inclusion and acceptance, where everyone is treated equally and without discrimination.

To promote an inclusive culture BP provides leadership training and supports employee-run advocacy groups in areas such as gender, ethnicity, sexual orientation, and disability. These groups support the company's recruitment programmes and provide feedback on the potential impact of policy changes.

It aims to ensure equal opportunity in recruitment, career development, promotion, training, and reward for all employees—regardless of ethnicity, national origin, religion, gender, age, sexual orientation, marital status, disability, or any other characteristic protected by applicable laws. Where existing employees become disabled, BP's policy is to provide continued employment, training, and occupational assistance where needed.

Employee engagement

Managers hold regular team and one-to-one meetings with their staff, complemented by formal processes through works councils in parts of Europe. BP regularly communicates with employees on factors that affect the company's performance, and seek to maintain constructive relationships with labour unions formally representing its employees.

To better understand how employees feel about BP, the company conducts an annual survey. The overall employee engagement score in 2018 was 66%. Pride in working for BP was at the highest level in a decade at 76% in 2018.

The area where employees scored the company as needing attention was in the efficiency of their processes and ways of working. It knows it still has work to do to streamline its processes and drive the benefits of digitization throughout BP.

Share ownership

BP encourages employee share ownership and has a number of employee share plans in place. For example, it operates a ShareMatch plan in more than 50 countries, matching BP shares purchased by its employees. It also operates a group-wide discretionary share plan, which allows employee participation at different levels globally and is linked to the company's performance.

Introductory case study questions

Think about the following questions as you read through the chapter. You may not yet be able to answer these questions, but as we progress through the chapter we will revisit them at key stages. By the end of the chapter, you should be confident in answering them.

Table 6.1 The number of employees between 2014 and 2018 across different categories

	Our people and ethics				
	2014	**2015**	**2016**	**2017**	**2018**
Number of employees—group	84,500	79,800	74,500	74,000	**73,500**
Number of employees—group leadership	501	431	394	394	**376**
Women in group leadership (%)	18	19	22	21	**24**
Women at management level (%)	27	28	29	30	**31**
People from racial minorities in UK and US group leadership (%)	9	10	11	11	**11**
People from beyond the UK and US in group leadership (%)	21	21	23	24	**24**
Employee engagement (%)	73	71	73	66	**66**
Employee turnover (%)	12	16	16	12	**12**
Concerns raised	1114	1158	1701	1612	**1712**
Dismissals for non-compliance and unethical behaviour	157	132	109	70	**50**

1. In what ways do you think people can contribute to the success of BP?

2. What decisions do you think will be made in relation to managing people at BP?

3. What do you think are the benefits of investing in training i) for BP, ii) for employees, iii) for society?

4. What do you think are the benefits of greater diversity i) for BP, ii) for employees, iii) for society?

5. What do you think are the benefits of greater employee engagement i) for BP, ii) for employees, iii) for society?

6. What do you think are the benefits of greater employee share ownership i) for BP, ii) for employees, iii) for society?

7. What do you think are the consequences of lower employee turnover i) for BP, ii) for employees, iii) for society?

Critical thinking

How useful do you think company reporting on equality, diversity, and inclusion is?

Do you think people matter more than profits for businesses such as BP?

Sources

bp.com. 2019. [online] Available at: <http://www.bp.com/en/global/corporate/sustainability/people/engagement-and-development.html> [Accessed 20 September 2020].

bp.com. 2020. [online] Available at: <https://www.bp.com/content/dam/bp/country-sites/en_gb/united-kingdom/home/pdf/bp-uk-gender-pay-gap-report-2019.pdf> [Accessed 20 September 2020].

▶

The importance of managing people effectively

People are a factor of production: they are essentially an input into the transformation process of a business (see Chapter 1 for an explanation of the transformation process). They are potentially one of the most challenging resources to manage but are also likely to be the factor of production that can create the most value. People can be difficult to manage because they can get demotivated, they can resist change, and they can leave. However, people can also add tremendous value to an organization through their ideas, their ability to solve problems and innovate, and the commitment they can show to get a job done. Managing people is, therefore, an important part of managing a business. This is particularly true these days when so many businesses rely on their employees to differentiate themselves—for example, management consultancies, film-makers, musicians, universities, sports teams, marketing agencies, and games designers all rely hugely on the expertise of their employees for their competitiveness. This chapter is focused on exploring the complexities and benefits of people management. The importance of the labour force as an input into the transformation process can be seen by the sheer scale of this resource. For example, according to the World Bank, in 2021 the labour force in China included over 791 million people, in India it was over 476 million, and in the US it was over 164 million.

6.1 Human Resource Management

Human Resource Management (HRM) refers to the management of people. If managed effectively the business will have the people it needs at an appropriate cost to develop and implement a competitive strategy and achieve its objectives.

Let us consider some definitions of Human Resource Management:

"The purpose of HRM is to ensure that the employees of an organization are used in such a way that the employer obtains the greatest possible benefit from their abilities and the employees obtain both material and psychological rewards from their work" (Graham 1978)

"HRM involves all management decisions and actions that affect the relationship between the organization and its employees, the human resources" (Beer et al. 1984)

"A distinctive approach to employment management which seeks to achieve competitive advantage through the strategic development of a highly committed and capable workforce using an integrated array of cultural, structural, and personnel techniques". (Storey 2001)

"A philosophy of people management based on the belief that human resources are uniquely important to sustained business success. HRM aims at creating capable, flexible, and committed people and rewarding their performance" (Price 2000)

In the past HRM was seen mainly as a set of administrative tasks. It focused on keeping records of aspects of human resources such as attendance levels and payments made. In recent years, however, HRM has increasingly been seen as more strategic—the way people are managed is seen as a vital part of the overall competitive strategy of the business. Re-read the definitions provided above and you will notice a change in the language used to describe HRM in the 1970–80s compared with the early 2000s. The management of people

Key concept

Human Resource Management refers to the management of people.

needs to fit with what the business as a whole is trying to achieve, as is shown in this definition by Armstrong (2016):

"Human resource management is a strategic, integrated, and coherent approach to the employment, development, and well-being of the people working in organizations."

Now we have a good understanding of how HRM is defined, let us consider the goals of HRM. According to Armstrong and Taylor (2015) the goals of HRM are to:

- support the organization in achieving its objectives by developing and implementing strategies that are integrated with business strategy;
- contribute to the development of a high-performance culture;
- ensure that the organization has the talented, skilled, and engaged people it needs;
- create a positive employment relationship between management and employees and a climate of mutual trust.

Keep these overall objectives in mind as we move through the chapter.

6.1.1 The Human Resource function

The Human Resource (HR) function of a business is often known as a 'staff' function. This means it advises and supports managers in other departments. Each area of the business such as marketing or finance will have people to manage; the HR function provides the expertise to enable them to make better decisions. For example, HR can help the marketing manager to plan ahead for her future people requirements, can help with the recruitment of a new member of staff, and can develop a suitable way of rewarding the employee. The day-to-day management of the marketing employee remains the responsibility of the marketing manager. The marketing manager is the line manager of the new employee; this means she has direct authority over that person. To have authority means she has legitimate power over that subordinate (within the context of the organization) because of her position. However, the marketing manager is supported in all decisions relating to people by the HR function.

In a small business the HR function is likely to be carried out by managers in other areas of the organization as an additional part of their job. In larger organizations, on the other hand, the HR function is likely to be a specialist department. Some of the main functions within an organization are shown in Figure 6.1.

Can you now answer this question from the introductory case study?

In what ways do you think people can contribute to the success of BP?

6.1.2 A framework for the analysis of HRM activities

Over the years there have been various models which have been used to analyse the different activities involved in Human Resource Management and the outcomes of these activities.

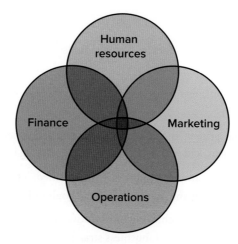

Figure 6.1 Some of the key functions of a business. *Source:* Author.

One of the most famous and well-regarded frameworks was developed by Beer and others at the Harvard Business School in 1984. This model is shown in Figure 6.2 and sets out the policy HR decisions that managers must make, the outcomes and consequences of these decisions, and the factors that influence why one decision is made rather than another. We will use this model to provide us with a framework to analyse the different aspects of Human Resource Management in this chapter.

HRM policy choices

The human resource policy choices that managers face include:

- Employee influence: this refers to decisions about how involved employees are in decisions.
- Human resource flow: this refers to the management of people from recruitment through to training, retention, and in some cases redeployment or redundancy.
- Reward systems: these choices refer to the way in which employees are rewarded and the levels of rewards between jobs within the business and relative to other businesses.
- Work systems: these choices refer to the way that jobs are designed, i.e. what tasks are included in a particular role.

HRM outcomes

The Human Resource (HR) outcomes show the effects of Human Resource policy decisions. They measure what happens as a result of particular decisions that are made in relation to the way people are managed.

Key concepts

The **functions** of a business describe the different areas of activities within it such as marketing, operations, finance, and human resources.

Authority occurs when someone has legitimate power over someone else.

A **line relationship** occurs when a superior has authority over a subordinate.

A **staff relationship** occurs when one person advises another but does not have direct authority over them.

In the Harvard model these HR outcomes are categorized by 4Cs, as you can see in Figure 6.2. The effectiveness of the HR policy decision will affect how committed employees are to their job and the organization. They will affect how well employees are trained and how well they do what to do; this in turn determines employees' competence. HR decisions such as the way in which people are rewarded and how involved they are in decisions will affect the extent to which employees' objectives and motivations fit with the overall objectives and strategy of the business; this is known as congruence. Lastly, HR decisions will affect the costs of employees to the business. This includes the costs of recruiting and training as well as the overall rewards employees receive.

Long-term consequences

The long-term consequences are the effects over time of the HR policy decisions that have been made. These examine the impact of HR decisions on employees themselves—for example, their earnings, their work–life balance, and their job satisfaction. Decisions also affect the business itself—they will affect the costs of the business as well as the productivity of employees and the revenue generated by the business. HR decisions will also affect society as whole—for example, they will affect how many people are employed and the income of the country. Any HR decision within a business can be analysed, therefore, on these three levels of the impact: the effect on the employees, the organization, and society as a whole.

We will now analyse the five different aspects of the Harvard Model: situational factors, stakeholders, policy choices, outcomes, and consequences in turn and in more detail.

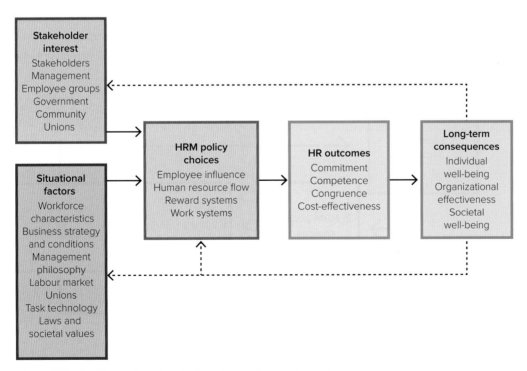

Figure 6.2 The Harvard model of HRM. *Source:* Beer *et al.* (1984).

Key concept

The **human resource policy choices** are decisions relating to employee influence, human resource flow, reward systems, and work systems.

6.2 Situational factors

The Human Resource decisions that are taken by a business will depend on the situational factors that exist. The role of situational factors in the Harvard model is shown in Figure 6.3. These factors in the business environment influence the HR decisions that managers take. For example, situational factors include:

- Business strategy. The strategy of a business is its long-term plan to achieve its objectives. The strategy that is chosen will influence the decisions made in the different functional areas including human resources. A decision to compete on customer service, for example, will require a well-trained workforce. Given the changes that can occur in the external and internal environment, a business will constantly review and develop its strategy. Jobs and the skills needed to do these jobs will change and HR will help the organization to manage this change successfully. In 2022 many tech companies such as Twitter and Meta needed to reduce costs to remain competitive; this involved significant job losses which involved the HR function.

- Workforce characteristics. For example, if the workforce is relatively inexperienced this may require a different management approach compared to a highly skilled and well-established workforce

- Management philosophy. Douglas McGregor was a management writer. In his book *The Human Side of Enterprise* (1960) McGregor outlined two theories of management: Theory X and Theory Y. Theory X managers believe that employees do not like

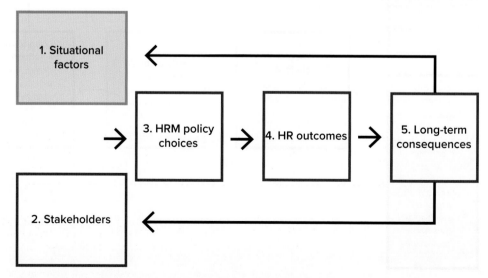

Figure 6.3 Situational factors in the Harvard model of HRM. *Source:* Beer *et al.* (1984).

work and therefore need to be supervised and controlled closely. Theory Y managers, by comparison, think employees value and enjoy work and therefore managers can be more trusting and delegate more.

- The state of the labour market. For example, if employees are readily available in the labour market then managers may be less concerned about retention compared to a situation where it would be very difficult to replace staff. According to the World Bank, in 2020 less than 16% of the number of females aged 15 and over in Algeria participated in the workforce; by comparison, it was nearly 70% in Vietnam.

- Task and technology: if the task is very repetitive and technology available means much of this can be automated then managers may be less concerned about managing people in a way that encourages and rewards creativity and innovation. The growth of artificial intelligence, for example, has affected many jobs.

- Laws. The management of people must take place within the legal framework that exists in a country. Employment laws exist to protect the rights of workers; the degree of protection and the rights of employees can vary significantly from one country to another. Examples of employment law can be seen in Figure 6.4.

Another important situational factor is the social expectations of the time. Social values about what is and what is not acceptable will also affect the HR decisions made. One issue commonly raised in the UK in managing people these days is that of ensuring people have an appropriate balance between their working life and their home lives. Some societies now expect businesses to consider whether employees are able to balance their time at work with other interests and demands. The argument is that if people work too hard without sufficient breaks or 'down-time' this can lead to stress. In the long-term working too hard may damage employees' health and productivity and so an appropriate work–life balance is in the interests of business as well as the individuals themselves.

Figure 6.4 Examples of employment laws. *Source:* Author.

Analysing the business data 6.1 Average working hours in different countries

Figure 1 shows the total hours worked by employees in 2019 in different countries. It shows considerable differences in the hours worked by employees around the world. This highlights how different the labour markets are globally.

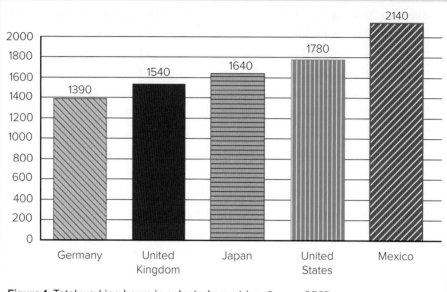

Figure 1 Total working hours in selected countries. *Source:* OECD.

Questions

What do you think determines how many hours people work?

Why do you think the average number of hours worked varies between countries such as Mexico and Germany (see above)?

What do you think is the impact of differences in the number of hours worked in these countries?

Source

data.oecd.org/emp/hours-worked.htm

Many societies are increasingly interested in the extent to which there is diversity within an organization and how a business ensures there is equality in the way it recruits, rewards, and promotes.

Having said this, societies will vary considerably in their view of how people should be managed. For example, in some countries there is not a minimum wage and child labour is still used in some places. Employee rights are relatively strong in the UK but in some countries the power is more clearly with managers; for example, it is easy to hire and fire staff. The difference in hours worked between countries is examined in Analysing the Business Data 6.1.

Different businesses will make different decisions relating to their human resources because the environment in which they operate is different and therefore the situational factors and the consequent HR decisions differ.

Key concepts

Theory X managers believe that employees do not like work and therefore need to be supervised and controlled closely.

Theory Y managers believe employees value and enjoy work and therefore managers can be more trusting and delegate more.

The **legal environment** refers to the laws that affect the activities of a business.

The **strategy** of a business is the long-term plan to achieve its objectives.

Think about it

Do you think you would be more of a Theory X or a Theory Y manager? Why?

Business insight 6.1 **Intel and diversity**

Intel says that its business is to help build a better world. To do this it says it feels it needs to lead the industry in diversity and inclusion. Intel says that when every employee feels they have a voice and a sense of belonging the company can be more innovative, agile, and competitive. According to Intel tapping into the skills of its diverse workforce is the key to driving future growth.

In 2020 racist behaviour by the police in the US led to mass demonstrations to support the Black Lives Matter campaign. Intel's Chief Executive sent a memo to employees saying that:

The senseless acts of racism and violence that took the lives of Ahmaud Arbery, Breonna Taylor, and George Floyd, and threatened Christian Cooper, are abhorrent and wrong.

Black lives matter. Period. While racism can look very different around the world, one thing that does not look different is that racism of any kind will not be tolerated here at Intel or in our communities.

To our black employees and communities inside and outside Intel, I hear you and see you. We stand with you and support you. Standing on the sidelines is not an option.

We strive to build a culture of belonging. We create a space where everyone can contribute to their fullest potential and deliver their best work. We welcome differences, knowing it makes us better. I challenge every one of us to ask ourselves the hard questions. Am I building an inclusive team? Am I making it possible for everyone to show up at work as their whole selves? Am I role-modeling humanity? What more can I do — especially right now?

Our 2030 corporate responsibility strategy and goals include a deep focus on diversity and inclusion, including working with other companies to accelerate adoption of inclusive business practices across industries by creating and implementing a global inclusion index open standard.

Intel is pledging $1 million in support of efforts to address social injustice and anti-racism across various non-profits and community organizations.

> Together we will change the world and enrich the lives of EVERY person on Earth.
>
> —Bob, Chief Executive

Questions

The degree of diversity within an organization has become a big issue for many managers. What situational factors do you think have led to this?

What benefits do you think greater diversity can bring to a business?

Sources

newsroom.intel.com/news/bob-swan-note-to-intel-employees/#gs.a9aysr

www.intel.co.uk/content/www/uk/en/diversity/diversity-at-intel.html

The five different aspects of HRM—situational factors, stakeholders, policy choices, outcomes, and consequences—will be examined in more detail in the following sections.

6.3 **Stakeholders**

Having analysed the situational factors in the business environment that affect Human Resource choices we now consider the influence that stakeholders can have. The influence of stakeholders on human resources policy choices is illustrated in Figure 6.5.

Stakeholders are individuals and groups that are affected by, and affect, the activities of a business. Stakeholders will influence the nature of HR decisions as shown in Figure 6.5. For example, if investors believe that people should be treated as an asset of the business this is likely to lead to relatively high rewards and investment in career development. If, however, investors regard employees as simply a cost of business they might focus on controlling this cost and looking for the short-term benefit they can get from employing someone rather

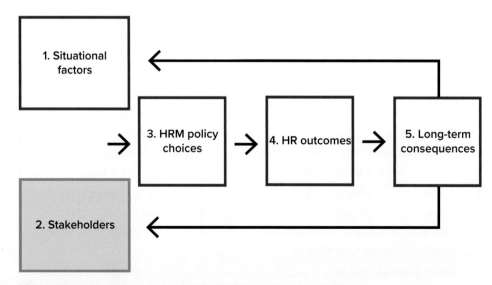

Figure 6.5 The role of stakeholders in the Harvard model of HRM. *Source:* Author.

Key concept

Stakeholders are individuals and groups that are affected by and affect the activities of a business.

than looking to develop them in the long term. Other important stakeholders include the employees themselves. Factors such as their education, their expectations and ambitions, and the extent to which they can organize themselves into trade unions will affect what they expect from work and how they expect to be treated. The government is another key stakeholder. Its policies will determine factors such as employee rights and have a major influence on how managers can treat employees and the legal constraints on any HR decision.

The different stakeholder groups linked to a business will each have their own objectives relating to the management of people. This will influence the decisions that a business makes. In the case of an employee co-operative, for example, the business is owned by employees and therefore this powerful stakeholder group should ensure employee-friendly policies. In some countries employees may have few rights giving the management stakeholder group considerable power to have policies that act in the interests of the business at the expense of employees.

6.4 Human Resource policy choices

The situational factors and the stakeholders that we have analysed so far will influence the Human Resource policy choices that are made. This is shown in Figure 6.6.

There will be many different policy choices that have to be made in relation to managing people; for example, how to recruit them, how to train them, how to reward them, and how to motivate them. For each of these decisions there are different options. To decide what to

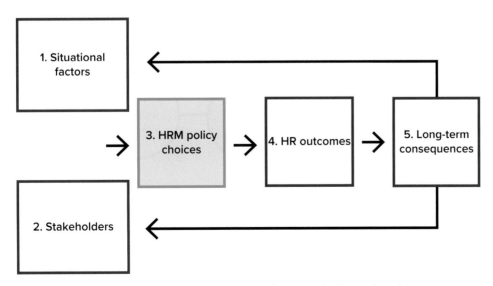

Figure 6.6 Human Resources Management policy choices in the Harvard model. *Source:* Author.

do managers will consider the influencing factors such as the underlying business strategy and nature of the work—for example, do we need staff who can innovate or just follow instructions? HR policy choices will have an impact on the HR outcomes for the business.

Human resource policy choices will include

1. The extent of employee influence within a business
2. Managing the human resource flow
3. Reward systems
4. Workforce systems.

These choices are shown in Figure 6.7.

The following sections consider these four different types of HR choices in more detail.

6.4.1 The extent of employee influence within a business

Managers will want to decide on the extent to which employees are involved in decision-making. Do they simply tell employees what to do or do they ask for employees' input on decisions? If so, in which areas do managers seek the input of employees and how do they do this? Do they consult with employees and ask their views or do they bargain and negotiate with employees? Whether employees are involved or not will depend on factors such as their experience and their interest in the success of the business, and the need for new ideas and approaches.

The ways in which managers may gain employee input include:

- A democratic management style which asks employees for their views and takes these into account when making decisions.

- Employee directors: these exist when employee representatives are elected on to the board of directors and contribute to decisions affecting the whole business.

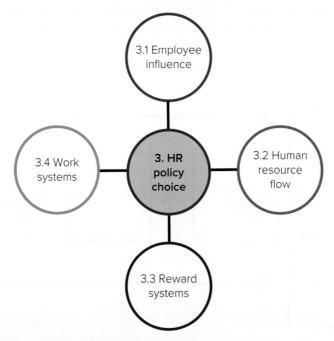

Figure 6.7 Types of Human Resource policy choices. *Source:* Author.

What would you do?

Your employees want to set up a committee of employees and managers to discuss key business decisions so they can have more input. Would you agree to this request?

Key concepts

A **works council** is a committee of managers and employees who discuss decisions that affect employees.

A **trade union** is an organization that represents employees.

- Works councils; these occur when employees elected from different parts of the business sit on a committee with managers to discuss issues that might affect employees. The prevalence of works councils varies from country to country. For example, according to the law firm DLA Piper they are a very common feature of working life in Germany, but this approach is not recognized in Sweden.

Analysing the business data 6.2 Global trade union membership

The membership of trade unions varies significantly from country to country. This highlights how labour markets vary between countries and therefore how labour market policy decisions will vary according to different situational factors. This can be seen in Figure 1.

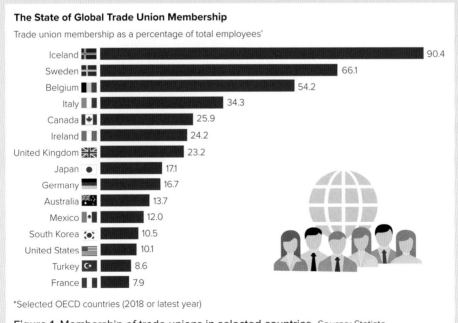

The State of Global Trade Union Membership

Trade union membership as a percentage of total employees'

Country	%
Iceland	90.4
Sweden	66.1
Belgium	54.2
Italy	34.3
Canada	25.9
Ireland	24.2
United Kingdom	23.2
Japan	17.1
Germany	16.7
Australia	13.7
Mexico	12.0
South Korea	10.5
United States	10.1
Turkey	8.6
France	7.9

*Selected OECD countries (2018 or latest year)

Figure 1 Membership of trade unions in selected countries. *Source:* Statista.

Questions

Why do you think trade union membership varies so much between countries?

What do you think the possible consequences of this is in terms of HR policies?

- The recognition of and negotiations with trade unions. A trade union is an organization which represents employees and aims to protect their interests. Unions provide a voice for employees; they can help managers understand the issues facing employees and the perspective of the workforce more effectively. The recognition of trade unions will vary from business to business depending in part on the legal environment in a country. For example, according to the law firm DLA Piper union representation in Brazil is mandatory, and all employees are subject to industry wide collective agreement, whereas unions are not common at all in Qatar and are illegal in Saudi Arabia.

- Various committees or staff groups that are set up to consult with employees.

6.4.2 Managing the human resource flow

The human resource flow refers to the movement of people into and out of the organization and the retention and development of them whilst they are working for the business. This is another example of the human resource choices that managers make. These choices are shown in Figure 6.8.

Managing the human resource flow includes managing:

- The recruitment and selection of staff

- The training of employees

- The motivating and engagement of employees

- The redeployment of staff

- Retirements, redundancies, and dismissals.

The activities relating to human resource flow are shown in Figure 6.9.

To manage the human resource flow managers must identify the requirements of the business and compare what is required in terms of human resources with what it has available.

Business insight 6.2 Netflix put people before process

Netflix has a highly distinctive approach to managing people. It focuses on the idea that employees are part of a team. In a team it expects high performance from individuals. If they cannot deliver they need to leave because they are no longer adding to the team. It values their integrity, respect, inclusion, and collaboration. People work together to achieve excellence. They share information, they are open and direct with each other, and they aim for a dream team—a team where everyone is extraordinarily good at what they do. When such a team is created you can trust people and you do not need lots of rules. The focus is on people and letting them do what they do well rather than creating lots of processes and rules.

Netflix compares its approach where you accept you may not always be on the team with a family approach which is more about 'unconditional love'. Netflix asks its staff to use the Keeper's Test. If you would not worry if someone said they were leaving, they shouldn't be there in the first place.

For those that get in the team, they are trusted. Netflix has no policy on holidays apart from 'take what you need'. It has no expenses policy apart from 'act in Netflix's best interests'. It has no spending controls apart from 'use your judgement'. Netflix says it does not need these because its employees are sensible enough to make good decisions. As an example of how you can trust people Netflix says it has no policy about what to wear to work and yet its employees manage to realize they shouldn't turn up naked!

Questions

What policy decisions does Netflix take in relation to its employees?

What situational factors do you think might have contributed to these decisions?

How does Netflix's approach differ from organizations where you have worked? Why do you think this is?

Why don't all organizations adopt Netflix's approach?

Source

Netflix.com

Can you now answer this question from the introductory case study?

What decisions do you think will be made in relation to managing people at BP?

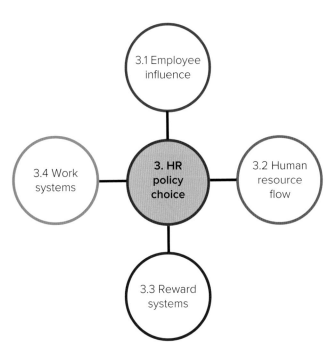

Figure 6.8 Types of Human Resource policy choices. *Source:* Author.

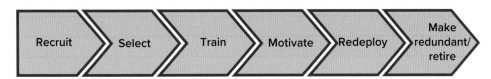

Figure 6.9 Managing the human resource flow. *Source:* Author.

This process is known as workforce planning. Workforce planning occurs when a business plans ahead to ensure the labour input is matched to the requirements of the organization. To undertake workforce planning a manager will:

- Assess the demand for the products and the implications of this in terms of the numbers of employees and skills required.
- Assess the existing supply of labour and adjust for any known changes such as staff retiring.
- Assess the external labour market, for example, the size of the labour market and the skills available.
- Determine HR plans to match the demand and supply of labour.

These stages of the workforce planning process are outlined in Figure 6.10.

By undertaking workforce planning a business can identify the different decisions relating to the human resource flow that need to be taken; for example, does the business need to recruit? Does it need to invest more in training? Do any actions need taking regarding employee engagement? Do individuals need redeployment? In the next few sections we analyse elements of managing the human resource flow, once workforce planning has been undertaken, in more detail.

The recruitment and selection of employees

If the demand for labour is greater than the existing supply a business may decide to recruit employees as shown in Table 6.2. The recruitment and selection process begins with a clear

Key concept

Workforce planning occurs when a business plans ahead and ensures the labour input is matched to the requirements of the organization.

Figure 6.10 The workforce planning process. *Source:* Author.

Table 6.2 Possible HR plans based on the demand and supply of labour

If the demand for labour exceeds the supply, then managers' HR plans may include:	If the supply of labour is greater than the demand managers' HR plans may include:
Training existing staff	Cutting pay so existing staff can be kept on
Recruiting employees from outside the organization	Reducing hours
Sub-contracting the work to others	Sharing work between existing staff
Using part-time or temporary employees	Voluntary retirements
Using overtime work	Incentives to leave
	Staff lay-offs

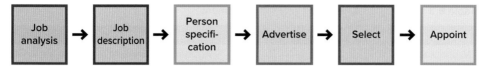

Figure 6.11 The recruitment and selection process. *Source:* Author.

understanding of the roles that need filling. This is achieved by undertaking a job analysis. The stages of the recruitment and selection process are shown in Figure 6.11.

Job analysis is the process through which a business determines the duties and skill requirements of a job and the kind of person who should be hired for it. According to the Chartered Institute of Personnel and Development (CIPD) (2018) 'Job analysis is the process of gathering together information about an existing job, establishing the activities to be performed, the expected outcomes of tasks, and the skills required.'

The analysis of the job leads to an outline of the job which is written up as a **job description**. A job description describes the requirements of the job to potential candidates, thus helping facilitate the recruitment process by providing clarity to those involved in the process (CIPD, 2018).

A job description typically includes:

- the title of the job
- who the jobholder reports to and is responsible for
- what the responsibilities of the role are.

Having produced a job description a business can identify the essential and desirable characteristics of the person needed to do the job; this is called a **person specification**.

The outline of the characteristics of a jobholder is shown in a person specification. The person specification relates to the desired criteria to be used for selection (CIPD, 2018). This will usually set out 'essential' and 'desirable' features of a jobholder. These may include:

- The qualifications required
- The experience needed
- The skills that are required
- Other relevant information, e.g. whether the person has a right to work in the country, whether they have a driving licence.

To fill any given vacancy a business may recruit internally or externally. Internal recruitment occurs when the person taking the new role is appointed from within the organization. This has the advantage that the person will already know the business and should be able to get started more quickly as a result. Internal recruitment may also motivate staff who know there are opportunities for promotion within the business. However, if a business only looks internally for candidates this does restrict the pool of people to choose from; this may reduce the potential quality of applicants. Also, by recruiting internally the business will then have to find someone else to undertake the previous job of the newly appointed person. External recruitment therefore opens up the job to more people which may make the process longer (and it will probably be more expensive to promote the role externally) but may lead to a bigger and better pool of applicants. A summary of the benefits of external recruitment compared to internal recruitment is shown in Table 6.3.

Table **6.3** Summary of external vs internal recruitment

External recruitment	Internal recruitment
More candidates to choose from	Appointing internally may motivate existing staff
May have better candidates and/or specialist skills that are not present within the business	Less time needed for employee to get to know the business

Think about it

If you have ever applied for a job think about the recruitment and selection process. What do you think was good about it? What could have been improved?

Key concepts

Job analysis is the process through which a business determines the duties and skill requirements of a job and the kind of person who should be hired for it.

A **job description** sets out what a job entails.

A **person specification** sets out the requirements of the jobholder.

Internal recruitment occurs when applicants are found from within the organization.

External recruitment occurs when applicants for a job are found from outside the organization.

The appeal of external recruitment will depend on:

- The size and quality of the pool of internal applicants relative to the requirements of the job
- The likely size and quality of external applicants
- The cost and time required to attract external applicants.

Having attracted applicants a business will usually shortlist candidates—this means they select a handful of the applicants to move to the next stage. The selection of a candidate from the shortlist may be via one or more of the following:

- Curriculum Vitae
- Interview—this may be an individual interview or a panel
- Letters of recommendation
- Tests
- Assessment centres.

Contracts of employment

When an employee is appointed to a job they will usually receive a contract of employment. This will set out the details of their employment including who they will report to, working hours, holiday entitlement, how they will be paid, and additional benefits.

Some employment contracts will be permanent. This means the person is employed and there is no fixed finish date. Other contracts may be temporary; this means they are for a set period. Some contracts will be full time; this means the employees work a full week—usually around 40 hours. Others will be part time, which means they do not work a full number of hours per week but instead work only some of them, such as 10 hours a week.

Training

The process of job analysis and person specification outline the requirements of the job and the jobholder. The business will then recruit what it hopes is the right person for the job. The recruit will need some training to introduce her to the business and the role and may need training to undertake the job successfully. Individuals will then require further training in their careers as their role evolves and as the nature of their work changes.

Training involves the use of systematic and planned instruction and development activities to promote learning. Training opportunities can increase staff commitment because they are gaining skills that can allow them to take on more challenging tasks and because it may make them more employable and give them greater earning power. If the training is based on an objective assessment of need, it can result in a more efficient and effective organization.

Training is intended to develop individuals' knowledge and skills so they can do theie existing jobs better and may be better prepared for their next role.

Types of training include

- Induction training. This is for new staff so they learn about how the organization works, who is who, and how to get things ordered and done.

- On-the-job training; this is training undertaken by people at the workplace.

- Off-the-job training; this occurs when people are trained away from the job itself. For example, they could be trained at an assessment centre.

When deciding whether to invest in training an organization should consider the need for it, the costs of it, the best way of delivering it, and ensuring that its effectiveness is evaluated to decide whether to repeat it or not. According to Statista, in 2020 the average spending worldwide per employee on training was $1270.

There are different ways in which people may be trained. Some training is 'on the job'—this means people learn as they do the work. Some parts of teacher training, for example, involve the trainee working in schools and learning as they teach. Usually people learn on the job with a mentor to supervise and support them; often on-the-job training involves shadowing an employee to understand the requirements of the job. The benefit of on-the-job training is that employees are working with someone who knows the job well. 'Off-the-job' training occurs when the training is away from the job itself. For example, some businesses have training centres; alternatively, people may be completing courses online or attending local colleges.

The benefits of training are that it enables employees to do their job more effectively. The standard of work should be higher and less mistakes should be made. Training should allow staff to do the work they do better and this may be more satisfying for them. The training will prepare them for future opportunities enabling them to progress. Society as a whole should also benefit from training, as an economy should do better with a better-trained workforce.

Can you now answer this question from the introductory case study?

What do you think are the benefits of investing in training i) for BP ii) for employees iii) for society?

 Key concept

Training involves the use of systematic and planned instruction and development activities to promote learning.

Employee motivation and engagement

Motivating people involves creating an environment and providing reward systems in which people have an inner drive to achieve certain tasks and behave in a certain way. Managers will want to motivate employees to align what they want to do with what the organization wants them to achieve.

The motivation of an employee will be affected by:

- intrinsic factors of the job—these are features of the job itself such as the nature of the tasks undertaken and the challenge it provides

- extrinsic factors—these are aspects related to a job but not linked to the tasks being undertaken itself such as the working conditions and the rewards available.

Extrinsic and intrinsic factors are shown in Figure 6.12.

Motivating employees is important because it will affect their drive and commitment. It will also affect their openness to change, their willingness to find solutions to problems, their willingness to come up with new ideas, and how likely they are to stay with the business. A motivated workforce can make a strong contribution to the success of a business.

 Key concept

Motivating people involves creating an environment and providing reward systems in which people have an inner drive to achieve certain tasks and behave in a certain way.

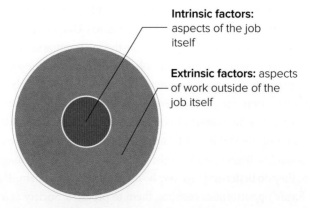

Figure 6.12 Intrinsic and extrinsic factors. *Source:* Author.

Theories of motivation

Given the impact that motivation (or demotivation) can have on the performance of a business it is no surprise that there have been many studies and theories about what motivates employees. Some of the most well-known studies on motivation are:

Taylor's scientific management

Frederick Winslow Taylor was an engineer who worked as a general manager and a consulting engineer to managers at the Bethlehem Steelworks Company between 1890 and 1893. He was employed to improve productivity. Taylor initially focused on the way that steel was being shovelled and lifted into wagons for transportation. At the time the way work at the company was undertaken was not very organized. People turned up each day hoping to be picked to work. They had their own shovels and would lift material in whichever way they wanted into one big wagon. Taylor studied the way that people worked and identified the best design of shovels and the best way of shovelling. The company was encouraged to buy shovels of the right design and store them; it also hired supervisors to train employees in how to shovel and measure their performance. The output of individual employees was measured for the first time. Taylor's studies enabled him to calculate the amount an employee should be able to shovel in a given time period using the methods he set out. If they did more than this they would receive a bonus. If they produced less than the target they could be retrained. Taylor's work was the beginnings of Scientific Management. Jobs are broken down into individual tasks and the best way of doing these is identified; employees are then trained in these methods. Employees follow the instructions and new ways of working as this helps them to be more productive. This can lead to higher profits for the business and higher earnings for staff. Taylor's work assumes that people will do as they are told for money; it assumes employees are rational economic beings motivated by money. It assumes that managers tell and workers 'do'. This approach can still be valid if employees are focused on earnings and accept management instructions and a 'tell' approach in return for greater productivity and rewards.

Maslow's hierarchy of needs

Abraham Maslow was an American psychologist. He identified the different levels of needs that employees might have in 1943 in his work *A Theory of Human Motivation*. These are (from the lowest need to the highest):

- Physiological needs—these are survival needs; for example, people need water and food to survive
- Security or safety needs—these include the need for shelter
- Social or belonging needs—these include the need to be part of a group
- Ego or esteem needs—this is the need to be recognized for what you do
- Self-actualization needs—this is the need to achieve for yourself; for example, to have a sense of self-worth because of what you do.

Maslow's hierarchy of needs is illustrated in Figure 6.13.

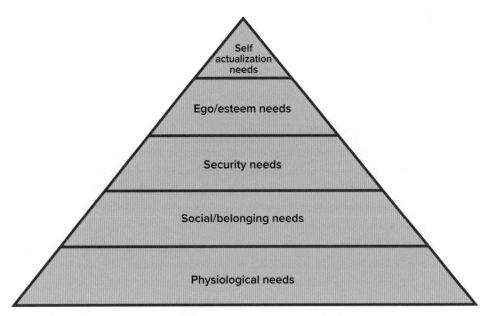

Figure 6.13 Maslow's Hierarchy of Needs. *Source:* Maslow, A.H. (1943).

The key points from Maslow's work are that:

- Different rewards meet different needs. For example, the opportunity for full-time employment rather than part-time may meet security needs; more teamwork may meet social needs; a new job title may meet ego needs and greater delegation of tasks may meet self-actualization needs.

- Needs are arranged in a hierarchy. When one level of need is fulfilled, individuals will be motivated by the possibility of the next level being met. For example, if an individual has met her social needs she will be motivated by the rewards that meet the next level such as praise being given to them for the work done (meeting ego needs). This means that individuals will be motivated by different rewards at different times in their lives depending on where they are on the hierarchy. For example, having just left school or university and taking their first job employees may want money to pay for their first rented accommodation. Later in life they may have their own house and be more interested in higher level needs.

- Self -actualization is the highest level of need and this cannot be completely fulfilled. There are always new ways in which individuals can find challenges and want to achieve them. There will always be new projects and new responsibilities that create the opportunity for a sense of achievement.

Herzberg's two-factor theory

Frederick Herzberg (1923–2000) was a US clinical psychologist who later became Professor of Management at Utah University. He had a strong interest in the mental health of employees.

Herzberg's two-factor theory (outlining hygiene and motivator factors) was first published in *The Motivation to Work* in 1959. Herzberg's work was based on a survey of managers. The findings of this survey are shown in Figure 6.14.

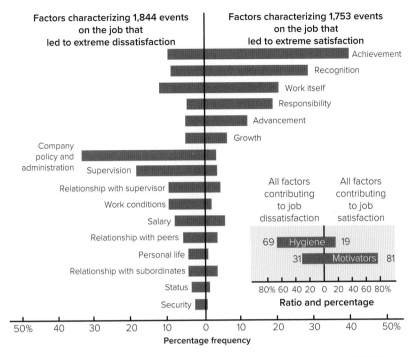

Figure 6.14 Findings from Herzberg's study. *Source: Harvard Business Review* (2023).

From this survey Herzberg identified the impact of different factors on employees' motivation. Herzberg identified three potential states of mind for employees:

- Dissatisfied
- Not dissatisfied
- Satisfied.

The different states of satisfaction and the role of hygiene and motivator factors is shown in Figure 6.15.

Some aspects of work tended to cause dissatisfaction if they were not present; if they are present, they remove the dissatisfaction but they do not in themselves satisfy. These factors are known as 'hygiene factors'. They include working conditions, working relationships, basic pay, and the rules of the organization. For example, if your working conditions are poor then you will be dissatisfied; if they are improved this removes the dissatisfaction but this does not in itself lead to satisfaction.

Figure 6.15 Herzberg's two factors and three potential states of mind. *Source: Harvard Business Review* (2023).

What do you think?

Staff retention at your business is poor due to a lack of motivation. You need to hold on to staff for longer as it is expensive to replace them and you are losing expertise. Should you increase the pay of all your employees to stop them leaving?

To motivate or satisfy employees managers must ensure hygiene factors are in place and then offer 'motivator factors'. These factors include the opportunity for achievement, the challenge provided by the job, and the opportunity to take on bigger tasks.

The significance of Herzberg's work is that it suggested that some aspects of work had to be in place to prevent employees being dissatisfied; other factors were necessary to be in place to actually motivate. His work also highlighted the importance of job design. He talked of job enrichment when jobs were designed in a way that made them more motivating—for example, giving an employee greater control over resources and how they schedule their work.

Employee engagement

These days managers often refer to how engaged employees are rather than how motivated they are. Employee engagement occurs when employees feel psychologically involved in, connected to, and committed to getting their job done. The higher the level of the management the more that employees understand and support the aims, values, and strategy of the business. This means they are aligned with what senior managers want the business to be and what they want it to achieve in the future.

In a 2008 *Harvard Business Review* article it was claimed that only 28% of US employees are engaged, or are actively pursuing top performance on behalf of their organizations, and that this has a direct impact on the profits of a business. Engaged employees lead to engaged customers, who in turn drive a company's growth, long-term profitability, and share price. The defining contribution of great managers is that they increase the engagement levels of the people who work for them (Harvard Management Update, 2008).

Key concepts

Taylor's Scientific Management aims to identify the one best way of doing a job. It assumes employees are rational and motivated by money.

Maslow outlined a hierarchy of needs from physiological to security to social to esteem to self-actualization.

Hygiene factors, according to Herzberg's work, prevent dissatisfaction.

Motivator factors, according to Herzberg's work, prevent dissatisfaction.

Employee engagement refers to being psychologically involved in, connected to, and committed to getting one's job done.

Can you now answer this question from the introductory case study?

What do you think are the benefits of greater employee engagement i) for BP ii) for employees iii) for society?

Redeployment, redundancy, and dismissal

If the demands for employees change this may require some employees to be retrained and redeployed—this means that their skills would be used in a different capacity within the business. If there is no longer the same level of demand for employees and they cannot be redeployed they may be made redundant.

Redundancy occurs when an individual loses his or her job because demand for it no longer exists. In 2023 the global management consultancy McKinsey announced it was making 2000 of its 45,000 workforce redundant. When making redundancies managers will need to follow the legal regulations in the country. These may include:

- Consulting with employees to see if there is a way of avoiding redundancy
- Giving employees time to find alternative employment
- Paying employees a redundancy payment, usually linked to the number of years worked at the business.

If demand for the job does exist but the business does not want a particular employee to do that work then he or she would be dismissed. Again, the regulations covering this will vary from country to country but are likely to include:

- Giving an employee time to improve
- Giving an employee a notice period.

An employee may also lose his or her job through a process of dismissal. Dismissal occurs when an individual is asked to leave because they are not competent for that role. With dismissal the job still exists but that particular person is not needed for it. For example, an employee may be dismissed for issues with attendance, for consistently poor work, or for offensive behaviour. Regulations will exist to define the rights employees have and the process involved in making a dismissal.

Of course, managers will hope to avoid dismissal. Underperformance should be identified in employee appraisals. Appraisals occur when an employee's performance is reviewed. Following an appraisal actions may be taken such as organizing further training or identifying targets for that individual.

Where are we now?

We have now looked at employee influence and human resource flow as aspects of HR policies. We now examine aspects of the remuneration policy of a business.

6.5 Reward (remuneration) systems

So far, we have considered employee influence and managing the human resource flow as part of the HR policy choices made. Managers will also have to make decisions regarding the reward systems used. The different policy choices are shown in Figure 6.16.

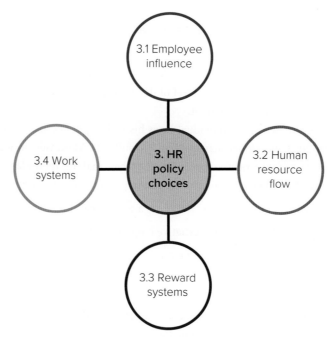

Figure 6.16 Types of Human Resource policy choices. *Source:* Author.

There are many different ways in which a business might reward (or remunerate) its employees. The rewards a business offers include financial and non-financial rewards.

When selecting a reward or 'remuneration' system managers will consider many factors such as:

- The likely costs of the system to the business. For example, what are employee costs as a percentage of turnover? In North America in 2020, according to the World Bank, employee compensation was just over 7% of total expenses, in the European Union it was just over 15%, and in Latin America and the Caribbean it was 32.5%.

- The impact of the system on employee behaviour.

- The impact on employee engagement, loyalty, and retention.

- What is perceived as fair within the organization and to the outside world. In recent years, for example, there has been increasing focus on the gender gap and the difference between the pay that male and female employees receive in some organizations.

- The legal environment. For example, there may be a national minimum wage that employees should receive. According to a UK parliamentary report in 2023, the minimum wage in Luxembourg for the year before was £10.72 an hour (adjusted for the costs of living); this was the highest in the OECD, the lowest being Mexico at £1.88 per hour.

Financial reward systems include:

- Wages. These are payments that are usually made weekly and are often based on an hourly rate or payment on output.

- Salaries. These are payments paid monthly, based on an annual salary figure.

- Commissions. This is where the employee (or group of employees) receives a percentage of the revenue.

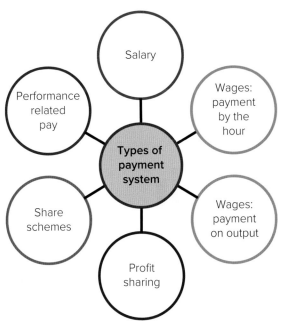

Figure 6.17 Examples of types of financial reward systems. *Source:* Author.

- Profit-related pay. This is where employees receive a percentage of profits.
- Performance-related pay. This is where employees are paid money depending on how well they meet certain performance-related criteria.
- Share ownership schemes. This is where employees are given shares in the business so become owners.

A number of different types of financial reward systems are outlined in Figure 6.17.

The choice of reward system can have a significant impact on employee behaviour. For example, imagine you reward the sales staff in your car salesroom on commission. This will make them very eager to sell (because that's how they gain rewards) but may mean they are very pushy with customers and end up trying to sell them a car even if it is not the right one for them. Commission schemes in the financial services industry have led to financial advisers mis-selling financial products to customers to try and earn the highest returns they can. If these employees were paid salaries, staff would be less focused on making sales to boost their earnings.

Analysing the business data 6.3 Remuneration at Goldman Sachs

In 2019 the investment bank Goldman Sachs allocated 35% of its revenue for staff compensation and benefits. This was the lowest that the ratio had been for a decade. The average Goldman employee earned $246,216 for the first nine months of 2019, less than half the $527,192 at the same point in 2009. According to a CNBC report in October 2019, Goldman Sachs has been working feverishly to create automated solutions in existing and nascent businesses which, it alleges, means clients will increasingly interact with software instead of expensive humans. The change in company compensations between 2009 and 2019 is shown in Figure 1.

▶

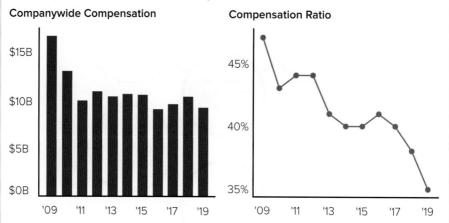

Goldman pay on the decline

The firm's "compensation ratio" – the share of total employee pay divided by total net revenues – is at a 10-year low.

Note: Total compensation includes both pay and benefits. All compensation numbers are year to date through Q3.

Figure 1 Pay at Goldman Sachs. *Source:* Son (2019).

Question

What do you think is the significance of the change in the compensation ratio shown above?

What would you do?

You are the manager of a chain of clothes stores. Would you pay your store assistants on commission or a salary?

Can you now answer this question from the introductory case study?

What do you think are the benefits of greater employee share ownership i) for BP, ii) for employees, iii) for society?

Business insight 6.3 EA's Core Values

EA produces some of the world's most famous computer games such as Command and Conquer, Fifa, and Star Wars Jedi. The company's mission is to 'Inspire the World to Play'. It aims to create amazing experiences for its players everywhere. It says that to create these transformational experiences requires constant innovation and 'brilliant, passionate people'. EA says that it develops great new games by bringing together great people that combine creativity, technology, and expertise to develop new ways to play.

The company's core values are:

- Creativity: it wants people need to bring their imagination, ideas, and excitement to what they do.

- Pioneering; it wants people to be curious and courageous.

- Passion; it wants people to do what they love.

- Determination: it wants people who are focused.

- Learning; it wants people to listen, and to be open to new ways of thinking.

- Teamwork: it wants people to be committed to each other, accountable, and to act with integrity.

Question

What Human Resource policy decisions do you think EA makes to ensure that its work-force contributes to the business success in the way it wants?

Analysing the business data 6.4 Average pay in different countries

The data in Figure 1 shows the average pay in different countries.

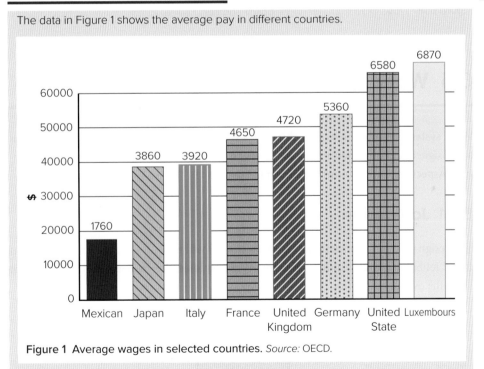

Figure 1 Average wages in selected countries. *Source:* OECD.

Question

1. Why do you think average pay varies from one country to another?

Where are we now?

We have now looked at employee influence, managing the human resource flow, and re-ward systems, and so we move on to the final set of human resource policy choices: work systems, as shown in Figure 6.18.

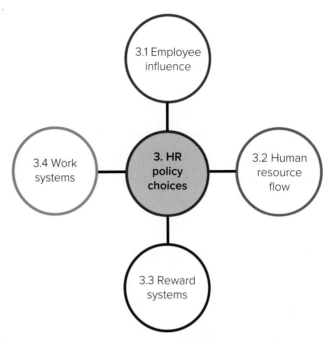

Figure 6.18 Types of Human Resource policy choices. *Source:* Author.

6.6 Work systems

Work systems refer to the way in which work is organized. These systems include how jobs are designed and how they are organized together in the form of the organizational structure. Aspects of work systems are shown in Figure 6.19.

6.6.1 Job design

The design of a job (i.e. exactly what the job entails) will have an impact on the motivation of the jobholder. Hackman and Oldham (1976) outlined the elements of job design that affect the overall motivating potential of a job. These elements are.

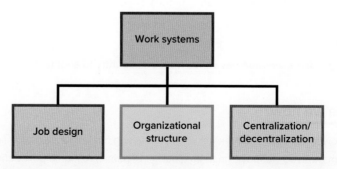

Figure 6.19 Aspects of work systems. *Source:* Author.

- The variety of tasks: if the tasks are very repetitive this is likely to be demotivating.
- The degree of task identity. This refers to whether the work of the employee can be identified directly. If an employee feels her work cannot be identified specifically or is not directly noticed they are less likely to be motivated.
- The degree of task significance. This refers to whether an employee appreciates how important their job is in relation to the business as a whole. If they do not feel their job matters much they are unlikely to be motivated.
- Autonomy. This refers to how much independence an employee has to undertake their work in the way they want and make decisions for themselves about how and when the work is done. If there is no autonomy an employee is likely to lack motivation because they are simply being told what to do.
- Feedback. This refers to whether an employee gets feedback on how she is doing. If there is no feedback then it seems as if no one cares and employees are not likely to be motivated very much.

The different elements of job design in Hackman and Oldham's model are shown in Figure 6.20.

Consider the job of a store assistant at Timpson. Timpson stores are located in city centres. They offer a wide range of services. Someone working there may fix shoes, repair watches, do some engraving on jewellery, or make nameplates for house names. This means that this job provides task variety. It is clear who does the work so there is a clear task identity and the store assistant can see the impact that the work has on the customer and why it matters—e.g. the shoes need repairing, the phone screen needs fixing—this means there is task significance. The store operative deals directly with customers so will get feedback—for example, thanks for a job well done. She also has the ability to deal with any customer requests or complaints and make decisions including friends' discounts up to a certain amount without asking the regional manager; this means there is autonomy. The combination of these factors mean that the nature of this job is potentially quite motivating.

Key concept

Work systems refer to the way in which work is organized.

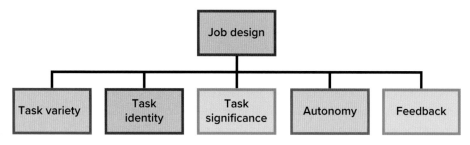

Figure 6.20 The different elements of job design in Hackman and Oldham's model. *Source:* Hackman and Oldham (1980).

6.6.2 **Organizational structure**

Part of the job of management is to decide how best to organize the people they have. This involves deciding on the tasks that need doing and deciding on how best to group these jobs. The way that tasks are grouped will affect the satisfaction of those that do them, the quality of service experienced by customers, and the effectiveness of the way they are undertaken. Managers must design each job and the responsibilities of the jobholders.

The combined effect of decisions relating to the grouping of jobs, the reporting relationships of jobs, and the authority of different jobs defines the structure of the organization. The structure will affect the costs and flexibility of the organization, which in turn will affect its competitiveness.

Having decided what jobs consist of, managers must decide on how to group them together and what reporting relationships exist. For example, these decisions include:

- The number of levels of authority in the business—these are called levels of hierarchy.

- How many people a manager should be directly responsible for. The span of control of a manager measures how many people report directly to her. A wider span of control will mean less levels of hierarchy are needed. This will reduce management costs. However, with wider spans it may be more difficult to control staff.

- How jobs are grouped together. For example, managers may group all the marketing roles in one division and all the finance jobs in another division. This is known as a functional approach to organizational structure.

Mechanistic v organic structures

A mechanistic organizational structure is one that has well-defined roles and reporting relationships. It is one where managers control from the top down. Spans of control are kept short so that a manager can easily supervise their work. There are clear chains of command. This type of structure can work well. In a routine environment with repetitive tasks and when there is a need to keep a tight control over decisions being made, perhaps because of high risk.

An organic organizational structure is more fluid with more cross-functional communication encouraged. Teams are often formed for particular purposes with the authority of an individual not being linked to their title or years of service, but to what individuals can contribute to the given task. An organic structure is well suited to a fast-changing environment where employees will benefit from collaboration to find innovative solutions to emerging challenges and opportunities. The typical features of organic and mechanistic structures are shown in Table 6.4.

Think about it

Imagine you go to a coffee shop: does one person serve you, make your coffee, and then bring it to your table, or are these jobs divided between different people. Think how the way that the work is organized might affect your experience as a customer. What about the job satisfaction of employees?

Table **6.4** Typical features of a mechanistic and an organic structure

Mechanistic	Organic
Well-defined hierarchy	Cross-functional teams
Centralized decision-making	Decentralized decision-making
Standardized processes	Flexible processes
Rules and procedures	
Specialized work	Broader job descriptions

Key concepts

Centralization refers to the extent to which decisions are made by senior managers.

A **mechanistic organization** is one with a clear organizational structure and many rules and procedures.

A **mechanistic organizational structure** is one that has well-defined roles and reporting relationships.

Authority occurs when one individual has legal power over another.

Accountability occurs when an individual is held responsible for an activity.

Centralization refers to the extent to which decisions are made by the senior managers.

Delegation occurs when a superior entrusts a subordinate with a task.

An example of an organic structure is W.L. Gore. This company is a highly innovative business making industrial products such as Gore-Tex outer wear. On its website the company says, 'At Gore's workplaces around the globe, there's a buzz in the air—an excitement for the work Gore does and the work each Associate brings to the enterprise.

It starts with that word, '"Associate". We're more than employees; we're trusted stewards of our business. Each of us makes commitments that help drive the business, and we work together in our lattice communications structure. In this structure, we collaborate and build connections without the constraints of traditional chains of command—giving us the freedom to encourage and support each other's growth and development. It's an environment in which highly motivated people thrive and where we are able to bring our unique talents and diverse perspectives to problem-solve and collectively get our work done.' You can see that W.L. Gore believes its fluid organic approach which empowers its associates is a key contributor to its innovation strategy.

organizational structure will be examined in more depth in Chapter 9.

6.7 The outcomes of HR policy decisions

We have now considered some of the policy choices made by managers and the factors that influence these decisions. In this section we consider the effect that these HR decisions have in terms of HR outcomes. This is shown in Figure 6.21.

Part 1

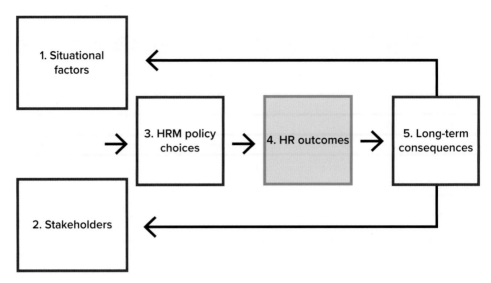

Figure 6.21 HR outcomes in the Harvard Model of HRM. *Source:* Author.

The effectiveness of managing people will ultimately be judged by whether the organization has the people it needs able to make the right contributions to the overall strategy of the business. This means HR should ensure that a business has the right people with the right skills and right values and behaviours.

The typical indicators of the success of Human Resources policy decisions include the following outcomes: labour productivity, labour turnover, staff retention, and employee engagement.

- Labour productivity.

  Labour productivity measures the output per employee. The more productive employees are, the more output per person there is. If there is more productivity with the same number of employees this means there is more total output and, assuming demand is there, this will lead to more sales. If the total output required remains constant and employees become more productive this means fewer people will be required which can reduce costs. Productivity will be measured in different ways depending on the nature of the work done. For example, in a garment factory productivity may be measured by the number of clothes produced per hour, in a supermarket checkout staff may be measured by number of items scanned per minute, for a delivery business it may be number of deliveries per hour; in other situations, productivity may be measured by sales per employee or profits per person. Using the value of the output produced at 2017 prices 'Our world in data' states that the highest labour productivity in 2019 was Ireland at over $125 an hour; by comparison, Cambodia was $3.43 an hour.

- Labour turnover.

  Labour turnover measures the percentage of people leaving a business over a given period. If labour turnover is unusually high this might suggest that there are problems causing people to leave. When staff leave they take with them their experience and the

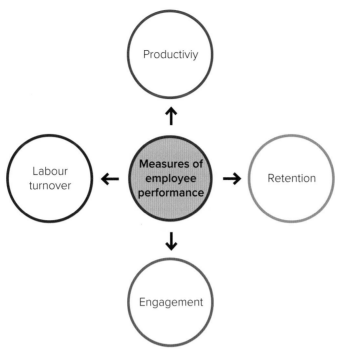

Figure 6.22 Outcomes of HR decisions. *Source:* Beer *et al.* (1984).

benefits of all the training they have had, and this can be expensive to replace. Labour turnover is linked to staff retention. Whereas labour turnover focuses on the numbers leaving; retention focuses on those staying. This measures how many staff are left after a given period of time after they have been recruited. For example, if 100 employees are recruited and 75 are left working at the business after a year then the retention rate at this point is 75%. A low retention rate might suggest that the recruitment policies are recruiting the wrong people or that they are not happy with the job once recruited—perhaps because it is not what they expected. This can be expensive for the business to replace the staff who are leaving.

- Employee engagement.
  Employee engagement measures whether employees identify with the objectives and values of the business and whether they feel they are well treated. This gives managers an insight into employees' state of mind and whether policies need to be changed to improve employees' engagement with the business and its strategy.

Some of the measures of the outcomes of HR decisions are shown in Figure 6.22.

Can you now answer this question from the introductory case study?

What do you think are the consequences of lower employee turnover i) for BP, ii) for employees, iii) for society?

Analysing the business data 6.5   Marks and Spencer's employee data

Table 1 shows the labour costs for Marks and Spencer plc (a retailer) for the financial year 2020–21. This data is taken from Marks and Spencer's annual report, which can be found on its website.

Table 1 Expense analysis for Marks and Spencer plc 2021

3 EXPENSE ANALYSIS	2022 Total £m	2021 Total £m
Revenue	10,885.1	9,155.7
Cost of sales	(7,130.3)	(6,244.1)
Cross profit	3,754.8	2,911.6
Selling and administrative expenses	(3,244.1)	(3,018.9)
Other operating income	80.1	12.4
Share of results of Ocado Retail Limited	(18.6)	64.2
Operating profit/(loss)	572.2	(30.7)

The figures above include £136.8m (last year: £252.9m) adjusting item charges within operating profit/(loss) (see note 5). These are further analysed against the categories of revenue (£nil; last year: £11.2m), cost of sales (£17.0m gain; last year: £86.3m gain), selling and administrative expenses (£155.9m; last year: £313.8m), other operating income (£34.6m; last year: £nil) and share of results of Ocado Retail Limited (£32.5m; last year: £14.2m).

The selling and administrative expenses are further analysed below:

	2022 Total £m	2021 Total £m
Employee costs[1,2]	1,420.6	1,339.1
Occupancy costs	344.3	223.9
Repairs, renewals and maintenance of property	122.2	95.8
Depreciation, amortisation and asset impairments and write-offs[3]	586.4	791.7
Other costs[4]	770.6	568.4
Selling and administrative expenses	3,244.1	3,018.9

Source: Marks and Spencer plc Annual Report 2021.

Questions

1. Calculate employee costs as a percentage of turnover for 2021.

2. Calculate employee costs as a percentage of total selling and administrative expenses in 2019.

3. Why might employee costs be an important HR outcome?

Key concepts

> **Labour productivity** measures the output per employee in a given period of time.

> **Labour turnover** measures the proportion of employees who leave a business in a given period, usually a year.

What would you do?

> You run a fast food chain. Your labour turnover is relatively high compared to other industries but you are not particularly concerned. Should you be?

Business insight 6.4 The successful management of people at Pal's

Pal's is a fast food restaurant in USA that sells burgers, hot dogs, chicken sandwiches, fries, and shakes. It has 26 stores in northeast Tennessee and southwest Virginia. Pal's is a drive-through restaurant. Customers drive up to a window and place their order; they then drive around to the other side of the building and collect their order. It usually takes about 18 seconds to place the order and 12 seconds to collect. This is four times faster than any other fast food drive through. Not only that, the service at Pal's is very accurate as well as fast. At Pals the number of mistakes is around one in every 3600 orders. That is ten times better than the average fast food business.

According to Pal's the key to this success is the way that it manages its people. Pal's employs over 1000 people, 90% of whom are part-time and 40% of whom are between the ages of 16 and 18. To make sure it employs the right people the company have developed a psychometric survey that assesses applicants' attitudes and attributes. Pal's has identified the characteristics of a great employee and matches any applicant's profile against these.

Once an employee starts at Pal's she will receive a lot of training. New employees have around 120 hours of training before they can work on their own, and in this time they need to have gained a certificate in the different aspects of their job. Every day on every shift in each of the restaurants a computer generates a couple of names of employees who are tested again on an aspect of their job.

The company places a lot of emphasis on training. It has a reading list for all of its managers. The list includes 21 classics, including Machiavelli's *The Prince*, through to highly technical books on quality and lean management. Every two weeks the Chief Executive invites five managers from different locations to discuss one of the books on the list. All leaders at Pal's are expected to spend 10% of their time on teaching, and to identify a target subject and a target student every day.

The result of Pal's focus on training is that labour turnover is incredibly low. In 33 years of operation, only seven store managers have left the company voluntarily. Annual turnover among assistant managers is 1.4 percent. Even among front-line employees, labour turnover is just one-third the industry average.

Question

How does the way in which people are managed contribute to the success of Pal's?

Source

hbr.org/2016/01/how-one-fast-food-chain-keeps-its-turnover-rates-absurdly-low?registration=success

6.8 Long-term consequences of HR decisions

As shown in Figure 6.23 the HR outcomes will have long-term consequences.

The HR policy decisions made by an organization will affect:

- The people actually doing the job. For example, whether they have permanent or temporary employment may affect the degree of job security they have and the level of rewards they get.

- The business itself. The way that people are managed can affect the costs of the business, the quality of the human resource input, and the ease and speed with which a business can respond to change.

- Society as a whole. The HR policy decisions will affect how many people are employed, the terms and conditions of employment, and the rewards received. This can affect the general sense of well-being in society. For example, if organizations are felt to reward senior managers but exploit more junior employees this can cause social discontent.

6.8.1 Soft v hard approaches to HRM

There are many different forms of HR strategy but a common distinction in approaches is to distinguish between soft and hard HRM. This distinction was made by John Storey

What would you do?

You are considering changing your employees' contracts to become zero-hours contracts to help the financial performance of the business. Do you think it would it be right to do this?

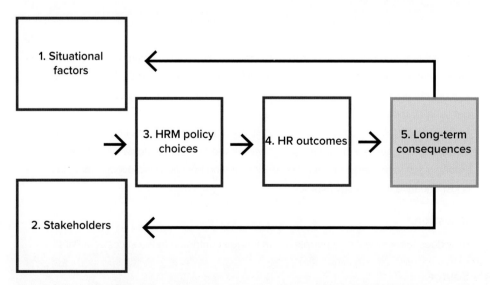

Figure 6.23 Long-term consequences shown in the Harvard Model of HRM. *Source:* Author.

(1989), in his book *New Perspectives on Human Resource Management*. Hard HRM regards employees as a resource to be controlled and managed closely.

Soft HR regards employees as an asset and believes that people can provide a competitive advantage through their commitment, innovation, and the quality of their ideas and work. Soft HR encourages teamwork, collaboration, motivation, and sharing of ideas. Managers will be willing to invest in training and take a long-term view of the value of investing and developing people.

6.8.2 Key performance areas for HR managers

According to the management consultancy, Deloitte, there are four key performance areas that HR managers should focus on.

Business insight 6.5 Working in an Amazon warehouse

As a sorter at Amazon's New York warehouse called JFK8 you work three 12-hour shifts a week. Your job is to inspect and scan 1800 Amazon packages an hour (30 a minute). These packages are sent through a chute and transported on a conveyor belt around the facility before going for delivery. In December 2019, 600 workers at the warehouse signed a petition to managers asking for an improvement in working conditions. The petition asked for two 15-minute breaks to be consolidated into a 30-minute one. This is because employees say it can take up to 15 minutes just to walk through the huge warehouse to the rest area. Workers also highlighted the high levels of injury which, they say, are three times the national average for warehouses, based on the company's injury reports to the Occupational Safety and Health Administration (OSHA). Dangers include being hit by forklifts and electric pallet jacks.

Problems include some packages being unsafely put on the conveyor belt and items breaking open and spilling. Staff have to clear up the mess whilst still hitting their targets. Staff say that workers are regularly sacked for missing their targets. One employee claimed that the business cares more about the robots in the warehouse than staff. The work rate of employees is constantly tracked by computers. An Amazon spokesperson told the *Guardian* newspaper in an email: 'Like most companies, we have performance expectations for every Amazonian and we measure actual performance against those expectations'. The spokesperson said coaching is provided to under-performing workers.

Amazon argues that because it records any incident (unlike some businesses) that it might seem as if it had a large number of injuries. It says it has a strong culture of safety.

Questions

Would you describe Amazon's approach to managing its employees as soft or hard HRM? Why?

Is a soft or hard approach to HR better do you think?

Source

www.theguardian.com/technology/2020/feb/05/amazon-workers-protest-unsafe-grueling-conditions-warehouse

6

These areas are:

- Customer Metrics

  Customer Metrics quantify a company's internal 'customer' satisfaction with HR services and HR's ability to meet its users' needs. These customer-focused metrics are effective at identifying improvement opportunities to enhance the quality of HR services and range from general (for example, overall employee satisfaction) to specific (for example, the percentage of leaders citing leadership training as a driver of satisfaction).

- Process Metrics

  Process Metrics measure the output and efficiency of HR processes and address high-level issues such as the effectiveness of process execution, the identification of opportunities to improve efficiency or reduce errors, and determining the overall volume of transactions being measured. Process Metrics include insights such as job offer acceptance rate, number of HR data errors, and variance from compensation guidelines. This type of metric is especially helpful in identifying opportunities to improve HR processes and delivery mechanisms.

- Talent Metrics

  Talent Metrics help to identify competency gaps in a company's workforce, recognize the implications of different hiring, attrition, and promotion strategies, and seek to understand which talent characteristics foster high performance. Talent Metrics include succession plan promotion rates, retention of high performers or critical segments, and the share of new hires who receive top performance ratings or leave within six months. Talent Metrics quantify the strength of the talent pipeline and identify improvement opportunities that will ultimately help with overall retention and employee productivity.

- Financial Metrics

  Financial Metrics quantify the cost and impact of HR processes and programmes, and include information such as the cost of turnover, training spend per employee, return on investment of an HR initiative, and the realization of business case savings from an HR Transformation project.

These different measures of HR performance are shown in Figure 6.24.

6.8.3 The changing HR environment

As with all aspects of business the HR environment is constantly changing. This creates new opportunities and challenges for the management of people. For example, changes in the HR environment in the UK include more flexible working, technology, and the nature of work.

- Flexible working

Flexible working involves contracts that are not permanent or full time. This enables a business to increase or decrease its labour supply relatively easily. It means that managers are not committed to employing people when demand for their services may not be there.

Examples of flexible working are shown in Figure 6.25.

Forms of flexible working (shown in Figure 6.25) include the use of temporary and part-time contracts but also zero-hours contracts. These occur when an employee can be

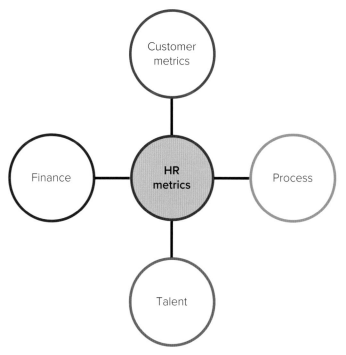

Figure 6.24 HR performance metrics. *Source:* Beer *et al.* (1984).

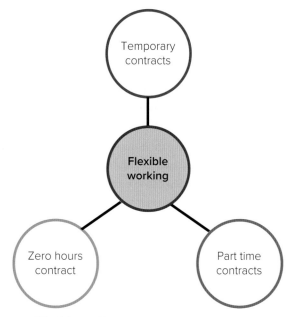

Figure 6.25 Forms of flexible working. *Source:* Author.

offered work when there is demand for her but she is not guaranteed any hours of work; their contract is for 'zero hours of work'.

Flexible working can benefit employees in that it can help them to balance work with other requirements on their time. However, for some it will mean they have a job but do not have the security they want in terms of a full-time permanent contract.

For the business flexible working can keep costs down because it is not committed to full-time salaries; this can help it to be price competitive.

One particular trend in flexible working is known as the 'gig economy'. This is where people work on freelance contracts for themselves rather than being employed by a business. In the gig economy, instead of a regular wage, people are paid for the 'gigs' they do, such as a food delivery or a car journey. A common feature of the gig economy is that there is a digital platform (such as Uber or Deliveroo) which connects employees with the work they do. The individuals are usually regarded as self-employed, although there are various court cases underway in which employees are arguing they are actually employed and therefore have more employment rights.

The gig economy gives individuals the flexibility to work as and when they want. They may be able to combine this job with other jobs or interests. It also gives the business a flexible workforce it can call on depending on demand levels. From a business perspective there are fewer costs and commitments if someone is self-employed. A self-employed person has no rights against unfair dismissal, no right to redundancy payments, and no right to receive the national minimum wage, paid holiday, or sickness pay.

However, there have been criticisms of this business model. Some claim that 'gig' workers are exploited because they do not have the same pensions, holiday, and sickness benefits as employed workers and because they are not guaranteed work.

- Technology

Technology has also affected the HR function. Developments in technology change the way some tasks are undertaken—for example, more first interviews may now be in the form of applicants responding to pre-recorded questions online. Artificial Intelligence (AI) can help provide employees with all the information relating to their employment that they need when they need it. For example, AI can provide many aspects of an induction programme answering employees' questions and helping them find out what they need to know. An AI programme can tell a new employee who she needs to contact in her first few weeks of employment and can organize where and when induction meetings will occur. New employees can be directed to follow online training guides and their progress could be monitored. New employees can ask questions via a chatbot and have their questions answered without a real person being involved. AI can also handle issues such as holiday requests or permission needed by employees. Developments in technology also enable much better tracking of the output of employees as well as changing the way they do their work. The pandemic of 2020 forced many people to work from home; this was possible due to developments in technology.

The HR environment will change over time. It also varies significantly between countries. The rights of employees, the legal environment, the attitudes to different professions, the education systems, the expectations of employees, average pay rates, labour markets, and many other aspects of HR will vary from country to country. Multinational businesses find it difficult to centralize the HR function because of major differences in the HR environment. Global businesses will want to make use of the differences in labour markets to benefit from differences in skills and costs but it is not necessarily possible to transfer across the same policies and systems into a new region.

6.8.4 The nature of work

The world of work is changing rapidly and this affects the jobs employees will be doing, the skills they will need to succeed, and the HR decisions that need to be made.

Changes that are occurring in the world of work include:

- Longer working lives. Improvements in healthcare and lifestyle mean that people are living longer. As a result, people are going to have to work longer to finance their retirement. In the UK the state retirement age will increase to 68 in 2037; it will rise to 67 in Germany in 2029.

- More portfolio careers. Employees are likely to have several careers at once. For example, they may have several part-time jobs or they may have a full-time job with one business but also be doing additional freelance work outside that.

- More use of digital skills. Employees are increasingly using digital skills to communicate, to collaborate online, to design, and to help collect and analyse data. Employees will need to ensure they are up to date with technological developments.

- Developments in technology such as artificial intelligence which mean that many jobs that currently exist will disappear in that they will be undertaken by computers not people. Employees need to develop the skills they need for the jobs that won't be replaced.

To protect themselves against being replaced by computers people need to show skills that are difficult for machines to develop. These include;

- Creativity

- Problem-solving skills

- People skills such as managing a team.

A study by EY, the management consultancy business, identified five major changes in the world of work. It also identified what it thought were the skills needed in this new environment. These changes were that in the future there would be four generations in the workplace at the same time. The jobs they were doing would be increasingly automated and five million jobs would be affected by the digital revolution that is occurring. Changes in technology mean that 60% of jobs require skills that only 20% of the population currently have. People would have more portfolio careers (i.e. they may have several different jobs at the same time) and there is a growing demand for greater agility and flexibility from employees.

These changes mean that employees need to be creative, they need emotional intelligence, they need to collaborate, and they need to be good at solving problems and juggling lots of issues at the same time.

 Now you should know

- Human Resource Management refers to the management of people.

- Authority occurs when someone has legitimate power over someone else.

- A line relationship occurs when a superior has authority over a subordinate.

Think about it

Can you think of any other changes happening in the HR environment?

- A staff relationship occurs when one person advises another but does not have direct authority over them.

- Human resource policy choices are decisions relating to employee influence, human resource flow, reward systems, and work systems.

- Theory X managers believe that employees do not like work and therefore need to be supervised and controlled closely. Theory Y managers believe employees value and enjoy work and therefore managers can be more trusting and delegate more.

- The legal environment refers to the laws that affect the activities of a business.

- The strategy of a business is the long-term plan to achieve its objectives.

- Stakeholders are individuals and groups that are affected by and affect the activities of a business.

- A works council is a committee of managers and employees who discuss decisions that affect employees.

- A trade union is an organization that represents employees.

- Workforce planning occurs when a business plans ahead and ensures the labour input is matched to the requirements of the organization.

- Job analysis is the process through which a business determines the duties and skill requirements of a job and the kind of person who should be hired for it.

- A job description sets out what a job entails.

- A person specification sets out the requirements of the jobholder.

- Internal recruitment occurs when applicants are found from within the organization.

- External recruitment occurs when applicants for a job are found from outside the organization.

- Training involves the use of systematic and planned instruction and development activities to promote learning.

- Motivating people involves creating an environment and providing reward systems in which people have an inner drive to achieve certain tasks and behave in a certain way.

- Taylor's Scientific Management aims to identify the one best way of doing a job. It assumes employees are rational and motivated by money.

- Maslow outlined a hierarchy of needs from physiological to security to social to esteem to self-actualization.

- Hygiene factors, according to Herzberg's work, prevent dissatisfaction.

- Motivator factors, according to Herzberg's work, prevent dissatisfaction.

- Employee engagement refers to being psychologically involved in, connected to, and committed to getting one's job done.

Review questions

Quick Check

1. Explain what is meant by Human Resource Management.

2. State two situational factors that might affect Human Resource policy decisions.

3. State two possible ways of measuring Human Resource performance.

4. State the five levels of need in Maslow's hierarchy.

5. Explain the difference between Herzberg's motivator and hygiene factors.

6. Explain what is meant by the gig economy.

7. State five elements of job design according to Hackman and Oldham.

8. Give one example of how an HR decision can affect i) the individual, ii) the businesses, and iii) society.

Analysis

1. Analyse two ways in which the management of people contributes to the success of a business.

2. Analyse how an ageing population might affect the HR function of a business.

3. Analyse the key elements of effective job design.

Evaluation

1. The way in which people are managed can vary significantly from one business to another. You may have experienced this from your own work experience. What do you think influences the Human Resource policy decisions in a business?

2. There has been much discussion recently about flexible employment contracts and whether they are ethical. What do you think?

3. An ongoing debate in business is how best to get employees to engage with the objectives. Do think it really matters if employees are engaged?

Find out more

- Herzberg
  You can watch Herzberg discussing his theory if you search for 'Jumping for Jelly Beans' on You Tube. There are two videos by Herzberg.
  You can read Herzberg's famous article at: hbr.org/2003/01/one-more-time-how-do-you-motivate-employees

- Netflix
  You can out more about Netflix's culture at jobs.netflix.com/culture. Why not search on a range of company websites to see how they explain their approach to managing people.

- For an excellent, brief overview of HRM you can read Wilkinson, A. (2022) *Human Resource Management: A very short introduction: Na.* New York, Oxford University Press.
- A classic book on what happens within organizations is 'Organizational behaviour' by Buchanan and Huczynski. Buchanan, D.A. and Huczynski, A. (2019). *Organizational behaviour.* Harlow, England.

Where are we now?

In this chapter we have analysed the human resource function of a business. We have now examined the functions of a business. In the next chapter we analyse the external environment of a business and then go on to consider strategic planning.

☰ Bibliography

3M (2020). Life with 3M. [online] Available at: <http://www.3m.com/3M/en_US/careers-us/working-at-3m/life-with-3m/> [Accessed 20 September 2020].

Alvesson, M. (2009). Critical Perspectives on Strategic HRM. In Storey, J., Wright, P. M., and Ulrich, D. (eds), *The Routledge Companion to Strategic Human Resource Management*, Abingdon, Routledge, pp. 52–67.

Andersen, T. J. and Minbaeva, D. (2013). The role of human resource management in strategy making. *Human Resource Management*, 52(5), 809–27.

Armstrong, M. (2008). *Strategic Human Resource Management: A Guide to Action*. London, Kogan Page.

Armstrong, M. (2016). *Armstrong's Handbook of Strategic Human Resource Management*. London, Kogan Page.

Armstrong, M. and Baron, A. (2002). *Strategic HRM: The Key to Improved Business Performance*. London, CIPD.

Armstrong, M. and Taylor, S. (2015). *Armstrong's Handbook of Human Resource Management Practice*. London, Kogan Page.

BBC News (2019). Mercedes-Benz owner Daimler to cut 10,000 jobs worldwide [online]. Available at: <http://www.bbc.co.uk/news/business-50598673> [Accessed 20 September 2020].

Beer, M., Spector B., Lawrence, P. R., Mills, D. Q., and Walton, R. E. (1984). *Managing Human Assets*. New York, The Free Press.

Chartered Institute of Personnel and Development (2014). *Survey report: Managing an age diverse workforce—employer and employee views.* CIPD (www.cipd.co.uk [Accessed 10 September 2018]).

Chartered Institute of Personnel and Development (2017). *Strategic human resource management.* CIPD (Factsheet available at www.cipd.co.uk).

Chartered Institute of Personnel and Development (2018a). *Workforce planning.* CIPD (Factsheet available at www.cipd.co.uk).

Chartered Institute of Personnel and Development (2018b). *What skills do I need.* CIPD (www.cipd.co.uk [Accessed 8 September 2018]).

Chartered Institute of Personnel and Development (2020). [online] Available at: <https://www.cipd.co.uk/Images/labour-market-outlook-autumn-2019_tcm18-67336.pdf> [Accessed 20 September 2020].

Confederation of British Industry and the National Union of Students (2011). *Working towards your future. Making the most of your time in higher education*. CBI/NUS.

Gore (n.d.). *Our story*. Available at: https://www.gore.co.uk/about/culture [Accessed 12 March 2023].

Graham, H. T. (1978). *Human Resources Management*. London, Macdonald and Evans.

Graham, H. and Bennett, R. (1998). *Human Resources Management*. London, Financial Times.

Guest, D. (2011). Human resource management and performance: still searching for some answers. *Human Resource Management Journal*, 21(1), pp. 3–13.

Hackman, J. R. and Oldham, G. R. (1976). Motivation through the design of work: Test of a theory. *Journal of Organizational Behavior and Human Performance*, 16(10), 250–279.

Hackman, J. R. and Oldham, G. R. (1980). *Work design*. Reading, MA, Addison-Wesley.

Harvard Management Update (2008). How great managers manage people. *Harvard Business Review*. Available at: <https://hbr.org/2008/02/how-great-managers-manage-peop-1> [Accessed: 27 October 2023].

Herzberg, F. (1959). The Motivation to Work. New York, John Wiley & Sons.

Herzberg, F. (1974). *Work and the Nature of Man*. London, Crosby Lockwood Staples.

House of Commons (2020). [online] Available at <http://publications.parliament.uk/pa/cm201617/cmselect/cmbis/219/219.pdf> [Accessed 20 September 2020].

Intel (2020a). [online] Available at: <http://www.intel.co.uk/content/www/uk/en/diversity/diversity-at-intel.html> [Accessed 20 September 2020].

Intel (2020b). [online] Available at: <http://newsroom.intel.com/news/bob-swan-note-to-intel-employees/#gs.a9aysr> [Accessed 20 September 2020].

Maslow, A. H. (1943). A Theory of Human Motivation. *Psychological Review*, 50 (4), 430–437.

McCarthy, N. (2020). *Infographic: The State of Global Trade Union Membership*. [online] Statista Infographics. Available at: <https://www.statista.com/chart/9919/the-state-of-the-unions/> [Accessed 20 September 2020].

McGregor, D. (1960). *The Human Side of Enterprise*. New York, McGraw-Hill.

McGregor, D. and Cutcher-Gershenfeld, J. (2008). *The Human Side of Enterprise*. New York, McGraw-Hill Professional.

Morse, J. and McGregor, D. (1974). *Theory X And Theory Y*. Santa Monica, CA, Salenger Educational Media.

OECD (2020). [online] Available at: <http://data.oecd.org/emp/hours-worked.htm> [Accessed 20 September 2020].

Price, A. (2000). *Principles Of Human Resource Management*. Oxford, Blackwell Business.

Son, H. (2019). Goldman Sachs is slashing employee pay as it ramps up new tech ventures like the apple card. Available at: https://www.cnbc.com/2019/10/17/goldman-is-slashing-employee-pay-as-it-ramps-up-tech-like-apple-card.html [Accessed 27 October 2023].

Storey, J. (1989). *New Perspectives on Human Resource Management*. Abingdon, Routledge.

Storey, J. (2007). *Human Resource Management: A Critical Text*. London, Thompson Learning.

Storey, J. (ed.) (2001). *Human Resource Management: A Critical Text* (2nd edn). London, Thomson.

Taylor, F. W. (1911). *The Principles of Scientific Management*. New York, Harper & Brothers.

Taylor, M., Marsh, G., Nicol, D., and Broadbent, P. (2017). *Good Work: The Taylor Review of Modern Working Practices*. London, Department for Business, Energy and Industrial Strategy.

The Guardian (2020). [online] Available at: <http://www.theguardian.com/technology/2020/feb/05/amazon-workers-protest-unsafe-grueling-conditions-warehouse> [Accessed 20 September 2020].

Ulrich, D. (1997). *Human Resource Champions*. Boston, Harvard Business School Press.

Ulrich, D., Younger, J., and Brockbank, W. (2013). The state of the HR profession. *Human Resource Management*, 52(3), May/June, 457–471.

6

Part 2

The external environment

Chapter 7

Analysing the external environment of business

Where are we now?

We have now studied the internal functions of business. We have considered what happens within a business. These functional decisions will be affected by what is happening outside of the organization and, in this chapter, we analyse the external environment of business. We will then go on in the next chapter to consider how this understanding of the external environment along with our insights into the internal environment combine to influence the strategy of the business.

Why am I studying this?

- You are interested in the ways in which government policy can affect business costs and demand. This chapter explains different types of government policy such as fiscal and monetary policy and the impact of such policies on business.
- You see and hear the news about your economy and want to know how it affects business decisions. This chapter analyses the impact of different economic variables such as unemployment, inflation, and economic growth.
- You can see society is changing and want to know how social change affects businesses. This chapter analyses the impact of some significant social changes such as changes to the population structure in some economies.
- You want to consider how technological change can present opportunities and threats for businesses. This chapter considers the effects of some technological changes on business activity.

Learning objectives

By the end of this chapter you should be able to

- Explain the meaning of the competitive environment and the macro-environment of business

- Analyse how changes in national income can affect a business

- Examine how changes in inflation can affect a business

- Analyse how changes in an exchange rate can affect a business

- Analyse how changes in interest rates can affect a business

- Explain the difference between fiscal and monetary policy

- Discuss how government policy can affect a business

- Examine why social change matters to business

- Analyse how technological change can affect businesses

- Discuss how businesses might use PEST analysis

Introductory case study Ford

In its annual report to investors in 2019 Ford, the automobile manufacturer, outlined the nature of the markets in which it operates and highlighted the risks it faces:

- Its market share (Table 1) is influenced by customers' perception of Ford vehicles compared to what is offered by other manufacturers. This perception is influenced by many factors such as the price, quality, styling, safety, and fuel efficiency of its vehicles as well as the company's reputation.

Ford vehicles. *Source:* Wikimedia/Otoparcasan.com.

Table 1 Retail sales, industry volume, and market share for Ford, 2019–2021

Retail Sales, Industry Volume, and Market Share

Retail sales, industry volume, and market share in each region and in certain key markets within each region during the past three years were as follows:

	Retail Sales (in millions of units)			Industry Volume (in millions of units)			Market Share (as a percentage)		
	2019	2020	2021	2019	2020	2021	2019	2020	2021
United States	2.4	2.0	1.9	17.5	14.9	15.4	13.8 %	13.7 %	12.4 %
Canada	0.3	0.2	0.2	2.0	1.6	1.7	14.6	15.1	14.3
Mexico	0.1	—	—	1.4	1.0	1.0	4.4	4.0	4.0
North America	2.8	2.3	2.2	21.1	17.6	18.4	13.2	13.2	12.0
Brazil	0.2	0.1	—	2.8	2.1	2.1	8.1	6.8	1.7
Argentina	0.1	—	—	0.5	0.3	0.4	11.4	9.7	7.9
South America	0.3	0.2	0.1	4.3	3.1	3.6	7.2	6.2	2.6
United Kingdom	0.4	0.2	0.2	2.7	1.9	2.0	13.0	12.9	11.8
Germany	0.3	0.2	0.2	4.0	3.3	3.0	8.3	7.4	5.7
EU20	1.3	1.0	0.9	17.9	13.7	13.7	7.4	7.1	6.4
Turkey	—	0.1	0.1	0.5	0.8	0.8	10.1	12.4	9.7
Europe	1.4	1.1	1.0	19.2	15.1	15.1	7.3	7.2	6.4
China	0.6	0.6	0.6	26.1	25.2	26.3	2.2	2.4	2.4
Australia	0.1	0.1	0.1	1.1	0.9	1.1	6.0	6.5	6.8
India	0.1	0.1	—	3.8	2.8	3.5	2.0	1.7	1.0
ASEAN	0.1	0.1	0.1	1.8	1.3	1.4	5.9	5.3	5.3
Russia	—	—	—	1.8	1.5	1.7	1.6	0.9	1.2
International Markets Group	0.4	0.3	0.3	21.2	17.5	18.7	1.9	1.7	1.8
Global / Total Company	5.5	4.5	4.2	91.9	78.5	82.1	6.0 %	5.8 %	5.1 %

- Its vehicles are durable goods and consumers and businesses have some flexibility in terms of deciding whether and when to replace an existing vehicle. The decision about whether or not to buy a vehicle will be affected by factors such as slower economic growth, the cost of borrowing money, and the cost of fuel. This means demand can change significantly from year to year. In addition, the automotive industry is very competitive with a huge amount of choice for consumers from a growing number of manufacturers. ▶

- The company purchases a wide variety of raw materials from suppliers around the world. Some of these are metals (such as steel and aluminium), some are energy (e.g. natural gas), and some are plastics. There are always risks with the availability and prices of such supplies.

- The company must meet government regulations. These include vehicle emission controls. Meeting these regulations affects product development, warranty costs, and vehicle recalls. New regulations such as the California requirements to produce zero emission vehicles (ZEV) are likely to increase the challenges and cost of future product development.

- In European markets, European Union ('EU') directives and related legislation limit the amount of regulated pollutants that may be emitted by new motor vehicles and engines sold in the EU. There is an increasing trend of restrictions on the access to cities for internal combustion engine powered vehicles.

- In an effort to achieve their targets as part of the Paris Accord, some countries are adopting yearly increases in CO_2 taxes. Some countries are publishing dates by when internal combustion powered vehicles may no longer be registered, e.g. Norway is 2025 and the Netherlands is 2030.

- The company's products must meet the vehicle safety standards of each country. European regulators are focusing on active safety features, such as lane departure warning systems, electronic stability control, and automatic brake assist. New safety and recall requirements are being introduced in Brazil, China, India, and Gulf Cooperation Council countries. E-Call (where there is an online emergency call if the vehicle is in an accident) is now mandatory in the UAE for new vehicles.

- There is a risk from the increasing interconnectedness of economies. Changes in one country spread through others—for example, a financial crisis, economic downturn or recession, natural disaster, or geopolitical crisis. Changes in international trade policy—for example, changes in taxes on foreign goods—can also have a substantial adverse effect on businesses. For example, recent U.S. government policy to apply or consider applying taxes on foreign automobiles, parts, and other products and materials have the potential to disrupt existing supply chains, create additional costs on parts, affect the demand for Ford's products, and make Ford less competitive. Ford may also suffer if other countries retaliate by imposing tariffs. This would increase the cost of Ford vehicles imported into these countries. According to Ford, China, in particular, presents unique risks to automakers due to its unique competitive and regulatory landscape. Changes in US–China trade policy and new or increased tariffs, as well as a further economic slowdown, may have an adverse effect on Ford's financial condition or results of operation. In Europe, the United Kingdom withdrew from the European Union effective as of 31 January 2020, and was in a period of transition until the end of 2020. An exit from the European Union is likely to result in a significant reduction in sales in the United Kingdom, greater taxes on UK imports and exports, and delays at the UK borders.

- Ford has operations in various markets with volatile economic or political environments and are pursuing growth opportunities in a number of newly developed and emerging markets. These investments may expose Ford to heightened risks of economic, geopolitical, or other events, including governmental takeover (i.e., nationalization) of its manufacturing facilities or intellectual property, restrictive exchange or import controls, disruption of operations as a result of systemic political or economic instability, outbreak of war or expansion of hostilities, and acts of terrorism.

- The demographic effect on pensions and other postretirement benefit plans could be worse than Ford had previously assumed.

- The company needs to make changes to its product cycle plan to improve the fuel economy of its petroleum-powered vehicles and to offer more propulsion choices, such as electrified vehicles, with lower GHG emissions.

- Ford companies continue to develop autonomous vehicle technologies. Governments are continuing to develop the regulatory framework that will govern autonomous vehicles.

- Ford and Ford Credit could be affected by the continued development of more stringent privacy, data use, and data protection laws and regulations as well as consumer expectations for the safeguarding of personal information.

Sources

annualreport.ford.com/files/doc_downloads/Ford-2019-Printed-Annual-Report.pdf
https://www.annualreports.com/HostedData/AnnualReports/f/NYSE_F_2021.pdf

Introductory case study questions

1. What do you think is meant by the external environment of business? Can you distinguish between the competitive environment and the macro-environment?

2. What political or legal factors might affect Ford's success?

3. What economic factors might affect Ford's success?

4. What social factors might affect Ford's success?

5. What technological factors might affect Ford's success?

6. How might an analysis of the external environment determine Ford's future strategy?

Critical thinking

1. How do you think the external challenges facing Ford may have changed over time?

2. Do you think the external challenges facing Ford are greater than those facing other businesses?

3. An annual report is a document produced by public companies each year for its current and potential investors. To what extent do you think Ford will reveal its true challenges in its annual report?

7.1 The external environment of business

Businesses operate within an external environment rather than in isolation. These means that business decisions will be affected by and effect the environment in which they operate. There are changes constantly going on in the wider world and businesses need to try and prepare for and be ready to respond to these. The 'right' strategy—or long-term plan—for the business will depend on what is happening in its environment. As the environment changes so must the strategy. For example, the growth of internet usage might require a business to move more of its retail operations online.

The external environment of business can be analysed in terms of:

- The competitive environment. This refers to the different stakeholder groups that a business deals with regularly such as suppliers, customers, and distributors. The competitive environment can be analysed using Michael Porter's Five Forces analysis.

- The macro-environment. This refers to changes in the wider business environment. It refers to factors in the business world which can have an impact on business decisions but which an individual business has little or no influence over. For example, changes in the economy. The macro-environment can be analysed using the PEST framework.

Some of the elements of the competitive and macro-environments are shown in Figure 7.1.

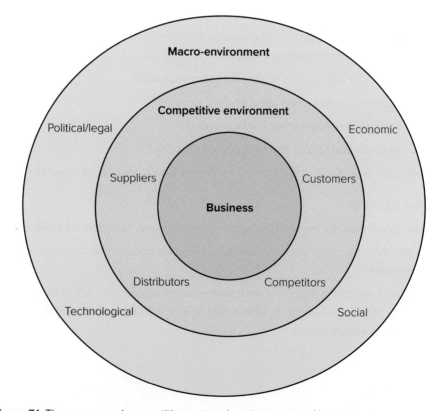

Figure 7.1 The macro- and competitive external environments of business. *Source:* Author.

The competitive environment will be examined first and then we will consider the macro-environment.

7.1.1 The competitive environment: five forces analysis

Five forces analysis was developed by Porter (1985) as a way of analysing the competitive environment of an industry. Porter identified five forces that determine the profitability of an industry. The five forces are illustrated in Figure 7.2.

The five forces in an industry are:

- **Rivalry.** The degree of rivalry in an industry refers to the competition between established businesses. The higher the degree of rivalry the more profits will be shared between competing businesses and the lower the likely return to any one business.

- **Buyer power.** This refers to the power that the immediate customers (who may not be the end customers) have in relation to the business. The greater the power of buyers the more they can push down prices. This means they get better value for money but the businesses in the industry get lower prices and profitability.

- **Supplier power.** This refers to the power of the suppliers of inputs such as labour, land, and materials. The greater the power of these suppliers the more they can push up prices. This means that the suppliers make more profits but the established businesses have lower profits due to higher costs.

- **Substitute threat.** This refers to the ease with which customers can switch to an alternative way of gaining the same benefit. A substitute performs the same or a similar function as an industry's product by a different means. Instead of flying to a particular destination, is it easy to rent a car or catch a train? The easier it is for customers to

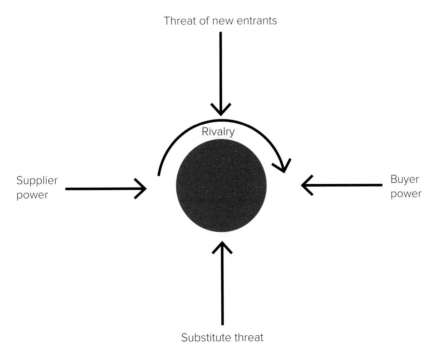

Figure 7.2 Porter's five forces. *Source:* Author.

Table 7.1 The impact of the five forces in profitability

Force	Impact
Entry threat	High entry threat reduces profitability
Substitute threat	High substitute threat reduces profitability
Rivalry	High rivalry reduces profitability
Buyer power	High buyer power reduces profitability
Supplier power	High supplier power reduces profitability

find substitutes, the more difficult it is for businesses to raise prices because customers will switch away. The greater the substitute threat the lower the likely profitability of businesses in the industry.

- **Entry threat.** This refers to how easy it is to enter an industry, i.e. how big is the threat of entry of other businesses? The easier it is, the more pressure there is on existing businesses to push down profits. Why? because if their profits are high and it is easy to enter the industry other firms will come in and the profits will have to be shared amongst more businesses.

The impact of these five forces on the profitability of an industry is shown in Table 7.1.

According to Porter (1985) the combination of forces in an industry determines the profitability that is likely to occur within it. This does not mean that businesses in that industry must accept the forces that exist: they can take actions to make them more favourable.

For example, a business may:

- merge with or take over another business to reduce the degree of rivalry
- try to get government protection against foreign competition to reduce the threat of entry by other businesses
- differentiate its product further to reduce the substitute threat.

These forces will change over time due to external factors. For example:

- measures by governments to protect domestic industries against foreign competition would reduce entry threat
- two or more suppliers combining would increase the supplier power.

7.1.2 Factors affecting the five forces

- **Entry threat**

  The threat of entry is low when there are high barriers to entry into an industry. Barriers to entry include:

  - High costs needed to enter an industry. For example, the costs of establishing a telecommunications network are significant which makes entry by new businesses less likely.

Think about it

How do you think greater use of the internet is affecting the five forces in an industry of your choice?

- The significance of experience. For example, a barrier to entering the banking sector is the expertise required to operate in such a highly regulated environment.

- Access to supply and distribution channels; if you cannot access key resources or get to key distribution outlets this makes entry difficult. For example, breaking into the film industry used to be difficult because you were so reliant on gaining access to cinemas to get the films shown. It is easier now with streaming services.

- Government restrictions; for example, licenses that may be required to provide a service. In some cities, for example, the number of taxis is closely controlled and there is a limited number of licences given out.

- The likely reaction of businesses if there were new entrants; for example, how fiercely they would compete to protect their existing sales.? If it is felt that new entrants might face an aggressive response this might put off any proposed entry.

- The degree of brand loyalty that exists already in the industry. It is difficult to enter the carbonated drinks market, for example, due to the brand loyalty to Pepsi and Coca-Cola.

- **The substitute threat**

  The substitute threat will be higher if a substitute offers similar or better value for money (i.e. the benefits offered relative to the price) than a product. For example, if you increasingly use your mobile phone to tell the time, this could put pressure on the watch industry.

- **Buyer power**

Buyer power is likely to be high when:

- there are relatively few buyers; this the business selling the product relies on these buyers. If, for example, you sell healthcare products and the main buyer is the government it will have a lot of power. If you are a supermarket, one buyer has relatively little power.

- it is easy for buyers to switch to other providers if they wish. For example, it has become easier in recent years to switch energy providers or banks online this increases the buyer power.

- buyers have the ability and resources to take-over the suppliers

- **Supplier power**

  Supplier power is likely to be high when:

- There are relatively few of them; this means their buyers will need them. For example, the airlines are very dependent on relatively few aircraft manufacturers. This increases the power of these manufacturers.

- They provide something quite specialized which means it is difficult for a business to switch to alternatives.

- Suppliers have the ability and resources to acquire the businesses they supply to.

Five forces analysis is a powerful tool that is used to:

- Identify how attractive an industry is to compete in

- Analyse the effect of different forces on the profitability of an industry

- Identify strategies businesses may wish to adopt to influence the impact of the forces.

Analysing the business data 7.1

Porter's work analysed the average return on investment in many different industries, as shown in Figure 7.1. In the soft drinks industry, for example, the profitability of businesses was 37.6%—relatively high. By comparison, the profitability of hotels and airlines was relatively low.

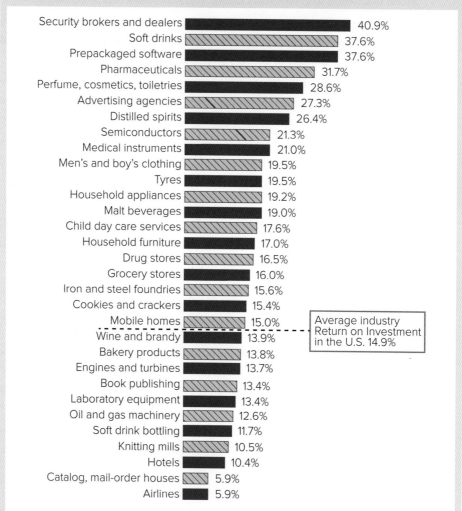

Figure 1 The profitability of different industries. *Source:* Porter, M. E. (1979). 'How Competitive Forces Shape Strategy' *Harvard Business Review*, 57(2) (March–April), 137–145.

Question

Can you use five forces analysis to explain why profitability might vary between industries as shown above?

What would you do?

You are Managing Director of a large US car manufacturer. What would you do to make the five forces more favourable to you in your home country?

Can you now answer these questions from the introductory case study?

What do you think is meant by the external environment of business?

Can you distinguish between the competitive environment and the macro-environment?

Business insight 7.1 Online food delivery

The internet has created many business opportunities, including the online ordering of food to be delivered to your door. In a relatively short space of time the industry has become extremely competitive, attracting big businesses such as Amazon and Alibaba. However, most of these businesses make a loss. Although some of the more established businesses such as Grubup in the US, and Takeaway and Just Eat in Europe have been profitable, many of the current competitors are not. The more established businesses had a simple model. They work with restaurants that have their own delivery services and simply provide online access in return for a percentage of the order. The newcomers, such as Meituan of China and Delivery Hero of Germany, Uber Eats, Ele.me (owned by China's Alibaba), and Deliveroo (UK), are different in that their main business is the delivery. They share the price paid with the delivery riders as well as the restaurants. This means they can offer a much wider range of foods (as the existing business does not need a delivery service) but profit margins suffer. These businesses have used low prices to attract customers and this has forced the established businesses to respond. Usually the established businesses have fought back with more advertising.

The market remains appealing because of its potential size. It is estimated that almost a third of the global restaurant industry is made up of home delivery, takeaway, and drive-throughs and that this could be worth $1trn by 2023. In 2018 delivery amounted to $161 bn, meaning there is room to grow.

Profits have been difficult to achieve, as they were with firms such as Uber in the passenger journey businesses. Food delivery is even more complicated. Meal-delivery firms must handle dishes that take different amounts of time to cook, while restaurants also deal with orders from in-house customers. Most importantly, the fee is split three ways: between delivery firms, restaurants, and riders, rather than just between the ride-hailing firms and their drivers. Add to this the fact that the most popular brands like McDonald's and Starbucks have the power to squeeze the delivery start-ups in exchange for access to millions of customers.

The markets are likely to get even more competitive as huge businesses such as Amazon enter.

Question

Use Porter's five forces model to analyse the factors affecting the profitability and established businesses in the food delivery industry.

Where are we now?

We have now analysed the competitive environment of business using five forces analysis. The next part of external analysis to consider the macro-environment. To do this we will use the PEST framework and examine Political, Economic, Social, and Technological factors in the macro-environment of business.

7.2 The political and legal environment

Businesses will be affected by the political decisions and the laws of the countries in which they operate. For example, political decisions may determine the level of government intervention in an economy. In a planned or command economy the government controls many of the resources in the country and provides many of the goods and services. By contrast, in a free-market economy most of resources are owned and used by the private sector. In a free market, businesses can decide what to produce, who to produce for, and what price to sell their products for. The degree of intervention by the state will depend on the government and the political system and can vary considerably; for example, China has a relatively high level of government intervention compared to the US. The amount of intervention can change over time as political parties and systems change. For example, the ravaging effects of the pandemic in 2020 have led to much more government intervention than in the past in many economies.

Government intervention may be justified to ensure the provision of essential goods and services such as education, health, water, or energy to the general public, either free or at affordable prices. By intervening a government can determine what is produced and therefore ensure the country focuses on the areas that it thinks are the priorities rather than leaving the decisions of what is produced to businesses and customers. Intervention also ensures there will be some services, such as the police and national defence, that would not be provided in a free market. Government intervention can also prevent customers being misled or exploited or sold dangerous products as profit-seeking businesses try to push down costs and persuade customers to buy their products. Governments may be needed to protect consumers, and indeed other businesses, from the behaviour of some firms. For example, you may want government regulation of the plastic surgery industry, dentistry, medical services, the sale of guns, or alcohol production.

On the other hand, government intervention can be inefficient. It can be more difficult for a central government to make decisions about how to use resources than leaving it to individual businesses and customers to decide in the market place. Gathering the huge quantities of information needed to run the economy and make decisions centrally can be bureaucratic and slow. Government involvement can lead to over- or under-production of some products relative to customer demand. It also removes the profit incentive. In the free market businesses are keen to innovate and find new and better ways of producing to increase profits. Competition between businesses can also be an important driver for new products and new process development. The advantages of government intervention and the free-market approach are compared in Table 7.2.

Governments will also pass laws which will regulate business activity. Laws are passed by a government to protect groups in society such as customers, employees, and businesses. According to the World Bank (2020) 'regulation aims to prevent worker mistreatment by

Think about it

Can you think of areas of business where you think the government should intervene more than it does?

Table 7.2 Advantages of a planned economy and a free market economy

Advantages of command/planned economy	Advantages of free-market economy
Government can provide essential items for all citizens	Competition between businesses can encourage innovation and efficiency
Government can determine the priorities of production and investment.	Desire for profit can lead to new product development, better processes, and good customer services
Government can prevent production of products it does not approve of	Businesses produce what customers want so this should avoid surpluses and shortages
Government may assess projects with a longer-term views and taking account of the impact on society not just profits	Resources will be used efficiently to generate the highest profit possible

Key concepts

A **command or planned economy** involves goods and services provided by the state.

A **free market** involves goods and services provided by privately owned businesses.

greedy employers (regulation of labor), to ensure that roads and bridges do not collapse (regulation of public procurement), and to protect one's investments (minority shareholder protections)'. Laws are necessary to control and regulate the activities of business. This is because without regulation businesses may behave in a way which is regarded as socially unacceptable. For example, managers may try to pay employees the least they possibly can even if this is not enough to live on. Managers may not invest enough in safety at work or in ensuring their products are safe because this increases costs. They may deliberately mislead customers to gain sales and may compete unfairly against rivals to win orders.

Legislation may involve:

- local laws—for example, local legislation on what can be built where or local taxes to finance the provision of local amenities such as libraries and waste collection
- national laws—for example, country-specific laws on the labelling of products and minimum wages
- international laws—for example, international agreements on trade.

Some of the different types of laws that affect business are shown in Figure 7.3.

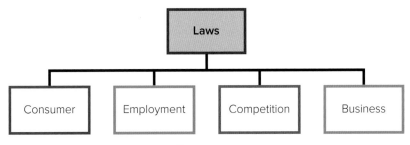

Figure 7.3 Different types of laws that affect business activity. *Source:* Author.

The legal environment includes:

- **Consumer laws**

  Consumer laws are designed to protect consumers. Laws exist to ensure that customers are informed appropriately and that these products are safe. For example, consumer laws may affect what is allowed to be used as ingredients in products, how products can be described and must be labelled, and the safety standards that must be met. Laws may protect consumers from dishonest advertising. They may also prevent some products being on sale at all (such as drugs) or may ensure that some services (such as healthcare) are made available to everyone.

One area of consumer protection that has become very significant in recent years is data protection—this is to prevent businesses selling on your data to others without your permission. You will notice when visiting websites that you are often asked for your permission to allow the 'cookies' on that site; this is part of the legislation in many countries that means you have the right to know what information is being collected and refuse for it to be held and used for other purposes.

- **Employment laws**

  Laws will exist in most countries to protect the rights of employees. These are needed because some employers may try to exploit staff to save costs. Employment laws can protect employees in many areas such as:

  - Employment rights. If an employee loses his or her job because of a lack of demand this is known as redundancy. Laws will determine the process by which an employee can be made redundant, if employees are entitled to redundancy payments, and the level of compensation they are entitled to.

  - Trade union rights. Trade unions are organizations that represent the rights of employees. They act as a counterbalance to management power. The role of trade unions includes trying to ensure the safety of employees, trying to ensure fair pay, and protect employment. Whether or not employees are allowed to join trade unions and the power they are allowed will be determined by the law of the country.

Business insight 7.2 Chickens

In the US chickens can be washed in chlorine and then sold. In the UK no chickens that have undergone this process can be sold. US farmers argue that using chlorine ensures the chickens do not have salmonella. The UK government argues that this process means that farmers are less concerned about the health of the chickens because they know they will be treated at the end.

When the UK left the European Union it was looking for new trading partners and was particularly eager to do a deal with the US. The ability of the UK to agree a trade deal with the US depended on negotiations about allowing chlorine-washed chicken into the UK. Similar arguments occurred over hormone-injected beef which is allowed in the US but not the UK.

Question

Why do you think the UK and US have different laws regarding what food can be sold in their countries?

- Maternity and paternity rights. These determine the time off work that someone can have and the pay they receive in this period when they have a child.

- Health and safety rights in the workplace. Laws can affect working conditions, the training and equipment provided to employees, and the maintenance and use of that equipment.

- Flexible working rights. These determine the rights of employees to ask for flexible working hours and how much an organization has to accept such requests.

However, it should not be assumed these rights are present in all countries. The International Trade Union Confederation report in 2020 stated that 85% of the 144 countries it studied had violated the right to strike. For example, strikes and demonstrations have been banned in Belarus, Guinea, Senegal, and Togo. The number of countries which restricted the registration of unions increased from 86 in 2019 to 89 countries in 2020. Sudan has suspended all trade unions and associations, and in Bangladesh, of the 1104 union registration applications examined between 2010 and 2019, 46% were rejected by the Department of Labour. According to this report, the ten worst countries for workers in 2020 were Bangladesh, Brazil, Colombia, Egypt, Honduras, India, Kazakhstan, the Philippines, Turkey, and Zimbabwe.

- **Competition laws**

  These laws affect how businesses can compete with each other. The regulations affecting how businesses compete may include:

  - Restricting the size of a business to prevent it dominating a market. When one business has a significant market share (such as a market share of 25% or more) this is known as a monopoly. A monopoly may abuse its power to push down prices from suppliers, to force out smaller competitors, and to provide poor quality products knowing that customers have limited alternatives. Typically, governments may restrict some businesses from getting too big through mergers or takeovers by having the right to prevent such deals or only allowing them under certain conditions.

  - Preventing unfair competition. In a free market, businesses may use what are regarded as unfair tactics in a market. In 2019 Google was fined €1.49 bn (£1.28 bn) by the European Union for blocking the adverts of rival online search advertisers. In 2020 charges were brought against Google in the US; the company was accused of anti-competitive behaviour by ensuring its search engine is the default on browsers and devices such as mobile phones. A business might also use low prices to try and force out a competitor. Or it might collaborate with other businesses in the same industry and work together and collude to set prices together so that consumers have to pay the price set. When businesses collude, this is called a cartel. Governments often pass laws to prevent secret agreements between businesses in a market because it is unfair to other businesses and consumers.

- **Business trading laws**

  These laws will affect what is required to trade in business. For example, business laws might set out the documentation required to set up a company, the regulations affecting company behaviour, and the information a company must provide to investors. There will be many different laws that will affect businesses when they are operating—for example, these will affect the purchase of property, planning permission, and contracts with suppliers.

These laws can also affect the handling of information by companies. This has been a big issue for many businesses, not least social media companies such as Facebook. In its 2020 Annual Report Facebook said 'We are subject to a variety of laws and regulations in the United States and abroad that involve matters central to our business, many of which are still evolving and being tested in courts, and could be interpreted in ways that could harm our business. These laws and regulations involve matters including privacy, data use, data protection and personal information, rights of publicity, content, intellectual property, advertising, marketing, distribution, data security, data retention and deletion, data localization and storage, data disclosure, artificial intelligence, electronic contracts and other communications, competition, protection of minors, consumer protection, telecommunications, product liability, e-commerce, taxation, economic or other trade prohibitions or sanctions, anti-corruption and political law compliance, securities law compliance, and online payment services.' From this you can see how significant the legal environment can be for businesses.

The laws in a country can affect how easy it is to set up in business and how easy it is to operate. This is highlighted in the World Bank's Doing Business league table. This annual report argues that governments in many economies adopt or maintain regulation that make it difficult for entrepreneurs. Whether deliberately or not, some regulations limit entrepreneurs' ability to freely operate a private business. The Doing Business table analyses regulation in 12 areas of business activity in 190 economies and considers the impact of these on processes on doing business in that region It considers areas such as how to get a business legally recognized, how to get a building permit, how to obtain an electricity connection, how to transfer property, how to get access to credit, the tax system, and how easy it is to enforce legal business contracts. The top five (the 'easiest countries in which to do business') and the bottom five ('the worst countries to do business in because of regulations') are shown in Table 7.3.

Key concepts

Redundancy occurs when an individual loses his or her job because it no longer exists.

Trade unions are organizations that represent the rights of employees.

A **monopoly** occurs when a business dominates a market —usually this means its sales have more than 25% market share.

A **cartel** occurs when businesses collude together to fix prices or output.

Think about it

How might changes in the law affect demand and supply conditions for a business?

Can you now answer this question from the introductory case study?

Analyse two political or legal factors that might affect Ford's success.

Table 7.3 The top five and bottom five countries in terms of ease of doing business in 2019 according to the World Bank

Rank	Country
1	New Zealand
2	Singapore
3	Hong Kong
4	Denmark
5	Republic of Korea
186	Libya
187	Yemen
188	Venezuela
189	Eritrea
190	Somalia

Source: http://data.worldbank.org/indicator/IC.BUS.EASE.XQ?end=2019&most_recent_value_desc=true&start=2019&view=bar

Can you now answer this question from the introductory case study?

What political or legal factors might affect Ford's success?

Where are we now?

Having analysed the Political environment in PEST analysis we now consider the Economic environment.

7.3 The economic environment

Another aspect of the external environment that has a big impact on business activity is the economic environment. Key elements of the economic environment are shown in Figure 7.4.

Key economic factors include:

- **National income**

  National income is usually measured by Gross Domestic Product (GDP). GDP measures the total value of the income earned within a country in a given period, usually a year. Typically, the GDP of a country will increase over a period of time due to factors such as improvements in technology, a better-skilled workforce, and greater capital investment. In some countries, such as China, GDP has grown fast at rates of 8–10% a year in recent years due to major investment and high levels of industrialization. In more mature economies the growth rates of the economy are more likely to be 1 to 2% a year. Sometimes, however, GDP might not grow; there can even be negative growth if the income of the economy is actually falling relative to last year. If there is negative income growth in an economy for six months or more this is known

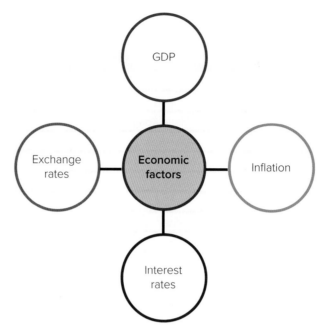

Figure 7.4 Key economic factors that affect a business. *Source:* Author.

as a recession. The pandemic in 2020 led to shut-downs in many countries forcing businesses to close; this caused recessions in many countries. Changes in world income growth are examined in Analysing the Business Data 7.2. There can be very significant differences in growth rates between countries depending on the size of the economy and local and global factors. According to the IMF, in 2022 growth rate of the UK was 0.3%; for Russia it was −2.3% as it was affected by sanctions as a result of the war in Ukraine, and for Macao it was over 56% as this small economy that is dependent on gambling and tourism experienced a resurgence as markets and travel opened up, after the pandemic.

Increasing GDP—or increasing the GDP per person—is a very common objective for governments because increasing the incomes of its citizens is usually popular politically. GDP per person is a typical measure of the standard of living in a country and so by increasing this, citizens are thought to be better off. However, the citizens of a country and its government may be interested not just in the average income per person in the country but also in how income is distributed. All governments reduce the difference between the very richest and the very poorest through the tax system and the benefits system. However, how much a government intervenes to do this varies between countries and over time.

Changes in national income and the income per person in a country will affect the demand for the products of a business. Some products will be very sensitive to changes in income. The demand for these products is called income elastic (or sensitive). For example, the demand for luxury yachts is probably sensitive to income changes. An income elastic demand means that the percentage change in demand would be bigger than the percentage change in income, assuming all other factors are constant. Other products are not so sensitive to income changes. The demand for these products is income inelastic. For example, household spending on salt is unlikely to be affected much by changes in demand. An income inelastic demand means that the percentage change in demand would be less than the percentage change in income, assuming all other factors are constant.

The elasticity (or sensitivity) of demand in relation to income is measured by the equation:

$$\frac{\text{Percentage change in quantity demanded}}{\text{Percentage change in income}}$$

A value of +2 means that a 10% increase in income leads to a 20% increase in quantity demanded. The change in quantity demanded is 2 × the change in income and both move in the same direction; in this case both increase. This is a 'normal' good and demand is income elastic because the change in quantity demanded is greater than the change in income.

Most products will be normal with demand increasing with more income and decreasing with less income. However, in some cases demand for a product may fall when income increases and vice versa. For example, when income increases people may switch from bicycles or buses to cars; with higher income demand may fall. When demand and income move in opposite directions these products are called 'inferior products'. A value of −0.5, for example, means that a 10% increase in income leads to a fall of 5% in quantity demanded. The change in quantity demanded is 0.5 × the change in income and they move in different directions; in this case income increases and quantity demanded falls. This is an 'inferior good' where demand is income inelastic because the change in quantity demanded is smaller than the change in income.

Increasingly the performance of governments is assessed using a wide range of indicators not just income—for example, some measures will try and estimate the quality of life or human happiness not just income. There has also been growing concern over environmental issues in recent years. This may mean that a government and its citizens are willing to accept slower economic growth if it is more environmentally friendly.

Understanding economic growth is important to business as it is likely to affect demand and may influence which markets are targeted and the nature of the product range offered.

Key concepts

GDP measures the total value of the income earned within a country in a given period usually a year.

A **recession** occurs when there is negative income growth in an economy for six months or more.

Income elastic demand occurs when a given percentage change in income leads to a more than proportionate change in demand, all other factors remaining unchanged.

Income inelastic demand occurs when a given percentage change in income leads to a less than proportionate change in demand, all other factors remaining unchanged.

Normal products are products for which demand increases as income increases.

Inferior products are products for which demand decreases as income increases.

What would you do?

You produce luxury watches which are very income elastic. How might this affect the activities of your marketing team?

Analysing the business data 7.2

The data in Figure 1 shows the growth rate of the world's national income since 1980.

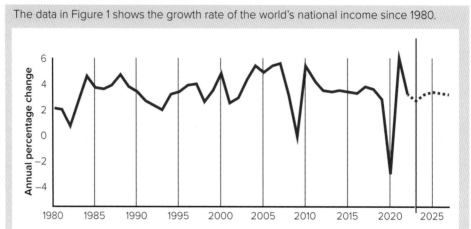

Figure 1 The growth rate of the world's national income since 1980. *Source:* IMF. Available at: http://www.imf.org/external/datamapper/PCPIPCH@WEO/WEOWORLD [Accessed 2 April 2023].

Questions

What would you estimate the average annual growth rate in world GDP was between 1980 and 2022?

In what years was world income growing particularly slowly or fast? Can you research to find out why?

Think about it

As a manager, do you think the following products are likely to be normal or inferior? Why?

a. cigarettes
b. health clubs
c. bicycles
d. cruise ship holidays

Do you think they are likely to be income elastic or inelastic? Why?

- **Inflation**

  Inflation occurs when there is a sustained increase in the general level of prices over a given period. For example, if inflation is 2% a year it means that the prices of products in general have increased by 2% over the year. In reality the prices of some products will have gone up by more than 2% and some may even have fallen but when the prices of a typical basket of goods are considered overall, prices in general are 2% higher. To measure inflation governments usually take a typical basket of products and measure the increase in price of the basket, taking into account the relative amount spent on different products so that some price changes have more significance than others. The world inflation rates between 1980 and 2020 are examined in Analysing the Business Data 7.3.

The two main causes of inflation are:

- Too much demand in the economy relative to supply. Excess demand in an economy pulls up prices; this is called demand pull inflation. When there are high levels of demand business will be eager to increase their ability to produce but this takes time. In the short term there will be too little capacity. This leads to shortages, queues, waiting lists, and higher prices.

- Costs rising. For example, costs may increase due to higher wages, higher import costs, or higher energy costs. These higher costs for the business are passed on to customers in the form of higher prices. This is called costs push inflation. Prices are pushed up by the higher costs. In 2022 many economies experienced high levels of costs push inflation caused by rising energy prices resulting from energy shortages that occurred with the Russian invasion of Ukraine.

Inflation can affect customers and businesses in various ways:

- Uncertainty about price changes can mean that households delay their spending decisions and businesses are reluctant to invest because they are not sure what their costs or revenues will be.

- Businesses will face inflation in their input prices. They have to consider how much of this they can pass on to customers; if they cannot pass it on they may have to accept lower profit margins.

- Inflation may affect some groups in society negatively. If, for example, some employees are not in a strong enough position to negotiate a wage increase as big as or higher than inflation they will be worse off. For example, if inflation is 3% and employees only receive a 1% pay increase this means they will be worse off in terms of what they can afford to buy. Although employees' nominal pay has increased by 1% (i.e. the amount they actually get), their real pay has decreased—this is because they have less purchasing power. Real income shows what has happened to nominal income adjusted for inflation; it shows the purchasing power of a given income.

If inflation is in the thousands of per cent or more then prices are rising at an incredible speed. This is known as hyper-inflation. In Zimbabwe in 2020 inflation reached nearly 700%!

Managers will be concerned about inflation because it will affect the price of inputs and therefore costs as well as affecting the price competitiveness of products abroad. Inflation can also erode the purchasing power of consumers if their incomes do not rise as fast; this can affect demand.

- **Deflation**

  Deflation occurs when the general level of prices is falling over a given period of time. This may be because demand is low or because costs are falling. When there is deflation customers and businesses may delay spending decisions because they want to wait for prices to fall further. This can reduce demand and cause the prices to then fall further. Deflation can, therefore, lead to a cycle of falling demand creating negative growth and

Analysing the business data 7.3

The data in Figure 1 shows the average world inflation rate since 1980.

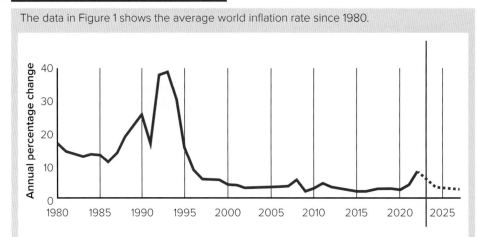

Figure 1 The average world inflation rate since 1980. *Source:* IMF. Available at: http://www.imf.org/external/datamapper/PCPIPCH@WEO/WEOWORLD [Accessed 2 April 2023].

Questions

What would you estimate the average annual inflation was between 1980 and 2021?

In what years was world inflation particularly high or low? Can you research to find out why?

What would you do?

Inflation is expected to reach 3% a year but demand for your products is very price elastic. How might this affect your business?

What actions might your human resources team have to take?

Key concepts

Inflation measures the rate of increase in the general price level over a period of time.

Deflation measures the rate of decrease in the general price level over a period of time.

high levels of unemployment in the economy. Deflation has been a problem in Japan in recent years.

- **Interest rates**

  An interest rate is the reward paid to those who are saving in a financial institution such as a bank. For example, if the interest rate for savers is 3% a year this means that if you deposit $100 in a bank you will receive $103 12 months later.

The interest rate is also a charge made to those who borrow money. For example, if the interest rate to borrowers is 4% a year this means that if you borrow $100 you will have to repay $104 a year later. Financial institutions, such as banks, offer an interest rate to attract savings; they then charge borrowers a higher interest rate and this is how they make a profit.

A low interest rate means that it is cheaper for households and businesses to borrow money. This is likely to encourage borrowing leading to more consumer spending and business investment. Lower interest rates are likely, therefore, to increase the demand in the economy (called 'aggregate demand'). This increase in aggregate demand should boost the output and growth of the economy provided the capacity exists to produce more.

By contrast, a higher interest rate makes it expensive to borrow and more attractive to save money. This is likely to decrease spending in the economy thereby reducing aggregate demand.

Between 2008 and 2020 interest rates in many countries were set at a low rate by many governments or their central banks in order to encourage borrowing and spending. This is because the uncertainty following the global financial crisis of 2008 and then later the effect of coronavirus in 2020 had led to low levels of demand around the world. In 2022 interest rates in many countries increased to limit the growing rates of inflation.

- **Exchange rates**

    An exchange rate is the price of one currency in terms of another—for example, the price of one US dollar in terms of Chinese yuan. There are, of course, many different exchange rates for any one currency, such as the dollar against the euro, the dollar against the pound, and the dollar against the yen.

    If the value of one currency decreases in terms of another, e.g. if the price of £1 falls to 7 yuan instead of 8 yuan, the pound is said to have got weaker or depreciated in value.

    If the value of one currency increases in terms of another, e.g. if the price of £1 rises to 9 yuan instead of 8 yuan, it is said to have got stronger or appreciated in value.

    If a currency appreciates this means that it is more expensive in terms of another currency. All other things unchanged, an appreciation of a currency means a country's products abroad would be more expensive in the other currency. This is likely to reduce the demand for them reducing the sales abroad (known as 'exports'). If the exchange rate increases from £1 to 8 yuan to £1 to 9 yuan then a £100 product in the UK now sells for 900 yuan not 800 yuan, all other things remaining unchanged.

What would you do?

The interest rate in your country has just fallen. Would you use this as an opportunity to borrow to expand your hotel business?

Think about it

If the gearing ratio of a business is high does this make changes in interest rates more or less significant? Why?

At the same time a stronger currency means that products from abroad (which are known as 'imports') will be cheaper in the domestic currency. For example, if the exchange rate increases from £1 to 8 yuan to £1 to 9 yuan then a 720 yuan product would have cost £90 but now will cost £80, all other things remaining unchanged. This reduces costs if the imports are inputs into the transformation process. This can lead to higher profit margins or may enable the business to cut prices. However, lower import prices can also make it more difficult for domestic producers to compete against international rivals in the local market as they may be relatively more expensive against cheaper foreign products.

A strong currency is, therefore, likely to lead to fewer exports and more imports into the country. This may lead to a trade deficit where the spending on imports is greater than the earnings from exports in a given period. By comparison, a weaker currency is likely to lead to more exports—because the country's products will be cheaper in foreign currency—and fewer imports because imports will be more expensive.

The extent to which currencies can change over time can be seen in Analysing the Business Data 7.4 where we examine the value of the pound against the dollar and the dollar against the renminbi.

Key concepts

The interest rate is the price of money; it is the cost of borrowing and the reward for saving.

Inflation occurs when there is a sustained increase in the general level of prices.

Real income shows what has happened to nominal income adjusted for inflation.

An **interest rate** is the reward paid to those who are saving in a financial institution such as a bank and the cost of borrowing.

The **exchange rate** is the price of one currency in terms of another.

Exports are products sold abroad.

Imports are products bought from abroad.

What would you do?

Your business sells furniture in your own country. It imports materials from abroad.

The exchange rate of your country has fallen significantly in the last few months and is expected to remain low in the foreseeable future.

What changes might you want to make within your business as a result?

Analysing the business data 7.4

The data in Figure 1 shows the value of the pound against the dollar over the last few years.

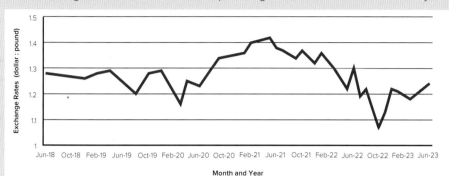

Figure 1 The value of the pound against the dollar. *Source:* British pound to US Dollar Exchange Rate Chart (no date) XE. Available at: https://www.xe.com/currencycharts/?from=GB-P&to=USD&view=5Y [Accessed 21 June 2023]. Adapted by the author.

The data in Figure 2 shows the value of the dollar against the Chinese renminbi over the last few years.

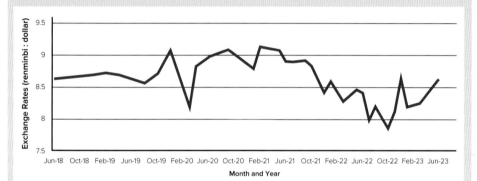

Figure 2 The value of the dollar against the renminbi. *Source:* British pound to Chinese yuan renminbi Exchange Rate Chart (no date) XE. Available at: https://www.xe.com/currency-charts/?from=GBP&to=CNY&view=5Y [Accessed 21 June 2023]. Adapted by the author.

Questions

Summarize what has happened to the pound in terms of the US dollar and Chinese yuan renminbi over the period shown above.

Explain how these changes might affect a UK business.

Where are we now?

So far, we have examined some economic factors that will affect business decision-making. Some of the effects of economic change are shown in Table 7.4. We now consider some of the economic policies used by governments to try and influence the economy.

Table 7.4 The impact of economic change on business

Economic change	Potential impact on the business
Higher national income	More demand for normal products, especially those that are income elastic
High inflation	May lead to higher costs; if these are passed on this may reduce demand and international competitiveness
Lower interest rates	Reduce the cost of borrowing making investment more affordable
Stronger exchange rate	Increases prices overseas of products (assuming all other factors remain unchanged); reduces domestic price of imports

7.3.1 Government economic policy

A government will have various policy instruments it can use to influence an economy. These include fiscal and monetary policy measures.

Fiscal policy involves using changes in government spending, taxation rates, and the benefit system to influence the demand and supply in the economy. For example, an increase in government spending will boost demand in the economy. Following the fall in spending when the coronavirus pandemic affected economies around the world many governments introduced major spending programmes to try and maintain demand. A decrease in income tax will increase the income households have to spend. A decrease in corporation tax means the company keeps more profits for investment or to pay to investors to spend. The government's budget position measures the difference between its spending and its revenue over a given period. When a government is using an expansionist fiscal policy its spending is likely to be greater than its revenue which means the government will have a budget deficit.

Monetary policy involves using interest rates to influence the borrowing in the economy. As we have seen, lower interest rates make it cheaper for businesses and households to borrow money. This is likely to increase spending by consumers and more investment by businesses.

Government policy can aim to affect the aggregate demand in the economy and the total output of products (called aggregate supply).

Aggregate demand is made up of:

C: this represents the consumption spending by households
+
I: this represents the investment spending by businesses
+
G: this represents the injection of government spending over and above the tax revenue taken out of the economy
+
X: this represents export spending, i.e. spending on a country's goods and services from abroad
−M: this represents the spending on imports, i.e. spending on goods and services overseas. This represents spending that leaves the economy which is why it is deducted from the other spending.

This means the total demand in an economy can be given by the equation:

$$AD = C + I + G + X - M$$

Government policy instruments can affect businesses in numerous ways. Examples include the impact of government policy on businesses as a result of changes in

- Corporation tax. This affects the proportion of profits a business can retain. Lower corporation taxes mean businesses have more of their own funds to finance investment.

- Business rates. These will affect the costs of operating. They represent a tax on property. With lower rates the profits of operating increase making it more feasible for businesses to open and run facilities.

- Interest rates. With lower interest rates this makes it cheaper to borrow and repay loans; this should encourage investment.

- Government spending can create more demand for goods and services in the economy.

Government policy will also influence the state of consumer and business confidence. If businesses think that the government is taking appropriate actions to encourage growth this will stimulate investment.

Government policy can also include trade agreements. We examine the impact of these on business next.

Global trade agreements

The ease with which businesses can trade abroad will be influenced by government policy. A government that believes in free trade will aim to make it easy to move goods, services, people, and money between countries. By contrast, a government that is protectionist will try to limit trade to protect its own domestic businesses. Protectionist measures include tariffs, which are taxes placed on foreign products, and quotas, which limit the number of foreign goods and services allowed into a country.

Trade and open markets allow businesses access to suppliers and markets all over the world. Greater freedom of trade in the last fifty years has led to businesses to be far more global in terms of where they buy components and materials, where they produce, and where they sell. This can lead to more choice when it comes to buying supplies and more markets to sell to when it comes to marketing activities.

The World Trade Organization (WTO) is a global international organization that deals with the rules of trade between nations. Its goal is to help producers of goods and services, exporters, and importers to reduce protectionism.

Examples of trading areas which are designed to encourage trade between member countries include:

- The Association of Southeast Asian Nations (ASEAN). The members of ASEAN are Brunei, Cambodia, Indonesia, Laos, Malaysia, Myanmar, the Philippines, Singapore, Thailand, and Vietnam.

- The African Continental Free Trade Area (AfCFTA) agreement. This is the largest free trade area in the world measured by the number of countries participating. The agreement covers 1.3 billion people across 55 countries.

- Mercosur. This is a South American trading bloc whose members are Argentina, Brazil, Paraguay, and Uruguay.

Key concepts

Fiscal policy involves using changes in government spending, taxation rates and the benefit system to influence the demand and supply in the economy.

Monetary policy involves using interest rates to influence the borrowing in the economy.

The **government's budget position** measures the difference between its spending and its revenue over a given period.

Protectionism involves policies by a government to protect domestic businesses from foreign competition.

Tariffs are taxes on foreign goods and services.

Quotas are limits on the number of foreign goods and services allowed into a country.

The relationship between a country and the rest of the world is subject to political change. For example, under President Trump the US pursued policies that protected US producers and introduced taxes on a number of Chinese products. In 2020 the United Kingdom left the European Union which changed some of the terms of trade between the UK and the trading bloc.

Can you now answer this question from the introductory case study?

Analyse two economic factors that might affect Ford's success.

Where are we now?

We have now analysed aspects of the political and economic environments as part of PEST analysis. Next, we consider the social environment of business.

7.4   The social environment

The social environment of business refers to the nature of the society in the markets in which a business operates. The social environment includes demographic factors and social values.

7.4.1 Demographic factors

Demographics refer to the study of the population of a country and includes factors such as the size of its population, the average family size, the age distribution, and composition in terms of gender and race.

The size of the population is affected by the birth rate in the country, the death rate, and net migration. Net migration measures the difference between emigration (which is the number of people leaving a country in a given time period) and immigration (those coming into a country.)

In the 1960s world population growth peaked at 2.1% a year; since then the growth rate of the world population has been declining. This decline in global population growth has been due to factors including:

- Falling fertility rates. As countries get richer there tends to be more birth control and lower birth rates.

- Government policies; for example, China's 'One Child Policy' had an effect on global population growth.

- Urbanization; there have been major movements from the countryside to cities in many countries in recent years. Those who live in the city tend to have fewer children.

The demographic structure of a population will affect the levels of demand for different products. For example, the age structure will affect the demand for housing, education, and medical care. Demographics will also affect the size and composition of the workforce which can affect how easy it is for business to recruit.

Despite a slowing growth rate the world's population is still projected to rise by more than 1 billion by 2030, to over eight billion. Almost all (97%) of this growth in the population will come from emerging or developing countries. This will affect the countries that businesses want to target and where they will recruit. Changes in the world's population can be seen in Analysing the Business Data 7.5.

One significant feature of demographic change is the increasing proportion of the older age groups within many populations. With longer life expectancy and people having fewer children, the fastest growing segment of the population is the over 65s—there will be 390 million more people in this age group in 2030 than in 2015. With an ageing population the dependency ratio is increasing. The dependency ratio measures the number of dependents aged 0 to 14 and over the age of 65, compared with the total population aged 15 to 65. With a higher dependency ratio there is likely to be an increase in demand for healthcare for the older population. This can be expensive for a government; it also potentially means there are fewer people working and more people receiving government benefits and pensions in Europe, Asia, and Latin America. In Asia, for example, there have been around nine people of working age to support each elderly person on average in recent years. By 2050 that ratio will fall to around four people. In Europe, it will be two. This can put a strain on a government's resources because it is paying more benefits. It also means that those working are likely to be taxed more to pay for those who are retired.

The impact of an ageing population is on businesses as well as governments. Businesses may struggle with their financial commitments if they are committed to paying past employees' pensions if employees live a lot longer than originally expected. In addition, an ageing population can create labour shortages unless managers develop appropriate recruitment policies to respond to the changing labour market. For example, businesses may

Key concepts

Demographics refers to the study of the population and includes factors such as its size, composition, family size, age, and gender and race composition.

Net migration measures the difference between emigration and immigration.

want to focus on increasing participation in the workforce by women and older people. To attract older people this might require the business to offer more flexible working patterns and be prepared to invest in training and development. To encourage women to come back into the labour market may require more support from the business with child care and attractive pay and working options. Greater participation from these groups can help to increase the workforce and offset a potential threat to the supply of labour. It also provides greater opportunity through diversity.

The differences between the demographic changes that are happening in different countries are quite noteworthy and are very important in terms of business strategic planning. According to the World Economic Forum (2020), the fastest growing region of the world is going to be Africa; its population is set to double by 2050. By comparison, Europe's population is projected to shrink. The average age in Japan in 2050 will be 53; in Nigeria it is likely to be 23. Changes in the age structure in different regions of the world are shown in Figure 1 in Analysing the Business Data 7.6.

All of these demographic changes create opportunities and threats; whether they are an opportunity or threat depends a great deal on how managers respond to them.

Social factors also include the values of society as well as demographic factors; these values will affect what customers, employees, and investors think is important and how they respond to business activities. These values will affect the demand for different products and also the willingness and desire of employees to work in certain sectors and or certain employees.

7.4.2 Social values

Social values are often linked to a particular age group. Many businesses are now aware of the values and attitudes of Generation Z (Gen Zs); this refers to the people born between 1995 and 2010. This group are known as 'digital natives'—this is because they have been using the internet, social media, and mobile technology all their lives.

Think about it

How might these demographic changes affect the human resource and marketing functions?

Key concept

The dependency ratio measures the number of dependents aged zero to 14 and over the age of 65, compared with the total population aged 15 to 65.

What would you do?

You want to attract more older people to come and work in your supermarket chain. How would you do this?

You want to attract more women back into your workforce to come and work in your supermarket. How would you do it?

Analysing the business data 7.5

The data in Figures 1 and 2 show the growth in the population of the world since 1750 and the trend in that growth since 1980.

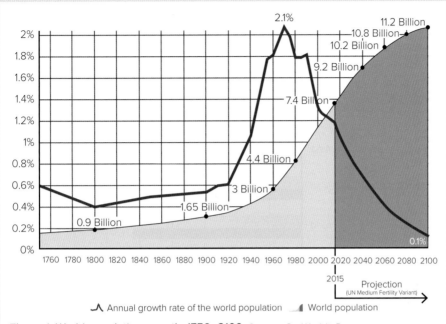

Figure 1 World population growth, 1750–2100. *Source:* OurWorldinData.org.

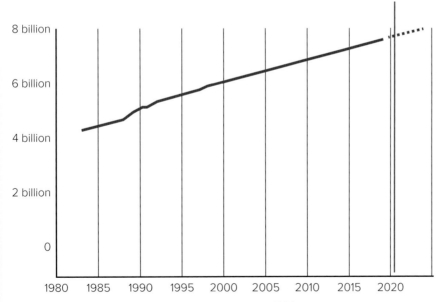

Figure 2 The trend of the world's population since 1980. *Source:* OurWorldinData.org.

Questions

What is the trend in terms of the world's population since 1980? Can you explain this trend?

What do you think the impact of this trend will be on businesses?

7

Analysing the business data 7.6

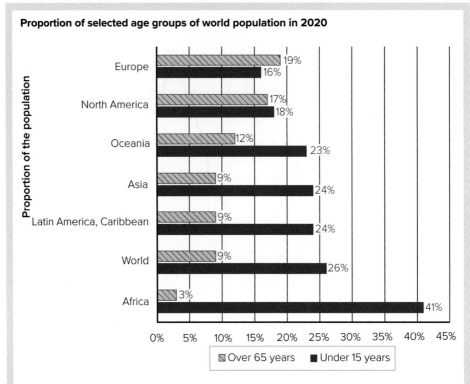

Proportion of selected age groups of world population in 2020

Figure 1 The proportion of selected age groups in world population 2020. *Source:*
Published by Statista Research Department and 20, O. (2022) World population by age and region
2022, Statista. Available at: https://www.statista.com/statistics/265759/world-population-by-age-
and-region/ [Accessed 2 April 2023].

Question

Discuss the significance of the above data for businesses operating in these different
regions.

The characteristics of Generation Zs include:

- They value individual expression and dislike being labelled. An example of this is
  gender fluidity; Generation Zs do not like to be defined. However, Gen Zs do defend
  the rights of individuals to be themselves. They are more interested than previous
  generations have been in human rights; in matters related to race and ethnicity; in
  lesbian, gay, bisexual, and transgender issues, and in feminism.

- They are concerned about ethical issues and the values an organization represents.

- They value online communities because they allow everyone to connect.

- They want access to products or services but not necessarily to own them. For example,
  they are keen to use car-riding services and video streaming services. This affects how
  businesses might want to operate. Car manufacturers, for example, are increasingly

renting out vehicles directly to consumers. Instead of selling many cars they may now 'sell the services' of one car many times over, so that instead of selling 1000 cars, these companies may sell one car 1000 times.

An important part of life for Generation Zs is the importance of showing their individual identity. Consumption is a way that they can express themselves as opposed to buying or wearing brands to be part of a group. Generation Zs want more personalized products and are willing to pay a premium for products that highlight their individuality.

Generation Zs are also attracted by brands that seem to have a view and take a stand. Generation Zs look at the brand, the company's behaviour, and also who it works with as partners and suppliers. For a Generation Z, a company's actions must match its stated values, and these values must be reflected in all its actions with stakeholders.

Social changes in recent years include a growing concern for environmental issues in many societies and greater interest in how businesses are responding to this. Customers, employees, investors, and the media are all focusing more on where businesses source their products, how they produce them, what packaging is used, and how customers can dispose of products with minimum environmental impact. This social change has affected the behaviour of existing businesses whilst creating new market opportunities for others.

One issue that been particularly high profile as a social concern is climate change. Without significant action by consumers, businesses, and governments across the world, it is estimated that average temperatures across the world will increase by more than two degrees Celsius. If this does happen it is likely that it will create irreversible changes to the environment. Amongst these changes are rising sea levels. This would see significant parts of land such as the east coast of China submerged under water. By the end of this century it is possible that up to 200 million people could have to leave the place where they are currently living because it will be under water.

Greater understanding of the dangers of climate change have led to political agreements about the need for action in this area; this puts pressure on businesses to change. The Paris Agreement in December 2015 involved governments from around the world agreeing to take the steps required to limit increased global warming to an average of two degrees. The 193 member states of the United Nations adopted the Sustainable Development Goals (SDGs) in 2015. These set 17 goals for sustainable economic development, covering a wide range of activities and their impacts across key areas including economic development, climate change, environmental improvement, water quality, and urban development. Climate change is also linked with the growing pressure on resources due to the world's increasing population.

What would you do?

You are the Marketing Manager of a clothes brand. You feel the business has not paid enough attention to the Generation Z target group. You are due to give a presentation in how targeting this segment might affect your business. What would you say?

Key concept

Generation Z (Gen Zs). This refers to the people born between 1995 and 2010.

What would you do?

You are the Chief Executive of a global hotel business.

What would you do to ensure your business responded appropriately to the growing environmental awareness in society?

Can you now answer this question from the introductory case study?

What social factors might affect Ford's success?

Where are we now?

So far, we have considered aspects of political, economic, and social change as part of PEST analysis. We now consider the impact of technological change.

7.5 Technological change

Technological change is a key part of business life. Technological changes have created new ways of reaching customers, new markets, and new ways of working. Consider how the internet has transformed many industries—for example, the computer games industry, the television and film industry, and the music streaming industry. It is amazing to think that the world wide web was only created in 1990. Just think how businesses and all our lives

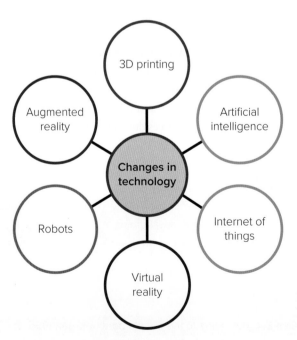

Figure 7.5 Examples of changes in the technological environment. *Source:* Author.

have been revolutionized in less than 40 years. Spotify was established in 2006; 14 years later it had 180m users, including 83m subscribers, across 65 markets. By 2020 Netflix had 130 million members in over 190 countries watching streamed TV series, documentaries, and feature films. Whole industries that did not exist 20 years ago, such as computer games, have been created by technological change and how items are produced, how information is collected and managed, and how we purchase and receive products are continually changing. Examples of technological change can be seen in Figure 7.5; these changes create new marketing opportunities but also affect all the other functions of a business. These technological changes were examined in detail in Chapter 4 on Operations.

Business insight 7.3 Moore's Law

Gordon Moore, a co-founder of the technology company Intel, predicted that the number of transistors incorporated in a chip would approximately double every 24 months. This has become known as Moore's Law. According to Intel this 'law' describes the basic business model for the semiconductor industry. Intel, through investments in technology and manufacturing, has made Moore's Law a reality (Figure 1). As the scale of transistors gets ever smaller Intel expects to continue to deliver on Moore's prediction well into the foreseeable future by using an entirely new transistor formula that alleviates wasteful electricity leaks creating more energy-efficient processors.

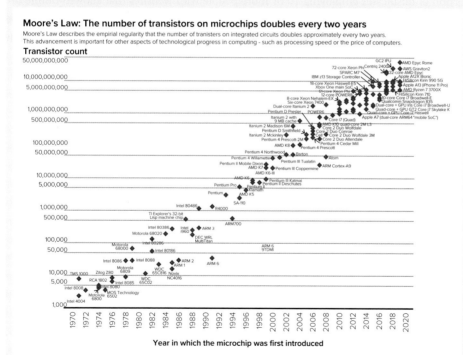

Figure 1 A logarithmic graph showing the timeline of how transistor counts in microchips are almost doubling every two years from 1970 to 2020; Moore's Law. *Source:* ourworldindata.org; Max Roser, Hannah Ritchie.

Question

What do you think are the implications of Moore's Law for business?

One of the ways in which the rate of change in technology is changing society is its impact on the way we communicate; this has been quite dramatic. It took 76 years for half of the homes in the US to have a telephone. The smartphone achieved the same household penetration in less than a decade. There are now estimated to be around seven times the number of connected devices as there are people on the planet. And these technological developments in communication change the business environment and business activities. For example, social media used to be an opportunity for friends to share stories—now it provides a powerful scrutiny of the actions of a business and is a highly influential marketing tool. Greater connectivity also brings increased vulnerability for businesses. Connecting devices makes them accessible to hacking and cyberattack; this is a major concern for many organizations and digital security is a critical business issues these days.

As ever in business change creates threats and opportunities. The threats from technological change are sometimes to those well-established businesses. Technology creates the chance for new businesses to create new models and new ways of doing things that can challenge the established models—think of AirBnB, Spotify, and Uber. This creates problems for businesses that do not adapt or make use of the opportunities that exist. Many retailers that have physical stores have found that customers have switched to online buying and have either had to close the stores or change them—for example, moving to offering click and collect.

Of course, the impact of technological change varies from business to business, industry to industry, and country to country. For example, according to the OECD, in 2019 the proportion of businesses employing 10 or more people with websites that allowed online ordering or reservations ranged from over 33% in Denmark to less than 8% in Turkey. The proportion of businesses using social media in the same year ranged from over 76% in Norway to under 37% in Poland.

Business insight 7.4 Disney

For many businesses the coronavirus pandemic of 2020 was a disaster. Businesses were closed overnight as people were forced to stay at home. However, for Disney the timing coincided with the launch of its streaming service in Europe in March 2020. With people stuck indoors the option of Disney on demand was very attractive. Disney reached more than 50 million subscribers in the first five months after it was launched. Disney originally set a target of 60 million to 90 million subscribers by the end of fiscal year 2024, when it was first launched in the US in November 2019. With no cinemas open and people not allowed to leave their homes in many countries streaming services were booming. In April Disney launched in India and gained 8 million subscribers in its first week. By comparison Netflix had over 167 million paying subscribers globally. Amazon had 150 million viewers at the time.

Disney's offer includes films and TV shows from Disney, Pixar, Star Wars, and National Geographic, and has achieved numbers that took Netflix five to seven years to acquire. Technology meant that the pandemic was a business opportunity for Disney.

Questions

Technology has completely changed the way we consume television and film content. What other industries can you think of where technology has changed the way businesses do business?

Source

www.bbc.co.uk/news/business-52211207

Business insight 7.5 Lego

In its annual report in 2019 Lego's managers claimed that they had managed to stay ahead of key trends such as e-commerce, digitalization, and global socio-economic shifts which they say are reshaping the toy sector.

Lego says that digitalization is changing the way people shop and also how people play. This creates the opportunity for Lego to bring together digital and physical play. It calls this 'fluid play'. For example, in 2019, the company launched LEGO® Hidden to integrate building and augmented reality. Lego has also invested in digital marketing and has adapted to the fact that roughly a third of all toys are now bought online.

Lego has also:

- Upgraded its e-commerce platform and opened almost 150 branded stores around the world, ending 2019 with 570 stores.

- Continued to expand overseas. In 2019, China continued to be a growth priority. Lego invested in building its brand presence and geographical reach and ended the year with 140 stores in 35 cities. It strengthened its partnership with local partners to broaden its reach on e-commerce and digital platforms. By 2032, 90% of the world's two billion children will live outside Europe and North America, with more than three quarters of these living in Eastern Asia. As a result, the company is stepping up investment in the growth markets of tomorrow.

Question

How have changes in the external environment affected Lego?

Source

www.lego.com/cdn/cs/aboutus/assets/blt55a9aaa4253b2fa5/Annual_Report_2019_ENG.pdf.pdf

Think about it

Can you think of examples of how technology is affecting the marketing, operations, finance, and human resource functions of a business?

Can you now answer this question from the introductory case study?

What technological factors might affect Ford's success?

Where are we now?

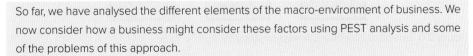

So far, we have analysed the different elements of the macro-environment of business. We now consider how a business might consider these factors using PEST analysis and some of the problems of this approach.

7.6 Undertaking PEST analysis effectively

PEST analysis occurs when managers consider the key macro-external factors in their business environment and how these factors might develop in the future. Managers gather data in many ways: for example, they watch trends in their markets, talk to experts, analyse market research, and listen to their customers. The changes happening in the outside world are then categorized under the headings Political/Legal, Economic, Social, and Technological factors, i.e. PEST factors.

The PEST framework is just that—a framework to help organize ideas. There are other versions of PEST—for example, managers may include Environmental factors as an additional heading and sometimes Legal is given a separate heading so this could become PESTLE analysis.

However, simply identifying factors in the external environment is not enough. Managers must make judgements about how significant they are for their business. The factors need to be ranked in terms of their relative importance so that planning can be focused around the key ones. Managers must use their judgement to prioritize the different factors based on the likelihood of them occurring and the impact on the business if they do.

Having identified the most critical factors in the macro-envrionment and also in the competitive environment, managers can compare these with the internal position of the business. Considering external changes and internal strengths and weaknesses should allow managers to identify opportunities and threats. These factors combine as part of a SWOT analysis (comparing internal Strengths and Weaknesses and external Opportunities and Threats) which should shape any strategy being developed.

A strategy is a long-term plan to achieve the objectives of the business. Its sets out the direction of the organization. Out of the overall corporate (business) strategy the different functional areas can determine their own plans and develop their functional strategies. This process of strategic planning is shown in Figure 7.6.

This process will be examined in more detail in the following chapter on strategic planning.

PEST analysis needs to be an ongoing process. External conditions can change rapidly: think about the sudden unexpected impact of 9/11, the speed with which the global recession of 2008 took effect, the effect of the Russian invasion of Ukraine in 2022, and the shutdown of businesses due to the COVID-19 virus in 2020, all of which would have been unimaginable only a few weeks before. It is important to keep revisiting the PEST framework and reviewing earlier judgements.

Figure 7.6 Business objectives linked to strategy. *Source:* Author.

7.6.1 Difficulties undertaking PEST analysis

There are some typical problems with undertaking PEST analysis that managers should be aware of:

- The quality of the information. The quality of the final decision made and strategy chosen will depend on the quality of the information available to make it. In computing there is a phrase GIGO (Garbage in, garbage out); if your information is poor, it's likely your decision will be as well!

- The composition and skills of the group of decision-makers. The quality of the decision will depend on who is making that decision. Often when bad decisions are made it is because those involved do not have the right combination of skills or experience to make it. Find a successful business and you will find a strong management team with the right mix of skills between them. The same is true of an outstanding hospital or school. One problem that can exist with a management team is that they all see things through a particular lens and are not open to different views. This can occur because managers are too similar in their thinking and do not challenge each other enough. They like each other because they think the same but this does not mean they make good decisions. In 1972 Irving Janis wrote about group-think and how it can lead to disastrous decisions. According to Janis group-think stands for an excessive desire amongst group members to conform and they come to value being part of the group more than making the right decision. With group-think people suppress any personal doubts because they don't want to upset the group as a whole. Another reason for poor decisions by a management team is that managers may have been successful with one approach in one environment and are slow to appreciate, and potentially reluctant, to appreciate that the world has moved on. Kodak used to dominate the sales of photographic film. Its senior managers built their careers on success in the film industry. Perhaps not surprisingly, they did not necessarily have the experience or willingess to appreciate that digital photography would destroy the industry as they had understood it. The same thing is happening with the collapse of the traditional petrol or diesel engine in the car industry as electric cars seize market share at a pace. It would not be surprising if some traditional manufacturers are slow to act when change is coming from new businesses and a technology that is developed outide of their industry.

Whilst the process of PEST analysis may seem simple, and indeed the technique is fairly straightforward, the difficulty lies in correctly identifying the key factors in the environment, correcty weighing up their relative importance, correctly choosing the strategy required, and correctly implementing it. That's a lot to get right and provides many opportunities to get it wrong! Too often we look back at a poor strategy and struggle to understand how a business could get it so wrong without appreciating the challenges at the time, identifying what did and did not matter, and then making the right choices.

Can you now answer this question from the introductory case study?

How might PEST analysis determine Ford's future strategy?

Now you should know

- A command or planned economy involves goods and services provided by the state.

- A free market involves goods and services provided by privately owned businesses.

- Redundancy occurs when an individual loses his or her job because it no longer exists.

- Trade unions are organizations that represent the rights of employees.

- A monopoly occurs when a business dominates a market—usually this means its sales have more than 25% market share.

- A cartel occurs when businesses collude together to fix prices or output.

- GDP measures the total value of the income earned within a country in a given period, usually a year.

- A recession occurs when there is negative income growth in an economy for six months or more.

- Income elastic demand occurs when a given percentage change in income leads to a more than proportionate change in demand, all other factors remaining unchanged.

- Income inelastic demand when a given percentage change in income leads to a less than proportionate change in demand, all other factors remaining unchanged.

- Normal products are products for which demand increases as income increases.

- Inferior products are products for which demand decreases as income increases.

- Inflation measures the rate of increase in the general price level over a period of time.

- Deflation measures the rate of decrease in the general price level over a period of time.

- The interest rate is the price of money; it is the cost of borrowing and the reward for saving.

- Inflation occurs when there is a sustained increase in the general level of prices.

- Real income shows what has happened to nominal income adjusted for inflation.

- The exchange rate is the price of one currency in terms of another.

- Exports are products sold abroad.

- Imports are products bought from abroad.

- Fiscal policy involves using changes in government spending, taxation rates, and the benefit system to influence the demand and supply in the economy.

- Monetary policy involves using interest rates to influence the borrowing in the economy.

- The government's budget position measures the difference between its spending and its revenue over a given period.

- Protectionism involves policies by a government to protect domestic businesses from foreign competition.

- Tariffs are taxes on foreign goods and services.

- Quotas are limits on the number of foreign goods and services allowed into a country.

- Demographics refers to the study of the population and includes factors such as its size, composition, family size, and age, gender, and race composition.

- Net migration measures the difference between emigration and immigration.

- The dependency ratio measures the number of dependents aged zero to 14 and over the age of 65, compared with the total population aged 15 to 65.

- Generation Z (Gen Zs) refers to people born between 1995 and 2010.

 ## Review questions

Quick Check

1. Identify Porter's five forces.

2. State two political factors in your country that can influence business.

3. Explain how a change in the economic environment can affect the profitability of a business.

4. Explain one social change that might affect business planning.

5. Explain how technological change can create opportunities and threats for business.

6. Explain one exanple of how external change can affect the marketing function of a business.

7. Explain one example of how external change can affect the operations function of a business.

8. Explain one example of how external change can affect the human resources function of a business.

Analysis

1 Analyse the possible impact of slow economic growth on a business.

2 Analyse the possible impact of a fall in the value of a country's currency on a business located within that country.

3 Analyse the value of PEST analysis to a business when undertaking strategic planning.

Evaluation

1. To what extent do you think the profits of a business depend on the external environment in which it operates?

2. Imagine you do a survey of the Chief Executives of the largest 100 companies in your country. What do you think are the top three items in the external environment that they are considering? Justify your choices.

∿ Find out more

- To find out more about how countries measure the welfare of their citizens you can search for search for 'Measuring Economic Well Being' to find different ways of measuring the performance of a country apart from income. The OECD and Office for National Statistics have articles on this: www.ons.gov.uk
- The UK uses a weighted index of goods and services in a 'typical' household shopping basket to measure inflation. This produces the Consumer Prices Index (CPI).
- You can find out more about how inflation is measured in the UK at the Office of National Statistics: www.ons.gov.uk
- To find out more about the concept of the circular economy you can visit The Ellen Macarthur Foundation at www.ellenmacarthurfoundation.org/
- You can find out more about the work of the World Trade Organization at www.wto.org
- You can watch Michael Porter's classic explanation of his five forces theory on You Tube. Search for Michael Porter 'The five forces that shape competitive strategy'.
- You can find out a huge amount of data about countries at the World Bank, International Monetary Fund, and OECD websites. You can find their websites at www.worldbank.org, www.imf.org and data.oecd

Where are we now?

In this chapter we have analysed the competitive and macro-environments of business. This external analysis is part of the process of strategic planning. In the next chapter we analyse how a business combines internal and external analysis to identify a potential strategy.

☰ Bibliography

World Economic Forum (2020). *Africa's population will triple by the end of the century even as the rest of the world shrinks*. Available at: https://www.weforum.org/agenda/2020/07/africa-population-triple [Accessed 27 October 2023].

Annualreports.com (2020a). www.annualreports.com/HostedData/AnnualReportArchive/f/NYSE_F_2021.pdf

Annualreports.com (2021b). [online] Available at: <https://www.annualreports.com/HostedData/AnnualReports/PDF/NASDAQ_FB_2020.pdf> [Accessed 2 April 2021].

Desjardins, J. (2020). *The World Population Pyramid (1950–2100)*. [online] Visual Capitalist. Available at: <https://www.visualcapitalist.com/world-population-pyramid-1950-2100/> [Accessed 29 December 2020].

Natixis (2019). Global Retirement Index: An in-depth assessment of welfare in retirement around the world. https://www.im.natixis.com/us/resources/global-%20retirement-index-2019-report.

OECD (n.d.). OECD statistics. Retrieved 4 April 2021, from https://stats.oecd.org/

Porter, M. E. (1979). How Competitive Forces Shape Strategy. *Harvard Business Review*, 57(2) (March–April), 137–145.

Porter, M. (1985). Competitive Advantage: Creating and Sustaining Superior Performance. New York: The Free Press

PwC (2019). 22nd Annual Global CEO Survey: CEOs' curbed confidence spells caution, https://www.pwc.com/gx/en/ceo-survey/2019/report/pwc-22nd-annual-global-ceo-survey.pdf

PwC (2019). New world. New skills. https://www.pwc.com/gx/en/issues/upskilling.html

Rankings (n.d.). Retrieved 3 April 2021 from http://www.doingbusiness.org/en/rankings

Schwab, K. (2019). Global Competitiveness Report 2019: How to end a lost decade of productivity growth, World Economic Forum, https://www.weforum.org/reports/how-to-end-a-decade-of-lost-productivity-growth.

Statista (2021). *World population by age and region 2020*. [online] Available at: <https://www.statista.com/statistics/265759/world-population-by-age-and-region/> [Accessed 2 April 2021].

The Economist (2019). Global warming 101: The past, present and future of climate change. https://www.economist.com/briefing/2019/09/21/the-past-present-and-future-of-climate-change.

World Bank (2020). Doing Business 2020. Available at: https://openknowledge.worldbank.org/entities/publication/130bd2f3-f4b5-5b77-8680-01e6d6a87222.

World Economic Forum (2020). World Economic Forum Annual Meeting 2020, http://www3.weforum.org/docs/WEF_AM20_Overview.pdf

7

Chapter 8

Business strategy

Where are we now?

In this chapter we will consider what we mean by a 'strategy' and how businesses decide on their strategies, having analysed the external and internal environment. We will consider how a business decides what products to offer, which markets to enter and how to position itself against rivals. We will also consider why strategies fail.

Why am I studying this?

- One day you hope to be in a management position. You will be given an objective and asked to produce a strategy to achieve it. This chapter will help you know how to go about deciding on your strategy.
- You read every week about some businesses succeeding and some failing because of their strategies. You want to understand why strategy matters so much.

Learning objectives

By the end of this chapter you should be able to

- Explain the meaning of strategy and the key features of a strategic decision
- Explain the elements of strategic management
- Consider how to undertake a SWOT analysis
- Analyse how to make strategic decisions
- Analyse how to choose a strategic position
- Analyse how to implement a strategy effectively
- Discuss why strategies fail

8

Introductory case study Tesla's business strategy

Tesla, based in the US, is a world-leading producer of electric cars and was established by the entrepreneur, Elon Musk. In 2006 Musk set out Tesla's strategy. He said that the initial product produced by Tesla would be a high-performance, premium-priced sportscar called the Tesla Roadster. The long-term plan, however, has always been to produce affordably priced electric cars. The overarching vision of the company is to move the world from a hydrocarbon economy towards a solar electric economy. Musk feels this is essential for the future of the planet.

Musk outlined from the beginning of Tesla that when a business develops new technology the unit cost of any product, including cars, is always very high. The only way to cover these high costs is to target the premium segment of a market—in this case by producing a sportscar and targeting the very wealthy. Over time, however, with experience and growing volumes of production the unit cost will fall and this enables lower-priced models. Eventually, when enough people switch to electric cars, the impact on the environment will be significant. The Tesla had a disruptive effect on the car industry, challenging even hybrid vehicles as being still too dependent on oil.

Therefore, from its very beginning Tesla's strategy has been:

1. build a sports car

2. use that money to build an affordable car

3. use that money to build an even more affordable car

4. while doing the above, also provide zero-emission electric power generation options.

However, whilst the strategy may be clear, the execution of it has not always been straightforward. The company has had many technical problems which have slowed production.

Tesla Roadster on the road in the Canary Islands. *Source:* Shutterstock/Mike Mareen.

For example, in 2019 Tesla began selling its Model 3 but production experienced many problems. The company was also hit by external difficulties such as strike action at the port of Zeebrugge in Belgium, which reduced exports to Europe and problems exporting into China due to problems with the labelling of certain parts.

The company has also suffered because of questions over the leadership of Musk and whether he has the right qualities to lead the business forward at this stage of its development.

Sources

www.bbc.co.uk/news/business-47817830

www.tesla.com/en_GB/blog/secret-tesla-motors-master-plan-just-between-you-and-me

Introductory case study questions

1. Tesla has a strategy. What do you think are the features of a strategic decision?
2. What factors in the external environment do you think influenced Tesla's strategy?
3. Analyse the strategic options open to Tesla using Ansoff's matrix.
4. Use the Bowman's strategy clock to analyse Tesla's strategy.
5. What problems might Tesla face when implementing its strategy?
6. Discuss the factors that you think will determine the success of this strategy.

Critical thinking

• Telsa appears to still be pursuing its original strategy. Why do you think most businesses end up changing their strategy over time?
• What would you think is the greatest threat facing Tesla?

8.1 What is strategy?

A strategy is a plan of action to achieve a given goal. The objective is the target, and the strategy is the method of achieving that target. This is shown in Figure 8.1. For any given objective there are many strategies that could be adopted to achieve it, just as there are many ways you might travel to get to a particular destination. Choosing the right strategy makes it more likely you will get to where you want to get to. The strategy of a business is crucial to its success. For example, is the business competing in the right markets with the right products? If it is, success may come. If it isn't, failure may occur.

According to Watkins (2007) a business strategy is 'a set of guiding principles that, when communicated and adopted in the organization, generates a desired pattern of

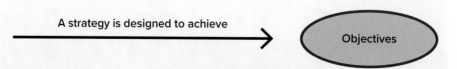

Figure 8.1 A strategy is a way of achieving the business objectives. *Source:* Author.

Key concept

A **strategy** sets out a plan to achieve the objectives of the business.

decision-making'. A strategy, therefore, affects how people throughout the organization should make decisions and allocate resources in order to accomplish its key objectives.

A strategy determines where a business is headed and how it is getting there. A strategy involves deciding where to compete, with what, how to do it, and what to use.

The highly respected management writer Michael Porter (2008) stressed that businesses will want to find a way of getting to their destination that is better than their rivals. Porter wrote about the importance of choosing a strategy that is competitive. This means that the strategy of a business determines how it is different from rivals; it involves 'deliberately choosing a different set of activities to deliver a unique mix of value'. This view of strategy stresses the need to make decisions that ensure the business is competitive relative to rivals.

An effective strategy provides a clear map of the way ahead for the business. It consists of a set of guiding principles or rules; these principles should define the actions that people in the business should take (and not take) and the things that they should prioritize (and not prioritize) to achieve the desired targets.

Diageo is a global drinks business. Its brands include J&B and Johnnie Walker Scotch whisky, Smirnoff vodka, Captain Morgan rum, Gordon's gin, and Guinness beer. In a recent annual report Diageo outlined its business strategy:

> The global spirits category has shown resilient, long-term growth. This is being driven by population and income growth, and the increasing penetration of spirits around the world. Our strategy is to support premiumisation in developed and emerging countries. Our broad portfolio means we can access different consumer occasions with our brands, across price points. In developed markets, we support premiumisation through our premium core and reserve brands. These enable consumers to trade up into luxury categories. In emerging markets, we aim to grow participation in international premium spirits. To support this, we participate in mainstream spirits so consumers can access our brands at affordable price points. This also enables us to shape responsible drinking trends in markets where international premium spirits is an emerging category.

Diageo is, therefore, very clear about the external factors driving growth in the spirits market such as population and income growth. It is also clear what its strategy is in this market—namely, to focus on getting people to trade up to its premium brands. People may not be drinking more but Diageo wants them to spend more when they do drink. The strategy of the company is to focus on developing its premium brands with higher profit margins.

In this chapter we will consider the features of a strategic decision compared to other more routine decisions and why strategic decisions are so important. We will examine the elements of strategic management: this involves an analysis of how strategies might be developed if a systematic and logical approach to planning is used. This will involve an understanding of SWOT analysis.

We will then consider the strategic choices being made about which market to enter and which products to offer using the Ansoff Matrix. We will also consider what is required to implement a strategy effectively. Finally, we will consider why strategies might fail.

8

8.1.1 The features of a strategic decision

A strategic decision will include a number of different features. Understanding these features helps us to understand how significant the strategy of the business is in terms of determining its success.

According to Johnson *et al.* (2020), the features of a strategic decision are that they affect:

The long-term direction of an organization, i.e. a strategy, sets out where the business is headed. For example, the energy business BP states 'We aim to be a very different kind of energy company by 2030 as we scale up investment in low carbon, focus our oil and gas production and make headway on reducing emissions. Our strategy kickstarts a decade of delivery towards our #bpNetZero ambition.'

- The scope of an organization's operations, i.e. a strategy, sets out the markets in which a business wants to compete. For example, Accell Group focuses on bicycles, bicycle parts, and cycle accessories. Bicycle brands in its portfolio include Haibike, Winora, Ghost, Batavus, Koga, Lapierre, Raleigh, Sparta, Babboe, and Carqon. XLC is its brand for bicycle parts and accessories. The scope of Accell's operations is therefore the bicycle market and not, for example, the scooter or skateboard market.

- Gaining an advantage over competitors, i.e. the strategy shows the competitive advantage the business will have. For example, Caterpillar, a leading manufacturer of construction and mining equipment, places a heavy emphasis on the services it provides once customers have bought its equipment. This covers everything from parts to maintenance to finance. Caterpillar regards the quality of its service as a competitive advantage.

- Addressing changes that occur in the business environment, i.e. a strategy must respond to external change. For example, H&M clothing closed over 1800 stores and invested heavily in its digital platforms during the pandemic of 2020 and 2021.

- Building on the resources and competences (capability) of the business, i.e. the strategy needs to be linked to what the business is good at.

- Meeting the values and expectations of stakeholders, i.e. the strategy must be informed by what stakeholders want. For example, in Japan the business philosophy of 'three way good' (for buyers, sellers, and society) is strong; this means that there is a greater expectation that businesses should act in the public interest than in many other countries.

- The nature of strategic decisions, as shown by the features above, means that they are likely to be complex in nature. They are not routine decisions that will have been made many times before. A strategic decision will be unusual and involve many different people and resources. A strategic decision is unlikely to be clear cut; it will have far reaching, long-term effects and some of the factors involved or the consequences of the actions taken will be unknown.

Strategies will also be difficult to reverse. Once a decision has been made and actions taken to put it into effect it will not be easy to turn it around. It is not easy to reallocate resources and funds once they are committed. For example, in 2021 both Panasonic and Hitachi committed billions of dollars to move their businesses into the growth areas of digital

Think about it

What sorts of decisions have you taken that have the characteristics of a strategic decision?

software. This was to reduce their reliance on their core business area of consumer electronic hardware because this sector has been growing slowly. Panasonic paid $7.1bn for Blue Yonder, a supply chain software specialist, and Hitachi paid $9.5bn for Global Logic, a Silicon Valley software engineering company. These strategic decisions are clearly very expensive and cannot easily be changed once made—they represent a major commitment by the buyers.

These features of strategic decisions highlight how important they are and how difficult they can be to bring about successfully. Not surprisingly then, strategic decisions are linked to the role of senior rather than junior managers. They are major, high-risk decisions that will affect the long-term competitiveness and success of the business.

Can you now answer this question from the introductory case study?

Tesla has a strategy. What do you think are the features of a strategic decision?

Where are we now?

We have already discovered that an organization's strategy can be complex, and involve several different features. We now consider why strategic decisions are often difficult to make.

8.1.2   Why are strategic decisions difficult to make?

Strategic decisions are difficult to make because they are not 'everyday' decisions. They are, by definition, major, high risk, and new. Examples of strategic decisions might be entering a new market, developing a new product, or taking over a competitor. Strategic decisions involve high levels of risk and uncertainty. When making this type of decision, managers cannot just rely on experience, or 'what worked last time', because each situation will be different. A significant amount of research and data gathering is usually involved when an organization sets its strategy. Think about the type of decisions you make: deciding whether you want to make a cup of tea of coffee in the morning is relatively straightforward because it is a decision you take every day. However, when you were deciding which course and university to apply for you probably took quite a long time and did quite a lot of research. This is because it is such a big decision which you won't have made before and which will have a very significant impact on your life. That is the difference between a 'routine' and a 'strategic' decision. An example of a strategic decision is shown in Business Insight 8.1.

A strategic decision is likely to face resistance from key stakeholders because they will be affected by the change. Strategic change will suit some stakeholders because they may gain from it, but because strategic decisions involve such considerable changes, some individuals and groups are likely to resist—this is because of the potential impact on their status, their rewards, and their power. For example, let's imagine an organization's strategy is to become more digitally focused. The organization might need to implement a restructure of its staff and hire people with different skillsets to those they already employ, such as web developers. It is likely that the restructure would involve some existing staff being made redundant, and/or the roles of others being changed. But without the web developers the organization cannot succeed with its strategy to become more digitally focused.

Managers will have to be prepared to overcome such resistance to get the strategy to succeed.

Business Insight 8.1 A strategic decision to build a new shopping mall in Bangkok

The Iconsiam shopping mall was opened in 2018 in Bangkok, Thailand. It was the biggest mall in Bangkok at the time and cost $1.63bn to build. Its floor space is twice that of New York's Empire State Building. The decision to build this mall was a high-risk move, investing so much in bricks and mortar when others were focusing on online sales. Siam Piwat, the owner of Iconsiam, has three other malls already in its portfolio. This compares to 30 malls owned by its rival Central Group and 11 by The Mall Group. Siam Piwat's other malls are Siam Paragon, one of Bangkok's most successful shopping centres, and two other locations in the city's central Siam district. The family-owned company was established in 1959 and developed Thailand's first five-star hotel, the Siam Intercontinental. Siam Piwat opened its first mall in 1973. The Iconsiam is in a relatively under-developed part of the city on the western side of Bangkok. For some customers it will be a lot more convenient than the stores in the centre of the city but, at the moment the mall is 1 km from the nearest SkyTrain station. However, Siam Piwat was confident at the opening that it would attract local and international visitors. It expected 40 to 45% of visitors to be from overseas, mainly China.

The risks facing Siam Piwat include the danger of lower than expected visitor numbers—the pandemic will not have helped here—in a city that already has 600 sq m of retail floor area, which is about 30% more than Tokyo. Siam Piwat's rivals also have plans to open more malls. A further risk is an assumption that the political situation in Thailand becomes more stable and does not deter overseas visitors.

E-commerce in Thailand in 2018 accounted for around 1% of total retail sales, well below the 20% in many developed countries. However, the government has been actively promoting digital business under its Thailand 4.0 strategy, and online sales are increasing.

Question

With reference to the features of a strategic decision we have outlined in this chapter, what are the features of the decision to construct the Iconsiam mall in Bangkok that make it a strategic decision?

The strategy that is selected by a management team will determine how and where the business will compete. It will determine who is given positions of responsibility, what the priorities of the business are, and where investments are made.

These decisions will then determine how competitive the business is relative to rivals. It is essential, therefore, that managers appreciate how crucial an organization's strategy is to its success.

Where are we now?

From what we have covered so far we know what a business strategy is, and we understand how crucial having a strategy is to the success of an organization. We now consider how strategy might be managed.

8.2 Strategic management

In this section we consider how strategies are developed.

Strategic management is the process of developing, implementing, and reviewing a strategy. It involves managing major decisions in a business such as new product development, expanding overseas or acquisitions. Effective strategic management means that everyone in the business knows where it is headed and that it is clear what the priorities are and what success looks like. This enables better planning and better resource allocation.

At this stage we will assume that a strategy is developed through a logical process of analysis and planning. This means it comes from a rational, systematic examination of the existing position of the business and a consideration of future developments in the external environment known as SWOT analysis. Managers must then make choices about where to compete and with what products and where to position the product. Lastly managers must implement the strategy.

A systematic approach to strategic management, therefore, involves:

- Undertaking a SWOT analysis to analyse the current position of the business and the future opportunities and threats.

- Making strategic decisions about which markets to compete on and what products to offer.

- Choosing a strategic position within the market.

- Implementing the strategy effectively.

- Reviewing the strategy and ensuring it remains 'fit for purpose'.

The process of strategic management is shown in Figure 8.2.

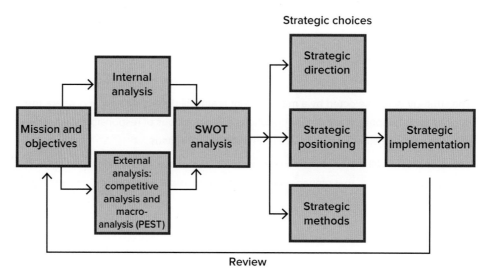

Figure 8.2 The process of strategic management. *Source:* Author.

 **Key concept**

Strategic management is the process of developing, implementing, and reviewing a strategy.

8.2.1 Using SWOT analysis

SWOT analysis is said to have been developed by Albert Humphrey who was leading a research project at Stanford University in the 1960s into the planning processes of leading companies at the time. It involves a logical process of analysing the internal and external environment of a business in order to decide on the right strategy for the business. In earlier chapters we have examined the internal functions of business and what is involved in an external analysis of the competitive and macro-environments of business. These are the building blocks of SWOT analysis. This is shown in Figure 8.3.

The analysis of the internal environment of a business will help it to identify its Strengths and Weaknesses. Strengths are positive aspects of a business, such as a strong brand name (e.g. Nike or Nintendo) or a high level of cash. Weaknesses are internal factors that detract from the ability of the business to achieve its objectives, such as poor quality production. An analysis of the external environment of a business will enable it to identify potential Opportunities and Threats.

Examples of the types of questions managers might ask when undertaking a SWOT analysis are given in Table 8.1.

Having undertaken a SWOT analysis, managers will analyse the findings to develop the strategy of the business. For example, a business may try to build on the strengths of the

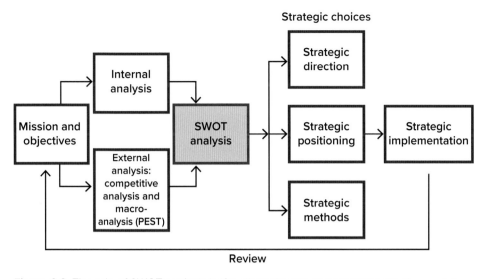

Figure 8.3 The role of SWOT analysis in the strategic management process. *Source:* Author.

Table 8.1 How to undertake a SWOT analysis

Internal	External
Strengths	**Opportunities**
Examples	*Examples*
• What are we good at? e.g. design or a strong brand	• What new technology is there we can make use of? e.g. new online processes
• What particular skills do our employees have? e.g. qualifications and training	• What markets might be opening up that we could enter? e.g. markets overseas with fast growth
• What are our financial strengths? e.g. good cashflow	• What opportunities are there to take over rivals? e.g. are there possible synergies if we acquire a competitor?
• What is our bargaining power with suppliers and others? e.g. are we able to negotiate good prices?	
Weaknesses	**Threats**
Examples	Examples
• What are we not good at?	• What might our competitors be able to do to that could be damaging to us? e.g. a price war
• e.g. high level of production defects	
• What financial problems do we have? e.g. high repayments in debt	• What new legislation might damage us? e.g. regulations that increase our costs
• What weaknesses are there with our employees? e.g. high levels of staff leaving	• What social changes might threaten us? e.g. a change in lifestyle that reduces demand for our product
	• How might changes in the economy affect us? e.g. a fall in consumers' incomes

8

Key concepts

Strengths are internal positive aspects of a business, such as a strong brand name.

Weaknesses are internal factors that detract from the ability of the business to achieve its objectives, such as poor quality production.

Opportunities refer attractive opportunities in the external environment.

Threats refer to risks that might emerge in the external environment.

Think about it

Think of a business you know well. What are its Strengths and Weaknesses? What are its Opportunities and Threats?

organization to exploit the opportunities that are there externally; alternatively, it may try to use these strengths to protect against or reduce the threats that exist.

Can you now answer this question from the introductory case study?

What factors in the external environment do you think influenced Tesla's strategy?

Given that internal and external conditions change managers must regularly undertake a SWOT analysis and review their strategy accordingly. Also, given that businesses often operate in several different markets and regions, they may need to undertake different SWOT analyses. For example, in 2021 the Sumitomo Corporation operated in 66 countries and was made up of 935 companies including logistics, metal, animal foods, and medicines. A business such as this would not undertake one SWOT analysis.

Although the framework for a SWOT analysis is relatively simple, undertaking it effectively is not. Managers need to identify what are genuine strengths, weaknesses, opportunities, and threats. They also need to decide on their relative importance—what matters most for this business? Which factors are most significant? What can happen is that managers allow their own assumptions to influence the factors they prioritize. When considering the strengths and weaknesses of the business, managers need to focus on the areas where they are significantly better or worse than competitors; there is no point analysing areas where they are the same. They also need to avoid bias; it is too easy to let preconceptions dominate judgements rather than evidence.

Can you now answer this question from the introductory case study?

Analyse the reasons why Tesla might have adopted the strategy that it did.

Business insight 8.2 How the strategy of Inditex is changing as the external environment changes

For many years the strategy of the Spanish clothes retailer, Inditex, focused on opening new stores (Figure 1). In the year 2000 it had around 740 stores; twenty years later this number had increased to around 7500. However, in 2020, for the first year ever, the company ended the year with fewer stores than it began with. Meanwhile, its online operations grew. This move was no doubt accelerated by the effects of the pandemic which created threats to physical stores and opportunities for online operations.

Figure 1 A Zara store in Saint-Petersburg, Russia. *Source:* Shutterstock/valerii eidlin.

To bring about this change from physical stores to greater online activity the company invested billions of dollars in its online operations. Technology, such as RFID (radio-frequency identification) chips, were introduced to allow the business to track exactly where items are at any moment.

This move online is appealing to companies in many ways not least because a store has many fixed costs, such as rent and staff salaries. By comparison, online sales may lead to lower prices because buyers can compare prices more easily but costs are lower.

However, the potential problem with this change in strategy is that growing the online business is at the expense of the existing stores—this makes it more difficult for them to be profitable. Until the stores are closed the business may be running online and physical stores and simply splitting the sales between the two.

Question

Do you think the growth of online sales means the end of physical stores?

Source

www.economist.com/business/2021/01/16/how-inditex-is-refashioning-its-business-model

Analysing the business data 8.1

The data in the graph in Figure 1 show the percentage of retail sales through e-commerce in different regions of the world in 2020 and the forecasted percentages for 2025. Take a close look at the differences in these figures for each region.

Regional e-commerce share of retail in 2020, with a forecast for 2025

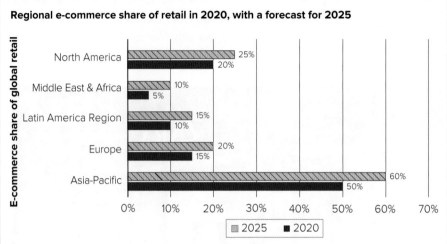

Figure 1 Regional E-commerce share of retail sales. *Source:* https://www.statista.com/statistics/1192717/ecommerce-share-of-retail-by-region/.

Question

Consider the implications of the above data for business strategy. For example, if you worked for an organization whose strategy was to grow e-commerce sales, which regions might you consider operating in?

Source

Statista.com

8.3 Making strategic choices

Having undertaken a SWOT analysis, managers should have the information they need to make strategic choices. The strategic choices made by a business involve decisions about:

- The strategic direction in which the business might move; this involves decisions about which markets to compete in and which products to offer. For example, Coca Cola focuses on drinks—it does not offer food. By comparison Pepsi, its famous rival, offers foods and beverages, including Walkers Crisps, Lays snacks, and Quaker Oats. The two companies have made different strategic choices.

- Its strategic positioning; this involves decisions about the benefits offered and price charged relative to competitors. For example, Southwest Airlines is a budget airline, whereas Qatar Airlines is a premium provider.

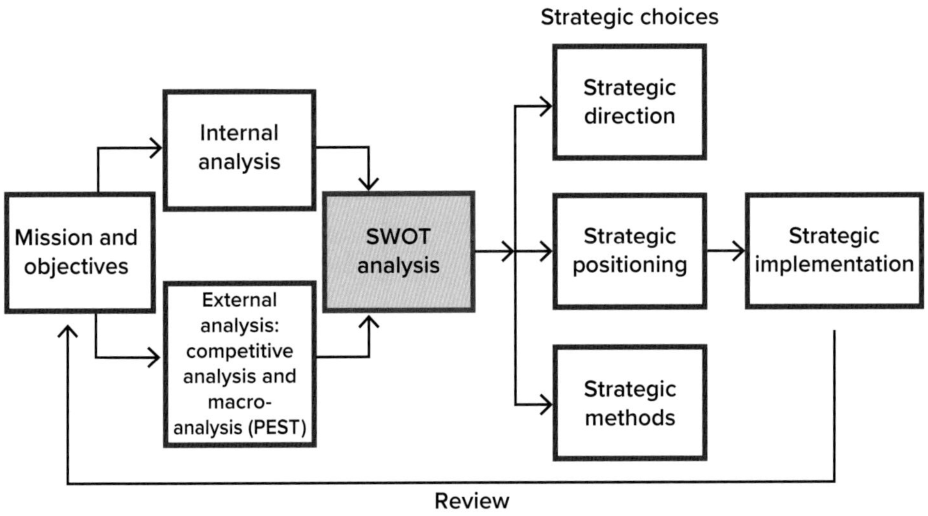

Figure 8.4 The role of strategic choices in the strategic management process. *Source:* Author.

- The strategic methods it wants to adopt; this involves decisions about how to pursue the chosen strategy. For example, do managers want to grow the business organically, by acquisition or through ventures? Alphabet (the parent company of Google) has grown not just organically but through acquisitions. It has made over 240 acquisitions since 2001 including YouTube (in 2006) and Fitbit (in 2021). By 2021 Spotify, which was set up in 2006, had made 22 acquisitions and 6 investments in a variety of sectors such as music technology and social platforms. Strategic methods will be examined in more detail in Chapter 9 where we consider how businesses grow.

When making strategic choices managers will consider where and how the business will be competitive. They will consider how they can compete in a way that offers value for customers and which is not easy for competitors to imitate. The role of strategic choices in the strategic management process is shown in Figure 8.4.

8.3.1 Choosing a strategic direction

The first strategic choice for managers involves deciding on the strategic direction of the business. Choosing the right strategic direction involves deciding which products and markets to focus on. This is important to the success of the business. If managers choose the wrong products the business will struggle. For example, in recent years there has been a major shift in demand towards electric cars. Vehicle producers still focused on diesel have needed to make rapid and significant changes to adapt. Similarly, if a business competes in the wrong markets it will again struggle. For example, businesses that relied heavily on sales in Venezuela in recent years will have suffered difficulties with demand given the economic decline there. Getting the right products in the right markets is the key to strategic success.

The role of choosing the strategic direction in the strategic management process is shown in Figure 8.5.

Strategic choices

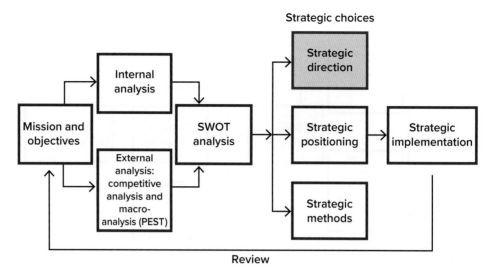

Figure 8.5 The role of choosing the strategic direction in the strategic management process. *Source:* Author.

Key concept

Strategic direction: choosing the strategic direction of a business involves deciding which products and markets to focus on.

Business insight 8.3 Nadella's strategic direction at Microsoft

In 2014 Satya Nadella (Figure 1) became the third Chief Executive of US-based Microsoft after its founder Bill Gates and his first successor, Steve Ballmer. Nadella revolutionized Microsoft with the new strategic choices he made for the company. Nadella stopped the company focusing on its Windows operating system as being at the heart of the business. Instead he drove Microsoft's shift to a more open and collaborative cloud-first strategy: Nadella defined the two main areas of opportunity—mobility and the cloud. He enabled Microsoft software to be shared with other operating systems including Google's and Apple's. Significantly he made Microsoft's cloud-computing arm, Azure, which was launched in 2010, central to the business. This strategy led to rapid revenue growth and a major increase in the company's market capitalization.

Nadella also addressed the issue of culture at Microsoft from one that was inherently confrontational ('us versus them') to one that was focused on collaboration, 'us *with* them'. He wanted Microsoft to be much more open to working with other businesses.

Nadella recognized that sales in the PC business were slowing and there was a need to change the company's strategy. The shift was not easy and competition remains fierce for Microsoft; for example, Azure competes fiercely with Amazon Web Services; Microsoft Teams competes with Zoom in terms of video calls. The company has also missed some opportunities—for example, it failed to gain control of Tik Tok and LinkedIn. Nevertheless, Nadella has been extremely successful at turning Microsoft around by changing the strategic direction and focus of the business by developing the cloud side of the business from almost nothing when he arrived. Nadella wrote in his book 'Hit Refresh' that 'Amazon was leading a revolution and we had not even mustered our troops,' when he arrived.

The graph in Figure 2 shows the value of Microsoft in terms of its shares and some key points in its history. You can see that in the few years after Nadella took over and changed the

Figure 1 Microsoft Vice-President of Business Solutions Satya Nadella delivers an address to the Microsoft Convergence conference on 12 March 2007 in San Diego, California. *Source:* Shutterstock/drserg.

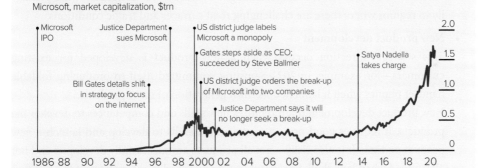

Figure 2 Microsoft Market capitalization. *Source:* How Satya Nadella turned Microsoft around (no date) The Economist. The Economist Newspaper. Available at: https://www.economist.com/briefing/2020/10/22/how-satya-nadella-turned-microsoft-around [Accessed: 2 April 2023].

focus of the strategic direction of the business the market capitalization increased. This suggests the strategy was well received by investors because the value of the business rose.

Question

What challenges might a new Chief Executive face when trying to change the strategic direction of a business such as Microsoft?

One way of analysing the strategic direction of a business was developed by Igor Ansoff. Ansoff was a Russian-American applied mathematician and business manager. In 1988 he set out four types of strategic direction in what has become known as the Ansoff matrix (Ansoff 1988).

These four directions are:

- **Market penetration**

  This strategic direction occurs when a business aims to increase the sales of its existing products in its existing markets. For example, this could be through more aggressive marketing campaigns. A market penetration strategy builds on the existing capabilities of the business. The business focuses on greater market share which can lead to more power with buyers and sellers; this can help push down unit costs. In 2021, for example, the sport business Adidas announced a new strategy called 'Own the Game' aimed at strengthening the brand and making the business more sustainable. The company's objective was higher sales, profitability, and market share by 2025 in its key segments of football, running, training, outdoor, and lifestyle. Adidas announced it would target customers more directly and focus on Greater China, EMEA (Europe, Middle East, and Africa), and North America.

- **Market development**

  This strategic direction occurs when existing products are targeted at new markets. These could be different market segments—for example, different age groups—or different geographic areas. In 2021, for example, Citroen developed a new supermini car (the New C3) to target the Indian and South American markets. The company set a target of 30% of its sales coming from outside of Europe by 2025. The New C3 was designed to be affordable, durable, and agile because it was designed for use primarily in regions where there are challenging road surfaces and traffic conditions.

- **New product development**

  This strategic direction occurs when a new product is developed for existing customers—for example, in 2021 Samsung committed itself to producing foldable handset phones when it launched its third generation of these products.

  New product development often requires new skills and competences to develop the products. It requires good project management skills to develop and launch a new product on time. It is also risky—not all products are successfully developed and not all succeed when launched. For example, Samsung had to delay the launch of its first foldable handsets in 2019 as the products were too weak at the hinges.

- **Diversification**

  This strategic direction occurs when a business develops a new product for a new market. For example, the Tata group is a global enterprise, headquartered in India, that includes 30 companies across ten divisions. The group operates in more than 100 countries across six continents, with a mission 'To improve the quality of life of the communities we serve globally, through long-term stakeholder value creation based on Leadership with Trust'. The Tata conglomerate includes Tata Consultancy Services, Tata Motors, Tata Steel, Tata Chemicals, Tata Global Beverages, Titan, Tata Capital, Tata Power, Tata Advanced Systems, Indian Hotels, and Tata Communications.

Another example of a diversification strategy is that of the tobacco giant, Philip Morris International (PMI). Given the decline in cigarette smoking with the increased awareness of the impact of it on health and greater government regulation and taxation, Phillip Morris has been busy investing heavily in nicotine alternatives. The company's 'statement of purpose' on its website states its appreciation of the toxicity of its key product, and its efforts towards 'a smoke-free future'. Philip Morris has set itself a goal of producing half its revenues from non-combustible products, like its heated tobacco, by 2025. In 2021 the company diversified even further by buying the UK inhaler business, Vectura, for around £1bn. This was somewhat surprising given that most of Vectura revenues are linked to smoking-related diseases.

The strategic direction of diversification comes with high risk because both the products and the customers are new to the business.

The four strategies of the Ansoff Matrix are illustrated in Figure 8.6.

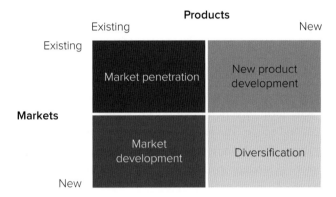

Figure 8.6 The Ansoff Matrix sets out strategic directions. *Source:* Ansoff, H. (1957). Strategies for Diversification. *Harvard Business Review*, 35(5), 13–124.

Business insight 8.4 **A strategy of diversifying**

Sajen Aswani joined the Tolaram Group in 1984. The company had been founded by his grandfather in 1948 as a textile retail shop in Indonesia, where he had moved from India. By the 1980s, the family had built Tolaram into an international business which traded textile and consumer goods and were expanding into manufacturing. Aswani, became the Chief Executive Officer in 2000.

By 2021, Tolaram earned over US$1.2 billion in annual revenues and employed 16,000 people across 15 countries. It is one of the most successful food companies in Africa, for instance, largely on the back of its instant noodles. The company's Indomie brand of noodles is a favourite national dish; its cheap 70-naira packets are eaten frequently by 200 million people. Meanwhile, Tolaram's core consumer goods business reaches consumers in nearly 80 countries, selling products such as paper goods, home and personal care products, and packaged food. Tolaram is now diversifying by moving into digital banking and infrastructure, building what will become the largest port in West Africa, off the coast of Lagos.

The company's strategy is to stick to its 3As. Make sure the product is affordable, make sure the product is acceptable [to the target population], and make sure the product is available.

Question

What do you think might be the reason why Tolaram is diversifying?
Bottom of Form

Source

Strategy Business, 'Tolaram's diversified strategy for growth in Africa' (2021)

Key concept

The **Ansoff matrix** analyses strategic direction in terms of the product a business offers and the markets it competes in.

A business may conduct any of the four strategies in the Ansoff Matrix at the same time and may well be pursuing combinations of all of them at the same time. For example, Lego has very successfully entered the Chinese market with its existing products, targeting families with growing incomes wanting educational toys for their children; this is an example of market development. At the same time Lego has developed new products specifically for this new market which is diversification. For example, it has produced a Chinese New Year's Eve dinner kit, with tiny red envelopes and *chunlian*, lucky rhymes on banners, and a dragon boat race set. This was the first time Lego had ever developed new products just for one region of the world.

Johnson and Scholes are two of the most well-known writers on strategy. In their book with Whittington and others called *Exploring Strategy* (2020), they state that a strategy determined the 'long-term direction of an organization formed by choices and actions about its resources and scope'. The strategy determines where a business is headed and how it is getting there. This definition of strategy stresses the idea of direction and the need to make choices. A strategy involves deciding where to compete, with what, how to do it and what to use.

The highly respected management writer Michael Porter (2008) stressed that businesses will want to find a way of getting to their destination that is better than their rivals. Porter wrote about the importance of choosing a strategy that is competitive. This means that the strategy of a business determines how it is different from rivals; it involves 'deliberately choosing a different set of activities to deliver a unique mix of value'. This view of strategy stresses the need to make decisions that ensure the business is competitive relative to rivals.

Decisions about the strategic direction of a business may, of course, include decisions not to compete in certain markets or even to stop competing in certain areas with certain products. An example of a strategic decision to withdraw from a market is shown in Business Insight 8.5 on HSBC withdrawing from the US market.

Business insight 8.5 HSBC withdraws from US

The British multinational banking business HSBC (Figure 1) changed its strategy in recent years and as a result withdrew from a number of markets where it was previously competing. In 2021 HSBC sold its US retail banking network. This effectively sold its North American business. This decision was part of an overall strategy of cutting costs by $4.5bn and reducing the numbers employed by the business by 35,000. The company said it lacked the ability to compete effectively in the US mass market because it did not have the scale to compete. At a time of low interest rates the company wanted to focus on higher profit margin segments. HSBC had, therefore, decided to focus its efforts more on investing in wealth management in mainland China and Hong Kong. The business retained some outlets in the US but these were to service the needs of its wealthy Asian clients.

Figure 1 HSBC building in the Canary Wharf financial centre. *Source:* Shutterstock/
William Barton.

On its website HSBC stated that it was building a dynamic efficient bank with a digital
focus. It said it was moving its investment into areas which have demonstrated the highest
returns—principally Asia and wealth.

In addition, the company aims to digitize at scale to adapt its operating model for the
future.

Question

At one point HSBC wanted to be a global bank with physical operations all around the
world. Why do you think it has changed its strategy?

Source

www.ft.com/content/d51df836-092b-4b6e-9b50-b5e8e6c98d96

Where are we now?

Once a business has decided on its strategic direction (i.e. which markets to enter and
which products to offer) it must decide on its positioning. We now examine the meaning
and significance of choosing a strategic position.

Can you now answer this question from the introductory case study?

Analyse the strategic options open to Tesla using Ansoff's matrix.

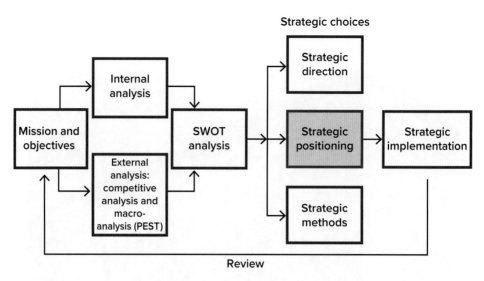

Figure 8.7 The role of positioning in the strategic management process. *Source:* Author.

Choosing a strategic position

The strategic positioning of a business refers to how it is perceived by customers relative to competitors. The role of positioning in the strategic management process is shown in Figure 8.7.

According to Porter (1980) a business can gain a competitive advantage by either positioning itself focusing on lower costs or by differentiating what it offers from rivals.

As part of deciding on its positioning a business will also choose the scope of its activities. If it focuses on a small segment of the market Porter calls this a 'focus strategy'. Alternatively, a business may adopt much broader strategy (which Porter called 'industry wide') which aims at the market as a whole.

A low-cost leadership strategy

This strategy involves winning market share by targeting price conscious consumers with low prices. To be profitable whilst offering a lower price than competitors a business must find ways of keeping costs lower than them.

Keeping costs lower than rivals may be achieved by:

- Using its assets more efficiently.

  For example, this may be a restaurant that turns tables around very quickly, or an airline that turns around flights very fast. In manufacturing, using assets efficiently usually involves high levels of capacity utilization and producing high volumes of output. These approaches mean fixed costs can be spread over a larger number of units of output, resulting in a lower unit cost.

- Achieving low operating costs.

  Reducing operating costs may be achieved by producing a basic product with 'no frills' in high volumes, using standardized components. A business may limit the number of models it offers so that production and maintenance is standardized. The low-cost airlines, for example, tend to fly the same type of plane so that it is easier to train ground staff and spare parts can be used in any plane. Businesses may also keep overheads down by paying low wages, locating premises in low-rent areas (e.g. Ikea's strategy in the past was always to locate out of town), or developing a culture where everyone seeks to keep costs low. Maintaining a low-cost strategy requires a continuous search for cost reductions in all aspects of the business such as production and marketing.

The fashion retailer Primark is an example of a business that pursues a cost leadership strategy. Whereas some fashion retailers such as Zara have competed through 'fast fashion' and manufacturing many of its products itself to allow a fast turnaround of products, Primark has changed its product ranges less often. Primark's strategy has always been to buy huge quantities of items from low-cost manufacturers abroad and gain benefits from economies of scale. Given that it is not trying to rapidly change its products to be fashionable, Primark can place its orders in the off-peak periods; this helps it gain better deals from suppliers. Primark can also use cheap, if slow, transportation methods because it is not aiming to be at the cutting edge of fashion trends. These savings can then be passed on to customers. According to *The Economist* (2021a), Primark's gross profit margins are typically 41% compared to Zara's 57% and H&M's 53%. However, by spending relatively little on marketing—unlike competitors, Primark spends almost nothing on advertising—Primark's final profit margin of 12% is in line with its competitors. To further reduce its costs Primark's stores are almost six times bigger than rivals and usually in low-rent, out-of-town shopping malls rather than on the high street. Clothes are displayed in large quantities on racks or display stands and the business sells ten times as many items as H&M per square metre. Furthermore, unlike its rivals, Primark has no online presence, avoiding all the costs involved in distribution and returns.

Cost leadership is likely to only be feasible for larger businesses that can benefit from economies of scale and that use their bargaining power. If a business can achieve lower costs it can match the benefits and price of rivals and make higher profits; alternatively, it can offer slightly lower benefits and charge slightly less but still make a profit because its costs are lower.

However, a cost leadership strategy may have the disadvantage of reducing customer loyalty, as price-sensitive customers will switch to another business if a lower-priced alternative is available. A focus on price may encourage brand switching.

A reputation as a cost leader may also result in a reputation for low quality, which may make it difficult for a firm to rebrand itself or its products if it chooses to shift to a differentiation strategy in future.

A differentiation strategy

A differentiation strategy is appropriate if the target customer is not price sensitive. A business may be able to differentiate in a number of ways. It may have employees with expertise or skills that are difficult for others to imitate or it may have a strong brand. For example, the Italian design company Prada says 'The Prada label has become one of the leading brands in the fashion and luxury goods industry. As one of the most innovative fashion brands, it is capable of redefining the norm by anticipating and setting new trends. This is because Prada constantly applies its creative approach not only to design development, but also to the most novel production techniques, to communications and to its distribution network.'

When a business is able to differentiate successfully it can charge a premium price for its products. In 2021 a white Prada T shirt was being sold for over £100; a Primark white T shirt was £3.99.

Think about it

Do you think cost leadership and differentiation are mutually exclusive?

In Porter's view only one strategic positioning approach should be adopted by a firm and the failure to do so results in the business being 'stuck in the middle'. This argument is based on the idea that differentiation incurs additional costs, which make a low-cost strategy impossible. An example of a business that failed by being caught in the middle was South Korea's LG Electronics In 2021 LG announced it would close its loss-making smartphone business after years of struggling to be competitive. The Seoul-based group announced that it would formally exit the industry and instead focus on growth areas such as vehicle components. LG had lost ground in smartphones as the global market had become more saturated. It faced pressure from cheaper Chinese competitors such as Huawei, Xiaomi, and Oppo in the low-to-mid end segment while being outcompeted by Apple and Samsung Electronics in the premium, differentiated segment of the market. LG's mobile phone business experienced cumulative losses of nearly $4.5bn between 2016 and 2021 and its global market share had fallen to about 2%, according to research provider Counterpoint.

According to Porter, cost leadership and differentiation strategic positionings are mutually exclusive. However, other strategy writers have questioned this view. According to Baden-Fuller and Stopford (1992) the most successful companies are the ones that can resolve what they call 'the dilemma of opposites'. For example, the retailer Ikea might argue it successfully offers a differentiated product at a low price.

Hill (1988) also challenged Porter's concept regarding mutual exclusivity of low cost and differentiation strategies and argued that successful combination of those two strategies will result in a sustainable competitive advantage.

Where are we now?

We have examined one approach to strategic positioning outlined by Porter. We now examine two other ways of analysing the positioning of a business. One is known as the 'strategy clock' and the other is called the blue ocean strategy.

Another approach to positioning was developed by two economists, Cliff Bowman and David Faulkner in 1977. This approach is usually called the Bowman Strategy Clock. The strategy clock shows a wider range of options than Porter's framework and focuses on the price charged to customers rather than the costs to producers.

Bowman analyses the strategy of a business in terms of the benefits customers think they provide relative to competitors and the price a business charges relative to its competitors.

The strategy clock is illustrated in Figure 8.8.

The strategy clock highlights a range of different strategies that a business can adopt. For example:

- Differentiation without price premium (shown as 4 on the diagram). This strategy occurs when the business offers what is perceived as more benefits than competitors for similar prices. This may be used to increase market share.

- Differentiation with price premium (shown as 5 on the diagram). This strategy occurs when the business offers what is perceived as more benefits than

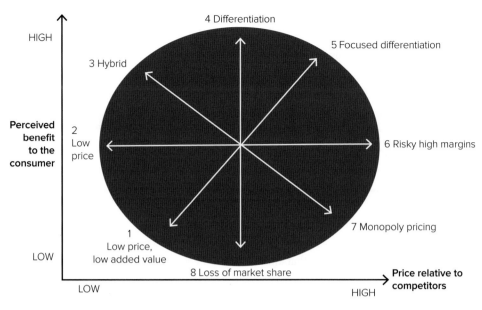

Figure 8.8 Bowman's strategy clock. *Source:* Bowman, C. and Faulkner, D. (1997). *Competitive and Corporate Strategy.* London, Irwin.

competitors. This justifies a higher price. This strategy may be used to increase profit margins.

- A low-price strategy (shown as 2 on the diagram). This strategy involves matching the quality of competitors at a lower price—for example, Walmart. This strategy is aimed at increasing market share. To pursue this strategy successfully a business needs a cost advantage.

- A 'no frills' strategy (shown as 1 on the diagram). This strategy focuses on price sensitive market segments—typified by low-cost airlines like Ryanair. It offers a basic product at a low price.

- A hybrid strategy (shown as 3 on the diagram). This strategy seeks to achieve both higher benefits and lower prices relative to those of competitors. Hybrid strategies may be used to enter markets and build market share quickly. This is aimed at gaining scale so that the business can benefit from cost advantages allowing it to combine high benefits with a low price and still be profitable. The risk is that the costs of higher benefits are so high or it does not gain the scale it needs and therefore makes losses.

Think about it

Why do you think strategy 6 on the Bowman clock is 'risky'?

Why do you think strategy 7 is called 'monopoly pricing'?

What would you do?

Sales of products in your existing markets are slow.

You are trying to decide whether a market development strategy is likely to be better than a diversification strategy. What would you do?

Can you now answer this question from the introductory case study?

Use the Bowman's strategy clock to analyse Tesla's strategy.

Table 8.2 Features of red ocean and blue ocean strategies

Red ocean strategy	Blue ocean strategy
Compete in an existing market	Find a new space in the market that is not contested
Out-compete rivals	Make the competition irrelevant
Gain more of the existing demand	Create a new demand

A third way of viewing strategic positioning was outlined by Professors W. Chan Kim and Rénee Mauborgne in 2005. Kim and Mauborgen developed the concept of a blue ocean strategy. This refers to a strategy that aims to find a space in the market where competition is minimized. In this model 'red oceans' are market spaces where there is already intense competition. The idea of blue ocean thinking is to find or create market spaces where competitors are not currently operating.

The features of red ocean and blue ocean strategies are shown in Table 8.2.

An example of blue ocean strategy is provided by Cirque du Soleil. This business was founded in 1984 by a group of street performers. It has since staged hundreds of performances all over the world which have been seen by millions of people. Cirque du Soleil distanced itself from traditional circuses by creating a completely different type of performance. The company says, rightly, that 'Cirque du Soleil has redefined how the world views the circus'. Another example the authors use to illustrate a blue ocean strategy is Yellow Tail wine. Yellow Tail eliminated factors in the industry that were unnecessary—in this case complicated terminology to describe the product. It also removed factors that created unnecessary costs—Yellow Tail kept its offering simple by offering 'only red' or 'white'. However, whilst reducing costs the company added value through creating a sense of fun and enjoyment buying wine with its Australian branding. By late 2003, Yellow Tail had become the United States' best-selling red wine in a 750-ml bottle—outstripping what had been the very well-established Californian wine labels.

Where are we now?

So far, we have considered what we mean by strategy, how a strategy may be developed, and what is meant by strategic direction and positioning. We will examine the strategic methods separately in Chapter 9. We will now consider how strategies are implemented.

8.3.2 Implementing a strategy

According to some managers, designing a strategy is the easy part of strategic management. The difficult part, they would say, is making sure the strategy is implemented successfully. Think about your career planning: we can all work out what we need to do to become a lawyer or doctor or successful entrepreneur, for example, but actually doing it can be the

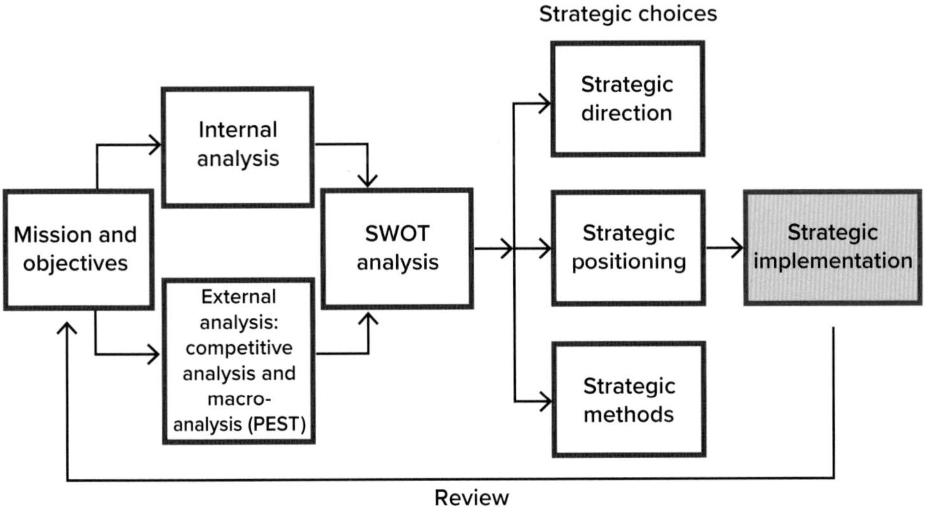

Figure 8.9 The role of implementation in the strategic management process. *Source:* Author.

difficult part! According to Deloitte (2021) 'a poor strategy well executed is better than a good strategy poorly executed.'

Effective strategy implementation involves coordinating people and resources, ensuring they are all informed and understand what they are supposed to do, how and when to do it, and making sure that employees have the skills, training, and resources they need to do it as intended. The role of implementation in the strategic management process is shown in Figure 8.9.

Succesful strategic implementation requires:

- Effective leadership; managers need to send clear messages on what is to be achieved, how it is to be achieved, and why it is important to achieve it. They also need to be clear what the targets are, what standards are to be met and what behaviours are or are not acceptable.

- An effective implementation plan of what needs to be done when and by whom.

- The allocation of appropriate budgets to the different elements of the plan.

- Reward and appraisal systems that ensure people are aligned to the objectives for each stage and each part of the plan.

- Effective communication; this is vital to ensure people are informed correctly (rather than making up their own interpretation of the objectives, goals, values, and methods).

- Effective resource allocation; this means that people have the resources they need when they need them.

- Effective systems to monitor and review progress and take action if progress is not on target.

In their research Neilson, Martin, and Powers (2008) identified two factors that were essential for the effective implementation of a strategy. Firstly, they said it is essential that it is clear who owns each decision and who is required to provide inputs to these decision-makers. Secondly, it is important the information flows easily and quickly to those who need it.

Can you now answer this question from the introductory case study?

What problems might Tesla face when implementing its strategy?

Where are we now?

Having examined the strategic management process from developing the strategy to implementing it, we now consider the need to review a given strategy and the need to change strategy as conditions change.

8.4 What causes a change in business strategy?

Strategies may need to change for a number of reasons. Often the business environment has changed requiring the organization to change what it is doing.

For example, in recent years:

- There has been a growth in the demand for bicycles as more people see this as a good way of keeping fit and of travelling environmentally. This led to a strategic decision by Japanese bicycle parts maker Shimano to invest about ¥20bn ($180m) to build a new plant in Singapore.

- There has been a growing concern for the environment by many stakeholders. This increasing focus on climate change led a Dutch court in 2021 to require the oil company, Shell, to change its strategy to reduce its emissions. The company was being made to change its strategy by law.

- There has been a growing middle class in several emerging economies. Companies, such as Unilever, are increasingly targeting these markets because of the growing demand for products such as cosmetics and dishwasher tablets.

External changes will often lead to strategic changes. In some cases, businesses are forced to respond to external factors; in other cases, they will be proactive.

Strategic change can also come from internal developments. For example, a new manager can identify an opportunity that be taken advantage of if the business changes its approach. A move into a new market or the acquisition of another business may be good examples of this. Often a newly appointed leader will want to change the direction of the business as Nadella did at Microsoft when he placed more focus on cloud computing (see Business Insight 8.3).

The need to review a strategy and re-evaluate in new conditions can be seen in Figure 8.10.

8.4.1 Planning for external change

Businesses should always be planning for the future and thinking how their strategy will need to evolve. Companies may change dramatically over time. From its origins in 1865 when it produced paper, the Finnish company Nokia's strategy has included producing rubber boots, tyres, televisions, and mobile phones.

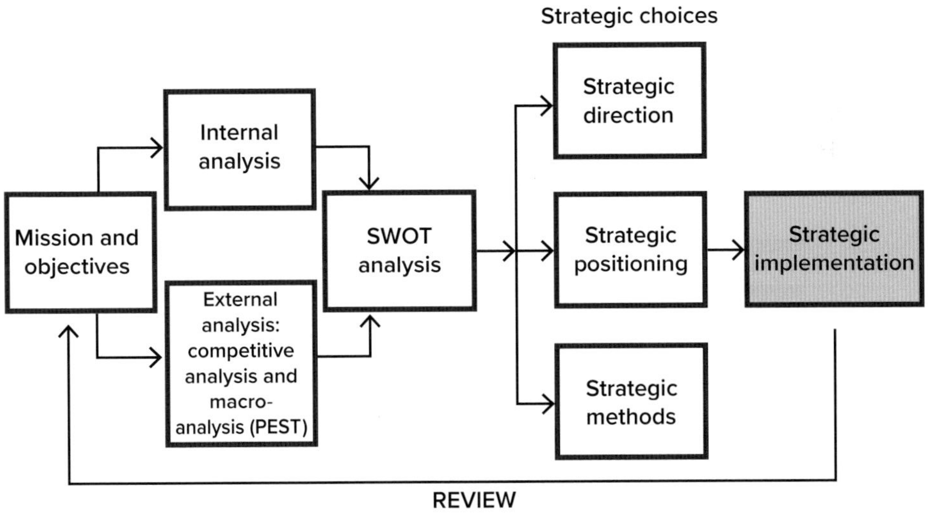

Strategic choices

Figure 8.10 The importance of review in the strategic management process. *Source:* Author.

Where are we now?

As we have seen, businesses will need to change their strategies as conditions change. Businesses will obviously want to anticipate such change so they are ready for it. They may also want to put in place plans in case conditions worsen unexpectedly. In this next section we consider how businesses plan for change.

Strategic planning involves producing a long-term plan for the coming years. The strategy will evolve to be based around expected changes in the external environment and, therefore, anticipating and forecasting will be important. A forecast is an estimate of future values of different variables in the business environment.

A forecast may be developed by:

- Examining past trends and projecting forward. This is known as extrapolation.
- Identifying key factors that affect demand and analysing how these may develop in the future. Correlation analyses examine the possible links between variables such as income and sales.
- Undertaking market research to estimate future trends.
- Gaining expert advice.
- Considering the plans of the business and how these might affect sales.

As well as forecasting a business might use scenario planning to help identify future changes and how this might affect strategic management. Scenario planning occurs when managers use experts to create possible views of what an industry might look like in future. Unlike a sales forecast which attempts to predict fairly accurately what the level of sales would be in the relatively near future, scenario planning focuses more on possible 'big picture' situations. They often create two or three possible scenarios depending on assumptions about how the world will change in the future.

According to Johnson et al. (2020) a scenario is '. . . a detailed and plausible view of how the business environment of an organization might develop in the future based on groupings of key environmental influences and drivers of change about which there is a

Analysing the business data 8.2

Analysing past trends in market and forecasting future trends can help identify opportunities for businesses. Looking at the data in Figure 1 we can see the growth in the halal food market. Halal food is that is prepared in a permitted way according to the Qu'ran.

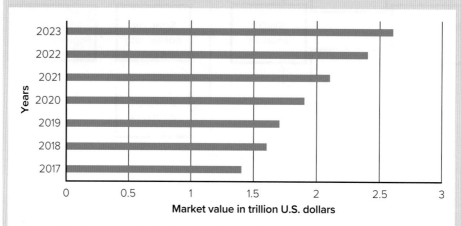

Figure 1 Market value of halal foods worldwide from 2017 to 2023. *Source:* Shahbandeh, M. (2018.) Global Market Value of Halal Food 2017–2023, Statista. Available at: https://www.statista .com/statistics/562857/market-value-of-halal-products-worldwide/ [Accessed 2 April 2023].

Questions

What is the forecasted percentage growth in the halal foods market globally between 2017 and 2023?

What do you think is driving this growth?

What might a food business consider before entering this market?

high level of uncertainty'. According to Schwartz (1991) in 'The Art of the Long View', scenarios are described as: 'Stories that can help us recognize and adapt to changing aspects of our present environment.' They are a way articulating the different pathways that might exist for a business in the future and finding appropriate ways down each of those possible paths.

Scenario planning has been used by some of the world's largest companies, including Royal Dutch Shell, Motorola, Disney, and Accenture. As a result of its scenario planning, the New York Board of Trade decided in the 1990s to build a second trading floor outside the World Trade Centre, a decision that kept it going after the 9-11 attacks. More recently Tik Tok has been using scenario planning to imagine how its industry might look in relation to government regulation in the future.

To undertake scenario planning a business uses a number of experts and gathers their views independently to start shaping a view of the future. It then uses experts again to refine and keep building and refining the view of how an industry might look. Many retailers used scenario planning to consider the world post pandemic.

Key concepts

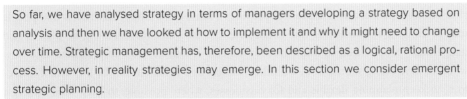

Strategic planning involves producing a long-term plan for the future.

Contingency planning involves planning for an unlikely event.

Scenario planning tries to build possible pictures (or scenarios) of how the world and the industry might loook in the future, perhaps 20 or 30 years from now.

The risk with scenarios is that experts will disagree (they often do!) or be heavily influenced by the way they would want the future to look.

Where are we now?

So far, we have analysed strategy in terms of managers developing a strategy based on analysis and then we have looked at how to implement it and why it might need to change over time. Strategic management has, therefore, been described as a logical, rational process. However, in reality strategies may emerge. In this section we consider emergent strategic planning.

8.5 Emergent strategic planning

The strategic planning process that has been described so far suggests that it is a logical, rational approach. Managers gather data, analyse it, and from this work out the 'right' strategy. In reality strategies may not be developed in this straightforward step-by-step approach.

We may find that the strategy that emerges is not necessarily the strategy that was originally intended. In 1987 Henry Mintzberg, a well-known business writer, distinguished between the 'deliberate strategy' of a business and the 'emergent strategy'. The deliberate strategy is the plan that managers produce and intend to make happen; the emergent strategy is the plan that comes into effect as people learn from the situation they are facing. In the case of an emergent strategy managers take actions, learn from the consequences, and adapt; as they do so the strategy develops. Managers may have an initial plan but they have to respond to what happens and gradually as decisions are made a pattern emerges and a strategy is formed. The concept of an emergent strategy recognizes that plans may be made up as managers face different situations, rather than there being a new grand plan that is developed and rolled out without changes.

According to Mintzberg (1987) we can compare a manager to a craftsperson. He writes 'Our potter is in the studio, rolling the clay to make a waferlike sculpture. The clay sticks to the rolling pin, and a round form appears. Why not make a cylindrical vase? One idea leads to another, until a new pattern forms. Action has driven thinking: a strategy has emerged.'

It is also important to be aware of all the stakeholders that are affect by a strategy and who will want to shape it. Employees, investors, suppliers, and others will all want to protect their interest. Managers may have a strategy in mind but what evolves may be

Think about it

Do you have a plan for the next 5 years? What about the next 10 years?
Do you think it will actually happen?

something of a compromise. Herbert Simon write about managers 'satisficing' different stakeholder groups.

It may even be that strategic planning that involves managers setting out a plan and then pursuing this no matter what could be highly risky for the business. This is because circumstances change so fast. What seemed sensible and well thought through one minute can seem outdated and misguided fairly soon after. If all planning centres on a long-term strategy that is outdated this can clearly cause problems for the business. The attraction of a clear strategic plan is that it appears to provides a sense of certainty—the risk is that people may be clinging to something that is obsolete. On the other hand, having no plan is also dangerous—people need to know how to allocate resources, how to prioritize, and how what they are doing should fit in with the business as a whole. It may be important, therefore, to keep planning flexible and for businesses, where possible, to keep their strategic options open.

Where are we now?

We have now considered how strategies are developed—in some cases they are planned in advance; in other cases, strategies emerge over time. What is important is that however they derive a strategy, managers need to monitor its success carefully and ensure they are ready to change it if needed and avoid strategic drift. In this section we consider how managers may keep their strategies flexible and how they can avoid them becoming irrelevant.

8.5.1 Agility and drift

When implementing a strategy there will be a need to be flexible and agile. Plans need to be reviewed and managers need to be prepared to review and make changes to the original plan.

This is because circumstances can change so quickly, and because plans rarely work the way they were imagined. Who could have predicted the impact of COVID-19 at the start of 2019? According to the Prussian military commander Helmuth van Moltke in 1880, 'No plan of operations reaches with any certainty beyond the first encounter with the enemy's main force.' Strategic planning these days may require agility and a willingness to change the plan rather than sticking to it regardless of whether it is still appropriate.

David Gillespie (2017) highlighted great deal of lessons that business organizations can learn from the military about building an agile organization.

Two practices stand out in the most agile parts of the military:

1. **Leaders should focus on decisions only they can make.** Great generals focus their time on the decisions that only generals can make. They resist the temptation to get

involved to solve a problem that someone else should be accountable for. Leaders should be absolutely clear about what decisions only they can make and push all other decisions as far down the organization as possible.

Managers will be surprised at how few decisions only they can make. Those decisions include choosing the team that directly report to them, authorizing spending over a certain limit, and updating the Board. Most other decisions can be made elsewhere in the organization, and preferably as close as possible to the customer.

Most companies, if they were to review their decision-making structure, would find too many situations where committees rather than individuals are tasked with gathering information, weighing options, and making decisions. This is a potential blocker of organizational agility. As a general rule, organizations should reduce decisions by committee and increase decisions by the individuals and teams who are closest to a particular issue.

By highlighting opportunities for a broader range of people to be decision-makers the business can reduce its reliance on bureaucratic hierarchies that depend solely on the most senior leaders for direction. Over time, people and teams will be empowered to be responsible for decisions within their authority, and will act rather than automatically escalate everything to senior leadership.

2. **Leaders should establish 'commander's intent'.** This means focusing on the 'why' and 'what', while leaving the 'how' to those closer to the front line. It means not micromanaging. The famous U.S. Army General George S. Patton is quoted as saying, 'Never tell people how to do things. Tell them what to do, and they will surprise you with their ingenuity.'

Examples of highly agile organizations are Amazon.com Inc. and Netflix Inc., which are guided by Amazon's Leadership Principles and Netflix's Principles of Chaos Engineering respectively. These organizations work with a speed and an experimental agility that traditional command-and-control organizations can only dream of. It's one reason why Amazon could deliver something as significant as Amazon Prime in only 111 days.

8.5.2 The danger of strategic drift

Strategic drift occurs when the strategy of a business is no longer linked appropriately to the external environment. Imagine there are changes in the environment but a business does not adapt its strategy accordingly; this means its strategy drifts from where it should be.

Strategic drift may occur because senior managers are too complacent. The senior managers of Kodak did not worry about digital photography—they had made their own careers in traditional photography and assumed that would continue to be the way forward.

Drift can also happen because managers do not look outward enough. 'Group think' was a phrase developed by Janis (1972) to describe what happened in the US over the Cuban Missile crisis. President Kennedy was surrounded by supporters who reinforced each other's views and did not challenge each other enough; this nearly led to a nuclear war. Janis' work highlights the importance of the quality and experience of the key decision-makers and the risk of group think. Other examples of group think highlighted by Janis included

Key concept

> **Strategic drift** occurs when the strategy of a business is no longer linked appropriately to the external environment.

the loss of the Challenger spacecraft in 1986. Managers at NASA ignored information about possible problems because they were convinced this could not be the case. The managers had illusions of invulnerability (they could not be wrong) and of unanimity (everyone agreed with each other); both of these are risks that managers must be aware of when making decisions.

8.5.3 Why do strategies fail?

Strategies often fail. There are many companies that were once successful that do not last. Companies such as Polaroid, Kodak, AOL, Tie Rack, Toys R Us, and Blackberry are examples of businesses that lost their dominance in their markets.

The failure of a strategy may be because the initial strategy was ill conceived; the wrong decision may have been made. Alternatively, the plan may have been appropriate at the time but because conditions changed the strategy needed to change as well. Another possibility is that the strategy was the right one but it was badly implemented; for example, with major technological projects the technology can be more difficult to achieve than anticipated.

An example of a failed strategy is Adidas' attempt to gain market share from Nike through the acquisition of Reebok. Adidas paid $3.8bn for Reebok in 2005 as part of a strategy to attack Nike head on its in main markets. However, in 2021 Adidas announced the sale of Reebok for €2.1bn to US-based clothing licensing group Authentic Brands. Although Adidas had managed to make profits with Reebok it did not win market share very successfully. Analysts say the positioning of Reebok was never clear—it was neither a go to brand for sports people nor for those wanting athleisure fashion and style. Reebok got 'caught in the middle' in terms of its positioning.

In 2019 a study by Meeks and Whittington in the *Business History Journal* showed that only 19 of 1,513 UK quoted companies had survived from 1948 to 2018. In most decades a listed company typically had only a 50–50 chance of making it through the next 10 years. The ones that survived changed their strategies at the right time; the ones that disappeared were either bought or did not change their strategy sufficiently or quickly enough. Interestingly some sectors have simply lost significance within the UK—in 1948 10 listed companies were leather and fur companies; 57 were brick and pottery-makers and so businesses in these industries failed due to declining need. The study concluded that developing the strategy to match the external environment was essential to survival. For example, over the past 30 years, Whitbread has moved from being a brewer to owning budget hotels (Premier Inn) and restaurants, having also owned sports clubs, pizza parlours, and coffee-shops (Costa) in between.

Analysing the business data 8.3

> The average lifespan of a U.S. Standard & Poor 500 company has fallen by 80% in the last 80 years (from 67 to 15 years), and 76% of UK FTSE 100 companies have disappeared in the last 30 years.
>
> Why do you think this is?

Can you now answer this question from the introductory case study?

Discuss the factors that you think will determine the success of Tesla's strategy.

 ## Now you should know

- A strategy sets out a plan to achieve the objectives of the business.
- Strategic management is the process of developing, implementing, and reviewing a strategy.
- Strengths are internal positive aspects of a business, such as a strong brand name.
- Weaknesses are internal factors that detract from the ability of the business to achieve its objectives, such as poor-quality production.
- Opportunities refer attractive opportunities in the external environment.
- Threats refer to risks that might emerge in the external environment.
- Strategic direction: choosing the strategic direction of a business involves deciding which products and markets to focus on.
- Strategic planning involves producing a long-term plan for the future.
- Contingency planning involves planning for an unlikely event.
- Scenario planning tries to build possible pictures (or scenarios) of how the world and the industry might look in the future—perhaps 20 or 30 years from now.

 ## Review questions

Quick Check

1. Distinguish between objectives and strategy.
2. State two features of a strategic decision.
3. What is meant by choosing a strategic direction?
4. Distinguish between a market development and diversification strategy according to Ansoff.
5. Explain what is meant by diversification.
6. Explain how stakeholder mapping can be used to analyse how to respond to the different groups.
7. Explain when a cost differentiation or cost leadership strategy might be more suitable for a business.
8. Explain the challenges of implementing a strategy.

Analysis

1. Analyse the reasons why a business may choose a market penetration strategy rather than market development.

2. Analyse how SWOT analysis may be used in business strategic planning.

3. Analyse the challenges facing a business wanting to change its strategy.

Evaluation

1. Given that so much is difficult to forecast and change can happen so fast do you think there is any value in strategic planning?

2. Do you think a strategy is best developed from the top and pushed down the organization or from the bottom and pushed up?

⌇ Find out more

- John Kay is an excellent and engaging writer on business strategy. Why not read his book: Kay, J. (1993). Foundations of Corporate Success: How Business Strategies Add Value. Oxford: Oxford University Press.
- Harvard Business Review is a source of many superb strategy articles. You could start with *HBR's 10 Must Reads: On strategy.* Boston, MA, Harvard Business Review Press. Classic Harvard articles include:
  - Neilson, G. L., Martin, K. L., and Powers, E. (2008). The Secrets to Successful Strategy Execution. *Harvard Business Review*, 86, 60–70.
  - Porter, M. (1996). What is Strategy? *Harvard Business Review*, 74(6), 61–78. © Harvard Business School Publishing.
- If you want to read more about red and blue ocean strategy then look at Chan, K. W. and Mauborgne, R. A. (2005). *Blue Ocean Strategy.* Harvard Business Review Press.

Where are we now?

In this chapter we have considered the importance of having an appropriate strategy and analysed how this strategy might be developed in a logical, analytical manner using techniques such as SWOT analysis. We have examined some of the elements required for the effective implementation of a strategy and considered some of the reasons why strategy fails. We have also discussed how strategy can evolve over time and how sometimes the strategy may become inappropriate given changed conditions internally and externally. In the next chapters we consider different aspects that can influence business strategy.

☰ Bibliography

Ansoff, H. I. (1988). *Corporate Strategy*. New York, Penguin.

Asia.nikkei.com/Business/Food-Beverage/Jollibee-aggressively-expands-globally-and-beyond-fast-food

Baden-Fuller, C. and Stopford, J. M. (1992). *The Mature Business: The Competitive Challenge*. London, Routledge.

Deloitte (2021). *Changing role of people management in the Digital Era–deloitte us*. Available at: https://www2.deloitte.com/content/dam/Deloitte/xe/Documents/human-capital/dme_hc_changing_role_of_people_management_in_the_digital_era.pdf [Accessed 27 October 2023].

Gillespie, D. (2017). What the military can teach organizations about agility. *MIT Sloan Management Review*. Available at: https://sloanreview.mit.edu/article/what-the-military-can-teach-organizations-about-agility/ [Accessed 12 March 2023].

Hill, C. W. L. (1988). Differentiation versus low cost or differentiation and low cost: a contingency framework. *Academy of Management Review*, 13, 401–412.

Janis, I. L. (1972). *Victims of Groupthink*. Boston, Houghton Mifflin Company.

Johnson, J., Whittington, R., Regnér, P., Angwin, D., and Scholes, K. (2020). *Exploring strategy*. New York, Pearson Education Limited.

Kim, W. and Mauborgne, R. (2005). Blue Ocean Strategy: From Theory to Practice. *California Management Review*, 47(3), 105–121.

Meeks, G. and Whittington, G. (2019). Death on the stock exchange: the Fate of the 1948 Population of Large UK Quoted Companies, 1948–2018 (March 21, 2019). Available at SSRN: https://ssrn.com/abstract=3423524 or http://dx.doi.org/10.2139/ssrn.3423524

Mintzberg, H. (1987). Crafting strategy. *Harvard Business Review*, 65, 66–75.

Neilson, Martin, and Powers (2008). The Secrets to Successful Strategy Execution. *Harvard Business Review*, 86, 60–70.

Porter, M. E. (2008). The Five Competitive Forces that Shape Strategy. *Harvard Business Review*, 86, 79–93.

Porter, M. E. (1980). *Competitive Strategy: Techniques for Analyzing Industries and Competitors*. Free Press, New York.

Schwartz, P. (1991). *The Art of the Long View*. New York, Doubleday.

Tesla (n.d.). *The Secret Tesla Motors master plan (just Between you and me)*. Available at: https://www.tesla.com/blog/secret-tesla-motors-master-plan-just-between-you-and-me [Accessed 27 October 2023].

The Economist (2020). www.economist.com/briefing/2020/10/22/how-satya-nadella-turned-microsoft-around

The Economist (2021a). *How Primark makes money selling $3.50 t-shirts*. Available at: https://www.economist.com/business/2021/08/21/how-primark-makes-money-selling-350-t-shirts [Accessed 27 October 2023].

The Economist (2021b). www.economist.com/business/2021/01/16/how-inditex-is-refashioning-its-business-model

Watkins D. (2007). Demystifying Strategy: The What, Who, How, and Why, *Harvard Business Review*.

8

Chapter 9

Growth and international business strategies

Where are we now?

In this chapter we examine why businesses might want to grow, and the advantages and challenges of such growth. We also focus on the benefits and challenges of becoming more international. These are both common strategies of businesses.

Why am I studying this?

- You want to know why growth seems so important to businesses. In this chapter we explore the reasons why businesses grow.
- You want to understand the attractions and risks for businesses of growing by joining with other businesses. In this chapter we consider the issues related to mergers and acquisitions.
- It is likely you will be working a business that operates internationally, so understanding the opportunities and challenges this creates would be useful. In this chapter we examine the ways in which businesses expand overseas.
- You are interested in how cultures may differ between countries and how that might affect business. In this chapter we explore cultural differences.

Learning objectives

By the end of this chapter you should be able to:

- Analyse why growth matters to a business
- Explain the advantages and disadvantages of organic and external growth
- Discuss the challenges of mergers and acquisitions
- Discuss why and how businesses can enter overseas markets

9

- Explain how national cultures may differ according to Hofstede
- Analyse the difference between a multi-domestic and a transnational strategy
- Analyse what is meant by protectionism and how it affects business

Introductory case study Netflix goes global

Netflix states that it is the world's leading entertainment service with over 139 million paying members in over 190 countries. Netflix streams TV series, documentaries, and feature films. The global growth of Netflix, the online streaming service, has been quite phenomenal. In 2015 it was operating in 50 countries: by 2017 this had grown to more than 190 countries. More than 70 million of its 130 million subscribers are now outside of the US, but up until 2010 the company only operated in the US. The overseas growth of Netflix has been rapidly accelerated in recent years. The key question is: how did they achieve this?

To expand abroad Netflix faces numerous barriers. For example, many countries limit the amount of foreign content that can be made available in local markets. In some countries there may be strong preferences for local language content. A further challenge in some markets is getting people to pay for streaming services when they are used to free services.

Netflix has also faced strong local competition in some countries, such as India and France, where there were already home language providers, or where it was competing with Amazon Prime which was already well established.

Netflix's strategy seems as though it was carefully planned. Netflix did not try to enter overseas markets in one go but grew one step at a time. It started with countries where the

Figure 1 Netflix booth at a Comic Con experience in Brazil. *Source:* Wikimedia/Fernando Cesar Nox.

culture was similar—for example, growing from the US to Canada—where there would be less sense of 'foreignness'. This focus on relatively lower-risk expansion at the start helped Netflix build the experience it needed for further growth overseas. In its second stage of expansion it targeted a wider variety of countries; it focused on regions with affluent consumers, good broadband access, and some similarities in tastes. This stage required more development of local content.

In its third, most rapid, phase Netflix used its growing expertise in big data and analytics; they now had more awareness of how content might be adapted for markets. It also started adding on languages through subtitles and developed more personal algorithms, so people could build their own library more easily. Netflix now focused on markets where mobile devices were the primary source of access to the internet—such as emerging economies. It put more emphasis on improving the mobile experience and developing local content. One of the company's sayings is that 'great storytelling transcends borders'. However, it now produces original content for nearly 20 countries and is sourcing more regionally produced content. Its streaming services now offer drama series from Korea, anime from Japan, Sundance films, and other films and television shows from countries such as the United Kingdom, China, and India, among others.

Netflix's strategy has focused on organic growth. It has not spent heavily at all on acquiring other businesses. One exception in recent years was the purchase of StoryBots, a media brand focused on educational shows for children. It has also bought Millarworld, a comic book publisher, and ABQ Studios, which is a production facility in Mexico. However, these acquisitions are extremely rare for Netflix and it has managed extremely fast growth without many mergers or takeovers.

As well as showing content developed by other producers Netflix has increasingly developed its own content. Shows such as The Crown, The Witcher, and Stranger Things are some of Netflix's most popular original content shows. Its core strategy is to grow its streaming membership globally whilst achieving suitable profit margin targets. It describes itself as a 'focused passion brand' rather than trying to be all things to all people. It says it is a 'Starbucks not a 7-Eleven'. The internet allows Netflix to offer a wide variety, and to have its user interface quickly learn and make recommendations based upon individual users' tastes. This means Netflix hopes, with new content, it can win more of its members' 'moments of truth'. A moment of truth is a decision point when people choose what to do with their time—imagine it's 7.30 in the evening, what will you do with your time? Netflix want more people to choose to watch its programmes.

Netflix started as an DVD rental-by-mail business. It used a monthly subscription model instead of a single-rental model that was typical in most other video rental stores. It spent many years spent fighting with Blockbuster in the US. With the growth of the internet in the mid-2000s, and significant improvements in bandwidth and internet speeds, Netflix started to explore the possibility of online video streaming services. In February 2007 Netflix started to offer streaming content and began moving away from its core DVD rental business. Its competitors now are other streaming service providers such as YouTube and Amazon, the streaming services of TV networks and Hollywood producers such as HBO and Fox Entertainment, and other similar competitors such as HOOQ and iFlix, among others.

Streaming has marked a major shift in the entertainment industry. Radio was the dominant home entertainment medium for nearly 50 years. Then 'linear' (traditional) TV took over in the 1950s and 1960s. Internet entertainment has created a new model in the last 20 years.

Internet entertainment has expanded rapidly because the internet is getting faster and more reliable, while penetration of connected devices, like smart TVs and smart phones, has also risen. Netflix has seized this opportunity, originally in the US, but increasingly all over the world.

Sources

www.netflix.com

www.vox.com/recode/2019/5/9/18538155/netflix-acquisition-storybots-kids-video-jibja

Brennan, L. (2018). How Netflix Expanded to 190 Countries in 7 Years, *Harvard Business Review*, October 12, 2018

Introductory case study questions

1. Why would Netflix want to grow?

2. Why does Netflix prefer organic growth to acquisitions?

3. Why would Netflix want to expand overseas?

4. What problems might Netflix face expanding internationally?

5. What might Netflix consider when choosing which country to target next?

Critical thinking

1. Netflix has avoided acquisitions. Do you think this would be good advice to all organizations?

2. Are the challenges facing Netflix when expanding abroad greater than for other businesses?

3. Do you think all businesses need to change what they offer when entering overseas markets?

9.1 Strategic methods of growth

In Chapter 8 we looked in detail at the process of strategic management, which is illustrated in Figure 9.1. If this management process is a logical and rational one (which it may not be!) the strategic planning of a business will be based on an internal and external analysis of its situation. Based on a SWOT analysis, as examined in Chapter 8, managers can identify various opportunities and threats and develop an appropriate strategy for the business. Managers will consider which markets to compete in, which products to offer and how to position itself against the competition. They will decide the strategic direction and positioning of the business.

Once managers have decided how and where to compete they must choose the method they want to use to grow the business. For example, do they want to grow by acquiring other companies? Are they willing to sell the rights to produce their products to other businesses? Do they want to grow within the home country or by selling more abroad? These decisions refer to the strategic method of growth. These strategic methods will be examined in this chapter.

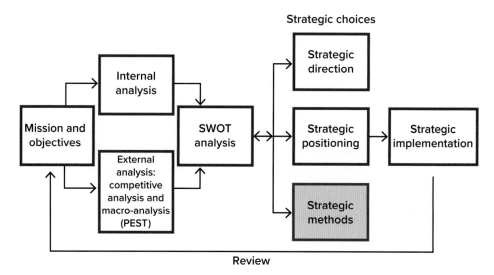

Figure 9.1 The strategic planning process. *Source:* Author.

9.1.1 Why do businesses want to grow?

Growth occurs when the size of a business increases. The size of a business may be measured in many ways such as:

- **The value of sales.**
  According to Fortune magazine in 2022 the largest three companies in the world were Walmart (US retailer with sales of over $572,000 million), Amazon (US retailer) with sales of over $469,000 million and State Grid (a Chinese electricity company) with sales of over $460,000 million.

- **The market share of the business.**
  Market shares measures the sales of one business as a percentage of the total sales in the market. For example, according to Statista, in 2022 Apple had over 24% of the global smartphone market, Samsung had over 19%, and Xiaomi had around 11%.

- **The number of stores or outlets.**
  This measure of size is often used in the retail sector. For example, there were 7,225 Starbucks outlets in 2003; by 2020 there were 32,660 in 80 countries. In 2022, according to the company website 7-Eleven had more stores than any other retailer in the world with over 83,000 across 19 countries.

- **The market capitalization of the business.**
  This measures the value of a company's shares. According to Statista in April 2022 the three largest companies in the world by market capitalization were Apple (over $2640 billion), the Saudi Arabian Oil Company (over $2292 billion), and Microsoft (over $2054 bn).

Chief Executives are often eager to grow a business so that it is bigger when they move on than when they joined; this would be regarded as a personal achievement and looks good on their CV! Growth is used as a common measure of a manager's success. Managers may

Table 9.1 Advantages of growth

Advantages of growth
Internal economies of scale
Market power
Brand reputation and prestige
Personal sense of achievement for managers
May be less vulnerable to a takeover

also want to increase the scale of their business because their earnings may be linked to its size. An example of a famous Chief Executive who was well rewarded for the growth of the business when he was in charge was Jack Welch. Welch was Chief Executive of GE (General Electric) and widely admired for the increase in shareholder value that happened under his leadership. With Welch at the helm for 20 years shareholders received returns of 5200%. Welch was called 'manager of the century' by Forbes magazine. When he retired in 2001 Welch received a pay-off of over $400 million from the company.

The growth in a business may also lead to **economies of scale**. As you may remember from Chapter 4 this means that unit costs fall as output increases. Economies of scale can help the business to be more competitive. This can allow a business to cut price but still retain its profit margins or allow higher profit margins at the same price. Another reason for growth is that by increasing in size, a business may also be less of a target for purchase by other businesses because it may be more expensive to buy. Managers may be protecting themselves by making their business less affordable for potential buyers.

The advantages of growth are shown in Table 9.1.

Can you now answer this question from the introductory case study?

Why would Netflix want to grow?

Internal and external growth

A business may grow internally or externally. Internal growth means expanding the business by growing the existing operations. This can be a relatively safe method of growth in that the business should understand what it is already doing—it just has to find ways to increase demand, and supply its output on a bigger scale. This is also called '**organic growth**'. Pinduduo, for example, was founded in 2015 in China and in the space of a few years has grown to be the biggest online market place for agricultural products in the country, working with over 16 million growers.

External growth occurs when a business grows by joining with another business. This is also called integration. External growth can occur through a merger or an acquisition. In 2021, for example, the Chief Executive of the online beauty retailer, THG, announced it would grow that year by making over £250m worth of acquisitions. Microsoft has also been expanding through acquisition. In 2016 Microsoft bought LinkedIn, a business-oriented social network, for $26bn. In 2018 it bought GitHub, a development platform for open-source programs, for $7.5bn. In 2021 it acquired Nuance, a speech-recognition specialist, for nearly $20bn in cash.

9

Where are we now?

So far, we have considered the different forms of growth. We now look at the challenges that face businesses as they grow internally.

Key concepts

Economies of scale occur when a business grows and its unit costs fall.

Organic growth occurs when a business grows by increasing sales internally.

Managing internal growth

When businesses grow they typically go through a number of stages which need to be managed. As a business gets bigger over time it will have opportunities because of its scale and experience but it will also face challenges and managers will need to respond to these.

The Greiner model of growth highlights a number the stages that businesses typically go through as they get bigger and older and grow internally. The Greiner model is shown in Figure 9.2. Greiner highlights some of the management challenges facing entrepreneurs if their business grows. When an entrepreneur starts a business, there is usually a period where there is considerable creativity. The founder or founders of the business tend to be very passionate about their idea; they each help to make it work and there is an energy to what is being done. At this stage, the business is small and flexible so decisions can be made quickly. This means the business can respond quickly to change. The entrepreneur/founder is willing to take risks and look for new opportunities to grow the business. However, at some point this approach may not be as suitable as it was at the beginning. The business may not be able to rely on the inspiration of the founder if it wants to keep growing; to move forward and expand the business may need better management skills to organize resources and people. The 'ideas' person who created the business may not

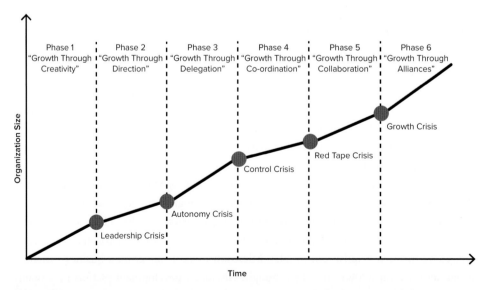

Figure 9.2 Greiner's model of growth. *Source:* Greiner, L. E. (1998). 'Evolution and Revolution as Organizations Grow', *Harvard Business Review,* 76(3), 55–67.

necessarily be a good planner or organizer. At this stage there may be a 'leadership crisis' (as shown on Figure 9.2) which requires managers to be brought into the business to run it more effectively. There may also be a need for more formality generally. Roles may need defining more clearly so, now there are more people, everyone knows who is responsible for what.

With a more formal structure and new leaders the business should have a clearer direction for a period of time. This is shown as 'Phase 2' in Figure 9.2. However, the focus is now on control and as the business continues to grow and operate in new markets with new products it may be that at some point in the future greater delegation is required. Staff may need to respond to local conditions and take their own decisions rather than require central approval. This is called an 'autonomy crisis'. The business may respond to these pressures by delegating more to local employees; however, this can mean that parts of the business are operating very differently from each other. Over time these differences may increase and, at some point, this may require intervention to coordinate what is happening across the business and bring in more uniformity.

The business will continue to grow through the stages of crisis. In each case, the business will aim to respond with solutions to the given crisis; this may solve the current problem but as growth continues new issues may emerge. The solution to one crisis may eventually create another set of challenges.

Greiner's model highlights that there is a constant tension in a business between the need to control what is happening, especially as the business grows, and the need to delegate as the operations become more complex and diverse. In the early stages of the business the challenge is often between creativity and control. In small businesses everyone knows everyone, people regularly talk and share ideas, and it's possible to keep track of what is happening informally. This is not the case as more people become involved and that's when some form of control systems and rules and procedures need to be introduced, hopefully without killing off the creativity that was at the heart of the enterprise to start with.

Where are we now?

We have now considered what internal growth is and explored some of the challenges associated with this using Greiner's model. In the next section we will look at how businesses manage external growth, and examine some of the issues related to this mode of growth.

Managing external growth

There are two main ways in which business can grow externally: through **mergers** or **acquisitions**. Mergers occur when two or more businesses join together to create a new business. For example, the giant pharmaceutical, GlaxoSmithKline plc (GSK) was formed in 2000 by a merger of GlaxoWellcome and SmithKline Beecham. An acquisition (or takeover) occurs when one business gains control of another; for example, it buys a controlling interest in the target company's shares. In 2021 the convenience retail giant 7-Eleven acquired Speedway, a US convenience store business that had approximately 3800 stores, for $21 billion.

To acquire another business the buyer will need to gain control of a majority of the shares of the target business. It may do this by paying cash for the shares or by offering shares in its own business (this is called a paper offer) or a combination of the two.

A **hostile acquisition** occurs when the target company's directors resist the bid and advise their shareholders not to sell. For example, in 2023 Kakao, one of South Korea's major internet businesses, made an attempt to make a hostile takeover of SM, the famous K-pop music agency.

A **friendly acquisition** occurs when the directors of the target company advise their shareholders to sell because it would be in their best interests. In 2014, for example, there was a friendly takeover of WhatsApp for $19 billion by Facebook.

Mergers and acquisitions can lead to a sudden increase in the scale of a business. This usually means there is much faster growth than can be achieved organically. When external growth works well it can lead to synergies—the businesses may share complementary skills and resources and both are better off as a result. A business may acquire skills, expertise, experience, products, and distribution channels that it might not have itself. For example, when Nippon Glass acquired Pilkington Glass in 2006 it gave Pilkington the ability to access Asian markets with its products more easily; it also gave Nippon access to Europe with its offerings. In 2021 Heineken made a bid in South Africa for Distell. Distell's ciders and alcopops were an attractive complement to Heineken's existing operations in the country.

An example of a company that has grown rapidly through acquisitions as well as organic growth is Unilever. For example, in 2019 alone Unilever acquired:

- Lenor Japan, a skin care business
- Astrix S.A, a Bolivian manufacturer of home and personal care brands
- Fluocaril and Parogencyl, oral care brands
- Graze, the UK's leading healthy snacking brand
- The Laundress, a global premium eco-friendly line of detergent, fabric care, and home cleaning products
- Tatcha, a Japanese-inspired skincare brand
- OLLY Nutrition, a US-based premium well-being business in the vitamins, minerals, and supplements (VMS) sector
- Garancia, a French cosmetic brand.

External growth can be a quick way to acquire technology, enter a market segment, or expand internationally. In January 2022, for example, Microsoft announced it would pay $69bn to take over Activision Blizzard, a video-game developer. Microsoft has been in the gaming industry already for two decades with its Xbox console. However, by acquiring Activision Blizzard, Microsoft suddenly became the third-largest video-gaming firm by revenue, behind only Tencent, a Chinese giant, and Sony. The deal gave Microsoft access to the content of Activision Blizzard such as 'Call of Duty', a best-selling series of military-themed games, 'Candy Crush', a popular pattern-matching mobile game, and 'Warcraft', a fantasy game. In 2022 Unilever announced another potential takeover when it offered to pay £50bn ($68bn) for the consumer health products division of GSK. Unilever was eager to expand quickly into consumer health prescription medicines—Unilever's Chief Executive sees the future of the company in health and hygiene products more than food, and this deal would have marked a further shift towards this goal. However, the bid was rejected by GSK's shareholders.

Key concepts

Internal growth means expanding the business by growing its existing operations.

External growth occurs when a business grows by joining with another business.

Mergers occur when two or businesses join together to create a new business.

An **acquisition or takeover** occurs when one business gains control of another.

A **hostile** acquisition is an unwelcome bid for a company.

A **friendly** acquisition is a welcome bid for a company.

Mergers and acquisitions obviously involve bringing two or more businesses together and means that the people within them have to work together. This can lead to a clash of priorities, and of corporate cultures; this can then lead to disagreements and inefficiency. AOL–Time Warner, HP–Compaq and Quaker–Snapple are some of the most famous mergers and acquisitions where there have been culture clashes and the deal has reduced shareholder value. The differences that can exist in culture are examined in Chapter 10.

The different forms of external growth can be categorized as:

- Vertical integration;
- Horizontal integration; and
- Conglomerate integration.

We will now look at each of these in turn.

Vertical integration

Vertical integration occurs when a business joins with another business at a different stage of the same production process. This is usually undertaken to gain control over supplies, to maintain the quality of these inputs, and to be able get supplies for less than if they were bought from an external business. Buying a supplier also enables better integration in areas such as design and deliveries. GoPuff is a US business that, unusually in the food delivery sector, is highly vertically integrated; it owns its inventory and manages its own warehouses as well as its logistics. In 2021 Gopuff operated a network of more than 250 micro-fulfilment centres—or 'dark stores'—each containing between 2500 and 3000 products that allowed it to deliver to customers in about 30 minutes of an order being placed. **Backward vertical integration** occurs when one business acquires another business that provides inputs for the current business. **Forward vertical integration** occurs when a business joins with another business closer to the customer in the supply chain. For example, a clothes manufacturer buys a retailer. This is usually to try and guarantee access to markets.

Horizontal integration

Horizontal integration occurs when one business joins with another business at the same stage of the production process. Examples of horizontal integration include Frit Lay joining with the Uncle Chipps snacks business, Hertz Car rentals acquiring Thrifty Dollar rentals and Pepsi buying Rockstar energy drinks. Horizontal integration is often undertaken to gain market power and economies of scale. Horizontal integration may also allow a business to gain access to brands and markets and benefit from synergies. There have been

9

many horizontal integrations in the car and pharmaceutical industries as businesses seek to benefit from internal economies of scale.

Conglomerate integration

Conglomerate integration occurs when a business joins with another business that operates in a different market. This may be undertaken to reduce risks. A downturn in one market may be offset by growth in another. In 2017, for example, Mars, which produces confectionery such as M&Ms (as well as dog food and vending machines), bought VCA, a veterinary business which owned about 800 animal hospitals. Meanwhile, the Tata Group is a large Indian conglomerate that has grown with acquisitions such as Corus Steel (acquired in 2007) and Jaguar LandRover (acquired in 2008). Another example of conglomerate integration is the Italian group Photo M International (PMI). PMI's primary business is photo booths (e.g. for passport photographs) but it also owns a launderette business and in 2021 acquired a pizza vending machine manufacturer. PMI's expansion plans include moving more into food, drink, and clothes washing machines. The company is also changing its name to ME Group, to reflect the shift from purely selling and operating photo booths.

Business insight 9.1 The growth of Amazon

In 2012 Amazon bought the film studio MGM (Figure 1) for $8.45bn. The deal gave Amazon access to a library of over 4000 movies including the James Bond films, the Terminator franchise, *The Good, the Bad, and the Ugly*, and *Silence of the Lambs*. It was an important deal because most of the Hollywood film studios had already been acquired. Warner Bros is part of AT&T, Fox is owned by Disney, Universal is part of Comcast, and Paramount belongs to ViacomCBS. Sony Pictures remains one of the few independent studios left. In the battles with companies such as Netflix in the streaming market having access to great

Figure 1 Metro Goldwyn Mayer. *Source:* Wikimedia/Carmelo Speltino.

content is key (think back to the opening case in this chapter); this is why MGM was so important to Amazon. Meanwhile, the deal was important to MGM because of the impact of the COVID-19 pandemic; the pandemic meant that the release of James Bond 'No Time to Die' was delayed four times in 2020, which affected its income.

Amazon was in a good position to buy other companies. It had raised $18.5 billion by selling bonds just a few weeks before and in 2020 it had a revenue of $386 bn and generated a cash surplus of $31 bn.

Questions

Why would Amazon want to buy a film studio?

How do you think Amazon would decide what to pay for MGM?

Sources

www-ft-com.ezproxy01.rhul.ac.uk/content/56beb2f4-10b3-4255-b4d9-362ed30bd3ce

www-ft-com.ezproxy01.rhul.ac.uk/content/d7257362-45a3-421b-b55f-cc496a144d2c

www-ft-com.ezproxy01.rhul.ac.uk/content/de672d37-1ebe-452e-956e-d170398606e5

Key concepts

Horizontal integration occurs when one business joins with another at the same stage of the same production process.

Vertical integration occurs when one business joins with another at a different stage of the same production process.

Conglomerate integration occurs when one business joins with another in a different production process.

What would you do?

You want to grow your business. How might this desire to grow the business relate to Maslow's hierarchy of needs which was studied in Chapter 6.

Possible disadvantages of growing through mergers and acquisitions

One of the appeals of external growth is that it enables a rapid increase in size. However, this can also bring with it a number of challenges. Growth brings with it the danger of internal diseconomies of scale. Problems with controlling more resources, with coordinating all the different factors of production, and with communicating across a bigger business can lead to inefficiency and higher unit costs.

A further problem with external growth is the cost involved in doing the deal. In an acquisition, for example, the bidder has to get the existing share owners to sell their shares. To do this they will typically pay a premium. This means that if the deal is successful the new owners will be seeking to cover these additional costs. In 2021, for example, the US fruit and vegetable producer Dole Food merged with the Ireland-based Total Produce. This merger created the world's largest fresh produce company with around $9.7bn revenue per year. The price paid by Dole for the shares was a premium of around 47% of Total Produce's share price at the time.

9

Table 9.2 The possible disadvantages of external growth

Possible disadvantages of growing through mergers and acquisitions
Communication problems
Control problems
Motivation problems
Investigation by competition authorities

If a business gets too big, or would become too big, through external growth it may be subject to competition laws within a country. Many governments will have agencies to investigate mergers or acquisitions that could lead to an abuse of power and a business acting against the public interest. For example, in 2020 the Competition and Markets Authority (CMA) in the UK investigated a proposed merger between two leading publishers of university textbooks: McGraw-Hill and Cengage. The CMA wanted to see if there would be competition issues in relation to student choice. The concern was that the coming together of two important suppliers in the UK could lead to students paying more for essential textbooks and educational materials. There were 379 courses where both companies offered textbooks. In the end, the publishers terminated their plans to merge. In Poland in 2019 the authorities blocked the takeover by Agora, the publisher of Gazeta Wyborcza, one of Poland's largest daily newspapers, of the radio group Eurozet. The country's competition authority argued that the transaction would restrict competition. In 2021 Facebook was being accused of being a monopoly. In the US the Attorney General stated that 'For nearly a decade, Facebook has used its dominance and monopoly power to crush smaller rivals and snuff out competition, all at the expense of everyday users'. This has led to calls to make Facebook reduce its market power. Some of the disadvantages of large-scale operations are shown in Table 9.2.

Business insight 9.2 Legislation in India limiting Chinese takeovers

In 2021 India introduced new legislation to limit Chinese takeovers. The Indian Ministry of Commerce brought in a law which meant that any potential investment from a country which has a land border with India required government approval before investing in an Indian company. The impact was greatest on Chinese businesses because there were already restrictions on investment from Bangladesh and Pakistan. Chinese investment had increased in India in recent years with significant purchases by internet companies such as Tencent and Alibaba.

Can you now answer this question from the introductory case study?

Why does Netflix prefer organic growth to acquisitions?

Where are we now?

So far, we have examined mergers and acquisitions as a method of external growth including the benefits and challenges associated with this approach. We will now consider franchising as an alternative form of external expansion.

The weak economy in India in 2020 and 2021 had reduced the value of many Indian companies; this had made them more attractive targets for oversea purchasers. The Indian government felt that domestic companies were vulnerable at this time and should be protected. The new legislation was intended to do this.

At the time Chinese companies were investors in two-thirds of Indian start-ups valued at over $1bn. For example, Alibaba was a large investor in Paytm, a fintech company, and food-delivery service Zomato. Tencent had invested in the car-hailing app Ola and Byju's, an education start-up. There was a concern within India and other countries at the idea that foreign investors from China would have access to companies dealing with sensitive personal data or critical technologies. This was another reason for greater government oversight and regulation.

Question

What do you think might be the consequences of restricting foreign takeovers of businesses within your country?

Sources

www-ft-com.ezproxy01.rhul.ac.uk/content/ad3f84b0-fb75-4588-97e8-4a657ad67883

www.iflr.com/article/b1lq7wrzcz9dbn/india-takes-steps-to-prevent-unwanted-chinese-takeovers

What would you do?

1. You are considering growing by acquiring a competitor. What factors would you take into account before deciding whether to go ahead?

2. You have been told that many mergers and takeovers are often unsuccessful. You want to grow by taking over a rival. What would you do to make yours successful?

9.1.2 Franchising

Franchising occurs when one business sells the right to use its name and sell its products to another business. The seller of the franchise is called the franchisor; the buyer is called the franchisee; this relationship is shown in Figure 9.3. For example, Paris Baguette is a bakery chain in South Korea owned by the SPC group. It has over 4000 franchises in many countries such as the United States, Vietnam, and Singapore. Other examples of international franchises include 7-Eleven, Subway, OvenClean, Costa Coffee, McDonalds, and Domino's Pizza.

The benefits of buying a franchise are that the franchisor is likely to have a proven track record; this means that the buyer can benefit from the reputation and awareness of the established brand. The franchisee will also be able to benefit from the experience and expertise of the franchisor. Established ways of operating, training, and equipment will often be available from the franchisor.

The benefits of selling a franchise are that this provides money for the business; the franchisee will pay for the franchise and will also pay a proportion of its annual revenue.

```
┌─────────────┐   Sells rights to use name to   ┌─────────────┐
│  Franchisor │  ──────────────────────────▶    │  Franchisee │
└─────────────┘                                  └─────────────┘
```

Figure 9.3 Franchisor sells to franchisee. *Source:* Author.

A Paris Baguette franchise in Singapore. *Source:* Shutterstock/Artorn Thongtukit.

This means that franchising enables faster growth than might be achieved if the business had to finance it all itself and generates an income. The returns may be relatively high because the franchisee is likely to be highly motivated; this is because it is their business and they keep the majority of the rewards. This motivates the franchisee; it should help the business grow and the brand to be well regarded.

However, there will be dangers when selling a franchise. This is because the business loses some control over its day-to-day operations. There will also be a risk because if there are problems with one franchisee this may affect the brand as a whole. The benefits and potential disadvantages of franchises are shown in Table 9.3.

Table 9.3 Benefits and potential disadvantages of selling a franchise

Benefits of selling a franchise	Disadvantage of selling a franchise
Some of the funds for growth are provided by franchisee	Do not have complete control over activities
Revenue received from a percentage of the sales	Poor performance by one franchisee affects brand as a whole
Motivation of franchisees should be high as they keep majority of profits	

Key concept

Franchising is the granting of a licence by one person (the franchisor) to another (the franchisee), which entitles the franchisee to own and operate their own business under the brand, systems, and proven business model of the franchisor.

What would you do?

You run a successful fast food chain selling food from Malaysia. You have been approached to sell a franchise so your business can open in overseas markets. Would you sell?

Where are we now?

So far, we have examined mergers, acquisitions, and franchising as strategic methods of growth. We now consider the opportunities and challenges of growing by targeting international markets.

9.2 Internationalization

Internationalization occurs when a business expands overseas and enters new markets abroad. A business may do this to reduce risk by selling in more than one region. It may also be able to grow faster because of more favourable conditions than in its existing markets. For example, the 32 clubs in the American National Football League (NFL) are keen to encourage a younger, more diverse audience base by promoting the game more widely abroad, particularly in Germany, the UK, and Canada.

When targeting overseas, managers will want to consider the different ways of entering these markets.

The ways a business might enter a market abroad include:

- Exporting
- Licensing or franchising
- Joint ventures
- Buying an overseas business
- Setting up an overseas business.

We will look at each of these in more detail in turn.

9.2.1 Exporting

Exporting occurs when a business sells products abroad from its home base. This is a relatively low-risk entry method. The business accepts orders as usual, but these happen to be from overseas. The advantages of this approach include potential economies of scale from larger domestic production. A disadvantage is that the business will have to deliver overseas which incurs transportation costs; it may also face trade barriers when exporting overseas. Brompton is a UK company that makes folding bicycles which are also sold abroad especially in Germany, France, and the US. It sells around 60,000 bicycles a year.

9.2.2 Licensing

Licensing occurs when a business sells the right to sell its products to another business overseas. McDonalds has nearly 39,000 stores around the world. The benefit of this approach is that it makes use of the local expertise and networks without requiring a deep understanding of the market abroad. However, the challenge comes in finding the right partner and terms of the deal.

9.2.3 Joint ventures

Joint ventures occur when a business joins with an international partner. For example, in 2021 the creation of the world's longest electricity cable that runs under the sea was the result of a joint venture between the UK's National Grid and Norway's Statnett. When the UK has excess power from offshore wind, the cable allows it to export power to Norway. On other days the UK can import electricity from Norwegian hydropower. The advantage of this entry method is that it is possible to benefit from the expertise and networks of the partner based abroad. The disadvantages of a venture include the problems of working collaboratively with a partner because there may be differences in objectives and ways of working, and the fact that profits will be shared.

9.2.4 Buying an overseas business

Buying an overseas business requires relatively high levels of investment and therefore involves quite a high degree of risk. However, if the acquisition is successful all the rewards stay with the business. For example, in 2021 the Russian based TMH (a producer of locomotives, freight cars, and subway cars) bought Bergen, a Norwegian engine business.

9.2.5 Setting up an overseas business

This way of entering an overseas market is high risk because there is no existing business and expertise. However, if successful the rewards all stay with the business.

The different ways of entering an overseas market and the significance of these in terms of the investment or commitment required and the market knowledge available are shown in Figure 9.4.

If we look at exporting first we can see in Figure 9.4 that this is a relatively low-risk entry method. This is because it does not require a great amount of market knowledge, or a great commitment to overseas markets.

Buying or setting up an overseas business and having full ownership of it, on the other hand, is a high-risk entry method and requires higher levels of investment. With this method the potential returns are higher but the business is taking the risk that it understands the market well enough and is having to commit relatively large sums.

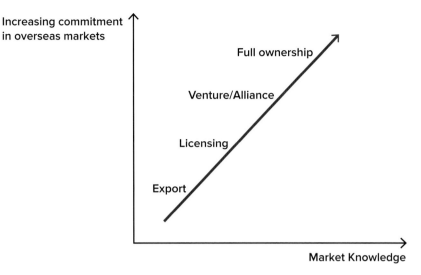

Figure 9.4 Ways of entering an overseas market. *Source:* Author.

Business insight 9.3 Vietnam's Vingroup aims to export cars

In 2021 Vietnam's biggest conglomerate, Vingroup, announced that it planned to sell VinFast, the country's first domestic car brand, overseas. The group had decided to launch a range of cars in the US; these included electric cars and autonomous self-driving vehicles. VinFast only began making cars in 2019, and sold only 30,000 in 2020.

VinGroup was founded in 1993 by Phạm Nhật Vượng. At first VinGroup focused on real estate and this remains its core business but it has since expanded into other areas such as retail (VinMart), phones and televisions (VinSmart), and new areas such as artificial intelligence, often with foreign partners.

VinFast is relatively new in the car industry but is developing high technology cars incorporating Artificial Intelligence. It already has three self-driving electric models and believes there is a window in the US to take market share before the fast-growing electric market gets too crowded.

Questions

Based on what you have read so far, how would you advise VinFast to enter the US market?

What challenges do you think Vinfast might face in the US?

Source

www.reuters.com/article/tech-ces-vinfast-idCNL1N2TM05A

When deciding on the best way of entering a market overseas, managers will consider the:

- costs—an acquisition will obviously cost more than just exporting products;
- the likely returns on the investment (ROI);

- the risk—exporting carries less risk than setting up operation overseas, for example;
- how much commitment the business wants to make—clearly, setting up its own operations is a long-term commitment compared to exporting.

When it comes to choosing a particular way of entering a market much may depend on managers' understanding of that region. A Chinese business entering Europe for the first time may involve less certainty than entering some other Asian countries, for example, because the social and cultural differences may be greater.

Business insight 9.4 The growth of Jollibee

Jollibee is the largest fast food chain in the Philippines and has over 1150 stores nationwide. The company has also been expanding rapidly abroad. It has over 270 international branches in the United States, Canada, Hong Kong, Macau, Brunei, Vietnam, Singapore, Malaysia, Saudi Arabia, United Arab Emirates, Qatar, Oman, Kuwait, Bahrain, Italy, and in the United Kingdom (Figure 1). In 2022 it had plans to open 500 stores in 2022, up from 398 in 2021.

Jollibee was founded by Tony Tan and his family as an ice cream parlour. It remains a family business and it very much targets other families, stressing the importance of family values in its promotional materials.

Jollibee believes its growth is due to its menu with items such as its Chickenjoy, its Yumburger, its Champ hamburger, and Jollibee Spaghetti. It says it has well-trained teams, a culture of integrity and humility, and a fun and family environment. Jollibee says that

Figure 1 The UK's first Jollibee store, Leicester Square, London, UK. *Source:* Shutterstock/cktravels.com.

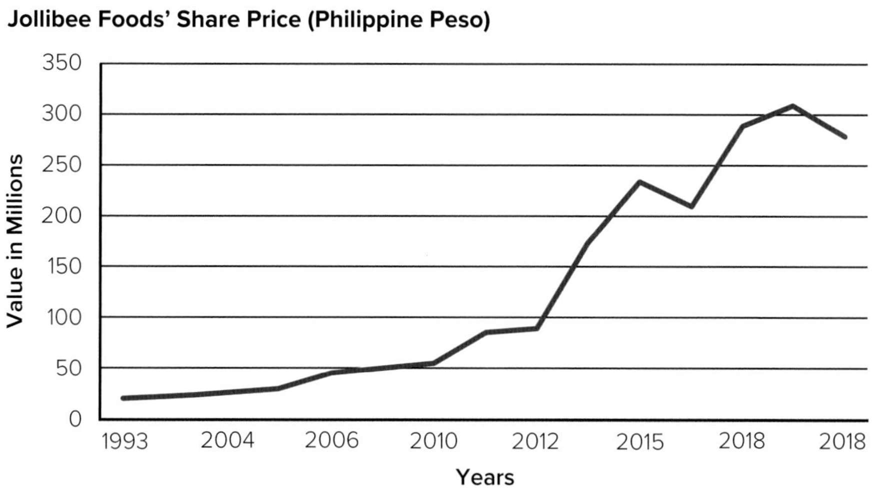

Jollibee Foods' Share Price (Philippine Peso)

Figure 2 The growth of Jollibee. *Source:* Ramos, G. and Reed, J. (2018). Philippines' Jollibee Foods plans expansion to rival KFC. *Financial Times*. Available at: https://www.ft.com/content/e65301a6-c85c-11e8-ba8f-ee390057b8c9 [Accessed 2 April 2023]. Adapted by the author.

every outlet welcomes customers with a clean and warm in-store environment and friendly and efficient service.

Jollibee entered the UK in 2021 and plans to open over 25 outlets there in the next five years. It sees the 300,000 Filipinos living in the UK as it main target group initially, but thinks it will gradually pick up a wider customer base and take customers away from rivals such as KFC. Jollibee is also targeting growth in Spain and the rest of Europe. The company's vision is to be a global brand.

Jollibee already owns most of the US chain Smashburger, operates Vietnam's Highlands Coffee and Pho 24 noodle chains, runs Dunkin' Donuts in some territories of China and operates the Burger King franchise in the Philippines.

Jollibee does not only grow through organic growth: it is also eager for acquisitions. It generally acquires small- to medium-sized companies in cash. For example in 2020 it paid $12.4m for 47% of Tortas Frontera, a Mexican chain. Jollibee's aim was to move into 'fast casual' dining as this has a higher price point than fast food. In 2017 Jollibee nearly bought Prêt à Manger but in the end felt the price was too high.

The chart in Figure 2 shows the share price of Jollibee as it acquired various franchises over the years.

Question

What factors might Jollibee consider when deciding which countries to target for expansion of its core business?

Sources

www-ft-com.ezproxy01.rhul.ac.uk/content/568c6a43-7e41-4ebb-8394-75661c3ebd86

www-ft-com.ezproxy01.rhul.ac.uk/stream/b739fded-d38a-4db4-a4fa-2880e12c7f9a

www-ft-com.ezproxy01.rhul.ac.uk/food-beverage

www.ft.com/content/8549e0e5-0dbe-4d94-bf23-b4d9863e35af

What would you do?

You have the opportunity to have a joint venture with an overseas business. They would produce your product and market your product abroad and you would take a percentage of revenue. What would you want to know before agreeing to the deal?

Can you now answer this question from the introductory case study?

Why would Netflix want to expand overseas?

Where are we now?

We have now considered various ways in which a business might expand overseas. In the next section we will examine some of the factors that may make these markets different from the domestic one.

9.3 Challenges of internationalization

Whilst selling abroad brings many opportunities it also brings challenges. Managers wanting to enter overseas markets will have to understand the competitive business environment and the business macro-environment within those countries. One key tool a manager can use to better understand the external business environment they are considering entering is a **PESTLE** analysis for each region. PESTLE is an acronym that stands for Political, Economic, Social, Technological, Legal, and Environmental. PESTLE analysis provides a framework to analyse the different aspects of the external business environment. We will now look at each of these in more detail.

9.3.1 Political factors overseas

There can be significant differences in political systems between countries. For example, systems vary between democracies (in which governments are elected by their citizens) and totalitarian systems (where the government retains complete control over society). In some countries there is relative political stability—in Germany, for example Angela Merkel was Chancellor for over 15 years up until 2021. In other countries, however, there is regular political change. Between 2011 and 2021, for example, there were ten different governments in Tunisia. In Turkey between 2019 and 2021 there were four different central bank governors as the government tried to tackle inflation. In the UK Liz Truss lasted just 50 days as Prime Minister in 2022.

The differences in political approaches can create very different environments in which businesses operate. For example, some countries have economies based mainly around the free market. In these areas, businesses are free to produce what they wish in response to consumer demand. The free market forces of supply and demand determine what is produced, who works where, and what they receive. By comparison, some economies are more of a centrally planned (or command) economy; in this situation the government determines more of what is produced, how it is produced, and who is employed where. All economies are mixed, i.e. they have a free-market element and government involvement, but there are significant differences in the extent to which the government determines what is produced.

Businesses will need to be aware of political changes and consider the implications for their strategy. For example, in February 2021, Cuba announced a big increase in the size of the private sector as the country faced a severe economic crisis. Previously, private businesses were only allowed in 127 professions; this was changed to more than 2000, keeping only 124 areas partly or wholly for the state. This created the opportunity for more start-ups and expansion into new business areas. By comparison, in 2021 the Chinese government unexpectedly announced that all private tutoring businesses would not be allowed to make profits. According to *The Economist* (2021) the shares of three big online tutors, TAL Education, New Orient, and Gaotu, quickly fell, reducing their shareholder value by $18bn. Business Insight 9.5 explores the political factors in India which have made it challenging for foreign businesses to succeed.

Political differences can also lead to changes in where businesses want to operate. Many US and European businesses stopped selling in Russia in 2022 following its invasion of Ukraine.

According to *The Economist*, Coca-Cola in 2023 did not make its products available in Russia, North Korea, and Cuba because of political differences.

Business insight 9.5 Facebook in India

In 2020 Facebook spent $5.7bn to acquire a 9.9% stake in Jio Platforms, the digital arm of Reliance Industries. Reliance Industries is the biggest business in India. Many other foreign businesses have also been investing in Jio Platforms. Since its launch in 2016, Jio has become the country's leading technology platform, with nearly 400m mobile subscribers, a broadband network, as well as entertainment, retail, and finance businesses. Overall foreign investors have around a 25% share of Jio Platforms. These investments seem to be because foreign businesses have decided they cannot succeed in India without a local partner. The general view of foreign businesses seems to be that overseas investment is welcome but foreign competition is not. In a speech in May 2021 India's prime minister referred to 'self-reliance' 17 times. He said that India must make 'the local the mantra of our life'.

Figure 1 shows the decline in the average tariff on imports into India which encourages exports to this country. It also shows the growth in foreign companies in India in recent years.

Foreign businesses that do not link with an Indian partner often seem to struggle. For example, by 2020 Amazon had spent over $6.5bn on its Indian operations, but had not made any profit in the country. Walmart's $16bn purchase in 2018 of a controlling stake in Flipkart, an Indian e-commerce firm, has also struggled. As foreign businesses Amazon and Walmart have an additional tax on transactions, and they are also limited in the size of the inventory they can hold and on the sales of their own brands.

In 2021 Ford announced that it was reviewing its operations and considering withdrawing completely from this market. Despite having tried to gain a foothold for over 30 years, by 2020 Ford had only achieved a 2% market share. Many global carmakers are attracted

▶

9

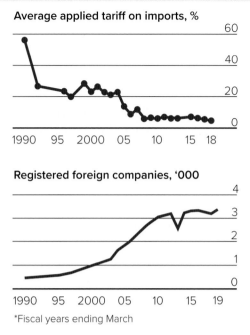

Figure 1 Average applied tariffs on imports into India. *Source:* 'Facebook bets on a different sort of e-commerce in India' (no date). *The Economist*. Available at: https://www.economist.com/business/2020/04/25/facebook-bets-on-a-different-sort-of-e-commerce-in-india [Accessed 2 April 2023].

by the size of the Indian market—the fifth largest in the world by volume in 2021—and by the fact that it is growing relatively fast. However, like Ford, most foreign carmakers have struggled to price their vehicles low enough to appeal to the majority of Indian customers. Rivals Toyota, Honda, and Renault have not done much better than Ford and only have 3% market share each. By comparison Maruti Suzuki, a 40-year-old Indian subsidiary of the Japanese carmaker, dominates the market with efficient, low-priced vehicles. Its market share is nearly 50% of the Indian market. The difference is that Maruti Suzuki has developed products specifically for India. Foreign companies such as Ford have generally tried to sell products in India that were developed for other markets. There has been no focused strategy of product development just for this country. As a result, most car companies have been criticized for selling too few models in India and not refreshing them often enough. Suzuki cars have been cheaper to buy and run, and given their well-established market position there are many garages able to undertake repairs and provide parts. This makes them a safer bet when it comes to buying a car. Other vehicle manufacturers have already abandoned India when they failed to achieve their sales targets. General Motors gave up in 2017, and motorcycle manufacturer Harley-Davidson announced in 2020 that it too would leave the country, after struggling to compete with local brands such as Royal Enfield.

Questions

Why do you think Indian businesses are appealing to outside investors?

Why might the Indian government be concerned about such investment?

Why might businesses from outside India struggle when operating in the country?

Sources

www.economist.com/business/2020/04/25/facebook-bets-on-a-different-sort-of-e-commerce-in-india

www-ft-com.ezproxy01.rhul.ac.uk/content/1d4885d2-09e8-403e-8c64-3bc49e912267

economictimes.indiatimes.com/tech/internet/facebook-buys-9-99-stake-in-reliance-jio-for-5-7-billion/articleshow/75283735.cms?from=mdr

www.ft.com/content/a844c3f2-bf12-4bdd-b730-d571c68e561b

9.3.2 Economic factors in overseas markets

As well as political factors, managers must also consider the economic environment in the countries where they are operating, or considering operating. For example, a business may be interested in the average income per person, the inflation rate, and the cost of borrowing money. Some countries may have favourable economic conditions stimulating demand or making operating there attractive. For example, low-cost borrowing, stable prices, fast economic growth, and a wide pool of skilled labour would be appealing for many businesses. On the other hand, some countries will have conditions which create challenges. For example, between 2015 and 2020 the Venezuelan economy shrank in size by 75%, inflation was over 6500% in one year, and the country's currency, the bolivar, became essentially worthless. Read Analysing the Business Data 9.1 for examples of other economic indicators that managers may want to consider as part of their PESTLE analysis.

Analysing the business data 9.1

The data in the following table shows some key economic indicators for July 2021 in select countries. These will all have an impact on businesses operating in or considering selling to, or buying from, these countries.

	National income growth % change on year before	Inflation % change on a year ago	Unemployment Rate %	Interest rates %
Britain	5.8	1.3	4.7	0.7
China	8.5	2.9	5.1	2.7
Russia	3.5	5.8	4.8	7.0
Peru	10.8	3.5	9.7	6.5
Turkey	5.6	16.6	10.4	16.8

Question

Discuss the possible implications of the above economic data for businesses considering entering these markets.

Source

www.economy.com

Think about it

Think of two countries you know. How do they differ in terms of the role of the government within them?

How has the role of the government changed in your country in the last ten years? Why?

Key concepts

Foreign Direct Investment refers to money invested in shares in other countries.

An **emerging economy** is typically defined as one where the income per person is low to medium and where the economy is moving towards becoming developed.

One economic feature a manager may wish to consider when examining the conditions in a country is the level of economic growth, and the impact of this on purchasing power and spending patterns. A particular group of countries of interest to many businesses are known as **emerging economies** because of the growth opportunities they offer. The term 'emerging economy' was first used in 1981 by Antoine W. Van Agtmael of the World Bank. There are many definitions of emerging economies but typically these focus on countries where the income per person is classed as low to medium, and where the economy is moving towards becoming developed. This usually means that reforms are happening to make it easier for private sector businesses to operate; this can lead to fast economic growth. India is a good example of an emerging economy. According to *The Economist* (2022) the India economy grew by 40% between 2014 and 2021; by 2027 India will become the world's fifth largest economy with a national income of approximately $5 trillion.

9.3.3 Social factors in overseas markets

As well as political and economic differences, there will likely be major differences in the social environment in different countries. For example, demographic data such as the population size, the average age of the population, the languages spoken, the main religions, and the culture of the country are likely to differ.

Other differences will include social norms: how business is 'done', how people behave, and how people expect to be treated can vary tremendously. These differences will influence lifestyles, beliefs, values, and attitudes. They can have a dramatic effect on the way people in a society act toward each other and towards those in other societies. They will affect how people are managed in the workplace, how products are marketed, what products to offer, and generally how to compete. Interestingly, when businesses expand abroad, they usually begin with countries nearby as they understand these regions best and they are often most similar to them culturally. Differences in national cultures are examined in more detail later in this chapter.

A good example of how important it is to understand the local market can be seen in the experience of Nestlé in Japan. Nestlé produces the KitKat bar which for many years has used the slogan 'have a break, have a KitKat' all over the world. In Japan, Nestlé was eager to target KitKat at students but its market research showed that these students

Analysing the business data 9.2

Figure 1 shows demographic data on China and India. Since 1950 India and China have contributed around 35% of the world's population growth. However, the strict rules on the number of children expected in China had a significant effect on its birth rate and by 2050 China's population will be 8% smaller than it was in 2023. Meanwhile India's population continues to grow and is expected to reach its highest level at 1.7bn in 2064, when it will be nearly 50% larger than the population of China. Between now and 2025 India will have over one sixth of the world's working age population between age 15 and 64.

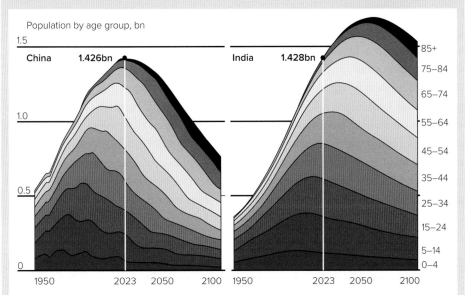

Figure 1 Demographic data on China and India. *Source:* www.economist.com/graphic-detail/2023/01/05/india-will-soon-overtake-china-as-the-worlds-most-populous-country.

Question

What do you think are the implications of the data above for business?

Source

www.economist.com/graphic-detail/2023/01/05/india-will-soon-overtake-china-as-the-worlds-most-populous-country

were so stressed by 'Juken'—their very high-pressure school exams—that what they wanted was to succeed in their exams not 'take a break' or have a chocolate bar! However, Nestlé noticed that the word KitKat sounded like the Japanese phrase 'kitto katsu' ('you will overcome') and that some students were giving each other the chocolate bar as a good-luck token whilst preparing for juken. Nestlé's managers in Japan started to put the phrase 'Kitto sakura saku yo!' ('wishes come true!') in their adverts. Nestle also changed the packaging and used much more vivid colours and innovative packaging than in any other country. Sales of KitKat grew extremely fast and the chocolate bar became regarded as an 'omamori'—a good-luck token sold at Shinto shrines and Buddhist temples. Nestlé has since boosted sales in Japan by producing more than 300 flavours in that country including strawberry, wasabi, soy sauce, sake, and even, in 2017, a limited-edition throat-lozenge flavour to soothe the throats of Japanese football fans cheering on the national team in the World Cup qualifying campaign. Whereas in most countries the range of KitKats stays stable, in Japan it has to be continually changed and modified to keep selling.

National cultures

One key social factor that should be considered is the national culture of a country or region. Geert Hofstede was a Dutch social psychologist who studied how cultures can differ between countries. These differences can affect how employees expect to be treated at work, what customers value, and how managers might want to manage. They also explain the challenges business people from different regions can face when trying to do business together simply because their ways of working are different. We examined some of these issues when considering cross-national mergers and takeovers. Hofstede developed a model of national culture which consists of six dimensions: power distance, uncertainty avoidance, individualism vs collectivism, masculinity vs femininity, long-term orientation, and indulgence. Hofstede believed that national cultures can be assessed through these six dimensions. We'll now take a closer look at each of these in turn.

The popular Japanese KitKit packaging that can be folded to create 'omamori' Japanese lucky charms in support of students preparing to take university and high school entrance exams. *Source:* City-Cost.

Business insight 9.6 The growth of US food in India

The demand for American style fast food has been growing rapidly in India in recent years. The interest in this sector was shown by the huge demand for shares in Burger King's India franchise when they were sold in 2020. Demand for its shares was 157 times higher than the number of shares that were on offer. Burger King only entered the India market in 2014; by 2020 it had 261 outlets and is aiming for 700 outlets by 2026. Other providers such as McDonald's, KFC, Domino's, and Wendy's are also planning to expand significantly. The fast food market in India is still mainly made up of independent restaurants serving local delicacies such as moms and samosas. However, weekend visits to the US outlets have become increasingly common for middle-class Indian families.

To be successful the international fast food businesses have had to adapt their menus in India very significantly. Their menus in this country look very little like they do in the US. This is because many Indians are vegetarian or rarely eat meat. Hindus make up almost 80% of the population and most do not eat meat, and the large Muslim minority avoid pork. US chains have therefore avoided ingredients such as beef and bacon and instead focused on chicken and mutton, as well as vegetarian alternatives that use Indian spices.

Question

Do you think there are any reasons why fast food restaurants should not change their menus in different countries where they operate?

Sources

www-ft-com.ezproxy01.rhul.ac.uk/content/7886c14c-1d1a-417b-8ae1-30ac94f5a712

- **Power distance**

  Power distance measures the extent to which there is a hierarchy within society and institutions. If there is a high power distance this means that it is accepted that power is not equally distributed within society- those at the 'top' of a business, for example, have much more than those at the bottom in terms of salaries and benefits. Those lower down the organization are expected to listen to those at the top and not challenge them. If power distance is low there is far less sense of 'top' and 'bottom' and the business is likely to be more of a meritocracy.

- **Uncertainty avoidance**

  Uncertainty avoidance measures the extent to which people can cope without knowing precisely what is going to happen or what they should do. If people are tolerant of this they are able to cope with uncertainty. If they have a low tolerance they would find ambiguity stressful and prefer to have clear instructions and tasks. Low uncertainty avoidance people like the detail; high uncertainty avoidance people can live with the big picture and general direction.

- **Individualism vs collectivism**

  Individualism occurs when there is a 'me' culture. People look after themselves and focus on doing what they do well, even if it is at the expense of their colleagues. Imagine a sales team where each person is trying to sell more than everyone else to

9

win a bonus. In a collectivist culture there is more of a team approach with people working with each other for a common goal.

- **Masculinity vs femininity**

  According to Hofstede, masculinity refers to the extent to which society values success, money, and material things. Femininity refers to the extent to which society values caring for others. Competing to win is less important and there is greater empathy for those who are not successful.

- **Long-term orientation**

  This refers to how long individuals plan ahead. Some societies are focused much more on the here and now.

- **Indulgence**

  In what Hofstede calls an 'indulgent' culture individuals like to be free and act on impulse. In a more restrained society there is a sense that life is difficult and that service to others is the normal way to behave.

Hofstede's dimensions of culture are shown in Figure 9.5.

According to Hofstede, regions of the world can be grouped in terms of similar national cultures. For example, he argues that Scandinavian cultures are based on collectivism and consensus. Japan, France, Belgium, Spain, and Italy have a large power distance. Germany, Switzerland, and Austria have a low tolerance for ambiguity.

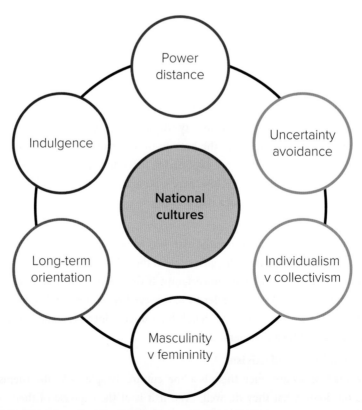

Figure 9.5 Hofstede's national cultures. *Source:* Hofstede (2011).

Differences in these aspects of culture can lead to very different ways of thinking and doing business. Someone with a collectivist view is likely to find someone with a more individualist approach as quite egocentric. Some managers may regard the long term as 10 to 15 years whilst others may regard three to five years as long term—this may lead to very different views of whether investment decisions are worth doing. In a high power distance culture the relationship between superiors and subordinates would be very different from in a culture where the difference is less. When dealing with managers and employees from around the world it is important to be aware of cultural differences and take account of this in when working together. Read Analysing the Business Data 9.3 for further exploration of how cultures can differ—in this example, between the US and China.

Analysing the business data 9.3 Cultural differences between the US and China

The data in Figure 1 shows how national cultures may differ in the USA and China according to Hofstede. The data is presented as index numbers ranging from 0 to 100. The higher the number, the stronger this dimension. You can see that there are some dimensions where these two countries are starkly different—individualism being one of them.

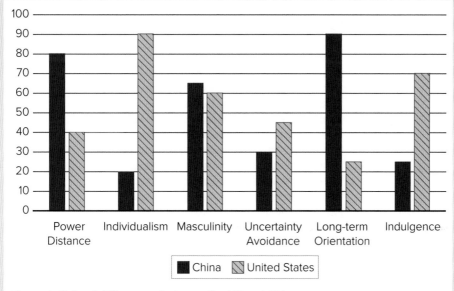

Figure 1 Cultural differences between the US and China. *Source:* The Culture Factor Group (2021). Hofstede Insights. Available at: https://www.hofstede-insights.com/product/compare-countries/ [Accessed 2 April 2023]. Adapted by the author.

Questions

What is the significance of the data above for a Chinese business wanting to take over a US business?

How might these differences affect the way a US manager manages its company's operations in China with local employees?

Source

www.hofstede-insights.com/product/compare-countries/

9.3.4 Technological factors in overseas markets

Moving on to the 'T' in PESTLE, technological factors also need to be considered by managers. The level of technology available within a country can vary considerably and this will affect the appeal of different regions. For example, access to the internet and the speed of internet access will affect how a business can operate in that market. The proportion of households with access to the internet around the world is shown in Analysing the Business Data 9.4.

Analysing the business data 9.4 Internet access around the world

The data in Figure 1 shows the proportion of the population in different regions that have access to the internet.

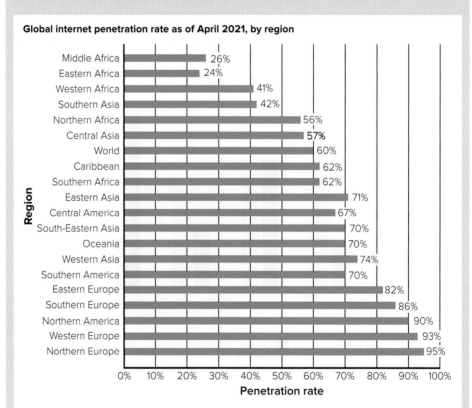

Global internet penetration rate as of April 2021, by region

Region	Penetration rate
Middle Africa	26%
Eastern Africa	24%
Western Africa	41%
Southern Asia	42%
Northern Africa	56%
Central Asia	57%
World	60%
Caribbean	62%
Southern Africa	62%
Eastern Asia	71%
Central America	67%
South-Eastern Asia	70%
Oceania	70%
Western Asia	74%
Southern America	70%
Eastern Europe	82%
Southern Europe	86%
Northern America	90%
Western Europe	93%
Northern Europe	95%

Figure 1 Internet access around the world. *Source:* Published by Petrosyan, A. (2023). Global internet penetration rate by region 2023, Statista. Available at: http://www.statista.com/statistics/269329/penetration-rate-of-the-internet-by-region/ [Accessed 2 April 2023].

Question

Discuss the significance of the data above for businesses and customers.

Source

www.statista.com/statistics/269329/penetration-rate-of-the-internet-by-region/

9.3.5 Legal factors

As well as technological factors, legal factors must be considered. The regulations facing businesses can vary significantly between countries. This will affect many aspects of a business' activity such as:

- Costs: laws will affect whether there is a minimum wage and if so what the minimum rate of pay is. Health and safety regulations will also add different costs for businesses around the world to be compliant.

- Flexibility: laws and regulations will determine how easy it is to hire and fire employees or how easy it is to set up and run a business. Delivery Hero and Just Eat Takeaway.com are two large food delivery businesses in Europe that have struggled to make the same returns as other similar businesses elsewhere in the world because of European labour laws and employee rights such as maternity leave, sickness pay, holiday entitlement, and redundancy which increase their costs.

- What can be produced or sold: some laws open up opportunities. For example, there are several countries, including Germany, which are about to legalize the sale of cannabis for recreational use. Several businesses including the large tobacco companies are investing heavily in preparation for this. Other laws limit options for businesses. For example, in 2017 the China Insurance Regulatory Commission banned insurance companies from offering insurance against acne, sleep deprivation, or smog.

The differences in legal systems will affect how easy it is to do business in a country. The Ease of Doing Business Index highlights how different it can be to try and operate in different regions of the world due to the amount of paperwork, the regulations, and the time taken to get permissions. The data on the Transparency Index in Analysing the Business Data 9.5 highlights how corruption levels can vary between countries; this again will influence the appeal of a country to business managers.

9.3.6 Environmental issues

Finally, managers must consider environmental factors—the 'E' of the PESTLE analysis. These refer to the growing concerns over the impact of business activity on the environment and how businesses need to consider this in their planning. Consumers, employees, investors, and government are all increasingly interested in the extent to which a business thinks about its environmental impact. Businesses need to think about where they produce, how they produce, what materials they use, where they are sourced, how their products are transported, and how they are disposed of. In 2021, for example, Apple announced it would provide parts for its products, making it possible for consumers to repair them and thereby reduce environmental waste. In 2022 the Serbian government revoked the Australian mining company Rio Tinto's licences to mine lithium. Rio Tinto was due to invest $2.4bn in a deal which would have made Serbia one of the world's largest producers of the metal that is key to producing batteries and in extremely high demand as many drivers switch to electric vehicles. The deal was cancelled because of the environmental impact of the mining.

In 2021, the United Nations Climate Change Conference (Known as C0P26) was held in Glasgow, UK. COP26 was a summit on environmental issues aimed at encouraging

Analysing the business data 9.5 Ease of doing business and transparency

The Ease of Doing Business Index is an annual report that covers 12 areas of business regulation. These include starting a business, dealing with construction permits, getting electricity, registering property, getting credit, protecting minority investors, paying taxes, trading across borders, enforcing contracts and resolving insolvency, regulation on employing workers, and contracting with the government. The overall ease or difficulty of these regulations in terms of businesses operating is shown in a ranking of economies. Listed in the following table are the top 10 countries in 2020 and the worst 10 countries in terms of the ease of doing business.

Rank	Economy	DB score
1	New Zealand	86.8
2	Singapore	86.2
3	Hong Kong SAR, China	85.3
4	Denmark	85.3
5	Korea, Rep.	84.0
6	United States	84.0
7	Georgia	83.7
8	United Kingdom	83.5
9	Norway	82.6
10	Sweden	82.0
180	Congo, Rep.	39.5
181	Timor-Leste	39.4
182	Chad	36.9
183	Congo, Dem. Rep.	36.2
184	Central African Republic	35.6
185	South Sudan	34.6
186	Libya	32.7
187	Yemen, Rep.	31.8
188	Venezuela, RB	30.2
189	Eritrea	21.6
190	Somalia	20.0

Transparency

Corruption is a major issue in business and it can make it difficult to enter a market or do business within a country. Corruption can take many forms: in some cases it is a government official taking millions to commission a particular project; in other situations, it is money paid to go to the top of a doctor's appointment lists. However, all forms of corruption damage society—they make it difficult to do business, which affects investment, jobs, and the standard of living. It is also unfair. The Corruption

Perception Index ranks 180 countries and territories by their perceived level of public sector corruption according to experts and businesspeople; the table shows the best and worst countries on that index in 2020.

Rank	Country	Region	
1	New Zealand	Asia Pacific	87
1	Denmark	Western Europe & EU	87
3	Finland	Western Europe & EU	86
4	Switzerland	Western Europe & EU	85
4	Singapore	Asia Pacific	85
4	Sweden	Western Europe & EU	85
173	Afghanistan	Asia Pacific	16
177	Yemen	Middle East and North Africa	15
178	Syria	Middle East and North Africa	13
179	South Sudan	Sub-Saharan Africa	12
180	Somalia	Sub-Saharan Africa	9

Source www.doingbusiness.org/en/reports/global-reports/doing-business-2020

Questions

What do you think is the significance of the above data for managers?

How do you think a government might make it easier to do business in its country?

How might corruption affect whether a business chooses to locate in a given country?

countries to deliver on the Paris Agreement goals of limiting global warming to 'well below' 2°C above pre-industrial levels. The drive towards significant improvements in business behaviour with regards to the environment is well underway although pressures and regulations do vary between countries. For example, the leaders of some countries such as Brazil, Iran, South Africa, Mexico, and Russia did not attend COP26. A report at the end of 2021 by Brazil's space research agency (Inpe) showed that deforestation in that country increased by 22% in a year. The Amazon rainforest provides an important store of carbon that slows down the pace of global warming. According to the latest data, some 13,235 sq km (5110 sq miles) was lost during the 2020–21 period, the highest amount since 2006.

The pressure on businesses to be more environmentally friendly does vary, therefore, between regions. Whereas some countries like Morocco and Gambia have been doing well in terms of reducing their emissions, others such as Russia, Ukraine, and Saudi Arabia have not, according to the *National Geographic* (2022).

9.3.7 Globalization

The significant differences that can exist between the PESTLE environment of countries adds a complexity to undertaking international business. This means that whilst operating overseas offers many opportunities, the challenges should not be underestimated.

Examples of businesses that have pulled out of overseas markets because they could not generate the returns required to make this viable include:

- Target, a US discount retailer store which withdrew from Canada having lost billions of dollars over two years;

- Home Depot, a huge DIY business which entered China in 2006 but after opening 12 stores it realized it has misread the market—in China people tend to employ contractors rather than try and do it themselves. Home Depot closed its stores in 2012.

- Walmart opened in Germany in 1997 but struggled with the regulatory environment and different shopping habits. It left Germany in 2006.

- Starbucks, the US coffee business, struggled in Australia after it entered in 2014 as customers preferred local stores. In 2014 Starbucks sold its remaining 24 shops.

- Hailo, the taxi finding app, lasted only a year and a half when entering the UK market in the middle of a price war between Uber and Lyft. It left the UK in October 2014.

- In 2009 Mattel entered China and built a huge Barbie store in Shanghai. Unfortunately, customers in China preferred more educational toys. The store closed two years later.

- Tesco entered the US market in 2007. This brand focused on fresh and organic food. However, when the US faced a recession, Fresh & Easy was wrongly positioned. After five years Tesco closed nearly 200 stores in the US.

As we can see from this list, success with overseas expansion is by no means guaranteed.

With growing levels of international business, organizations are very interlinked across the world. **Globalization** refers to this growing interdependence of businesses around the world. International business is not new—it has been occurring for hundreds of years. However, the growth of international business in recent years and the current scale of it nowadays is what leads people to talk about globalization.

Although globalization can bring many benefits as it becomes easier to work with businesses around the world, it does also bring risks. The fact that the world is so interlinked means that a problem in one country have a knock-on effect on others. Ian Goldin, a professor of globalization and development at Oxford University, co-wrote 'The Butterfly Defect, How Globalization Creates Systemic Risks, And What To Do About It'. According to Goldin and Mariathasan (2015) there are various risks that have been created due to globalization; for example, the credit crunch and banking crisis of 2008, and the vulnerability of the internet to cyber-attacks. Goldin argues that although the new global economic system brings huge benefits, there are also enormous risks. In his book he highlights the dangers of contagion both financial and medical.

 Can you now answer this question from the introductory case study?

What problems might Netflix face expanding internationally?

 Where are we now?

Using the PESTLE analysis tool, we have now considered some of the factors that create different business environments around the world and how national cultures may differ. We will now examine the reasons why international business has been growing.

9.4 Why has international business increased?

The importance of international business has generally been growing in recent years; businesses have increasingly seen opportunities overseas for expansion.

This growth in international business has been for a number of reasons including:

- **The appeal of economies of scale**
  By operating globally a business can experience lower unit costs and bring down prices. This may enable it to win market share in some markets. According to Theodore Levitt (1983) in the *Harvard Business Review*: 'The result is a new commercial reality: the emergence of global markets for standardized consumer products on a previously unimagined scale of magnitude. Corporations geared to this new reality benefit from enormous economies of scale in production, distribution, marketing, and management. By translating these benefits into reduced world prices, they can decimate competitors that still live in the disabling grip of old assumptions about how the world works.'

- **Lower transportation costs**
  Improvements in transportation and logistical systems have brought down the costs of moving products around the world. For example, the rise of containerization has increased efficiencies in road and sea transport and has made a significant contribution to the growth in world trade.

- **More powerful and more affordable technology**
  Developments in telecommunications have facilitated faster and easier communication around the world. They have made it easier to run businesses abroad, to order materials, to arrange sales, and to coordinate the supply and distribution channels.

- **Less protectionist measures,** such as tariffs and quotas, have generally made international trade easier.

- **Greater competitive pressures**
  Increased competition has forced businesses to find lower costs and better-quality inputs. This has made managers more willing to look further afield for resources.

- **Greater similarity in markets and tastes**
  With the growth of the internet, for example, people around the world can share music, fashion, films, and ideas. This brings people closer together and makes it easier to target markets all over the world.

What would you do?

You have built a successful construction business in your own country specializing in major road systems. However, government cutbacks and increasing competition have affected demand in recent years. How would you convince your Board of Directors of the potential that overseas expansion may bring?

Analysing the business data 9.6 Growth in exports as a percentage of world income

Figure 1 shows the value of exports as a percentage of world national income (GDP). The growth in this figure shows a growth in the significance of trade in the world.

Figure 1 Value of exported goods as a percentage of world income. *Source:* Ortiz-Ospina, E. (2018). *We've updated our entry on trade and Globalization*, Our World in Data. Available at: https://ourworldindata.org/weve-updated-our-entry-on-trade-and-globalization [Accessed 2 April 2023].

Questions

Why do you think the value of exported goods has risen as a percentage of world income?

Consider the possible causes of the trend in exports as a percentage of national income in China. What do you think the main causes are?

- **More trade agreements between countries**

  Within these trading areas (or 'blocs') safety, trading, and quality standards and regulations are often agreed between member countries making it easier for businesses to trade.

9.4.1 Trading areas

One feature of recent years that has led to more international business has been the growth of trading areas organized by different countries. Governments of these countries have come together to agree rules of trade amongst themselves to make it easier for businesses

Think about it

Why do you think that most international trade is between businesses in countries that are physically close to each other?

amongst members to trade amongst themselves. These trading agreements are usually between countries which are geographically close to each the as the majority of international trade tends to be with nearby countries. Examples of trading areas (or 'blocs') are Mercosur (which consists of Argentina, Brazil, Paraguay, and Uruguay) and Asean (which includes Indonesia, Malaysia, the Philippines, Singapore, and Thailand).

The growth in global trade has been helped by the work of the Word Trade Organization (WTO). The WTO was established in 1995 to promote trade between countries. The WTO deals with the rules of trade among member countries and tries to reduce or remove any barriers to trade.

Analysing the business data 9.7 Exports

Figure 1 shows the countries that have the highest value of exports in the world.

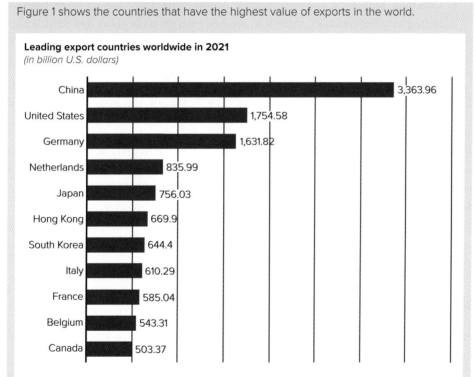

Figure 1 Leading export countries worldwide. *Source:* Published by Statista Research Department (2022). Leading export countries globally 2021, Statista. Available at: https://www.statista.com/statistics/264623/leading-export-countries-worldwide/ [Accessed 2 April 2023].

Questions

Why do you think these countries have such high exports?

How could a government encourage more exports?

Why might exporting be good for a country?

What would you do?

Imagine a country is considering joining the European Union. How would you outline the potential benefits of this to your company's shareholders?

These trade areas can lead to trade creation, which occurs when joining a trading area leads to the growth in trade between the member countries, and trade diversion, which occurs when joining a trading agreement leads to a fall in trade with non-member countries.

There are different types of trading area. These include:

- **Free Trade Areas**. In free trade areas barriers to trade (such as tariffs or quotas) among member countries are removed. An example of this is NAFTA, the North American Free Trade Agreement.

- **Customs Union**. A customs union occurs when there are no tariffs between member countries and there is a common trade policy towards non-member countries.

- **Common Market**. A common market occurs when there are no trade barriers among member countries, there is a common external trade policy and there is also freedom of movement of factors of production among member countries.

- **Economic Union**. An economic union has no trade barriers, a common external policy, freedom of movement of, and also agreement and integration of, economic policies between members. The European Union is an example of an economic union.

Membership of these trading blocs will change over time due to political changes. For example, for many years it looked like there would be a Trans Pacific partnership. This was a proposed trade agreement between Australia, Brunei, Canada, Chile, Japan, Malaysia, Mexico, New Zealand, Peru, Singapore, Vietnam, and the US. However, in 2017 President Trump decided that the US would not go ahead with this deal. Meanwhile on 31 January 2020 the UK officially left the European Union. The UK decided that it wanted to be free to create its own trading agreements outside of the European Union.

9.4.2 Multinational Enterprises (MNEs)

A multinational enterprise is a business which has a production base in more than one country.

A business may want to have these bases abroad for several reasons. For example, it may want to be closer to their markets and reduce transportation costs. It may also be able to make use of local resources or gain subsidies or tax advantages from governments wanting to attract foreign investment.

An example of a multinational enterprise is Orbia. Orbia describes itself as 'a purpose-led company' that aims to 'advance life around the world'. It aims to reduce food and water scarcity, improve access to healthcare, improve the global data infrastructure, and reinvent cities and homes. Originally a Mexican commodities producer called Mexichem the company now operates in 41 countries and employs more than 22,000 people worldwide.

Why governments may want to attract multinational enterprises

A government may welcome multinational businesses to its country because:

- they bring jobs and finance into the country
- they pay taxes (and so do their employees) which provides income to the government
- they bring technology, expertise, and ways of working which can benefit other businesses in the country
- they train local employees.

However, a government may be reluctant to welcome multinationals in some cases because these foreign businesses may exploit local resources but share relatively little expertise and technology. They may also use accounting techniques to ensure profits are recorded outside of the country and so little tax is paid to the host country. For example, the government of Ireland has attracted multinational investment with low taxes; however, in 2021 the Parliamentary Budget Office raised concerns that there was a dual economy in the country with multinationals making large profits while small domestic companies are less likely to (*The Irish Times* 2021).

Although businesses do operate globally, generally multinational enterprises continue to earn most of their revenues in domestic markets. Typically, they operate within their own region. Professor Alan Rugman has written extensively about the importance of the Triad. The Triad refers to the key regions of the European Union, America, and Japan. The largest multinationals tend to have their sales and operations focused within the region where they originated.

The activities of multinational enterprises are mainly linked to trade and **foreign direct investment (FDI)**. Foreign Direct Investment refers to money invested in shares in other countries. According to the World Bank (2020) around 50% of all trade and 80% of Foreign Direct Investment is made by the world's largest 500 multinational enterprises. Inward FDI flows occur when money comes into a country from foreign-owned MNEs to their subsidiaries. Outward FDI flows occur when money flows out of a country from businesses to their subsidiaries in other countries.

In 2020 China overtook the US as the world's top destination for new foreign direct investment according to a report from the United Nations Conference on Trade and Development (UNCTAD). This reflected China's growing economic importance in the world. China had inflows of $163bn (£119bn) in 2020, compared to $134bn flowing into the US. In 2019, the US received $251bn in new foreign direct investment while China received $140bn.

Foreign Direct Investment normally involves one company taking over another; one of the consequences of the COVID-19 pandemic was less foreign investment flow and a significant fall in FDI globally.

9.4.3 Managing an international business: Global or local?

Businesses that operate with bases abroad must decide on how best to manage these. To do this, managers will consider the extent to which products need to be adjusted to local conditions, and the extent to which there are advantages running the business as a global operation or as separate units.

Regarding the extent to which the products of the business need to be adjusted to local conditions: some products may be global—they can be sold all over the world in essentially the same format. For example, oil, cigarettes, cameras, watches, and razors. The advantage of keeping the product the same all over the world is that the business can benefit from economies of scale through larger-scale production. However, it is important to meet regional needs and this may require adaptation. Some products may need some adaptation for different markets—for example, some clothing and drinks may need to be changed for different regional conditions and tastes. Some products that may need to be adapted quite significantly for different countries include advertisements, education, and food. As we saw with Nestlé's KitKat it may be necessary to treat some markets very differently than others and this is where a regional organizational structure may be appropriate,

Regarding the extent to which there are advantages running the business as a global operation or as separate units, are there benefits in each base recruiting and training its own staff or could this be done in a more centralized way and staff moved around the world? Is there a benefit in centralizing all research and development or is this best done locally? There answer is there will be a balance: market research may be done better in regional markets whereas major investment decisions may be better done with a global perspective. The decision is about what decisions are made where. Some staff may be better recruited locally whereas you may want a team of senior managers who have global experience and are chosen and deployed centrally.

Decisions about local responsiveness and integration lead to four types of strategy when managing an international business. These are shown in Figure 9.6.

Think about it

Can you think of more examples of products that are global? What about those that have to be adapted for local markets?

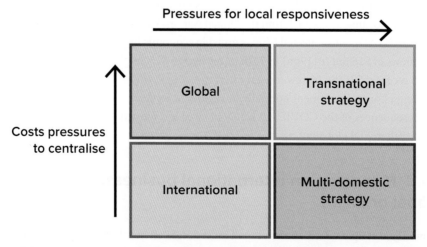

Figure 9.6 International strategies adapted from Bartlett and Ghoshal. *Source:* Bartlett, C. and Ghoshal, S. (1987). Managing across borders: New organizational responses. *Sloan Management Review*, 29(1), 43–53.

- **An export strategy**

  This approach occurs when the business remains very domestically focused. The products are left as they are in the domestic market but this may transfer well for the right products if the brand is strong. For example, Brompton folding bicycles are made in the UK but exported to many countries around the world.

- **A multi-domestic strategy**

  This approach allows different parts of the business to operate independently in different markets. Products are adapted to local tastes and there is little global overview of the business. Businesses are flexible to their local markets but there are no global synergies. For example, 7-Eleven tailors the products stocked, the payment methods, and marketing to each country in which it operates.

- **A global strategy**

  This approach occurs when there is little adaptation of the product for local needs. Products are standardized for all markets (e.g. commodities) and there are seen to be benefits from thinking on global lines (e.g. economies of scale for research and development). Gillette is an example of a business that sells the same product globally. Bic is another global business selling similar lighters and stationery products all over the world. In 2021 23.7 million Bic products were produced daily.

- **A transnational strategy**

  This approach is a complex strategy in which products are responsive to local conditions but managers also seek to benefit from a global coordination of key activities. The aim is to share learning and resources across the global units. The consumer goods business, Unilever, is an example of a transnational company. Writing in the *Harvard Business Review* in 1992 the co-chairman and CEO of Unilever wrote that the company was a transnational business that thinks globally but acts locally. He said that the very nature of its products requires proximity to local markets but the company also wanted to benefit from economies of scale in head office departments.

Protectionism

Whilst international trade brings opportunities it also brings threats. Some businesses and some governments will want to protect themselves against foreign competition. Protectionism occurs when governments try to protect their domestic industries against foreign competition. This may be through taxes placed on foreign products (called tariffs), limits on the quantity of foreign imports (called quotas), or other ways of making it difficult for foreign businesses to enter or compete in the domestic market. For example, in 2018 the US and China entered a major protectionist war in which tariffs were imposed on many different products. The US President Donald Trump accused China of unfair trading practices and intellectual property theft. He argued that many US innovations were illegally adopted in China. By 2020 the US had imposed tariffs on more than $360 bn (£268 bn) of Chinese goods, and China had retaliated with tariffs on more than $110 bn of US products.

Protectionist measures can affect the revenue of businesses by making overseas markets more difficult or more expensive to access. Protectionism can also affect the costs and quality of a business by making it more difficult or more expensive to get foreign supplies.

Protectionism may be introduced for many reasons by governments. For example, it may want to protect key industries, to retaliate against unfair foreign competition, or to support industries that need time to develop and grow. However, the consequences of protectionism are higher prices and less choice for customers. Those who believe in free trade (i.e. they are against protectionism) argue that trade brings businesses and customers more products at lower prices from all over the world. The World Trade Organization is an international organization that deals with the rules of trade among member countries. It aims to reduce protectionism between its members and settle any disputes.

The reasons for and against protectionism are shown in Table 9.4.

Table 9.4 Reasons for and against protectionism

Reasons for protectionism	Arguments against protectionism
Protect industries as they are still developing	Reduces choice for producers and consumers leading to poor quality and higher prices
Protect against unfair competition from abroad	Allow domestic producers to be inefficient and survive

Business insight 9.7 Russian food prices

In 2021 the Russian government stated that it was going to continue its restrictions on exports of key food products. The government was worried by recent price rises at home and intervened to limit the domestic price of staple items such as sugar and flour. The government said it would consider how best to support its food exports whilst protecting domestic consumers from price increases. In recent years Russia has been one of the world's largest exporters of grain.

Food prices are a very significant political issue for the Russian government given that 20 million people, or around one in seven Russians, live below the poverty line, and rationing and hyperinflation occurred in the country not that long ago. In December 2020, President Vladimir Putin ordered temporary price controls on key foodstuffs such as sunflower oil and pasta. A wheat export quota was announced in early 2021 and export taxes added later. The government said that these policies were needed because of years of falling incomes that have made essential goods unaffordable for many. The government also introduced subsidies for some products, such as bread and flour.

Russia only began exporting key foodstuffs such as wheat after 2014, when it banned most western food imports in response to US and EU sanctions, and then began heavily developing its domestic agriculture. Agricultural goods, such as wheat, accounted for almost 8% of Russia's $419 bn of exports in 2019, according to World Trade Organization data. However, the country does not have the infrastructure to stockpile food on the same level as the US or Europe. If it did have sufficient warehousing it could stockpile in the good years and release the surplus when there were shortages.

Officials in Russia blamed higher food prices in the country on the greed of producers and retailers. This led to fears of government action to punish these groups. According to a presidential survey more than three quarters of Russian businessmen felt unsafe from unfounded criminal prosecution by the state.

Question

Do you think protectionist measures such as those above in Russia are good for business?

Source

Financial Times (2022). www-ft-com.ezproxy01.rhul.ac.uk/content/07378501-0ab9-4eef-ad13-eb72adff1838

Where are we now?

Growth is a very common business objective. It provides the opportunity for economies of scale and greater market power. Managers must decide on the form of growth—for example, internal or external—and how to manage the challenges of growth. International business creates many opportunities in terms of producing abroad and selling to different markets. Expanding overseas provides growth opportunities that may not be available domestically. However, expanding internationally brings many challenges due to differences in the business environment and culture. Businesses must decide how best to expand overseas and how to manage their international operations.

In the next chapter we consider the challenges and opportunities that change can provide to a business. We also examine the determinants and importance of business culture and how the structure of a business affects its performance.

 ## Now you should know

- Economies of scale occur when a business grows and its unit costs fall.
- Organic growth occurs when a business grows by increasing sales internally.
- Internal growth means expanding the business by growing its existing operations.
- External growth occurs when a business grows by joining with another business.
- Mergers occur when two or businesses join together to create a new business.
- An acquisition or takeover occurs when one business gains control of another.
- A hostile acquisition is an unwelcome bid for a company.
- A friendly acquisition is a welcome bid for a company.
- Horizontal integration occurs when one business joins with another at the same stage of the same production process.

9

- Vertical integration occurs when one business joins with another at a different stage of the same production process.

- Conglomerate integration occurs when one business joins with another in a different production process.

- Franchising is the granting of a licence by one person (the franchisor) to another (the franchisee), which entitles the franchisee to own and operate their own business under the brand, systems, and proven business model of the franchisor.

- Foreign Direct Investment refers to money invested in shares in other countries.

- An emerging economy is typically defined as one where the income per person is low to medium and where the economy is moving towards being developed.

Review questions

Quick check

1. Describe what is meant by franchising.

2. State three reasons why a business might want to grow.

3. Outline the difference between organic and external growth.

4. State three ways a business might enter an international market.

5. Explain one possible problem for a business of an acquisition.

6. Explain one reason why a business might want to expand internationally rather than domestically.

7. Explain one benefit and one potential disadvantage of a business growing through franchising.

8. Explain one reason a government might want to attract multinationals to its country.

Analysis

1. Analyse the reasons why growth is a common business objective.

2. Analyse the factors a business might consider before expanding internationally.

3. Analyse the factors a business might consider before expanding through franchising.

Discussion

1. According to Levitt (1983) globalization has led to 'needs and desires being irrevocably homogenized'. He suggests the world has become one global market. Do you agree with this view?

2. To what extent do you think your government should try to attract more multinationals?

3. To what extent do you think business growth is driven more by ego than commercial reality?

∿➤ Find out more

- You can find out more about franchising at the British Franchising Association website https://www.thebfa.org/what-is-franchising/ or the International Franchising Association www.franchise.org
- Hofstede is regarded as an expert on national cultures. You can find out more about Hofstede's work at www.hofstede.com and by searching for 'Hofstede on culture' on You Tube.
- You might be interested in these *Harvard Business Review* articles: Levitt's 'The Globalization of Markets' in 1983 and Hamel, G. and Prahalad,C. 'Do you really have a global strategy' in July 1985.
- You might visit these websites for more information:
  World Trade Organization www.wto.org
  World Bank www.worldbank.org

☰ Bibliography

7-Eleven (n.d.). *About 7-Eleven corporate*. Available at: https://sites.7-eleven.com/corp/about [Accessed 22 March 2023].

Agarwal, S. and Ramaswami, S. (1992). Choice of foreign market entry mode: Impact of ownership, location and internalization factors. *Journal of International Business Studies*, 23(1), 1–27.

Agrawal, A., Jaffe, J. F., and Mandelker, G. N. (1992). The post-merger performance of acquiring firms: A re-examination of an anomaly. *Journal of Finance*, 47(4), 1605–1621.

Bartlett, C. and Ghoshal, S. (1989). *Managing Across Borders: The Transnational Solution*. Boston, Harvard Business School Press.

Bartlett, C. and Ghoshal, S. (2000). *Transnational Management: Text and Readings* (3rd edn). New York, McGraw-Hill/Irwin.

Birkinshaw, Julian (2000). *Entrepreneurship in the Global Firm*. London, Sage.

BBC News (2022). Brazil: Amazon sees worst deforestation levels in 15 years. [online] Available at: <https://www.bbc.com/news/world-latin-america-59341770> [Accessed 12 February 2022].

Dyvik, E. H. (2022). *Biggest companies in the world by Market Capitalization 2022, Statista*. Available at: https://www.statista.com/statistics/263264/top-companies-in-the-world-by-market-capitalization/ [Accessed 22 March 2023].

Financial Times (2022a). Serbia pulls plug on planned Rio Tinto lithium mine. [online] Available at: <https://www.ft.com/content/423077d0-949e-4793-81a8-ee8e2982623e> [Accessed 12 February 2022].

Financial Times (2022b). www-ft-com.ezproxy01.rhul.ac.uk. 2022. [online] Available at: <https://www-ft-com.ezproxy01.rhul.ac.uk/content/6c4e4ea6-d263-11e6-9341-7393bb2e1b51> [Accessed 12 February 2022].

Goldin, I. and Mariathasan, M. (2015). *The Butterfly Defect: How Globalization Creates Systemic Risks, and What to Do about It*. Princeton, Princeton University Press.

Greiner, L. E. (1998). Evolution and Revolution as Organizations Grow. *Harvard Business Review*, 76(3), 55–67.

Hofstede, G. (2011). Dimensionalizing Cultures: The Hofstede Model in Context. *Online Readings in Psychology and Culture*, 2(1).

Laricchia, F. (2023). Smartphone market shares by vendor 2009–2022. Available at: https://www.statista.com/statistics/271496/global-market-share-held-by-smartphone-vendors-since-4th-quarter-2009/ [Accessed 22 March 2023].

Levitt, T. (1983). The globalization of markets. *Harvard Business Review*, 93–94.

Maljers, F. A. (2021). Inside Unilever: The Evolving Transnational Company. *Harvard Business Review* [online] Available at: <https://hbr.org/1992/09/inside-unilever-the-evolving-transnational-company> [Accessed 27 October 2021].

National Geographic (2022). World climate change report card: These countries are meeting goals. [online] Available at: <https://www.nationalgeographic.com/environment/article/climate-change-report-card-co2-emissions> [Accessed 12 February 2022].

New York Times (2021). *U.S. and States Say Facebook Illegally Crushed Competition*. [online]. Available at: <https://www.nytimes.com/2020/12/09/technology/facebook-antitrust-monopoly.html> [Accessed 27 October 2021].

Orbia.com (2021). Advance Life Around the World [online]. Available at: <https://www.orbia.com/our-purpose/> [Accessed 27 October 2021].

Porter, M. (1990). *The Competitive Advantages of Nations*. New York, Free Press.

Rugman, A. M. (1985). The Comparative Performance of U.S. and European Multinational Enterprises, 1970–79. *Management International Review*, 23(2), 4–14.

9

Singh, H. and Montgomery, C. A. (1987). Corporate acquisition strategies and economic performance. *Strategic Management Journal*, 8(4), 377–386.

Stigler, G. (1950). Monopoly and oligopoly by merger. *American Economic Review*, 40(2), 23–34.

Sudarsanam, S. (2003). *Creating Value from Mergers and Acquisitions*. Harlow, Essex, U.K., Pearson Education.

The Culture Factor Group (n.d.) Country comparison tool. Available at: https://www.hofstede-insights.com/country-comparison-tool [Accessed 27 October 2023].

The Economist (2021). *China's crackdown on the online-education business marks a turning-point*. [online] Available at: <https://www.economist.com/leaders/2021/07/31/chinas-crackdown-on-the-online-education-business-marks-a-turning-point> [Accessed 27 October 2021].

The Economist (2022a). [online] Available at: <https://www.economist.com/business/why-microsoft-is-splashing-69bn-on-video-games/21807242> [Accessed 12 February 2022].

The Economist (2022b). India is likely to be the world's fastest-growing big economy this year. Available at: https://www.economist.com/briefing/2022/05/14/india-is-likely-to-be-the-worlds-fastest-growing-big-economy-this-year [Accessed 27 October 2023].

The Irish Times (2021). *State has 'dual economy' between multinationals and domestic firms, budget office says*. [online] Available at: <https://www.irishtimes.com/business/economy/state-has-dual-economy-between-multinationals-and-domestic-firms-budget-office-says-1.4675133> [Accessed 27 October 2021].

World Bank (2020). Available at: <https://thedocs.worldbank.org/en/doc/c9af-0143184de77cb58ddd5adf024508-0350012021/original/Chapter-1-An-Investment-Perspective-on-Global-Value-Chains.pdf>

Chapter 10

Change, culture, and organizational structure

 Where are we now?

Change is a constant feature of business. Some change is planned, some is unexpected, some is internal, some is external, some is fast, some is slow—there are many forms of change. But, whatever the form, we know change is inevitable. In this chapter we will examine the importance of change, why people often resist it, and what business leaders can do to manage it effectively. We will also consider the importance of the culture of a business in terms of its performance. 'How we do things around here' affects the priorities of employees and how they behave; this can have a big impact on employee performance. Lastly, we consider the way that a business is structured, for example, how are jobs grouped together and who reports to whom? The structure of an organization can affect many aspects of its performance, such as its costs and speed of decision-making.

Why am I studying this?

- When you are working in a business you will need to make changes and know how best to respond to change; what does this involve and how could you overcome resistance to change? In this chapter we will consider how to manage change.
- You know from your friends that the businesses they work for have different expectations of what employees do and how they behave; why is this and why does it matter? In this chapter we examine the culture of businesses.
- Businesses often talk about restructuring—what does this mean and why does it matter? In this chapter we explore the different aspects of organizational structure.

10

- You have seen several businesses announce they were restructuring to improve performance and you want to understand why this matters. In this chapter we consider the benefits of different approaches to organizational structure.

Learning objectives

By the end of this chapter you should be able to:

- Analyse different forms of change
- Apply force field analysis to managing change
- Analyse why people might resist change and how to overcome resistance to change
- Analyse types of culture
- Analyse job design
- Discuss different forms of organizational structure
- Examine the advantages and disadvantages of centralization and decentralization
- Explain Peters and Waterman's features of an excellent organization

Introductory case study Culture at 3M

3M is an American multinational business that focuses on innovation. It has bases in over 70 countries across the world and global sales of over $32 billion. It has 93,500 employees globally and sells its products in around 200 countries. More than 60,000 3M products are used in homes, businesses, schools, hospitals, and other industries. One third of the company's sales come from products invented within the past five years.

The business aims to create an inclusive environment where employees feel safe, engaged, and free to create and innovate. It wants everyone to be valued regardless of experience, ethnicity, sexual orientation age, gender, faith, personality, or styles. It says that different cultures, nationalities, backgrounds, insights, and physical and mental abilities of employees generates the creativity it needs as a business and keeps the company progressing.

3M says that that its culture supports and appreciates differences, and at the same time provides fair and equal opportunities for all employees. Inclusion, it believes, leads to employee engagement which in turn supports collaboration, creativity, and innovation that are the key to the company's long-term growth. 3M encourages employees to ask 'what if?'. It considers all employees leaders and provides opportunities for them to develop throughout their career. It prides itself on its ethical approach. It says that honesty and integrity are at the heart of the business. It believes it has the ability to drive positive change in the business community and in societies all over the world.

As part of its approach, 3M has what it calls a unique 15% Culture. This encourages employees to set aside 15% of their work time to proactively cultivate and pursue innovative ideas that interest them. This gives employees space to pursue projects that they believe have potential and allow them to challenge the status quo. Employees are encouraged to create new teams and innovate. It has a flexible approach to working. It aims to find the working patterns that enables employees to find the best pattern for them to maximize their productivity.

In 2019 3M announced a new streamlined organizational structure in a programme which it called Transformation. Transformation has included a move from five to four business groups; safety and industrial products, transportation and electronics, healthcare, and consumer. These business groups now have full responsibility for all aspects of strategy, product portfolio development, and the allocation of resources. These groups are responsible for domestic and international operations. Previously country teams were responsible for setting priorities in their regions. The aim of these structural changes was to improve the value provided to customers and increase business efficiency.

3M continues to abide by the principles of William McKnight who was president of the company in 1929. These include placing great value on initiative and autonomy. McKnight said that as the business grew it became more important to delegate responsibility and encourage men and women to use their initiative. McKnight recognized that mistakes would be made but said that if the person is essentially the right person for the job the mistakes they make will not be as serious in the long run as mistakes that are made if their managers try to tell them exactly how to do their job. McKnight's approach was to hire good people and then leave them alone! McKnight also believed it was important to challenge the existing ways of doing things and give people the space to question.

Employees at 3M are encouraged to follow what are described as the 'key behaviours of leaders'; namely:

- Play to win
- Prioritize and execute
- Foster collaboration and teamwork
- Develop others and self
- Innovate
- Act with integrity and transparency.

According to a Sloan Review study the most frequently discussed value at 3M is agility.

3M also has a Code of Conduct for employees. These expect employees to:

- Be good
- Be honest
- Be fair
- Be loyal
- Be accurate
- Be respectful.

For some the culture of 3M is important to its success and can create a competitive advantage. As the company's Chief Technology Officer said in an article in WARC: 'Cultures are unique and extraordinarily difficult to duplicate. And it takes a real effort to sustain them.'

Sources

www.3m.co.uk/3M/en_GB/company-uk/about-3m/

multimedia.3m.com/mws/media/1787775O/3m-corporate-brochure-ner.pdf

sloanreview.mit.edu/culture500/company/c101/3M

www.warc.com/newsandopinion/news/unique-culture-key-for-3m/28353

You Tube video on 15% culture www.youtube.com/watch?v=1D3DqIMLntM

Introductory case study questions

1. Summarize the features of 3M's culture. How does 3M's culture help the business to succeed?

2. Do you think 3M is likely to be centralized or decentralized ? Why?

3. Why does 3M have a Code of Conduct?

4. Why might 3M have restructured the business?

5. Why might there have been some resistance to the change in organizational structure at 3M?

6. How might 3M have overcome any resistance to this change?

7. Why do you think change is important to 3M?

8. Why do you think culture is difficult to duplicate?

9. How do you think culture can be a competitive advantage for a business?

Critical thinking

1. Many businesses, such as 3M, say that they want to be inclusive and yet there remain many cases of discrimination in business. Why do you think discrimination continues? How can businesses make sure they live up to their stated intentions?

2. The organizational change called Transformation at 3M sounds very positive. Why might some take a different view of it?

10.1 Change

Change is a constant of business. Change can be incremental or sudden; it can be expected (such as the ongoing ageing of the population in countries such as Japan and Italy) or unexpected (such as the COVID-19 pandemic). It can be external—changes in the macro- or the competitive environment. For example, new laws, new government policies, changes in society, or the 2022 war in Ukraine are all factors that could affect the costs or demands of a business. Change can also be internal—for example, new managers, new values, and new objectives can affect how and where a business wants to compete, or how it operates. For example, in its survey of Chief Executive Officers (CEOs) in 2022 IBM found that 37% more CEOs rated sustainability as a top priority than the year before.

Whatever form it takes, the one thing that is certain is that change will happen and that it will create opportunities and threats. Employees must therefore be looking ahead to try to anticipate what changes might occur and, where appropriate, prepare for this. The ability to have a view of where the business might need to be, or should be, in the future is a key factor in effective leadership. Depending on how significant the change is it may affect all or most employees within a business, not only the leaders. Increasingly, organizations are seeking employees who are resilient and adaptable—these attributes help an individual to respond well to change, and as change becomes more frequent, it is very important for organizations to have staff who are able to deal with change.

Key concepts

Organizational inertia occurs when a business stays as it is and is slow to change.

A failure to respond to change is called **organizational inertia** and this is usually very risky. The need to explore the opportunities of change and/or mitigate the risks is important for a business to be successful. In many cases managers will need to lead change and this will often involve overcoming the resistance to it; whilst some may benefit from any given change, others may well be worse off (or perceive they will be worse off) and this will lead to people resisting the change even if it may be better ultimately for the organization as a whole.

10.1.1 Change and Lewin's force-field analysis

Kurt Lewin (a German-American psychologist) produced a study of change in 1947 which highlighted that at any moment there will be forces for change and forces against change. It is known as the force-field analysis. If these forces are equally balanced the situation will stay as it is. If a manager wants to bring about change they must increase the pressures to change and/or reduce the forces preventing it.

The different forces in Lewin's force-field analysis are illustrated in Figure 10.1.

Imagine, for example, a business wants to move more of its operations online. The forces for change (called driving forces) may be:

- The need to reduce costs
- The growing use of the internet by customers
- The growth of online sales by competitors.

The factors resisting change (called restraining forces) may be:

- A lack of investment in IT (meaning the infrastructure is poor)
- A lack of skills in the workforce
- A reluctance to change an approach which has been successful in the past.

These driving and restraining forces may counterbalance each other, leading the business to carry on as it is unless the forces for change become stronger or the forces against

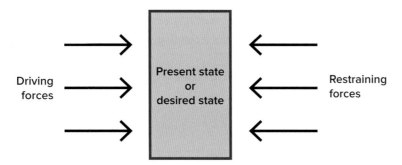

Figure 10.1 Lewin's force-field analysis model highlighting driving and restraining forces for change. *Source:* Lewin, K. (1951). *Field Theory in Social Science*. New York, Harper and Row.

Key concepts

Driving forces are factors in a situation that push for change.
Restraining forces are factors in a situation that prevent change.

become weaker. For example, imagine the COVID-19 pandemic led a government to close the stores in a country to reduce the number of people gathering together. This would immediately increase the forces for change when it comes to moving the operations of a business online, because it removes any idea that carrying on without a robust online operation could work. This could shift the situation and bring about rapid change, as indeed it did. To bring about change, therefore, a shift in the balance of driving and restraining forces needs to occur or needs to be made to occur.

What would you do?

You need to make redundancies at your business but are facing major resistance from trade unions.
  How might you increase the forces for change or reduce the forces against change?

According to Lewin (1947), if managers want to bring about change there are three stages in the process. Firstly, managers must 'unfreeze' the existing behaviour. This means they must increase the dissatisfaction with the current position and/or increase the willingness to change.

Secondly, managers must help to move behaviour to the new desired location. This means that managers must be clear what the objective is and must bring about the necessary changes to move the business there. Change does not happen immediately—it is a process of transition.

Lastly, managers must 're-freeze'. This means they need to get the new behaviours accepted. To re-freeze managers could, for example, ensure the reward and appraisal systems reinforce the desired behaviour and do not reward the old behaviour. It is important to 're-freeze' the change to stop behaviour reverting back to where it was.

Imagine that a business wants to introduce new technology. To help bring about this change the managers might highlight factors such as falling profits or higher costs than rivals as driving forces. This could help unfreeze the existing behaviours and increase the relative strength of the driving forces over the restraining forces. To further help unfreeze behaviours managers could evidence the costs and benefits of using the new technology, and show in their plans how this could help to maintain sales and jobs. This can help the move to the new position. Managers can then re-freeze the new situation by showing the halt to the decline in sales as a result of the technology to reinforce that this was the right decision.

The three stages of change can be seen in Figure 10.2.

What would you do?

You want to move your head office out of the capital which is where it has always been located. How would you unfreeze employees' views? How would you move and then refreeze them?

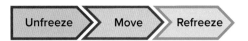

Figure 10.2 Lewin's three stages of change. *Source:* Lewin, K. (1951). *Field Theory in Social Science.* New York, Harper and Row.

 Can you now answer this question from the Introductory case study?

What forces might bring about change at 3M?
What forces might resist change?

Where are we now?

Now we've covered what change is and the forces which drive and restrain change, we will move on to look at how change can be managed.

10.1.2 Managing change

When managing change managers should consider the following questions:

1. **Why is change wanted or needed?**

   Managers need to be able to explain to themselves, and others, the key forces driving the change so that the need for it is understood.

2. **What type of change is needed?**

   There are different ways a problem may be solved or an opportunity exploited. Managers should consider whether their focus is on changing the organization itself, individuals within it, the way that work is done, or the way that teams work together.

3. **Will there be resistance to the change and, if so, how best can this be managed?**

   Managers should identify the stakeholders of the business, how they will be affected, and how they might react. Managers must assess which groups they are most concerned about and which groups are most likely to resist and delay the change. They will then need to decide on the best way to manage this change. Employee resistance to change and how to overcome it is examined in the next sections in more detail.

4. **Who will be responsible for managing the change process?**

   The person or team put in charge of managing the change will need to have the right skills. They will need experience, they will want a clear vision of what they are aiming to achieve, and they need to be good organizers. Change will usually involve setting objectives, allocating budgets, and coordinating people and other resources.

A key part of successful change is effective communication—organizations need to make sure people know what is happening, why it is happening, and how it will come about. It is

10

important to ensure everyone knows what their role in the change is and have a chance to raise their concerns or fears. People need to be kept informed on how things are progressing and what the final destination looks like. For those at the centre of change it can be stressful and, in some cases, very fast-changing; it can be easy in these circumstances to be so focused on making the change happen that communication with others less directly involved in decision-making is neglected.

When trying to manage change it is important to remember that people will react in different ways. For some, change may be seen as an opportunity to prove themselves; for others, it may threaten an existing and previously successful way of working. People bringing about change must be sensitive to, and plan for, different reactions by different stakeholders.

10.1.3 Employee resistance to change

There are many reasons why employees might resist a particular change. According to Kotter and Schlesinger (1979) these reasons for resistance can be grouped under four headings:

- **Parochial self-interest**

  This means that people will resist a change if they think they will be worse off as a result of it. Perhaps they think they will lose their job or have lower status.

- **Misunderstanding and lack of trust**

  People may resist change if they do not understand the reasons behind it or why it is occurring.

- **Different assessments**

  People may resist change if they think it is wrong and will not lead to the outcomes intended. People may have a different assessment of what actually needs to be done to achieve the end result required.

- **Low tolerance for change**

  Some people like things the way they are. They do not want to change because they prefer to just keep the existing ways of doing things.

These reasons why people resist change are shown in Figure 10.3.

Can you now answer this question from the Introductory case study?

Why might there have been some resistance to the change in organizational structure at 3M?

10.1.4 Overcoming resistance to change

To overcome resistance to change managers need to understand what lies behind the resistance. They need to consider the factors identified in Figure 10.3 and from this determine the appropriate methods to resolve them.

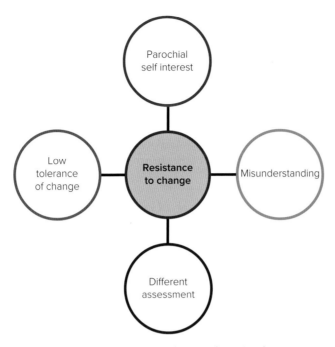

Figure 10.3 Kotter and Schlesinger's reasons why people resist change. *Source:* Kotter, J. P. and Schlesinger, L. A. (1979). 'Choosing Strategies for Change.' *Harvard Business Review*, 57(2), (March–April).

Analysing the business data 10.1

One way that employees sometimes respond to change is to take industrial action and strike. The data in Figure 1 compares the average annual number of strike days in different countries.

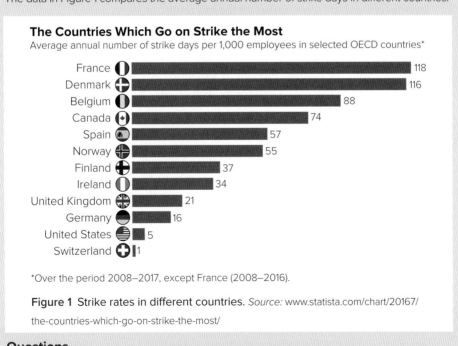

The Countries Which Go on Strike the Most
Average annual number of strike days per 1,000 employees in selected OECD countries*

France	118
Denmark	116
Belgium	88
Canada	74
Spain	57
Norway	55
Finland	37
Ireland	34
United Kingdom	21
Germany	16
United States	5
Switzerland	1

*Over the period 2008–2017, except France (2008–2016).

Figure 1 Strike rates in different countries. *Source:* www.statista.com/chart/20167/
the-countries-which-go-on-strike-the-most/

Questions

1. What factors do you think might influence the number of strike days in a country?

2. Do you think a strike is an effective way of resisting change?

According to Kotter and Schlesinger (1979) the ways in which managers might overcome resistance include:

- **Education and communication**

  By educating people about the need for change this can gain greater acceptance. By communicating effectively to people it can give them the understanding they need to thrive in the changed world and remove fears that they won't know what to do or have the skills to do it. Educating and communicating with people can take time but should led to greater acceptance of the change.

- **Participation and involvement**

  This happens when people are involved in the change—their ideas are welcomed and they can help shape the way that the change occurs. Discussion and consultation can take time but can help build a sense of shared outcomes. Employee involvement in change has been highlighted as important by many writers. The participation can lead to high-quality change and overcome resistance in the implementation stage according to Vroom and Yetton (1973). By involving employees in a change, a variety of information and ideas may be generated, which may contribute to making the change effective and suitable and create greater employee commitment in implementing the change (Cummings and Molloy 1977). However, the value of participation will depend in part on the skills and usefulness of employees' ideas.

- **Negotiation and agreement**

  This approach occurs when managers negotiate with those who might resist the change—for example, with a trade union—so that the resistance of employees is acknowledged and has some impact on the end result.

- **Facilitation and support**

  This occurs when managers provide training, resources, and support to staff to help them cope with the change. This can be welcomed by employees who fear they are not able to adapt otherwise. However, facilitation may be an expensive way of overcoming resistance to change.

- **Coercion**

  Coercion occurs when managers simply force people to do something. This can be appropriate if time is very short—managers may just tell people to do it and even threaten them if they don't—for example, they may threaten to make them redundant. In the short term this may make people change but it won't make them understand why or make them feel better about it. There will still be underlying resistance—it has just been ignored. If the change happens and works then over time people may come to accept that it was the right decision. According to the *New York Times* when Elon Musk became the new owner of Twitter, he gave employees a deadline to decide if they wanted to work for him. He asked those who did not share his vision to leave their jobs, in his latest shock treatment of the social media company. He had already dismissed half of Twitter's 7500 workforce.

www.nytimes.com/2022/11/16/technology/elon-musk-twitter-employee-deadline.html

- **Manipulation and co-optation**

  Manipulation occurs when information is used selectively to distort the picture presented and win people over. For example, managers may only reveal some information that is favourable.

  To help overcome resistance the managers could bring some of those likely to oppose into the team bringing about the change; this is called co-option. This is not the same as consultation because managers are not really interested in the views of those opposing the change but simply trying to get them to endorse it to help convince others.

The different ways that resistance to change may be overcome are shown in Figure 10.4. These different ways of dealing with the resistance to change are analysed in Table 10.1. How any individual reacts to change will depend on their personal circumstances, their own perception of whether the change is necessary, the quality of the plan that is in place and the management running it, how they will be personally affected, and the extent to which they think it is being forced on them.

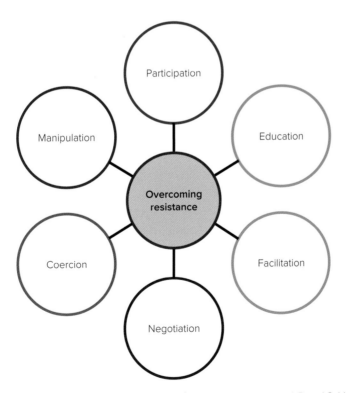

Figure 10.4 Ways of overcoming resistance to change. *Source:* Kotter, J. P. and Schlesinger, L. A. (1979). 'Choosing Strategies for Change.' *Harvard Business Review*, 57(2), (March–April).

10

Table 10.1 Ways of overcoming change

Method	Involves	When appropriate	Comments
Education	Explain reasons for changes	If employees lack information	Can be time-consuming but gains understanding
Participation	Involve employees in the change	If employees can make useful contributions	Can be time-consuming but gains commitment
Facilitation	Provide training and resources to support employees	If employees fear they will not cope with the change	Can be time-consuming and expensive
Negotiation	Offer incentives to change	If employees may lose out through change and are in a strong position to resist	May be expensive
Coercion	Forces change through	If change needs to happen quickly	May be resented
Manipulation and co-option	Manipulating information and people	If managers do not care about the ethics of such as approach	Risky—if the manipulation of information becomes clear or if people find out the real motives behind why they have been involved in the change team

Business insight 10.1 Strikes in French schools

In 2022 thousands of teachers in France walked out of their classrooms in opposition to government policy in relation to COVID-19. Trade unions said that 75% of primary teachers walked out and 62% of secondary teachers, although the government figures were significantly lower. The French prime minister responded by agreeing to meet the French trade unions to reach an agreement. The unions said they had been trying to discuss the issue but had not been listened to. They were striking because of the lack of consultation by the government. Teachers felt they were told about government policy changes at the last minute and that their views were not listened to.

Problems occurred because of the rising COVID infections which meant that many staff and pupils were away from school isolating. In January 2022 about 10,000 classes were closed in France due to infections. Recently there had been huge queues outside of pharmacies as parents and pupils have been trying to get tested to keep up with current government requirements if someone in the class is infected. The rules on testing had changed several times in the previous weeks. Rules about wearing masks had also changed.

Teachers said that government policies were not effective and there was not sufficient cover if teachers were infected. The result was that pupils were not learning effectively, they said.

Unions were also demanding that the government provided the more protective FFP2 face masks for staff, as well as CO_2 monitors to check whether classrooms were sufficiently ventilated.

Unusually France's largest parents' group, the FCPE, supported the strike.

Questions

What stakeholders were involved in this strike?

With reference to Kotter and Schlesinger's theory, why do you think the teachers in France were opposing changes in government policy?

With reference to Kotter and Schlesinger's theory of overcoming resistance to change, what actions do you think the French government could have taken?

Source

www.theguardian.com/world/2022/jan/13/half-of-french-primary-schools-expected-to-close-teachers
-strike-protest-covid-education

What would you do?

You want to change working patterns so that employees are much more flexible about how many hours are worked in any given week rather than a fixed number of hours.

Outline the reasons why this change might be necessary.

Why might people resist the change?

How might you overcome this resistance?

Can you now answer this question from the Introductory case study?

How might 3M have overcome any resistance to this change?

Where are we now?

So far, we have considered some of the reasons why people resist change and how best to manage this. We will now examine the meaning and significance of organizational culture. The culture of a business will affect the extent to which employees are open to change and how they respond to it. Culture itself may be something that managers may want to change and we examine why in the next section.

10.2 Organizational culture

What is organizational culture?

The culture of an organization refers to the values, attitudes, and beliefs of its employees and how they behave. Culture was referred to by Balogun and Johnson (2004) as 'the way we do things around here'.

10

According to Drennan (1992) the culture of an organization Is 'what is typical of the organization, the habits, the prevailing attitudes, the grown-up pattern of accepted behaviour.' We can see from this definition how culture determines what is acceptable—this influences how people behave in any situation.

Key concepts

Organizational culture refers to the values, attitudes and beliefs of its employees and how they behave.

Think about it

Why might cultures of different departments differ within a business?

Think of an organization where you have worked or studied. How would you describe its culture?

Schwartz (2006) describes culture as 'a pattern of beliefs and expectations shared by the organization's members. These beliefs and expectations produce norms and powerfully shape the behaviour of individuals and groups in the organization.' The use of the word 'powerfully' in this definition highlights the importance of culture—it shapes the way people in the business respond to situations and the actions they take,

Another definition by Edgar Schein, a professor at the MIT Sloan School of Management focusing on organization management, describes culture as 'the pattern of shared assumption—invented, discovered, or developed by a given group as it learns to cope with its problems of external adaptation and internal integration—that has worked well enough to be considered valid and therefore to be taught to new members as the correct way to perceive, think, and feel in relationship to those problems' (Schein 1985). This definition highlights that culture influences these new to the business as well as those already in it and that it shapes what people think is the 'correct' way of acting.

Culture is important, therefore, because it determines how people within the organization behave. It influences, for example, whether they work collaboratively or more individually, whether they are proactive or more passive, or whether they focus on quality or costs. Culture determines how people respond to a given decision, what decisions they make, and what they prioritize.

Many organizations clearly define their culture so you know what it is like if you work there and you know how to behave once employed. For example, Naspers is a highly successful South African technology investment business. On its website it says its values are entrepreneurship, empowerment, pushing for performance, and doing the right thing (no exceptions). It is clear that if you work here the goals will be challenging and you will be expected to grow and deliver. This will appeal to some; but not everyone.

10.2.1 What determines the culture of a business?

The culture of a business will be influenced by many factors including the values of the owners/founders/leaders, the reward systems, and employees' own values. We'll now look at each of these factors in turn.

- **The values of the owners, founders, and/or the senior leadership team**

  These groups will often shape who is recruited and set the example in terms of what is expected from other employees. For example, 'The HP Way of doing things' at Hewlett-Packard runs through the business and is directly linked to the way that the founders Dave Packard and Bill Hewlett thought and behaved. The HP Way consists of five fundamental values: 1) The Hewlett-Packard company exists to make a technical contribution, and should only pursue opportunities consistent with this purpose; 2) The Hewlett-Packard company demands of itself and its people superior performance—profitable growth is both a means and a measure of enduring success; 3) The Hewlett-Packard company believes the best results come when you get the right people, trust them, give them freedom to find the best path to achieve objectives, and let them share in the rewards their work makes possible; 4) The Hewlett-Packard company has a responsibility to contribute directly to the well-being of the communities in which its operates; 5) Integrity, period. At Amazon, the founder, Jeff Bezos, believed that the company should be completely customer-focused. Senior meetings still have an empty chair to represent where the customer sits so that they are never forgotten.

- **The reward systems**

  People tend to value the things that they will be rewarded for doing. This means the remuneration system and the appraisal system will influence employees' behaviour. If people are assessed and rewarded on the sales they make they will pursue sales; if they are assessed on the profits they make they will be more interested in costs as well as sales. In his book *Jack: Straight from the Gut* (2001) Jack Welch, a highly successful Chief Executive of GE, describes how he graded top executives into A, B, and C grades. 'A' grade executives had the following characteristics: they were filled with passion, they made things happen, they were open to ideas from anywhere, they had high energy levels and energized others. 'B graders are important to the business because they are the biggest category but they are not especially driven. 'C' graders do not energize others and prevaricate. Welch's approach was to reward 'A' graders very well indeed. 'C' graders were removed from the business. Clearly at GE under Welch there were significant incentives to show the characteristics of an 'A' grader!

- **Employees' own values**

  These will be influenced by many things such as their own backgrounds and experiences and those of the society in which they live. Increased concerns over environmental issues, for example, can often be seen in the values of employees joining a business.

Note that whilst so far we have talked of the culture of a business, in reality there may be many different cultures (or sub-cultures) within the business as a whole. Cultures will vary between regions, divisions, and departments. Similarly, whilst students at your university may have some general shared values there will usually be differences between faculties, sites, and year groups.

10.2.2 Understanding the culture of an organization

Schein (1985) highlighted that culture forms over a period of time. New employees will bring their values and beliefs and this may influence and shape the culture. To understand the culture of an organization, Schein identified three levels of culture that could be analysed.

Business insight 10.2 Johnson and Johnson

Johnson and Johnson is famous for 'our credo' which is a statement of what it believes in. This was first written in 1943 by the company's founder Robert Wood Johnson, Chairman from 1932 to 1963. What is interesting is the order in which the company lists its responsibilities to different stakeholders with its responsibilities to shareholders coming last. This is interesting given that this was written many years before anyone wrote about Corporate Social Responsibility.

Our Credo

We believe our first responsibility is to the patients, doctors, and nurses, to mothers and fathers and all others who use our products and services. . .

. . .Customers' orders must be serviced promptly and accurately. Our business partners must have an opportunity to make a fair profit.

We are responsible to our employees who work with us throughout the world. We must provide an inclusive work environment where each person must be considered as an individual. We must respect their diversity and dignity and recognize their merit. They must have a sense of security, fulfilment, and purpose in their jobs. Compensation must be fair and adequate and working conditions clean, orderly, and safe. We must support the health and well-being of our employees and help them fulfil their family and other personal responsibilities. Employees must feel free to make suggestions and complaints. There must be equal opportunity for employment, development, and advancement for those qualified. . .

We are responsible to the communities in which we live and work and to the world community as well. We must help people be healthier by supporting better access and care in more places around the world. We must be good citizens—support good works and charities, better health and education, and bear our fair share of taxes. We must maintain in good order the property we are privileged to use, protecting the environment and natural resources.

Our final responsibility is to our stockholders. Business must make a sound profit.

The credo was tested in 1982 when seven people died from taking a Tylenol capsule (a Johnson and Johnson painkiller product) contaminated with cyanide. The company immediately recalled Tylenol from all stores in the US costing millions of dollars.

Questions

What do you think is the purpose of Johnson and Johnson publishing Our Credo?

What actions could managers at Johnson and Johnson take to ensure that Our Credo is followed and drives behaviour?

Sources

www.jnj.com/credo/

Schein stated that the culture of an organization could be understood by examining its **artefacts, stated values, and assumed values.** We will now look at each of these in turn.

Artefacts

Artefacts are aspects of the business that can be easily seen or heard. For example, what people wear, how people address each other, and what the offices look like. The artefacts are the visible aspects of a culture. In 2020 Google published its plans for its headquarters at Mountain View in Silicon Valley. The redesigned 40-acre campus includes a network of parks, retail space, a public swimming pool, and a sports field. The ultra-modern design of the campus and the inclusion of subsidized homes and fitness and well-being centres, are intended to show the company's concern for employees and local residents. In an interview with the *Financial Times* (2021) the architect involved in this development, Thomas Heatherwick, said that 'We used to get briefs for buildings which were all about efficiency, treating people like they were nothing more than cogs in a machine. But that forgot that we are all intelligent, emotional, sensing beings. The real opportunity now is for workplaces to be temples of the values of each organization, not just logistically calculated grunt work factories.'

Stated values

The stated values of the business are what it claims its employees believe and what determines how they act. This may be stated as the values or 'what we believe' or expressed in a Code of Conduct. Stated values are what the business wants employees to believe. This should be reinforced by the rules and reward system. At the management consultancy PWC 'Speaking up' is an important aspect of the company's values. The company says: 'Speaking up is crucial to our culture and our long-term results—it is a living example of our values. Speaking up when something doesn't seem right demonstrates our integrity and that we have the courage to do the right thing. Speaking up helps to prevent mistakes and misconduct and foster innovation. Speaking up shows that we care about each other and our business. And speaking up to get things right or keep them on track helps us live up to our commitment to deliver high quality outcomes.'

Assumed values

The shared basic assumptions with the organization are the deeply embedded, taken-for-granted behaviours. These are usually unconscious, but constitute the essence of culture. These assumed values may be reflected in the stated values but not necessarily. One business where the assumed values seem to be reflected in the actual behaviour is Zappos. Zappos is well-known for its customer service culture. The company says: 'Twenty years ago, we began as a small online retailer that only sold shoes. Today, we still sell shoes—as well as clothing, handbags, accessories, and more. That "more" is providing the very best customer service, customer experience, and company culture. We aim to inspire the world by showing it's possible to simultaneously deliver happiness to customers, employees, vendors, shareholders, and the community in a long-term, sustainable way.' The founder of Zappos, Tony Hsieh, says 'Our number one priority is company culture. Our whole belief is that if you get the culture right, most of the other stuff like delivering great customer service or building a long-term enduring brand will just happen naturally on its own.'

Key concepts

Artefacts are aspects of the business that can be easily seen or heard.

The **stated values** of the business are what it claims its employees believe and what determines how they act.

Assumed values. The shared basic assumptions with the organization are the deeply embedded, taken-for-granted behaviours.

Can you now answer this question from the Introductory case study? <<<

Why does 3M have a Code of Conduct?

Schein's analysis of culture focuses on the outward signs of culture in the form of artefacts and then the state and assumed values that lie beneath these. Another way of analysing culture is known as the cultural web.

10.2.3 The cultural web

The cultural web model was developed by Johnson in 1992. It shows the different aspects of culture that reflect and shape the key values of the organization. The cultural paradigm is what all the different elements of the web add up to—it is a summary of the culture of the organization (see Figure 10.5).

The elements of the cultural web are:

- **The stories that are told in a business**

  What people talk about and remember as important moments in what has happened or what happens in the business reveal what the people in the organization value. Who the 'heroes' of a business are and what they did to earn that status (and equally who are the people regarded with disdain and why) show what is regarded as important in that business.

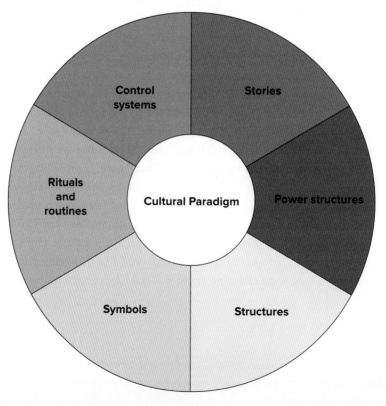

Figure 10.5 Johnson and Scholes cultural web. *Source:* Johnson, G., Whittington, R., Scholes, K., Angwin, D., and Regnér, P. (2014). *Exploring Strategy Text & Cases* (10th edn). Harlow, Pearson, pp .154–157.

- **The symbols of a business are objects or artefacts**

  These symbols show something about the values of the business. For example, how its offices are decorated or laid out reveal something about what matters. As soon as you walk into a business you get a sense of what it is like from the location, the design, what is on the walls, and what people wear. Open plan offices, for example, suggest that collaboration and openness are valued. Hubspot, the software business, says that 'We believe businesses can grow with a conscience, and succeed with a soul.' As part of its approach the business values everyone's input and so has an open-door policy; any employee can go and see any other to ask them questions and all opinions are said to be valued.

- **Every business will have rituals and routines**

  The rituals and routines of a business could include award ceremonies or annual employee 'away' days. Rituals and routines again reveal what the business thinks is important—who goes, where they go, and what is celebrated tell the people involved something about the organization's values. At Gusto's, a US human resources software business, there is a 'no shoes' policy in its office. Its founders all grew up in 'no shoes indoors' households, so when they started the business in a house in Palo Alto in 2012, they adopted this approach. By the time the company moved to its first real office, this had become part of the rituals of the business. The company believes people feel more themselves and more comfortable with their shoes off. Meanwhile at another software business, Culture IQ, everyone ends the week with a round of handshakes and thank-yous for their colleagues. At Amazon, Jeff Bezos, the founder and Chief Executive, leaves one chair empty at meetings to represent the customer. Whenever a decision is made it is important to consider what the empty chair would think. At Zappos there is 'the face game'. When an employee logs on a picture of a colleague shows on the screen. If you cannot guess the name of the person their biography shows up.

- **The nature of a structure shows what is important to the organization**

  Some organizations have clear, well-defined structures and chains of command. This helps maintain control and ensure that pre-determined outcomes occur. By comparison, Spotify, the music and video streaming company, says that it does not operate with the traditional corporate structure. It has 'squads', 'tribes', and 'guilds', which function as different ways of organizing and performing work with more accountability and autonomy. Its core organizational unit is an autonomous squad of no more than 8 people. Each squad is accountable for a discrete aspect of the product; it has the authority to decide what to build, how to build it, and who they need to work with. There is no single appointed leader of a squad; the leadership role emerges and is informal. Every few weeks, squads evaluate what is going well and what needs to improve. Meanwhile 'tribes' are made up of several squads which are linked together through a 'chapter'. A 'chapter' links the squads by providing support in areas such as quality assurance and web development. Leadership within the squad is self-determined, while the chapter leader is a formal manager who focuses on coaching and mentoring. Guilds are communities of people interested in an aspect of the business whose primary purpose is to share knowledge in areas that cut across chapters and squads, such as leadership, continuous delivery, and web delivery.

10

Key concepts

The cultural paradigm is what all the different elements of the web add up to—it is a summary of the culture of the organization.

- **Control systems**

  The control systems within a business show how people are managed and what matters to the business. When it comes to budget setting, what is allowed and what is not, for example. When it comes to staff appraisals, what is being assessed and what happens to those who do not do well in these areas? Is control mainly through reward or punishment? Do managers micromanage or do employees have considerable freedom when it comes to decision-making? Again, the answers to these questions show those within the organization what matters and what their priorities should be.

- **Power structures**

  This refers to where the power actually lies within an organization. There may be various committees, for example, which exert a great deal of power over the use of resources or particular functional areas may receive much higher status than others. Does the decision-making power lie with marketing or operations, for example? The power base will not be shown on an organizational chart but those within the business will know who really makes the decisions.

  The cultural web is illustrated in Figure 10.5.

What would you do?

Your boss tells you he wants you to adopt the 10-foot rule that Walmart has through all the stores you manage. This rule was developed by the founder of Walmart, Sam Walton. He told employees to take a pledge that said 'I solemnly promise and declare that every customer that comes within 10 feet of me, I will smile, look them in the eye, greet them, and ask if I can help them.' What would this ritual tell your staff about the culture of your business?

Where are we now?

We have examined what is meant by culture and the elements of culture by exploring Schein's model and the cultural web. We now consider different types of culture.

10.2.4 Types of culture

The culture of a business has such a powerful impact on its performance that it is no surprise that it is studied extensively. Some managers want to change culture, some want to preserve it, some just want to understand it better. As a result, there are many models which attempt to classify different types of culture. By categorizing culture it becomes easier to analyse it. In this section, we will examine two in detail: Deal and Kennedy's types of culture, and Handy's types of culture.

10.2.5 Deal and Kennedy's types of culture

One of the first cultural models proposed was by Deal and Kennedy (1982). They believed the culture of an organization could be analysed in terms of the risks involved in the task being carried out and how long it takes for an employee to assess the impact of their work through feedback. These factors will vary from business to business, creating different cultures. Four categories of culture identified by Deal and Kennedy (as shown in Figure 10.6) are:

- **The 'tough guy, macho' culture**
  In this culture employees tend to be risk takers and there is quick feedback on results. This culture may exist in the police force.

- **A 'work hard/play hard' culture**
  This environment has low risks and quick feedback on performance such as a sales business.

- **The 'bet your company' culture**
  This is characterized by high risks and a long period to realize if a project is working, e.g. aircraft engine development or a pharmaceutical company. Investment into a project is very high risk but it will not be clear for many years whether it has worked so you are 'betting the company' by going ahead.

- **The 'process' culture**
  This business environment has low risks and slow feedback, e.g. insurance companies. Any one transaction is unlike to make or break the business and it will be many years before it is clear whether or not it is profitable.

10.2.6 Handy's types of culture

Another typology is offered by Charles Handy (1976) who identified four types of culture in a model he developed. These are:

- **Power culture**
  This type of culture occurs when power is focused on a few key people at the centre of an organization. Decisions are made at the centre. This is often found in start-ups where the entrepreneur has a clear vision and makes the key decisions. Others ask the advice and guidance of those in the centre.

- **Role culture**
  This occurs when individuals have clearly defined jobs and where there is a clear structure and set of reporting relationships. There are clear rules and procedures setting out who does what. This type of culture is common as businesses grow and introduce a functional business structure with policies and routines.

- **Task culture**
  This occurs when the focus is on getting job done. The importance of people depends on what they can contribute to the given task. The emphasis is on completing the job or project. People are brought together depending on what they can contribute to the project. In a role culture your job title, age, qualifications, and years with the business are all likely to be regarded as important and influence what you get involved in. In a task culture what matters is what you can do regardless of anything else. In

10

advertising agencies, for example, what matters on the creative side is the quality of the ideas and designs not how many qualifications you have.

- **Person culture**

  This type of culture occurs where individuals have considerable freedom to do their work the way they want to. They have an experience or expertise that means they are allowed to run their own area with little direction from elsewhere. The individual is the central focus. This culture may be found with lawyers, doctors, and academics where each person specializes in a part aspect of their profession.

10.2.7 Why does organizational culture matter?

As we have seen, organizational culture determines what people prioritize, how they make decisions, and which stakeholders they think matter. The culture underpins how people in the business behave and act. The importance of culture is evident in a speech given by the Chief Executive of Microsoft, Satya Nadella, to the company's investors in 2015. According to *The Economist* (2020) Nadella said that the company's ability to change its culture was the 'leading indicator'of its future success. If an organization gets its culture wrong, none of its other plans matter. Nadella had taken over as Chief Executive the year before and wanted to remove the bureaucracy and make the business more agile.

The culture of a business can create positive behaviour that lies behind its success—for example, it can encourage initiative and innovation, it can lead to an obsession with customer service, or it can lead to a focus on continuous improvement. Building a culture where employees are aligned and working together towards the same goals and with the same values can be very powerful and provide a competitive advantage, Importantly for a business, its culture is difficult for others to imitate. Competitors may be able to buy similar machinery, replicate certain features of a product, or match prices but it is very difficult to replicate the culture of a business because it depends so much on the people in the organization and their values.

Culture can help a business to succeed. Hard work may be seen as the norm, customer service may be valued highly, and quality may be seen as a priority. Many businesses believe their culture is the core reason for their success. Southwest Airlines, for example, was a pioneer in the low-cost airline sector. It says its strength comes from its focus on employees. Southwest says its philosophy is simple: 'When your employees are happy, your customers are happy. When your customers are happy, your profits are healthier, which means your shareholders are happy too.'

The clothing business Patagonia also believes its culture is critical to what it does. Its founder Yvon Chouinard says 'We're in business to save the planet'. Its culture focuses on responsible sourcing of products and sustainable business practices—this attracts employees, customers, and investors. Patagonia believes in treating its employees well and ensuring they have a good work–life balance. The company is famous for its founder's saying 'Let my people go surfing' meaning they can take time off work to pursue their passions.

A strong culture can, therefore, have a significant positive influence within an organization. However, culture can also create problems. For example, if the culture within an

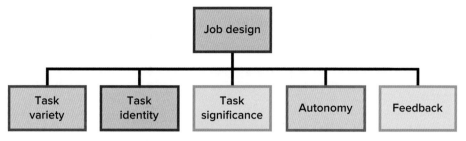

Figure 10.6 Hackman and Oldham's elements of job design. *Source:* Hackman, J. and Oldham, G. (1980). *Work redesign.* Reading, MA, Addison-Wesley Publishing Company.

organization encourages people to pursue profits and not worry too much about ethics, that's what people will do. Similarly, if the culture of a business encourages people to protect their own colleagues even if this means hiding their offences, that's what they will do. Whenever there are instances of unethical behaviour by businesses, or where employees take excessive risks, this is usually down to the culture of the organization. The leadership, the control systems (or lack of), the reward systems, and the behaviour of others have all contributed to the creation of a negative culture. For example, in 2008 there was a global financial crisis which was caused by excessive lending by banks. Studies into why this happened have blamed amongst other things the culture of the banks. Employees were encouraged to lend even if this lending was clearly high risk; they were rewarded for the lending rather than how sustainable it was in the long term. The culture was short-termist and risk taking. It encouraged aggressive sales techniques with large bonuses for those who hit ambitious targets. There was little concern for how these targets were achieved. The Financial Conduct Authority (FCA), which oversees the banking system in the UK, stated 'We believe that a firm's culture is a key driver of staff behaviour and, in many cases, where things have gone wrong in a firm, a cultural issue was a key part of the problem'. The remuneration and appraisal systems in the banking system encouraged unethical risk taking.

New chief executives often face the challenge of changing culture. For example, when Bill Michael became the chairman of the consultancy KPMG in 2017, one of his challenges was to change the culture at the business from one where it did not seem to matter what you did provided you were generating enough revenue. Mr Michael said he wanted to end a 'corrosive' mentality which seemed to believe that making large amounts of money excused any behaviour. In 2021 Facebook was heavily criticized for a culture that put increasing the number of people using its platform above any sense of the responsibility to protect them. A former Facebook employee testifying in front of the Senate said that the company failed to protect children's mental health and that the use of the platform created divisions in society which threatened democracy.

Culture and integration

Culture is a very important consideration when businesses integrate through acquisition or merger. If the cultures of the businesses are very different this can lead to clashes. There are some well-known examples of major culture clashes which led to inefficiency and poor performance. Such culture clashes following a merger or acquisition include AT&T–Time Warner, Disney–Fox, and CVS–Aetna. An example of the problems created by a culture clash following a merger is highlighted in Business Insight 10.3 on the Daimler–Chrysler deal.

Business insight 10.3 Comparing the stated cultures of ByteDance, Etsy, Tencent, and Shoprite

ByteDance	Etsy	Tencent	Shoprite
ByteDance is the parent company of TikTok. Its other products include Douyin (mobile videos in China), Toutiao (a content platform where visitors can explore different topics in China), Helo (social media platforming, India) and Lark (a collaboration tool, in Japan and Singapore).	Etsy is the global marketplace for unique and creative goods.	Tencent is a Chinese internet and technology company. It is the biggest video gaming company in the world and runs QQ.com, one of China's biggest web portals.	Shoprite is Africa's largest fast-moving consumer goods retailer. Our purpose is to be Africa's most affordable, accessible, and innovative retailer, and our customers are at the heart of what we do—the reason for our business.
Aim for the highest Raise the bar. Wait for bigger gains Find the best solutions by widening our perspectives Be attentive. Distill ideas down to their fundamental truths Keep learning and growing	**We commit to our craft** Our work has the power to change lives. That's why we strive to learn continuously and excel at what we do.	**Integrity** Uphold principles, ethics, openness, and fairness.	**Put our customers first.** We do this through excellent service. Our employees are empowered to make sure our customers leave our stores happy.
Be candid and clear Dare to share your honest opinions It's ok to make mistakes. Own it when you do. Stick to the facts, identify the issues, and avoid 'leader pleasing' Be accurate and forthright; be methodical and focused	**We minimize waste** Time, resources, and energy are precious, so we focus only on what will have the greatest impact.	**Proactivity** Pursue positive contributions, volunteer for responsibility, and push for breakthroughs.	Act with **integrity**. We strive to treat everyone with respect. We are accountable for our actions and we behave in an ethical way to build trust with our stakeholders.

ByteDance	Etsy	Tencent	Shoprite
Be open and humble	**We embrace differences**	**Collaboration**	**Make a difference**
- Trust yourself, trust each other - Be willing to offer and ask for help. Collaboration creates value - Approach problems with the big picture in mind - Be mindful and check your ego; stay pen to different ideas	Diverse teams are stronger, and inclusive cultures are more resilient. When we seek out different perspectives, we make better decisions and build better products.	Be inclusive and collaborative, strive to progress and evolve.	beyond our own doors. Through job creation, affordable products, hunger relief, and other programmes, we work to create shared value for our communities.
Be grounded and courageous	**We dig deeper**	Creativity	Relentlessly focus on **keeping costs low**
- Make your own discoveries, Dive deep into facts - Stay level headed, Focus on impact - Assume ownership, take risks, break the mould - Rapid iterations, multiple possibilities	The best solutions to meaningful challenges are rarely easy or obvious. We stay curious, balance our intuition with insights, and decide with confidence.	Push for breakthrough innovations, explore the possibilities of the future.	and aim to become more efficient. We know where and how every rand is spent. Our business and operational processes are set up to manage the use of resources by reducing waste and minimizing harm to the natural environment.
	We lead with optimism		Help where we can. We have a specific focus on **food security**. When we
	We believe in our mission, and we believe in each other. We see the world as it is, set ambitious goals, and inspire one another with generosity of spirit. Together, we reimagine what is possible.		have surplus food or resources, we distribute them to people in need.

10

Questions

Compare and contrast the stated cultures of the businesses above.

Why do think differences occur?

How would these differences affect how you behave as an employee?

Sources

www.bytedance.com/en/

www.shopriteholdings.co.za/group/our-purpose-values.html

www.tencent.com/en-us/about.html#about-con-6

//careers.etsy.com/global/en/guiding-principles

 Where are we now?

We have seen how culture is important to the success of a business. It is also a key issue when businesses are merging or one business takes over another because this involves bringing two different cultures together.

In her book *Rule Makers, Rule Breakers: How Tight and Loose Cultures Wire Our World* (2018), Professor Gelfand outlines research on 6000 significant mergers in more than 30 countries taking place from 1980 to 2013. She focused specifically on comparing the effect of bringing together 'tight' cultures (which are about command and control) and 'loose' cultures (where there is more freedom for individuals to make decisions in their own way). Gelfand found that significant differences in the tight vs loose cultures of the businesses involved resulted in a lower-than-average share price, and much lower returns for the investor than in a typical deal. The largest gaps analysed resulted in a loss of $30m of the market value of the business within five days of the announcement of the deal, which, according to Gelfand, indicates that markets understand cultural gaps even when buyers themselves do not.

10.2.8 Culture and doing business abroad

Differences in national business cultures can include:

- **Different ways of communicating**

  The way we communicate can vary significantly around the world and managers should be alert to such differences to ensure they do not misinterpret others' actions. For example, according to Hult International Business School (2017), some countries such as Finland expect a direct and brief approach when having a conversation in a meeting whereas managers from India may be more nuanced in their communication. Non-verbal communication is also important: a firm handshake or direct eye contact may send positive signals in some countries but be regarded as offensive in others. Even how close people tend to stand to each other can vary. Sometimes people may seem quite aggressive by standing close when someone else may seem rather distant by standing so far back.

Business insight 10.4 **DaimlerChrysler**

In 2007 the automotive businesses, Daimler and Chrysler, joined together to benefit from synergies and greater scale. Or at least that was the intention. In reality the merger never worked and they never formed a cohesive business unit. The potential benefits that had been expected simply did not occur because of a clash of cultures.

One of the underlying issues was the differences between the way the managers thought and worked. The mainly German senior managers of Daimler and the mainly US managers of Chrysler did not work well together. The Germans wanted clarity and precision. They wanted precise instructions to be given and plans made; the US managers were more tolerant of ambiguity—they were happier knowing what the general goal was and working out for themselves how to get there. The Germans had a greater sense of hierarchy than the Americans and so felt the way some of the US junior managers behaved towards their senior managers was inappropriate. Even language was an issue. A sarcastic 'sure, that will work' by the Americans could be interpreted as a sincere 'sure that will work' by the Germans.

Although the deal was supposed to be a 'merger of equals' it soon became apparent that it was takeover of Chrysler by Daimler and this started the mistrust that continued in the coming months. The teams also differed hugely in their strategies. If sales were falling Daimler would look to increase quality, Chrysler would look to cut price.

Question

1. How might managers reduce cultural clashes when a merger occurs?

Source

Ft.com. 2022. *Car industry has poor history on alliances.* [online] Available at: <https://www.ft.com/content/c0c949ce-5d77-11e1-869d-00144feabdc0> [Accessed 3 June 2022].

- **Different workplace etiquette**

  There will be considerable variations in what is regarded as the 'normal way of doing business' in different countries: for example, in Asian countries such as South Korea, China, and Singapore people tend to use the formal 'Mr./Mrs. Surname', when they meet whereas Americans and Canadians tend to use first names. Other examples of differences include:

  - In some countries it is common to use two hands when handing over a business card; in others it is just one hand.

  - In some countries you are expected to turn up exactly on time for a meeting; in others it is normal to be late.

  - In some countries working long hours is seen as a sign of commitment to the job; in others it may be regarded as a lack of efficiency.

The working culture of South Korea is examined in Business Insight 10.4.

- **Differences in the importance of organizational hierarchy**

There can be significant differences in how hierarchical businesses are in different countries. In Japan, for example, senior managers tend to expect that junior members of staff

Can you now answer this question from the Introductory case study?

Summarize features of 3M's culture. How does 3M's culture help the business to succeed?

Think about it

One of the concerns about the pandemic and the consequent shift to working from home was the impact that this would have on company culture. Many companies—including technology businesses Google and Microsoft, accountants EY, KPMG, and PwC, and law firms Clifford Chance and Freshfields—committed to having working from home as a more permanent feature of their way of doing business. However, this has led to concerns over how less face-to-face contact and fewer chats around the water cooler would affect the extent to which values are shared and the consequent implications for behaviour.

In Japan businesses refer to 'gemba'. The word gemba literally means 'the real place' but is taken to mean that people have to be physically there in the office to deal with issues together. If you are 'in gemba' this means you are undertaking an activity that adds value. It means that you are there when key decisions are made or there are key learnings to gain.

Following the pandemic there has been greater pressure for flexible working. Businesses need to consider how to adapt to this flexibility whilst finding ways of keeping 'in gemba'.

Do you think the increasing number of people who are working from home threatens the culture of businesses?

Where are we now?

So far we have looked at different types of culture within organizations, but cultures can also vary significantly from one country to another, and this is important for managers to be aware of when doing business abroad.

respect them because of their seniority. In meetings superiors would not expect to be challenged in any way by their subordinates. The senior managers would enter the room first, sit down first, and not expect to be interrupted by anyone junior. By comparison, in Scandinavian countries, such as Norway, hierarchy is not as important and it would be usual for an employee to talk directly to and question a superior.

Examples of differences in national cultures were highlighted by Cheng and Groysberg (2020) in their *Harvard Business Review* article. Based on their research these writers stated that businesses in Western Europe and North America tend to place a great emphasis on results; people are goal oriented and stress the importance of achievement. By comparison, in South America enjoyment is regarded as a particularly important aspect of work. Employees have a propensity towards fun and value a light-hearted work environment. On the other hand, businesses in Asia, Australia, and New Zealand have workplaces that focus on *caring*, and stress the importance of safety and planning. In Asia in particular many businesses emphasize order and promote a cooperative, respectful, and rule-abiding culture.

Think about it

Why do these cultural differences between countries matter to managers?

Business insight 10.5 South Korean working culture

South Korean culture is heavily influenced by Confucian principles. Confucianism supports group harmony, respect for elders and authority, the importance of family, friendship, and tradition. Maintaining their 'kibun' (face, honour, personal dignity) is generally highly important for Koreans. Confrontation should be avoided at all costs because once 'kibun' is lost it cannot be regained.

A 15° bow is used when meeting someone of the same age while a 30–45° bow is preferred when meeting someone new, a boss, or an elderly person. If a superior (in age or status) initiates a handshake, the other person should take it with both hands without standing straight. It is usual to address a counterpart by their surname followed by their title and 'Nim', as for example 'Kim Director Nim'. Koreans usually use titles, rather than personal names. At work, co-workers are addressed with a combination of title and family name.

The work culture in South Korea is notoriously intense. South Koreans put in an average of 2024 hours in 2017, the second-most after Mexico among members of the Organisation for Economic Cooperation and Development (OECD). There has long been an acceptance of *gapjil*, which describes the authoritarian attitude of senior managers who feel able to shout at subordinates, who may expect all-nighters or weekend work to get a project completed and who often insist that junior employees go out drinking for hours. Status in Korea is very important, and respected in workplace and society.

In 2018 the government introduced a new labour law imposing a cap on working hours in an effort to improve employees' work–life balance. The law required companies with more than 300 employees and public institutions to cut the maximum weekly work hours from 68 to 52.

Question

How might an understanding of South Korean culture be useful to a business trading with a South Korean business?

Sources

www-ft-com.ezproxy01.rhul.ac.uk/content/54379f02-7db1-11e8-bc55-50daf11b720d

www-ft-com.ezproxy01.rhul.ac.uk/content/54379f02-7db1-11e8-bc55-50daf11b720d

www.economist.com/asia/2021/07/08/south-korean-tech-workers-are-having-a-lousy-time-at-work

10

Where are we now?

We have considered the meaning and importance of culture, types of culture, and differences in culture across countries. We will now move on to consider why changing culture can be difficult and what managers should consider when trying to change it.

10.2.9 Changing the culture

A culture is built on peoples' attitudes and beliefs. If managers are trying to change the culture of a business they are challenging what people believe in. These beliefs may be very well ingrained. They form an important part of what people think is 'normal' behaviour and they could have shaped what people have been doing for many years. Trying to change culture requires people to rethink what they believe in. Furthermore, many people will have done well in a given culture and so changing it may threaten them.

Furthermore, any change may be resisted unless people understand why it is happening and are convinced the change will work.

To change the culture of a business, managers must be clear why it needs changing and what they want to change it to. They should have a clear vision that they can explain of what they want the culture to be. Managers must develop systems that reward the behaviour they want and that do not reward behaviours they don't want to see. Managers may need to change some employees to remove those whose behaviour is too fixed; changing staff can take time.

What would you do?

You have been appointed as a team leader at a retail outlet. The culture of your team seems to be that 'ok is good enough'. Customer service has worsened and sales have fallen. You are determined to develop a culture where excellent customer service is always strived for. How would you do this?

Business insight 10.6   Japanese business culture

Although it is changing, the Japanese way of doing business has tended to be very different from the Western approach.

According to the *Financial Times* (2017) features of culture in Japanese businesses have included:

Lifelong employment

Joining a business was seen as committing yourself to an organization and becoming a 'family member'. In return the family would look after you during your working life in return for your loyalty.

Promotion based on length of service

This approach avoids some of the negative consequences of competition between employees. The more Western individualistic culture encourages competition; the danger of this that people try to prove themselves at the expense of others. The Japanese culture is more collectivist—it encourages people to work in teams and share the same values and objectives. If it is clear that the person who will be promoted is the person who has served the longest this removes any need or desire to win at the expense of others. It helps to create an environment where people can work together and again rewards loyalty.

Training and education

The Japanese approach has tended to focus on the long term and so businesses have invested heavily in training and education. People are seen as an important asset of the business and therefore spending on training is regarded as an investment not a cost.

Collaborative decision-making

The Japanese approach focuses on consultation and the involvement of others to hear their views and benefit from their perspective. The ringi system of decision-making in-volves extensive discussion and consultation with everyone who might be affected by the decision. The result of the ringi process is that decision-making is relatively slow but when a decision is made it is right because it has been debated extensively by everyone. The execution of the decision can therefore be relatively fast because the potential problems have already been thought through.

Questions

1. Summarize some of the key features of Japanese business culture.

2. Why are the potential benefits of this culture?

3. Why might this culture make it difficult for overseas businesses to do business in Japan?

4. Would you like to work in this culture? Explain your answer.

5. Why might managers want to change this culture? What problems might they have doing so?

Think about it

From your own experience can you think how cultures may differ between parts of the world? Or between different parts of an organization such as a university?

Where are we now?

So far we have examined culture and the importance of this to a business. We now examine the way that the business is organized—i.e. the organizational structure. We will see the two are closely linked—the way you organize your business depends on in part on what you value.

10.3 Organizational structure

10

The structure of an organization defines who does what, who reports to whom, and what responsibilities and authority a particular job has. It defines how work is divided, how it is supervised, and how it is coordinated.

The structure of an organization will depend on:

- how the different tasks that need to be undertaken are grouped into jobs
- how the jobs are grouped into departments or teams

Key concepts

The **organizational structure** defines who does what, who reports to whom, and what responsibilities and authority a particular job has.

- how many people are directly managed by a manager (this is called the span of control)
- the authority given to a particular job
- the extent to which reporting relationships are fixed and prescribed.

10.3.1 Job design

When designing the various jobs within the organization, managers will need to consider the tasks that need to be undertaken and the impact of putting them together in different ways on the customer, the employee, and the business. For example, in a restaurant you could have staff specializing in taking the orders, others focused on making the orders, and others specializing in delivering the orders to the customers' tables. Or each member of staff would be responsible for taking the order, making the drink, and taking it to the table. Staff could be trained to do all jobs or just specialize in single tasks.

The design of a job will affect:

- The service a customer receives (for example, an employee whose work covers a range of tasks may be able to provide a more complete service for customers rather than having to passing them on to others to deal with an issue).
- Productivity and the speed of service. For example, having people specialize in particular tasks may lead to greater efficiency and faster service.
- Training requirements. These will be less if jobs are specialized and so individuals have to be trained in fewer tasks. This can make it easier to recruit and replace staff if needed.
- Job satisfaction. Staff may be bored and less motivated if they simply undertake a limited number of tasks time and time again.
- Costs. If several different people are employed to specialize in different aspects of a job this may be more expensive than one person undertaking several jobs.

Hackman and Oldham (1976) considered the following aspects of the design of a job:

- **Task variety:** this describes how much variety there is in a job in terms of the nature of tasks.
- **Task significance**: this describes whether the jobholder understands and believes that what they do is important to the overall success of the business.
- **Task identity**: this describes whether what the jobholder does is easily identifiable; can that person see what they personally do?
- **Autonomy**: this describes how much independence a person has in their job; what can they decide for themselves without getting permission from others?
- **Feedback**: this describes the extent to which someone doing this job knows how well they are doing. Do they get feedback from their customers or their managers to keep them informed about how well they are doing?

Think about it

Have you ever had a job? How did it rate on the features in the Hackman and Oldham model?

These aspects are shown in Figure 10.6.

According to Hackman and Oldham, the different aspects of a job can be analysed and rated to give an overall motivating potential score. A job with high levels of variety, significance, and identity and with high levels of autonomy and feedback is going to be motivating. By comparison, a job where you have little independence of action and rarely receive any feedback is unlikely to motivate someone.

10.3.2 The span of control and levels of hierarchy

One thing which needs to be taken into consideration in the structure of an organization is something known as the **span of control**. The span of control measures the number of subordinates reporting directly to a superior. A wide span of control means that there is relatively high number of people reporting to a superior; a narrow span means relatively few.

A small span of control has the advantage of enabling the superior to keep close control over subordinates as there are not many of them. This is important if there is a high level of risk, if employees lack experience or skills and need monitoring, or if the task needs small numbers of people to interact closely with each other. Start-up organizations, for example, often have small spans of control. The disadvantage of a small span of control is that subordinates may feel micromanaged and lose some motivation; it is also likely to increase management costs as there will be more managers.

If a business narrows the span of control then, for a given number of employees, this means more managers will required. If there are a large number of managers these might themselves need managing and so the business has created an additional level of hierarchy. A level of hierarchy occurs when there is a level of authority in a business. All other things being equal a smaller span increases the number of levels of hierarchy. The fast fashion business Shein says on its website that 'our organization is deliberately flat and de-tiered with no cumbersome reporting or formalism. Every voice matters at Shein and is encouraged to speak up.'

A business with small span of control and many levels of hierarchy is called a tall and narrow organization. A business with a wide span and relatively few levels of hierarchy is called a short, wide organization.

What would you do?

You are looking to make cost savings by increasing the span of control within your business and reducing the number of managers. What might you consider before doing this?

Key concepts

The **span of control** is the number of people directly reporting to a manager.
A **level of hierarchy** is a level of management responsibility.

Analysing the business data 10.2

Decisions about the span of control and levels of hierarchy will affect the shape and structure of organization. For example, consider the following situation:

The span of control in a business is 10. There are 1000 employees at the lowest level of hierarchy in the organization.

In the business there would be three levels of hierarchy as shown in Figure 1.

How many levels of hierarchy would be needed to manage around 1000 employees at the base level if the span was four?

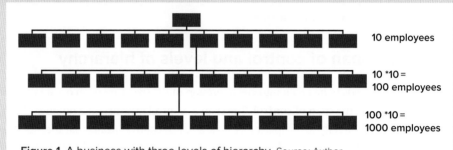

10 employees

10 *10 = 100 employees

100 *10 = 1000 employees

Figure 1 A business with three levels of hierarchy. *Source:* Author

Can you now answer this question from the Introductory case study?

Do you think 3M will have small or wide spans of control in general? Why?

10.3.3 Types of organizational structure

- **Functional structure**

The structure of a business will include grouping jobs into departments. As we discussed when examining the Greiner model in Chapter 9, when businesses first start out jobs are often ill defined. People do what has to be done. Sometimes this means tasks are duplicated; on other occasions tasks may not be completed because it is assumed that someone else is doing them. As a business grows it becomes necessary to formalize responsibilities more clearly with the aim of making it clearer for both the superior and subordinate what the responsibilities of a job are.

Businesses will typically group jobs by **function** when they first start to formalize their structure. This means, for example, that all the marketing jobs are in one section, finance jobs are in another, and operations jobs are in another. This type of structure is shown in Figure 10.7. Note that this is a simplified version in terms of the functions shown. If you look at the global tyre maker, Pirelli's organizational structure, for example, it shows functions including operations, human resources, corporate and brand image, digital, legal, finance, tax, administration, real estate and facilities, information security, and sustainability.

One advantage of a functional structure is that all the expertise and experience in one aspect of business is grouped together. Those involved in marketing can learn from each other. A potential disadvantage is that people stay focused within their functional areas and do not

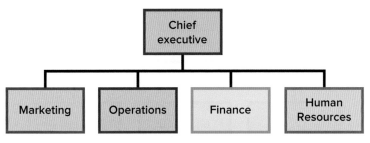

Figure 10.7 A functional structure. *Source:* Author.

collaborate with other functions; this is known as 'the silo effect'. This means, for example, that operations staff may consider issues only from an operations perspective and not try to understand the marketing, financial, or human resource implications of a decision. The huge Indian conglomerate Reliance Industries states on its website that it aims to 'nurture innovation by breaking silos, encouraging cross-fertilization of ideas and flexibility of roles and functions'. This may not suit a functional structure.

- **A product or regional structure**

As a business grows and develops more products and enters more markets, the functional structure may not be appropriate. The marketing required in different regions or for a range of products may be so varied that having all the marketing jobs in one department may mean that is not enough flexibility to deal with different conditions. Similarly, the nature of operations may vary considerably if a business operates in different product areas.

At this stage a business might adopt a product or regional structure. This means all the different jobs relating to a particular product or region are grouped together. The product or the specific demands of the region provide the focus of activities. The advantage of these structures is that jobs have a clear focus on the particular demands of a product (or type of product) or region. In the case of a regional structure it may also mean there is a better understanding of and responsiveness to the culture of a region. The disadvantage of A product or regional structure is that jobs may be duplicated—for example, there may be similar marketing jobs in many different countries. A product structure is shown in Figure 10.8; a regional structure is shown in Figure 10.9.

Of course, the 'right' organizational structure will change over time as the business evolves and decides what is best for its environment and strategy. For example, in 2020 the French food company Danone announced it was restructuring to improve business performance. The company, which makes various food and drink products, including Evian bottled water and Activia yoghurts, said the changes would save €1 bn within 2 years. This change reduced the number of jobs by 2000 which was about 2% of its workforce. The restructuring aimed to give more power to regional managers and involved changing from a product-based approach to a regional structure. The company needed to improve performance because some of its biggest brands' sales had been hit by the pandemic—for example, bottled water sales fell with the closure of restaurants and working from home. There were also significant longer-term issues for Danone—for example, its baby milk business had been hit by declining birth rates, especially in its key market of China. Although Danone's competitors, such as Nestlé, mainly had regional structures, some say this may be more suitable for them because they have a much wider product portfolio.

10

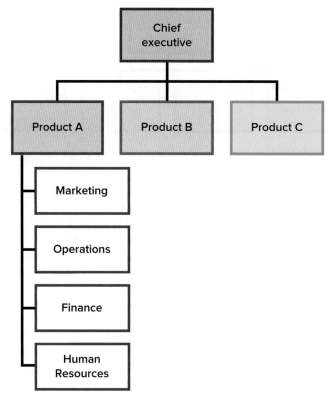

Figure 10.8 Product organizational structure. *Source:* Author.

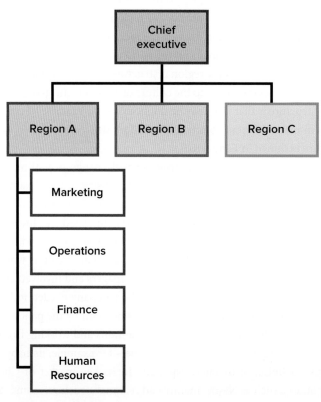

Figure 10.9 A regional organizational structure. *Source:* Author.

Key concepts

A **functional** organizational structure groups jobs by their business function.
A **regional** organizational structure groups jibs by their geographical focus.

What would you do?

The Swiss food group Nestlé has many different products sold all over the world. These include baby foods (such as Gerber), cereal (such as Cheerios and Lion), water (such as Perrier and S. Pellegrino), chocolate (such as Aero and KitKat), coffee (such as Nescafé), drinks (such as Nesquik), ice cream (Haagen Dazs), and petcare (such as Felix).

What form of organizational structure would you recommend for Nestlé? Why?

Where are we now?

We have looked at job design, spans of control, and outlined different ways of grouping jobs within a structure. We will now consider where authority lies within the organization by analysing how authority is delegated and the degree of centralization in a business.

10.3.4 Delegation

Delegation occurs when authority is transferred from a superior to a subordinate. The benefits of delegating are that it frees up the superior's time to focus on other (often more valuable) activities, such as strategic issues (see Chapter 8). Delegation will make use of the skills of subordinates and their specialist expertise. It may also motivate employees because it is giving them greater responsibility.

However, delegation involves risks. Managers are handing down authority which has the potential to be abused. Managers must therefore decide on what tasks they want to delegate, how they will keep overall control (because they remain ultimately responsible for what is done), and how they ensure the work is done in the way they would like (for example, following the Code of Conduct of the business).

The extent to which managers delegate will depend on:

- The nature of the task; simple low risks tasks can be delegated easily, for example.

- The personality and experience of the superior; for example, if she has a low tolerance of ambiguity she will want to keep control herself.

- The training and skills of the subordinates; what can they do for themselves and what are they capable of doing well or even better than the superior?

- The pressure on managers to free time for other tasks.

What would you do?

In your recent appraisal it was suggested that you are too hands on and need to delegate more. Justify your approach.

10

Do you think extensive delegation is common at 3M? Why?

Delegation focuses on a particular relationship between a superior and a subordinate and considers the extent to which one passes on task to the other. Decentralization focuses on the business as a whole and the extent to which decisions are taken at lower levels within the organization. The greater the degree of delegation by employees the more decentralized a business will be.

10.3.5 Centralization v decentralization

Centralization occurs when decisions are made by senior managers. Those at the top of the organization retain a high degree of control. Decentralization occurs when authority is passed down an organization and decisions are made extensively at lower levels.

Centralization keeps decision-making in the hands of experienced decision-makers. It means decisions are taken by those with a good overview of the business as a whole. This means it can hopefully ensure a consistent approach.

However, the problems of centralization include the fact that decisions may not take account of local conditions sufficiently. Managers and employees lower down the organization may be demotivated as they are not involved in decision-making. Furthermore, decision-making can be slow as information has to be passed up to the top for a decision to be made and then this decision has to be passed down various levels of hierarchy to be implemented.

An example of decentralization occurred in 2020 when ABB, a Swiss engineering business, announced plans to break up its existing four strategic divisions—electrification, industrial automation, motion, and robotics—into 18 autonomous businesses. These divisions are fully responsible for their own profit and loss account and balance sheets and their managers are completely accountable for the performance of their division. According to Jones (2020) the new Chief Executive at ABB, Mr Rosengren, thought this decentralization would avoid the complacency that had occurred in recent years. Meanwhile, as part of the decentralization strategy the number of employees at head office is due to be cut from 18,000 to just 1000 in the coming years.

Of course, decentralization is not always appropriate. The value of decentralizing depends on the skills and experience of staff and the benefits and risk of more decisions being made locally as opposed to senior management with an overview of the business.

10.3.6 Why does organizational structure matter?

The structure of a business is an important element of its success. It determines how jobs are organized, who reports to whom, and what powers different jobs have. This can affect the speed of decision-making—if a question has to go up through many levels of hierarchy or discussed in numerous committees to get a decision this will slow up any response. The structure can also affect the overall costs of a business. The use of short spans of control with many levels of management is likely to add additional overhead costs. A well-designed structure is efficient, enables jobholders to focus on the key issues, and ensures they are not overburdened. A poor organizational structure may lead to sluggishness and jobs not being designed appropriately to the needs of the business.

Think about a football team. The success of the team will depend on the individual players but also how they are organized for a match—what formation do they play? The 'right' formation will depend on the players you have, how the opposition is likely to be organized, and what result you are looking for. If a draw would give you enough points to win the league your formation is likely to be different than if you need to win. The same is true of the organizational structure—it is not just about the jobs and who does them, it is about how they are organized to work together. The right organizational structure depends on factors such as the business environment, what competitors are doing, and what the business itself wants to achieve. For example, W.L. Gore and Associates is a highly innovative enterprise (it prefers to be called an enterprise rather than 'company' or 'business'); it produces a wide range of products including medical equipment, waterproof clothing, and guitar strings. To ensure there is an innovative culture no-one at W.L. Gore talks of hierarchy—because there isn't one. Everyone is an 'associate' and everyone is encouraged to lead a project or be part of someone else's project. If you have an idea it is up to you to find others who want to work with you on it. According to the *Financial Times* the current Chief Executive argues that this approach works well for those who are self-driven and self-motivated but not for those who want to be told what to do. Qualifications, experience, and job titles count for nothing at W.L. Gore; what matters is what you can contribute to a given project. This approach to organizational structure leads to empowered employees and a project-based approach; it encourages associates to have and develop ideas and this is what leads the business to be so innovative.

The structure of a business will affect:

- The employee; for example, the structure will affect how many people you manage or report to; this can affect your workload and motivation.

- The organization; for example, wider spans of control may lead to fewer levels of hierarchy and lower management costs.

- The customer; for example, how tasks are organized will affect the customer experience. When dealing with your bank, for example, do you have to contact different departments to review your savings, your insurance policy, and your mortgage, or can one customer advisor help with everything?

Getting the structure of the business right is, therefore, an important decision that affects competitiveness and many stakeholder groups. Over time, as condition and objectives change, so will the structure. A change in structure is called a restructuring.

Businesses may decide to **restructure** if it is felt the existing structure is not appropriate or there are driving forces pushing for change. A common form of restructuring occurs when businesses look to lose layers of management; this is called delayering. By doing this it reduces management costs and it means there are fewer levels of management between the 'front line' and headquarters. In 2022, for example, the household products conglomerate Unilever

10

Think about it

The way in which an organization is structured will affect its costs, its speed of response, its responsiveness to local conditions, the quality of service, and the engagement of employees.

Why do you think this is?

Key concepts

Delegation occurs when authority is transferred from a superior to a subordinate.

Centralization occurs when decisions are made by senior managers.

Delayering occurs when a layer of management is removed from an organizational structure.

Restructuring occurs when the organizational structure of a business is changed.

announced it was restructuring and dividing the business into five units. These changes involved a reduction of 1500 management roles. A driving force for the restructuring was pressure from shareholders, who wanted better financial performance after a failed takeover bid for GlaxoSmithKline's consumer health division. The five new business units at Unilever are beauty and well-being, personal care, home care, nutrition, and ice cream. One possibility that arises from this restructuring is that a division could be more easily sold off in future. Each of the five divisions is responsible for its own strategy, growth, and performance. The company believes these changes will help the business as a whole meet its overall target of growth.

Business Insight 10.7 explores another example of restructuring which occurred at Pandora in 2020.

Business insight 10.7 Pandora

Pandora designs, manufactures, and markets hand-finished jewellery made from high-quality materials at affordable prices. Pandora jewellery is sold in more than 100 countries. In 2020 Pandora stated that it needed to make certain structural changes to ensure it remained a consumer-focused organization and was able to support future growth ambitions.

Its strategic reorganization—called Programme NOW—was intended to bring Pandora closer to its consumers and ensure the company could act more quickly and have more impact with its products and its marketing.

The company decided to close its three regional organizations and thereby remove an organizational layer between global headquarters and the local market. It wanted a flatter structure. The 100-plus markets where Pandora operated were grouped into 10 clusters, each headed by a General Manager. The General Manager is now based in the largest market in the cluster. The General Managers report to a newly established Chief Commercial Officer (CCO) position.

In the new structure the CCO reports to the President & Chief Executive Officer and is part of Pandora's Executive Leadership Team (Figure 1). The CCO is responsible for a retail centre of excellence to improve Pandora's global retail skills including global merchandising, store development, planning, and execution. The aim is to ensure greater impact in product development and marketing and a more consistent consumer experience across different markets. One Global Business Unit is responsible for the core products including Moments, Charms, and collaborations; another Global Business Unit will drive the newer product categories and innovations.

Pandora is already investing in developing stronger global functions including Marketing, Digital, Merchandising, and Business Intelligence. A Global Business Services centre will be established to deliver efficient and scalable transactional processes and drive efficiencies through standardization and higher quality.

Alexander Lacik
Chief Executive Officer
(CEO)

Anders Boyer
Chief Financial Officer
(CFO)

Byron Clayton
Chief HR Officer (CHRO)

David Walmsley
Chief Digital &
Technology Officer
(CDTO)

Mary Carmen Gasco-Buisson
Chief Marketing Officer
(CMO)

Stephen Fairchild
Chief Product Officer
(CPO)

Massimo Basei
Chief of Retail
Operations (CRO)

Jeerasage Puranasamriddhi
Chief Supply Officer
(CSO)

Figure 1 Executive leadership team at Pandora as of May 2023. *Source:* https://pandoragroup.com/investor/corporate-governance/executive-leadership-team [Accessed 22 May 2023].

The overall purpose of the restructuring is to bring the global headquarters closer to the local markets. It aims to reduce organizational complexity to allow Pandora to act with more speed and agility.

Questions

Why do you think Pandora is making the changes above to its organizational structure?

What challenges might it face?

What would you do?

You are the Chief Executive of a supermarket where decisions have been made centrally. You want to decentralize. What would you do to justify your decision to the Board?

Can you now answer these questions from the Introductory case study?

Do you think 3M is likely to be centralized or decentralized? Why?

Why might 3M have restructured the business?

Where are we now?

We have now examined the meaning and significance of organizational culture and organizational structure. We now examine in more detail how these two aspects of a business are interlinked.

10.4 Structure and culture

The structure and culture of a business are closely linked. This can be seen by analysing two extreme versions of organization: a **mechanistic organization** and an **organic organization**. The terms 'mechanistic' and 'organic' were introduced by the sociologists Burns and Stalker (1961). A mechanistic organization is intended to work like a machine. The structure is designed so that everyone has a clear place within it. It is clear who reports to whom, who does what, and what the boundaries of any role are. There are rules and procedures set out so that the response in any situation is clear. In this type of organization people are seen as replaceable; you can move someone else into a role and it is so well defined it is clear what they have to do. A mechanistic organization is designed by senior managers to deliver an outcome in a known and defined way. It focuses on control.

A mechanistic structure works well in a stable, routine environment where a predictable outcome is required. A mechanistic structure and the culture associated with it is often focused on doing what has been set out to be done in as efficient a way as possible. It may concentrate on volume production of standardized products, for example.

However, in a fast-changing environment an organic structure and a culture open to change may be more appropriate. In an organic structure, roles are less clearly defined and there are fewer rules and procedures. Delegation is more common and people are encouraged to make decision for themselves and work with whoever helps them to complete the task. Whereas a mechanistic structure has a role culture the organic focuses on getting things done. The relationships between people change depending on the contribution they can make to the task in hand. This type of structure is better suited to a creative world where the business cannot predict and does not want to predict the outcomes in advance. An organic structure and the culture that goes with this focuses on diversity, innovation, flexibility, and creativity.

When there is a need for creativity it is likely, therefore, that an organic structure will be most suitable. At Dreamworks—the studio behind the Shrek and Madagascar film franchises—there is no rigid organizational structure because the company wants employees' diverse perspectives to collectively solve problems. Similarly, at Pixar, the animation studio, the company believes it needs a structure that can live with ambiguity, that generates innovation and brings about creative ideas through collaboration. Haier, the Chinese producer of appliances and consumer electronics, states that it has moved away from the traditional hierarchical structure towards teams that are agile and emerge as the need arises. With better and faster communication and information systems comes the ability to decentralize and have empowered autonomous teams. Haier describes its approach as ecosystems held together by a clear set of values and purpose. Other organizations also talk of the benefits of a 'highly aligned, loose fit' approach—what the business wants to do and how

Table 10.2 Mechanistic v organic structures

Feature	Mechanistic organization	Organic organization
Span of control	Small	Wide
Levels of hierarchy	Many	Few
Rules and procedures	Many	Few
Delegation	Limited	Extensive
Culture	Role	Task
Communication	Mainly vertical	More horizontal
Outcome	Predictable and predetermined	Unpredictable

it wants it done is clear; how you do it is down to you. The global brewer AnBev, with brands such as Budweiser, Corona, Becks, Cass, Aguila, and Leffe, says on its website that its employees will 'have the freedom to grow without the traditional boundaries of role, function or location'. This organic approach is to encourage innovation which the company says is central to its success.

Rosabeth Moss Kanter was a professor at Harvard Business School. In her book *The Change Masters* (1983), she looked at ways in which change can be successfully brought about by examining six companies. She argued that companies have open communications systems and decentralization of resources. In *When Giants Learn to Dance* (1989), Kanter likened the world of global competition to a 'corporate Olympics'. The winners in these 'games' would be non-hierarchical, co-operative, and focused on processes—the way things are done. This is an organic type of organization.

The differences between a mechanistic and organic organization are shown in Table 10.2.

According to McKinsey, the management consultancy, to be competitive in the future a business needs to be much more organic than in the past. McKinsey advise organizations to:

- Remove as many layers of hierarchy as they can. It says that with digital technology it often sees spans of up to 30. Even the largest organizations these days tend to have only have six layers of hierarchy; the most agile tend to have three.

- Create a team-based approach where these groups can form and dissolve as needed; this enables rapid responses to an ever-changing situation.

- Ensure that there is good communication with those on the front line. These employees need to be empowered to speak up because they are closest to where value is being created and where there are risks if changes in the market are not spotted.

- Ensure people are clear about their responsibilities and roles and that there is delegation so they can make decisions as and when they are needed.

10

What would you do?

You have taken over a fast food chain where sales have been declining in recent months. You think there needs to be more decentralization within the business. Explain your thinking to the rest of your team.

Key concepts

A **mechanistic structure** focuses on control, clearly defined jobs, and well-defined lines of authority and communication.

In an **organic structure**, there are fewer rules and procedures, and roles and responsibilities are fluid as teams evolve to get tasks done.

10.4.1 The structure and culture of 'Excellent' organizations

In 1982 Tom Peters and Robert Waterman wrote the book *In Search of Excellence*. This is one of the biggest selling and most widely read business books ever. Peters and Waterman worked at the famous management consultancy McKinsey, based in the San Francisco office. They examined 43 of Fortune 500's top performing companies and found eight common themes which they claimed contributed to the success of the chosen businesses.

They found a strong link between excellence in the form of good performance and organizational structure and culture. These are shown in Figure 10.10.

Peters and Waterman identified eight key attributes of excellent organizations. These were:

1. A bias for action: these businesses were able to respond quickly to change and get on with it.

2. Closeness to the customer: these businesses were driven by their desire to meet customer needs.

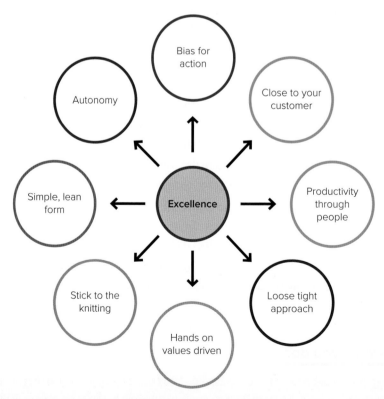

Figure 10.10 Features of an excellent business. *Source:* Peters, T.J. and Waterman, R.H. (1982). *In Search of Excellence*. London, Harper and Row.

3. Autonomy and entrepreneurship: these businesses delegated and encouraged employees to use their initiative.

4. Productivity through people: these businesses appreciated the importance of people to the success of a business.

5. Hands-on, value-driven: these businesses have clear, strong values that employees understand and agree with.

6. Stick to the knitting: these businesses focus on what they are good at.

7. Simple form, lean staff: these businesses have lean organizational structures that enable quick decision-making; for example, they often have minimal head office staff.

8. Simultaneous loose–tight properties: these businesses have centralized values but high levels of delegation. This means that whilst employees are empowered to make decisions for themselves they know the underlying values and strategy of the business and so have something to refer to.

We can see from this study that organizational structure and culture are closely linked and that they play a big role in the success of an organization. As with so much in business there is no right answer and what is appropriate at one moment in time in one context may not be right in another situation. Some of the excellent companies in Peters and Waterman (1982) still thrive; others do not, arguably because their culture and structure have not adapted to changes in internal and external conditions. One example of this is the growth in interest in social responsibility which does not figure directly in Peters and Waterman's original book. Take the luxury business LMVH which includes Dior. It seeks to develop an organization which is 'reactive and innovative', which 'delivers excellence', which 'cultivates an entrepreneurial spirit'—this sounds very much like Peters and Waterman's features of an excellent organization. However, LMVH also wants to be 'committed to positive impact', which is increasingly a feature of successful businesses.

Those in business therefore need to be constantly reviewing their culture and structure and be prepared to make and manage change.

Where are we now?

In this chapter we have analysed some very important aspects of organizations. We have considered how change can come about and why employees may resist such change. We have examined ways of overcoming such resistance. We have then discussed the nature and significance of organizational culture. Lastly, we have analysed the different elements of organizational structure and how the structure is closely linked with the culture. These areas of study are extremely important for organizations that need to get the right way of grouping and organizing tasks and the right underlying values to succeed in their markets. In such competitive times businesses need a structure that is fit for purpose and the ability to be proactive and reactive to change. In the next chapter we consider the responsibilities a business might think it has in relation to society and some of the ethical issues individuals face in a business.

Now you should know

- Organizational inertia occurs when a business stays as it is and is slow to change.

- Organizational culture refers to the values, attitudes, and beliefs of its employees and how they behave.

- The cultural paradigm is what all the different elements of the cultural web add up to—it is a summary of the culture of the organization.

- Driving forces are factors in a situation that push for change.

- Restraining forces are factors in a situation that prevent change.

- Artefacts are aspects of the business that can be easily seen or heard.

- The stated values of the business are what it claims its employees believe and what determines how they act.

- Assumed values. The shared basic assumptions within the organization are the deeply embedded, taken-for-granted behaviours.

- The organizational structure defines who does what, who reports to whom, and what responsibilities and authority a particular job has.

- The span of control is the number of people directly reporting to a manager.

- A level of hierarchy is a level of management responsibility.

- A functional organizational structure groups jobs by their business function.

- A regional organizational structure groups jobs by their geographical focus.

- Delegation occurs when authority is transferred from a superior to a subordinate.

- Centralization occurs when decisions are made by senior managers.

- Delayering occurs when a layer of management is removed from an organizational structure.

- Restructuring occurs when the organizational structure of a business is changed.

- A mechanistic structure focuses on control, clearly defined jobs, and well-defined lines of authority and communication.

- In an organic structure, there are fewer rules and procedures, and roles and responsibilities are fluid as teams evolve to get tasks done.

Review questions

Quick check

1. Identify Lewin's three stages of change.

2. Identify three features of job design according to Hackman and Oldham.

3. Distinguish between span of control and levels of hierarchy.

4. Outline two types of organizational culture.

5. Distinguish between a mechanistic and an organic organizational structure.

6. Explain the meaning of delayering.

7. Explain the difference between a centralized and decentralized business.

8. Explain the factors that might determine the culture of a business.

9. Explain why employees might resist the introduction of a new way of working.

Analysis

1. Analyse the ways in which a manager may overcome resistance to change.

2. Analyse the factors that influence the culture of a business.

3. Analyse the ways in which the structure of a business might affect its competitiveness.

Discussion

1. To what extent do you think the culture of a business determines it success?

2. Look at the structure of your university. How is it organized? Why do you think it is organized in this way? How might it be improved?

3. What do you think is the best way to manage change?

∿▶ Find out more

The topics covered in this chapter are part of an important area of study in business known as Organizational Behaviour (OB).

The classic texts in this area are:

Mullins, L. (2020). *Organisational Behaviour in the Workplace* (12th edn). Harlow, Pearson.

King, D. and Lawley, S. (2019). *Organizational Behaviour*. Oxford, Oxford University Press.

- To find out more about Tom Peters' many stimulating insights into business visit his You Tube channel or visit his website tompeters.com. You might also want to read Tom Peters and Robert H Waterman Jr *In Search of Excellence*.

- To find out more about managing change why not search for Kotter and Schlesinger's (1979) classic article in the *Harvard Business Review*, re-published in 2013, called 'Choosing Strategies for Change'. https://hbr.org/1979/03/choosing-strategies-for-change-2 You could also search for Kotter's article 'Leading Change: why transformation efforts fail' in the *Harvard Business Review*, January 2007.

- Kotter also has some excellent videos on change on You Tube. Visit his You-Tube channel www.youtube.com/channel/UCUxHbdpSMeT3ckJ7iZPDc1Q

- To find out more about the importance of culture you can watch Johnson and Scholes explain the importance of culture on You Tube. Watch 'Johnson: The role of organizational culture'. https://www.youtube.com/watch?v=8lVxC6XRvtY

☰ Bibliography

Alvesson M., Sveningsson S. (2008). *Changing Organizational Culture: Culture Change. Work in Progress*. London, New York, Routledge.

Anheuser-Busch (n.d.) Our Culture. wwww. ab-inbev.com, www.ab-inbev.com/careers/working-with-us/our-culture/.

Balogun, J. and Johnson, G. (2004). Organizational Restructuring and Middle Manager Sensemaking. *Academy Of Management Journal*, 47(4), 523–549.

Beckhard R. and Harris R. (1987). *Organizational Transitions: Managing Complex Change*. Reading, MA, Addison Wesley Publishing Company.

Burke, W. (2008). *Organization Change: Theory and Practice*. Thousand Oaks, CA, Sage.

Burnes B. (2004). *Managing Change: A Strategic Approach to Organizational Dynamics* (4th edn). Harlow, Prentice Hall.

Burns, T. and Stalker, G. M. (1961). *The Management of Innovation*. London, Tavistock.

By, R. T. (2005). Organizational change management: A critical review. *Journal of Change Management*, 5, 369–380.

Cameron K., Dutton, J., and Quinn R. (2003). *Positive Organizational Scholarship: Foundations of a New Discipline*. New York, Berrett Kohier.

Carr, D. K., Hard, K. J., and Trahant, W. J. (1996). *Managing the Change Process: A Field Book for Change Agents, Consultants, Team Leaders, and Reengineering Managers*. New York, McGraw-Hill.

Cheng, J. Y.-J. and Groysberg, B. (2020). How Corporate Cultures Differ Around the World. [online] *Harvard Business Review*. Available at: https://hbr.org/2020/01/how-corporate-cultures-differ-around-the-world.

Cummings, T. and Molloy, E. (1977). Improving Productivity and the Quality of Work Life. New York, Praeger.

Deal, T., and Kennedy, A. (1982). *Corporate Cultures: The Rites and Rituals of Organizational Life*. Reading, MA, Addison-Wesley.

Denison, D.R. (1990). *Corporate Culture and Organizational Effectiveness*. New York, John Wiley & Sons.

Drennan, D. (1992). *Transforming Company Culture*. London, McGrawHill.

Drucker, P. (1997). *Managing in a Time of Great Change*. Oxford, Butterworth-Heinemann.

Financial Conduct Authority (2022). Culture in banking. [online] Available at: <https://www.fca.org.uk/publication/foi/foi4350-information-provided.pdf> [Accessed 4 June 2022].

Financial Times (2022a). *What do we mean when we talk about workplace culture?*. [online] Available at: <https://www.ft.com/content/8239d8e4-7add-4db1-b64e-99afc2e749bb> [Accessed 3 June 2022].

Financial Times (2022b). *How to future-proof company culture*. [online] Available at: <https://www.ft.com/content/39db7e82-3947-11ea-ac3c-f68c10993b04> [Accessed 4 June 2022].

Financial Times. (2022c). *Japan is starting to question its working habits*. [online] Available at: <https://www.ft.com/content/8dcbe3ee-7089-11e7-aca6-c6bd07df1a3c> [Accessed 4 June 2022].

Gelfand, M. (2018). *Rule Makers, Rule Breakers: How Tight and Loose Cultures Wire Our World*. New York, Scribner.

Hackman, J. R. and Oldham, G. R. (1976). Motivation through the design of work: Test of a theory. *Journal of Organizational Behavior and Human Performance*, 16(10), 250–279.

Hackman, J. R. and Oldham, G. R. (1980). *Work design*. Reading, Massachusetts, Addison-Wesley.

Handy, C. (1976) Understanding Organisations. London, Penguin.

Hult International Business School (2017). *How cultural differences impact international business in 2017*. [online] Available at: <https://www.hult.edu/blog/cultural-differences-impact-international-business/> [Accessed 4 June 2022].

Johnson, G. (1992). Managing Strategic Change—Strategy, Culture, and Action. *Long Range Planning*, 25, 28–36.

Jones, S. (2020). How Switzerland's ABB plans to shake off ugly duckling image. *Financial Times*. [online] 29 Jun. Available at: https://www.ft.com/content/941ff99e-0a5d-4e51-a054-a955b096fab6 [Accessed 28 October 2023].

Kanter, R. M. (1983). *The Change Masters*. New York, Simon and Schuster.

Kanter, R. M. (1989). *When Giants Learn to Dance*. New York, Simon and Schuster.

Kotter, J. P. and Schlesinger, L. A. (1979). 'Choosing Strategies for Change.' Harvard Business Review, 57(2), (March–April).

Leetaru, L. (2019). The Wrong Ways to Strengthen Culture. *Harvard Business Review*, 97(4), July/August, 21–24.

Lewin, K. (1947) Group decision and social change. In: Newcomb, T. M., Hartley, E.L. (eds), *Readings in Social Psychology*. New York, Henry Holt, pp. 330–344.

Lewin K. (1951). *Field theory in social science*. New York, Harper & Row.

LVMH (2022). Values. www.lvmh.com/group/about-lvmh/values-lvmh/.

Martin, K. (2020). *How to future-proof company culture*. [online] www.ft.com. Available at: https://www.ft.com/content/39db7e82-3947-11ea-ac3c-f68c10993b04.

McKinsey (2021). [online] Available at: <https://www.mckinsey.com/business-functions/people-and-organizational-performance/our-insights/organizing-for-the-future-nine-keys-to-becoming-a-future-ready-company> [Accessed 25 October 2021].

McKinsey (2022). [online] Available at: <https://www.mckinsey.com/business-functions/people-and-organizational-performance/our-insights/the-organization-blog> [Accessed 3 June 2022].

Mintzberg, H. (1989). *Mintzberg on Management: Inside our Strange World of Organizations*. New York, Free Press.

Ostroff, C., Kinicki, A. J., and Muhammad, R. S. (2013). Organizational Culture And Climate. In Schmitt, N.W., Highhouse, S., and Weiner, I.B. (eds), *Handbook of Psychology: Industrial and Organizational Psychology*. Hoboken, NJ, John Wiley & Sons, 643–676).

Patagonia (2022). Culture & Life at Patagonia. [online] Available at: <https://eu.patagonia.com/gb/en/culture.html> [Accessed 4 June 2022].

Peters T. and Waterman R.H. (1982). *In Search of Excellence: Lessons from America's Best Run Companies*. London, Harper & Row.

Pricewaterhouse Coopers (2018). Where Organizational Culture is Headed (Global Survey). www.pwc.com.

PWC (2021). PWC's Code of Conduct. [online] Available at: <https://www.pwc.com/gx/en/about/ethics-business-conduct/code-of-conduct.html> [Accessed 25 October 2021].

PWC (2022). Why a Speak Up culture is important. [online] Available at: <https://www.pwc.co.uk/who-we-are/our-purpose/empowered-people-communities/why-a-speak-up-culture-is-important.html> [Accessed 3 June 2022].

Rehn, A. (2019). *Has Your Organisation Turned into a Monoculture?* People Management (Online). 5 July.

Schein, E.H. (1985) *Organizational Culture And Leadership*. San Francisco: Jossey-Bass.

Schein, E. H. and Schein, P. A. (2019). A New Era For Culture, Change And Leadership: A Conversation Between Edgar H. Schein And Peter A. Schein. *MIT Sloan Management Review*, 60(4), 52–58.

Schwartz, S.H. (2006). A theory of cultural value orientations: Explication and applications. *Comparative Sociology*, 5, (2), 137–182.

Shaw, J. (2019) *How Businesses Can Bounce Back After A Challenging Period*. People Management (Online). 26 June.

Shein Group (2022). Careers. [online] Available at: <https://sheingroup.com/careers//> [Accessed 5 June 2022].

Southwest Airlines (2022). Careers. [online] Available at: <http://careers.southwestair.com/culture> [Accessed 4 June 2022]

Todnem, R. (2005). Organizational change management: A critical review. *Journal of Change Management*, 5, 369–380.

The Economist (2020). www.economist.com/briefing/2020/10/22/how-satya-nadella-turned-microsoft-around

Vroom, V., and Yetton, P. (1973). *Leadership and Decision-Making*. Pittsburgh, PA, University of Pittsburgh Press.

10

Chapter 11

Business ethics and corporate social responsibility

Where are we now?

In earlier chapters there has often been a focus on the rewards to shareholders and the importance of profit as the objective of businesses. In this chapter we consider broader responsibilities that businesses may assume and the possible significance of business ethics to individuals making decisions. The areas of business ethics and social responsibility are very topical ones—managers need to think carefully about the relationship between their business and society.

Why am I studying this?

- You may be surprised by some aspects of business behaviour and want to know how it could happen. This chapter aims to explain more about business ethics.
- You may be impressed by other aspects of business behaviour where organizations seem to work actively to help society. You are interested in what drives these choices. This chapter examines social responsibility.
- You want to understand more about the different groups that have an interest in a business, and how a business might respond to them. This chapter examines the relationship between a business and its stakeholders.
- You want to understand the different views of how a business should relate to the environment in which it operates. This chapter explores the stakeholder and shareholder view of business.

Learning objectives

By the end of this chapter you should be able to:

- Explain the meaning of business ethics and ethical dilemmas
- Explain the difference between a utilitarian and deontological view of ethics

- Explain why people may behave unethically

- Explain the importance of a Code of Conduct or Code of Ethics

- Apply a stakeholder map to analyse how businesses respond to stakeholders

- Explain the meaning of Corporate Social Responsibility

- Analyse the reasons why Corporate Social Responsibility is an important concept these days

- Assess how to measure Corporate Social Responsibility

- Evaluate the benefits to a business of a socially responsible approach

- Explain reasons that might limit the move to being more socially responsible

Introductory case study Sony

Sony is a Japanese multinational business that produces games, entertainment programmes, movies, TVs, digital cameras, audio equipment, and smartphones. In its 2020 Annual Report Sony says its purpose is to 'fill the world with emotion, through the power of creativity and technology'. The company's Group Code of Conduct (shown in more detail in Appendix 1) states that it is a key responsibility of Sony to innovate, to have sound business practices, and to contribute to a more sustainable society.

Sony says that it considers the impact of its business activities on the interests of its stakeholders—including shareholders, customers, employees, suppliers, business partners, local communities, other organizations—and the global environment. Sony also says it is important to engage in dialogue with stakeholders to build trust and get input on its decisions.

Based on these principles, Sony aims to create long-term sustainable social and economic value by working with its stakeholders to pursue sustainability and human rights.

The company provides information on its activities to highlight how it performs in many areas, not just financial and how it works with its stakeholders.

Appendix 1: The Sony Group Code of Conduct

The Sony Group Code of Conduct ('the Code') underpins the company's ethics and compliance programme. The Code applies to all Sony board members, officers, and employees.

Sony says that it is committed to ethical and responsible business conduct. Sony's culture is built on its core ethical values of Fairness, Integrity, Honesty, Respect, and Responsibility. These are intended to guide how Sony personnel work with each other, with business partners, and with the communities in which Sony does business.

Sony says that it recognizes its responsibility as a member of a global society and the Code reflects principles set out in global ethical guidelines, which include (among others):

- **Organisation for Economic Co-operation and Development (OECD) Guidelines for Multinational Enterprises**

- **The United Nations Global Compact**

- **The United Nations Universal Declaration of Human Rights**

▶

- **The Guiding Principles on Business and Human Rights and Sustainable Development Goals (SDGs).**

Sony also participated in the formulation of (and updates of) and observes the standards in the Charter of Corporate Behavior of Keidanren (Japan Business Federation), an alliance of Japan's leading corporations.

Sony's Code of Conduct includes guidance on key areas of risk such as:

- **Accurate recordkeeping**
- **Anti-corruption/bribery**
- **Antitrust/fair competition**
- **Avoiding conflicts of interest**
- **Diversity/anti-discrimination/equal employment opportunity/fair labour and employment practice/proper workplace conduct**
- **Fair dealing (fair business practices)**
- **Privacy (e.g., data privacy of employees, customers, consumers) and cyber security**
- **Protection of human rights**
- **Financial integrity and anti-fraud**
- **Speaking up/no retaliation**
- **Tax compliance**
- **Workplace health and safety.**

You can see from this list how areas of risk exist throughout the business—for example, tax compliance in the finance function and diversity and workplace health and safety in human relations.

All Sony Group employees are required to complete comprehensive Code of Conduct training within 90 days of hire or the commencement of provision of service and refresher Code of Conduct training periodically thereafter. In addition, Sony provides in-depth training on key risk areas at least once per year.

Sony believes that a 'speak-up' culture—where employees are encouraged to raise concerns and feel confident that they can do so without fear of retaliation—is a key to early detection and prevention of ethical and regulatory problems. Sony has an open reporting programme and provides many different types of resources to employees to enable them to raise concerns, including the Sony Group Ethics & Compliance Hotline ('the Hotline'). All information provided to the Hotline is handled confidentially. Calls to the Hotline are not recorded or traced, and reporters may remain anonymous to the extent permitted by law.

Sony believes it is important to listen to and communicate with those its activities affect (called stakeholders).

Sources

www.sony.net/SonyInfo/csr/library/reports/SustainabilityReport2020_E.pdf

www.sony.net/SonyInfo/csr_report/about/

Introductory case study questions

1. Why would Sony have a Code of Conduct?

2. Why might this Code of Conduct need reviewing from time to time?

3. Why does Sony want a 'speak up' culture?

4. Who are Sony's stakeholders?

5. How might Sony benefit from engaging with stakeholders?

6. With reference to a stakeholder map, how might Sony engage and communicate with the different stakeholder groups?

7. What might be the benefits to Sony of a socially responsible approach?

8. Based on the data provided, would you say Sony is behaving in a socially responsible way?

9. Evaluate the ways that Sony is measuring its social responsibility

Critical thinking

1. Companies are often very proud of their Code of Ethics or their Code of Conduct and proudly show these on their websites as Sony has done. Even so there are plenty of examples of poor behaviour by employees in businesses. Why do you think this is?

2. The information above is published by Sony on its website. Do you think you can trust the information about social responsibility that a business puts on its website?

Introduction: business ethics and corporate social responsibility

Business activity affects many different groups such as investors, employees, customers, the local community, and even future generations. The groups affected by business are called stakeholders and businesses need to consider the responsibilities they have to them. In this chapter we will examine the extent to which a business should accept responsibility for its impact on stakeholders and also the extent to which a business might seek to actively improve society. This consideration of the role of a business within society as whole is known as Corporate Social Responsibility. A key consideration for a business is how much responsibility it wants to accept for the impact on others over and above what the law dictates. To decide on their responsibilities managers will consider the following types of questions:

- Does it feel responsible for the working conditions of its suppliers?

- What about the working conditions of the suppliers of the suppliers? Is the business responsible for these?

- Should the business be concerned about the environmental impact of its activities?

- Does it matter if the business is discharging waste into local rivers if the government says it can?

- What about the product the business makes and how it makes it? For example, if there is a legal and profitable market for palm oil, should a business producing it care about the deforestation it can lead to unless a government makes it?

- What about the impact of its product on society? For example, should YouTube and Facebook care if some posts distort the truth or are alleged to lead to harmful behaviour?

11

Owners and managers have to decide what they think their responsibilities are, not just to shareholders but to wider groups in society, i.e. how socially responsible the business should aim to be and what they decide is acceptable behaviour.

At an individual level, employees are also grappling with decisions over what is the right or wrong thing to do. For example, imagine that a close colleague asks you to write an overly glowing reference so they can get a new job—would you do it? What if some of your existing clients are paying more for your service than the price now being offered to new customers—would you tell them if you knew your profits would drop as a result? Would you register your company abroad even though all its activities are in this country, if it reduced your tax bill? In each of these cases employees will need to decide what they think is right. These are ethical decisions.

In this chapter we will consider the issues related to ethical decision-making and the impact of these issues for the decision-maker and the business. We will start by exploring the area of business ethics.

11.1 Business ethics and decision-making

According to the Institute of Business Ethics: 'Business ethics is the application of ethical values to business behaviour. Business ethics is relevant both to the conduct of individuals and to the conduct of the organization as a whole. It applies to any and all aspects of business conduct, from boardroom strategies and how companies treat their employees and suppliers to sales techniques and accounting practices.'

Ethical behaviour goes beyond the legal requirements for a company and is, therefore, about discretionary decisions and behaviour that is influenced by an individual's values rather than government regulations. All business will be subject to regulatory requirements and all businesses should follow these. However, there are many decisions which may be legal but where there may be a question of what the right thing to do actually is.

Decisions in all the different functions of a business are likely to have an ethical perspective.

For example:

- In operations, managers may decide to use overseas suppliers because they are cheaper than domestic ones. This will benefit investors and may be a perfectly sensible decision on purely financial grounds, but, at the same time, may damage the local economy. Furthermore, the transportation of the products from further afield may be environmentally harmful. There is, therefore, an ethical dimension to this decision which is whether it is right to benefit another community rather than the one you are based in and whether it is right to increase the negative impact of operations on the climate. At what point do these considerations outweigh the financial gains? What if you are personally judged on the profits you generate—what will you prioritize when making a decision: profit, community, or the environment?

- Imagine that the marketing function of a business is considering developing facial recognition technology to sell to other organizations. This technology will be used to track the movement of customers around their stores. This will lead to better insights into shopping behaviour and better data on the impact of different promotions of various customer groups. However, this data might also be accessed by governments wanting to track individuals' movements more closely; this could infringe on their personal liberties. Does this matter? Should the business be concerned about how their product will be used? Does it make a difference if the government of the country had a track record of monitoring citizens' personal data and of human rights abuse?

- In human resources a business may face ethical issues in terms of what to pay its employees. For example, according to the International Labour Organization, in Mexico in 2021 the minimum wage was $1.05 an hour. Would it be right for a UK company to pay this wage per hour if it had a base there? According to the International Labour Organization, in 2022 there was no minimum wage in 10% of countries around the world including Eritrea, Somalia, or the United Arab Emirates. Should a company worry about doing business in these countries where wages are so low?

- In finance, an example of an ethical issue is when a manager is under pressure to improve the liquidity of the business and is considering renegotiating payments with suppliers to achieve this. If the business is a big buyer it may have the power to force suppliers to accept less favourable payment terms. For some of the suppliers this could create significant cashflow problems. According to the *Financial Times* (2022), in 2020 official data showed it took an average of 54 days for Chinese private manufacturers to get paid by the government in the first three quarters of the year. This was up from 45 days in 2019 and 27 days five years before. We can see the business logic of this decision, particularly if the government finance manager is being asked to improve their liquidity position, but that does not necessarily make it right. Another example of an ethical issue in finance is whether to allow payment in bitcoins. This might attract new customers but creating bitcoins uses huge amounts of fossil fuel energy. According to the *Financial Times*, mining bitcoin, which accounts for half of all crypto currencies, uses the same amount of energy annually as the Netherlands did in 2019. Scientists warn that this threatens the Paris climate goals. Interestingly, in 2021 Tesla said it would stop accepting bitcoin payments because of the environmental impact. A further issue linked to using bitcoins to trade is that you cannot track ownership and so it can be used to move money earned illegally. In 2021 El Salvador became the first country to make bitcoins an official currency, according to PWC; this might help the economy but does mean that money made illegally may be used within El Salvador relatively easily.

We can see that many—if not all—decisions in business will have an ethical aspect to them and that there is no simple answer in terms of what someone should do in that situation. When deciding what is the right thing to do the context matters—what might seem right in one situation may seem wrong in another. This was highlighted in a recent study on personal ethics in which individuals were given what was supposedly a lost wallet by someone who had to dash off and so left the person with it (Aberystwyth University 2019). The study analysed the number of people who then handed in the wallet. One interesting finding was that the more money that was left in the wallet the more people were likely to hand it in; the context of a situation can have a big impact on what people think is the right thing to do.

11

Think about it

1 Imagine you found a wallet and were considering whether to hand it in to the police. Would it make any difference if:
   - There was a driver's licence so you knew who owned it?
   - It was owned by a pensioner?
   - It had £20 in it?
   - It had £200 in it?
   - You found it in a busy shopping area with lots of people around?
     Why do you think these factors matter?

2 Imagine that:
   - your colleague has told you they need time off to see their daughter in a school play but have no official leave left so they will pretend to be ill.
   - you know that a colleague—who is also a friend—is going to be made redundant but you are asked not to say anything to them about this.
   - a supplier whose contract is up for renewal gets you tickets for you to see your favourite band.
     What do you think you would do in these situations?

The fact that there are often different perspectives and that what is the right thing to do may not be clear is known as an ethical dilemma.

11.1.1 Ethical dilemmas

An ethical dilemma occurs when someone faces a decision where there is more than one view of what is right. For example, when deciding whether to close down a local business to relocate overseas to a low-wage economy, a manager may consider issues such as the impact on local jobs, the impact on employment and earnings overseas, the morality of paying much lower wages abroad than domestically, and the impact on the profits of the business. Managers may face an ethical dilemma in that they don't want to take jobs away from their own communities, but if they don't, there may not be jobs for anyone because the business could fail. In 2018 the well-known American brand, Harley Davidson, faced criticism when it announced it was moving some of its production to Europe to avoid tariffs, according to the *New York Times*. Arguably, if it didn't move, more employees' jobs would have been lost so there were no easy answers. Sometimes one decision may end up being right because the alternative is worse. In 2022 there was widespread criticism of Russia's invasion of Ukraine. Companies with business interests in Russia had to consider whether to shut these down to protest against this invasion even if it meant some staff had to be made redundant.

Ethical dilemmas can be stressful for employees because it means they are balancing different views of the same action. Telling a potential customer that they can get a better deal from a competitor may feel the honest thing to do but it may harm the sales of the business and put jobs at risk. Some people, therefore, would think it was the right thing to do to tell the customer; others wouldn't.

Think about it

1. Search engines such as Google have been criticized for taking little responsibility for what is on the websites that can be found through their services. Do you think they should take more responsibility?

2. Elon Musk argues that filtering comments on Twitter can threaten free speech. Do you agree. What rules would you have?

3. When was the last time you had to think to yourself whether something was right or not? What made you choose to do what you did in the end?

What would you do?

1. On 24 April 2013 a fire at an eight-storey garment factory in Rana Plaza on the outskirts of Dhaka in Bangladesh killed over 400 people and injured many more, according to a UK government report. Local police and an industry association had previously warned that the building was unsafe. Well-known global brands such as Primark and Loblaw were accused of exploiting low-paid workers and failing to care enough about safety.

If you were the manager of one of these brands with the job of getting the best value for money when ordering products would you:

• Ignore the criticism and carry on benefiting from low costs by using the same suppliers?

• Move production to somewhere else where conditions may be more socially acceptable?

• Try to engage with government agencies to improve regulations, pay, and conditions in Bangladesh?

Key concept

Business ethics refer to what is regarded as right or wrong when making a business decision.

Where are we now?

We now appreciate how complex decisions concerning ethics can be, and, when deciding what is 'right' or 'wrong', individuals may use different criteria. There are various frameworks an individual might have in their minds that leads them to one decision or another. Two examples of such frameworks are: utilitarian ethics and deontological ethics. We will now look at each of these in turn.

11

11.1.2 Ethical decision-making frameworks

Utilitarian ethics

This is an approach to ethics that is based on the outcomes of an action; it is known as a consequentialist theory because it focuses on what happens if a decision is made. A utilitarian approach to ethics asks the questions: 'How will my decision affect others? What are the consequences for others of my actions?'. Using this approach, a manager looks at the outcomes of a decision and considers its impact on others. He or she would then decide what is the best decision overall in terms of selected criteria such as happiness or income. Achieving 'the greatest good for the greatest number' is the aim of utilitarian decision-making, although what is meant by 'good' is obviously subjective. Taking a utilitarian approach, a manager might, for example, add up the financial costs and benefits of a decision and see whether the overall outcome is positive. A utilitarian approach recognizes that the options involved in any decision may have good and bad effects; the best decision is the one that does the greatest good for all those affected.

Deontological ethics

This is known as a duty-based approach to ethics. 'Deontological' means the study (or science) of duty. This approach is commonly associated with the philosopher Immanuel Kant (1724–1804). Kant argued that doing what is right is not about the consequences of an action (something over which we ultimately have no control) but about having the right intention when deciding to perform the action. Kant argued that humans could use their unique ability to reason to determine what their ethical duty is in any situation. For Kant there are some ethical duties which cannot be sacrificed for 'the greater good'. For example, when working with a team to achieve a goal Kant argued that the end does not justify the means. Respect for individuals within the team is what Kant calls a 'categorical Imperative'. The people in the team are not just a means to an end, they are an end in themselves, according to this approach.

The most basic form of the imperative is: 'Act only according to that maxim by which you can at the same time will that it should become a universal law'. For instance, lying is unethical because we could not universalize an approach that said, 'One should always lie'. We can, however, universalize the maxim, 'Always speak truthfully' without running into a logical contradiction. This means we should act truthfully whatever the consequences. A utilitarian may argue that in some situations acting truthfully brings more costs than benefits.

Whilst adopting a particular ethical framework is one way that individuals may help themselves to make a decision, businesses may make it easier for employees by having a code of conduct or ethics.

11.1.3 Code of conduct or code of ethics

Employees may have their own view of what is 'right' or 'wrong'. The managers of the organization may also have a view of what they think is ethically correct. The views of employees and the senior leaders of the organization may or may not be aligned. To ensure employees understand what the organization believes is the right thing to do in any situation and to help provide guidelines to help people make decisions, a business may produce a Code of Ethics or a Code of Conduct. This is a written statement that sets out the principles that the business believes should govern how employees behave. These Codes provide employees with a view of what the business considers to be ethical conduct, and a guide as to how employees should behave. They may also outline the expected behaviour and conduct of suppliers or other partners.

An ethical code may include the importance of:

- Integrity: competing in a fair and honest way; for example, the business should not mislead customers, or engage in bribery.

- Honesty: being transparent in what you do and why.

- Not harming others: for example, not causing undue stress on employees by pressurizing them to get a job done.

- The importance of speaking up if there is any behaviour within the organization which causes you concern.

An example of a business with an ethical code is the electronics company, Texas Instruments, a semiconductor manufacturing company based in the US.

According to Texas, the code provides the following ethical advice to employees:

- 'Is the action legal? . . . If not, stop immediately.

- Does it comply with our values? . . . If it does not, stop.

- If you do it would you feel bad? . . . Ask your own conscience if you can live with it.

- How would this look in the newspaper? . . . Ask if this goes public tomorrow, would you do it today?

- If you know it's wrong . . . don't do it.

- If you are not sure . . . ask; and keep asking until you get an answer.

A code of ethics (or code of conduct) sets out the expectations that the company has in relation to how employees should behave in any given situation, to assist with decision-making.

So, for example, if an employee is offered a gift in return for a contract, they will be able to refer to the code of ethics to see whether or not that would be in line with the organization's policy.

Another example of how a code of conduct can help employees make the right choices is given in Business Insight 11.1 on GSK plc (formerly GlaxoSmithKline plc).

As well as providing guidance to staff, codes of conduct or business ethics can reassure customers, investors, suppliers, partners, and even competitors about the expected integrity of how business is conducted.

A code of business ethics reflects how the organization operates its business model—how it relates to the communities in which it does business and how it expresses the corporate values it considers important. The code of ethics of an organization sets out what it considers to be acceptable ways of conducting its affairs.

What would you do?

According to the *Japan Times* newspaper, in 2021 government officials at Japan's communications ministry were treated to dinner on 54 occasions by the Tohokushinsha Film Corp. between November 2015 and December 2020. The film company covered all the costs. The company also gave gifts of tickets to basketball games. Do you think this behaviour is acceptable?

Business insight 11.1 **GSK plc says how you achieve your objectives matters as much as the objectives themselves**

GSK is a global pharmaceutical business. It believes that what is important is not just what it achieves but how it achieves it. It believes it is important for its employees to make good choices. This means going beyond simply following laws and rules.

According to GSK its values are:

A focus on the patients and always doing the right things for them

Transparency to build trust by being open and honest

Respect, which means supporting diversity and individuality

Integrity, which means colleagues have the highest ethical standards of behaviour.

The implications for not following these values include disciplinary action, potentially including dismissal or termination of contract. For senior managers there might also be financial penalties for significant misconduct.

Figure 1 outlines the questions GSK employees should ask themselves when considering the ethics of a particular action.

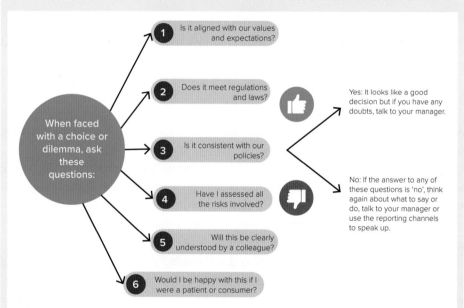

Figure 1 Questions employees should ask when faced with a choice or dilemma.

Source: Press release: Sanofi-GSK first to report a successful efficacy study against Omicron with COVID-19 beta-containing vaccine (no date) Sanofi. Available at: https://www.sanofi.com/en/media-room/press-releases/2022/2022-06-24-05-29-02-2468538 [Accessed 2 April 2023].

Source: www.gsk.com/media/4800/english-code-of-conduct.pdf.

Questions

1. What sorts of ethical issues do you think might occur at GSK?

2. What do you think will determine whether employees actually behave in the way set out by GSK?

However, simply having a code of conduct or a code of ethics does not mean it necessarily has an impact on what employees do. If the code in a business is to influence employees' behaviour it must be supported in a number of areas:

- there must be suitable communication of the Code and training for employees on what the Code means in practice
- the organization's managers must show commitment to the Code and follow it themselves
- they must be prepared to invest to support the Code and its enforcement
- there must also be suitable processes such as effective communication, training to change behaviour, and that behaviour should be monitored to ensure that employees are held accountable for their actions.

Can you now answer this question from the Introductory case study?

1. Why would Sony have a Code of Conduct?
2. Why might this Code of Conduct need reviewing from time to time?

The various elements involved in building an ethical culture are highlighted in Figure 11.1.

What would you do?

1 You are the new Chief Executive of a government department that commissions building projects. There is not a Code of Ethics at the moment but you want to introduce one.

You need to explain to the Board of Directors why a Code of Ethics is important. What would you say?

2 In 2022 the UK government announced it would not use the global management consultancy Bain & Company for any government contracts for three years. According to the *Guardian* this was because of Bain's 'grave professional misconduct' in state corruption in South Africa (Guardian 2022). Is there any business you would not buy from or work for because of ethical reasons?

3 China has a population of over 1.4 bn people. According to *The Economist*, in 2021 China accounted for a quarter of global sales of clothes, nearly a third of jewellery and handbags, and around two-fifths of cars, plus a major share of packaged food, beauty products, pharmaceuticals, electronics, and more You have concerns about some of the Chinese government's policies towards protesters, the Uighurs, and Taiwan. Would you avoid trading with this country?

Source: www.economist.com/business/2022/11/24/multinational-firms-are-finding-it-hard-to-let-go-of-china

The IBE Business Ethics Framework

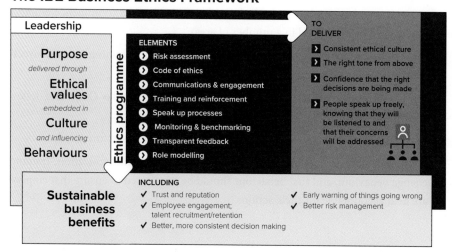

Figure 11.1 Elements required to build an ethical culture. *Source:* The Institute of Business Ethics www.ibe.org.uk/knowledge-hub/ibe-business-ethics-framework.

Where are we now?

A code of ethics may help individuals to know how to behave in any situation but this does not mean that they will. Organizations will generally want to create a culture whereby if someone sees or hears something that they think is not acceptable behaviour they will speak up. We now look at 'whistle-blowing', which is when people highlight their concerns.

11.1.4 Whistle-blowing

An organization's code of ethics may include information on how employees can report any concerns they have. Organizations may set up confidential 'hotlines' (as we've seen in the opening case study with Sony's 'speak up, listen up' policy) where employees can raise their concerns confidentially. The code may also encourage employees to be 'whistle-blowers'. This means that where employees feel as though they are unable to raise concerns through a specific channel, they are encouraged to raise those concerns in other ways.

According to a 2021 survey by the Institute of Business Ethics over half of the employees surveyed said their organizations had a Speak Up mechanism to report misconduct confidentially.

Whistle-blowing occurs when an individual feels that something that is being done within the business is wrong and that they have to tell others about what is happening. For example, a whistle-blower may tell the media. An example of whistle-blowing could occur if the business was holding information back which an employee felt it was in the public interest that it was known. For example, in 2021 Frances Haugen became a well-known whistle-blower revealing inside secrets from her time at Facebook. According to the *New York Times*, Haugne's allegations included the fact that Facebook knew its products were damaging teenagers' mental health and was guilty of putting 'astronomical profits before people'. In 2022, the *Guardian* newspaper published allegations following a leak from a whistle-blower that some of Credit Suisse bank's clients had made their money from drug trafficking, money laundering, corruption, and other serious crimes. It was claimed the

Key concepts

> A **code of ethics** sets out the expectations that the company has for how employees should behave in any given situation, to assist with decision-making.
>
> **Whistle-blowing** occurs when an individual within a business reveals information that highlights illegal or unethical behavior by others within the organization.

bank had failed to do due diligence on those depositing money, although the bank rejected the claims, saying the information had been taken out of context and was largely historical.

In some situations, employees may be reluctant to speak up about unethical behaviour occurring within the business because of pressure from others. There may be a sense of group loyalty which prevents people making public what is actually happening. There may also well be a fear of what will happen if they speak up. Indeed, according to the Institute of Business Ethics survey of 2021, the most common reasons why people do not speak up are that they are concerned that they might jeopardize their job (34%) and that they do not believe that their organization would take corrective action (34%). 43% of employees who said they had spoken up about misconduct say that they experienced retaliation as a result.

An extreme example of people responding to a whistle-blower occurred in 2022 in Johannesburg when Babita Deokaran was shot dead. As acting financial officer at Gauteng Provincial Government Department of Health, Babita had been a whistle-blower, and a key witness in an investigation into alleged corruption involved in the procurement contracts of COVID-19 protective clothing.

In many countries, laws exist to protect whistle-blowers. This is to encourage people to speak up. Governments also use the information of whistle-blowers to act against businesses. For example, in December 2021 the US Department of Labor said it was investigating Apple over claims that it retaliated against an employee who complained of workplace harassment and unsafe working conditions. According to the *Financial Times*, Ashley Gjovik, 35, had been a senior engineering program manager for six years at Apple when she was fired in September for allegedly leaking confidential information. Gjovik has written regularly on Twitter about her allegations of harassment, surveillance, and workplace safety issues. She has alleged that she was dismissed under a false pretext following numerous complaints that led to more than a dozen instances of retaliation including job reassignment.

Can you now answer this question from the Introductory case study?

> Why does Sony want a 'speak up' culture?

11.1.5 Why do people act unethically?

People may act unethically for their own personal gain or to avoid an undesirable outcome. For example, a salesperson may mislead customers to increase their commission or to ensure sales targets are met and to make sure they keep their job. Unethical behaviour is often

Business Insight 11.2: Opioids and ethics

In 2019 the US-based pharmaceutical company, Purdue Pharma, was accused of encouraging doctors to prescribe painkillers (opioids) in return for financial benefits. When giving the prescriptions to patients it is claimed that doctors downplayed the dangers of addiction or overdose. It is claimed that between 1999 and 2016 over 200,000 deaths in the US could be linked to the prescription of opioids. Purdue introduced the painkiller OxyContin in 1996 and had sales of $48m. By 2001 Purdue's sales of opioids had reached $1.1 bn.

According to the National Bureau of Economic Research, OxyContin has accounted for 65% of the national growth in overdose death rates in the US since 1996.

McKinsey, the management consultancy, was fined in 2021 for its role in promoting opioids. The prosecutors in the trial claimed that McKinsey had worked on strategies to 'turbocharge' the sales of OxyContin advising Purdue to increase sales calls to doctors known to be high prescribers and to 'subvert' government restrictions on higher dosages. The legal prosecutors said McKinsey used cynical and calculated marketing tactics by targeting those doctors they knew would overprescribe opioids.

Questions

Even if Purdue's actions were legal, do you think they were ethical?

Why do you think employees of Purdue would have done this?

Sources

www.theguardian.com/us-news/2019/may/22/purdue-pharma-opioid-world-health-organization-painkiller-global-sales

---

linked to a business under pressure to increase profits; employees look to cut costs or find new ways of increasing revenue and, as a result, their own standards are dropped to achieve a profit target. In the 2021 Institute of Business Ethics survey 48% of employees in organizations with ethics programmes said that their line managers rewarded employees who get good results even if they use practices that are ethically questionable. The dangers of creating a culture where results matter more than ethics can be seen in Business Insight 11.2 about the promotion of opioids in the US, in recent years.

People may also act unethically because the culture of the business may support, or at least not challenge, unethical behaviour. The energy business Enron was one of the biggest examples of corporate failure ever, with staff publishing false profits; this ultimately led to the bankruptcy of the business in 2001. The company had grown fast, employing many graduates whose first experience was working at Enron—they knew no different and assumed that risk taking and misleading investors was an acceptable way to behave.

The ability and willingness of someone to act unethically will depend, in part, on how that individual views the likelihood of being caught and the consequences of their actions. It will also depend on how clear they are about what they should be doing.

The CCAB (an institute of chartered accountants in England and Wales) outlines some of the threats to ethical behaviour that exist in its industry:

- self-interest: the threat that a financial or other interest will inappropriately influence your judgement or behaviour

- self-review: the threat that you will not properly evaluate the results of a previous judgement made or service performed by you (or someone else within your practice) when forming a judgement as part of providing a current service
- advocacy: the threat that you will promote a position (usually your client's) to the point that your objectivity is compromised
- familiarity: the threat that, due to a long or close relationship with someone, you will be too sympathetic to that person's interests, or too accepting of their work
- intimidation: the threat that you will be deterred from acting objectively because of actual or perceived pressures, including attempts to exercise undue influence over you.

Cannon (2012) identified some of the factors that undermine any standards set by the business and are likely to lead to unethical behaviour, compared to those factors that reinforce these standards. These are set out in Table 11.1.

Table 11.1 Undermining and reinforcing factors for ethical behaviour

Undermining factors	Reinforcing factors
Pressure for profits	Reward systems that reward ethical behaviour
Focus on quantity not quality	Emphasis on quality
Uncertainty about ethical standards	Clearly communicated ethical standards
Group-think or group loyalty	Frequent reinforcement of standards
Social bullying and fear	Standards committees
Secrecy or closed-door decision-making	Openness

What would you do?

Look at the following examples and decide whether you would speak up:

- A colleague uses their company computer to check their social media accounts and order some of their shopping online.
- Your manager is having a relationship with one of the team who has recently been promoted.
- Your team is researching a new drug for heart disease. After some encouraging initial results recent tests have been disappointing but your chief executive does not want this information to leak out or it will affect funding and the whole project will stop.
- Your company has signed a contract with an overseas supplier who uses child labour. This is legal in the country where they are based.

Where are we now?

So far, we have considered what might be right or wrong in a given situation. However, there is a broader debate about the role of any organization and the extent to which the owners and managers think the business should aim to improve society as whole. This debate is over the extent to which a business accepts that it has responsibilities to the various groups it deals with and affects; these individuals and groups affected by a firm's behaviour are known as stakeholders.

11

11.2 **Stakeholders**

According to Freeman (1984) a stakeholder is: 'Any group or individual who can affect or [be] affected by the achievement of an organization's objectives'.

For example, in its 2021 annual report the food and drink business, Nestlé, identifies the following groups as fundamental to its continuing business success:

- Academia

- Communities

- Consumers and the general public

- Customers

- Employees and their representatives

- Governments

- Industry and trade associations

- Intergovernmental organizations

- Non-governmental organizations (NGOs)

- Reporting agencies

- Shareholders and the financial community

- Suppliers (including farmers and smallholders).

Every business decision will have an impact on its stakeholders. The growth of a business, for example, may generate higher returns for investors, more tax revenue for the government, more jobs or overtime for employees, and higher spending by employees in the local area. However, not all the effects will be positive. The growth of one business may be at the expense of another, affecting its profits and leading to a loss of jobs there. Growth may require more deliveries and lead to more congestion in the area. This means that any business decision may affect some stakeholders positively but may have a negative impact on others.

The above highlights the fact that different individuals and groups may have a different perspective of any decision a business takes. Stakeholders will have their own needs and objectives and, in some cases, these will overlap with each other and the objectives of the business, but in other situations they will clash. The power of stakeholders will vary between regions and over time. For example, changes in the law may change the ability of employees to strike. Examples of stakeholder objectives are shown in Table 11.2.

Table 11.2 Examples of stakeholder objectives

Stakeholder	Example of needs
Employees	Job security, fair pay, career development
Suppliers	Repeat orders, payment on time, fair price
Investors	Accurate financial reporting, share price increase, dividends
Government	Legal activities; tax revenue, job creation; environmentally friendly
Community	Job creation; environmentally friendly
Customers	Good value for money; safe products

Key concept

The **stakeholders** of a business are individuals or groups who affect or are affected by its activities.

Can you now answer these questions from the Introductory case study?

- Who are Sony's stakeholders?
- How might Sony benefit from engaging with stakeholders?

The relationship between managers and their stakeholders will depend, in part, on factors such as the power and interest of these different groups. The more interest that a particular stakeholder group has in what a business is doing, and the more power they have to affect the success of the business, the more managers will want to meet their needs and keep them happy.

The power of stakeholders will depend on what actions they can take to influence the actions of managers. Investors may have power, for example, through their ability to vote to replace managers; employees have power by their ability to take industrial action.

The way in which managers are likely to treat different stakeholders can be analysed using stakeholder mapping. One version of stakeholder mapping was developed by the academic, Aubrey Mendelow in 1991. The aim is to identify which stakeholders have the most influence on the decisions of a business. The influence a stakeholder has depends on its interest in the activities of the business and its power. The level of interest reflects how much a stakeholder cares about what a business is doing. The level of power reflects how much a stakeholder can affect and change the activities of a business. According to Mendelow (1991):

$$\text{Influence} = \text{power} \times \text{interest}$$

The position of any stakeholder group will influence how managers respond to them. For example, the stakeholders in quadrant A in Figure 11.2 do not have much interest in the business or much power to influence what the businesses does. Managers will pay limited attention to these stakeholders. By comparison, the stakeholders in quadrant C are powerful and very interested in what is happening at the business; managers will involve these stakeholders in their decisions and ensure that their needs are taken into consideration. The stakeholders in quadrant B are interested in what happens but are not particularly powerful; managers will make sure they are kept informed but do not need to adapt what the business is doing to meet their needs. In quadrant D the stakeholders are powerful and therefore have to be listened to but they are not particularly interested in the activities of the business, so whilst stakeholder needs have to be met the business may not have to change many of its activities.

The position of stakeholders in terms of their interest or power is not fixed; it may change over time. For example, changes in legislation may give employees more power. Employees might also gain more power by joining together to form or join a trade union. This can give them more bargaining power. Equally, one shareholder may buy more shares from others and become more powerful. Managers must be aware that the positions of

11

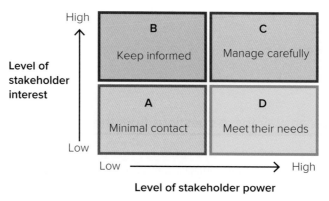

Figure 11.2 A stakeholder map showing interest and power. *Source:* Author.

Key concept

> **Stakeholder mapping** categorizes different stakeholder groups according to their power and their level of interest.

stakeholders on the map will change over time and need to adjust their approach accordingly. The power of different stakeholders will vary considerably from one organization to another. Consider that, according to the International Labour Organization, unionization rates in Iceland in 2019 were 91.4% compared to 3.3% in Thailand.

Whilst the interest and power of different groups are important influences on how managers respond, their overall attitude will depend on the nature of the relationship they want with their stakeholders. This, in turn, will depend on managers' view of why their business exists and whether they think they have a duty to try and improve the world around them. Managers will consider: should the business should simply aim to behave in a way which is legal; or should it seek to be a 'force for good'?

 Can you now answer this question from the Introductory case study?

> With reference to a stakeholder map, how might Sony engage and communicate with the different stakeholder groups?

One way of analysing the spectrum of possible approaches by businesses, in terms of their relationship with their stakeholders and society in general, is shown using Archie Carroll's pyramid.

Carroll's (1991) model outlines four different approaches listed below from the lowest to the highest in his pyramid:

- **An economic approach**

  This approach by business focuses on making profits. Managers would argue that without profits the business would cease to exist. Businesses need to generate income to pay their employees and provide a return on investment for their shareholders. This is essential to survival.

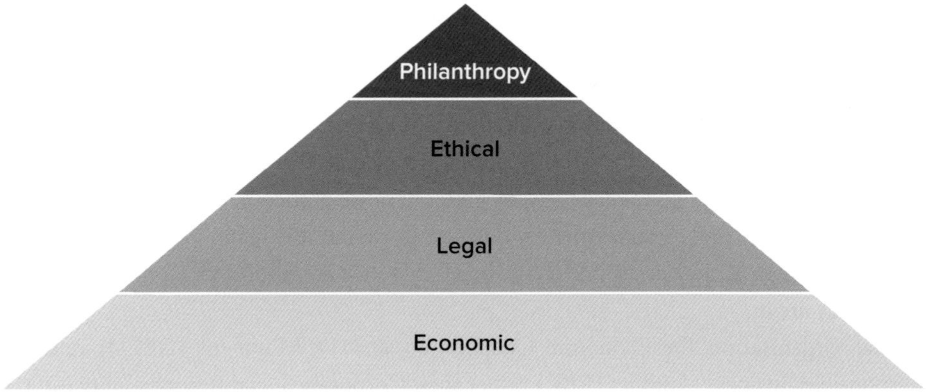

Figure 11.3 Carroll's Corporate Social Responsibility pyramid. *Source:* Carroll, A. B. (1991). 'The pyramid of corporate social responsibility: Toward the moral management of organizational stakeholders.' *Business Horizons*, 34(4), 39–48.

- **A legal approach**

  This approach occurs when a business meets its legal requirements but does not seek to do more than do what it has to. For example, in 1970 the well-known management writer Milton Friedman said that, 'There is one and only one social responsibility of business—to use its resources and engage in activities designed to increase its profit. . . In a free-enterprise, private-property system, a corporate executive is an employee of the owners of the business. He has direct responsibility to his employers. That responsibility is to conduct the business in accordance with their desires, which generally will be to make as much money as possible while conforming to their basic rules of the society, both those embodied in law and those embodied in ethical custom' (Friedman 1970).

- **An ethical approach**

  This occurs when a business tries to do what is right and avoid causing harm.

- **A philanthropic approach**

  This occurs when a business sees itself as a corporate citizen and wants to give back to society. The business will donate resources to charitable, educational, and humanitarian institutions to improve the quality of life. It is a proactive approach—it seeks to do good rather than simply avoid causing harm.

Carroll's CSR pyramid is shown in Figure 11.3:

The highest level of the pyramid, which is labelled 'philanthropy', has come to be known as Corporate Social Responsibility.

11.3 Corporate social responsibility (CSR)

Corporate Social Responsibility occurs when a business believes that it has responsibilities to society over and above the pursuit of profit. One of the earliest definitions of CSR was given by Howard Bowen. It defined CSR as 'the obligations of businessmen to pursue those policies, to make those decisions, or to follow those lines of action which are desirable in terms of the objectives and values of our society' (Bowen 1953). More recently, CSR is defined by the World Business Council for Sustainable Development as the commitment by organizations to 'behave ethically and contribute to economic development while improving the quality of life of the workforce and their families as well as the local community and society at large'. Notice the focus on improving society. CSR occurs when businesses do more than they have to do to make society better because of their actions. Our view of CSR has developed in recent years, whereby businesses are not just being philanthropic—they are building their strategies around a core belief that they are responsible for improving the world they are in.

The Organisation for Economic Cooperation and Development (OECD) refers to Responsible Business Conduct (RBC) rather than Corporate Social Responsibility (OECD 2021). The OECD has defined RBC as 'making a positive contribution to economic, environmental, and social progress with a view to achieving sustainable development and avoiding and addressing adverse impacts related to an enterprise's direct and indirect operations, products or services'. Again, the focus is on businesses making a positive contribution to society.

Areas where questions of Corporate Social Responsibility commonly arise are:

- **In the workplace**

    Managers may consider the best way to look after employees; for example, they might want to consider the quality of employees' working life, the extent to which individuals can develop their careers with the organization, and the degree of job security they provide.

- **In the market in which the business operates**

    Managers may want to consider the impact that their products have in the market. For example, according to Centers for Disease Control and Prevention in 2019, the largest tobacco companies spent $8.2 billion marketing cigarettes and smokeless tobacco in the United States. This amount translates to about $22.5 million each day, or nearly $1 million every hour. These companies may want to consider whether this is the right thing to do.

- **In the supply chain**

    Managers may want to consider how their businesses select, manage, and support their suppliers. For example, coffee shop chains such as Starbucks aim to ensure that coffee farmers receive a fair price for their products.

- **The environment**

    Managers may consider the impact of the business on the environment and the extent to which their operations are sustainable. For example, My Green Home is an award-winning business in Rwanda that recycles plastic and combines this with sand to produce materials for the construction industry.

- **The community**

    Managers may consider the impact of their activities on the communities in which they operate. For example, in 2020 Coca-Cola stated in its annual report that it had returned the equivalent of 160% of water used in finished beverages back to communities and nature as of 2019. It also claimed it had improved the lives of more than 10.6 million people globally through its water, sanitation, and hygiene programmes.

Other successes claimed by the company included reformulating nearly 1000 beverages between 2017 and 2019. This resulted in removing approximately 350,000 tons of added sugar from beverages on an annualized basis in 2019. In 2019 80% of its packaging was recyclable and 20% was made of recycled material. Coca-Cola refilled, recycled, or collected 60% of its bottles and cans.

The textile industry has also been heavily criticized for its water usage; Figure 11.4 illustrates why these concerns exist.

Some businesses that are widely recognized as socially responsible include:

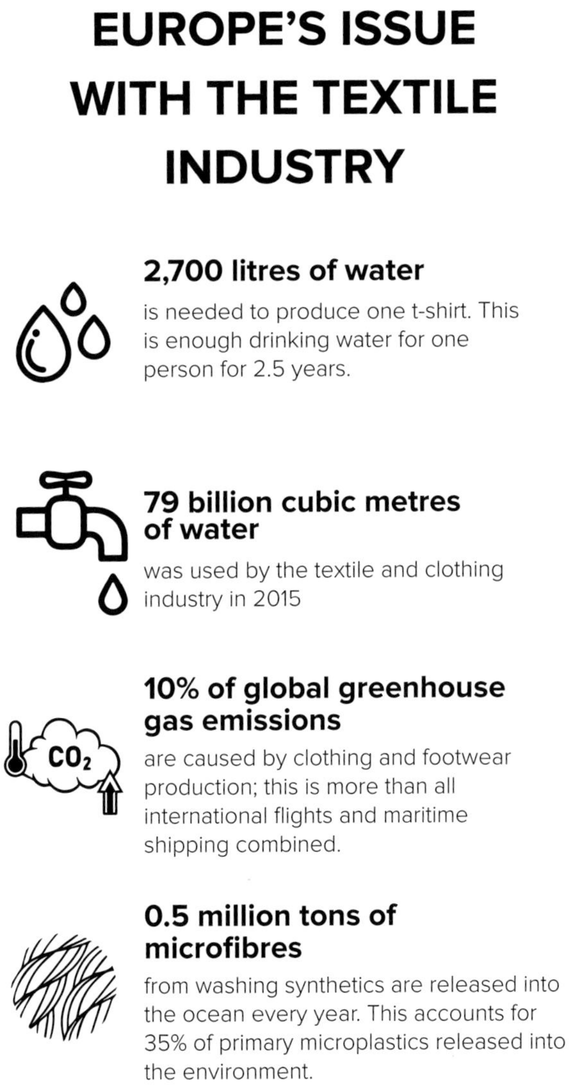

EUROPE'S ISSUE WITH THE TEXTILE INDUSTRY

2,700 litres of water
is needed to produce one t-shirt. This is enough drinking water for one person for 2.5 years.

79 billion cubic metres of water
was used by the textile and clothing industry in 2015

10% of global greenhouse gas emissions
are caused by clothing and footwear production; this is more than all international flights and maritime shipping combined.

0.5 million tons of microfibres
from washing synthetics are released into the ocean every year. This accounts for 35% of primary microplastics released into the environment.

Figure 11.4 The environmental impact of the European textile industry. *Source:* Chakraborty, S., Hoang, L., and Yiu, P. (2022). From China to India, Asia Braces for EU plan to kill fast fashion, *Financial Times*. Available at: http://www.ft.com/content/e8439ef1-c588-4ad2-9579-0eac0d5d07a0 [Accessed 2 April 2023].

- **Patagonia**

  This outdoor clothes business makes all its products from sustainable or recycled materials, and gives the equivalent of 1% of all sales to environmental organizations globally. Patagonia is considered 'an activist company', because you can find opportunities to support good causes directly on its website.

- **Toms**

  The shoes produced by Toms are made from sustainable materials and the company is very transparent about its supply chain so you know the conditions under which the products were made. The company promises to donate at least one-third of its annual net profits to its grant fund, which it distributes to good causes at grassroots level. Toms currently invests in three key issue areas. These are promoting mental health, increasing access to opportunity, and in the US, ending gun violence.

- **Warby Parker**

  This company specializes in affordable eyewear. Appreciating that 15% of the world's population lack access to glasses, when you buy a pair of glasses from it, Warby Parker gives a pair of glasses free to someone in need.

11.3.1 Social enterprises

As part of a growing focus on social responsibility there have been an increasing number of social enterprises. These are businesses that have a clear social and/or environmental mission. They usually aim to make a profit but this profit is used to have a positive social impact; for example, the profits may be reinvested back into the local community. Social enterprises are identified by the OECD as 'any private activity conducted in the public interest, organized with an entrepreneurial strategy, whose main purpose is not the maximization of profit but the attainment of certain economic and social goals, and which has the capacity for bringing innovative solutions to the problems of social exclusion and unemployment'.

The European Commission has defined a social enterprise as being 'an operator in the social economy whose main objective is to have a social impact rather than make a profit for their owners or shareholders. It operates by providing goods and services for the market in an entrepreneurial and innovative fashion and uses its profits primarily to achieve social objectives. It is managed in an open and responsible manner and, in particular, involves employees, consumers and stakeholders affected by its commercial activities.'

An example of a social enterprise is a Nigerian organization called Babban Gona (which means 'Great Farmer' in Hausa). Babban Gona's main goal is to support small Nigerian farmers improve their crop yields and earn enough to survive.

11.3.2 B Corps

Some of the businesses that are socially responsible have been awarded 'B Corps' status. Oddbox, the fruit and vegetable delivery service, and Ben & Jerry's, the ice-cream maker, are just a few of the 4000-plus companies in more than 70 countries with B Corp status. This means they have met certain standards set out by the B Lab organization.

B Lab promotes stakeholder governance. This means that the actions of what is known as a B Corps company must benefit all stakeholders—customers, employees, suppliers, communities, and investors. Stakeholder governance aims to ensure that businesses are accountable to people and planet. It seeks to ensure that businesses do not create problems such as inequality and environmental damage that often come when profits for shareholders are put as the dominant objective. Following B Lab's lead, some 51 jurisdictions around the world, including Italy, Colombia, France, Peru, Rwanda, Uruguay, Ecuador, British Columbia, and Canada, as well as 44 US states, Puerto Rico, and the District of Columbia (Washington, D.C.), have some laws promoting some degree of stakeholder governance statutes.

11.3.3 Shared values

A big advocate of involving stakeholders in decision-making in the way that Unilever has is the well-known management writer Michael Porter. In 2011 Porter wrote in the *Harvard Business Review* about a 'shared value' approach: 'The concept of shared value can be defined as policies and operating practices that enhance the competitiveness of a company while simultaneously advancing the economic and social conditions in the communities in which it operates. Shared value creation focuses on identifying and expanding the connections between societal and economic progress' (Porter and Kramer 2011).

Porter thinks businesses should be willing to invest in each other to support each other's success. The focus is not on sharing out existing rewards more fairly, but working together to create more value for all those involved.

Porter uses the example of fair trade. Fair trade, according to Porter, aims to increase the proportion of revenue that goes to low-income farmers by paying them higher prices for their crops. It is, therefore, about redistribution rather than increasing the total amount of value created. A shared value perspective, instead, focuses on improving growing techniques and improving suppliers and other institutions to increase farmers' efficiency, yields, product quality, and sustainability. This leads to more revenue and profits that benefits both farmers and the companies that buy from them.

11.3.4 Corporate activism

Increasingly, businesses are being asked to consider their relationships with different stakeholders and their stance on different issues. It is not enough to be behaving well in its day-to-day activities; businesses are being questioned about the actions they are taking to address big issues in society. For example, what is the position of the business in relation to trading with countries that have a poor human rights record? What about its position on climate change? Inequality? Diversity? Deforestation? It is increasingly difficult for businesses to ignore such issues or to avoid taking a stance. According to the Financial Times

What would you do?

A major supplier has complained that you keep trying to push down its prices and threatening it with moving your order to other suppliers. It wants a more collaborative approach and has asked you to share costs for investment in new equipment, arguing that both businesses will benefit. Should you take a more collaborative approach?

11

(2021b) the Public Affairs Council in the US reported that in 2021 nine out of 10 companies reported that they had experienced pressure from stakeholders to engage in social issues and most expected this pressure to increase further.

Examples of how businesses can engage with major social issues include the decision—reported in Reuters—of Paypal in 2017 to end its plans to open a global operations centre in Charlotte, North Carolina. It made this decision because of a state law that required transgender people to use bathrooms that corresponded to their gender at birth. Another example of a business engaging social activism occurred when in 2018 Delta Air Lines announced that it would no longer offer discounts to members of the National Rifle Association flying to the lobby group's annual meeting. This decision was made, according to the *Financial Times*, after a shooting left 14 students and three staff dead at Marjory Stoneman Douglas High School in Florida.

Another example of a business being socially active is Tony's Chocolonely; this is outlined in Business Insight 11.3.

Business Insight 11.3: Chocolate with social impact

Tony's Chocolonely is a Dutch company that sells chunky bars of chocolate. It makes these chocolate bars, it says, by paying farmers properly, working with farmer cooperatives, and not using producers who use slave labour. The company says that its product is incidental to its mission. It says that it is not a chocolate company—it is 'an impact company that makes chocolate'. The chunky chocolate bars are targeted at young and affluent buyers, who expect firms to do more for society than simply pay their taxes.

According to research by McKinsey, nine out of ten consumers born between 1995 and 2014 (Generation Zers) believe companies have a responsibility to address environmental and social issues. However, companies that make such claims about their social responsibility will be open to close scrutiny. For example, in 2020 Oatly, an oat-milk producer that argues that its products are a more sustainable alternative to dairy, was boycotted by some customers after part of the company was sold to Blackstone, a private-equity firm whose CEO and co-founder had donated money to Republican politicians, including Donald Trump. Tony's was also under close scrutiny after Slave Free Chocolate, a pressure group, removed it from its list of ethical producers. It claimed that the beans used in Tony's bars are processed by Barry Callebaut, a company that is being taken to court in America by representatives of eight former child-workers on cocoa plantations in Ivory Coast. On its website, Barry Callebaut pledges to 'eradicate child labour from our supply chain' by 2025.

Questions

What do you think Tony's Chocolonely means when it says it is an impact company not a chocolate company? How might this affect the decisions it takes?

Sources

www.mckinsey.com/industries/consumer-packaged-goods/our-insights/
true-gen-generation-z-and-its-implications-for-companies
www.tonyschocolonely.com/nl/nl
www.theguardian.com/food/2020/sep/01/oatly-vegan-milk-sale-blackstone
www.economist.com/1843/2021/04/14/tonys-chocolonely-the-risks-of-being-a-woke-brand

11.3.5 The growth of Corporate Social Responsibility (CSR)

Whilst there remain significant differences between businesses in terms of their approach to, and commitment to, Corporate Social Responsibility, the general trend in most countries has been for businesses to become more socially responsible. The move towards a greater acceptance of obligations to society was highlighted by the statement made by the Business Roundtable in the US in 2019.

The Business Roundtable is a collection of large US businesses. In 2019 these businesses announced that they felt that businesses should serve their stakeholders not just their shareholders. This was quite a shift from the focus that Roundtable businesses had previously placed on making profits. For some this shift of approach from the Roundtable businesses was seen as 'the death of capitalism'.

According to the *New York Times* the Business Roundtable businesses agreed to commit to:

- **investing in employees**

  This starts with compensating employees fairly and providing important benefits. It also includes supporting staff through training and education that help develop new skills for a rapidly changing world. Businesses should aim to foster diversity and inclusion, dignity and respect.

- **dealing fairly and ethically with suppliers**

  These businesses said they were dedicated to acting as good partners to the other companies, that they worked with.

- **supporting the communities in which they work**

  The Roundtable businesses said that organizations needed to respect the people in their communities and protect the environment by embracing sustainable practices across their businesses.

- **generating long-term value for shareholders, who provide the capital that allows companies to invest, grow, and innovate.**

  The Roundtable businesses said that they were committed to transparency and effective engagement with shareholders.

This change in approach by Roundtable businesses may lead to different decisions being made in the future; for example, the response of businesses to the alleged use of forced labour in Xinjiang province, as outlined in Business Insight 11.4, might be different now than, say, 10 years ago.

The growth of interest in CSR by business has no doubt been influenced by greater awareness of the consequences of business activity—for example, in terms of the impact on the environment—and greater concern by stakeholders. For example, change can be brought about by pressure from investors and consumers. According to a poll by Interactive Investor in 2021, 70% of 1000 retail investors surveyed said they back a greater emphasis on climate concerns. An identical proportion of the surveyed investors said that they believed company chairs and chief executives should be held to account on environmental, social, and governance issues. An example of this, according to the *Financial Times*, was the

11

Business Insight 11.4 XPCC and alleged forced labour

The Xinjiang Production and Construction Corps (XPCC) is a huge Chinese conglomerate. It produces a wide range of products, including pyjamas and tomatoes. Its 400,000 farmers harvest around one third of China's cotton. The company has been accused of using forced Uighur labour according to the US government. Some retailers, such as PVH Corp, whose brands include Calvin Klein and Tommy Hilfiger, decided to stop working with Xinjiang, because of concerns over how its employees are treated. Other businesses are still deciding whether to work with Xinjiang.

Xinjiang supplies a large proportion of China's cotton, yarn, and textile industry. It produces fabric that is whiter and less knotty than other sorts, making it a favourite for dress shirts sold around the world. It contains spinning factories belonging to some of China's most advanced shirtmakers, which produce shirts for Western brands. The problem these brands face is the difficulty they have sending anyone to audit the factories as these visits are not welcomed by the producers. To make life more difficult, Xinjiang cotton is mixed with other cotton from other regions so whatever cotton businesses buy it may well have some produced from the Xinjiang region.

Questions

Do you think a Roundtable business would buy cotton from the Xinjian province? Could this be justified?

Source

www.economist.com/business/2020/08/22/forced-labour-in-china-presents-dilemmas-for-fashion-brands

resignation in 2020 of the chief executive of Rio Tinto mining company. The chief executive was forced to resign after a scandal regarding the company's expansion of an iron ore mine that destroyed a cave containing ancient artefacts including a 4000-year-old hair plait (Smyth and Hume 2020).

However, not all socially responsible actions are a response to pressure—some business leaders bring about change themselves and whilst some managers are reactive others have undoubtedly been leaders in the area of social responsibility and driven their businesses forward in this area. For example, in 1988, Bob Langert took over as chief executive at McDonald's and set out to make the business more socially responsible and environmentally friendly. Under Langert, McDonald's made many changes to improve its behaviour; for example, it now only buys eggs from suppliers that give hens 72 square inches of space, compared with an industry average of 48 square inches. It has stopped using 'trans fats' in its cooking as these increase heart disease and has added more salads and healthy options.

Satya Nadella, chief executive of Microsoft, is another leader who wanted his business to act with a sense of purpose and win the trust of all its stakeholders. He said: 'As technology becomes so pervasive in our lives and society, we as platform companies have more responsibility, whether it's ethics around artificial intelligence, cyber-security or privacy. There is a moral obligation.'

Another great business leader who took a liking to corporate social responsibility was Paul Polman, who was Chief Executive at the conglomerate Unilever from 2009 to 2019.

Under Polman Unilever put Corporate Social Responsibility at the heart of its planning. Its vision became one of growing by serving society and the planet. The company believes that sustainable business drives superior performance and that this is the only way to create long-term value for all its stakeholders. Unilever says that it is convinced that businesses that will thrive in the future will be those that are driven by purpose for the benefit of stakeholders.

Unilever's Sustainable Living Plan sets out to decouple its growth from its environmental footprint, while increasing its positive social impact. It has three goals:

- To improve the health and well-being of more than 1 billion people through better health and hygiene and improving nutrition.

- To reduce the environmental impact by half the environmental footprint of the making and use of our products. Unilever will do this by reducing waste, water use, reducing greenhouse gases, and more sustainable sourcing.

- To enhance the livelihoods of millions through fairness in the workplace, opportunities for women, and operating an inclusive business.

11.3.6 The benefits of Corporate Social Responsibility (CSR)

The fundamental benefit of a CSR approach is that it is 'the right thing to do'. It benefits the world in which we live and aims to leave it in a better place after business activity than before it. However, CSR can be good for business as well. This is because consumers and other businesses often want to work with socially responsible businesses. So do employees—'good behaviour' by a business can attract and help retain the best staff. According to a Nielsen poll in 2018, 85% of Millennials and 80% of Gen Z rank the way businesses treat the environment at the top of their list when deciding which companies they will engage with.

Key concept

Corporate Social Responsibility (CSR) is defined by the World Business Council for Sustainable Development as the commitment by organizations to 'behave ethically and contribute to economic development while improving the quality of life of the workforce and their families as well as the local community and society at large'.

Think about it

Do you care about the behaviour of a business when you go to buy a product from it? What if you were offered a job there?

Where are we now?

We have now covered the concept of Corporate Social Responsibility. Responsibilities can cover many different areas of business. One area that has attracted increasing attention in recent years is sustainability. In the next section we consider the meaning and significance of this to business these days.

11

11.4 **Sustainability**

The environmental agenda is a clear example of where socially responsible businesses need to review what they do and take action in the interests of society as a whole. This is increasingly important because of growing pressure from consumers and investors and because of greater regulatory pressure. If businesses do not do more themselves, they are likely to be made to do so in the coming years. The scale of destruction to natural habitats and to animal species is clear to all now and climate change means that extreme hurricanes, flooding, and wildfires seem increasingly the norm. As a result, businesses are being expected by many to take action and achieve zero net emissions as soon as they can. It is increasingly argued that businesses should aim to remove any negative effect that they might have on the environment. More than that, the socially responsible view would be that businesses should be sustainable and aim to have a positive long-term impact on the environment and society. The impact of sustainability on operations was examined in Chapter 4.

Examples of businesses taking action to be more sustainable include developing a more environmentally friendly supply chain, increasing recycling, reducing water usage, and reducing the use of plastic bags in shops. For example, the management consultancy, PricewaterhouseCoopers (PwC) introduced new waste hubs and has achieved its target of zero to landfill since 2012. It sends its food waste to anaerobic digestion or commercial composting. Any old staff uniforms at the company are shredded (to make insulation for the automotive industry). It has remanufactured all its old laptops. It has also eliminated all unnecessary plastic and encouraged reusable water bottles. PwC now eliminates its residual carbon footprint with verified, certified offsets, primarily in high-value global biodiversity hotspots so that they both protect biodiversity and enable the company to be carbon neutral. Furthermore, it has encouraged more sustainable lifestyles both at work and at home, as part of being a responsible business; for example, through firm-wide campaigns such as Cycle to Work and Veganuary.

By 2020, PwC, according to its 2021 annual report, had achieved the following:

- 86% of the electricity it procured was renewable
- 80% of all its energy (including gas) was from renewable sources
- it recycled or reused 90% of all its waste.

A recent report by the management consultancy, KPMG, highlighted that climate risk is a strategic issue that needs to be considered by businesses at board level. The need for change is driven by increasing pressure from investors, governments, employees, competitors, customers, and suppliers. By taking the time to think about climate risks and creating various scenarios, businesses can identify the opportunities that exist and prepare themselves for the potential threats. According to the *Guardian*, Mark Carney, who used to be Governor of the Bank of England, has warned that companies which do not move towards zero carbon emissions will be punished by investors and go bankrupt (Guardian 2019). The interest in sustainability is certainly much greater than it was. In 2020, the management consultancy KPMG reported that 80% of companies worldwide now report on sustainability; 96% of the world's largest 250 companies do such reporting. Sustainability reporting is highest in Japan, Mexico, Malaysia, India, US, Sweden, Spain, France, South Africa, and the UK. This highlights that the focus on different CSR issues varies between countries as shown in Analysing the Business Data 11.1; this also shows how the focus can change over time.

The significance of sustainability to investors can be seen in Business Insight 11.5 on Black Rock.

Business insight 11.5 Black Rock stresses the importance of climate change and business purpose

The US investment fund Black Rock had assets of nearly $10 trillion in 2020. Its chief executive, Larry Fink, is a major proponent of social purpose and action against climate change. This is his 2021 letter to Chief Executives.

Dear CEO,

. . . We have long believed that our clients, as shareholders in your company, will benefit if you can create enduring, sustainable value for *all* of your stakeholders. . .Despite the darkness of the past 12 months [*of the pandemic*], there have been signs of hope . . . We saw businesses rapidly innovate to keep food and goods flowing during lockdowns. Companies have stepped up to support non-profits serving those in need . . . Many companies also responded to calls for racial equity, although much work remains to deliver on these commitments. And strikingly, amid all of the disruption of 2020, businesses moved forcefully to confront climate risk . . . The pandemic has presented such an existential crisis . . . that it has driven us to confront the global threat of climate change more forcefully and to consider how, like the pandemic, it will alter our lives . . . In the past year, people have seen the mounting physical toll of climate change in fires, droughts, flooding, and hurricanes . . . No issue ranks higher than climate change on our clients' lists of priorities.

In 2020, the EU, China, Japan, and South Korea all made historic commitments to achieve net zero emissions. With the US commitment to rejoin the Paris Agreement, 127 governments—responsible for more than 60% of global emissions—are considering or already implementing commitments to net zero.

There is no company whose business model won't be profoundly affected by the transition to a net zero economy—one that emits no more carbon dioxide than it removes from the atmosphere by 2050, the scientifically established threshold necessary to keep global warming well below 2°C. As the transition accelerates, companies with a well-articulated long-term strategy, and a clear plan to address the transition to net zero, will distinguish themselves with their stakeholders—with customers, policymakers, employees, and shareholders—by inspiring confidence that they can navigate this global transformation . . . Companies that are not quickly preparing themselves will see their businesses and valuations suffer, as these same stakeholders lose confidence that those companies can adapt their business models to the dramatic changes that are coming.

. . . a successful transition . . . will require both technological innovation and planning over decades. And it can only be accomplished with leadership, coordination, and support at every level of government, working in partnership with the private sector to maximize prosperity . . .

In 2018, I wrote urging every company to articulate its purpose and how it benefits all stakeholders, including shareholders, employees, customers, and the communities in which they operate. Over the course of 2020, we have seen how purposeful companies, with better environmental, social, and governance (ESG) profiles, have outperformed their peers . . . It is clear that being connected to stakeholders—establishing trust with them and acting with purpose—enables a company to understand and respond to the changes happening in the world. Companies ignore stakeholders at their peril—companies that do not earn this trust will find it harder and harder to attract customers and talent, especially as young people increasingly expect companies to reflect their values. The more your company can show its purpose in delivering value to its customers, its employees, and its communities, the better able you will be to compete and deliver long-term, durable profits for shareholders.

Sincerely,

Larry Fink

Chief Executive

Question

Do you agree with Larry Fink's view as outlined in the letter above?

Source

www.blackrock.com/corporate/investor-relations/larry-fink-ceo-letter#:~:text=Larry%20Fink%20CEO%20Letter%20%7C%20BlackRock&text=Access%20BlackRock's%20Q3%202021%20earnings%20now.

Of course, whilst being more sustainable may be socially desirable, it does not mean it is easy. It is especially difficult for some businesses whose whole existence is challenged. For example, oil companies such as BP and Shell are widely denounced and attacked because of the impact of fossil fuel use on the environment. They also face legal challenges. In May 2021, according to Bloomberg, Shell was ordered by a Dutch court to cut its emissions of greenhouse gases (ghgs) by 45% below the levels in 2019 by the end of this decade, a ruling that the company is challenging in a higher court. In response to growing demands from stakeholders Shell has been trying to adapt rapidly. According to Bloomberg, Shell says that its spending on renewable energy and low-carbon technologies will make up a quarter of its budget by 2025. It is putting money into hydrogen, carbon capture and sequestration, and other non-oil linked projects. It is also slowly shrinking its petroleum footprint, selling off some $4.7 bn worth of refineries and hydrocarbon assets in the first half of 2021. However, the difficulties facing Shell show some of the problems a company can face when becoming socially responsible. Shell is trying to change its approach—which can be slow and expensive—at the same time as investors demand ever higher short-term financial returns.

https://www.bloomberg.com/news/articles/2021-06-04/what-a-dutch-court-ruling-means-for-shell-and-big-oil-quicktake

11.4.1 Measuring Corporate Social Responsibility

In Chapter 5 we analysed the financial ratios that can be used to evaluate the financial performance of a business. Whilst such analysis remains an important part of the work of investment funds, most of these organizations now analyse a broad range of data about business performance—not just the financials—to recommend investments.

Analysing the Business Data 11.1

The charts in figure 1 show the views of chief executive officers (CEOs) in 2020 in a survey by the management consultants PWC. It highlights that chief executives believe more strongly that there are opportunities arising from the growing pressures on businesses to respond to prevent climate change than they did in the past. These opportunities include having a better reputation (or preventing a reputation worsening), opportunities for new products, and the possibility of benefiting from government incentives.

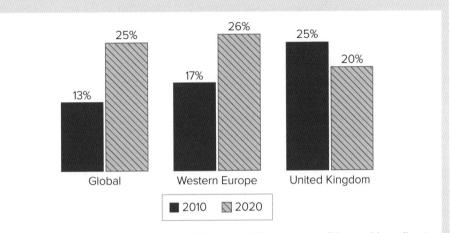

Figure 1 The views of Chief Executive Officers in different parts of the world on climate change initiatives. *Source:* PWC (no date). Available at: https://www.pwc.com/gx/en/ceo-survey/2020/trends/pwc-ceo-trends-insurance-infographic-2020.pdf [Accessed 2 April 2023].

The research showed that chief executive officers in countries which were at the forefront of the campaign to halt climate change ten years ago—France, the UK, Canada—were slightly less enthusiastic about new product and service opportunities. Having encountered many challenges to reducing climate change they were less optimistic about the options open to them. In the US, chief executives were the most sceptical about the opportunities around climate change. A possible explanation lies in the success of the shale revolution over the past decade. Having unleashed massive supplies of natural gas and oil, fracking moved the US into the position of a world leader in fossil fuel production. This development may have reduced any sense of urgency to shift to 'green' energy technologies.

Questions

What opportunities do you think climate change can bring businesses?
What do you think are barriers to these opportunities?
Why might some businesses resist a more sustainable approach?

Source

www.pwc.com/gx/en/ceo-survey/2020/reports/pwc-23rd-global-ceo-survey.pdf

11

Can you now answer this question from the Introductory case study?

What might be the benefits to Sony of a socially responsible approach?

A common framework that is used is to assess the performance of a business in relation to Environmental, Social, and Governance (ESG) factors. The performance of a business in these areas will affect whether investments are recommended or not rather than the focus being purely on areas such as profitability, gearing, and liquidity. ESG funds are investment funds that aim to invest only in organizations that have a positive social impact. The governance aspect (the G) of a business is important because the leadership of the organization will drive its agenda, set the priorities, and be responsible for ensuring that what they say is going to happen, does. The importance of governance was examined in Chapter 1. The increasing expectation that the shares of business that rate highly in the areas of ESG compared to other shares is shown in Analysing the Business Data 11.2.

Given the interest from investors and other stakeholders in the environmental, social, and governance activities of a business, many companies now produce reports including this information. According to Datamaran, in 2020 around 58% of companies in America's S&P 500 index (i.e. the largest 500 companies in the US) publish some form of CSR report. These reports contain information such as the environmental and social impact of the business and the corporate governance of the business.

Many businesses have adopted the approach of the author and entrepreneur, John Elkington, in their reporting. Elkington proposed in 1994 what he called 'triple bottom line reporting' in which businesses reported not just on their profits but also their impact on people and the planet. The triple bottom line is, therefore: People, Planet, and Profit. Elkington (1999) describes the triple bottom line as a sustainability framework that examines a company's social, environment, and economic impact.

However, precisely what businesses measure when trying to assess their social responsibility can vary enormously. Businesses can decide what matters to them and what they want to publish. This makes it very difficult for investors to compare; businesses can select the information that they want to share and hide the information they want to keep private. Given this ability to be selective with information, several businesses have been criticized for 'greenwashing'—i.e., highlighting the things they do well in relation to the environment and hiding what is not so good. For example, a business may highlight its use of recycled materials but not disclose how far those items are transported and the impact of this on the environment. Similarly, what about a business that actively promotes the fact it uses vegan leather in its products but ignores the fact its executives use private jets to travel?

To try and bring about greater consistency in the measurement of social responsibility, governments are beginning to develop reporting systems to provide some degree of standardization. For example, European Union law now requires large companies to disclose certain information on the way they operate and manage social and environmental challenges. This helps investors, consumers, policy makers, and other stakeholders to evaluate the non-financial performance of large companies with more than 500 employees and encourages these companies to develop a responsible approach to business.

The European Union non-financial reporting directive (NFRD) requires large companies to report on:

- environmental protection
- their social responsibility and treatment of employees
- their respect for human rights

- their anti-corruption and bribery policies
- the degree of diversity on their boards (in terms of age, gender, and educational and professional background).

Other institutions such as the Sustainability Accounting Standards Boards (SASB), the Global Reporting Initiative (GRI), and the Task Force on Climate Related Financial Disclosure (TCFD) are also working to agree standards that enable greater consistency of reporting and the easier comparison of data across companies around the world.

Whatever the form of reporting, it is likely that some aspects of what a business does may be regarded as socially responsible, whereas other elements may not. British American Tobacco (BAT), for example, highlights its social responsibility in the way it treats its tobacco plantation farmers and employees; however, some would argue that given that the business produces tobacco, it cannot possibly be regarded as socially responsible.

As with financial analysis, investors and other stakeholders will need to weigh up the relative importance of different data. They are also likely to keep pushing for more data than

Can you now answer this question from the Introductory case study?

Evaluate the ways that Sony is measuring its social responsibility.

Analysing the business data 11.2

The data in Figure 1 shows investors views of how shares in businesses that have a positive social impact (i.e., strong performance in relation to Environmental, Social, and Governance factors) will perform relative to other share portfolios.

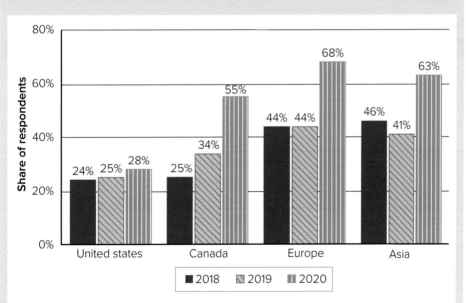

Figure 1 Expectations that ESG portfolios will outperform other portfolios worldwide 2018–2020. *Source:* Published by Statista Research Department (2022). Performance expectations of ESG portfolios 2021, Statista. Available at: https://www.statista.com/statistics/755758/performance-expectations-of-esg-portfolios/ [Accessed 2 April 2023]. *Source:* www.statista.com/statistics/755758/performance-expectations-of-esg-portfolios-2018-2020/.

11

many companies currently produce. For example, according to *The Independent* newspaper, in 2021, the investors of Amazon were under pressure to disclose how much of its plastic packaging ends up in the environment (Independent 2021). According to the *Guardian* newspaper, a report by Oceana, a conservation group, estimated that Amazon had generated 210,000 tonnes (465m lbs) of plastic packaging waste in 2019, including enough air pillows to circle the Earth 500 times. It calculated that up to 10,000 tonnes of plastic generated by Amazon entered freshwater and marine ecosystems in one year. Amazon rejected these figures but said it would review its packaging. This provides another example of how society is putting pressure on businesses to be more socially responsible.

Although exactly what is measured can vary, some of the typical measures businesses use to report on their activities relative to social responsibility are shown in Table 11.3.

What would you do?

You produce fashion clothing. Many of your directors think that behaving in a more socially responsible manner is expensive and will reduce profits. They argue they cannot afford to be socially responsible. How would you make the case that they cannot afford not to act socially responsibly.

Table 11.3 Typical measures related to social responsibility

Stakeholder group	Typical measures related to social responsibility
Employees	Diversity
	Average length of service
	Accident rates
	Employee engagement
	Average spending on training per employee
Suppliers	Average payment period
	Number of repeat contracts
	Number of new contracts
Customers	Customer satisfaction
	Customer complaints
Environment	Fuel usage
	CO_2 emissions
	Waste
	Water usage
	Paper usage
	Air travel
Community	Donations
	Grants
	Volunteers

Think about it

Can you think of situations where there might be a conflict between meeting the needs of shareholders and meeting the needs of other stakeholders?

11.4.2 What limits the move towards being more socially responsible?

Some managers would argue that their responsibility is to the owners of the business. This is known as the shareholder view (as opposed to a stakeholder view). In this approach managers would say that they are there to generate profits. For this group, the idea of CSR is a distraction that takes away from their main focus. They would argue that if society wants to change their behaviour they can always change the law and this will force businesses to do things differently.

The case of such managers against CSR is even stronger if it involves extra costs or limits activities that would otherwise be profitable. So, for some, CSR is simply not central to what they do and, in some cases, it may be seen as working against what they want to achieve. Whilst this view persists, we have seen how there is a significant move in recent years to adopt a more socially responsible approach, which some companies such as Unilever have been adopting for many years. Some of this change is driven by businesses themselves; some is because of regulatory change. Business Insight 11.6 shows that regulatory change can sometimes have unintended consequences.

Where are we now?

We have seen the reasons why the interest in CSR has grown in recent years and how the behaviour of businesses now faces greater scrutiny. We have also seen how the way the performance of business is assessed is now broader than it used to be, including Environmental, Social, and Governance indicators. Whilst some businesses embrace the CSR movement, others remain less enthusiastic. Some try to suggest their CSR credentials are stronger than they are. This is known as 'greenwashing'.

Business Insight 11.6 The dangers of forcing companies to be socially responsible

Kitex garments is one of the largest private companies in Kerala in India. The company is a great believer in Corporate Social Responsibility (CSR). In the financial year ending March 2021 Kitex gave 5.3% of its profit to public roads, schools, housing, and safe drinking water projects. This is more than is required under a 2013 Indian law which requires Indian companies to allocate at least 2% of their annual profits to CSR projects.

Whilst this law has increased contributions to good causes, there have been some unwelcome side effects. Of the 2152 companies that gave more than 5% of profits before the

11

law went through, their average contributions fell by half. The motives for CSR usually include: genuine altruism, a desire by managers to support their own interest, and an attempt to meet growing demand from consumers and employees for better behaviour. If the first two were the driving motives you would not expect to see a fall following the 2013 legislation. However, if the motive was to attract attention and support and the new law means that giving to CSR is seen as 'normal' and there is an 'expectation' it is undertaken by all companies, then perhaps there is not an additional benefit in terms of customers and employees in giving 5%+ of profits instead of 2%.

Interestingly many Indian businesses are family-controlled. Their CSR contributions often go from the companies to charitable entities also controlled by the families. For example, India's largest company, Reliance Industries, gave 94% of its 2019 contributions to the Reliance Foundation, chaired by the wife of Reliance's largest shareholder and chief executive.

Question

Given the experience above in India do you think governments should leave it up to businesses to decide how they want to behave or should they try to make them more socially responsible?

Source

www.economist.com/business/2021/01/09/what-happens-when-firms-have-to-stump-up-for-good-causes

Summary

Historically, businesses have been regarded by many as organizations created to generate a profit for their owners. Provided the business acted legally, it was widely accepted that the objective of most businesses was to earn the largest financial returns possible. Nowadays, there is much greater awareness of what businesses do, how they do it, and the consequences of what they do. There is much greater awareness of the stakeholders involved in the transformation process and greater consideration of the impact of business activity on them. Climate change has been a good example of raising awareness of the potential dangers and short-sightedness of a purely profit-focused approach that does not think about how business is undertaken and who and what it affects.

There has in recent years been a growing interest in whether individuals are behaving ethically—are they doing the right thing—and whether businesses as a whole think of themselves as corporate citizens trying to improve the society in which they live. Obviously, not every business sees all its stakeholders as partners all the time and not every business sets out to be socially responsible, but there has definitely been a shift and growing consciousness that partnership may bring rewards for all. This pressure comes from individuals within businesses themselves but also from consumers, would-be employees, and governments.

Now you should know

- Business ethics refer to what is regarded as right or wrong when making a business decision.

- A code of ethics sets out the expectations that the company has for how employees should behave in any given situation, to assist with decision-making.

- Whistle-blowing occurs when an individual within a business reveals information that highlights illegal or unethical behaviour by others within the organization.

- The stakeholders of a business are individuals or groups who affect or are affected by its activities.

- Corporate Social Responsibility (CSR) is defined by the World Business Council for Sustainable Development as the commitment by organizations to 'behave ethically and contribute to economic development while improving the quality of life of the workforce and their families as well as the local community and society at large'.

Review questions

Quick check

1. Identify three stakeholders of a business.

2. Outline the difference between the utilitarian and deontological approach to ethical decisions.

3. Outline the difference between the stakeholder and the shareholder view of a business.

4. State the four levels of Carroll's pyramid of social responsibility.

5. Explain what is meant by an ethical dilemma.

6. Explain what is meant by whistle-blowing.

7. Explain why a business would produce a Code of Ethics.

8. Explain what is meant by Corporate Social Responsibility.

Analysis

1. Analyse the reasons why a business might want to be more socially responsible.

2. Analyse why people within a business might act unethically.

3. Analyse the benefits to a business of stakeholder mapping.

Evaluation

1. Do you think CSR is a passing trend?

2. Do you think that CSR is just good business?

3. Do you think unethical behaviour in business is inevitable?

11

➤ Find out more

For more on Business Ethics you might read:

Crane *et al.* (2019). **Business Ethics** (5th edn). Oxford, Oxford University Press. *This textbook provides a comprehensive overview of business ethics and corporate social responsibility, including different ethical theories, stakeholders (shareholders, employees, consumers, suppliers, civil society, and governments) and the management of business ethics.*

If you are interested in the shareholder approach why not read Friedman's world-famous article *The Social Responsibility of Business is to Increase its Profits* in full; Milton Friedman, *The New York Times Magazine,* 13 September 1970.

Having read this, do you think that 'the business of business is business' . . . or not?

You might also be interested in listening to Paul Polman, ex Chief Executive of Unilever discuss how essential it is for businesses to work with their stakeholder partners.

www.youtube.com/watch?v=JJEmG5q3m4A

You can read more about the shared-value approach and how Porter argues it can build long term competitive advantage here:

Kramer, M.R. and Pfitzer, M.W. (2016). The ecosystem of shared value. *Harvard Business Review,* 94(10), 80–89.

Kramer, M.R. and Porter, M. (2011). *Creating shared value* (Vol. 17). FSG.

Porter, M.E. and Kramer, M.R. (2006). The link between competitive advantage and corporate social responsibility. *Harvard Business Review,* 84(12), 78–92.

Elkington's focus on far broader measures of performance than just the financials has had a major impact on business reporting. Why not read his book on the Triple Bottom Line approach?

Elkington, J. (1999). *Cannibals with forks: the triple bottom line of 21st century business.* Oxford, Capstone.

A big movement in recent years has been the circular economy (as outlined in Chapter 4 on Operations). This focus on rethinking how we design and produce products to reduce waste and conserve resources is outlined here:

McDonough, W. (2002). *Cradle to cradle: remaking the way we make things.* New York, North Point Press.

☰ Bibliography

Aberystwyth University (2019). *Majority of people return lost wallets—here's the psychology and which countries are the most honest—.* [online] Available at: <https://www.aber.ac.uk/en/news/archive/2019/06/title-224299-en.html> [Accessed 7 May 2022].

Abu-Shakra, E. (2021) *Three-quarters of institutional investors say they may divest from companies with Poor Environmental Track Records.* Available at: https://www.ey.com/en_gl/news/2021/11/three-quarters-of-institutional-investors-say-they-may-divest-from-companies-with-poor-environmental-track-records [Accessed 14 January 2023].

ACCA Global (2021). *All about stakeholders—part 2.* Available at: <https://www.accaglobal.com/pk/en/student/exam-support-resources/professional-exams-study-resources/strategic-business-leader/technical-articles/all-about-stakeholders-part-2.html> [Accessed 29 December 2021].

Alphabet Investor Relations (2021). *Alphabet Investor Relations.* [online] Available at: <https://abc.xyz/investor/other/google-code-of-conduct/> [Accessed 28 December 2021].

BBC News (2019). [online] Corporate leaders scrap shareholder-first ideology (19 Aug). Available at: https://www.bbc.com/news/business-49400885.

BBC News (2021). [online] Available at: <https://www.bbc.co.uk/news/business-55735108> [Accessed 28 December 2021].

BlackRock (2021). *Larry Fink CEO Letter| BlackRock*. [online] Available at: <https://www.blackrock.com/corporate/investor-relations/larry-fink-ceo-letter> [Accessed 28 December 2021].

Bowen, H.R. (1953). *Social Responsibilities of the Businessman*. New York, Harper & Brothers.

BP Global (2021). *Sustainability|Home*. [online] Available at: <https://www.bp.com/en/global/corporate/sustainability.html> [Accessed 28 December 2021].

Brown.edu (2022). *A Framework for Making Ethical Decisions|Science and Technology Studies*. [online] Available at: <https://www.brown.edu/academics/science-and-technology-studies/framework-making-ethical-decisions> [Accessed 8 May 2022].

Business Roundtable (2019). *Business Roundtable Redefines the Purpose of a Corporation to Promote 'An Economy That Serves All Americans'*. [online] Available at: <https://www.businessroundtable.org/business-roundtable-redefines-the-purpose-of-a-corporation-to-promote-an-economy-that-serves-all-americans> [Accessed 28 December 2021].

Cannon, T. (2012). *Corporate Responsibility*. Harlow, Pearson Education UK.

Carroll, A. (1991). The pyramid of corporate social responsibility: Toward the moral management of organizational stakeholders. *Business Horizons*, 34(4),39–48.

Centers for Disease Control and Prevention (2022). *Economic trends in tobacco*. Available at: https://www.cdc.gov/tobacco/data_statistics/fact_sheets/economics/econ_facts/index.htm [Accessed 14 January 2023].

Chakraborty, S., Hoang, L., and Yiu, P. (2022). From China to India, Asia Braces for EU plan to kill fast fashion. *Financial Times*. Available at: http://www.ft.com/content/e8439ef1-c588-4ad2-9579-0eac0d5d07a0 [Accessed 2 April 2023].

Cisco, A. (2021). *Cisco Corporate Social Responsibility*. [online] Cisco. Available at: <https://www.cisco.com/c/en/us/about/csr/impact/csr-priorities.html#~stickynav=2> [Accessed 28 December 2021].

De George, R. (2014). *Business Ethics*. Harlow, England, Pearson Education.

Deloitte (2021). *Deloitte UK|Audit, Consulting, Financial Advisory and Tax services*. [online] Available at: <https://www2.deloitte.com/uk/en.html> [Accessed 28 December 2021].

Desjardins, J. (2020). *An introduction to Business Ethics* (6th edn). New York, McGraw-Hill.

Deutsche Welle (2022). *Africa's whistleblowers pay a high price for their courage*. [online] Available at: <https://www.dw.com/en/africa-whistleblowers-pay-high-price-for-truth/a-61146475> [Accessed 7 May 2022].

Disney (2021). [online] Available at: <https://thewaltdisneycompany.com/social-responsibility/> [Accessed 28 December 2021].

ec.europa.eu/growth/industry/sustainability/corporate-social-responsibility_en

Elkington, J. (1999). *Cannibals with forks: the triple bottom line of 21st century business*. Oxford, Capstone.

Ethics Unwrapped (2022). *Lost Wallet, Found Honesty—Ethics Unwrapped*. [online] Available at: <https://ethicsunwrapped.utexas.edu/lost-wallet-found-honesty> [Accessed 7 May 2022].

Friedman, M. (1970). 'The Social Responsibility of Business is to Increase its Profits', *The New York Times Magazine;* 13 September, 1970.

Financial Times (2021a). *How one founder meets the challenge of staying ethical and profitable*. [online] Available at: <https://www.ft.com/content/d7551de1-e402-4996-a27b-f0a209fc8f3d> [Accessed 29 December 2021].

Financial Times (2021b). *Stakeholder collaboration will help companies and society thrive*. [online] Available at: <https://www.ft.com/content/8f6f9bc8-2e81-43d0-ad2a-b387de41e0f5> [Accessed 29 December 2021].

Financial Times (2021c). *Sustainable businesses should be 'long-term greedy'*. [online] Available at: <https://www.ft.com/content/bd-30c5ec-20a9-11e9-a46f-08f9738d6b2b> [Accessed 28 December 2021].

Financial Times (2022). *Chinese companies waiting twice as long for payments as in 2015*. [online] Available at: <https://www.ft.com/content/0b831a12-6101-4420-8629-8d73f1dded91> [Accessed 2 January 2022].

Foreign and Commonwealth Office (2014). *The Rana Plaza disaster*. Available at: https://www.gov.uk/government/case-studies/the-rana-plaza-disaster [Accessed 14 January 2023].

Freeman, R. E. (1984). *Strategic Management: A Stakeholder Approach*. Bath, Pitman.

Gelles, D. and Yaffe-Bellany, D. (2019). *Shareholder value is no longer everything, top C.E.O.s say*, *The New York Times*. The New York Times. Available at: https://www.nytimes.com/2019/08/19/business/business-roundtable-ceos-corporations.html [Accessed 14 January 2023].

Halpern, S. (2021). *The Facebook whistleblower's testimony and the Tech Giant's Very Bad Week*, *The New Yorker*. Available at: https://www.newyorker.com/news/daily-comment/the-facebook-whistle-blowers-testimony-and-the-tech-giants-very-bad-week [Accessed 14 January 2023].

Harvard Business Review (2021). *The Social Responsibility of Business Is to Increase . . . What Exactly?*. [online] Available at: <https://hbr.org/2012/04/you-might-disagree-with-milton> [Accessed 18 December 2021].

International Labour Organization (n.d.) *Statistics on union membership. ILOSTAT*. Available at:

11

https://ilostat.ilo.org/topics/union-membership/ [Accessed 14 January 2023].

Johnson, G. and Scholes, K. (2002). *Exploring Corporate Strategy, Text and Cases* (6th edn). Prentice Hall, Pearson Education Limited.

Johnston, E. (2021) *Communications Ministry scandal puts Focus on Japan's broadcast act. The Japan Times.* Available at: https://www.japantimes.co.jp/news/2021/03/23/national/communications-ministry-scandal-broadcast-act/ [Accessed 14 January 2023].

KPMG (2022). [online] Available at: <https://assets.kpmg/content/dam/kpmg/xx/pdf/2020/12/the-time-has-come-executive-summary.pdf> [Accessed 8 May 2022].

Mendelow, A. (1983). Setting corporate goals and measuring organizational effectiveness—a practical approach. *Long Range Planning*, 16(1).

Mendelow, A. L. (1991). Environmental scanning: The impact of the stakeholder concept. In *Proceedings from the second international conference on information systems*. Cambridge, MA.

Michiganstateuniversityonline.com. 2021. [online] Available at: <https://www.michiganstateuniversityonline.com/resources/leadership/common-ethical-issues-in-the-workplace/> [Accessed 28 December 2021].

Murray, S. (2022). When should business take a stand? *Financial Times*. [online] 9 Mar. Available at: https://www.ft.com/content/5ceffa36-899a-4457-919f-b70902162f64. [Accessed 14 January 2023].

Nestlé Global (2021). *Stakeholder engagement.* [online] Available at: <https://www.nestle.com/csv/what-is-csv/stakeholder-engagement> [Accessed 28 December 2021].

NielsenIQ (2018). *Was 2018 the year of the influential sustainable consumer?* (2018) Available at: https://nielseniq.com/global/en/insights/analysis/2018/was-2018-the-year-of-the-influential-sustainable-consumer/ [Accessed 14 January 2023].

OECD (2021). *Guidelines for MNEs - Organisation for Economic Co-operation and Development.* [online] Oecd.org. Available at: https://mneguidelines.oecd.org/.

Porter, M. and Kramer, M. (2011). How to fix capitalism? Creating shared value. *Harvard Business Review*, 63, 67.

PWC (2021). [online] Available at: <https://www.pwc.co.uk/who-we-are/our-purpose/strategy/stakeholders.html> [Accessed 28 December 2021].

Rappeport, A. (2018). *Harley-Davidson, blaming E.U. tariffs, will move some production out of U.S. The New York Times.* Available at: https://www.nytimes.com/2018/06/25/business/harley-davidson-us-eu-tariffs.html [Accessed 14 January 2023].

Reuters (2016). *PayPal pulls North Carolina plan after transgender Bathroom Law* Thomson Reuters. Available at: https://www.reuters.com/article/north-carolina-transgender-paypal-hldg-idUSL2N1780TU [Accessed 14 January 2023].

Smyth, J. and Hume, N. (2020). Rio Tinto CEO quits after backlash over Aboriginal site destruction. *Financial Times*. Available at: https://www.

ft.com/content/dd75d6da-f047-49d4-9b2e-cfc2ef95df00 [Accessed 14 January 2023].

Temple-West, P. and McGee, P. (2021) *Apple faces probe over whether it retaliated against whistleblower, Subscribe to read\Financial Times.* Financial Times. Available at: https://www.ft.com/content/973aae8d-21d9-4e84-8912-ead071c7935d [Accessed 14 January 2023].

Texas Instruments (n.d.) *Living our values TI's ambitions, values and code of conduct* (no date). Available at: https://www.ti.com/lit/ml/szzb178/szzb178.pdf?ts=1650727334418 [Accessed 14 January 2023].

The Economist. 2021. *Can Johnson & Johnson put the taint of scandal behind it?.* [online] Available at: <https://www.economist.com/business/2021/12/04/can-johnson-and-johnson-put-the-taint-of-scandal-behind-it> [Accessed 28 December 2021].

The Economist. 2021. *Forced labour in China presents dilemmas for fashion brands.* [online] Available at: <https://www.economist.com/business/2020/08/20/forced-labour-in-china-presents-dilemmas-for-fashion-brands> [Accessed 28 December 2021].

The Economist (2019). *Big Business is beginning to accept broader social responsibilities.* Available at: https://www.economist.com/briefing/2019/08/24/big-business-is-beginning-to-accept-broader-social-responsibilities [Accessed 14 January 2023].

The Guardian (2019). Firms ignoring climate crisis will go bankrupt, says Mark Carney. *The Guardian*. Available at: https://www.theguardian.com/environment/2019/oct/13/firms-ignoring-climate-crisis-bankrupt-mark-carney-bank-england-governor [Accessed 17 January 2023].

The Guardian (2021a). *Grovelling apologies fail to get Rio Tinto out of a Hole.* Guardian News and Media. Available at: https://www.theguardian.com/business/2021/apr/04/grovelling-apologies-fail-to-get-rio-tinto-out-of-a-hole [Accessed 11 December 2022].

The Guardian (2021b). *Amazon shareholders to vote on revealing retailer's plastic footprint.* Guardian News and Media. Available at: https://www.theguardian.com/environment/2021/may/26/amazon-shareholders-to-vote-on-revealing-retailers-plastic-footprint [Accessed 11 December 2022].

The Guardian (2021c). *Frances Haugen: 'I never wanted to be a whistleblower. But lives were in danger'.* [online] Available at: <https://www.theguardian.com/technology/2021/oct/24/frances-haugen-i-never-wanted-to-be-a-whistleblower-but-lives-were-in-danger> [Accessed 28 December 2021].

The Guardian (2021d). *FTSE leaves coal and oil firms and G4S on ethical investment list.* [online] Available at: <https://www.theguardian.com/business/2019/dec/22/ftse-leaves-coal-and-oil-firms-and-g4s-on-ethical-investment-list> [Accessed 29 December 2021].

The Guardian (2021e). *Nestlé baby milk scandal has grown up but not gone away.* [online]

Available at: <https://www.theguardian.com/sustainable-business/nestle-baby-milk-scandal-food-industry-standards?view=mobile> [Accessed 30 December 2021].

The Guardian (2022a). *New study deems Amazon worst for 'aggressive' tax avoidance*. [online] Available at: <https://www.theguardian.com/business/2019/dec/02/new-study-deems-amazon-worst-for-aggressive-tax-avoidance> [Accessed 7 May 2022].

The Guardian (2022b). *Purdue Pharma accused of 'corrupting' WHO to boost global opioid sales*. [online] Available at: <https://www.theguardian.com/us-news/2019/may/22/purdue-pharma-opioid-world-health-organization-painkiller-global-sales> [Accessed 7 May 2022].

The Guardian (2022c). *Bain & Co barred from UK government contracts over 'grave misconduct' in South Africa*. Guardian News and Media. Available at: https://www.theguardian.com/business/2022/aug/03/bain-and-co-barred-from-uk-government-contracts-over-grave-misconduct-in-south-africa [Accessed 11 December 2022].

The Guardian (2022d). *Revealed: Credit Suisse leak unmasks criminals, fraudsters and corrupt politicians*. Guardian News and Media. Available at: https://www.theguardian.com/news/2022/feb/20/credit-suisse-secrets-leak-unmasks-criminals-fraudsters-corrupt-politicians [Accessed 11 December 2022].

The Independent (2021). *Amazon's plastic packaging could circle the planet 800 times. can it be stopped?* (2022). Independent Digital News and Media. Available at: https://www.independent.co.uk/climate-change/news/amazon-package-waste-plastic-christmas-b2248580.html [Accessed 17 January 2023].

Unilever PLC (2022). *Our history: Unilever global company website—2010–2020, Unilever*. Unilever PLC. Available at: https://www.unilever.com/our-company/our-history-and-archives/2010-2020/ [Accessed 14 January 2023].

Vetter, D. (2022). *Sustainability In Africa: How Rwanda's Young Innovators Are Building a Circular Economy*. [online] Forbes. Available at: <https://www.forbes.com/sites/davidrvetter/2021/05/27/sustainability-in-africa-how-rwandas-young-innovators-are-building-a-circular-economy/?sh=240c83207910> [Accessed 8 May 2022].

World Economic Forum (2021). *Agenda*. [online] Available at: <https://www.weforum.org/agenda> [Accessed 28 December 2021].

Worldpopulationreview.com (2022). *Minimum Wage by Country 2021*. [online] Available at: <https://worldpopulationreview.com/country-rankings/minimum-wage-by-country> [Accessed 2 January 2022].

11

INDEX